THIRD EDITION

# *Income Tax*
# PLANNING
## *for Financial Planners*

Thomas P. Langdon

E. Vance Grange

Michael A. Dalton

# Income Tax

# PLANNING

## for Financial Planners

### THIRD EDITION

Thomas P. Langdon

E. Vance Grange

Michael A. Dalton

YOUR MONEY EDUCATION RESOURCE.™

115 JAMES DRIVE WEST
SUITE 140
ST. ROSE, LA 70087
888-295-6023

Printed in the U.S.A.

ISBN-10: 0-9801299-6-6
ISBN-13: 978-0-9801299-6-0
Library of Congress Card Number: 2009940890

# ABOUT THE AUTHORS

**Thomas P. Langdon, JD, LL.M., CFA, CFP®**
- Associate Professor of Business Law, Gabelli School of Business, Roger Williams University, Bristol, RI.
- Principal, Langdon & Langdon Financial Services, LLC (Connecticut-based tax planning & preparation firm).
- Former Professor of Taxation at The American College, Bryn Mawr, PA.
- Former Adjunct Professor of Insurance and Economics at The University of Connecticut Center for Professional Development.
- Former Member (and Chair) of the CFP Board's Board of Examiners.
- Master of Laws (LL.M.) in Taxation from Villanova University School of Law.
- Juris Doctor, from Western New England College School of Law.
- Master of Science in Financial Services from The American College.
- Master of Business Administration from The University of Connecticut.
- Bachelor of Science in Finance from The University of Connecticut, Storrs, CT.
- Chartered Financial Analyst (CFA), Certified Financial Planner (CFP), Chartered Life Underwriter (CLU), Chartered Financial Consultant (ChFC), Accredited Estate Planner (AEP), Certified Employee Benefits Specialist (CEBS), Chartered Advisor in Senior Living (CASL), Registered Employee Benefits Consultant (REBC), Registered Health Underwriter (RHU), Associate in Life & Health Claims (ALHC), and Fellow of the Life Management Institute (FLMI).
- Co-author of *Estate Planning for Financial Planners* (1st - 5th editions).

**E. Vance Grange, PhD, CPA, CFP®**
- Director of Tax and Personal Financial Planning Programs in the School of Accountancy at Utah State University.
- Teaches courses in income taxation, personal financial planning, retirement planning, and estate planning.
- Bachelor's degree in English from Brigham Young University.
- Master's of Accountancy degree from Utah State University.
- Ph.D. in Accounting (Taxation) from the University of Texas at Austin.
- Licensed CPA in the state of Utah.
- Investment advisor associate of Beacon Financial Planning, LLC, a registered investment advisory company in Utah.
- Former member Board of Examiners of the Certified Financial Planner Board of Standards and a member of the CFP Board of Governors.
- Former chair of the Board of Examiners.
- Participated in the Model Curriculum project of the Academy of Financial Services and CFP Board.

- Has worked with CFP Board staff and other researchers to identify determinants of success on the CFP® Certification Examination since 1999.
- Has served as faculty advisor for numerous national finalist teams in the Deloitte Tax Case Study Competition, including a graduate team for 2007.

### Michael A. Dalton, Ph.D., JD, CFP®

- Principal of Cobalt Financial Solutions, L.L.C.
- Former Chair of the Board of Dalton Publications, L.L.C.
- Associate professor of Accounting and Taxation at Loyola University in New Orleans, Louisiana.
- Adjunct faculty in Financial Planning at Georgetown University in Washington, D.C.
- Former Senior Vice President, Education at BISYS Group.
- Ph.D. in Accounting from Georgia State University.
- J.D. from Louisiana State University in Baton Rouge, Louisiana.
- MBA and BBA in Management and Accounting from Georgia State University.
- Former board member of the CFP Board's Board of Examiners, Board of Standards, and Board of Governors.
- Former member (and chair) of the CFP Board's Board of Examiners.
- Member of the *Journal of Financial Planning* Editorial Advisory Board and Editorial Review Board.
- Member of the LSU Law School Board of Trustees (2000 - 2006).
- Author of *Dalton Review for the CFP® Certification Examination: Volume I – Outlines and Study Guides, Volume II – Problems and Solutions, Volume III - Case Exam Book, Mock Exams A-1 and A-2 (1st - 8th Editions)*.
- Author of *Retirement Planning and Employee Benefits for Financial Planners (1st - 5th Editions)*.
- Co-author of *Estate Planning for Financial Planners (1st - 5th Editions)*.
- Co-author of *Dalton CFA® Study Notes Volumes I and II (1st - 2nd Editions)*.
- Co-author of *Dalton's Personal Financial Planning Series – Personal Financial Planning Theory and Practice (1st - 3rd Editions)*.
- Co-author of *Dalton's Personal Financial Planning Series – Personal Financial Planning Cases and Applications (1st - 4th Editions)*.
- Co-author of *Cost Accounting: Traditions and Innovations* published by West Publishing Company.
- Co-author of the *ABCs of Managing Your Money* published by National Endowment for Financial Education.

## ABOUT THE CONTRIBUTORS

**Phyllis Duhon** made a significant contribution to this text by her thoughtful and meticulous reading, rewriting, and editing throughout the book. She provided many valuable suggestions and improvements to both the text and instructor materials that significantly improved this edition. We are extremely grateful for her contributions. Phyllis is an attorney and received her J.D. from Loyola University New Orleans College of Law and a B.S. in Business Administration/Finance from the University of New Orleans. She is a contributor to *Estate Planning for Financial Planners* by Money Education.

**Allison Dalton McCammon** made a significant contribution to this text by reviewing and editing many chapters in the first two editions. Allison is an attorney and personal financial planner specializing in Small Business Planning and Estate Planning. She received her J.D. from Georgetown University Law Center, an Executive Certificate in Financial Planning from Georgetown University, and a B.A. in International Studies from Rhodes College. She is a contributor to *Retirement Planning and Employee Benefits for Financial Planners* by Money Education.

## ABOUT THE REVIEWERS

We owe a special thanks to several key professionals for their significant contribution of time and effort with this text. These reviewers provided meticulous editing, detailed calculation reviews, helpful suggestions for additional content, and other valuable comments, all of which have improved this edition.

**Michelle Bertolini** is an professor in the Barney College of Business at the University of Hartford. She has a J.D. from Stetson University College of Law in St. Petersburg, Florida and a LLM in International Taxation from Thomas Jefferson School of Law in San Diego, CA. Ms. Bertolini is a licensed attorney and CPA in the state of Florida. She is a contributing author for a text book on SEC Audits and has published articles in various tax journals.

**Brad Childs** is an Associate Professor of Accounting at Belmont University, where he does research in taxation and financial planning fields. He has a Ph.D. from Purdue University and a J.D. from Suffolk University. He is currently a licensed attorney in Tennessee, a licensed CPA in Ohio, and a CFP Certificant.

**E. L. "Skip" Lloyd** graduated from the University of Mississippi with a BBA in accounting in 1976. He practiced in the area of income and estate taxation for 28 years in public accounting. Mr. Lloyd moved to New Orleans in January 2007 and is currently a senior tax analyst for Postlethwaite & Netterville, APAC in their Metairie office.

**Kristi M. Tafalla** is an attorney and personal financial planner specializing in income tax and estate planning. She teaches estate planning, income tax planning and comprehensive case courses through various CFP Board-Registered Programs as well as comprehensive reviews for the Certified Financial Planner designation. She is a contributor to Money Education's *Estate Planning for Financial Planners* and *Retirement Planning and Employee Benefits for Financial Planners*.

**Bill Yurkovac** has a private practice in Florida focusing on asset management and estate planning considerations for his clientele. Mr. Yurkovac holds a Master's Degree in Education, has more than twenty-five years experience in the financial services arena, and enjoys serving as an instructor for candidates preparing for the CFP® Certification Examination. Current community involvement includes assisting and counseling several non-profit organizations and a chair on the local Estate Planning Council's Board of Directors.

**Laurence J. Whalen** is a senior judge of the United States Tax Court. He graduated from Georgetown University, received his J.D. and LL.M. from Georgetown University Law Center. He is a member of Oklahoma Bar Association, District of Columbia Bar Association, and American Bar Association. He was appointed by President Reagan as Judge, United States Tax Court, on November 23, 1987, for a term ending November 22, 2002. Judge Whalen retired on November 23, 2002, but continues to perform judicial duties as Senior Judge on recall.

## ACKNOWLEDGEMENTS & SPECIAL THANKS

We are most appreciative for the tremendous support and encouragement we have received throughout this project. We are extremely grateful to the instructors and program directors of CFP Board-Registered programs who provided valuable comments during the development stages of this text. We are fortunate to have dedicated, careful readers at several institutions who were willing to share their needs, expectations, and time with us.

A special thanks to the students in Ken Picerno's tax class at the University of North Texas CFP Board-Registered Program. After using the 1st Edition in their income tax planning course, they provided valuable feedback on where improvements could be made for the 2nd edition.

Thanks to Chris White, Randall Martinez, and Ken Picerno for their meticulous editing, detailed calculation reviews, helpful suggestions for additional content, and other valuable comments with the previous editions of this text.

Chris teaches in the CFP Board-Registered Programs at Xavier University in Cincinnati and at Bellarmine University in Louisville. He is vice president of the National City Private Client Group, a board member and past president of the Greater Cincinnati Chapter of the Financial Planning Association and an instructor for comprehensive reviews for the CFP® Certification Examination.

Randy is a personal financial planner specializing in personal financial planning, estate, and individual income tax planning. He teaches retirement planning, estate planning, and income tax planning through various CFP Board-Registered Programs as well as comprehensive reviews for the Certified Financial Planner designation.

Ken is a practicing Certified Public Accountant and Certified Financial Planner. He specializes in providing tax and financial planning solutions for individuals and businesses. Mr. Picerno is an adjunct professor at the University of North Texas in Denton, Texas where he teaches the tax course in their CFP Board-Registered Program.

Thanks also to Patricia Heckler and Sherri Knoepfler for their manuscript reviews and thoughtful feedback. Their thorough editing, detailed calculation reviews, helpful suggestions for additional content, and other valuable comments, improved this text. We extend our deepest gratitude and appreciation to them.

Developing a textbook that is aesthetically pleasing and easy to read is a difficult undertaking. We would like to pay special thanks to Robin Meyer and Donna Dalton who managed the project, formatted the entire text, performed numerous reviews, and provided invaluable feedback throughout the entire project. This book would not have been possible without their extraordinary dedication, skill, and knowledge.

We have received so much help from so many people, it is possible that we have inadvertently overlooked thanking someone. If so, it is our shortcoming, and we apologize in advance. Please let us know if you are that someone, and we will make it right in our next printing.

## PREFACE

*Income Tax Planning for Financial Planners* is written for graduate and upperdivision undergraduate level students interested in acquiring an understanding of income tax planning from a professional financial planning viewpoint. The text is intended to be used in an Income Tax Planning course as part of an overall curriculum in financial planning. The text is also intended to serve as a reference for practicing professional financial planners.

This text was designed to meet the educational requirements for an Income Tax Course in a CFP Board-Registered Program. Therefore, one of our goals is to assure CFP Board-Registered Program Directors, instructors, students, and financial planners that we have addressed every relevant topic covered by the CFP Board Exam Topic List and the most recent model curriculum syllabus for this course. The book will be updated, as needed, to keep current with any changes in the law, exam topic list, or model curriculum.

### *Special Features*

A variety of tools and presentation methods are used throughout this text to assist the reader in the learning process. Some of the features in this text that are designed to enhance your understanding and learning process include:

- **Key Concepts** – At the beginning of each subsection are key concepts, or study objectives, each stated as a question. To be successful in this course, you should be able to answer these questions. So as you read, guide your learning by looking for the answers. When you find the answers, highlight or underline them. It is important that you actually highlight/underline and not just make a mental note, as the action of stopping and writing reinforces your learning. Watch for this symbol:

- **Quick Quizzes** – Following each subsection you will find a Quick Quiz, which checks and reinforces what you read. Circle the answer to each question and then check your answers against the correct answers supplied at the bottom of the quiz. If you missed any questions, flip back to the relevant section and review the material. You will also find explanations to the false questions at the end of each chapter. Watch for this symbol:

- **Examples** – Examples are used frequently to illustrate the concepts being discussed and to help the reader understand and apply the concepts presented. Examples are identified in the margin with the following symbol:

  **EXAMPLE**

- **Exhibits** – The written text is enhanced and simplified by using exhibits where appropriate to promote learning and application. Exhibits are identified with the following symbol:

  **EXHIBIT**

- **Key Terms** – Key terms appear in **boldfaced type** throughout the text to assist in the identification of important concepts and terminology. A list of key terms with definitions appears at the end of each chapter.

- **End of Chapter Questions** – Each chapter contains a series of discussion questions and multiple choice problems that highlight the major topics covered in the chapter. The questions test retention and understanding of important chapter material and can be used for review and classroom discussion.

- **Quick Quiz Explanations** – Each chapter concludes with the answers to the Quick Quizzes contained in that chapter, as well as explanation to the "false" statements in each Quick Quiz.

- **Glossary** – A compilation of the key terms identified throughout the text is located at the end of the book.

**VISIT OUR WEBSITE AT
WWW.MONEY-EDUCATION.COM
FOR UPDATES TO THE TEXT**

# Table of Contents

## 3. FUNDAMENTALS OF INCOME TAX

## 4. GROSS INCOME FROM PERSONAL AND INVESTMENT ACTIVITIES

## 5. GROSS INCOME FROM EMPLOYMENT

## 6. INTRODUCTIONS TO DEDUCTIONS

## 7. ITEMIZED DEDUCTIONS

## 8. OTHER DEDUCTIONS, PENALTIES, AND LOSS DISALLOWANCE

## 9. TAX CREDITS

# 10. BASIS RULES, DEPRECIATION, AND ASSET CATEGORIZATION

# 11. THE TAXATION OF CAPITAL ASSETS

# 12. BUSINESS ASSETS

## 13. NONTAXABLE EXCHANGES

## 14. PASSIVE ACTIVITY RULES

## 15. THE ALTERNATIVE MINIMUM TAX

## 16. BUSINESS ENTITY SELECTION AND TAXATION

## APPENDICES

# Introduction to Income Tax Planning

## INTRODUCTION

Taxes play a significant, although sometimes subtle, role in the daily lives of most Americans. Although some people may only think about the taxes that they file once a year, Americans actually encounter taxes on a daily basis. For example, when someone buys a cup of coffee on his way to work, he generally pays sales tax. When that person fills up his fuel tank on the way home, he pays a federal gasoline excise tax. And of course, if that person is employed, the wages that he earns during the day are subject to federal income taxes, and generally to Social Security and Medicare taxes.

Although most people would agree that taxes are pervasive in our country, not everyone would agree on whether that is a good thing. Oliver Wendall Holmes, Jr., a U.S. Supreme Court Justice, believed that "Taxes are what we pay for a civilized society." Winston Churchill, on the other hand, is known for stating that "There is no such thing as a good tax." Regardless of how one feels about taxes, they cannot be avoided. Income taxes have an impact on almost every topical area of financial planning, every type of entity, every individual who earns income of any kind, and on most financial transactions. The federal government imposes income taxes on the taxable income of individual taxpayers at rates up to 35 percent and most states add additional state income taxes at rates up to 9.5 percent.

## HISTORICAL PERSPECTIVE

Over time, the federal, state, and local tax systems in the United States have changed significantly. These changes have occurred as a result of changes in society and in the role of the government. Some changes have been the result of specific events, while others have occurred more gradually. Regardless of how these changes occurred, it is clear that the types and amounts of taxes collected are vastly different than they were even 50 years ago.

## COLONIAL TIMES

Prior to the Revolutionary War, the most common types of taxes were excise taxes, tariffs, and customs duties. In 1765, England imposed a series of taxes on the American colonies because it needed revenues to pay for its wars against France. Colonists were forced to pay these taxes even though they were not represented in the English Parliament. Consequently, the belief that "taxation without representation is tyranny" became closely associated with the American Revolution and established a persistent wariness regarding taxation as part of the American culture.

## THE POST REVOLUTIONARY ERA

Despite their wariness regarding taxation, the writers of the Constitution recognized that the federal government needed a source of revenue, and as a result, the federal government was given the power to raise taxes. However, most of the taxes imposed by Congress were similar to the taxes that existed prior to the Revolutionary War (i.e., excise taxes or tariffs).

In the late 1790s, the federal government imposed the first direct taxes on the owners of houses, land, slaves, and estates. Direct taxes are recurring taxes paid directly by the taxpayer to the government based on the value of certain items. When Thomas Jefferson was elected president in 1802, direct taxes were abolished and for the next 10 years there were no internal revenue taxes other than excise taxes.

To raise money for the War of 1812, Congress imposed additional excise taxes, raised certain customs duties, and raised money by issuing Treasury notes. In 1817 Congress repealed these taxes, and for the next 44 years the federal government collected no internal revenue. Instead, the government received most of its revenue from high customs duties and through the sale of public land.

## THE CIVIL WAR

Congress passed the Revenue Act of 1861, which restored earlier excise taxes and imposed a tax on personal incomes, as a result of the outbreak of the Civil War. The income tax was levied at three percent on all incomes greater than $800 a year. This tax on personal income was a new direction for a federal tax system based mainly on excise taxes and customs duties. Certain inadequacies of the income tax were quickly acknowledged by Congress and thus none was collected until the following year. By the spring of 1862, it was clear that the federal government had significant revenue needs and Congress passed many new excise taxes as a result.

After the war ended, the need for federal revenue fell sharply and most taxes were repealed. By 1868, the main source of government revenue was derived from liquor and tobacco taxes. The income tax was abolished in 1872. From 1868 to 1913, almost 90 percent of all revenue was collected from the remaining excise taxes.

## THE 16TH AMENDMENT

Under the Constitution, Congress could impose direct taxes only if they were levied in proportion to each state's population. Thus, when a flat rate federal income tax was enacted in 1894, it was quickly challenged. In 1895, the U.S. Supreme Court ruled that the federal income tax was unconstitutional because it was a direct tax not apportioned according to the population of each state.

Eventually, a constitutional amendment was proposed that would allow the federal government to impose tax on individuals' incomes without regard to the population of each state. By 1913, 36 states had ratified the 16th Amendment to the Constitution. Congress subsequently passed a new income tax law with rates beginning at one percent and rising to seven percent for taxpayers with income in excess of $500,000. Less than one percent of the population paid income tax at that time. Form 1040 was introduced as the standard income tax reporting form and, though changed in many ways over the years, remains in use today.

## WORLD WAR I AND THE 1920'S

The entry of the United States into World War I greatly increased the need for revenue and Congress responded by passing the 1916 Revenue Act. The 1916 Act raised the lowest income tax rate from one percent to two percent and raised the top rate to 15 percent on taxpayers with income in excess of $1.5 million. The 1916 Act also imposed taxes on estates and excess business profits. However, the federal government's need for revenue was still not met, and as a result, the War Revenue Act of 1917 lowered income tax exemptions and greatly increased income tax rates. In 1916, a taxpayer needed $1.5 million in taxable income to face a 15 percent rate. By 1917, a taxpayer with only $40,000 faced a 16 percent rate and the individual with $1.5 million faced a tax rate of 67 percent.

Another revenue act was passed in 1918, which hiked income tax rates once again, this time raising the bottom rate to six percent and the top rate to 77 percent. These changes increased revenue from $761 million in 1916 to $3.6 billion in 1918, which represented about 25 percent of Gross Domestic Product (GDP). Even in 1918, however, only five percent of the population paid income taxes, and yet the income tax funded one-third of the cost of the war.

The economy boomed during the 1920s and increasing revenues from the income tax followed. These increasing revenues allowed Congress to cut the income tax rates five times, ultimately returning the lowest tax rate to one percent and reducing the top income tax rate to 25 percent. These tax cuts reduced the federal tax burden as a share of GDP to 13 percent. As income tax rates and tax collections declined, the economy was strengthened.

In October of 1929 the stock market crash marked the beginning of the Great Depression. As the economy shrank, government receipts also fell. In the face of rising budget deficits which reached $2.7 billion in 1931, Congress followed the prevailing economic wisdom at the time and increased income tax rates once again. By 1936 the lowest income tax rate had reached four percent and the top rate was 79 percent.

## THE SOCIAL SECURITY TAX

The state of the economy during the Great Depression led to the passage of the Social Security Act in 1935. This law provided payments known as "unemployment compensation" to workers who lost their jobs. Other sections of the Act gave public aid to the aged, the needy, the handicapped, and to certain minors. These programs were financed by a two percent payroll tax, one-half of which was subtracted directly from an employee's paycheck and one-half was collected from employers on the employee's behalf. The tax was levied on the first $3,000 of the employee's salary or wages.

## WORLD WAR II

Even before the United States entered World War II, increased defense spending led to the passage of two income tax laws in 1940 that increased individual and corporate taxes, and they were followed by another income tax hike in 1941. By the end of the war, reductions in exemption levels meant that taxpayers with taxable incomes of only $500 faced a bottom income tax rate of 23 percent, while taxpayers with income over $1 million faced a top income tax rate of 94 percent.

## DEVELOPMENTS AFTER WORLD WAR II

Throughout the 1950s, tax policy was increasingly seen as a tool for raising revenue, for changing the incentives in the economy, and also as a tool for stabilizing macroeconomic activity. The economy remained subject to frequent boom and bust cycles and many policymakers readily accepted the new economic policy of raising or lowering income taxes and spending to adjust aggregate demand and thereby smooth the business cycle. Even so, however, the maximum income tax rate in 1954 remained at 87 percent of taxable income. While the income tax underwent some revision or amendment almost every year, certain years marked especially significant changes.

Beginning in the late 1960s and continuing through the 1970s, the United States experienced persistent and rising inflation rates, which ultimately reached 13.3 percent in 1979. Combined with rising inflation and a heavy regulatory burden, the high income tax rates caused the economy to under-perform badly, all of which laid the groundwork for the Reagan tax cut, also known as the Economic Recovery Tax Act of 1981.

## THE REAGAN TAX CUT

The Economic Recovery Tax Act of 1981, which enjoyed strong bipartisan support in Congress, represented a fundamental shift in the course of federal income tax policy. The Act featured a 25 percent reduction in individual income tax rates, phased in over three years, and indexed the rates for inflation thereafter. This brought the top income tax bracket down to 50 percent.

As inflation came down and as more and more of the tax cuts from the 1981 Act went into effect, the economy began a strong and sustained pattern of growth. Though the painful medicine of disinflation slowed and initially hid the process, the beneficial effects of marginal rate cuts and reductions in the disincentives to invest took hold as promised.

EXHIBIT 1.1

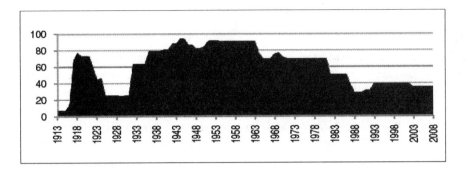

## THE TAX REFORM ACT OF 1986

Following the enactment of the 1981, 1982, and 1984 tax changes, there was a growing sense that the income tax was in need of a more fundamental overhaul. In his 1984 State of the Union speech, President Reagan called for a sweeping reform of the income tax so it would have a broader base and lower rates and would be fairer, simpler, and more consistent with economic efficiency.

The culmination of this effort was the Tax Reform Act of 1986, which brought the top statutory income tax rate down from 50 percent to 28 percent while the top corporate income tax rate was reduced from 50 percent to 35 percent. The number of tax brackets was reduced and the personal exemption and standard deduction amounts were both increased and indexed for inflation, thereby relieving millions of taxpayers of any federal income tax burden. However, the Act also created new personal and corporate alternative minimum taxes.

The 1986 Tax Reform Act was roughly revenue neutral; that is, it was not intended to raise or lower overall tax revenues, but it shifted some of the tax burden from individuals to businesses. Much of the increase in the tax on businesses was the result of an increase in the tax on business capital formation. From a broader perspective, the 1986 Tax Reform Act represented the penultimate installment of an extraordinary process of tax rate reductions. Over the 22-year period from 1964 to 1986 the top individual income tax rate was reduced from 91 to 28 percent. However, because upper-income taxpayers increasingly chose to receive their income in taxable form, and because of the broadening of the tax base, the progressivity of the tax system actually rose during this period.

Between 1986 and 1990 the federal tax burden rose as a share of GDP from 17.5 to 18 percent. Despite this increase in the overall tax burden, persistent budget deficits due to even higher levels of government spending created near constant pressure to increase taxes. Thus, in 1990 Congress enacted a significant tax increase featuring an increase in the top income tax rate to 31 percent. Shortly after his election, President Clinton insisted on, and Congress enacted, a second major tax increase in 1993 in which the top income tax rate was raised to 36 percent and a 10 percent surcharge was added, leaving the effective top income tax rate at 39.6 percent.

The Taxpayer Relief Act of 1997 made additional changes to the income tax code providing a modest tax cut. The centerpiece of the 1997 Act was a significant new tax benefit to certain families with children through the child tax credit. The 1997 Act launched the modern proliferation of individual tax credits and especially refundable credits that are in essence spending programs operating through the tax system.

## THE BUSH TAX CUT

By 2001, the total tax take had produced a projected unified budget surplus of $281 billion, with a cumulative 10-year projected surplus of $5.6 trillion. Much of this surplus reflected a rising tax burden as a share of GDP due to the interaction of rising real incomes and a progressive income tax rate structure. Consequently, Congress halted the projected future increases in the tax burden by passing the Economic Growth and Tax Relief and Reconciliation Act of 2001. The centerpiece of the 2001 tax cut was to regain some of the ground lost in the 1990s in terms of lower marginal income tax rates. Though the rate reductions are to be phased in over many years, ultimately the top income tax rate fell from 39.6 percent to 35 percent.

## INCOME TAXES AND THE IRS

The Internal Revenue Service, a bureau of the United States Department of the Treasury, is charged with the daunting task of providing America's taxpayers with top quality service by helping them understand and meet their tax responsibilities and by applying the tax law with integrity and fairness to all. The IRS has over 100,000 employees and based on the number of tax returns filed each year, it is easy to see why the IRS requires so many employees.

| EXHIBIT 1.2 | NUMBER OF RETURNS FILED, BY TYPE OF RETURN, FISCAL YEARS 2007 AND 2008 |

| TYPE OF RETURN | 2007 | 2008 | PERCENTAGE CHANGE |
|---|---|---|---|
| **United States, Total** | **235,438,000** | **250,379,000** | **6.3%** |
| Income Tax | 183,091,000 | 197,409,000 | 7.8% |
|   Individual | 138,894,000 | 154,346,000 | 11.1% |
|     Forms 1040, 1040A, 1040EZ | 138,131,000 | 153,308,000 | 11.0% |
|     Forms 1040NR, 1040NR-EZ, 1040-SS, 1040C | 763,000 | 1,038,000 | 36.0% |
|   Individual Estimated Tax | 29,996,000 | 28,782,000 | -4.0% |
|   Estate and Trust | 3,718,000 | 3,075,000 | -17.3% |
|   Estate and Trust Estimated Tax | 780,000 | 922,000 | 18.2% |
|   Partnership | 3,097,000 | 3,307,000 | 6.8% |
|   S Corporation | 4,099,000 | 4,440,000 | 8.3% |
|   C or other Corporation | 2,508,000 | 2,538,000 | 1.2% |
| Estate Tax | 50,000 | 46,000 | -8.0% |
| Gift Tax | 253,000 | 252,000 | -0.4% |
| Employment Taxes | 30,740,000 | 30,683,000 | -0.2% |
| Tax-Exempt Organization | 901,000 | 901,000 | 0% |
| Excise Taxes | 907,000 | 865,000 | -4.6% |
| Supplemental Documents | 19,496,000 | 20,221,000 | 3.7% |

*Source: Internal Revenue Service Data Book, 2008*

As shown in Exhibit 1.2, the IRS is responsible for processing and reviewing many types of tax returns. In addition to receiving or processing a large number of tax returns (in excess of 235,000,000), the IRS also pursues a significant amount of collections. As shown in Exhibit 1.3, the IRS collected more than $2.3 trillion dollars in 2007. Note that individual income taxes make up both the largest number of returns and the largest amount of net collections. This is consistent with data from the Office of Management and Budget indicating that individual income taxes make up more than 40 percent of the revenues of the federal government.

**INTERNAL REVENUE COLLECTIONS AND REFUNDS, BY TYPE OF TAX (2008)**  EXHIBIT 1.3

| Type of Tax | Gross Collections* | | 2008 Refunds | Net Collections* | |
|---|---|---|---|---|---|
| | 2008 | Percentage of 2008 Total | | 2008 | Percentage of 2008 Total |
| United States, Total | $2,745,035,410 | 100.0% | $428,838,202 | $2,316,197,206 | 100.0% |
| Corporation Income Tax | $354,315,825 | 12.9% | $53,569,392 | $300,746,433 | 13.0% |
| Individual Income Tax | $1,425,990,183 | 52.0% | $366,132,092 | $1,059,858,091 | 45.8% |
| Employment Taxes | $883,197,626 | 32.2% | $5,713,515 | $877,484,111 | 37.9% |
| Estate and Gift Taxes | $29,823,935 | 1.1% | $1,021,742 | $28,802,193 | 1.2% |
| Excise Taxes | $51,707,840 | 1.9% | $2,401,462 | $49,306,378 | 2.1% |

*Money amounts are in thousands of dollars*
*Source: Internal Revenue Service Data Book, 2008*

## OVERVIEW OF FEDERAL INCOME TAXATION

Prior to introducing the technical rules governing income taxation, an overview of the basic themes that will consistently emerge in the text is helpful. Having a broad overview of the income tax system may make some of the specific rules of taxation a bit easier to understand. This section is arranged in three primary parts: (1) the three tax systems; (2) basic rules of income taxation; and (3) the triads of income taxation. Many of the major issues encountered in income taxation will come in sets of three, hence the *triads of taxation*. While we have not included all of the possible sets of three in this section, the ones included are intended to give a brief introduction and understanding of how the tax system works.

When reviewing these rules, keep in mind that there will always be exceptions. Tax law is often structured so that while a general rule applies, which covers most situations encountered, special circumstances are covered by exceptions to that general rule. To make things even more confusing, there are even some exceptions to the exceptions (which brings you back to the general rule). Some, but not all, of the major exceptions to the general rules covered below are presented here. Remember that the purpose of this section of the text is to give a broad overview of how our tax law is structured; it is not intended to be an exhaustive review of the rules – that is what the rest of the text is for.

## THE THREE TAX SYSTEMS

In the United States, there are three separate and distinct tax systems that are relevant to financial planning: (1) the income tax system, (2) the estate and gift tax system, and (3) the generation skipping transfer tax system. While many individuals assume that the Internal Revenue Code is one set of rules that all work together, this is not the case. There are three tax systems, and those systems do not always fit together perfectly. It is important for tax professionals and financial planners to understand which tax system they are dealing with when engaging in a transaction. It is possible, for example, for one single transaction to be treated as a gift for income tax purposes and as a sale for estate and gift tax purposes. The tax consequences for income tax purposes and for estate/gift tax purposes will, therefore, differ. This text covers income tax rules. The gift and estate tax system, and the generation skipping transfer tax system, are covered in *Estate Planning for Financial Planners* by Michael A. Dalton and Thomas P. Langdon.

## BASIC RULES OF INCOME TAXATION

As you study income taxation, you will find that two primary rules apply that can often be used to determine the income tax consequences of a transaction. These two rules are:

1. All accretions to wealth, from whatever source derived, constitute income; and
2. For every deduction taken for income tax purposes, there must be an inclusion in income. (But keep in mind there are exceptions even to these two rules.)

## ALL ACCRETIONS TO WEALTH CONSTITUTE INCOME

Generally, any accretion (increase) in wealth, from any source and in any form, is subject to income taxation. U.S. citizens are subject to income tax on their worldwide income whether or not that income is reported to the IRS on a tax form (such as a W-2 or 1099). Income is not limited to cash compensation – it can be received in many forms, including cash, property, or even as an exchange of services (a bartering transaction) or as forgiveness of a debt that is due. Generally, any time someone's wealth has measurably increased, they will have to pay income tax on that increase in wealth. There are some limitations that apply to this principle. An individual will not have to pay tax on income that is not yet measurable, or realized. For example, if a taxpayer purchases a stock today, and its value increases by $10 by the end of the year, the taxpayer will not have to pay income tax on the increased value. The value of the stock could increase or decrease by the time the stock is sold, so the taxpayer's actual increase in wealth is not measurable until the stock is sold or transferred. In this case, the gain on the stock will be realized on sale.

The courts, and Congress, have classified certain types of increases in wealth as something other than income, thereby exempting those amounts from income tax. Continuing our example from above, when the taxpayer sells the stock that she purchased, the amount that she paid for the stock, or her taxable basis, will be received income tax free. Basis represents previously taxed income that is invested in an asset, and is exempt from tax to prevent the taxpayer from being subject to a double tax on the same income. In this example, if basis were not received income tax free on the sale of an asset the basis would be taxed twice - once when it was originally earned and once when the asset it was used to purchase was sold. The tax-free return of basis is sometimes referred to as the capital recovery doctrine.

Another example of an exclusion from income is the receipt of life insurance proceeds upon the death of the insured. The receipt of the tax-free death benefit is certainly a good thing for the family of the deceased individual, but it is also good for society. By exempting life insurance proceeds from income tax, Congress is encouraging individuals to purchase life insurance to protect their families in the event of their untimely death. To the extent that these risks are privately funded, there is less likelihood that the surviving family members will need to receive government assistance through welfare type payments. Congress is said to pass these types of exclusions for public policy reasons. Keep an eye out for this as you study the income tax rules – many of the exceptions to the general rules (such as the tax-free receipt of death benefits from a life insurance policy) are enacted to serve various public-policy purposes.

## FOR EVERY DEDUCTION, THERE MUST BE AN INCLUSION

The second basic rule governing our income tax system is that for every deduction taken on an income tax return, there must be an inclusion in income somewhere in the tax system. This principle is important for two reasons: (1) to be entitled to deduct something on a tax return, a taxpayer must have included that amount in income; and (2) if a taxpayer claims a deduction, that deduction should be income (and therefore subject to income tax) on someone else's return.

A common example of the requirement that taxpayers can only deduct what is already included in their gross income comes into play in charitable giving. Many individuals volunteer time to charitable causes that are important to them, and sometimes they do this in lieu of working for compensation. Since the taxpayer's time is valuable, and represents forgone income, taxpayers often ask if they can deduct the value of their time. The answer, of course, is no. The taxpayer cannot deduct the value of time as a charitable deduction because the value of time was not first included in income.

When a taxpayer claims a deduction, that deduction usually results in income for someone else. For example, if a taxpayer purchases supplies and equipment, or purchases services in furtherance of some business activity, the taxpayer is entitled to a deduction, but the person from whom the goods or services were purchased now has income. Likewise, when a taxpayer pays mortgage interest to a bank, a mortgage interest deduction is generally available, but the bank has mortgage interest income upon receipt of the interest payment.

The major exceptions to this principle are found in retirement planning and charitable planning.

When a taxpayer makes a gift of cash or property to a charity, a charitable deduction can be claimed on their income tax return, but the charity, as a tax exempt entity, is not required to pay income tax on the amount received. In addition, a special exception applies when a taxpayer makes a gift of appreciated property to a charity, and has met the long-term holding rule requirement with respect to that property. The value of the charitable deduction is the fair market value of the property contributed, even though the taxpayer is not required to recognize the gain on the property and include that gain in income.

When a business makes a contribution to a qualified retirement plan on behalf of its employees, it is entitled to an income tax deduction for the amount contributed. The employees, however, will not report the income in the current year – they will report and pay tax on the income when they take distributions from the qualified plan many years later.

These exceptions to the general rule both facilitate public policy objectives of Congress. Private funding of charitable organizations serves the public interest, as does the funding of qualified plans that will provide retirement income for workers. The general rule, in these cases, is thus modified to achieve Congress' public policy objectives.

## TRIADS OF INCOME TAXATION

As mentioned earlier, income tax rules tend to come in threes. Exposure to these triads of income taxation should help you understand the purpose of the specific income tax rules that are presented in the chapters that follow. In summary, the triads covered here include:

- three types of income
- three types of tax accounting
- three key tax principles
- three components for classifying gains
- three types of assets
- three uses of assets
- three types of rental real estate
- three methods of tax planning
- three anti-abuse provisions
- three types of administrative rulings
- three types of final regulations
- three courts to resolve disputes

### *Three Types of Income*

In the U.S. income tax system, there are three types of income: (1) active (ordinary) income, (2) portfolio income, and (3) passive income. Every bit of income earned by a taxpayer must be classified into one of these three categories.

Active income is income derived from labor, and income connected with the active conduct of a trade or business. Portfolio income is income derived from investments, such as interest, dividends, and capital gains. Passive income is income derived from dealings in real estate and from the conduct of a trade or business in which the taxpayer does not participate.

Categorization of income is important for two reasons: (1) different tax consequences apply to each type of income; and (2) the "bucket rule" limits a taxpayer's ability to write off losses in one income bucket only to the gains in that same bucket.

Active income (and loss) is subject to ordinary income tax rates, which are the highest tax rates in our system. Some types of portfolio income are subject to favorable income tax rates, such as the 15 percent rate that applies to long-term capital gains and qualified dividends. Passive income is subject to a host of anti-abuse rules, and therefore constitutes a separate category of income.

The "bucket rule" limits losses in one bucket to gains in the same bucket. For example, if a taxpayer incurred $5,000 in investment gains and $20,000 in investment losses, $5,000 of the loss could offset the investment gain but could not, under the bucket rule, be used to offset other types of income (such as ordinary or passive income). As in all other areas of tax law, there are exceptions to this rule. In the case of portfolio losses, up to $3,000 of net losses in the portfolio bucket can be used to offset either active or passive income. These rules will be discussed more fully in the chapters on the taxation of property transactions.

## Three Types of Tax Accounting

For income to be reported properly, taxpayers must follow some method to account for income. There are three methods of accounting that are used for federal income tax purposes: (1) the cash method, (2) the accrual method, and (3) the hybrid method.

The cash method of accounting is the method used by most individuals and small businesses. Under the cash method, income is taxed when it is received, and allowable deductions are claimed when they are paid. Understanding the cash method is particularly important for financial planners, who are typically providing financial advice and planning to individuals and small businesses.

The accrual method of accounting is the method frequently used by larger businesses. Under the accrual method of accounting, income is taxed when it is earned (whether or not it has been received), and deductions are claimed when they are incurred (whether or not they have been paid).

Any method of accounting other than the cash method or accrual method that is approved by the IRS is referred to, collectively, as the hybrid method. The hybrid method is used by some businesses to better reflect their economic income on their income tax returns

Chapter 3 reviews the methods of tax accounting in more detail, and covers the exceptions to the general rules governing each accounting method listed above.

## Three Key Tax Principles

Three key tax principles underlie personal income taxation. They are: (1) the doctrine of constructive receipt, (2) the economic benefit doctrine, and (3) the doctrine of the fruit and the tree.

While most individuals account for their income using the cash method, certain circumstances may arise that will subject income that has not yet been received to current taxation. The doctrine of constructive receipt states that if income is permanently set aside in an account for the benefit of a taxpayer, or if a taxpayer is given the choice to receive income now or defer it to the future, that income will be taxed to the taxpayer currently even if he does not receive it until sometime in the future. For example, consider interest that is earned on a three-year certificate of deposit. Even though a taxpayer does not receive the interest until the certificate of deposit matures, he is taxed on the earned interest currently, since the interest earnings are permanently set aside in an account for the taxpayer's benefit.

The doctrine of constructive receipt (income that is permanently set aside in an account for the taxpayer's benefit) is a special exception to the cash-basis method of income tax accounting. The doctrine states that even if you have not actually received the income, if you have constructively received it, then it is income. For example, if a taxpayer goes to his mailbox on December 31st and sees a check made out to that taxpayer for work he performed, immediately closes the mailbox, and comes back to get the check on January 1st, the income is reported as of December 31st. In fact, the doctrine of constructive receipt is at the cornerstone of retirement planning, and constructive receipt must be avoided if a taxpayer wishes to defer income and taxes into the future to fund his or her retirement.

You may recall from our discussion above that all income received by a taxpayer, in any form, is subject to income tax. The economic benefit doctrine simply states that if a taxpayer receives an economic benefit as income, the value of that benefit will be subject to tax. For example, if a taxpayer is provided group term life insurance by an employer, the value of that group term insurance is subject to income tax, since it is an economic benefit received in return for labor. Congress has, however, for public policy reasons, exempted part of the value of group term life insurance from income tax, but excess amounts are taxable under the economic benefit doctrine.

The third key principal of income taxation is that income is taxed to either, (1) the person who earns it; or (2) the person who owns the asset that produced the income. This principle is referred to as the doctrine of the fruit and the tree. He who owns the tree pays income tax on the fruit that the tree produces. This doctrine is really an anti-abuse provision. It is designed to prevent taxpayers from assigning income to a family member in a lower income tax bracket while retaining the asset that produces the income.

### Three Components for Classifying Gain

When property is sold, the manner of taxation will depend on (1) the type of asset that was held; (2) the use to which the asset was put; and (3) the holding period (how long the asset was held). Two of these criteria are specified in their own sections, below. The holding period requirement will be discussed in more detail in Chapter 11 on property transactions.

### Three Types of Assets

In the U.S. income tax system, there are only three types of assets: (1) capital assets, (2) ordinary income assets, and (3) IRC Section 1231 assets. To properly determine the tax consequences upon the sale or disposition of property, the taxpayer must first know what type of property was sold. Each type of asset has different income tax consequences and rules. Depending on the type of asset, different income tax rates may apply, or different loss limitation rules may be imposed. The first step that a financial planner should take in determining the tax consequences of a sale of property is to identify the property by its asset type. The rules concerning property transactions are covered in detail in Chapters 11, 12, and 13 of the text.

### Three Uses of Assets

Another factor that impacts the tax treatment associated with a sale or disposition of property is how that asset was used by the taxpayer. Individuals can use an asset in three ways: (1) they can use it for personal purposes; (2) they can use it in the active conduct of a trade or business; or (3) they can use it for the production of income. Personal use assets include such things as personal residences, cars, furniture, and the like. Business assets include any assets used in the active conduct of a trade or business, such as machinery, equipment, and real estate. Production of income assets include stocks and bonds and other assets held for investment. When attempting to determine the tax consequences resulting from the sale of property, a planner should (1) determine the type of asset, and (2) determine how that asset was used by the taxpayer. The tax rates and loss limitation rules may differ depending on the use to which a taxpayer puts an asset as well as the type of asset that is sold. The rules concerning property transactions are covered in detail in Chapters 11, 12, and 13 of the text.

### Three Types of Rental Real Estate

Real estate has always received special attention in both our legal and tax systems. When real estate is held for rental purposes, it is considered trade or business property because of the for profit purpose. The tax consequences on the sale of rental real estate, however, will depend on how that rental real estate was used. There are three types of rental real estate activities: (1) tax-free rental activities, (2) rental use activities, and (3) mixed use activities. The income inclusion and deduction rules differ depending on the use to which the rental real estate was put. The tax rules concerning rental activities are covered in detail in Chapter 8.

### Three Methods of Tax Planning

Planners need to know the income tax rules so they can help clients minimize exposure to taxation while achieving their desired goals. There are three primary ways to engage in this type of planning. The planner and client can (1) legally avoid taxation; (2) deduct expenses to reduce taxable income and take tax credits to reduce taxes due; or (3) defer income and thus defer taxation. In addition to these three primary ways to engage in tax planning, two additional methods should be considered. The planner may be able to help clients (4) shift income to related taxpayers in lower income tax brackets, or (5) realize income in a form that is taxed at lower tax rates (long-term capital gains or qualified dividends).

### Three Anti-Abuse Provisions

While tax planning is useful in assisting taxpayers to minimize their income tax liability, too much tax planning could lead to wealthy individuals paying very little tax compared to the rest of the population. Congress has imposed three sets of anti-abuse rules that limit the benefits that can be obtained from tax minimization planning. The three sets of anti-abuse rules are (1) the alternative minimum tax (AMT), (2) the at-risk rule limitations, and (3) the passive activity rules. The AMT is discussed in Chapter 15, and the at-risk rule limitations and passive activity loss rules are discussed in Chapter 14. These rules are designed to ensure that everybody pays a fair share of income tax on an annual basis.

### Three Types of Administrative Rulings

In an attempt to administer the tax system efficiently, and provide taxpayers with information about how to treat various transactions, the Internal Revenue Service issues three types of written rulings: (1) Revenue Rulings, (2) Private Letter Rulings, and (3) Determination Letters. These rulings are important for tax research, and are covered in more depth in Chapter 2.

### Three Types of Final Regulations

The Treasury also gives guidance to taxpayers in the form of Treasury Regulations. Once finalized, the Treasury Regulations take one of three forms: (1) Procedural Regulations, (2) Interpretative Regulations, and (3) Legislative Regulations. From a tax-research standpoint, the Treasury Regulations provide a wealth of knowledge about how the statutory law enacted by Congress will be enforced. Some of the regulations constitute law in and of themselves. The types and uses of Treasury Regulations are covered in more depth in Chapter 2.

### Three Courts to Resolve Disputes

Sometimes, when the IRS and a taxpayer cannot agree on how to treat a certain transaction for income tax purposes, an independent third party is necessary to resolve the dispute. There are three courts that may resolve income tax matters: (1) the U.S. Tax Court, (2) the U.S. District Court, and (3) the U.S. Court of Federal Claims. The requirements for bringing a case to the various courts will be discussed in detail in Chapter 2.

## SUMMARY

While this review is not intended to be a substitute for the detail that follows in the subsequent chapters, it does present a summary of some of the overriding themes that present themselves in a Federal Income Tax course. Understanding these basic principles may assist you in developing a deeper understanding of the more complex rules of Federal Income Taxation.

## PERSPECTIVE OF THE TEXT

The perspective of this text is that of a professional tax planner and financial planner who is providing professional services to clients with a variety of needs, including income tax planning needs. This textbook presents an essential foundation of income tax principles, concepts, and rules and focuses on income tax planning in a manner that will be useful for tax professionals and financial planners. This focus on the practical application of tax principles and concepts is a distinguishing characteristic of the book.

Although many financial planners are not tax specialists, a competent financial planner should understand the basic principles of income taxation and be able to recognize tax planning opportunities available to each client. In addition, a competent financial planner must know enough about income taxation to avoid giving bad advice because of ignorance of tax laws. Most financial planners who are not tax specialists work with Certified Public Accountants (CPAs), tax attorneys and other tax specialists to assure that each client's tax planning needs are adequately considered. This is part of a team approach that is often used in comprehensive financial planning. Even financial planners who are very knowledgeable about taxation frequently work cooperatively with other professionals in tax and other financial fields to best serve the needs of the client.

Income tax planning is a process that matches a client's goals, needs, attitudes, and financial circumstances with available tax planning options. It is an integral part of financial planning, and income tax planning opportunities pervade the financial planning process. Effective income tax planning requires that the financial planner understand (1) the client's goals and needs (both personal and financial), (2) the client's attitudes (including risk tolerance), (3) the client's financial circumstances, (4) the basic principles of income taxation, (5) the details of the income tax rules related to financial planning topics, and (6) the tax planning opportunities available with respect to the various topical areas addressed in financial planning. This understanding or knowledge base must then be used by the financial planner to identify, recommend, and assist in the implementation of useful tax planning strategies for the client.

EXHIBIT 1.4

- Chapter 2: Working with the Tax Law
- Chapter 3: Fundamentals of Income Tax
- Chapter 4: Gross Income from Personal and Investment Activities
- Chapter 5: Gross Income from Employment
- Chapter 6: Introduction to Deductions
- Chapter 7: Itemized Deductions
- Chapter 8: Other Deductions, Penalties, and Loss Disallowance
- Chapter 9: Tax Credits
- Chapter 10: Basis Rules, Depreciation, and Asset Categorization
- Chapter 11: The Taxation of Capital Assets
- Chapter 12: Business Assets
- Chapter 13: Nontaxable Exchanges
- Chapter 14: Passive Activity Rules
- Chapter 15: The Alternative Minimum Tax
- Chapter 16: Business Entity Selection and Taxation

Chapter 2 introduces concepts related to working with the tax law. The various sources and types of tax law are described. This chapter also covers the basics of the audit process and the various penalties to which a taxpayer may be subject if he does not follow the tax laws. Finally, the framework within which tax controversies are resolved is described, including taxpayers' options for appealing the decision of a court or administrative body.

Chapters 3 through 9 describe the income tax system and the calculation of gross income and tax liability. Chapter 3 first introduces the basic concepts of income taxation, including how to determine a taxpayer's filing status, how to determine the appropriate number of personal and dependency exemptions, and how to calculate the tax liability based on a given level of taxable income. Chapter 4 then provides in-depth coverage of various personal and investment activities that generate items that are included and excluded from gross income. Chapter 5 also deals with inclusions and exclusions from gross income, but focuses on items that are related to employment. Chapter 5 includes an extensive discussion of the taxation of fringe benefits. Chapter 6 introduces the concept of a deduction and discusses above-the-line deductions or adjustments to income. Chapter 7 takes this discussion a step further and examines the various itemized deductions to which a taxpayer may be entitled. Chapter 8 considers the limitations on deductions that can be taken against income. Finally, Chapter 9 discusses the tax credits that may be available to help taxpayers reduce their tax liability, or even create an income tax refund.

Chapters 10 through 14 examine the taxation of property transactions including sales and other dispositions. Chapter 10 introduces the concepts of basis, depreciation, and how assets should be categorized for tax purposes. Chapter 11 further examines the tax consequences of transactions involving capital assets. Chapter 12 delves into the tax consequences of transactions involving business assets. Chapter 13 discusses nontaxable exchanges, or transactions that may result in no tax assuming that the specified requirements are met. Chapter 14 contains a discussion of the passive activity rules, which limit a taxpayer's ability to recognize losses associated with the passive activities.

Chapter 15 explores the alternative minimum tax, the stated purpose of which is to prevent taxpayers with high incomes from paying little or no income tax by taking advantage of various preferences in the tax code. However, the number of taxpayers who are affected by the AMT is increasing.

Finally, Chapter 16 discusses the characteristics and taxation of various legal entities, including C corporations, S corporations, partnerships, and LLCs. This discussion is particularly useful to financial planners whose clients may be considering starting a business. Entity selection can affect not only the taxation of the business, but the taxation of the business owner as well.

# Working with the Tax Law

## INTRODUCTION

To many, the tax law seems to be an endless maze of confusing rules and exceptions. Understanding how these rules and exceptions fit together and how they can be used for financial planning purposes seems to be a daunting task. Once the structure of the rules is understood, however, the laws are easier to navigate and their significance for financial planning becomes apparent. The purpose of this chapter is to present the basic structure of our tax system, and how various components of that system can be used by taxpayers in their planning.

## SOURCES OF TAX LAW

There are three primary sources of tax law: statutory sources, administrative sources, and judicial sources. These sources of law reflect the structure of our political system.

Before we elaborate on the direct sources of tax law, however, it is important to understand the origin of our income tax system. As originally adopted, the U.S. Constitution did not give the federal government the ability to collect a tax on income. At the founding of our nation, there was a great deal of suspicion surrounding the new, federal, centralized government, and the states did not want the power of the federal government to get out of hand. Consequently, they imposed limitations on the federal government's ability to impose taxes. As time went on, however, and as the federal government began to assume a more active governance role, a source of revenue was

### Key Concepts

**Underline/highlight the answers to these questions as you read:**

1. Identify the three primary sources of tax law.

2. Describe the legal basis for the modern income tax.

3. Explain the process through which statutory tax law is established.

4. Identify the sources of administrative tax law.

needed to fund the cost of these activities. While Congress had enacted an income tax on several previous occasions, these taxes were either temporary, or were declared unconstitutional by the Supreme Court. With the obvious need for revenue, and the Supreme Court's decree that a federal income tax was unconstitutional, it became clear that a constitutional amendment would be needed to grant the Congress the power to lay and collect taxes on income.

On February 25, 1913, the **16th Amendment** to the U.S. Constitution was adopted. This short amendment stated, "The Congress shall have power to lay and collect taxes on income, from whatever source derived, without apportionment among the several States, and without regard to any census or enumeration."

The Constitution, through enactment of the $16^{th}$ Amendment, became the foundation for of income tax law in the United States. Two clauses of the $16^{th}$ Amendment are particularly important in developing an understanding of our income tax system: (1) the "power to lay and collect taxes on income," and (2) the clause "from whatever source derived."

As you will see from the in-depth definition of "income" in Chapter 3, the term "income" is not as easily interpreted as it may first seem. Generally, any accretion to an individual's wealth is income, and is therefore subject to taxation. However, when certain proposals seem to have gone too far, limitations on the definition of income have been imposed by various branches of the government. Exemptions and exclusions also allow some accretions to wealth to avoid income taxes altogether. We will discuss these items more specifically in future chapters.

As the second important clause from the $16^{th}$ Amendment indicates, a U.S. citizen is subject to income tax on income "from whatever source derived." In other words, the worldwide income of U.S. citizens from any source is subject to taxation by the U.S.

| EXHIBIT 2.1 | SOURCES OF TAX LAW |
| --- | --- |

| SOURCE | AUTHORITY | LAW |
| --- | --- | --- |
| **Statutory** | Congressionally derived law through legislative power provided by the $16^{th}$ Amendment to the U.S. Constitution. | Internal Revenue Code of 1986, as amended. |
| **Administrative** | • **Treasury Department:** Executive authority of law enforcement delegated to the Treasury Department. <br><br> • **Internal Revenue Service:** Tax collection authority delegated by the Treasury Department to the Internal Revenue Service. | • **Treasury Regulations:** <br>  a. Proposed Regulations <br>  b. Temporary Regulations <br>  c. Final Regulations <br> • **IRS Determinations:** <br>  a. Revenue Rulings <br>  b. Private Letter Rulings <br>  c. Determination Letters <br>  d. Revenue Procedures |
| **Judicial** | Judicial authority to determine if tax laws enacted by Congress and enforced by the President are constitutional. Also, decides whether a regulation or IRS position follows the intent of Congress. | **Case Law:** Usually a case or controversy between a taxpayer and the IRS resulting in case law expressed in the opinion of a court. |

## STATUTORY SOURCES OF TAX LAW

While the 16th Amendment gave Congress the authority to "lay and collect" an income tax, it did not actually impose an income tax on the citizenry. Shortly after the passage of the 16th Amendment, Congress passed the Revenue Act of 1913 - the first version of the law that would become known as the Internal Revenue Code.

Since 1913, the entire body of statutory law concerning income taxation has been codified three times: 1939, 1954, and 1986. The present Internal Revenue Code is referred to as the "Internal Revenue Code of 1986, as amended."

The Internal Revenue Code (the "Code") is the statutory source of law on taxation. Since the 16th Amendment to the Constitution gave Congress the power to collect and levy taxes on income from whatever source derived, the Code must be adhered to unless the courts declare that a provision of the Code is unconstitutional. Given that the 16th Amendment permits Congress to impose a tax on income, but does not impose any restrictions on that power, it is rare to find circumstances where provisions of the income tax code as enacted by Congress will be found unconstitutional by the courts. The relatively few cases that have been heard by the courts on this matter tend to deal with the definition of income. Certainly, if something is not legally classified as income, Congress does not have the power to tax it under the 16th Amendment.

Only Congress can amend the Code, since it is the source of statutory law in the United States. Sometimes, administrative agencies get overzealous in enforcing the provisions of the Code, and attempt to fix holes left by Congress by enacting regulations that go beyond the language of the statute and the intent of Congress. While the administrative agency's intent may seem proper, its action is not – the administrative branch of government cannot change statutory law without congressional action.

Income tax legislation begins as a revenue bill. All revenue bills must arise in the lower house of Congress, the House of Representatives, and may not be initiated by the executive branch, judiciary branch, or Senate. The House Ways and Means Committee has jurisdiction over tax legislation in the House of Representatives. Once tax legislation has passed the House Ways and Means Committee, the entire House of Representatives can consider the tax bill. If the tax bill receives a favorable vote in the House, it is then sent to the Senate for further consideration. The Senate Finance Committee will review the bill, and, if it passes through that Committee, the entire Senate may debate and vote on the proposed legislation.

It is rare to see a proposed tax bill adopted in exactly the same form in both the Senate and the House. Before the bill can be sent to the White House for the President's action, the bill passed by both houses of Congress must be identical. When the versions of the bill differ, the legislature will form a conference committee consisting of representatives from both the House and the Senate whose purpose is to come to a mutually agreeable version of the legislation. In some cases, the House and Senate cannot agree, and the proposed tax legislation fails. In other cases, a workable compromise is reached, and the revised bill is sent to both houses of Congress for further action. If both houses pass the revised legislation, the bill is then sent to the President of the United States.

When tax legislation arrives at the oval office, the President has three options: (1) sign the bill and enact it into law, (2) veto the legislation, or (3) refuse to sign the bill. If the President signs the bill, the new legislation is now part of the body of tax law and is incorporated into the Code. If the President vetoes the bill, Congress can override the President's veto by passing the bill with a two-thirds majority in both houses. If the override is successful, the legislation becomes part of the Code. Overriding a presidential veto is usually a difficult task for Congress, since it is rare to solicit enough support to achieve a two-thirds majority vote in both houses of Congress. If the President fails to sign the bill within 10 days, it becomes law without his signature. If Congress is in adjournment and the President fails to sign the bill within the 10 days allowed by the Constitution, however, the bill does not become law. The latter failure to sign and the resulting failure of the bill to become law is called a pocket veto.

The Internal Revenue Code is the only statutory source of federal tax law, and is the starting point for tax determination and research.

## ADMINISTRATIVE SOURCES OF TAX LAW

The President of the United States is the Chief Executive Officer of the U.S. Government. One of the President's primary duties is to enforce the law. As such, the President is responsible for the collection of taxes in the manner set forth in the Internal Revenue Code.

The President has delegated this authority to the Treasury Department, which in turn created, and delegated tax-collection authority to the Internal Revenue Service.

While enforcement of the Internal Revenue Code has been delegated to the Internal Revenue Service (IRS), the Treasury Department remains involved in the interpretation and clarification of tax law from an administrative standpoint by adopting Treasury regulations. The **Treasury regulations** are official interpretations of the Internal Revenue Code (IRC), and give taxpayers insight into how the Code provisions will be enforced by the IRS. Provided that the Treasury regulations are consistent with the literal provisions of the Internal Revenue Code and Congressional intent at the time the law was passed, the regulations are deemed by the courts to have the full force and effect of law.

There are several types of Treasury regulations, which are easily classified based upon the stage of adoption and the function of the regulation. Those classified based upon the stage of adoption include proposed regulations, temporary regulations, and final regulations. Procedural regulations, interpretative regulations, and legislative regulations indicate the function served by the regulation.

### Stage of Adoption

**Proposed regulations** have been drafted by the Treasury, but have not yet gone through the process of adoption. To adopt the regulation, the Treasury must comply with the provisions of the Administrative Procedures Act (APA). Under the APA, public comments must be solicited, public hearings must be held, and, after taking into consideration the input from the public, the

Treasury will redraft and adopt the regulations. Proposed regulations may be thought of as a first draft of final regulations. They have no legal precedence and are not binding on taxpayers (until the regulations become final).

**Temporary regulations** are issued when the Treasury feels that guidance must be provided quickly to taxpayers. They are typically issued when the regulations will impact a large number of taxpayers, and the IRS wishes to give taxpayers guidance on how a particular provision of the tax code will be interpreted. Unlike proposed regulations, temporary regulations have the same authority as final regulations and are binding on taxpayers once issued. Issuing temporary regulations does not relieve the Treasury of the obligation to satisfy the requirements of the Administrative Procedures Act – temporary regulations are just that…temporary. Temporary regulations are binding on taxpayers pending the adoption of final regulations in concert with the Administrative Procedures Act.

**Final regulations** began as proposed or temporary regulations, but have been adopted formally after compliance with the requirements of the Administrative Procedures Act. Final regulations have the full force and effect of law provided that they are consistent with the Internal Revenue Code provisions they interpret. Final regulations let taxpayers know how the Treasury and IRS will interpret and enforce the tax law. Once issued, they are binding on taxpayers and the Treasury (unless the Treasury takes action to amend the regulations). Courts, however, are not bound by final regulations. To the extent that a court determines that the regulation is not consistent with the Code, that the regulation exceeds the intent of Congress when enacting the Code, or that the regulation is unconstitutional, a Court can invalidate a Treasury regulation.

## Function of Regulation

**Procedural regulations** are merely housekeeping instructions indicating how the Treasury and IRS will conduct their affairs. They are useful to a taxpayer, for example, when the taxpayer would like to request a ruling from the IRS and needs to know how to do so. Procedural regulations do not deal with substantive issues of tax law. Instead, they deal with administration of the tax system.

Most Treasury regulations are **interpretative regulations**. That is, they provide an official interpretation of the Internal Revenue Code. Taxpayers may rely on interpretive regulations in tax planning. If, however, the regulations are not consistent with the Code or do not express the intent of Congress, a taxpayer may take a position in opposition to the regulations. Most likely, when this happens the issue will wind up in court, and the court will have to determine whether the regulation appropriately interprets the law. If the court finds that the regulation is not consistent with Congressional intent, it may invalidate the regulation.

The final type of regulation, a **legislative regulation**, permits the Treasury to determine the details of the law. Legislative regulations have the full force and effect of law as if Congress had passed them. Sometimes when Congress enacts tax legislation, Congress has a general idea of what it would like to accomplish, but has not yet worked out all of the details. Instead of waiting until the details are worked out, it passes the legislation, and includes language to the effect that "the Treasury shall promulgate regulations to effectuate the intent of Congress." When Congress does this, it is delegating part of its law-making authority to the Treasury. Provided that the delegation of authority was limited in scope, was definite, and was not overly broad, when the

Treasury enacts legislative regulations, they are treated as if they were passed by Congress and signed by the President. Unlike interpretative regulation, which can be overturned by the Courts if the Courts determine that the regulations were inconsistent with the intent of Congress, legislative regulations may only be overturned by the Courts if they are determined to be unconstitutional.

### The Internal Revenue Service

Regulations issued by the Treasury are one source of administrative law. Another administrative source of tax law comes from the Internal Revenue Service in the form of (1) revenue rulings, (2) private letter rulings, (3) determination letters, and (4) revenue procedures.

**Revenue rulings** are based on a set of facts that are common to many taxpayers, and are issued to the public to give taxpayers insight into how the IRS will treat certain transactions. Once issued, a revenue ruling is binding on the IRS. Therefore, a taxpayer can rely on a revenue ruling when engaging in tax planning. If the taxpayer engages in the same activity covered by the revenue ruling, the IRS must treat the transaction in the manner prescribed in the revenue ruling. Of course, if the taxpayer does not agree with the IRS' position described in the revenue ruling, he or she may take a contrary position. When this happens, the taxpayer and the IRS will likely end up in Court, and the Court will decide whether or not the revenue ruling is consistent with the Code. If the Court finds that the revenue ruling is inconsistent with the Code, or is unconstitutional, it may strike down the revenue ruling. All newly adopted revenue rulings are published weekly in the Internal Revenue Bulletin (which is published by the IRS).

Unlike a revenue ruling, which covers facts applicable to a large number of taxpayers, a **private letter ruling** is issued at the request of an individual taxpayer who would like to know how the IRS would treat an individual transaction that the taxpayer plans to engage in. The advantage of requesting a private letter ruling is that the taxpayer can solicit advice from the IRS on the tax consequences of a proposed transaction before the taxpayer enters into the transaction. Once issued, the private letter ruling binds the IRS with respect to that transaction for that taxpayer. The IRS may, however, change its mind when another taxpayer requests a private letter ruling proposing the same transaction, so it is possible that the tax results for taxpayers entering into the same transaction may differ. Private letter rulings, therefore, cannot be relied on for tax planning purposes, but are helpful in ascertaining IRS thinking on the proposed transaction. If a taxpayer can find a series of private letter rulings covering his or her proposed transaction, and those rulings all come to the same conclusion, there is a substantial likelihood that the IRS will follow its prior rulings, but it is important to remember that the IRS could change its mind. Private letter rulings are only valid for the taxpayer requesting the private letter ruling and only to the facts and law prescribed. If the requesting taxpayer changes the facts or transaction the private letter ruling is no longer valid. Unlike revenue rulings, private letter rulings are persuasive evidence of how a transaction will be treated for tax purposes, but a taxpayer may not rely on the result of a private letter ruling as precedent.

Unlike a private letter ruling, which covers a proposed transaction, a **determination letter** may be requested from the district director of the IRS if the taxpayer has already engaged in the transaction. The application must be made to the district director for the district in which the taxpayer's tax return will be filed. The district director will issue a determination letter only if the resolution of the tax issue is clearly covered by statute, Treasury decision or regulation, or a ruling or opinion of a Court decision published in the Internal Revenue Bulletin. If the taxpayer's tax return does not report the transaction in concert with the advice given in the determination letter, there will likely be an audit of the return. The IRS will look for consistent tax treatment when the tax return is filed, so taxpayers may wish to seek tax determination advice from their tax preparers or financial planners instead of the district director of the IRS to avoid further IRS scrutiny of their tax returns. Since a determination letter may be issued only if the matter is settled in law, there is no need to rely on determination letters for tax planning purposes.

In addition to issuing rulings and determination letters, the IRS also issues **revenue procedures**, which detail internal practices and procedures within the IRS, and make important announcements to taxpayers. For example, all of the inflation-adjusted thresholds (standard deductions, income tax tables, phaseouts, etc.) for a given tax year are announced in a Revenue Procedure, as are the applicable federal rates used for various tax planning techniques. Revenue Procedures are also published in the Internal Revenue Bulletin.

## JUDICIAL SOURCES OF TAX LAW

If all provisions of the Code were clearly stated, so that there were no ambiguity and everyone who read it interpreted it the same way, there would be little need for the courts to review the adequacy of the tax law. In reality, however, there are often disagreements between taxpayers and the IRS concerning the meaning of a Code provision, or how a particular transaction should be treated for tax purposes. The role of the courts in our tax system is to interpret ambiguous provisions of the Code, and ensure that the laws enacted by Congress and enforced by the President are constitutional.

The courts are not permitted to review the law on their own initiative and issue advisory opinions. A court can only review tax law when a case or controversy exists between two parties (most likely in this context, between the taxpayer and the IRS). In considering the case or controversy presented, the court can review the law that applies to the facts of the case, and determine whether or not the regulation cited by the IRS is consistent with the intent of Congress, or whether the law itself is constitutional.

When a court issues an opinion on a case or controversy brought before it, that opinion becomes part of the body of the law, since the

### Quick Quiz 2.1

**Highlight the answer to these questions:**

1. The 16th Amendment imposed the income tax on U.S. citizens.
   a. True
   b. False

2. The Internal Revenue Code is one of many sources of statutory tax law.
   a. True
   b. False

3. All Treasury regulations are either proposed, temporary, or final regulations.
   a. True
   b. False

4. Private letter rulings are binding on the IRS with respect to all taxpayers, but revenue rulings are only binding on the IRS with respect to the transaction and taxpayer discussed in the ruling.
   a. True
   b. False

False, False, True, False.

courts have the obligation and duty to state what the law means. Once a court has entered its interpretation on a given case, all lower courts in the same jurisdiction must comply with the opinion of the court. Obviously, once the U.S. Supreme Court has ruled on an issue, all U.S. courts, and the administrative branches of government, must comply with its decision. Congress must also comply, but can always enact legislation which, if signed by the President, would change how similar transactions are treated in the future.

The body of decisions from U.S. courts is commonly referred to as "case law." Case law is an important resource for tax planning, and reported decisions can be relied on by the taxpayer as law unless the case has been overturned by a higher court or the law relevant to the case has been changed by Congress. See Exhibit 2.9 Court System Summary.

## ADMINISTRATION OF THE TAX SYSTEM

### ROLE OF THE IRS

The IRS was created by the Treasury Department to enforce the Internal Revenue Code and collect the taxes imposed by Congress. In fulfilling its role, the IRS receives and audits tax returns of individual taxpayers, and participates in the administration of the tax system by issuing revenue rulings, private letter rulings, determination letters, and revenue procedures. In addition, the IRS also manages conflict with taxpayers in the early stages of the dispute resolution process.

### STATUTE OF LIMITATIONS

Under Section 6501, the **statute of limitations** for IRS examination of income tax returns is generally three years from the date a tax return is filed. This means that the IRS must review and contest the information submitted in the return within three years of the filing date in order to have a cause of action against a taxpayer.

**Key Concepts**

**Underline/highlight the answers to these questions as you read:**

1. Explain the IRS' role in the administration of the U.S. tax system.

2. Describe the statute of limitations applicable to tax returns in various situations.

3. Identify the noncompliance penalties.

Remember that tax returns for a given tax year are typically filed in the subsequent year. Cash basis taxpayers (such as individual taxpayers), have a calendar-year tax period, and must file their individual income tax returns by the 15th day of the 4th month following the close of the year (April 15, for a calendar year taxpayer). Therefore, individuals will file their tax return for 2010 on or before April 15, 2011 (unless an extension has been granted). Assuming that the taxpayer does not receive an extension to file, the statute of limitations begins to run on April 15, 2011. This means that the statute of limitations for the 2010 tax year will expire and the return will no longer be open for inspection after April 15, 2014. Under Section 6513, returns that are received by the IRS on or before the due date of the return are deemed to be filed on the due date. Therefore, if an individual taxpayer decides to file before the April 15 deadline, the statute of limitations does not begin to run until April 15. Filing early has the effect of giving the IRS a longer period of time to review the tax return.

If a taxpayer does not file by the due date of the income tax return, the statute of limitations does not begin to run until the return is actually filed. This extension of the statute of limitations applies even when the taxpayer has requested an automatic extension of time to file his tax return. If a return is never filed, the statute of limitations never starts and the IRS can review the information at any time.

The statute of limitations is extended to six years if there is a **substantial omission** of gross income on the tax return, defined as an omission of more than 25 percent of the gross income reported on the tax return. As with the normal three-year statute of limitations, the statute of limitations starts with the due date of the return, or the actual filing date of the return if the return was filed after the due date (without extensions).

If a taxpayer commits **fraud** when filing his tax return, the statute of limitations never closes.[1] If the IRS ever discovers the fraud, it can open the return for examination, assess additional taxes, and impose interest and penalties without regard to the number of years that have passed since the return was filed. Fraud implies that the taxpayer intentionally disregarded tax rules or misstated information included on the return. Because the legal standard for fraud is intent, fraud is difficult to prove, but once proven, can result in significant fines and penalties, and possibly the imposition of criminal sanctions on the taxpayer. Planners should always encourage clients to truthfully report their income and deductions on their tax returns.

In the event that the IRS assesses a tax deficiency on a taxpayer after auditing a tax return, the statute of limitations for collection of that deficiency is 10 years under Section 6502. Once an assessment is made, the IRS has a relatively long time to collect the tax due. If the IRS had issued an erroneous refund to a taxpayer, however, the statute of limitations for the IRS to file a suit to recover that refund is only two years. Section 6532 extends this time frame to five years if the erroneous refund given to the taxpayer was induced by fraud.

Yet another statute of limitations applies to taxpayers who wish to claim a refund of tax. The statute of limitations for claiming a refund is three years from the date the return was filed, or two years from the date the tax was paid, whichever is later. If no tax return is filed by the taxpayer, the limitation under Section 6511 is two years from the time the tax was paid.

**STATUTE OF LIMITATIONS**

EXHIBIT 2.2

| | |
|---|---|
| General Statute of Limitations under Section 6501 | 3 years |
| Substantial Understatement of Income >25% | 6 years |
| Fraud | None |
| Collection of Deficiency by IRS | 10 years |
| Refund Claim by Taxpayer | 3 years |

---

1.  IRC Section 6501.

## INTEREST AND PENALTIES FOR NONCOMPLIANCE

Taxpayers who choose not to comply with the filing requirements are subject to a series of penalties, including the failure to file penalty, the failure to pay penalty, and the accuracy related penalty.

If a taxpayer fails to file his income tax return on time, the **failure to file penalty** under Section 6651 applies. The penalty is five percent of the unpaid tax balance for each month or part thereof that the tax return is late. The maximum failure to file penalty is 25 percent of the unpaid tax balance (or, alternatively stated, the failure to file penalty will reach its maximum once five months have passed). If a tax return is filed more than 60 days late, the minimum failure to file penalty is the lower of $100 or the amount of tax due. Since the failure to file penalty applies to the unpaid balance, no penalty is due if the taxpayer who files late is due a refund or has no income tax burden. If the failure to file the tax return is due to fraud, the failure to file penalty is increased to 15 percent per month, up to a maximum penalty of 75 percent of the tax due.

If a taxpayer fails to pay the tax due on the due date, Section 6651 also imposes a **failure to pay penalty**. The failure to pay penalty is 0.5 percent per month or part thereof that the balance due remains unpaid. The maximum failure to pay penalty is 25 percent of the tax liability. Unlike the failure to file penalty, which will stop accruing after five months, the failure to pay penalty will continue to accrue for up to 50 months!

If a taxpayer is subject to both the failure to file penalty and the failure to pay penalty, the failure to file penalty is reduced by the failure to pay penalty. Effectively, this creates a maximum potential 25 percent penalty for the initial five months with the 0.5 percent per month failure to pay penalty continuing thereafter for up to 50 months.

Section 6662 imposes an **accuracy-related penalty** on taxpayers who file incorrect returns as a result of (1) a failure to make a good faith effort to comply with the tax law, (2) a substantial understatement of tax liability (generally more than 10 percent of the correct tax liability and at least a $5,000 deficiency) (3) a substantial valuation understatement, or (4) a substantial estate or gift tax valuation understatement. The penalty imposed is generally 20 percent of the underpayment amount, and can be increased to 30 percent for understatement of tax liability due to undisclosed listed transactions (certain transactions listed by the IRS as tax-shelter devices).

The stakes are even higher for those who commit fraud while failing to file or pay, and those who intentionally understate their tax liability. A fraud penalty of 75 percent of the underpayment of tax may be imposed under Section 6663. If a frivolous or incomplete income tax return has been filed, a $500 penalty may be imposed under Section 6702 regardless of tax liability. Intentional actions constituting fraud, or a willful failure to file or pay the tax liability that is due can rise to the level of criminal offenses. A willful failure to file an income tax return or pay the tax due is a misdemeanor under Section 7203, carrying penalties of up to $25,000 in fines and up to one year in prison, or both. A willful attempt to evade tax is a felony under Section 7201, with fines up to $100,000 and jail sentences up to five years, or both. If a taxpayer willfully makes a false return, he or she can be guilty of a felony under Section 7206, carrying a fine of up to $100,000 and jail sentences up to three years, or both. For obvious reasons, taxpayers should properly report their income and deductions on their tax returns, file them in a timely fashion, and pay the tax liability when due.

Several years ago, Clark failed to file a tax return or pay his taxes. Clark owed $5,000 in taxes. Clark's tax return and his tax payment are both now 22 months overdue. Clark is subject to a failure to file penalty of $1,250 (maximum 25% penalty x $5,000). Clark is also subject to a failure to pay penalty of $550 (0.5% x 22 months x $5,000). Fortunately for Clark, because he is subject to both the failure to file and failure to pay penalties, the first five months of delinquency is subject to the maximum 25% penalty. Thereafter, the $5,000 unpaid balance is still subject to the 0.5% failure to pay penalty of $425 (0.5% x 17 months x $5,000), for a total combined penalty of $1,675 ($1,250 + $425).

## PENALTIES FOR UNDERPAYMENT OF ESTIMATED TAX

Taxpayers are required to make payments of tax ratably throughout the year, either through employer withholding or through estimated payments. Self-employed individuals and individuals with large amounts of investment income should determine the amount of tax that needs to be paid annually, and make adjustments to withholding from their employment income, or make quarterly estimated tax payments so that their required payment is made. If a taxpayer underpays estimated taxes, an underpayment of estimated tax penalty applies. When calculating the appropriate amount to pay each year, income, Social Security, and other taxes reported on an individual income tax return must be taken into account.

Estimated tax payments are not required if a taxpayer has no tax liability for the prior year, was a U.S. Citizen or resident alien for the entire year, and the prior tax year covered a 12-month period.

Individuals who will owe $1,000 or more for the current tax year, after subtracting income tax withholding and credits from tax liability, may have to make estimated tax payments. When an individual owes tax liability at the end of the year, the IRS will impose two tests on that income to determine if a penalty is appropriate. First, the IRS will check to see if the total amount of tax withholding and credits was at least 90 percent (66 1/3 percent for farmers and fishermen) of the tax due for the year. If the tax payments were less than 90 percent, a penalty will be imposed. Alternatively, the IRS will check to see if the income tax withholding was at least 100 percent of the tax shown on the prior year tax return. If it was, no penalty will be due. For high income taxpayers (those with adjusted gross income over $150,000 in 2009) to avoid a tax penalty using the second test, the tax payments must have been at least 110 percent of the prior year tax liability. Provided that the taxpayer made payments of an amount necessary to meet one of these tests, no penalty will be applied.

The penalty that applies if the correct amount of tax payment has not been made is really an interest charge on the underpayment. Since the government did not have use of the money on the required quarterly payment dates, it will charge interest for failing to pay the required amount on a quarterly basis even if the tax liability is paid in full by the due date of the return.

For taxpayers who are employees and also have either self-employment or investment income, quarterly tax payments may not be necessary if adjustments to withholding on employment income are made such that the income tax withheld meets the requirements of the tests discussed above. Quarterly payments are due in April, June, September, and January, and if a taxpayer elects to make quarterly estimated payments, interest penalties may be applied if enough was not paid in on each quarterly payment due date. Withholding from employment income, however, is deemed to be ratably withheld from taxpayer income throughout the year regardless of when the withholding is deducted from the taxpayer's paycheck. If a taxpayer will owe an additional tax liability for the current year, instead of making payments in April, June, and September, he or she could wait until near the end of the tax year and then instruct his or her employer (using Form W-4) to withhold additional amounts for federal income tax. This approach allows the taxpayer to have use of the funds until the end of the year, while still avoiding an IRS penalty for underpayment, since the withheld payments are deemed to have been made ratably throughout the year.

## Quick Quiz 2.2

**Highlight the answer to these questions:**

1. The statute of limitations for the IRS to examine an income tax return is generally three years.
   a. True
   b. False

2. A substantial understatement of income is an omission of more than 10% of gross income.
   a. True
   b. False

3. If a taxpayer is subject to both the failure to file penalty and the failure to pay penalty, the failure to file penalty will be reduced by the failure to pay penalty.
   a. True
   b. False

4. Willfully filing a false return is a felony.
   a. True
   b. False

True, False, True, True.

**EXAMPLE 2.2**

Last year, Ryan's federal income tax liability was $28,000, and his adjusted gross income was $130,000. He expects his tax liability this year to be $35,000 due to a particularly profitable year in his consulting practice, which he operates as a sole proprietorship. In addition to being a self-employed consultant, Ryan is a college professor at Murphy State University. Based on a review of Ryan's pay stubs, you calculate that Murphy State University will withhold $26,000 from Ryan's employment income this year. Ryan will have to make tax payments totaling $28,000, however, in order to avoid a tax penalty (the lower of 100% of his prior year tax liability, $28,000, or $31,500 (current year tax liability of $35,000 x 90%). Ryan can make quarterly payments of $500 in April, June, September, and January to cover the shortfall. Alternatively, he could fill out a form W-4 with his employer and request that an additional $2,000 be withheld from his last paycheck of the year. In either case, Ryan would have paid in enough to avoid an underpayment of estimated tax penalty for the year.

## PREPARER PENALTIES

In addition to tax penalties that may be assessed on taxpayers, tax preparers may also be subject to penalties. IRC Section 6694(a) states that if a tax preparer takes an unrealistic position on a tax return and the preparer knew or reasonably should have known of the position, then the penalty is the greater of $1,000 or 50 percent of the income derived by the preparer for preparing the return. If the understatement was due to willful or reckless conduct, the penalty is the greater of $5,000 or 50 percent of income derived by the preparer for the return.

Other penalties may also be assessed, including penalties for failure to sign a return prepared by the tax preparer (IRC Section 6695(b)), failure to provide a copy of the tax return to the taxpayer (IRC Section 6695(a), failure to keep a copy of the return (IRC Section 6695(d)) and a client list, and failure to comply with due diligence requirements when claiming the earned income credit (IRC Section 6695(g)).

Treasury Circular 230 establishes standards of conduct for tax preparers, and those who plan to prepare tax returns should become familiar with its content. These are included in Treasury Department Circular No. 230 (Revised 4-2008). Financial Planning practitioners who prepare tax returns should keep abreast of the changes in this area, and make sure that their actions will not subject them to penalties.

## SUMMARY OF PENALTIES

EXHIBIT 2.3

| Failure to File | 5% per month or part thereof to 25% maximum |
|---|---|
| Failure to Pay | 0.5% per month or part thereof to 25% maximum |
| Accuracy Related | 20% of underpayment to 30%* |
| Fraud | 15% per month up to 75% of underpayment |

*40% if due to substantial valuation misstatement, substantial overstatement of pension liabilities, or substantial estate or gift tax valuation understatement.

## AUDITS

In the United States, taxpayers self-report their income and deductible expenses, and also calculate the amount of tax due. While the government presumes that most individuals will properly report their taxable transactions and pay the correct amount of tax, an audit system encourages compliance by selecting tax returns for review. The primary purpose of an audit is to test whether or not the tax return filed by the taxpayer truthfully reflects their income and allowable deductions. There are several ways that tax returns are chosen for audit.

The most common type of audit today is a computer generated audit, referred to as the "Discriminant Inventory Function" or DIF. Once filed, a tax return is checked against information sources reported to the IRS. These information sources include employer-filed W-2 forms which disclose the amount of money a taxpayer made during the year as well as withholding for income and payroll taxes. Firms that hire independent contractors file Form 1099, disclosing gross payments made to independent contractors. Banks and brokerage firms file Form 1099 forms with the IRS disclosing the amount of interest, dividends, and gross proceeds from the sale of securities. If a tax return filed by a taxpayer does not include at least the amounts reported to the IRS through the above-mentioned information sources, the return is flagged for review. In addition, the DIF assigns scores to each tax return based on estimated degree of compliance. The formulas used to develop this score are highly confidential, but are known to be based, at least partially, on averages for particular income categories. If a return filed by a taxpayer includes items that are significantly different from the norm, or represents areas of known abuse, the computer will assign a high DIF score to the return. A high DIF score increases the likelihood that the return will be selected for audit.

| EXHIBIT 2.4 | **EXAMINATION COVERAGE: RETURNS EXAMINED RESULTING IN REFUNDS, BY TYPE AND SIZE OF RETURN, FISCAL YEAR 2008** |

| Type and Size of Return | Taxable Returns Examined (in thousands) | | | Recommended Refunds (in thousands of dollars) | | |
|---|---|---|---|---|---|---|
| | Total | Field | Correspondence | Total | Field | Correspondence |
| Individual Income Tax Returns | 49,907 | 19,423 | 30,484 | 617,908 | 495,432 | 122,476 |
| Corporation Income Tax Returns (except Form 1120S) | 2,882 | 2,844 | 38 | 8,679,036 | 8,671,598 | 7,438 |
| Estate & Trust Income Tax Returns | 283 | 132 | 151 | 27,770 | 27,127 | 643 |
| Estate Tax Returns | 674 | 674 | 0 | 146,889 | 146,889 | 0 |
| Employment Tax Returns | 411 | 411 | 0 | 44,765 | 44,765 | 0 |

Source: Internal Revenue Service Data Book, 2008

Other methods of choosing returns for audit include related party audits, targeted compliance audits, subsequent claims for refund, or financial status audits. A related party audit occurs when the IRS audits a tax return of one individual, and that individual has claimed deductions for payments made to another person. The IRS may audit the return of the recipient to verify that all income was reported. Targeted compliance audits result in checking the tax returns of members of a particular profession (usually professions that have a high potential for engaging in tax evasion, such as cash-basis businesses) to test compliance with the tax laws.

Even when a tax return was not selected for audit under one of the above methods, a subsequent claim for refund may prompt the IRS to take a closer look at the return. The justification for such an audit is that the taxpayer apparently did not carefully file their first return, resulting in the need to file an amended return, or claim for refund. Finally, financial status audits look at the lifestyle of the taxpayer to determine if the income reported on the taxpayer's tax return is sufficient to fund their current lifestyle. Lifestyle audits are used sparingly, and are only permissible under Section 7602 in cases where the IRS has reason to believe that there is a likelihood that the taxpayer has unreported income. Lifestyle audits are typically used with high profile criminal cases when criminals do not report high income, yet live lavishly.

Once selected for audit, an income tax return will be examined by the IRS, and adjustments will be made to correct the tax liability for the taxpayer according to the perspective of the IRS. If the taxpayer does not agree with the findings in the audit, the dispute resolution process between the IRS and the taxpayer will begin.

## Math Errors on Tax Returns, 2008

**Exhibit 2.5**

| Type of Math Error | Number | Percentage |
|---|---|---|
| Tax calculation/other taxes | 954,853 | 26.0% |
| Exemption number/amount | 573,548 | 15.6% |
| Earned income tax credit | 578,337 | 15.8% |
| Standard/itemized deduction | 416,270 | 11.3% |
| Adjusted gross/taxable income amount | 316,271 | 8.6% |
| Child tax credit | 238,733 | 6.5% |
| Refund/amount due | 198,488 | 5.4% |
| Other credits | 86,717 | 2.4% |
| Filing status | 97,215 | 2.7% |
| Withholding or excess Social Security payments | 74,794 | 2.0% |
| Adjustments to income | 76,703 | 2.1% |
| Other | 58,142 | 1.6% |
| TOTAL | 3,670,071 | 100.0% |

Source: Internal Revenue Service Data Book, 2008

## DISPUTE RESOLUTION

Dispute resolution with the IRS takes two forms. The first is an internal appeals process that permits taxpayers to request a second review of their case from the IRS Office of Appeals, which is separate from the IRS examination division that conducted the initial audit. Additionally, a taxpayer may choose the second dispute resolution process, which involves the use of the U.S. court system.

After an audit, if the taxpayer and the IRS do not agree on the amount of tax that should be imposed for a given tax year, the IRS will issue a 30-day letter, and will provide a copy of the examination report that explains the changes proposed by the IRS. Once the 30-day letter is issued, the taxpayer has 30 days to appeal the IRS' decision to the IRS Office of Appeals.

If, during the 30 day period after the issuance of the 30-day letter, the taxpayer decides that the IRS report is correct and pays the tax, the process ends there, and the matter is settled. When the taxpayer does not agree with the IRS examination report, he or she can take advantage of an internal appeals process within the IRS to resolve the dispute. The appeals office is separate from and independent of the IRS office that examines the taxpayer's return. The internal appeals process is very informal, and conferences with appeals office personnel may be held by correspondence, telephone, or in person. An appeal is requested by filing Form 12203 (Exhibit 2.6) within the appropriate time period. In addition to requesting an appeals conference, the taxpayer may have to file either a formal written protest or a small case request. If the taxpayer and the IRS do not agree after the appeals conference, the taxpayer can still take advantage of dispute resolution in the U.S. court system.

If the taxpayer does not respond to the IRS' 30-day letter, and no agreement has been reached with the IRS during this period, the IRS will issue a 90-day letter, also known as a statutory notice of deficiency. Once the 90-day letter is issued, the taxpayer has 90 days to petition the Tax Court for a hearing. If a petition is not made within the 90-day period, the IRS may assess the tax, and begin collection efforts.

Alternatively, taxpayers who receive a 90-day letter may pay the tax due under the notice of deficiency and file an immediate claim for refund. In this case, the IRS generally will not act on the claim for refund. If the IRS fails to respond to the claim for refund within six months, the taxpayer may file a suit for refund against the U.S. in the U.S. District Court, or the U.S. Court of Federal Claims.

For a taxpayer to bring any tax action in the U.S. District Court or the Court of Federal Claims, the tax deficiency asserted by the IRS must be paid in advance. Tax payers are not required to pay the deficiency in advance of bringing their action in the U.S. Tax Court.

## Request for Appeals Review

Please complete the information in the spaces below, including your signature and the date.

| Taxpayer name(s) | Taxpayer Identification Number(s) |
|---|---|
| Mailing address | Tax form number |
| City | Tax period(s) ended |
| State · ZIP Code | |

Identify the item(s) (for example: filing status, exemptions, interest or dividends) you disagree with in the proposed change or assessment report you received with the enclosed letter. Tell us why you disagree. You can add more pages if this is not enough space.

| Disagreed item | Reason why you disagree |
|---|---|

| Disagreed item | Reason why you disagree |
|---|---|

| Disagreed item | Reason why you disagree |
|---|---|

| Disagreed item | Reason why you disagree |
|---|---|

| Signature of Taxpayer(s) | Date |
|---|---|
| | Date |

Name and signature of authorized representative (**If a representative is signing this form, please attach a copy of your completed Form 2848, Power of Attorney and Declaration of Representative.**)

Name

| Signature | Date |
|---|---|
| Your telephone number | Best time to call |

Form **12203** (Rev. 4-2004)     Cat. No. 27136N     www.irs.gov     Department of the Treasury - Internal Revenue Service

EXHIBIT 2.7   DIAGRAM OF DISPUTE RESOLUTION

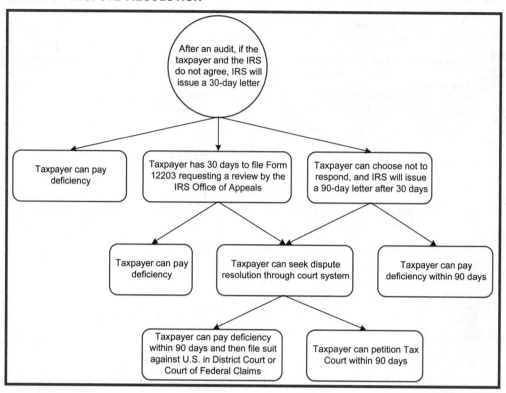

## COURT SYSTEM

There are three trial courts that may hear tax-related matters: the Tax Court, the U.S. District Court, and the U.S. Court of Federal Claims. In order to bring an action in the U.S. District Court or the U.S. Court of Federal Claims, the taxpayer must pay the tax deficiency alleged by the IRS. If the taxpayer cannot pay the deficiency, or does not want to pay the deficiency before the matter is resolved, the only option available is to bring an action for redetermination of tax liability in the U.S. Tax Court. If a taxpayer cannot pay the deficiency, or does not want to pay the deficiency before the matter is resolved, the only option available is to bring an action for redetermination of tax liability in the U.S. Tax Court. A cash bond payment may be used in court in lieu of payment of the tax deficiency.

The **Tax Court** is a special purpose court – it only hears tax matters. Any taxpayer who has an ongoing dispute with the IRS after the issuance of a statutory notice of deficiency (a 90-day letter) may bring his or her dispute to the Tax Court. The Tax Court sits in Washington, D.C., but the judges travel (go "on circuit") to hear cases around the country. Typically, a Tax Court case will be held in the state where the taxpayer resides. The special nature of the Tax Court – that it only hears tax cases - may be an advantage or disadvantage to the taxpayer, depending on the issue that is being contested, and the facts of the case. This fact may be a consideration in choosing to bring the case to the U.S. District Court or the U.S. Court of Federal Claims. Decisions of the Tax Court may be appealed if either party – the taxpayer or the IRS – does not like the outcome.

If the amount in controversy is $50,000 or less, the taxpayer can elect to bring the case to the small claims division of the tax court. The advantage of bringing the case to the small claims division is that the hearing is not as formal as a full tax court proceeding, and does not strictly follow all of the formal rules of legal procedure. Many small claims cases are heard by special trial judges. Since formal rules of procedure are not used, the taxpayer may not need to be represented by a lawyer. Enrolled Agents are members of the tax court bar and can represent clients in tax court, and, in some cases (provided that there is no objection from the opposing party), a CPA may be permitted to describe the positions taken by the taxpayer to the court. Furthermore, small claims cases tend to get resolved faster and easier than full Tax Court proceedings. If a taxpayer chooses to bring a case to the small claims division of the Tax Court, however, there are no appeal rights. The decision of the Tax Court judge is binding on both the taxpayer and the IRS.

If the taxpayer would like to have a jury trial, the dispute must be brought to the **U.S. District Court**. The U.S. District Court is the trial court in the federal system, and there is at least one district per state (some large states, such as Pennsylvania, have Eastern and Western District Courts). Unlike the Tax Court, which specializes in hearing tax-related cases, the U.S. District Court is a court of general jurisdiction. The presiding judge and the members of the jury will not be experts on tax law, which may have a bearing on whether or not the case should be brought to this court. Decisions of the U.S. District Court may be appealed if either party – the taxpayer or the IRS – does not like the outcome.

The final option for trial is to bring the controversy to the **U.S. Court of Federal Claims**. This court sits only in Washington, D.C., and unlike the Tax Court, the judges of the U.S. Court of Federal Claims do not go on circuit. Cases brought in front of this court must be litigated in Washington, D.C. Despite the inconvenience of traveling to Washington to litigate the case, if enough money is at stake, and the prior decisions of the U.S. Court of Federal Claims are more favorable to the taxpayer than the decisions of the U.S. District Court (comparing the decisions of different courts to determine what court to bring the suit to is referred to as 'forum shopping' by lawyers), it may make sense to bring the tax dispute there. The only type of trial available in this court is a bench trial – jury trials on tax matters are reserved for the U.S. District Court. Decisions of the U.S. Court of Federal Claims may be appealed if either party – the taxpayer or the IRS – does not like the outcome.

If a trial court decision is appealed, it goes to the U.S. Court of Appeals for the Circuit that covers

## Quick Quiz 2.3

**Highlight the answer to these questions:**

1. The most common type of audit is a lifestyle audit.
   a. True
   b. False

2. Any deficiency must be paid prior to bringing a dispute before the Tax Court.
   a. True
   b. False

3. The U.S. District Court is the only venue for tax controversies that provides jury trials.
   a. True
   b. False

False, False, True.

the District Court where the trial was brought, or the state where the Tax Court case was heard. Appeals from the U.S. Court of Federal Claims always go to the U.S. Court of Appeals for the Federal Circuit, which sits in Washington, D.C. Either the taxpayer or the IRS can appeal the case to the Circuit Court. Usually, the last step in the dispute resolution process is the decision issued by the Circuit Court. Once a Circuit Court rules on a tax-related issue, all district courts in that Circuit must abide by the decision announced by the Circuit Court. Other Circuit Courts outside the Court of Appeals circuit, other appellate courts, and the Supreme Court, are not bound by the decision.

| EXHIBIT 2.8 | **THE U.S. FEDERAL CIRCUIT COURTS** |

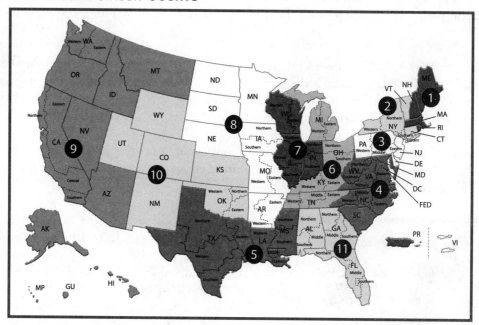

Source: Administrative Office of the U.S. Courts, http://www.uscourts.gov/courtlink

The U.S. Supreme Court rarely hears cases dealing with tax matters. A party may request the Supreme Court to review a decision of a Circuit Court, a process called petitioning for a *writ of certiorari*, but the Supreme Court will only hear the case if it has the potential to affect a large number of taxpayers, or if it feels that it needs to settle a point of law that is in dispute among the circuits. There is always the possibility, but not the probability of having your case heard in the Supreme Court. If the Supreme Court does decide to hear a tax case, once its decision is announced it is binding on all parties, and all U.S. Courts must follow the ruling in deciding similar cases.

EXHIBIT 2.9

|  | Tax Court | Tax Court - Small Claims | U.S. District Court | U.S. Court of Federal Claims |
|---|---|---|---|---|
| What kinds of cases? | Tax Only | Tax Only | All Types | Claims Against U.S. Government |
| Is the taxpayer required to pay the tax? | No | No | Yes | Yes |
| What is the maximum amount of the claim? | N/A | $50,000 | N/A | N/A |
| Is a jury trial available? | No | No | Yes | No |
| Where is court located? | Around U.S. | Around U.S. | Around U.S. | D.C. Only |
| To what court are appeals brought? | U.S. Court of Appeals | No Appeals | U.S. Court of Appeals | U.S. Court of Appeals - Federal Circuit |

## TAX RESEARCH

There are several sources of tax information for practitioners. Primary sources of information include the Internal Revenue Code, Treasury regulations, court opinions, the IRS Manual, and IRS rulings and determination letters. Many of these resources can be obtained from free sources on the internet. Some of the most used sites are the IRS website (www.irs.gov), and TaxAlmanac, a free online resource (www.taxalmanac.com). These sources of tax law are used primarily by attorneys and accountants, but may be helpful to financial planning professionals as well.

From a financial planning standpoint, the best way to get information about tax-related topics is to use practice aids and journals.

Practice aids index the tax law, making relevant provisions easier to find. The Research Institute of America (RIA), Commerce Clearing House (CCH), and Bureau of National Affairs (BNA) publish internet-based practice aids that can be accessed for a fee.

### Key Concepts

**Underline/highlight the answers to these questions as you read:**

1.  Identify sources of tax law available to practitioners.

2.  Identify the sources of secondary tax materials available to practitioners.

Journal articles are perhaps the best source of information for practitioners since they describe the use of the tax law provisions in a planning oriented context, illustrating the direct application of the concepts to client problems. Some journals focus on the legal aspects of tax planning. Journals of this type include *Federal Tax Articles* by CCH, *The Journal of Taxation*, the *Monthly Digest of Tax Articles*, and *Tax Notes*. Other journals focus directly on practical applications that can be useful for practitioners. Some of these journals include: *Estate Planning*, *Trusts & Estates*, *The Journal of Financial Planning*, and *The Journal of the Society of Financial Services Professionals*. Practitioners who are recommending tax-planning strategies to clients should regularly read one or more of these journals to keep up with new developments.

When new tax legislation is adopted by Congress, summaries of that information are often available on accounting firm websites and websites such as TaxAlmanac.com. For those who would like to understand the reasons for the tax law changes, Congressional committee and conference committee reports describing the details of the legislation may be found at the Library of Congress legislative information website at www.thomas.gov.

One of the hallmarks of professionalism is to know when to call in an expert. Nobody can be an expert in everything, and if the situation facing your client is complex enough, it may be wise to bring in another advisor that has experience and knowledge in the matter facing the client. A financial planner typically acts as the captain of the planning team, coordinating the efforts of team members, including accountants, lawyers, trust officers, estate planners, and insurance specialists. For many tax-related problems a client may encounter, either the financial planner or an existing member of the planning team will be able to resolve the issue. When the issue is beyond the scope of the current team members' research and application skills, however, call in an expert!

## CONCLUSION

While at first the tax law in all of its forms (legislative, administrative, and judicial) may seem daunting, repeated exposure to the sources of law and how they apply to client problems will remove the mystique. To successfully navigate through the myriad sources of law, you need to develop a basic understanding of our tax system and how it works. The remaining chapters will walk you through the tax system.

# Key Terms

**16th Amendment** - Amendment to the U.S. Constitution adopted on February 25, 1913 that gave Congress the power to lay and collect taxes on income.

**Accuracy-Related Penalty** - A penalty of 20 percent of the underpayment amount imposed on taxpayers who file incorrect tax returns in certain situations.

**Determination Letter** - A letter issued by a district director of the IRS advising a taxpayer on how to report a transaction for tax purposes.

**Discriminant Inventory Function System** - A computer program used by the IRS to identify tax returns for audit.

**Failure to File Penalty** - A five percent penalty of the unpaid tax balance for each month or part thereof that a tax return is late.

**Failure to Pay Penalty** - A penalty of 0.5 percent per month or part thereof that a taxpayer fails to pay tax that is owed.

**Final Regulations** - Regulations issued by the Treasury that have been adopted formally after compliance with the requirements of the Administrative Procedures Act.

**Fraud** - Implies that the taxpayer intentionally disregarded tax rules or misstated information included on the return.

**Interpretive Regulations** - Official interpretations of the Internal Revenue Code by the Treasury.

**Legislative Regulations** - Regulations in which the Treasury determines the details of the law.

**Private Letter Ruling** - Rulings issued by the IRS that are binding on the IRS only with respect to the transaction and the taxpayer that are the subject of the ruling.

**Procedural Regulations** - Housekeeping instructions indicating how the Treasury and IRS will conduct their affairs.

**Proposed Regulations** - Regulations that have been drafted by the Treasury, but have not yet been adopted.

**Revenue Procedures** - Statements issued by the IRS which details internal practices and procedures within the IRS and makes important announcements to taxpayers.

**Revenue Rulings** - Rulings issued by the IRS based on a set of facts common to many taxpayers and binding on the IRS.

# Key Terms

**Statute of Limitations** - Specified time within which the IRS may examine an income tax return.

**Substantial Omission** - An omission from a tax return of more than 25 percent of the gross income reported.

**Tax Court** - A special purpose court that sits in Washington, D.C. and only hears tax cases. The judges within the court travel throughout the U.S. to hear the cases.

**Temporary Regulations** - Regulations that have the same authority as final regulations and are issued when guidance must be provided quickly to taxpayers.

**Treasury Regulations** - An administrative source of tax law that are official interpretations of the Internal Revenue Code and give taxpayers insight as to how the Code will be enforced by the IRS.

**U.S. Court of Federal Claims** - Court that may preside over tax controversies and only hears cases in Washington, D.C.

**U.S. District Court** - Trial court of the federal judicial system which has general jurisdiction and is the only option for tax controversies in which the taxpayer would like a jury trial.

## DISCUSSION QUESTIONS

1. What are the three primary sources of tax law?

2. What is the legal basis for today's income tax?

3. What are the statutory sources of tax law?

4. What are the administrative sources of tax law?

5. Compare and contrast proposed regulations, temporary regulations, and final regulations.

6. What is the difference between a procedural regulation and an interpretive regulation?

7. Discuss the two types of rulings issued by the IRS.

8. When can a determination letter be issued?

9. What is the general statute of limitations before which the IRS may examine a tax return?

10. Under what circumstances is the statute of limitations extended?

11. What are the penalties for noncompliance?

12. What are the two forms of dispute resolution with the IRS?

13. What are the three trial courts that may hear tax-related matters and what are the requirements of each?

1.  The first constitutionally permitted income tax was imposed by:

    a.  The Constitution.

    b.  The 16th Amendment.

    c.  The Revenue Act of 1913.

    d.  The Internal Revenue of 1986, as amended.

2.  Hank filed his 2009 tax return on time on April 15, 2010. When preparing his return, Hank accidentally stated that his income was $50,000 when it was really $500,000. What is the statute of limitations prior to which the IRS may examine Hank's return?

    a.  3 years.

    b.  6 years.

    c.  10 years.

    d.  There is no statute of limitations.

3.  Allison filed her tax return on April 15. At that time, she owed $800 on a total tax liability of $10,000 and she submitted a check for $800 with her tax return. Which of the following penalties will apply to Allison?

    a.  Failure to file.

    b.  Failure to pay.

    c.  Underpayment of estimated tax.

    d.  None of the above.

4.  Anthony recently filed his tax return. He failed to file a proper extension and filed 80 days after the due date. Along with his return he remitted a check for $4,000, which was his tax liability without penalties. What is Anthony's total penalty?

    a.  $60.

    b.  $540.

    c.  $600.

    d.  $660.

5. Marques is considering a business transaction. After speaking with his accountant he has determined that the Internal Revenue Code is not clear on the tax treatment of his business transaction. Because the tax dollars at stake are substantial, Marques is not comfortable completing the transaction without first knowing how the transaction will be treated by the IRS. Which of the following would give Marques the most peace of mind prior to completing this transaction?

   a. Private Letter Ruling.
   b. Determination Letter.
   c. Revenue Ruling.
   d. Technical Advice Memoranda.

6. Caroline's husband, Drew, died last year. Before his death, Drew exercised a substantial amount of ISOs. Before they could pay the tax, the stock decreased in value, leaving them no cash to pay the alternative minimum tax (AMT) that resulted from the exercise. Caroline would like to challenge the amount due in court, as she has already exhausted the IRS process. Her lawyer believes that the facts of the case may help Caroline if she has a sympathetic audience. However, she is unable to pay the claim currently and her top priority is to utilize a court that does not require her to pay up-front. She does want to be able to appeal if the lower court does not render a decision in her favor. Which court is most appropriate for Caroline?

   a. U.S. District Court.
   b. U.S. Court of Federal Claims.
   c. U.S. Tax Court.
   d. U.S. Tax Court: Small Claims Division.

7. The maximum accuracy-related penalty is:

   a. 20 percent of the underpayment.
   b. 25 percent of the underpayment.
   c. 30 percent of the underpayment.
   d. 75 percent of the underpayment.

8. The failure to file penalty is reduced by which one of the following?

   a. The failure to pay penalty.
   b. Estimated tax payments.
   c. 20 percent of the underpayment penalty.
   d. The fraud penalty.

9. Which of the following cannot be relied upon by the public for legal precedence?

    1. Proposed Regulations.

    2. Revenue Rulings.

    3. Private Letter Rulings.

    4. Temporary Regulations.

        a. 1 and 3.

        b. 2 and 4.

        c. 2 and 3.

        d. 1, 2, and 3.

# Quick Quiz Explanations

## Quick Quiz 2.1

1. False. The 16th Amendment gave Congress the power to impose an income tax, but the amendment itself did not impose an income tax.
2. False. The Internal Revenue Code is the only statutory source of federal tax law.
3. True.
4. False. A private letter ruling binds the IRS with respect to the particular transaction and taxpayer discussed in the letter. A revenue ruling, on the other hand, is binding on the IRS with respect to all taxpayers.

## Quick Quiz 2.2

1. True.
2. False. A substantial understatement of income is an omission of more than 25% of gross income.
3. True.
4. True.

## Quick Quiz 2.3

1. False. The most common type of audit today is a computer generated audit, referred to as the "Discriminant Inventory Function."
2. False. A taxpayer is not required to pay any tax deficiency prior to bringing a claim before the Tax Court.
3. True.

# Fundamentals of Income Taxation

## TAX FORMULA FOR INDIVIDUAL TAXPAYERS

### INTRODUCTION

Prior to delving into the details of income tax rules, it is helpful to get an overview of how the federal income tax is calculated, and to get an introduction to some of the fundamental income tax concepts that are important in determining tax liability. This chapter begins with an overview of the tax formula for individual taxpayers. The chapter then identifies some of the major categories of income, exclusions, deductions, and credits that are common to income taxation. All of these items will be discussed at length in subsequent chapters of the text. Remember that the important task to accomplish here is to get a general understanding of how the tax formula works.

After discussing the individual income tax formula, the chapter turns to fundamental concepts of income taxation that are important for planners to know. Topics such as accounting periods and methods, filing status, personal and dependency exemptions, the calculation of the standard deduction for a dependent, the kiddie-tax rules, and return filing requirements are discussed in detail. The chapter ends with an overview of basic tax-planning strategies that can be used by taxpayers to help manage their tax liability. Many of the techniques used to achieve these planning goals are discussed at length in future chapters.

In very general terms, a taxpayer is required to pay a federal income tax on taxable income. **Taxable income** is determined by subtracting allowable deductions from income:

Income – Deductions = Taxable Income

Taxable income is multiplied by the income tax rate to determine the tax liability:

Taxable Income x Tax Rate = Tax Liability

## Key Concepts

**Underline/highlight the answers to these questions as you read:**

1. Explain the basic tax formula.

2. Define income.

3. Identify items excluded from gross income.

4. Identify items included in gross income.

Federal income tax rates are progressive in nature. Higher tiers of income are taxed at higher rates. For example, a single taxpayer with income of $30,000 and deductions of $10,000 has taxable income of $20,000 ($30,000 - $10,000). Using the 2009 tax rate schedule for the single filing status (See Appendix A), the taxpayer's tax is $2,598.75, as calculated below.

$$= (($8,350 \times 10\%) + ($11,650 \times 15\%))$$

$$= $2,582.50$$

Note: The tax calculation for 2010 would be as follows:

$$= (($8,375 \times 10\%) + ($11,625 \times 15\%))$$

$$= $2,581.25$$

As illustrated, higher levels of income are taxed at higher rates.

There is a more extensive tax formula for individual taxpayers than the simple tax calculation presented above. The more complete formula includes exclusions from income, different types of deductions, and tax credits. In addition, there are intermediate calculations (such as adjusted gross income) that can be important considerations in tax planning. Each of these items will be discussed in this chapter and throughout the remainder of the textbook.

| | |
|---|---|
| **Income Broadly Defined** | $xx,xxx |
| Less: Exclusions | (x,xxx) |
| **Gross Income** | $xx,xxx |
| Less: Deductions for Adjusted Gross Income (*above-the-line deductions*) | (x,xxx) |
| **Adjusted Gross Income** | $xx,xxx |
| Less: Deductions from Adjusted Gross Income: Greater of Standard or Itemized Deductions (*below-the-line deductions*) | (xx,xxx) |
| Less: Personal and Dependency Exemptions | (xx,xxx) |
| **Taxable Income** | $xx,xxx |
| | |
| Tax on Taxable Income | $x,xxx |
| Less: Credit for Taxes Withheld | (x,xxx) |
| Less: Credit for Estimated Tax Payments | (x,xxx) |
| Less: Other Tax Credits | (x,xxx) |
| **Tax Due or (Refund Due)** | $xxx |

individuals report their income, deductions, exemptions, and other information required for the calculation of the federal tax liability on one of the following three forms:

- Form 1040EZ,
- Form 1040A, or
- Form 1040.

Form 1040EZ may be used by single or married taxpayers filing jointly who do not have any dependents and whose taxable income is less than $100,000 for 2009. Note that Form 1040EZ may not be used by individuals claiming Head of Household status or by married individuals who file separately. Form 1040A may be used by taxpayers of any filing status, but the taxpayer's taxable income must be less than $100,000 for 2009, the taxpayer must not itemize his deductions, and the taxpayer must only take certain tax credits. Taxpayers must also meet other requirements in order to use Form 1040EZ or Form 1040A. Form 1040, which is the most complex form of the three, can be used by any taxpayer and is shown in Exhibits 3.2 and 3.3.

## INCOME

**Income**, broadly defined, means the gross amount of money and the fair market value of property, services, or other accretion to wealth received, but it does not include borrowed money or a return of invested dollars (sometimes referred to as return of capital or return of adjusted taxable basis).

During the year, David borrowed $20,000 from a bank and sold an investment for $12,000. He had no other cash inflows. He purchased the investment five years earlier for $5,000. Since the loan and the return of his $5,000 investment are not income, his income for the year is $7,000 ($12,000 sales price - $5,000 investment).

## EXCLUSIONS

**Exclusions** are income items that are not subject to income tax. Each exclusion must be specifically authorized by Congress and set forth in the Internal Revenue Code (IRC) or must be determined by the courts to be outside the definition of income as it is used in the 16th Amendment to the U.S. Constitution. Most exclusions from gross income are allowed by IRC Sections 101 through 150. A more detailed discussion of exclusions is included in Chapters 4 and 5. Some of the more common exclusions permitted by the Code are listed in Exhibit 3.1.

### PARTIAL LIST OF EXCLUSIONS

| | |
|---|---|
| • Interest income from municipal bonds | • Cash or property received by gift |
| • Child support payments received from a former spouse | • Deferral contributions to certain retirement plans |
| • Cash or property received by inheritance | • Gain on the sale of a principal residence |
| • Specified employee fringe benefits | • Scholarship or fellowship |
| • Qualifying distributions from a Roth IRA during retirement | • Life insurance proceeds received because of the death of the insured |

EXHIBIT 3.2   FORM 1040

Form **1040**   Department of the Treasury—Internal Revenue Service
**U.S. Individual Income Tax Return**   20**09**   (99)   IRS Use Only—Do not write or staple in this space.

| For the year Jan. 1–Dec. 31, 2009, or other tax year beginning | , 2009, ending | , 20 | OMB No. 1545-0074 |

**Label**
(See instructions on page 14.)
**Use the IRS label.**
Otherwise, please print or type.

L A B E L   H E R E

| Your first name and initial | Last name | | Your social security number |
| If a joint return, spouse's first name and initial | Last name | | Spouse's social security number |
| Home address (number and street). If you have a P.O. box, see page 14. | | Apt. no. | ▲ You **must** enter your SSN(s) above. ▲ |
| City, town or post office, state, and ZIP code. If you have a foreign address, see page 14. | | | Checking a box below will not change your tax or refund. |

**Presidential Election Campaign**   ▶ Check here if you, or your spouse if filing jointly, want $3 to go to this fund (see page 14) ▶   ☐ You   ☐ Spouse

**Filing Status**
Check only one box.

1 ☐ Single
2 ☐ Married filing jointly (even if only one had income)
3 ☐ Married filing separately. Enter spouse's SSN above and full name here. ▶
4 ☐ Head of household (with qualifying person). (See page 15.) If the qualifying person is a child but not your dependent, enter this child's name here. ▶
5 ☐ Qualifying widow(er) with dependent child (see page 16)

**Exemptions**

6a ☐ **Yourself.** If someone can claim you as a dependent, **do not** check box 6a . . . . .
b ☐ **Spouse** . . . . . . . . . . . . . . . . . . . .

| c **Dependents:** | | (2) Dependent's social security number | (3) Dependent's relationship to you | (4) ✓ if qualifying child for child tax credit (see page 17) |
| (1) First name | Last name | | | |
| | | | | ☐ |
| | | | | ☐ |
| | | | | ☐ |
| | | | | ☐ |

If more than four dependents, see page 17 and check here ▶ ☐

Boxes checked on 6a and 6b ____
No. of children on 6c who:
• lived with you ____
• did not live with you due to divorce or separation (see page 18) ____
Dependents on 6c not entered above ____
Add numbers on lines above ▶ ____

d   Total number of exemptions claimed . . . . . . . . . . . . . . . .

**Income**

Attach Form(s) W-2 here. Also attach Forms W-2G and 1099-R if tax was withheld.

If you did not get a W-2, see page 22.

Enclose, but do not attach, any payment. Also, please use Form 1040-V.

| 7 | Wages, salaries, tips, etc. Attach Form(s) W-2 . . . . . . . . . | | 7 | |
| 8a | **Taxable interest.** Attach Schedule B if required . . . . . . | | 8a | |
| b | **Tax-exempt** interest. **Do not** include on line 8a . . . | 8b | | |
| 9a | Ordinary dividends. Attach Schedule B if required . . . . . | | 9a | |
| b | Qualified dividends (see page 22) . . . . . | 9b | | |
| 10 | Taxable refunds, credits, or offsets of state and local income taxes (see page 23) . . | | 10 | |
| 11 | Alimony received . . . . . . . . . . . . . . . . | | 11 | |
| 12 | Business income or (loss). Attach Schedule C or C-EZ . . . . . . . | | 12 | |
| 13 | Capital gain or (loss). Attach Schedule D if required. If not required, check here ▶ ☐ | | 13 | |
| 14 | Other gains or (losses). Attach Form 4797 . . . . . . . . . | | 14 | |
| 15a | IRA distributions . | 15a | b Taxable amount (see page 24) | 15b | |
| 16a | Pensions and annuities | 16a | b Taxable amount (see page 25) | 16b | |
| 17 | Rental real estate, royalties, partnerships, S corporations, trusts, etc. Attach Schedule E | | 17 | |
| 18 | Farm income or (loss). Attach Schedule F . . . . . . . . . . | | 18 | |
| 19 | Unemployment compensation in excess of $2,400 per recipient (see page 27) . . . | | 19 | |
| 20a | Social security benefits | 20a | b Taxable amount (see page 27) | 20b | |
| 21 | Other income. List type and amount (see page 29) _____ | | 21 | |
| 22 | Add the amounts in the far right column for lines 7 through 21. This is your **total income** ▶ | | 22 | |

**Adjusted Gross Income**

| 23 | Educator expenses (see page 29) . . . . . . . | 23 | | |
| 24 | Certain business expenses of reservists, performing artists, and fee-basis government officials. Attach Form 2106 or 2106-EZ | 24 | | |
| 25 | Health savings account deduction. Attach Form 8889 . | 25 | | |
| 26 | Moving expenses. Attach Form 3903 . . . . . | 26 | | |
| 27 | One-half of self-employment tax. Attach Schedule SE . . | 27 | | |
| 28 | Self-employed SEP, SIMPLE, and qualified plans . . | 28 | | |
| 29 | Self-employed health insurance deduction (see page 30) | 29 | | |
| 30 | Penalty on early withdrawal of savings . . . . . . | 30 | | |
| 31a | Alimony paid   b Recipient's SSN ▶ _____ | 31a | | |
| 32 | IRA deduction (see page 31) . . . . . . . . | 32 | | |
| 33 | Student loan interest deduction (see page 34) . . . | 33 | | |
| 34 | Tuition and fees deduction. Attach Form 8917 . . . | 34 | | |
| 35 | Domestic production activities deduction. Attach Form 8903 | 35 | | |
| 36 | Add lines 23 through 31a and 32 through 35 . . . . . . . . . | | 36 | |
| 37 | Subtract line 36 from line 22. This is your **adjusted gross income** . . . . . ▶ | | 37 | |

**For Disclosure, Privacy Act, and Paperwork Reduction Act Notice, see page 97.**   Cat. No. 11320B   Form **1040** (2009)

Form 1040 (2009)

Page **2**

| | | | | |
|---|---|---|---|---|
| **Tax and Credits** | 38 | Amount from line 37 (adjusted gross income) . . . . . . . . . . . . . | 38 | |
| | 39a | Check if: ☐ **You** were born before January 2, 1945, ☐ Blind. ☐ **Spouse** was born before January 2, 1945, ☐ Blind. **Total boxes checked** ▶ 39a | | |
| **Standard Deduction for—** ● People who check any box on line 39a, 39b, or 40b **or** who can be claimed as a dependent, see page 35. ● All others: Single or Married filing separately, $5,700 Married filing jointly or Qualifying widow(er), $11,400 Head of household, $8,350 | b | If your spouse itemizes on a separate return or you were a dual-status alien, see page 35 and check here ▶ 39b ☐ | | |
| | 40a | **Itemized deductions** (from Schedule A) **or** your **standard deduction** (see left margin) . . | 40a | |
| | b | If you are increasing your standard deduction by certain real estate taxes, new motor vehicle taxes, or a net disaster loss, attach Schedule L and check here (see page 35) . ▶ 40b ☐ | | |
| | 41 | Subtract line 40a from line 38 . . . . . . . . . . . | 41 | |
| | 42 | **Exemptions.** If line 38 is $125,100 or less and you did not provide housing to a Midwestern displaced individual, multiply $3,650 by the number on line 6d. Otherwise, see page 37 . . | 42 | |
| | 43 | **Taxable income.** Subtract line 42 from line 41. If line 42 is more than line 41, enter -0- . . | 43 | |
| | 44 | **Tax** (see page 37). Check if any tax is from: **a** ☐ Form(s) 8814 **b** ☐ Form 4972 . | 44 | |
| | 45 | **Alternative minimum tax** (see page 40). Attach Form 6251 . . . . . . | 45 | |
| | 46 | Add lines 44 and 45 . . . . . . . . . . . . . ▶ | 46 | |
| | 47 | Foreign tax credit. Attach Form 1116 if required . . . . | 47 | | |
| | 48 | Credit for child and dependent care expenses. Attach Form 2441 | 48 | | |
| | 49 | Education credits from Form 8863, line 29 . . . . | 49 | | |
| | 50 | Retirement savings contributions credit. Attach Form 8880 | 50 | | |
| | 51 | Child tax credit (see page 42) . . . . . . . | 51 | | |
| | 52 | Credits from Form: **a** ☐ 8396 **b** ☐ 8839 **c** ☐ 5695 | 52 | | |
| | 53 | Other credits from Form: **a** ☐ 3800 **b** ☐ 8801 **c** ☐ | 53 | | |
| | 54 | Add lines 47 through 53. These are your **total credits** . . . . . . . | 54 | |
| | 55 | Subtract line 54 from line 46. If line 54 is more than line 46, enter -0- . . . . . ▶ | 55 | |
| **Other Taxes** | 56 | Self-employment tax. Attach Schedule SE . . . . . . . | 56 | |
| | 57 | Unreported social security and Medicare tax from Form: **a** ☐ 4137 **b** ☐ 8919 . . | 57 | |
| | 58 | Additional tax on IRAs, other qualified retirement plans, etc. Attach Form 5329 if required . . | 58 | |
| | 59 | Additional taxes: **a** ☐ AEIC payments **b** ☐ Household employment taxes. Attach Schedule H | 59 | |
| | 60 | Add lines 55 through 59. This is your **total tax** . . . . . . . . . . ▶ | 60 | |
| **Payments** If you have a qualifying child, attach Schedule EIC. | 61 | Federal income tax withheld from Forms W-2 and 1099 | 61 | | |
| | 62 | 2009 estimated tax payments and amount applied from 2008 return | 62 | | |
| | 63 | Making work pay and government retiree credits. Attach Schedule M | 63 | | |
| | 64a | **Earned income credit (EIC)** . . . . . . . | 64a | | |
| | b | Nontaxable combat pay election 64b | | | |
| | 65 | Additional child tax credit. Attach Form 8812 . . . . . | 65 | | |
| | 66 | Refundable education credit from Form 8863, line 16 . . . | 66 | | |
| | 67 | First-time homebuyer credit. Attach Form 5405 . . . . | 67 | | |
| | 68 | Amount paid with request for extension to file (see page 72) . | 68 | | |
| | 69 | Excess social security and tier 1 RRTA tax withheld (see page 72) | 69 | | |
| | 70 | Credits from Form: **a** ☐ 2439 **b** ☐ 4136 **c** ☐ 8801 **d** ☐ 8885 | 70 | | |
| | 71 | Add lines 61, 62, 63, 64a, and 65 through 70. These are your **total payments** . . . . ▶ | 71 | |
| **Refund** Direct deposit? See page 73 and fill in 73b, 73c, and 73d, or Form 8888. | 72 | If line 71 is more than line 60, subtract line 60 from line 71. This is the amount you **overpaid** | 72 | |
| | 73a | Amount of line 72 you want **refunded to you.** If Form 8888 is attached, check here . ▶ ☐ | 73a | |
| | ▶ b | Routing number ▶ c Type: ☐ Checking ☐ Savings | | |
| | ▶ d | Account number | | |
| | 74 | Amount of line 72 you want **applied to your 2010 estimated tax** ▶ 74 | | |
| **Amount You Owe** | 75 | **Amount you owe.** Subtract line 71 from line 60. For details on how to pay, see page 74 . ▶ | 75 | |
| | 76 | Estimated tax penalty (see page 74) . . . . . . . . 76 | | |

| **Third Party Designee** | Do you want to allow another person to discuss this return with the IRS (see page 75)? ☐ **Yes.** Complete the following. ☐ **No** |
|---|---|
| | Designee's name ▶ _____ Phone no. ▶ _____ Personal identification number (PIN) ▶ ☐☐☐☐☐ |

| **Sign Here** Joint return? See page 15. Keep a copy for your records. | Under penalties of perjury, I declare that I have examined this return and accompanying schedules and statements, and to the best of my knowledge and belief, they are true, correct, and complete. Declaration of preparer (other than taxpayer) is based on all information of which preparer has any knowledge. |
|---|---|

| Your signature | Date | Your occupation | Daytime phone number |
|---|---|---|---|
| Spouse's signature. If a joint return, **both** must sign. | Date | Spouse's occupation | |

| **Paid Preparer's Use Only** | Preparer's signature ▶ | | Date | Check if self-employed ☐ | Preparer's SSN or PTIN |
|---|---|---|---|---|---|
| | Firm's name (or yours if self-employed), address, and ZIP code ▶ | | | EIN | |
| | | | | Phone no. | |

Form **1040** (2009)

## GROSS INCOME

**Gross income** includes all income items that must be reported on the federal income tax return and that are subject to the federal income tax. It includes all income as broadly defined, less exclusions. Gross income is discussed in more detail in Chapters 4 and 5. Some of the most common gross income items are listed in Exhibit 3.4.

| EXHIBIT 3.4 | ITEMS INCLUDED IN GROSS INCOME |
| --- | --- |

- Gains from the sale of assets
- Distributions from retirement plans
- Rental income
- Unemployment compensation benefits
- Royalty income
- Compensation (salaries and wages, etc.)
- Interest income
- Dividend income
- Alimony received
- Gross income from self-employment

## DEDUCTIONS

**Deductions** are subtracted from gross income in arriving at taxable income. For individual taxpayers, deductions are divided into two categories: Deductions *for* (before) adjusted gross income and deductions *from* (after) adjusted gross income. Deductions for adjusted gross income are called **above-the-line deductions**, and deductions from adjusted gross income are called **below-the-line deductions**, itemized deductions, or Schedule A deductions. These types of deductions are discussed in more detail in Chapters 6 and 7. A small sample of deductions for adjusted gross income (above-the-line deductions) is listed in Exhibit 3.5.

Quick
Quiz 3.1

**Highlight the answer to these questions:**

1. Income includes a return of invested capital.
   a. True
   b. False

2. Property obtained by inheritance is not included in gross income.
   a. True
   b. False

False, True.

| EXHIBIT 3.5 | PARTIAL LIST OF DEDUCTIONS FOR ADJUSTED GROSS INCOME |
| --- | --- |

- Alimony paid
- Contributions to traditional IRAs
- Tuition for higher education
- Interest paid on student loans
- Business expenses
- Rental or royalty income expenses
- Losses from the sale of business property
- Moving expenses

## ADJUSTED GROSS INCOME (AGI)

Adjusted gross income (AGI) is gross income reduced by above-the-line deductions. When determining whether deductions are taken above the line (for AGI) or below the line (from AGI), "the line" is AGI. Adjusted gross income is also used to determine limitations on several below-the-line deductions, on several income tax credits (discussed later in this chapter), and on a few other items on the tax return. Adjusted gross income is a concept that applies to individual tax returns; it does not apply to corporate or other entity tax returns.

### Deductions from Adjusted Gross Income

Deductions from adjusted gross income (below-the-line deductions) are those deductions that are subtracted from AGI. They consist of the greater of the standard deduction or certain allowable itemized deductions and the deduction for personal and dependency exemptions.

**Key Concepts**

Underline/highlight the answers to these questions as you read:

1. Define adjusted gross income.

2. Explain the difference between the standard deduction and itemized deductions.

3. Explain when a taxpayer is not permitted to use the standard deduction.

### Standard Deduction

An individual taxpayer is allowed to deduct the greater of the standard deduction or allowable itemized deductions. In recent years, approximately 70 percent of individual taxpayers have used the standard deduction. The **standard deduction** is a standard amount used to offset AGI that is specified by Congress. The standard deduction is adjusted for inflation on an annual basis. The total standard deduction includes a basic standard deduction plus additional standard deduction amounts for taxpayers age 65 or older and for taxpayers who are blind. The basic standard deduction amounts depend on the taxpayer's filing status (discussed below). The 2009 and 2010 standard deduction amounts for nondependents are listed in Exhibit 3.6. The standard deduction for a dependent is different and is discussed below.

## STANDARD DEDUCTION

EXHIBIT 3.6

| Filing Status | 2009 | 2010 |
|---|---|---|
| Married Filing Jointly | $11,400 | $11,400 |
| Married Filing Separately | $5,700 | $5,700 |
| Surviving Spouse | $11,400 | $11,400 |
| Head of Household | $8,350 | $8,400 |
| Single | $5,700 | $5,700 |

### Additional Standard Deduction

An additional standard deduction is allowed for a taxpayer or spouse (not for a dependent) who is 65 years of age or older or blind. The age of the taxpayer is determined as of the end of the year. It is therefore possible for an unmarried taxpayer to receive one or two additional standard deductions and for a married couple to receive up to four additional standard deductions. The amounts allowed for each additional standard deduction are adjusted for inflation and depend upon the filing status of the taxpayer. The 2009 and 2010 additional standard deduction amounts are listed in Exhibit 3.7.

**EXHIBIT 3.7** **ADDITIONAL STANDARD DEDUCTION**

| Filing Status | 2009 | 2010 |
|---|---|---|
| Married Filing Jointly | $1,100 | $1,100 |
| Married Filing Separately | $1,100 | $1,100 |
| Surviving Spouse | $1,100 | $1,100 |
| Head of Household | $1,400 | $1,400 |
| Single | $1,400 | $1,400 |

**EXAMPLE 3.2**

Trevor (age 66) and Susan (age 67) file a joint return for 2009. Their standard deduction is $13,600 (basic standard deduction of $11,400 plus two additional standard deductions of $1,100 for age). If Susan were blind, their standard deduction would be $14,700 (basic standard deduction plus three additional standard deductions). Note that the calculation remains the same for 2010.

**EXAMPLE 3.3**

Alberto (age 65) and Stephanie (age 58) are raising their grandson, Jackson, who qualifies as their dependent. Jackson is blind. Their standard deduction on a joint return for 2009 is $12,500 (basic standard deduction of $11,400 plus one additional standard deduction of $1,100 for Alberto's age). They do not receive an additional standard deduction for Jackson's blindness because additional standard deductions for age and blindness are allowed only for the taxpayer and spouse, and not for their dependents. It should be noted, however, that a dependent's additional standard deductions can be claimed on the dependent's own tax return. Note that the calculation remains the same for 2010.

**EXAMPLE 3.4**

Jessica is 34 years of age, blind, and unmarried as of the end of 2009. She uses the single filing status for her tax return. Her standard deduction is $7,100 (basic standard deduction of $5,700 plus an additional standard deduction of $1,400 for blindness). Note that the calculation remains the same for 2010.

**Itemized Deductions**

A taxpayer may choose to deduct specific allowable itemized deductions rather than the standard deduction. Below-the-line ("itemized") deductions are claimed (on Schedule A) when they exceed the total standard deduction and thus reduce taxable income more than the standard deduction. Itemized deductions are explained in more detail in Chapter 7. A partial list of itemized deductions is presented in Exhibit 3.8.

## PARTIAL LIST OF ITEMIZED DEDUCTIONS

EXHIBIT 3.8

- Miscellaneous expenses that exceed 2% of AGI
- Charitable contributions
- Tax return preparation fees
- Home mortgage interest
- Unreimbursed employee expenses
- Investment interest expense
- Medical and dental expenses in excess of 7.5% of AGI
- State and local income taxes
- Real property taxes on home
- Property taxes based on the value of a car
- Certain investment expenses
- Casualty losses in excess of 10% of AGI

EXAMPLE 3.5

Michael (age 52) and Karen (age 50) have no dependents. During 2009, they paid $5,000 in state income taxes, $2,000 in charitable contributions, $4,000 in home mortgage interest, and $1,500 in property taxes on their home. The total of their itemized deductions is $12,500. Their standard deduction is $11,400. Therefore, they should itemize deductions rather than use the standard deduction. Note: For 2010, their standard deduction is $11,400. Michael and Karen's best option for 2010 is to itemize deductions if their total itemized deductions remain higher than the standard deduction.

In three situations, a taxpayer is not allowed to use the standard deduction and *must* itemize deductions:

1. A married individual who files a separate return (married filing separately filing status) cannot use a standard deduction if that person's spouse itemizes deductions.
2. A nonresident alien and a dual-status alien is not allowed to use a standard deduction.
3. An individual who files a tax return for less than 12 months because of a change in annual accounting period is not allowed to use a standard deduction (not common for individual taxpayers).

### Personal and Dependency Exemptions

Personal and dependency exemption amounts are also deductions from adjusted gross income. A **personal exemption** is allowed for the taxpayer and the taxpayer's spouse on a tax return. A **dependency exemption** is allowed for each person who qualifies as a dependent of the taxpayer. Normally, the child of a taxpayer qualifies as the taxpayer's dependent, but many other people may qualify as dependents and in some cases the taxpayer's own child does not qualify as a dependent. The inflation-adjusted amount allowed as a deduction for each personal and dependency exemption is $3,650 for 2009 and 2010.

**Key Concepts**

Underline/highlight the answers to these questions as you read:

1. Define personal and dependency exemptions.

2. Explain how the tax on taxable income is calculated.

3. Identify various tax credits.

## TAXABLE INCOME

Taxable income is the tax base on which the income tax is calculated. It is calculated after reducing AGI by the greater of the standard deduction or itemized deductions and the allowable personal and dependency exemptions.

## TAX ON TAXABLE INCOME

The income tax on taxable income is determined by applying certain tax rates to taxable income. The tax rates currently range from 10 percent to 35 percent. The amount of taxable income subject to tax at each rate (each tax bracket) depends on the filing status of the taxpayer. These rates are shown in Appendix A.

**EXAMPLE 3.6**

Scott is 32 years of age and unmarried. His taxable income for 2009 is $80,000. Using Tax Rate Schedule X – Single, his tax on taxable income can be computed.

| If taxable income is over-- | But not over-- | The tax is: |
|---|---|---|
| $0 | $8,350 | 10% of the amount over $0 |
| $8,350 | $33,950 | $835 plus 15% of the amount over $8,350 |
| $33,950 | $82,250 | $4,675 plus 25% of the amount over $33,950 |
| **$82,250** | **$171,550** | **$16,750 plus 28% of the amount over $82,250** |
| $171,550 | $372,950 | $41,754 plus 33% of the amount over $171,550 |
| $372,950 | no limit | $108,216 plus 35% of the amount over $372,950 |

For taxable income over $33,950 but not over $82,250, the income tax is $4,675 plus 25% of the amount over $33,950. [($80,000 – $33,950) x 25% = $11,512.50]. The tax is therefore $16,187.50 or $4,675 + $11,512.50.

The total tax consists of:

1. $8,350 taxed at 10%
   $8,350 x 10% = $835

2. $25,600 taxed at 15%
   [($33,950 – $8,350) x 15% = $3,840]

3. $46,050 taxed at 25%
   [($80,000 – $33,950) x 25% = $11,512.50]

Scott's total tax is $16,187.50.

Scott's marginal tax rate, the rate on the next dollar of taxable income, is 25%.

For 2010, Scott's total tax is $16,181.25 and his marginal tax rate is 25%. The 2010 tax rate schedule is available in Appendix A.

Although the tax can be determined by directly applying the tax rates from the tax rate schedules to taxable income (as shown in the example above), taxpayers are required to determine the tax using tax tables provided by the Internal Revenue Service, if possible. These tax tables, published by the Internal Revenue Service in the instructions for individual income tax returns, show small ranges of taxable income and the amount of tax for taxable income within each range.

## EXCERPT FROM 2009 AND 2010 TAX TABLES

EXHIBIT 3.9

| Excerpt from 2009 Tax Table | | | | | | Excerpt from 2010 Tax Table | | | | | |
|---|---|---|---|---|---|---|---|---|---|---|---|
| If taxable income is - | | And you are - | | | | If taxable income is - | | And you are - | | | |
| At least | But less than | Single | Married filing jointly | Married filing separately | Head of a household | At least | But less than | Single | Married filing jointly | Married filing separately | Head of a household |
| | | Your tax is - | | | | | | Your tax is - | | | |
| **80,000** | | | | | | **80,000** | | | | | |
| 80,000 | 80,050 | **16,194** | 12,381 | 16,539 | 14,859 | 80,000 | 80,050 | **16,188** | 12,369 | 16,529 | 14,854 |
| 80,050 | 80,100 | 16,206 | 12,394 | 16,553 | 14,871 | 80,050 | 80,100 | 16,200 | 12,381 | 16,543 | 14,866 |
| 80,100 | 80,150 | 16,219 | 12,406 | 16,567 | 14,884 | 80,100 | 80,150 | 16,213 | 12,394 | 16,557 | 14,879 |
| 80,150 | 80,200 | 16,231 | 12,419 | 16,581 | 14,896 | 80,150 | 80,200 | 16,225 | 12,406 | 16,571 | 14,891 |
| 80,200 | 80,250 | 16,244 | 12,431 | 16,595 | 14,909 | 80,200 | 80,250 | 16,238 | 12,419 | 16,585 | 14,904 |
| 80,250 | 80,300 | 16,256 | 12,444 | 16,609 | 14,921 | 80,250 | 80,300 | 16,250 | 12,431 | 16,599 | 14,916 |
| 80,300 | 80,350 | 16,269 | 12,456 | 16,623 | 14,934 | 80,300 | 80,350 | 16,263 | 12,444 | 16,613 | 14,929 |
| 80,350 | 80,400 | 16,281 | 12,469 | 16,637 | 14,946 | 80,350 | 80,400 | 16,275 | 12,456 | 16,627 | 14,941 |
| 80,400 | 80,450 | 16,294 | 12,481 | 16,651 | 14,959 | 80,400 | 80,450 | 16,288 | 12,469 | 16,641 | 14,954 |
| 80,450 | 80,500 | 16,306 | 12,494 | 16,665 | 14,971 | 80,450 | 80,500 | 16,300 | 12,481 | 16,655 | 14,966 |
| 80,500 | 80,550 | 16,319 | 12,506 | 16,679 | 14,984 | 80,500 | 80,550 | 16,313 | 12,494 | 16,669 | 14,979 |
| 80,550 | 80,600 | 16,331 | 12,519 | 16,693 | 14,996 | 80,550 | 80,600 | 16,325 | 12,506 | 16,683 | 14,991 |
| 80,600 | 80,650 | 16,344 | 12,531 | 16,707 | 15,009 | 80,600 | 80,650 | 16,338 | 12,519 | 16,697 | 15,004 |
| 80,650 | 80,700 | 16,356 | 12,544 | 16,721 | 15,021 | 80,650 | 80,700 | 16,350 | 12,531 | 16,711 | 15,016 |
| 80,700 | 80,750 | 16,369 | 12,556 | 16,735 | 15,034 | 80,700 | 80,750 | 16,363 | 12,544 | 16,725 | 15,029 |
| 80,750 | 80,800 | 16,381 | 12,569 | 16,749 | 15,046 | 80,750 | 80,800 | 16,375 | 12,556 | 16,739 | 15,041 |
| 80,800 | 80,850 | 16,394 | 12,581 | 16,763 | 15,059 | 80,800 | 80,850 | 16,388 | 12,569 | 16,753 | 15,054 |
| 80,850 | 80,900 | 16,406 | 12,594 | 16,777 | 15,071 | 80,850 | 80,900 | 16,400 | 12,581 | 16,767 | 15,066 |
| 80,900 | 80,950 | 16,419 | 12,606 | 16,791 | 15,084 | 80,900 | 80,950 | 16,413 | 12,594 | 16,781 | 15,079 |
| 80,950 | 81,000 | 16,431 | 12,619 | 16,805 | 15,096 | 80,950 | 81,000 | 16,425 | 12,606 | 16,795 | 15,091 |

EXAMPLE 3.7

Using the 2009 tax table above, Scott's federal income tax for 2009 is $16,194. This is $6.50 more than the $16,187.50 determined from the tax rate schedules. In the tax table, Scott's tax is based on taxable income of $80,025, the midpoint between the $80,000 lower limit and $80,050 upper limit for the small bracket he must use from the tax table. Scott is required to use the amount from the tax table. If Scott's taxable income were higher than the amounts listed in the tax tables, he would use tax rate schedules to determine his tax.

For 2010, Scott's federal income tax (using the 2010 tax table excerpt) is $16,188. This is $6.75 more than the $16,181.25 calculated from the tax rate schedule. (See Appendix A.)

## CREDIT FOR ESTIMATED TAX PAYMENTS

The income earned by a self-employed person, and certain other business and investment income is not subject to tax withholding by an employer. Nevertheless, Congress would like to collect the taxes throughout the year. Therefore, a taxpayer with income not subject to withholding must pay quarterly **estimated tax payments** to the Treasury Department (through the Internal Revenue Service) on April 15, June 15, September 15, and January 15 of the following year. Estimated payments must also be made (on different dates) by regular corporations. As with taxes withheld by the employer, the taxpayer can claim a credit against the calculated tax for these quarterly estimated tax payments. Penalties may be imposed if estimated tax payments for the year are insufficient or late. (See Chapter 2 for more specific information on the underpayment penalty.)

## OTHER TAX CREDITS

Various other tax credits are allowed to reduce the tax calculated on taxable income. These credits are discussed in more detail in Chapter 9. Exhibit 3.10 provides a partial listing of some popular tax credits.

## Quick Quiz 3.2

**Highlight the answer to these questions:**

1. A nonresident alien taxpayer is allowed to use the standard deduction.
   a. True
   b. False

2. Personal and dependency exemptions are deducted for AGI.
   a. True
   b. False

3. Tax credits increase the amount that the taxpayer owes.
   a. True
   b. False

4. Tax credits are available for child and dependent care expenses.
   a. True
   b. False

False, False, False, True.

EXHIBIT 3.10

| |
|---|
| Foreign tax credit |
| Credit for child and dependent care expenses |
| Credit for the elderly or disabled |
| Education Credits (American Opportunity Tax Credit, Lifetime Learning Credit) |
| Retirement savings contribution credit |
| Residential energy credits |
| Child tax credit |
| Earned income credit |
| Additional child tax credit |
| Various business and investment credits |

## USING THE TAX FORMULA: THE ANDERSON FAMILY

Paul Anderson (age 35) is a school teacher. He participates in two retirement plans and receives medical insurance and other fringe benefits from his employer. His wife, Stacey (age 33), works part-time as an office manager for a small business. Her company provides no retirement plan or other fringe benefits. They are the parents of one child, Amanda, who is almost three years old. Stacey's mother cares for Amanda at no cost while Stacey works. They live in Smithfield, Utah. During 2009, they had the following income and expenses that may be relevant in filing their joint tax return:

| | | Item |
|---|---|---|
| Paul's gross salary | $36,400 | 1 |
| Paul's payment to his 401(k) retirement plan (withheld from his pay by his employer) | $2,400 | 2 |
| Stacey's gross salary | $18,000 | 1 |
| Stacey's cash gift from her mother | $5,000 | 1, 2 |
| Interest income from a joint savings account | $100 | 1 |
| Federal income taxes withheld from their paychecks | $2,500 | 4 |
| State income taxes withheld from their paychecks | $1,680 | |
| Charitable contributions (cash) paid to several charities | $6,000 | |
| Rent paid for apartment | $10,000 | |
| Contribution to a traditional IRA by Stacey | $2,000 | 3 |

Their federal income tax for 2009 and 2010 is calculated as follows:

| Item | | 2009 | 2010 |
|------|------|------|------|
| 1 | Income Broadly Defined | $59,500 | $59,500 |
| 2 | Less: Exclusions | ($7,400) | ($7,400) |
| | **Gross Income** | **$52,100** | **$52,100** |
| 3 | Less: Deductions for Adjusted Gross Income | ($2,000) | ($2,000) |
| | **Adjusted Gross Income** | **$50,100** | **$50,100** |
| | Less: Deductions from Adjusted Gross Income: Greater of Standard or Itemized Deductions (Standard Deduction) | ($11,400) | ($11,400) |
| | Less: Personal and Dependency Exemptions (3 Exemptions) | ($10,950) | ($10,950) |
| | **Taxable Income** | **$27,750** | **$27,750** |
| | Tax on Taxable Income (from tax rate schedule) | $3,328 | $3,325 |
| 4 | Less: Credit for Taxes Withheld | ($2,500) | ($2,500) |
| | Less: Credit for Estimated Tax Payments | $0 | $0 |
| | Less: Other Tax Credits (Child Credit) | ($1,000) | ($1,000) |
| | **Tax Due or (Refund Due)** | **($172)** | **($175)** |

*Income broadly defined* (1) includes Paul's gross salary ($36,400), Stacey's gross salary ($18,000), Stacey's gift from her mother ($5,000) and the interest income ($100).

*Exclusions* (2) include Paul's deferral of salary (contribution) into his 401(k) retirement plan ($2,400) and Stacey's gift from her mother ($5,000).

*Gross income* includes the taxable portion of Paul's salary ($36,400 – $2,400 = $34,000), Stacey's gross salary ($18,000), and the interest income ($100). These amounts are reported on the tax return.

*Deductions for adjusted gross income* (3) include only Stacey's deductible contribution to a traditional IRA ($2,000).

The Andersons' *standard deduction* for 2009 and 2010 is $11,400, the basic standard deduction on a joint return. This amount is greater than the total of their itemized deductions, $7,680 (state income taxes of $1,680 plus charitable contributions of $6,000). The apartment rent is a personal expense that is not allowed as an itemized deduction.

A deduction for *personal and dependency exemptions* is allowed for 2009 and 2010 in the amount of $10,950 (3 x $3,650). Personal exemptions are allowed for Paul and Stacey, and a dependency exemption is allowed for Amanda.

The *tax on taxable income* can also be determined from tax tables provided in the instructions for Form 1040.

A credit (4) of $2,500 is allowed for the amount of federal income taxes withheld from the salaries of Paul and Stacey.

Other tax credits ($1,000) is a child tax credit for Amanda.

Based on their income, filing status, and use of the standard deduction, the Andersons are eligible to use Form 1040A, rather than the more complicated Form 1040.

## INTRODUCTION TO INDIVIDUAL INCOME TAXATION

The tax formula for individual taxpayers provides a roadmap for the remainder of this book. Each item in the tax formula will be examined in much more detail, but for now, several fundamental topics will be addressed in this chapter.

### TAX ACCOUNTING PERIODS

A tax year, for tax reporting purposes, may be the calendar year, a fiscal year that ends on the last day of a month other than December, or a 52-53 week year that ends on a specified day of the week (such as Friday) that occurs in the last week of the last month of the tax year. The 52-53 week **tax year** may also end on the specified day of the week that falls closest to the last day of the last month of the tax year. A taxpayer normally chooses a tax year by simply filing his first tax return using the desired tax year for reporting purposes.

If a taxpayer wishes to have a tax year other than the calendar year, books and records must be maintained on the basis of the taxpayer's tax year. Since most individual taxpayers do not maintain books and records, their default tax year is the calendar year. Even individuals who do keep accounting records commonly use a calendar year because most tax reporting documents, such as Forms W-2 and 1099, report income on a calendar year basis.

**Key Concepts**

**Underline/highlight the answers to these questions as you read:**

1. Identify the tax accounting periods that can be used by individual taxpayers.

2. Compare and contrast the various accounting methods.

3. Identify the different filing statuses.

4. Describe the requirements for each filing status.

A tax year must be used consistently unless a formal change in accounting period is approved by the Internal Revenue Service. When this happens, special rules apply to the short tax year that results from the change.

### TAX ACCOUNTING METHODS

An overall accounting method must be selected by each taxpayer for tax reporting purposes. This method must be used consistently from year to year unless a formal change in accounting method is made. Such changes normally require (1) the approval of the IRS, and (2) income adjustments in the year of the change.

A taxpayer who owns more than one business is allowed to select a different overall accounting method for each business, but taxable income must be computed using the methods normally used in keeping accounting records for each business. Additionally, a taxpayer may use different methods to account for business income and for nonbusiness income and deductions.

There are three accounting methods that are available for reporting income and deductions:
1. the cash receipts and disbursements method (cash method),
2. the accrual method, and
3. the hybrid method.

### Cash Receipts and Disbursements Method

Most individual taxpayers use the **cash receipts and disbursement method** (cash method) of accounting when filing their income tax returns. Under this method of accounting, income items (or revenues) are reported on a tax return for the year in which they are received in cash and expenses are deducted in the year in which they are paid with cash. For this purpose, cash includes currency, checks, and similar payments. Payments with credit cards issued by financial institutions are treated the same as paying with cash at the time of purchase, but paying with a credit card issued by a store (such as Sears, Wal-Mart, Home Depot, and the like) is not treated as a cash disbursement until the credit card bill is paid.

While cash method taxpayers normally recognize income when it is received in cash or cash equivalent, exceptions do apply. Among the more common exceptions that apply to the cash method of accounting are:
1. the doctrine of constructive receipt,
2. original issue discount bonds, and
3. cash received with an obligation to repay.

The **doctrine of constructive receipt** states that a cash method taxpayer must report income when it is constructively received. Constructive receipt occurs when income is credited to a taxpayer's account or when it is made available to the taxpayer without restriction. A taxpayer need not take possession of income for it to be constructively received. For example, interest income may be credited to the taxpayer's account after the bank closes on the last day of the tax year, or a client may offer to give the taxpayer a check for services already provided while attending a New Year's Eve party. In either case, constructive receipt has occurred and the taxpayer's gross income must include these amounts. The doctrine of constructive receipt underlies most of the retirement planning rules, and must be avoided to allow deferral of income.

A special application of constructive receipt is an **original issue discount (OID) bond**, more commonly known as a **zero coupon bond**. The interest that accrues on the bond each year (determined by a financial calculation that takes into consideration the difference between the maturity value of the bond and its purchase price), is deemed to be constructively received by the taxpayer, and is included in the taxpayer's income. Since the bond does not actually make the interest payment that year, but the taxpayer must include the imputed interest in income, zero coupon bonds generate "phantom income." As interest is reported in income, the taxpayer's basis in the bond increases by a like amount. The tax treatment of OID bonds will be more fully discussed in Chapter 4.

Finally, if a taxpayer receives cash, but has an obligation to repay the payor, the cash is not included in gross income. This may occur when a landlord receives a deposit for an apartment. If the landlord has an obligation to return the deposit when the renter moves out (provided, of course, that the apartment is left in good condition), the cash received is not included in gross income, since it does not represent an accretion to wealth. If the deposit is really a form of prepaid rent, however, it must be recognized as gross income.

A taxpayer who uses the cash receipts and disbursements method for reporting most items on a tax return may use an accrual or hybrid method for reporting self-employment income or other business income from a proprietorship (on Schedule C), farm (Schedule F), or partnership (Schedule E).

## Accrual Method of Accounting

Many businesses use the **accrual method** of accounting, since it provides a better match between income and the expenses associated with producing that income than the cash receipts and disbursements method of accounting. Under the accrual method, income (revenue) is normally reported when it is earned, and expenses are normally deducted when they are incurred.

The "all events" test is commonly used to determine income inclusion under the accrual method of accounting for income tax purposes. Income is includible when all events have occurred that, (1) fix the taxpayer's right to receive the income, and (2) allow the amount of income to be determined with reasonable accuracy.

There are several exceptions to the accrual method of accounting. Some of the more common exceptions that apply in a financial planning context are:
- Prepaid income,
- Advance payment for goods,
- Advance payment for services, and
- The claim of right doctrine.

For financial accounting purposes, prepaid income is not reported under the accrual method until goods or services are provided to the customer. For tax purposes, the federal government wants to collect taxes, even from an accrual basis taxpayer, when the taxpayer has the cash (the wherewithal to pay). Therefore, prepaid income, such as prepaid interest and prepaid rent, must be included in income when the payment is received.

When a business owner receives advance payment for goods to be delivered in the future, financial accounting rules normally require an accrual basis seller to report the revenues only when delivery of the goods is made and the revenues are earned. For tax purposes, the seller is generally allowed similar treatment if the seller elects such treatment and if the same method is used for both tax and financial reporting purposes.

An unusual rule applies when advance payments are received for services to be performed in the future. According to Revenue Procedure 2004-34, an accrual method taxpayer is allowed to use the regular accrual method for the year in which the prepayment is received, but the remainder of the prepayment must be included in gross income for the following year.

| **EXAMPLE 3.8** | Brittany is the owner of a cleaning and custodial business. On November 1 of Year 1, Brittany receives $2,400 ($100 per month) for custodial services to be provided from November 1 of Year 1 through October 31 of Year 3. She uses the normal accrual method for Year 1 and therefore reports $200 of the revenues in Year 1. The remaining $2,200 must all be recognized in Year 2. She is not permitted to defer recognition of the $1,000 (for January through October of year 3) until Year 3. |
| --- | --- |

### The Claim of Right Doctrine

When an accrual method taxpayer earns income, that income is normally included in gross income. There are circumstances, however, under which the situation is not so clear cut. For example, consider an accrual method taxpayer who sells tires. What happens if the customer is not satisfied? If the customer refuses to pay, the taxpayer is not required to report the contested portion of the bill because the taxpayer's income is in question. The disputed portion of the bill will be reported only when the dispute is settled.

For situations in which the customer pays and then requests or sues for a full or partial refund, courts have established the claim of right doctrine. Under this doctrine, the taxpayer must report the entire payment in gross income in the year of the payment even though part or all of the payment may have to be repaid to the customer. If the customer is repaid in a later year, the taxpayer is allowed a tax deduction in the year of the repayment.

### *The Hybrid Method*

The **hybrid method** of accounting includes any other method of reporting that is permitted by the Code and regulations as long as it is deemed to clearly reflect income. A common hybrid method of accounting involves use of the accrual method for inventories and property, plant, and equipment and the cash method for everything else. A taxpayer who owns more than one trade or business is allowed to use a different overall accounting method for each business.

Hybrid methods are commonly used in conjunction with special types of transactions or arrangements, such as with long-term contracts. Long-term contracts are contracts that are entered into during the year, but will not be completed within that year. Building, construction, installation, and certain manufacturing contracts are often long-term contracts. The costs associated with a long-term contract are deducted from the revenues generated by that contract under one of two hybrid methods: the completed contract method or the percentage of completion method.

The completed contract method states that no revenue from a contract is included in the taxpayer's income until the contract is completed. The percentage of completion method, on the other hand, requires that a portion of the expected revenues of the contract must be included in the taxpayer's income at regular intervals based upon the percentage of completion of the work. Because revenues from the contract are included in the taxpayer's income, the taxpayer is also allowed to deduct a pro rata share of the expenses during the same period based on the percentage completion method.

## FILING STATUS

The filing status of a taxpayer is used to determine the amount of the taxpayer's standard deduction, the tax rate schedule (or tax table) to be used, and the eligibility of the taxpayer to use various tax benefits. A list of filing statuses is presented in Exhibit 3.11.

### FILING STATUS FOR INDIVIDUALS

EXHIBIT 3.11

| Married Filing Jointly |
| --- |
| Married Filing Separately |
| Surviving Spouse |
| Head of Household (Including an Abandoned Spouse) |
| Single |

### Marital Status

The determination of whether a taxpayer is married is normally made as of the close (the last day) of the tax year. However, if a taxpayer's spouse dies during the year, the marital status of the taxpayer is determined on the date of the spouse's death. A married person normally has two filing status options: married filing jointly or married filing separately.

> Juan Martinez married Charlotte Johnson on December 31st of this year. They will have to file as married filing jointly or married filing separately for the year.

EXAMPLE 3.9

If a person is not married, then he or she may qualify for the surviving spouse, head of household, or single filing status. A very rare situation is discussed below which may allow a married person to file as a single taxpayer. A taxpayer who is legally separated from his spouse under a decree of divorce or of separate maintenance is not considered to be married for federal income tax purposes.

### Married Filing Jointly

Married taxpayers are allowed to choose either married filing jointly or **married filing separately status**. Most married taxpayers use the **married filing jointly filing status**. This filing status allows a married couple to combine their gross income and deductions. If they do not itemize deductions, the basic standard deduction when filing jointly is double the size of the basic standard deduction for a married taxpayer filing separately. Each tax bracket (the 15 percent tax bracket, for example) for joint filers is twice as broad as for a married taxpayer filing separately, subjecting twice as much income to the lower rates. In addition, a married couple is required to file jointly in order to be eligible for certain benefits such as the earned income credit (discussed in Chapter 9).

### Married Filing Separately

A married taxpayer can elect to file separately for any reason. This may be necessary if the husband and wife are separated at the end of the year, or if the taxpayer is not sure that his spouse is accurately reporting income. It may also be used for tax minimization purposes, by permitting one spouse to deduct more of his unusually large medical expenses or employee business expenses for the tax year.

For a taxpayer whose spouse dies during the year, a joint return can be filed. The joint return will include the income and deductions of the taxpayer for the full year and the income and deductions of the spouse for the part of the year that the spouse lived. If the surviving taxpayer remarries before the end of the year, she will be able to file a joint return with the new spouse but not with the deceased spouse. In this situation, the final income tax return for the deceased spouse must use the married filing separately filing status.

**EXAMPLE 3.10**

> Jared Kruger died in April. His surviving spouse, Susan, married Thomas in November of the same year. Susan will be able to file as married filing jointly with Thomas. A tax return for Jared for the part of the year he lived will have to use the married filing separately filing status.

### Abandoned Spouse

There is one situation in which a legally married taxpayer will be allowed to use a filing status (head of household) generally reserved for unmarried taxpayers. As discussed below, the head of household status is more favorable than filing as married filing separately and when an individual cannot locate his spouse, and does not want to file a tax return with him, it may be available. To be eligible to file as an abandoned spouse (and therefore use the head of household filing status), the taxpayer must meet *all* of the following requirements:

- The taxpayer must be married;
- Must file a separate tax return from the spouse;
- Must maintain as his/her home a household which for more than one-half of the taxable year is the principal place of abode of a child who can be claimed as a dependent;
- Must furnish over one-half of the cost of maintaining the household; *and*
- The spouse must not be a member of the household during the last six months of the tax year.

**EXAMPLE 3.11**

> Bonnie Simpson is married to Howard Simpson, but Howard moved to another state during March of the current year. Bonnie hasn't talked to Howard since he moved out. She works as a school teacher and has paid all of the costs of providing for herself and her two minor children who live with her. She will file her own tax return for the year. Although she is legally married at the end of the year, she will be allowed to file using the head of household filing status, a filing status normally used by unmarried taxpayers.

## Unmarried Taxpayers

A taxpayer who is not married on the final day of the tax year may be able to file as surviving spouse, head of household, or single. The tax benefits for the surviving spouse filing status are most favorable, those for head of household are next, and those for the single filing status are the least favorable.

### Surviving Spouse

The **surviving spouse filing status** affords the same basic standard deduction and tax rates as the married filing jointly filing status. However, eligibility for this filing status is not something that most people desire. To be eligible, the spouse of the taxpayer must have died within the two preceding tax years of the taxpayer. Specifically, a taxpayer must meet all of the following requirements to qualify:

- The taxpayer's spouse must have died during either of the two preceding tax years;
- The taxpayer must maintain (pay more than half the cost of) a household as his home which is also the principal place of residence of a dependent child (son, stepson, daughter, or stepdaughter);
- The taxpayer has not remarried; and
- The taxpayer and spouse were eligible to file a joint return for the spouse's year of death.

**EXAMPLE 3.12**

Todd Williamson died in 2007. His wife, Diane, filed a joint return with Todd for 2007. Diane did not remarry in 2008, 2009, or 2010, but she maintained a home for herself and her two minor children during those years. During 2008 and 2009, Diane is eligible to use the surviving spouse filing status. In 2010, she will probably be eligible to use the head of household filing status (see below).

It should be noted that the filing status called surviving spouse in the Internal Revenue Code and Treasury Regulations is referred to as the qualifying widow(er) filing status in IRS publications. Surviving spouse and qualifying widow(er) are alternate names for the same filing status.

### Head of Household

The **head of household filing status** provides a basic standard deduction and tax bracket sizes that are less favorable to the taxpayer than those for the surviving spouse, but more favorable than those for the single filing status. Head of household filing status can be used by an unmarried taxpayer who is not a surviving spouse and who meets the following requirements:

- The taxpayer must maintain (pay more than half the cost of) a household as his home, which is also the principal place of residence for more than half the year for:

- a qualifying child of the taxpayer who is claimed as a dependent (discussed later in this chapter) of the taxpayer,
- an unmarried qualifying child who lives with the taxpayer but is not a dependent of the taxpayer (e.g., a taxpayer's child or grandchild who lives in the taxpayer's household but is claimed as the dependent of another person), or
- a qualifying relative (discussed later in this chapter) who is (1) claimed as a dependent of the taxpayer, and (2) actually related to the taxpayer.

If a married child of the taxpayer lives with the taxpayer but cannot be claimed as a dependent of the taxpayer either because the child (1) files a joint return (married filing jointly) with her spouse or (2) fails to meet a citizenship or residency test, the taxpayer is not allowed to use the head of household filing status.

**EXAMPLE 3.13**

Joan, who is not married, rents a home for herself and her two young children. She qualifies to use the head of household filing status.

**EXAMPLE 3.14**

Hector is not married. He maintains a household for himself and his dependent son. During the year, Hector's son lived with him during the summer (three months) and lived in an apartment at a distant university during the rest of the year. Even though Hector's son did not live with him for more than half the year, Hector will be allowed to use head of household filing status because his son's absence is considered to be temporary. The taxpayer and the dependent are considered to occupy the household even during temporary absences due to special circumstances such as illness, education, business, vacation, military service, or a custody agreement under which the dependent is absent for less than six months during the tax year.

**EXAMPLE 3.15**

Tiffany, who is unmarried, rents an apartment for herself and for her 14-year-old daughter who lives with her. Under the terms of Tiffany's divorce decree, her daughter is claimed as a dependent by her father. Tiffany is allowed to use head of household filing status even though she doesn't claim her daughter as a dependent, because she maintains the home for her daughter.

**EXAMPLE 3.16**

Christopher, who is unmarried, maintains a home in which he and his uncle live. He properly claims his uncle as a dependent. Christopher is allowed to use the head of household filing status because he claims his uncle as a dependent and because his uncle is actually related to him.

EXAMPLE 3.17

Elizabeth is unmarried. She maintains a household in which she and her best friend's daughter live. Her friend's daughter, Jill, is 8 years old. Jill's parents, who died in an automobile accident two years earlier, had requested that Elizabeth raise Jill if they were to die prematurely. Since Jill meets the definition of a qualifying relative (explained below), Elizabeth is allowed to claim Jill as a dependent, but she will not be able to use the head of household filing status because Jill is not actually related to Elizabeth. If Elizabeth were to adopt Jill, she would be allowed to use the head of household filing status.

EXAMPLE 3.18

Jared, unmarried, owns a large house. He allows his 18-year-old son, Todd, to live in the basement of the home with his wife, Allison. Generally Jared will not be allowed to claim Todd as a dependent because Todd files a joint income tax return with his wife. Jared must use the single filing status rather than head of household.

### Special Rule for the Father or Mother of the Taxpayer

In order to use the head of household filing status, a qualifying child or a qualifying relative must normally live with the taxpayer. However, a taxpayer may also qualify for the head of household status by maintaining a separate household for the father or mother of the taxpayer who qualifies as the taxpayer's dependent.

EXAMPLE 3.19

John provides more than half of the cost of maintaining an apartment (or house or accommodations in a retirement home, etc.) for his mother this year. John properly claims his mother as a dependent. John is eligible to use the head of household filing status.

### Single

The **single filing status** must be used by an unmarried taxpayer who is not eligible to use the surviving spouse nor head of household filing status. It provides the least desirable basic standard deduction and tax brackets for an unmarried taxpayer.

## PERSONAL AND DEPENDENCY EXEMPTIONS

A taxpayer is allowed to take a deduction (from AGI) for the exemption amount for the taxpayer, the taxpayer's spouse, and for each dependent. Therefore, a married taxpayer with two dependent children is allowed to take a deduction for four exemption amounts. The exemption amounts for 2009 and 2010 are listed in Exhibit 3.12.

EXHIBIT 3.12 **PERSONAL AND DEPENDENCY EXEMPTION AMOUNTS**

| 2009 | 2010 |
|------|------|
| $3,650 | $3,650 |

When a taxpayer's adjusted gross income exceeds specified threshold amounts, the amount of the deduction for personal and dependency exemptions is gradually reduced. Exemptions are reduced or phased out by two percent for each $2,500 (or fraction thereof) that a taxpayer's adjusted gross income exceeds a threshold amount. The inflation-adjusted threshold amounts for 2009 and 2010 are:

| Threshold Amounts | 2009 | 2010 |
|-------------------|------|------|
| Married Filing Jointly and Surviving Spouse | $250,200 | $0 |
| Head of Household | $208,500 | $0 |
| Single | $166,800 | $0 |
| Married Filing Separately | $125,100 | $0 |

This reduction is being phased out from 2006 through 2009. Before 2006, the entire reduction was subtracted from the exemption amount. For 2006 and 2007, only two-thirds of the calculated reduction must be subtracted from the exemption amount. For 2008 and 2009, only one-third of the calculated reduction must be subtracted from the exemption amount. For years after 2009, the reduction is scheduled to go away so that the full deduction for personal and dependency exemptions will be allowed even for taxpayers with very high incomes.

EXAMPLE 3.20

For 2009, Connie's AGI exceeds the threshold by $20,200 ($187,000 - $166,800). Therefore the dependency exemption calculations are as follows:

$20,200/$2,500 = 8.08, rounded up to 9.

2% x 9 = 18%.

Connie's deduction, taking into account the 1/3 phaseout is:

$3,650 x 18% = $657

$657 x 1/3 = $219

Therefore, the exemption for 2009 is $3,431 ($3,650 - $219).

As indicated above, the full deduction for personal and dependency exemptions is allowed for 2010.

## Personal Exemptions

Each taxpayer is normally allowed to claim a personal exemption deduction. A married couple using the married filing jointly filing status is allowed to claim two personal exemptions.

However, only one exemption amount can be claimed for each individual. A person who can be claimed as a dependent by another taxpayer is not allowed to take a personal exemption deduction on his own tax return.

A married taxpayer who uses the married filing separately filing status normally claims only one personal exemption (plus exemptions for dependents), but may claim a personal exemption for the spouse as well if the spouse has no gross income and is not the dependent of another taxpayer.

### Key Concepts

**Underline/highlight the answers to these questions as you read:**

1. Define personal exemption.

2. Define dependency exemption.

3. Describe the requirements for claiming a qualifying child as a dependent.

4. Describe the requirements for claiming a qualifying relative as a dependent.

Note that in identifying the taxpayer and the spouse, the taxpayer is simply the individual whose name appears first on the tax return.

## Dependency Exemptions

The rules for dependency exemptions were significantly changed beginning in 2005. Currently, a taxpayer is allowed to claim a dependency exemption for each person who is considered a qualifying child or a qualifying relative. These terms can be confusing, however, because a qualifying child might not be the taxpayer's child at all and a qualifying relative in some cases is not a relative of the taxpayer.

## Qualifying Child

A **qualifying child** must meet *all* of four tests:
- A relationship test,
- An abode test,
- An age test, and
- A support test.

These rules for a qualifying child relate not only to dependency exemptions, but also to the definition of a child for purposes of head of household filing status, the earned income tax credit, the child tax credit, and the credit for child and dependent care expenses.

### Relationship Test

In order to satisfy the relationship test, a qualifying child of a taxpayer must be:

- the taxpayer's child,
- a descendant of the taxpayer's child,
- the taxpayer's brother, sister, stepbrother, stepsister, half brother, half sister, or
- a descendant of the taxpayer's brother, sister, stepbrother, stepsister, half brother, or half sister.

Stated differently, a qualifying child is a descendant of the taxpayer, the taxpayer's sibling, or a descendant of the taxpayer's sibling. Note that a cousin is not a qualifying child.

A taxpayer's child may be a natural child, a stepchild, an adopted child, or an eligible foster child.

**EXAMPLE 3.21**

Elizabeth and Warren McConkie have a remarkably diverse family. In addition to Elizabeth and Warren, the family includes:

1. Matt, Elizabeth's 10-year-old son from a prior marriage,
2. Amy, Elizabeth's 15-year-old sister,
3. Andrei, their 6-year-old son adopted from Russia,
4. Zoe, their 4-year old daughter, and
5. Carlos, a 2-year-old foster child placed with them by a state agency.

Each of the five children meets the relationship test as a qualifying child of Elizabeth.

### Abode Test

To meet the abode test, a qualifying child must live with the taxpayer for more than half the year. The taxpayer and the dependent are considered to occupy the household even during temporary absences due to special circumstances such as illness, education, business, vacation, or military service.

**EXAMPLE 3.22**

The 18-year-old son of Bill and Melinda Bates lived at home during the first five months of the year and then entered military service. Since military service is considered to be a temporary absence due to special circumstances, the son meets the abode test for the year.

### Age Test

A qualifying child must either be under the age of 19 as of the end of the calendar year or a student under the age of 24 as of the end of the calendar year in order to satisfy the age test. To be considered a student, the child must be a full-time student at an educational institution during five months of the calendar year. Most primary and secondary schools, colleges, universities and similar educational institutions are acceptable for this purpose.

**EXAMPLE 3.23**

Marilyn's 21-year-old son finished his third year of college in May of this year. He spent the remainder of the year serving as a volunteer in a program to assist the victims of a flood. If the son was a full-time student during part or all of the first five months of the year, he meets the age test.

## Support Test

The support test is satisfied if a qualifying child does not provide more than one-half of his or her own support during the year. If a child is the taxpayer's child and is a full-time student, amounts received as scholarships are not considered to be support.

Frank and Alice provide $10,000 toward the support of their son, Edward. Edward provides $2,000 toward his own support and receives a scholarship worth $12,000 from the university he attends. Edward is not considered to provide more than one-half of his own support because the scholarship is not considered to be support provided by Edward.

If more than one person is eligible to claim another person as a dependent under the qualifying child rules, the tie-breaker rules shown in Exhibit 3.13 apply:

## TIE-BREAKER RULES

| Eligible Taxpayers | Taxpayer Allowed to Claim the Dependency Exemption |
|---|---|
| Both parents | The parent with whom the child lived longer |
| Both parents and the child lives with each for the same amount of time | The parent with the higher adjusted gross income |
| Only one is a parent | The parent |
| Neither is a parent | The taxpayer with the higher adjusted gross income |

## Children of Divorced or Separated Parents

Because of the abode test, a child of divorced or separated parents is normally the qualifying child of the custodial parent. If all four of the following requirements are met, however, the child will be treated as the qualifying child of the noncustodial parent:

1. The parents are divorced or legally separated under a decree of divorce or separate maintenance, are separated under a written separation agreement, or they live apart at all times during the last six months of the year;
2. The child receives over one-half of his support for the year from his parents;
3. The child is in the custody of the parents for more than half the year; and
4. The custodial parent signs a statement that he will not claim the child as a dependent for the year, and the noncustodial parent attaches the statement to his return (may use Form 8332).

For the signed statement or written declaration in requirement four above, the custodial parent may use Form 8332 or a similar statement that contains the same information. The statement may apply to the current year, several years, or to all future years. For divorce or separation agreements after 1984, the requirement for a signed statement can be met by attaching certain pages from the decree or agreement to the tax return of the noncustodial parent. If pages from the decree or agreement are used, they must specify that the noncustodial parent can claim the child as a dependent, that the custodial parent will not claim the child as a dependent, and the years for which the noncustodial parent is allowed to claim the child. Different rules apply to divorce decrees and separation agreements before 1985.

<table>
<tr><td>

**EXAMPLE 3.25**

</td><td>

Edward and Janet were divorced three years ago. Janet was given custody of their daughter, Jessica, and Edward was given visitation rights on alternate weekends and other specified times. The divorce decree states that Edward will be allowed to claim Jessica as a dependent each year. Edward will be able to claim Jessica as a dependent, but he will be required to attach pages from the divorce decree to his income tax return each year. If the right to claim Jessica as a dependent had not been given to Edward in the divorce decree, Janet could allow him to claim Jessica by giving him a signed Form 8332 to attach to his tax return.

</td></tr>
</table>

### Qualifying Relative

In addition to the joint return test and the citizenship or residency test (discussed later), a **qualifying relative** must meet the following four tests to qualify as a dependent of a taxpayer:
- Relationship test,
- Gross income test,
- Support test, and
- Not a qualifying child test.

### Relationship Test

To satisfy the relationship test for a qualifying relative, the potential dependent of the taxpayer must be:
- the taxpayer's child or a descendant of a child (grandchildren, etc.),
- the taxpayer's brother, sister, stepbrother, or stepsister,
- the taxpayer's father, or mother, or an ancestor (grandparent, etc.),
- the taxpayer's stepfather or stepmother,
- a son (nephew) or daughter (niece) of a brother or sister of the taxpayer,
- a brother (uncle) or sister (aunt) of the father or mother of the taxpayer,
- a son-in-law, daughter-in-law, father-in-law, mother-in-law, brother-in-law or sister-in-law of the taxpayer, or
- any other individual (may be a totally unrelated person) who, for the taxable year of the taxpayer, has the same principal place of abode as the taxpayer and is a member of the

taxpayer's household. A person who was married to the taxpayer during part of the year does not qualify.

A child of the taxpayer who does not meet the requirements to be a qualifying child may still meet the requirements to be a qualifying relative of the taxpayer. Note that not all relatives of a taxpayer (a cousin, for example) meet this relationship test. Significantly, individuals who are not actually related to the taxpayer may meet the relationship test if they live with the taxpayer as a member of the taxpayer's household. An unrelated person does not qualify in certain limited circumstances.

### Gross Income Test

To meet the gross income test, a dependent's gross income must be less than the exemption amount ($3,650 for 2009 and 2010) for the year. This contrasts with a qualifying child, for whom there is no such test.

| | |
|---|---|
| During 2009, Craig and Malia Franklin provide more than half the support of Malia's mother, who lives with them. Malia's mother receives $4,000 (included in gross income) per year from a retirement plan and a small monthly Social Security benefit check. The Social Security is not included in gross income because her other income is so low. Malia's mother fails the gross income test because her gross income is not less than $3,650 for 2009 and 2010. | **EXAMPLE 3.26** |
| Phillip provides more than half the support of his son, David. David is a 25-year-old doctoral student at a university. David's only income is a $12,000 fellowship to pay tuition. Even though David is not under 24 years of age and is therefore not a qualifying child, he may be claimed as a qualifying relative if he meets the gross income test. Since a fellowship or scholarship is normally excluded from gross income, Phillip is allowed to claim David as a dependent. | **EXAMPLE 3.27** |

### Support Test

To satisfy the support test, the taxpayer must provide more than one-half of the support of a dependent. Support normally includes providing housing, food, clothing, education, and medical treatment, among other things. Income received by a dependent does not count as support provided by the dependent unless it is actually expended for that purpose. For example, if income earned by an elderly parent is deposited in a savings account rather than expended for his own support, it does not count as support provided by the parent.

### Not a Qualifying Child Test

In order to be claimed as a qualifying relative, a dependent cannot be a qualifying child of any taxpayer for the tax year.

Special rules apply to a person who can be claimed as a dependent by another taxpayer. Such a person (1) is not allowed to claim a personal exemption deduction, (2) may have a reduced basic standard deduction, and (3) is required to file a tax return based on different rules from the gross income test used by taxpayers who cannot be claimed as a dependent. An overview of these issues is presented in the section on calculating the standard deduction of a dependent, which follows.

Only one exemption amount is allowed for each taxpayer. Therefore, a taxpayer who can be claimed as a dependent by another taxpayer is not allowed to take a deduction for a personal exemption on his or her own tax return.

In addition to the four tests for a qualifying child or the four tests for a qualifying relative, anyone who may be claimed as a dependent under the qualifying child or qualifying relative classifications must meet the following two tests:
- A joint return test, and
- A citizenship or residency test.

**Joint Return Test**

To satisfy the joint return test, a married dependent must not file a joint return with a spouse unless a tax return is filed only to claim a refund for tax withheld, if neither spouse is otherwise required to file a tax return, and if no tax liability would exist for either taxpayer on separate returns.

| **EXAMPLE 3.28** | George and Francesca wish to claim their married daughter, Elena, as a dependent. They meet all of the tests to claim her except the joint return test. Elena and her husband file a joint tax return for the year to reduce their income tax liability. They owe money on their joint return and each would have owed money on a separate return. George and Francesca are not eligible to claim Elena as a dependent. |
|---|---|

**Citizenship or Residency Test**

A dependent must be a citizen or national of the United States or a resident of the United States, Canada, or Mexico during some part of the year. This test does not apply for certain adopted children.

*Multiple Support Agreements*

Sometimes, no individual taxpayer provides more than one-half the support of a potential dependent. Under these circumstances, over one-half of the support is deemed to be paid by one taxpayer if:
1. The taxpayer provides more than 10 percent of the potential dependent's support;
2. Two or more persons who individually provide more than 10 percent of the potential dependent's support also provide more than 50 percent of the individual's total support and meet all other requirements to claim the individual as a dependent; and
3. The qualifying persons in item 2 above (other than the taxpayer) sign a statement (Form 2120 can be used) agreeing not to claim an exemption for the potential dependent for the year.
4. The taxpayer attaches the signed Form 2120 to her tax return.

EXAMPLE 3.29

No one provides more than half the support of Mary Johnson for the year. She is currently unmarried and lives alone in a small apartment, but she only provides 25% of her own support. The remainder of her support is provided by her son, Thomas (10%), her daughter, Paula (22%), her son, David (30%), and a friend and neighbor, Marsha (13%). The qualifying persons are Paula (22%) and David (30%) if they meet all other requirements to claim Mary as a dependent. Each of them provides more than 10% of Mary's support and together they provide more than 50% of her support. Either one of them can claim a dependency exemption for Mary for the year if the other person signs an appropriate statement. Thomas is not a qualifying person because he does not provide more than 10% of Mary's support. Marsha is not a qualifying person because she doesn't meet the relationship test as a qualifying relative.

## CALCULATION OF THE STANDARD DEDUCTION FOR A DEPENDENT

An individual who can be claimed as a dependent by someone else cannot use the regular basic standard deduction, as discussed above. The basic standard deduction for someone who can be claimed as a dependent by another taxpayer is determined using a three-step process:

- The minimum basic standard deduction is $950 (2009 and 2010);
- If larger, the basic standard deduction is equal to the earned income (wages, salary, self-employment income, or taxable scholarships or fellowships) of the taxpayer plus $300 (2009 and 2010); and
- The maximum basic standard deduction is equal to the normal basic standard deduction for the taxpayer's filing status.

Any additional standard deductions for age or blindness are added to the basic standard deduction.

**Quick Quiz 3.5**

**Highlight the answer to these questions:**

1. A taxpayer is entitled to a dependency exemption for anyone who lives in his house.
   a. True
   b. False

2. A qualifying child must live with the taxpayer for more than half of the year.
   a. True
   b. False

3. A qualifying relative, unlike a qualifying child, is subject to a gross income test.
   a. True
   b. False

False, True, True.

EXAMPLE 3.30

Samantha is 17 years old and can be claimed as a dependent by her parents. She earned $500 in wages during 2009. Her basic standard deduction is $950. She has no taxable income for 2009 ($500 - $950). She also has no taxable income for 2010 ($500 - $950).

**EXAMPLE 3.31**

Trevor is 17 years old and can be claimed as a dependent by his parents.

- He earned $3,000 in wages and $400 in interest income during 2009 (assume the same for 2010).

- His basic standard deduction is $3,300 ($3,000 of earned income + $300).

- His taxable income for 2009 is $100 (the same for 2010).

|  | 2009 |
|---|---|
| Wages | $3,000 |
| Interest Income | 400 |
| Less Personal Exemption | (0) |
| Less Standard Deduction | ($3,300) |
| **Taxable Income** | **$100** |

**EXAMPLE 3.32**

Brandon is 17 years old and can be claimed as a dependent by his parents.

- He earned $7,000 in wages during 2009 (assume the same for 2010).

- His basic standard deduction for 2009 is $5,700 (the regular basic standard deduction for the single filing status).

- His taxable income for 2009 is $1,300 (the same for 2010).

|  | 2009 |
|---|---|
| Wages | $7,000 |
| Less Personal Exemption | (0) |
| Less Standard Deduction | ($5,700) |
| **Taxable Income** | **$1,300** |

**EXAMPLE 3.33**

Martha is 72 years old and can be claimed as a dependent by her daughter.

- She has $3,000 of interest income during 2009 (assume the same for 2010).

- Her basic standard deduction for 2009 is $950.

- Her total standard deduction is $2,350 ($950 basic standard deduction + $1,400 additional standard deduction for age for 2009).

- Her taxable income is $650 for 2009 (the same for 2010).

|                                    | 2009      |
| ---------------------------------- | --------- |
| Interest Income                    | $3,000    |
| Less Personal Exemption            | (0)       |
| Less Basic Standard Deduction      | ($950)    |
| Less Additional Standard Deduction | ($1,400)  |
| **Taxable Income**                 | **$650**  |

Martha would receive another additional standard deduction if she were blind.

## KIDDIE TAX

Unearned income includes interest, dividends, royalties, pension distributions, capital gains distributions, and gains from dealings in property. Unearned Income essentially includes all income that is not generated from work related activities.

Unearned income of a child under the age of 19, or a child under the age of 24 who is a full time student and is claimed as a dependent by his parents, may be subject to income tax at the parent's marginal tax rate. The portion of unearned income taxed at the parent's marginal tax rate is referred to as the **net unearned income (NUI)** of the child. NUI is determined by subtracting the greater of (1) two times the minimum basic standard deduction for a dependent; or (2) an amount equal to the minimum basic standard deduction for a dependent plus deductible expenses incurred in producing the income from the child's unearned income.

*Key Concepts*

**Underline/highlight the answers to these questions as you read:**

1. Explain the purpose of the kiddie tax.

2. Define net unearned income (NUI).

3. Identify the time period for filing a tax return.

4. Identify the taxpayers required to file a tax return.

To calculate the amount of income that will be subject to income tax at the child's rate, three steps are required. The first step is to calculate the child's taxable income. When making this calculation, remember the rules for determining the standard deduction of someone who is claimed as a dependent of another. Second, calculate the child's NUI, as described above. Finally, subtract the NUI (which will be taxed at the parent's marginal tax rate) from the child's taxable income to arrive at the amount of income that will be subject to taxation at the child's tax rate.

**EXAMPLE 3.34**

Tate is 17 years old, and is claimed as a dependent by his parents. He earned wages of $4,000 and interest income of $3,000 during 2009. Tate had no expenses related to producing the income. How much of Tate's income will be subject to tax at his marginal rate, and how much will be subject to tax at his parent's marginal tax rate?

**Step 1:** Calculate Tate's taxable income. Tate has gross income of $7,000 ($4,000 in wages plus $3,000 in interest income). His standard deduction is the greater of (1) the basic standard deduction for a dependent of $950 (in 2009 and 2010), or (2) earned income plus $300, but is capped at the normal standard deduction amount for the year. Since Tate has $4,000 of earned income, his standard deduction will be $4,300. Consequently, his taxable income is $2,700 ($7,000 - $4,300).

|  | 2009 |
|---|---|
| Wages | $4,000 |
| Interest Income | 3,000 |
| Less Personal Exemption | (0) |
| Less Standard Deduction | (4,300) |
| **Taxable Income** | **$2,700** |

**Step 2**: Calculate Tate's net unearned income. Since Tate does not have deductible investment expenses for the year, his NUI will equal his gross unearned income reduced by $1,900 (in 2009 and 2010), which is two times the minimum basic standard deduction amount. In this example, Tate's NUI is $1,100 ($3,000 - $1,900). Tate's NUI of $1,100 will be subject to income tax at his parent's marginal tax rate.

**Step 3**: Calculate the portion of Tate's taxable income that will be subject to tax at his marginal tax rate. Since Tate's taxable income is $2,700, and $1,100 will be subject to tax at his parents marginal tax rate, the difference of $1,600 will be subject to tax at Tate's tax rate.

Even though some of the tax is computed at the parents' marginal tax rate, the tax can be reported on a tax return for the child using Form 8615. Under certain circumstances, the child's tax can be reported on the parents' tax return.

For a child of divorced parents, the custodial parent's tax rate is used to calculate the tax on the NUI. For a child of married parents filing separately, the tax rate of the parent with the higher marginal tax rate is used to calculate the tax on the NUI.

Although the Internal Revenue Code does not refer to it by that name, this tax on NUI is popularly called the **kiddie tax**. The tax was enacted to discourage the shifting of investment income from parents to their minor children (in lower tax brackets) through the gifting of investments to the children.

The first $1,900 for 2009 (and 2010) of the unearned income of a child is not taxed at the parents' tax rate. Modest gifting of investment assets to a child can therefore effectively shift the income to the child. Some of that income may not be subject to income tax at all and some may be taxed at the lower rates of the child.

Some investment assets do not produce current income. These assets include stocks that do not pay dividends or raw land. Such assets could be given to a child and sold after the child reaches the age of 19 (or 24, if a full-time student).

## Filing the Tax Return

If an individual taxpayer is required to file a federal income tax return, the return must normally be submitted and any tax due must be paid by April 15 (within 3½ months after the end of the tax year or, alternatively stated, by the 15th day of the 4th month following the close of the tax year) to avoid any penalties. Taxes can be paid by check, money order, or credit card. A taxpayer who files electronically before the due date of the return is allowed to schedule an automatic withdrawal by the IRS from the taxpayer's checking or savings account at a future date. If the due date of the return falls on a weekend or holiday, the tax return is due the following business day. If any tax is due, failing to file on time may result in the imposition of both a failure to file penalty and a failure to pay penalty.

An automatic six-month extension of time to file is normally available to a taxpayer who files a Form 4868 (Application for Automatic Extension of Time to File U.S. Individual Income Tax Return) by the due date of the return. However, an extension of time to file does not grant an extension of time to pay. A taxpayer is expected to estimate the amount of tax due and submit payment with the extension form. A taxpayer who files for an extension without paying the tax due is not normally subject to a failure to file penalty but is subject to a failure to pay penalty until any tax due is paid. Special rules apply to a taxpayer who is out of the country on the due date of the return. Basically, two additional months are allowed to file and pay any taxes due, but interest may be charged on any taxes due from the normal due date of the return until the taxes are paid.

The Internal Revenue Service encourages taxpayers to file tax returns electronically. However, many tax returns are still filed by mail. A tax return is considered to be filed in a timely manner if it is postmarked by the due date of the return. The return must be mailed to the Regional Service Center specified in instructions provided by the Internal Revenue Service. Forms, instructions, publications and other information can be obtained from the website of the Internal Revenue Service at www.irs.gov.

A taxpayer is allowed to file using Form 1040EZ, Form 1040A, or Form 1040, depending on the complexity of the tax return. Additional forms are attached to the return as needed.

## TAXPAYERS REQUIRED TO FILE A RETURN

The requirement to file is normally based on the gross income of the taxpayer. If the gross income of a taxpayer is equal to or greater than the deductions allowed for personal (not dependency) exemptions, the basic standard deduction, and any additional standard deduction(s) for age (not blindness), then the taxpayer must file a tax return.

**EXAMPLE 3.35**

Enrique and Maria are married and normally file a joint return. Enrique is 66 years old and Maria is 64. They must file a return if their gross income is $19,800 or more in 2009 and 2010.

|  | 2009 and 2010 |
|---|---|
| Personal exemption | $7,300 |
| Basic standard deduction | $11,400 |
| Enrique's additional standard deduction for his age | $1,100 |
|  | **$19,800** |

EXAMPLE 3.36

Harold is unmarried, age 68, and blind. He must file a return if his adjusted gross income is $10,750 or more for 2009 (and 2010).

|  | 2009 and 2010 |
|---|---|
| Personal exemption | $3,650 |
| Basic standard deduction | $5,700 |
| Harold's additional standard deduction for his age only (note blindness does not count in this calculation) | $1,400 |
|  | $10,750 |

## CREDIT FOR TAXES WITHHELD

Although income taxes could (in theory) all be paid at the time the tax return is filed, Congress has decided that federal income taxes should be withheld by an employer from the employee's wages or salary and sent to the government during the year. This not only provides the government with revenues throughout the year, but it also taxes the employee when the employee has the wherewithal (the cash) to pay. This withholding is merely a prepayment of income tax. Therefore, the employee is allowed to subtract any federal income taxes withheld during the year from the tax on taxable income when a tax return is filed. When an amount is subtracted from a tax, it is called a credit or a **tax credit**.

As discussed in Chapter 2, Congress is so intent on receiving tax revenue throughout the year that taxpayers may be subject to an underpayment penalty for not having enough federal income tax withheld from their earnings.

## *FICA*

The Federal Insurance Contributions Act (FICA) provides for old-age, survivors, disability, and hospital insurance. This coverage is financed by Social Security and Medicare taxes. Employers are required to withhold Social Security and Medicare tax from an employee's wages with the employer paying a matching amount of tax. The Social Security tax has a wage base limit of $106,800 for 2009 (and 2010), and a rate of 6.2 percent to an employee, and is matched by a tax of 6.2 percent paid by the employer (12.4% total). The required Medicare tax is collected from an employee at a rate of 1.45 percent of their salary or wages, with a matching tax of 1.45 percent collected from the employer (2.9% total). The Medicare tax is not subject to a wage base limit.

Employers who are required to withhold income tax and FICA tax must file a federal return each quarter on Form 941 (see Exhibit 3.14). This form must be filed by the last day of the month that follows the end of the previous quarter.

## *FUTA*

The Federal Unemployment Tax Act (FUTA) exists in concert with state unemployment systems to pay unemployment compensation to employees who have become unemployed. This tax is paid by the employer only and is taxed at a rate of 6.2 percent (2009) on the first $7,000 that an employer pays in each employee's wages (note: the state wage base may be different). FUTA tax is reported annually on federal Form 940 (See Exhibit 3.15). A credit is allowed for unemployment taxes paid to states. The net FUTA rate is normally 0.8 percent.

### Self-Employment Tax

A self-employed individual pays income tax as well as self-employment FICA tax (15.3%) on his earnings up to the wage base of $106,800 for 2009 (and 2010) and 2.9 percent beyond the wage base for Medicare. However, the self-employed worker is not required to pay FUTA tax on himself. In addition, a self-employed person can take a FICA deduction for adjusted gross income on his own tax return, in the amount of one-half of his total FICA taxes paid.

**EXAMPLE 3.37**

Rosalyn is self-employed and has one employee, Richard. Rosalyn personally earned $125,000 in wages and paid Richard $28,000 in salary. The FICA tax and FUTA tax calculations are below:

| ROSALYN'S FICA CALCULATION | |
|---|---|
| | **2009 AND 2010** |
| Net self-employment income | $125,000 |
| Reduction of 7.65% self-employment tax | 92.35% |
| Net earnings subject to Social Security tax | $115,438 |
| Social Security wage limit | $106,800 |
| Self-employment Social Security rate | 15.3% |
| | $16,340 |
| Excess over wage limit | $8,638 |
| x Medicare rate | 2.9% |
| | $250.50 |
| Total Social Security tax for Rosalyn | $16,590.50 |

| RICHARD'S FICA CALCULATION | |
|---|---|
| | **2009 AND 2010** |
| Salary | $28,000 |
| FICA rate (7.65% employer and 7.65% employee) | 15.3% |
| Total FICA tax for Richard | $4,284 |

| RICHARD'S FUTA CALCULATION | |
|---|---|
| Wages subject to FUTA | $7,000 |
| FUTA rate | 6.2% |
| Total FUTA* tax for Richard | $434 |
| *$7,000 is the limit on FUTA. No FUTA on Self-employed. | |

For more information on payroll and withholding taxes, see Circular E, Employer's Tax Guide, published by the Internal Revenue Service.

# BASIC TAX PLANNING PRINCIPLES

A financial planner must have a basic understanding of both income tax rules and the related tax planning strategies that can be beneficial to clients. A planner may also be a tax specialist, but if not, the planner should work with accountants, attorneys and other tax experts to provide meaningful tax planning strategies to clientele. In doing so, it is important to remember that legal tax avoidance is fully acceptable, but tax evasion is illegal and must be completely avoided.

Income tax planning is emphasized throughout this book. The following tax planning principles provide the foundation for many tax planning strategies:

1. Receive income in a tax-exempt (excludible) form.
   *Examples:* Income from a Roth IRA, gain on the sale of a personal residence, or employer-provided health insurance.

2. Shift income to a related taxpayer with a lower marginal tax rate (tax bracket).
   *Example:* Gift assets to a child so that future income generated by the assets can be taxed at the child's tax rates. Beware of the kiddie tax.

3. Generate income that is taxed at favorable capital gains rates.
   *Example:* Sell investment assets held for more than one year or buy investments that pay qualified dividends.

4. Defer income taxes until later.
   *Example:* Invest in a Traditional IRA or participate in an employer-sponsored retirement plan.

5. Use tax credits to reduce tax liability.
   *Example:* Qualify for education tax credits or energy tax credits.

EXHIBIT 3.14  FORM 941

**Form 941 for 2009:** Employer's QUARTERLY Federal Tax Return
(Rev. April 2009)
Department of the Treasury — Internal Revenue Service

950109

OMB No. 1545-0029

**(EIN)**
Employer identification number ☐☐ – ☐☐☐☐☐☐☐

Name *(not your trade name)*

Trade name *(if any)*

Address
  Number   Street   Suite or room number
  City   State   ZIP code

**Report for this Quarter of 2009**
(Check one.)

☐ 1: January, February, March
☐ 2: April, May, June
☐ 3: July, August, September
☐ 4: October, November, December

Read the separate instructions before you complete Form 941. Type or print within the boxes.

**Part 1: Answer these questions for this quarter.**

1  Number of employees who received wages, tips, or other compensation for the pay period including: *Mar. 12* (Quarter 1), *June 12* (Quarter 2), *Sept. 12* (Quarter 3), *Dec. 12* (Quarter 4) **1**

2  Wages, tips, and other compensation . . . . . . . . . . . **2**

3  Income tax withheld from wages, tips, and other compensation . . . . . . . . **3**

4  If no wages, tips, and other compensation are subject to social security or Medicare tax ☐ Check and go to line 6.

5  Taxable social security and Medicare wages and tips:

|  | Column 1 | | Column 2 |
|---|---|---|---|
| 5a Taxable social security wages | ☐ | × .124 = | ☐ |
| 5b Taxable social security tips | ☐ | × .124 = | ☐ |
| 5c Taxable Medicare wages & tips | ☐ | × .029 = | ☐ |

5d  Total social security and Medicare taxes (*Column 2*, lines 5a + 5b + 5c = line 5d) . **5d**

6  Total taxes before adjustments (lines 3 + 5d = line 6) . . . . . . . . **6**

7  **CURRENT QUARTER'S ADJUSTMENTS,** for example, a fractions of cents adjustment. See the instructions.

7a  Current quarter's fractions of cents . . . . . . . . . .

7b  Current quarter's sick pay . . . . . . . . . . . .

7c  Current quarter's adjustments for tips and group-term life insurance

7d  **TOTAL ADJUSTMENTS.** Combine all amounts on lines 7a through 7c . . . . . . **7d**

8  Total taxes after adjustments. Combine lines 6 and 7d . . . . . . . . **8**

9  Advance earned income credit (EIC) payments made to employees . . . . . . . **9**

10  Total taxes after adjustment for advance EIC (line 8 – line 9 = line 10) . . . . . . **10**

11  Total deposits for this quarter, including overpayment applied from a prior quarter and overpayment applied from Form 941-X or Form 944-X . . . . . . . . . . . . . . . . .

12a  COBRA premium assistance payments (see instructions) . . . . . .

12b  Number of individuals provided COBRA premium assistance reported on line 12a . . . . . . . .

13  Add lines 11 and 12a . . . . . . . . . . . . . **13**

14  **Balance due.** If line 10 is more than line 13, write the difference here . . . . . . . **14**
For information on how to pay, see the instructions.

15  **Overpayment.** If line 13 is more than line 10, write the difference here  ☐ Check one  ☐ Apply to next return.  ☐ Send a refund.

▶ You **MUST** complete both pages of Form 941 and **SIGN** it.  Next ➡

For Privacy Act and Paperwork Reduction Act Notice, see the back of the Payment Voucher.   Cat. No. 17001Z   Form **941** (Rev. 4-2009)

The 2008 form was the latest available at the time of printing. Please visit our website at money-education.com for updates.

Form **940 for 2008:** Employer's Annual Federal Unemployment (FUTA) Tax Return

850108

Department of the Treasury — Internal Revenue Service

OMB No. 1545-0028

**(EIN)**
Employer identification number ☐☐ – ☐☐☐☐☐☐☐

Name (not your trade name)

Trade name (if any)

Address

Number    Street                          Suite or room number

City                     State    ZIP code

**Type of Return**
(Check all that apply.)

☐ **a.** Amended

☐ **b.** Successor employer

☐ **c.** No payments to employees in 2008

☐ **d.** Final: Business closed or stopped paying wages

Read the separate instructions before you fill out this form. Please type or print within the boxes.

**Part 1: Tell us about your return. If any line does NOT apply, leave it blank.**

1  If you were required to pay your state unemployment tax in ...

    **1a One state only,** write the state abbreviation . . . . **1a** ☐☐

    - OR -

    **1b More than one state** (You are a multi-state employer) . . . . . . . . . **1b** ☐ Check here. Fill out Schedule A.

    **Skip line 2 for 2008 and go to line 3.**

2  If you paid wages in a state that is subject to CREDIT REDUCTION . . . . . . . . . **2** ☐ Check here. Fill out Schedule A (Form 940), Part 2.

**Part 2: Determine your FUTA tax before adjustments for 2008. If any line does NOT apply, leave it blank.**

3  Total payments to all employees . . . . . . . . . . . . **3**

4  Payments exempt from FUTA tax . . . . . . . **4**

    Check all that apply:  **4a** ☐ Fringe benefits   **4c** ☐ Retirement/Pension   **4e** ☐ Other
                 **4b** ☐ Group-term life insurance   **4d** ☐ Dependent care

5  Total of payments made to each employee in excess of $7,000 . . . . . . . . . . **5**

6  Subtotal (line 4 + line 5 = line 6) . . . . . . . . . . . . **6**

7  Total taxable FUTA wages (line 3 – line 6 = line 7) . . . . . . . . . **7**

8  FUTA tax before adjustments (line 7 × .008 = line 8) . . . . . . **8**

**Part 3: Determine your adjustments. If any line does NOT apply, leave it blank.**

9  If ALL of the taxable FUTA wages you paid were excluded from state unemployment tax, multiply line 7 by .054 (line 7 × .054 = line 9). Then go to line 12 . . . . . . . . . **9**

10  If SOME of the taxable FUTA wages you paid were excluded from state unemployment tax, OR you paid ANY state unemployment tax late (after the due date for filing Form 940), fill out the worksheet in the instructions. Enter the amount from line 7 of the worksheet onto line 10 . . **10**

    **Skip line 11 for 2008 and go to line 12.**

11  If credit reduction applies, enter the amount from line 3 of Schedule A (Form 940) . . . . . **11**

**Part 4: Determine your FUTA tax and balance due or overpayment for 2008. If any line does NOT apply, leave it blank.**

12  Total FUTA tax after adjustments (lines 8 + 9 + 10 + 11 = line 12) . . . . . . . . **12**

13  FUTA tax deposited for the year, including any payment applied from a prior year . . . . **13**

14  Balance due (If line 12 is more than line 13, enter the difference on line 14.)
    ● If line 14 is more than $500, you must deposit your tax.
    ● If line 14 is $500 or less, you may pay with this return. For more information on how to pay, see the separate instructions . . . . . . . . . . . . . . . . . . . . . **14**

15  Overpayment (If line 13 is more than line 12, enter the difference on line 15 and check a box below.) . . . . . . . . . . . . . . . . . . . . **15**

    Check one: ☐ Apply to next return.
                    ☐ Send a refund.

▶ You **MUST** fill out both pages of this form and **SIGN** it.

Next ➡

For Privacy Act and Paperwork Reduction Act Notice, see the back of Form 940-V, Payment Voucher.   Cat. No. 11234O   Form **940** (2008)

# Key Terms

*Above-the-Line Deductions* - Deductions for adjusted gross income, also known as adjustments to income.

*Accrual Method* - An accounting method under which income is reported when it is earned rather than when it is received in cash, and expenses are reported when they are incurred rather than when they are paid.

*Adjusted Gross Income* - Gross income less above-the-line deductions.

*Below-the-Line Deductions* - Deductions from adjusted gross income. Also known as itemized deductions.

*Cash Receipts and Disbursements Method* - An accounting method under which income items are reported for the tax year in which they are received in cash and expenses are deducted in the year in which they are paid with cash.

*Deductions* - Items that are subtracted from gross income, either below or above the line, in order to arrive at taxable income.

*Dependency Exemption* - A deduction from adjusted gross income that is allowed for each person who is a qualifying child or qualifying relative of the taxpayer.

*Doctrine of Constructive Receipt* - A cash method taxpayer must report income when it is credited to the taxpayer's account or when it is made available without restriction.

*Estimated Tax Payments* - Quarterly payments that are paid to the IRS and may be claimed as a credit against tax.

*Exclusions* - Income items that are specifically exempted from income tax.

*Gross Income* - All income from whatever source derived unless it is specifically excluded by some provision of the Internal Revenue Code.

*Head of Household Filing Status* - A filing status that provides a basic standard deduction and tax bracket sizes that are less favorable to the taxpayer than those for the surviving spouse status, but more favorable than those for the single filing status.

*Hybrid Method* - An accounting method that includes any other method of reporting that is permitted by the Code and regulations as long as it is deemed to clearly reflect income.

*Income* - Broadly defined as the gross amount of money, property, services, or other accretion to wealth received, but it does not include borrowed money or a return of invested dollars.

*Kiddie Tax* - A tax at the parent's marginal rate on the net unearned income of a child.

# Key Terms

**Married Filing Jointly Filing Status** - A filing status that allows married couples to combine their gross incomes and deductions.

**Married Filing Separately Filing Status** - A filing status used when married couples do not choose to file a joint return.

**Net Unearned Income (NUI)** - The amount of unearned income of a child that is subject to tax at the parents' rate. NUI is equal to the unearned income of the child, less $950 (minimum basic standard deduction) and the greater of $950 or the amount of the deductions allowed in producing the unearned income (2009 and 2010 thresholds).

**Original Issue Discount (OID) Bond** - A bond that is issued for a price that is less than its face amount or principal amount on which interest is usually paid only at maturity.

**Personal Exemption** - A deduction from adjusted gross income that is allowed for the taxpayer and the taxpayer's spouse.

**Qualifying Child** - A person who meets the relationship test, abode test, age test, support test, joint return test, and citizenship test, and may be claimed as a dependent of the taxpayer.

**Qualifying Relative** - A person who meets the relationship test, gross income test, support test, joint return test, and citizenship test; is not a qualifying child of any other taxpayer; and may be claimed as a dependent by the taxpayer.

**Single Filing Status** - A filing status used by an unmarried taxpayer who does not qualify as a surviving spouse or head of household.

**Standard Deduction** - A standard amount that is specified by Congress and includes inflation adjustments. Taxpayers may deduct the greater of the standard deduction or allowable itemized deductions.

**Surviving Spouse Filing Status** - A filing status for a surviving spouse with a dependent child that affords the same basic standard deduction and tax rates as the married filing jointly status.

**Tax Credit** - An amount that reduces the calculated tax liability of the taxpayer.

**Tax Year** - Normally a period of 12 months.

**Taxable Income** - Determined by subtracting allowable deductions from income.

**Zero Coupon Bond** - A bond that is sold at a deep discount, pays no coupons, and matures at its face value.

1.  How is income defined?

2.  What are exclusions and where do they come from?

3.  Define gross income.

4.  List some examples of items that would be included in gross income.

5.  What are the two types of deductions?

6.  What is adjusted gross income and what is its significance?

7.  How much can an individual deduct from his AGI?

8.  Under what circumstances may a taxpayer be entitled to an additional standard deduction?

9.  Under what circumstances will a taxpayer be required to itemize his deductions?

10. What types of accounting periods are available to taxpayers?

11. What is the cash receipts and disbursements method of accounting?

12. What is the accrual method of accounting?

13. What is the all events test?

14. What are the different filing statuses available to taxpayers?

15. How is marital status determined for the purpose of selecting a filing status?

16. When is a married taxpayer allowed to file using the head of household filing status?

17. What are the requirements to file as a surviving spouse?

18. For whom is a dependency exemption allowed?

19. What tests must a qualifying child meet?

20. What tests must a qualifying relative meet?

21. How is the standard deduction calculated for someone who can be claimed as a dependent by another taxpayer?

22. What is the kiddie tax?

23. Who must file a tax return?

.. Franco, a consultant, uses the cash method of accounting for his business. Franco recently provided consulting services to his best customer Nicky. When should Franco recognize income from this service?

   a. When Nicky writes a check, made out to Franco.
   b. When Franco deposits Nicky's check.
   c. When Nicky gives the check to Franco.
   d. When Nicky receives an invoice from Franco for the service.

2. Which of the following is not an available filing status?

   a. Qualified dependent child.
   b. Married filing jointly.
   c. Head of household.
   d. Surviving spouse.

3. Which of the following is not a test that must be satisfied in order to meet the criteria for a qualifying child dependency exemption?

   a. Whether the dependent has lived with the taxpayer for more than half the year.
   b. If the qualifying child dependent is a descendant of the taxpayer, the taxpayer's sibling, or a descendant of the taxpayer's sibling.
   c. If the dependent's gross income is less than the exemption amount for the year.
   d. Whether the qualifying child does not provide more than one-half of his or her own support during the year.

4. Rita and Roberto were married on September 1 of this year. Following a honeymoon in Tahiti, Roberto died of a heart attack. Neither Rita nor Roberto had any dependents. What filing status can Rita use this year?

   a. Rita must use the single filing status because she was not married as of the end of the year.
   b. Rita will be able to file as married filing jointly as long as she would have qualified for this filing status if Roberto had survived.
   c. Rita may use the head of household filing status.
   d. Rita will be eligible to file as a surviving spouse.

5. Tommy, who sells trucks, uses the accrual method of accounting for his business. Tommy just sold a truck to Jimmy. Under the accrual method of accounting, Tommy recognizes income when:

    a. The bill for the truck is received by Jimmy.

    b. The truck is delivered to Jimmy and Tommy gives the invoice to Jimmy.

    c. Tommy gets ready to deliver the truck to Jimmy.

    d. Tommy receives the truck from the manufacturer.

6. Which of the following is not excluded from gross income?

    a. Gifts.

    b. Scholarships.

    c. Interest income from municipal bonds.

    d. Dividend income.

7. Tina (age 70) and Ike (age 74) are married to each other and file a joint return in 2010 for tax year 2009. Tina is blind. Ike and Tina do not have any dependents. What is their standard deduction for 2009?

    a. $11,400.

    b. $13,600.

    c. $14,700.

    d. $15,600.

8. Which of the following is not an allowable itemized deduction from adjusted gross income?

    a. Alimony paid.

    b. Medical expenses in excess of 7.5% of AGI.

    c. Charitable contributions.

    d. Home mortgage interest.

9. Under which of the following circumstances must a taxpayer itemize his deductions?

    1. When the taxpayer has been married for less than one year.

    2. When the taxpayer is married and files a separate return and the taxpayer's spouse itemizes his or her deductions.

    3. When the taxpayer is a nonresident alien.

    a. 1 and 2.

    b. 1 and 3.

    c. 2 and 3.

    d. 1, 2, and 3.

0.  Ella is 16 years old. She earned $3,000 during 2009 working at an ice cream store. She also had $4,000 of interest income this year. Ella is claimed as a dependent by her parents. How much of Ella's income will be taxed at her parent's highest marginal tax rate?

     a.  $1,600.

     b.  $2,100.

     c.  $3,700.

     d.  $7,000.

# Quick Quiz Explanations

## Quick Quiz 3.1

1. False. Income, broadly defined, means the gross amount received, but it does not include borrowed money or a return of invested dollars.
2. True.

## Quick Quiz 3.2

1. False. A nonresident alien is not allowed to use a standard deduction and must itemize his deductions.
2. False. Personal and dependency exemption amounts are allowed as deductions from adjusted gross income, not for adjusted gross income.
3. False. Credits reduce the amount of tax that the taxpayer owes.
4. True.

## Quick Quiz 3.3

1. False. Although most individual taxpayers report their income and expenses on a calendar year basis, individuals are permitted to choose another tax year under certain circumstances.
2. True.

## Quick Quiz 3.4

1. False. The determination of whether a taxpayer is married is normally made as of the close (the last day) of the tax year. However, if a taxpayer's spouse dies during the year, the marital status of the taxpayer is determined on the date of the spouse's death.
2. True.

## Quick Quiz 3.5

1. False. Multiple requirements must be met in order to claim a dependency exemption for someone living in the taxpayer's house.
2. True.
3. True.

## Quick Quiz 3.6

1. True.
2. True.
3. False. An automatic six-month extension of time to file is normally available to a taxpayer who files a Form 4868 (Application for Automatic Extension of Time to File U.S. Individual Income Tax Return) by the due date of the return.

# Gross Income From Personal and Investment Activities

## INTRODUCTION

Now that some general rules of income taxation and the tax formula have been covered in the text, a review of the specific planning issues that impact the calculation of an individual's tax liability is required. This chapter covers three areas:

1. Determination of when income is taxed;
2. Income and exclusions from investment activities; and
3. Income and exclusions from personal activities.

The question of when income is taxed begins with a review of the tax year and accounting rules covered in Chapter 3. Next, the concepts of realization and recognition of income are covered, followed by an overview of the types of gross income and exclusions, as well as the potential sources of income.

Finally, income and exclusions from investment related activities are covered, followed by income and exclusions associated with personal activities. Income and exclusion items associated with employment will be the subject of Chapter 5.

**Gross income** is defined in the Internal Revenue Code as all income from whatever source derived unless it is specifically excluded by some provision of the Internal Revenue Code. In other words, all income is subject to income tax unless Congress states that it is not. Further, the federal income tax is a global income tax since it is imposed on income earned anywhere unless Congress states otherwise.

Although income is not specifically defined in the Internal Revenue Code, a reading of the Code and related court decisions makes it clear that income as broadly defined includes the value of benefits received in the form of cash, property, services or any other form. Not all cash inflows are considered income, however. Courts have held that borrowed money and the return of invested dollars to the taxpayer are not forms of income. Borrowed money is not income because it must be repaid. The return of invested dollars (cost or tax basis) is simply the return to the taxpayer of dollars that have already been subject to income taxation.

## SUBJECTING GROSS INCOME TO TAXATION

### TAX YEAR AND ACCOUNTING METHOD

Gross income must be reported according to the tax year and the tax accounting method of the taxpayer. Most individual taxpayers use the calendar year as their tax year and the **cash receipts and disbursements method** (the cash method) as their accounting method. Basically, gross income of a cash method taxpayer is reported in the tax year in which cash is received or a benefit is conferred in the form of a cash equivalent. Cash includes currency, coin, or a check. Cash equivalents include non-cash property, services, other benefits, or even the value of a promissory note. However, in some circumstances a cash method taxpayer may have to report income when it is constructively, as opposed to actually, received. Constructive receipt is reviewed later in this chapter.

**Key Concepts**

Underline/highlight the answers to these questions as you read:

1. Identify the permissible accounting methods.

2. Describe when gains are normally taxed.

3. Explain the taxation of barter transactions.

While some taxpayers are allowed to use a fiscal, rather than a calendar tax year, it is rare for individuals to do so.

A taxpayer may choose to use one of several methods of accounting for reporting gross income and deductions. As discussed in Chapter 3, permissible methods include the cash receipts and disbursements method, the accrual method, or a hybrid method. Under the cash receipts and disbursements method (the cash method), gross income is normally reported as indicated above. Businesses with average gross receipts for the prior three years in excess of $5 million (IRC Section 448(b)(3)) are not eligible to use the cash method of accounting. Under the **accrual method**, gross income is normally reported when it is earned rather than when it is received. A hybrid method is simply a method other than the cash method or the accrual method. For example, under a hybrid method, a taxpayer might report the sale of goods using the accrual method and other types of income using the cash method. Under certain circumstances, the accrual method is required. For example, if inventories are an income-producing factor, the accrual method must be used to account for inventory items unless the taxpayer is a qualifying taxpayer with average annual gross receipts of $1 million or less.

### GAINS NORMALLY TAXED WHEN REALIZED

Gains on property are normally taxed when they can be objectively determined through a sale or exchange. A gain that is objectively determined is said to be realized. Unrealized gains are those that cannot yet be objectively determined and are not normally taxable until objectively determined.

EXAMPLE 4.1

Jared bought some stock at the beginning of the current year for $1,000 (his cost basis). At the end of the year, the stock had a value of $1,300. Jared is not required to report the $300 unrealized gain on his tax return for the current year. If he sells the stock next year for $1,450, he will report the $450 realized gain on his tax return for next year.

## Barter Transactions

**Bartering** is an exchange of property and/or services for other property and/or services. The value of goods or services received in a barter transaction must be included in gross income. The value received can be offset by the cost or other tax basis of goods given up in the transaction. When goods or services are received by a taxpayer in exchange for services, the services provided by the taxpayer normally have a tax basis of zero. When barter transactions are made through a barter club or exchange, an organization established to facilitate the trading of goods and services, the transaction must be reported to the taxpayer and the Internal Revenue Service by the barter club or exchange.

# TYPES OF GROSS INCOME AND EXCLUSIONS

Types of gross income that are specifically identified in the Internal Revenue Code are presented in Exhibit 4.1. Exhibit 4.1 lists the various inclusion items, as well as the form upon which each item of income should be reported and the IRS publication in which the item of income is discussed. Some specific exclusions from gross income are presented in Exhibit 4.2. All of these items are specifically excluded from gross income in the Internal Revenue Code.

## GROSS INCOME INCLUSION ITEMS

EXHIBIT 4.1

| Item | IRC Section | Reported On | IRS Publication |
|---|---|---|---|
| Capital Gains | 61(a)(3) & 1001 | Schedule D & Form 4797 | 550/544 |
| Interest Income | 61(a)(4) | Schedule B | 550 |
| Interest from Original Issue Discount Obligations | 1271-1275 | Schedule B | 550 |
| Dividend Income | 61(a)(7) | Schedule B | 550 |
| Mutual Fund Distributions | 61 | Schedule D | 564 |
| Rental Income | 61(a)(5) | Schedule E (pg. 1) | 527 |
| Royalty Income | 61(a)(6) | Schedule E (pg. 1) | 17 |
| Income from Annuities | 72 | Form 1040 | 939 |
| Income from Life Insurance and Endowment Contracts | 72 | Form 1040 | 525 |
| IRAs (Traditional IRAs) | 408(d) | Form 1040 | 590 |
| Income from Partnerships | 61(a)(13) | Schedule E (pg. 2) | 525 |
| Income from S Corporations | 1366(a) | Schedule E (pg. 2) | 525 |
| Income from Trusts and Estates | 61(a)(15) | Schedule E (pg. 2) | 559 |
| Prizes and Awards | 74 | Form 1040 | 17 |
| Alimony and Separate Maintenance Payments | 71 | Form 1040 | 504 |
| Imputed Interest on Below-Market Loans | 7872 | Schedule B | 550 |
| Income from Discharge of Indebtedness | 61(a)(12) | Form 1040 | 17 |
| Other Income | 61 | Form 1040 | 17 |

EXHIBIT 4.2 | EXCLUSIONS FROM GROSS INCOME

| Item | IRC Section | IRS Publication |
|---|---|---|
| Interest Income from Certain State and Local Government Obligations | 103 | 550 |
| Life Insurance Proceeds | 101 | 525 |
| Accelerated Death Benefits | 101(g) | 525 |
| Income from Roth IRAs (Qualified Distributions) | 408A | 590 |
| Educational Savings Bonds | 135 | 550 |
| Qualified Tuition Program/Educational Savings Plan | 529 | 970 |
| Coverdell Savings Account | 530 | 970 |
| Improvements by Tenant to Landlord's Property | 109 | -- |
| Exclusion (50%) of Gain from Sale of Certain Small Business Stock | 1202 | 550 |
| Gifts | 102 | 559 |
| Inheritances | 102 | 559 |
| Scholarships (Tuition and Fees) | 117 | 970 |
| Compensation for Injuries and Sickness | 104 | 17 |
| Child Support | 71(c) | 504 |
| Property Settlements from Divorce | 1041 | 504 |
| Income from Discharge of Indebtedness (Under Bankruptcy) | 108 | 908/17 |
| Gain on the Sale of Residence (Up to $250,000 or $500,000) | 121 | 523 |
| Amounts Received Under Insurance Contracts for Certain Living Expenses | 123 | 547 |
| Qualified Foster Care Payments | 131 | 17 |
| Disaster Relief Payments | 139 | 547 |
| Tax Benefit Rule | 111 | 17 |

## Quick Quiz 4.1

**Highlight the answer to these questions:**

1. Gains on property are normally taxed upon sale or exchange.
   a. True
   b. False

2. Barter transactions are not reportable for income tax purposes.
   a. True
   b. False

True, False.

Since this chapter focuses on gross income and exclusions related to investments and personal activities, only those items are listed in Exhibits 4.1 and 4.2. Chapter 5 focuses on gross income and exclusions related to employment and self-employment. The exclusions center around gifts (gifts, inheritances, proceeds of life insurance), making one whole (compensatory bodily damage), property transactions where basis is transferred (property transferred in divorce), and other statutory exclusions (tax free interest income from municipal bonds).

# SOURCES OF INCOME

Income can be received from:
1. investments,
2. personal activities, and
3. employment and self-employment.

Investments typically generate dividend income, interest income, gains from the sale of property, and other types of income. This is an application of the Doctrine of the Fruit and the Tree (introduced in Chapter 1). Income from personal activities might include items such as the receipt of alimony from a former spouse or receipt of prizes and awards. Wages, salaries, commissions, fringe benefits, and other types of income can be earned by providing services to an employer. Engaging in the conduct of a trade or business generates self-employment income.

## Key Concepts

**Underline/highlight the answers to these questions as you read:**

1. Identify the various sources of income.

2. Describe the effect of community property laws on the taxation of income.

3. Identify the types of relief available under Section 66.

## INVESTMENT INCOME

Income from investments is normally taxable to the owner of the investment. The owner of the investment cannot attribute the income to another person simply by having the income paid to another person.

## INCOME FROM PERSONAL ACTIVITIES

Gross income generated from personal activities is normally taxable to the recipient. For example, alimony is taxable to the person who receives it.

## EMPLOYMENT INCOME

Gross income from services provided to an employer or from self-employment is normally taxable to the person who performs the services. For example, income earned by a child actor is taxable to the child rather than to the parent of the child. Gross income cannot normally be assigned to another person by the person who earns it. Employment income and related deductions are discussed in Chapter 5. The taxation of business income is discussed in Chapter 16.

## SPECIAL ISSUES FOR PERSONS LIVING IN COMMUNITY PROPERTY STATES

Most of the states in the United States follow the common law system for property ownership. However, nine states in the United States use some form of community property regime. These states include Arizona, California, Idaho, Louisiana, Nevada, New Mexico, Texas, Washington, and Wisconsin. Spouses in Alaska can choose to follow community property rules. In **community property** states, one half of the income earned (wages, salaries, etc.) by a spouse is deemed to be earned by each spouse and one half of the income earned from community property is deemed to be the income of each spouse. If a married couple files as married filing jointly, this division of income makes no difference since income is added together. It may make a significant difference, however, if the couple files as married filing separately or if they divorce during the year. If they file as married filing separately, the community property income (earned from employment and community property assets) is divided equally, but any separate property income is reported by the spouse owning the separate property. After divorce, there is no community property regime and thus no community property income.

| EXHIBIT 4.3 | **COMMUNITY PROPERTY STATES** |
|---|---|

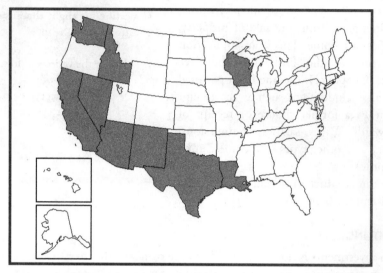

Community property includes property acquired by a married couple after their marriage. Property acquired before the marriage or acquired by gift or inheritance before or after the marriage is generally considered to be the separate property of the spouse. In four states, Idaho, Louisiana, Texas, and Wisconsin, income from separate property is deemed to be community income; in the other community property states, income from separate property is deemed to be the separate income of the spouse who owns the property. In allocating income from separate property, it should be noted that gains and losses or a nontaxable return of investment from separate property are not considered to be income that must be allocated.

| EXAMPLE 4.2 | Mary and Jim are married and live in Texas (a community property state). During the year, Mary sold some stock that she had inherited from her father five years earlier. The stock resulted in a long-term capital gain of $12,000. The stock had paid a cash dividend of $500 shortly before the sale. The stock is Mary's separate property because it was inherited. In Texas, the dividend income is treated as community income, but the gain on the sale is allocated to Mary because it is considered to be a gain from her separate property rather than income from community property. |
|---|---|

The reporting of community income earned through the personal services of either spouse can be complicated or even impossible if the spouses do not live together or if one spouse refuses to completely disclose his earnings. Section 66 of the Internal Revenue Code provides the following solutions for these circumstances.

## Separated Spouse Relief

For income earned through personal services, community property laws are ignored and each spouse reports his or her own earned income for federal income tax purposes if the married couple lives apart at all times during the year, they do not file a joint return with each other, and none of the earned community income is transferred between them during the year.

### Quick Quiz 4.2

**Highlight the answer to these questions:**

1. In community property states, half of the income earned from community property is deemed to be the income of each spouse.
   a. True
   b. False

2. The only relief available under Section 66 is innocent spouse relief.
   a. True
   b. False

True, False.

## Innocent Spouse Relief

A married taxpayer with community income from a spouse may be able to exclude that income if the taxpayer does not file a joint return, does not include in gross income an item of community income of the spouse, establishes that he or she did not know of or have reason to know of that community income, and it is inequitable to include that community income in the taxpayer's gross income. Innocent spouse rules are provided in Internal Revenue Code Section 66(a).

## Equitable Relief

Even if the requirements for separated spouse relief or innocent spouse relief are not met, the Internal Revenue Service is authorized to allow a taxpayer not to report half of the community income of the taxpayer's spouse if, taking into account all of the facts and circumstances, the failure to grant such relief would be "inequitable."

## Disallowance of Community Property Treatment

The Secretary of the Treasury is given authority in Internal Revenue Code Section 66(d) to disallow the benefits of any community property law (i.e., the splitting of income) to any taxpayer who acts as if he is solely entitled to the community income and who fails to notify his spouse about the income before the due date (including extensions) for filing a tax return for the year.

## INCOME FROM INVESTMENT ACTIVITIES

Many different types of investments are available to investors, but most of them involve the ownership of assets or the lending of money. Each type of investment has the potential to generate some type of income and/or gain that must be included in gross income and subjected to income taxation. Typically, owning assets carries greater risk of financial loss than loaning money, but the potential rewards are also greater with asset ownership. Some of the more common types of gross income from investment activities are discussed in this section.

Congress has chosen to tax some types of investment income or gain more favorably than other types. Capital gains are normally taxed at lower rates than ordinary income. Planners need to be aware of how each type of investment income is taxed.

## ITEMS INCLUDED IN GROSS INCOME

### Capital Gains

Most investments, including stocks, bonds, and mutual funds fit into the capital asset category. Gains from the sale or exchange of capital assets must be included in gross income and they are generally taxed at favorable capital gains rates. The taxation of capital gains is discussed in detail in Chapter 10.

### Interest Income

**Interest income** is generated by a variety of debt instruments, including bank accounts, money market instruments, corporate bonds, government agency securities, Treasury securities, and municipal bonds. Interest income must normally be included in gross income when it is actually or constructively received by a cash basis taxpayer or when it is earned by an accrual basis taxpayer. A cash basis taxpayer is deemed to have constructively received interest income from a savings account or certificate of deposit when it is credited to his account, even if it is not readily available for withdrawal until the next year. Interest income of $10 or more per year is normally reported to a taxpayer on Form 1099-INT by the payor of the interest, but the interest must be recognized by the taxpayer even when this form is not received or when the interest income is less than $10.

| EXHIBIT 4.4 | FORM 1099-INT |
|---|---|

| | | |
|---|---|---|
| ☐ CORRECTED (if checked) | | |

| PAYER'S name, street address, city, state, ZIP code, and telephone no. | Payer's RTN (optional) | OMB No. 1545-0112 | |
|---|---|---|---|
| | **1** Interest income $ | **20**09 Interest Income | |
| | **2** Early withdrawal penalty $ | Form **1099-INT** | |
| PAYER'S federal identification number / RECIPIENT'S identification number | **3** Interest on U.S. Savings Bonds and Treas. obligations $ | | **Copy B** **For Recipient** |
| RECIPIENT'S name | **4** Federal income tax withheld $ | **5** Investment expenses $ | This is important tax information and is being furnished to the Internal Revenue Service. If you are required to file a return, a negligence penalty or other sanction may be imposed on you if this income is taxable and the IRS determines that it has not been reported. |
| Street address (including apt. no.) | **6** Foreign tax paid $ | **7** Foreign country or U.S. possession | |
| City, state, and ZIP code | **8** Tax-exempt interest | **9** Specified private activity bond interest | |
| Account number (see instructions) | $ | $ | |
| Form **1099-INT** | (keep for your records) | Department of the Treasury - Internal Revenue Service | |

Interest income from most municipal bonds can be excluded from federal gross income. It may also be excludable for state income tax purposes. This topic is covered in detail later in this chapter as part of our discussion on exclusions from gross income.

Interest income from U.S. savings bonds and Treasury obligations (bills, notes, and bonds) must normally be included in federal gross income, but is excluded from gross income for state and local income tax purposes.

## Original Issue Discount (OID) Bonds

Some debt instruments are issued at a discount from the stated redemption price at maturity. The difference between the redemption price at maturity and the purchase price is called **original issue discount**. The original issue discount is really interest that will be received at maturity by the taxpayer. An accrual basis taxpayer reports this interest as it is earned. Without any special rules on the matter, a cash basis taxpayer would be permitted to report all of the original issue discount as interest income when cash is received at maturity. For debt instruments with maturities of more than one year, taxpayers (including cash basis taxpayers) must report the interest on the accrual basis, using a constant yield method (or effective interest rate method) of calculation. For debt instruments issued before July 2, 1982, a straight-line method was used. A cash basis taxpayer must therefore report a portion of the interest each year even though no cash is received during the year. This approach is consistent with the doctrine of constructive receipt, which requires cash basis taxpayers to recognize income when it is permanently set aside in an account for their benefit. The amount of the interest to be included in gross income is calculated by the issuer of the debt instrument and is reported to the taxpayer on Form 1099-OID. Treasury Regulation 1.1272-1(j) provides examples of the calculation of the interest income that must be reported each year.

> Goldilocks buys a 30-year, zero coupon $1,000 Treasury bond yielding 8% annually. She pays $99.38 for the Treasury bond on January 1, 2009. Because this bond has an original issue discount, Goldilocks must impute the interest on this bond on an annual basis. For 2009, Goldilocks will report $7.95 of imputed interest ($99.38 x 0.08). In addition, her basis at the beginning of 2010 will be $107.33 ($99.38 + $7.95) since the OID was included in her income and she paid income tax on that amount.

**EXAMPLE 4.3**

Although series E and series EE U.S. government savings bonds are original issue discount debt instruments, a taxpayer may elect to recognize all of the interest income when the bonds mature. A taxpayer may also choose to recognize the interest each year as with other original issue discount instruments. The method elected must be used for future purchases of savings bonds as well.

### Gifting of Debt Instruments

When a debt instrument is transferred by gift, the donor and the donee must report the related interest income based on the number of days that each owned the instrument during the year.

**EXAMPLE 4.4**

Todd owned bonds that paid interest of $600 on the first day of January each year. Exactly in the middle of the current year, Todd gave the bond to his daughter, Julie. When Julie receives the $600 of interest next year, Todd will be required to include $300 of interest in his gross income and Julie will be required to include the remaining $300. If Todd is an accrual basis taxpayer (unlikely), he will report his $300 for the current year. If he is a cash basis taxpayer, he will report his $300 of interest income on his tax return for next year, the year in which he would have received the interest if he had retained the bond.

### Dividend Income

A C corporation is taxed on its taxable income. A portion of the corporation's after-tax income is often paid to shareholders in the form of cash dividends. **Dividend income** in the form of cash received by shareholders of a C corporation must be included in the shareholder's gross income to the extent that the issuing corporation has earnings and profits (a concept very similar to retained earnings). If a C corporation makes distributions to shareholders in excess of earnings and profits, the excess is treated as a nontaxable return of invested dollars until the shareholder's entire tax basis in the stock has been recovered; any distribution in excess of the shareholder's basis generates capital gain income to the shareholder. A dividend distribution to a shareholder in the form of property other than cash is treated the same as a cash distribution.

**Quick Quiz 4.3**

**Highlight the answer to these questions:**

1. Interest income of less than $10 per year does not have to be included in gross income.
   a. True
   b. False

2. Dividend income is reported to a taxpayer on Form 1099-DIV.
   a. True
   b. False

False, True.

Dividend income of $10 or more per year is normally reported to a taxpayer on Form 1099-DIV by the corporation or the pass-through entity (such as a mutual fund) that pays the dividend.

| PAYER'S name, street address, city, state, ZIP code, and telephone no. | | 1a Total ordinary dividends $ | OMB No. 1545-0110 2009 Form 1099-DIV | Dividends and Distributions |
|---|---|---|---|---|
| | | 1b Qualified dividends $ | | |
| | | 2a Total capital gain distr. $ | 2b Unrecap. Sec. 1250 gain $ | Copy B For Recipient |
| PAYER'S federal identification number | RECIPIENT'S identification number | | | |
| RECIPIENT'S name | | 2c Section 1202 gain $ | 2d Collectibles (28%) gain $ | This is important tax information and is being furnished to the Internal Revenue Service. If you are required to file a return, a negligence penalty or other sanction may be imposed on you if this income is taxable and the IRS determines that it has not been reported. |
| | | 3 Nondividend distributions $ | 4 Federal income tax withheld $ | |
| Street address (including apt. no.) | | | 5 Investment expenses $ | |
| City, state, and ZIP code | | 6 Foreign tax paid $ | 7 Foreign country or U.S. possession | |
| Account number (see instructions) | | 8 Cash liquidation distributions $ | 9 Noncash liquidation distributions $ | |

Form **1099-DIV**          (keep for your records)          Department of the Treasury - Internal Revenue Service

Historically, dividends from C corporations were taxed the same as interest income or other ordinary income. Beginning in 2003, **qualified dividends** are taxed at the five percent and 15 percent rates that apply to long-term capital gains. Qualified dividends are not added to long-term capital gains nor do they offset capital losses; they are simply taxed at the five percent (for individuals with a marginal tax rate of 10% or 15%) or 15 percent (for individuals with a marginal tax rate of 25%, 28%, 33%, or 35%). The five percent rate for qualified dividends is reduced to zero percent after 2007. Some dividends do not qualify for this favorable treatment. To achieve favorable tax status, qualified dividends must meet all three of the following requirements:

1. They must be paid by a U.S. corporation or a qualified foreign corporation;
2. The dividend must not be a type of dividend excluded by law from the definition of a qualified dividend such as capital gain distribution, dividends on bank deposits, ESOP dividends, etc.; and
3. The shareholder must meet a holding period requirement of 60 days during the 121 day period beginning 60 days before the ex-dividend date.

Qualified dividends are identified by and reported to the shareholder by the payor of the dividends. Dividends that are not qualified dividends are taxed as ordinary income at regular tax rates. The tax rates for qualified dividends are shown in Exhibit 4.6.

EXHIBIT 4.6     QUALIFIED DIVIDEND TAX RATES

| Regular Tax Rates | Qualified Dividend Tax Rates |
|---|---|
| 10% and 15% | 5% (Reduced to 0% beginning in 2008) |
| 25%, 28%, 33%, and 35% | 15% |

The most common types of distributions from mutual funds are qualified dividends, ordinary dividends (taxed at ordinary income rates) that are not qualified dividends, and capital gain distributions. The qualified dividends and ordinary dividends are included in gross income and are taxed as explained in the preceding paragraph. Capital gain distributions are treated as long-term capital gains. If these mutual fund distributions are reinvested in more shares of the same fund, the income tax basis of the taxpayer in the mutual fund's shares is increased by the amount of the distributions that is included in gross income.

Unlike interest income, dividends do not accrue ratably over time. When stock is sold, the dividend is normally included in the gross income of the person who is listed as the owner of the stock on the record date. Court decisions are inconsistent about whether the donor or donee is to be taxed when the donor gifts stock after the declaration date but before the record date. When stock is gifted before the declaration date, the donee must normally include the dividends in gross income.

Dividends paid on life insurance policies are treated much differently than dividends paid to owners of corporations. A dividend paid to a policy holder by a life insurance company is considered a rebate of part of the premium paid on the policy, and is therefore not subject to income tax. Keep in mind that premiums paid on life insurance policies are paid with after-tax dollars, so a rebate of part of the premium (a life insurance dividend) is a return of capital, not a distribution of income.

### Rental and Royalty Income

Rents received from rental real estate and royalties from oil, gas, mineral properties, copyrights, and patents must be included in gross income as ordinary income. Related expenses are subtracted on Schedule E and the net amount is reported on Form 1040. As discussed later in this chapter, prepaid rent must be included in the gross income of both cash and accrual method taxpayers in the year the rent is received.

### Income from Annuities

Many individuals purchase commercial annuity contracts from insurance companies with after-tax dollars for the purpose of generating retirement income on a tax-deferred basis. This type of annuity contract is often referred to as a nonqualified annuity. While money invested in an annuity contract has already been subjected to income taxation, income or gains generated inside the contract are taxable when distributions are received from the annuity, which will presumably occur during retirement. An annuity is an ordinary income asset, and income generated from an annuity must be reported as ordinary income regardless of how the income was generated (for example, interest, dividend, or capital gain) inside the annuity. The timing of the recognition of gross income depends on whether the taxpayer annuitizes the contract, surrenders the contract, or simply takes distributions as needed from the contract.

## Annuitizing

An annuity contract is **annuitized** when regular periodic (such as monthly or annual) payments begin for life or for a specified period of time in excess of one year. When a contract is annuitized, each payment is deemed to include both a portion of nontaxable return of invested capital and a portion of gross income. The amount of each payment that is a nontaxable return of invested capital is determined using the exclusion ratio in the following formula:

$$\text{Excluded Amount} = \frac{\$ \text{ Investment in the Contract}}{\$ \text{ Expected Total Return}} \times \text{Distributions (Payments) Received}$$

The investment in the contract is the total amount of after-tax dollars invested in the contract. The expected return is the total amount of dollars distributions expected under the contract.

EXAMPLE 4.5

Thomas invested $100,000 in an annuity contract. Many years later, he annuitized the contract. The insurance company agreed to pay him $1,388.89 per month for 15 years. His total dollar expected return is $250,000.20 (15 years x 12 months x $1,388.89 per month). Using the formula above, the exclusion ratio (the central component of the formula) is 0.40 ($100,000/$250,000.20) and the excluded amount is $555.56 for each payment received.

$$\text{Excluded Amount} = \frac{\$100,000}{\$250,000.20} \times \$1,388.89 = \$555.56$$

$$\text{Exclusion Ratio} = \frac{\$100,000}{\$250,000} = 40\%, \text{ Therefore the Inclusion Ratio is} = 60\% \ (1 - 0.40)$$

Therefore, the amount excluded from gross income in a twelve month period would be $6,666.67 (12 x $1,388.89 x 0.40) and the amount excluded over the entire 15 years would be $100,000 (15 x 12 x $1,388.89 x 0.40). The amount included in gross income is the inclusion ratio (60% times each payment received).

EXAMPLE 4.6

David invested $100,000 in an annuity contract. Many years later, he annuitized the contract. The insurance company agreed to pay him $1,388.89 per month for the rest of his life. Using tables provided by the Internal Revenue Service, David's life expectancy was determined to be 15 years. As in the preceding example, the expected return is $250,000.20

(15 x 12 x $1,388.89) and the amounts excluded from and included in gross income are the same.

### Annuity Payments Received Beyond the Expected Period

In Example 4.6, if David receives annuity payments for 15 years, he will have recovered his entire investment in the contract (the entire $100,000 basis) free of income taxes. Therefore 100 percent of each payment he receives after 15 years will be included in his gross income.

### If an Annuitant Dies Before Recovering His Investment

In Example 4.6, if David dies after receiving payments for only 10 years, he will have recovered only $66,666.72 (10 x 12 x $1,388.89 x 0.40) of his investment in the contract free of income taxes. Therefore, a miscellaneous itemized deduction, not subject to a two percent of AGI limitation, of $33,333.28 can be deducted on his final federal income tax return for the unrecovered portion of his investment in the annuity.

### Joint Life Expectancies

In Publication 939, the Internal Revenue Service provides actuarial tables to determine life expectancies used in calculating the expected return from an annuity when payments are to be made for life or for the joint lives of two annuitants. Publication 939 also provides other tables and information to determine the expected return when a refund feature or other features are attached to the annuity.

### Surrender of an Annuity

If an annuity is surrendered to an insurance company for its cash surrender value, the difference between the total amount received and the total amount invested in the contract is included in gross income as ordinary income. If the annuity contract has not been owned for the required number of years specified in the annuity contract, the insurance company may impose a surrender charge. Surrender charges are usually specified as a percentage of the contract value and they decrease over time until they are eliminated entirely. The surrender charge period is usually five to seven years.

Whenever gross income is received from an annuity before the recipient (annuitant) reaches the age of 59½, a 10 percent penalty tax (10 percent of the gross income) is imposed unless certain requirements are met, such as payments made for life under IRC Sections 72(t) or 72(q). This penalty is waived on account of disability or death of the annuitant.

# SCHEDULE E
## (Form 1040)

Department of the Treasury
Internal Revenue Service (99)

# Supplemental Income and Loss
### (From rental real estate, royalties, partnerships, S corporations, estates, trusts, REMICs, etc.)
▶ **Attach to Form 1040, 1040NR, or Form 1041.** ▶ **See Instructions for Schedule E (Form 1040).**

OMB No. 1545-0074

**20 09**

Attachment
Sequence No. **13**

Name(s) shown on return

Your social security number

**Part I** **Income or Loss From Rental Real Estate and Royalties Note.** If you are in the business of renting personal property, use **Schedule C or C-EZ** (see page E-3). If you are an individual, report farm rental income or loss from **Form 4835** on page 2, line 40.

**1** List the type and address of each **rental real estate property:**

A _____

B _____

C _____

**2** For each rental real estate property listed on line 1, did you or your family use it during the tax year for personal purposes for more than the greater of:
- 14 days **or**
- 10% of the total days rented at fair rental value?
(See page E-3)

|   | Yes | No |
|---|---|---|
| A |   |   |
| B |   |   |
| C |   |   |

| Income: | | Properties | | | Totals (Add columns A, B, and C.) |
|---|---|---|---|---|---|
|   |   | **A** | **B** | **C** |   |
| **3** Rents received | **3** |   |   |   | **3** |
| **4** Royalties received | **4** |   |   |   | **4** |
| **Expenses:** | | | | | |
| **5** Advertising | **5** |   |   |   |   |
| **6** Auto and travel (see page E-4) | **6** |   |   |   |   |
| **7** Cleaning and maintenance | **7** |   |   |   |   |
| **8** Commissions | **8** |   |   |   |   |
| **9** Insurance | **9** |   |   |   |   |
| **10** Legal and other professional fees | **10** |   |   |   |   |
| **11** Management fees | **11** |   |   |   |   |
| **12** Mortgage interest paid to banks, etc. (see page E-5) | **12** |   |   |   | **12** |
| **13** Other interest | **13** |   |   |   |   |
| **14** Repairs | **14** |   |   |   |   |
| **15** Supplies | **15** |   |   |   |   |
| **16** Taxes | **16** |   |   |   |   |
| **17** Utilities | **17** |   |   |   |   |
| **18** Other (list) ▶ _____ | **18** |   |   |   |   |
| **19** Add lines 5 through 18. | **19** |   |   |   | **19** |
| **20** Depreciation expense or depletion (see page E-5) | **20** |   |   |   | **20** |
| **21** Total expenses. Add lines 19 and 20 | **21** |   |   |   |   |
| **22** Income or (loss) from rental real estate or royalty properties. Subtract line 21 from line 3 (rents) or line 4 (royalties). If the result is a (loss), see page E-5 to find out if you must file **Form 6198**. | **22** |   |   |   |   |
| **23** Deductible rental real estate loss. **Caution.** Your rental real estate loss on line 22 may be limited. See page E-5 to find out if you must file **Form 8582.** Real estate professionals **must** complete line 43 on page 2 | **23** | ( | )( | )( | ) |

**24** **Income.** Add positive amounts shown on line 22. **Do not** include any losses . . . . . . . . . | **24** | |

**25** **Losses.** Add royalty losses from line 22 and rental real estate losses from line 23. Enter total losses here . | **25** |( | )|

**26** **Total rental real estate and royalty income or (loss).** Combine lines 24 and 25. Enter the result here. If Parts II, III, IV, and line 40 on page 2 do not apply to you, also enter this amount on Form 1040, line 17, or Form 1040NR, line 18. Otherwise, include this amount in the total on line 41 on page 2 . . . | **26** | |

**For Paperwork Reduction Act Notice, see page E-8 of the instructions.** Cat. No. 11344L **Schedule E (Form 1040) 2009**

### Taking Distributions as Needed

When distributions (withdrawals) are taken from an annuity before annuitizing, every dollar distributed must be included in gross income until all of the gain in the contract has been distributed. Only then is a tax-free return of invested dollars allowed. This is a LIFO (last-in, first-out) approach to income reporting in which the gain in the contract (generated from the investment made in the contract) must be fully distributed before a tax-free return of basis may be received. However, annuities issued prior to August 14, 1982 receive FIFO (first-in, first-out) treatment.

### Other Annuity Issues

When distributions are made from a variable annuity, the payments may vary while the expected number of payments remains the same. In such a situation, the amount excluded from gross income from each payment is determined by dividing the investment in the contract by the number of periodic payments expected under the contract.

**Quick Quiz 4.4**

**Highlight the answer to these questions:**

1. All dividends paid by U.S. corporations are qualified dividends subject to favorable tax treatment.
   a. True
   b. False

2. Nonqualified annuity payments include both a nontaxable return of invested money and gross income.
   a. True
   b. False

3. Surrendering an annuity may result in gross income.
   a. True
   b. False

False, True, True.

---

**EXAMPLE 4.7**

Tom purchased a variable annuity at a total cost of $120,000. He starts receiving variable annuity payments for life at the age of 65. According to the appropriate actuarial table, his life expectancy at age 65 is 20 years. His annual exclusion amount from the annuity contract is $6,000 ($120,000/20). If he receives $9,000 in the current year, he will be allowed to exclude $6,000 and will include the remaining $3,000 in his gross income. If his payments from the contract are less than $6,000 for a given year (due to investment return fluctuations), he will be able to exclude all of the payments for the year and may choose to allocate his unused exclusion for that year to the remaining years of his life expectancy.

Gross income from an annuity is reported to the taxpayer on Form 1099-R (See Exhibit 4.8).

Gross income from private and commercial annuities is determined in the same manner as above. Private annuities are non-commercial annuities between two private parties, and are often used to achieve estate planning benefits.

---

# FORM 1099-R

EXHIBIT 4.8

| | VOID | CORRECTED | | |
|---|---|---|---|---|

| PAYER'S name, street address, city, state, and ZIP code | 1 Gross distribution $ | OMB No. 1545-0119 2009 Form 1099-R | Distributions From Pensions, Annuities, Retirement or Profit-Sharing Plans, IRAs, Insurance Contracts, etc. |
|---|---|---|---|
| | 2a Taxable amount $ | | |
| | 2b Taxable amount not determined ☐ | Total distribution ☐ | Copy 1 For State, City, or Local Tax Department |
| PAYER'S federal identification number | RECIPIENT'S identification number | 3 Capital gain (included in box 2a) $ | 4 Federal income tax withheld $ | |
| RECIPIENT'S name | | 5 Employee contributions /Designated Roth contributions or insurance premiums $ | 6 Net unrealized appreciation in employer's securities $ | |
| Street address (including apt. no.) | | 7 Distribution code(s) / IRA/SEP/SIMPLE ☐ | 8 Other $ % | |
| City, state, and ZIP code | | 9a Your percentage of total distribution % | 9b Total employee contributions $ | |
| | 1st year of desig. Roth contrib. | 10 State tax withheld $ $ | 11 State/Payer's state no. | 12 State distribution $ $ |
| Account number (see instructions) | | 13 Local tax withheld $ $ | 14 Name of locality | 15 Local distribution $ $ |

Form **1099-R**

Department of the Treasury - Internal Revenue Service

## *Income from Life Insurance and Endowment Contracts*

When the owner of a life insurance policy surrenders a life insurance policy to the issuing insurance company in exchange for the cash surrender value of the policy, the owner of the policy must recognize gross income equal to the amount of total money received minus the owner's adjusted basis (cost) for the policy. The gain is recognized as ordinary income. The owner's adjusted basis in the policy is equal to the total premiums paid on the policy less any refunded premiums, rebates, dividends, or existing loans against the policy.

An **endowment contract** is a type of insurance contract that pays a specified death benefit to a beneficiary upon the death of the insured owner, but has the added feature of paying the specified benefit (in lieu of the death benefit) to the owner of the policy if the insured person lives to a specified age or date. If the policy matures and the endowment proceeds paid to the owner of the policy exceed the owner's adjusted basis in the policy, the excess must be recognized as ordinary income. If the owner chooses to receive endowment proceeds in installments, the payments are taxed as an annuity with the proceeds being the initial basis.

Other gross income issues related to life insurance and endowment contracts are discussed later in this chapter.

### Traditional IRAs

Generally, a contribution to a traditional IRA is deductible in determining adjusted gross income (AGI), the income earned inside the IRA is tax deferred (taxed later), and distributions are taxed at ordinary income tax rates (regardless of the type of investments purchased inside of the IRA). Early distributions (before age 59½) may also be subject to a 10 percent penalty tax unless the distributions are made upon the death or disability of the owner or for certain other specified reasons.

Under certain circumstances, contributions to traditional IRAs may be only partially deductible or not deductible at all. When this occurs, each IRA distribution will consist of both a tax-free return of investment and taxable gross income.

### Income from Partnerships

A partnership is not subject to income tax on its income. Instead, the income of the partnership is passed through the entity to the partners and is subject to income taxation on the partners' individual income tax returns. Each partner's distributive share of partnership income is determined based upon the profit and loss sharing percentages of the partner. Distributions of cash or other property from the partnership to the partner during the year have no effect on the partner's income from the partnership unless cash distributions to the partner exceed the partner's basis in her partnership interest.

| | |
|---|---|
| **EXAMPLE 4.8** | ABC Partnership has $100,000 of ordinary income for the year. Charles has a 40% interest in the profits of ABC partnership. He received $30,000 of cash distributions during the year. Charles must report $40,000 of ordinary income from the partnership for the year. The cash distributions do not affect his current income recognition because they represent either income on which he has already been taxed or money that he invested in the partnership. |

### Income from S Corporations

The tax treatment of the income from an S corporation is similar, but not identical, to that of a partnership. Each stockholder is subject to income taxation on his pro-rata share of the S corporation's income. If the stockholder owns 10 percent of the stock of the corporation, he must report 10 percent of the corporation's income on his individual income tax return. Cash distributions from the corporation to the shareholder are not normally taxable because they represent income that has already been taxed.

The taxation of the income of S corporations and partnerships is discussed more fully in Chapter 16.

### Income from Limited Liability Companies

A limited liability company (LLC) is normally taxed as a partnership. Therefore, the income of the LLC is usually passed through the LLC to the members and is subject to income taxation on their individual income tax returns. Under check-the-box regulations discussed in Chapter 16, an LLC may elect to be taxed as a corporation if certain requirements are met.

## Income from Trusts and Estates

Individuals and C corporations (corporations that have not made an election under subchapter S) pay tax on their own income. Partnerships and S corporations are tax reporting entities that pass their income through to their owners. For income tax purposes, the term partnership includes LLCs, LLPs, and all other unincorporated entities with more than one owner. Trusts and estates may pay tax on their own income, pass through their income to their beneficiaries, or a combination of both. If a trust or estate retains all of its income for the year, it must pay income taxes on its income. If it pays out all of its income to beneficiaries during the year, it simply reports the income and passes it through to the beneficiaries. In this case, each beneficiary must report her share of the income. In some cases, some of the income for the year is retained by the trust or estate and some is paid to beneficiaries. When this happens, the trust or estate must pay income taxes on the income retained and the beneficiaries must pay income taxes on the income paid to them.

## INCOME TAX RATE SCHEDULE FOR ESTATES AND TRUSTS (FOR 2009)                EXHIBIT 4.9

| If taxable income is: | The tax is: |
| --- | --- |
| Not over $2,200 | **15%** of taxable income |
| Over $2,200 but not over $5,150 | $330.00 plus **25%** of the excess of such amount over $2,200 |
| Over $5,150 but not over $7,850 | $1,067.50 plus **28%** of the excess of such amount over $5,150 |
| Over $7,850 but not over $10,700 | $1,823.50 plus **33%** of the excess of such amount over $7,850 |
| Over $10,700 | $2,764.00 plus **35%** of the excess of such amount over $10,700 |

## INCOME TAX RATE SCHEDULE FOR ESTATES AND TRUSTS (FOR 2010)                EXHIBIT 4.10

| If taxable income is: | The tax is: |
| --- | --- |
| Not over $2,300 | **15%** of taxable income |
| Over $2,300 but not over $5,350 | $345 plus **25%** of the excess of such amount over $2,300 |
| Over $5,350 but not over $8,200 | $1,107.50 plus **28%** of the excess of such amount over $5,350 |
| Over $8,200 but not over $11,150 | $1,905.50 plus **33%** of the excess of such amount over $8,200 |
| Over $11,150 | $2,879 plus **35%** of the excess of such amount over $11,150 |

**EXAMPLE 4.9**

The Samantha Simpson Irrevocable Trust earned $25,000 of income during the year and paid $10,000 in cash to one beneficiary of the trust during the year. The trust must report $15,000 of the income and the beneficiary must report the remaining $10,000.

Income from a grantor trust is taxable to the trust's grantor (the person who established and funded the trust) rather than to the trust itself or to the trust beneficiaries. A revocable living (or inter vivos) trust is one type of grantor trust that is often used to avoid probate. If a Crummey provision is used to qualify a transfer to a trust for the gift tax annual exclusion, the trust may be partially or wholly beneficiary defective, causing some or all of the income to be reported on the beneficiary's income tax return.

## INVESTMENT-RELATED ITEMS EXCLUDED FROM GROSS INCOME

Relatively few types of investment income can be excluded from gross income, but the exclusion of municipal bond interest, life insurance proceeds, and distributions from Roth IRAs can provide meaningful tax planning opportunities for many taxpayers. The remaining exclusions provide more targeted or limited benefits.

### Interest Income from Certain State and Local Government Obligations

**Municipal bonds** are debt instruments issued by states and their political subdivisions (counties, cities, school districts, etc.). Interest income on municipal bonds issued to finance government operations is generally excluded from federal gross income. This tax-exempt status of bonds allows state and local governments to issue bonds at lower stated interest rates than the rates paid on taxable bonds of comparable quality because the net after-tax return is near or equal.

Municipal bonds are generally more appropriate for taxpayers with high marginal tax rates than for those with lower marginal rates. A comparison of the after-tax interest rate available on taxable bonds to tax-free municipal bonds can be made using the following formulas:

$$\text{Equivalent Tax-Free Rate} = \text{Taxable Rate} \times (1 - \text{Marginal Tax Rate})$$

$$\text{Equivalent Taxable Rate} = \frac{\text{Tax-Free Rate}}{1 - \text{Marginal Tax Rate}}$$

**EXAMPLE 4.10**

Jacob's marginal tax rate is 35%. He wants to invest in either a taxable bond with an interest rate of 6% or a tax-exempt municipal bond of comparable risk and quality, with an interest rate of 4%. The equivalent tax-free rate for the taxable bond is 3.9%.

$$\text{Equivalent Tax-Free Rate} = 0.06 \times (1 - 0.35) = 3.9\%$$

The equivalent taxable rate for the municipal bond is 6.15%.

$$\text{Equivalent Taxable Rate} = \frac{0.04}{1 - 0.35} = 6.15\%$$

Therefore, the municipal bond provides a higher after-tax return for Jacob. The comparison can be after-tax (4% vs. 3.9%) or pre-tax (6.15% vs. 6%). Under both methods, the municipal bond is superior in terms of after-tax yield.

Use the facts from the preceding example. If Jacob's marginal tax rate were 25% rather than 35%, which bond would provide a better after-tax return? The equivalent tax-free rate for the taxable bond is 4.5% (6% x 0.75). The equivalent taxable rate for the municipal bond is 5.33% (4%/0.75). Therefore, the taxable bond would provide a higher after-tax return (4.5% vs. 4.0%).

EXAMPLE 4.11

Interest income from municipal bonds is also excluded from gross income by many states. Some states exclude the interest earned from municipal bonds issued by entities within that state and tax the interest earned on bonds issued by state and local governments of other states. When comparing interest rates for taxable and tax-exempt bonds, the impact of state income tax laws should be included in the analysis.

The interest on some state and local bonds is taxable. Interest on some federally guaranteed bonds, some mortgage revenue bonds, some private activity bonds, and arbitrage bonds must be included in gross income.

The income tax exemption applies only to the interest on municipal bonds. Capital gains realized on the sale of municipal bonds must be included in gross income. Some municipal bonds are private activity bonds and create an AMT preference item. This is discussed further in Chapter 15.

## Life Insurance Proceeds

Life insurance proceeds paid to a beneficiary because of the death of the insured person are normally excluded from gross income. The entire death benefit is excludable regardless of the amount received. A beneficiary of a life insurance policy may choose to receive the death benefit in periodic installment payments, in which case the insurance company will pay interest on the proceeds that it retains. If the periodic installment payment option is selected, part of each payment received by the beneficiary will be excluded from income (the part that represents the death benefit received), and part will be included in income as interest income.

Paul died during the year. The $500,000 death benefit on his life insurance policy was payable to Beth, his wife and sole beneficiary. Rather than receiving a lump-sum payment of $500,000, Beth chose to receive $5,500 per month for a

EXAMPLE 4.12

period of 120 months. The excludable portion of each payment is $4,166.67 ($500,000/120), the death benefit divided by the number of payments. The remaining $1,333.33 from each payment must be included in gross income as the interest component.

Life insurance proceeds must be included in gross income of the new owner if the life insurance policy is sold ("transferred for value") by the original owner of the policy. This exception to the general rule that life insurance proceeds are exempt from income tax if received by reason of the death of the insured is known as the transfer for value rule.

| | |
|---|---|
| **EXAMPLE 4.13** | Brad owned a life insurance policy on his own life. Since he didn't need the policy any longer, he sold the policy to Joseph, his uncle, for $30,000. Joseph paid $20,000 in additional premiums over a period of years. When Brad died, Joseph received the death benefit of $400,000. Since the policy was transferred for value, Joseph must recognize $350,000 of ordinary income ($400,000 death benefit - $50,000 investment in the contract). |

There are five exceptions to the transfer for value rule. The death benefit is received income tax free by the beneficiary if the policy is transferred for valuable consideration to:

1. the insured;
2. a corporation in which the insured is a shareholder;
3. a partnership in which the insured is a partner;
4. a partner of the insured; or
5. a transferee who takes the transferor's basis.

| | |
|---|---|
| **EXAMPLE 4.14** | Jacob is a key employee at a large international manufacturing company. The company purchased a life insurance policy on Jacob's life several years ago to provide compensation to the company for the loss of Jacob's services in the event of his early death. Jacob is retiring this month and the company no longer wants to maintain the life insurance policy on his life. Jacob, however, could use the policy in his estate plan. The value of the policy is $95,000. If Jacob purchases the policy from the company for $95,000 a transfer for value has occurred, but the death benefit will not be subject to income tax because the life insurance policy was transferred for valuable consideration to the insured. |

| | |
|---|---|
| **EXAMPLE 4.15** | Kasey has a life insurance policy on his life that he purchased years ago, and does not really need it any longer. Last year, Kasey and two colleagues started a business in corporate form, and so far business has been booming. The shareholders would like to set up an entity type buy sell agreement whereby the corporation will purchase the shares of the |

deceased owner upon the owner's death. If Kasey sells his life insurance policy to the corporation to fund the buy-sell agreement, a transfer for value has occurred. The death benefit received by the corporation, however, will not be subject to tax since transfers for valuable consideration to a corporation in which the insured is a shareholder is an exception to the transfer for value rule.

Olivia has a life insurance policy on her life that she purchased years ago, and does not really need it any longer. Last year, Olivia and two colleagues started a business in partnership form, and so far business has been booming. The partners would like to set up an entity type buy sell agreement whereby the partnership will purchase the interest of the deceased owner upon the owner's death. If Olivia sells her life insurance policy to the partnership to fund the buy-sell agreement, a transfer for value has occurred. The death benefit received by the partnership, however, will not be subject to tax since transfers for valuable consideration to a partnership in which the insured is a partner is an exception to the transfer for value rule.

EXAMPLE 4.16

Odin has a life insurance policy on his life that he purchased years ago, and does not really need it any longer. Last year, Odin and his golf buddy, Christopher started a business in partnership form, and so far business has been booming. The partners would like to set up a cross-purchase type buy sell agreement whereby the surviving partner will purchase the interest of the deceased owner upon the owner's death. If Odin sells his life insurance policy to Christopher to fund the buy-sell agreement, a transfer for value has occurred. The death benefit received by Christopher, however, will not be subject to tax since a transfer for valuable consideration to a partner of the insured is an exception to the transfer for value rule.

EXAMPLE 4.17

Keli sold a life insurance policy that she owned on her own life to a grantor trust that she created a few years ago. The sale of the life insurance policy is a transfer for value. The trust, however, will have a basis in the life insurance policy equal to Keli's basis, since the sale to the trust is disregarded for income tax purposes due to its status as a grantor trust. Since, in this case, the transferee (the trust) will take the transferor's (Keli's) basis, the last exception to the transfer for value rule has been met.

EXAMPLE 4.18

A taxpayer may get a loan (or a series of periodic loans) from the life insurance policy t supplement retirement income or for any other purpose. Since the cash value in the polic secures the loan, the interest rates are normally very favorable for the borrower. Since a loan mus be repaid and is therefore not considered to be income, no gross income must be recognized b the borrower. Policy loans and any related accrued interest are often paid off with some of th tax-free proceeds of the policy upon the death of the insured owner of the policy. If the lif insurance policy is deemed to be a modified endowment contract (MEC), a policy loan is treate as a distribution of income to the extent of all of the deferred income in the policy. I determining the nature of the distribution for a MEC, a last-in, first-out (LIFO) approach i used in which all income (the last money going into the policy) is deemed to be distribute before the invested premiums (the first dollars into the policy) are deemed to be distributed.

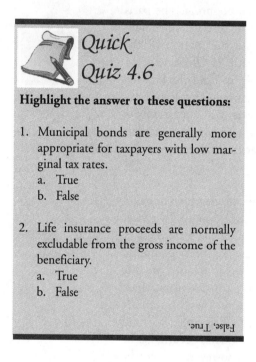

**Quick Quiz 4.6**

**Highlight the answer to these questions:**

1. Municipal bonds are generally more appropriate for taxpayers with low marginal tax rates.
   a. True
   b. False

2. Life insurance proceeds are normally excludable from the gross income of the beneficiary.
   a. True
   b. False

False, True.

### Accelerated Death Benefits

Accelerated death benefits are benefits paid to person who is terminally ill when the policy ha an accelerated death benefits rider. Accelerated death benefits paid by an insurance company under a life insurance policy before the death o the insured are excluded from gross income if th insured person is terminally ill. A person i deemed to be terminally ill if a physician certifie that he is reasonably expected to die from th illness or physical condition within 24 months The same tax treatment applies if the policy i sold or assigned to a qualified viatical settlemen provider.

Accelerated death benefits paid by an insurance company or a viatical settlement provider to a chronically ill individual are excluded from income to the extent that they are used to pay long-term care costs. Chronically ill individuals are people who are unable to perform two of the five activities of daily living (eating, bathing, dressing, toileting, transferring (walking), and continence) that would qualify the individual for benefits under a long-term care policy. Accelerated death benefits in excess of these costs are includible in income.

Without the special rules excluding certain types of accelerated death benefits from income, these benefits would be taxable because the payments are not paid to a beneficiary upon the death of the insured person.

### Roth IRAs

The tax treatment of Roth IRAs is very different from that for traditional IRAs. Distributions from Roth IRAs are normally excluded from gross income, while distributions from traditional IRAs are normally included in gross income. In order to avoid income taxation of the distributions from a Roth IRA, the owner must contribute after-tax dollars to the Roth IRA. In addition, distributions must be qualified distributions, which means that the taxpayer must leave he account open for at least five years from the beginning of the year for which the first contribution is made to the account, and receive a distribution:

1. after age 59½,
2. after the death of the owner,
3. after the disability of the owner, or
4. of up to $10,000 for a first-time home purchase.

In addition to qualified distributions, amounts contributed to the Roth IRA (on an after-tax basis) may be distributed at any time without including the distribution in gross income. Distributions from Roth IRAs are first deemed to come from the contributions to the plan rather than from income (a first-in, first-out or FIFO assumption). Part or all of any other distributions may be includible in gross income and may be subject to a 10 percent penalty tax if they do not meet the requirements of a qualified distribution.

If certain requirements are met, a taxpayer can convert a traditional IRA to a Roth IRA. For tax years before 2010, taxpayers are permitted to convert traditional IRAs to Roth IRAs if their AGI is less than or equal to $100,000. Under the Tax Increase Prevention and Reconciliation Act of 2005 (TIPRA 2005), however, the $100,000 AGI ceiling is eliminated for tax years after 2009. In the year of conversion, the taxpayer must normally include the entire value of the converted traditional IRA in gross income. Individuals who convert their IRAs in 2010, however, can elect to recognize the conversion income in 2010 or they can average the conversion income over the next two years (2011 and 2012). Only part of the value of the converted traditional IRA will be included in gross income if nondeductible contributions have been made to traditional IRAs.

## Educational Savings Bonds

Part or all of the interest income from the redemption of qualified U.S. savings bonds is excludable from gross income if the taxpayer pays for qualified higher educational expenses during the same year. The amount of interest that can be excluded is based on the following formula:

$$\frac{\text{Qualified Education  Expenses}}{\text{Bond Redemption Proceeds}} \times \text{Interest Income} = \text{Excludable Interest}$$

To exclude interest from income, qualified savings bonds must meet the following requirements: (1) the bonds must be series EE bonds issued after December 31, 1989, or Series I bonds; (2) the bonds must be issued in the name of the taxpayer or the names of the taxpayer and the taxpayer's spouse; and (3) the bond owner(s) must be at least 24 years of age on the issue date of the bonds. **Qualified education expenses** must be paid to an eligible institution. Qualified education expenses include tuition and fees paid for the taxpayer, spouse, or dependent, contributions to a qualified tuition program (discussion follows), or contributions to a Coverdell Education Savings Account (discussion follows). Qualified expenses do not include any expenses for room and board nor for courses related to sports, games, or hobbies that are not part of the student's degree or certificate program. Qualified expenses must be reduced by any scholarships or other tax-free sources of education funding and for expenses used to calculate either of the education tax credits discussed in Chapter 9.

EXAMPLE 4.19

After 1989, Tatiana purchased series EE savings bonds for $2,500 at the age of 25. This year she redeemed the bonds for $5,000 and paid qualified higher educational expenses in the amount of $4,000 for her daughter. The $2,500 difference between the redemption proceeds of $5,000 and the cost of $2,500 would all be taxable as interest income this year if she had not paid for the qualified expenses during the year. Since she did pay for the education expenses, she is allowed to exclude $2,000 [($4,000/$5,000) x $2,500] of the interest income. She will be required to include only $500 of the interest in gross income. If she had paid $5,000 or more for qualified education expenses, she would have been able to exclude all of the interest income from the savings bonds.

The amount of interest that can be excluded from gross income may be reduced or completely eliminated if the taxpayer's modified adjusted gross income (MAGI) exceeds specified amounts.

**EXHIBIT 4.11** **PHASEOUT LEVELS FOR SAVINGS BOND INTEREST EXCLUSION**

| Filing Status | 2009 | 2010 |
|---|---|---|
| Married Filing Jointly, Surviving Spouse | $104,900 - $134,900 | $105,100 - $135,100 |
| All Other | $69,950 - $84,950 | $70,100 - $85,100 |

### Qualified Tuition Programs/529 Plans

**Qualified tuition programs**, often called Section 529 plans, permit a taxpayer to save for post-secondary education of family members in a tax-favored manner. 529 plans come in two varieties: prepaid tuition programs and college savings plans. Prepaid tuition plans entitle a designated beneficiary (a student) to a waiver or a payment of qualified education expenses. No benefits or distributions are taxable unless the amounts distributed exceed the beneficiary's qualified education expenses. College savings plans allow taxpayers to earn income that will never be subject to income taxes if used to pay for future qualified education expenses for designated account beneficiaries.

Prepaid tuition plans allow parents to prepay future tuition at state educational institutions at today's rates. They are sometimes guaranteed by the sponsoring states. The states that sponsor prepaid tuition plans often allow the custodian of the account to transfer the value of a contract to an out-of-state or even a private school. Prepaid tuition plans can be sponsored by states, by a higher education institution, or by a group of such institutions.

College savings plans offer greater variety and flexibility than prepaid tuition plans, but they do not offer guarantees. To enjoy the tax benefits of a college savings plan, a donor (often a parent or grandparent) invests after-tax dollars in a college savings plan account for a family member (often the donor's child or grandchild) who is named as the account beneficiary. The donor selects from the available investments in the plan and the investment grows on a tax-deferred basis. When distributions are made by the donor to fund the beneficiary's postsecondary education, each distribution consists of a nontaxable return of investment and income. The income portion of the distribution is excluded from the beneficiary's gross income if the entire distribution is less than or equal to the amount of qualified education expenses for the year. If the distribution exceeds the qualified education expenses for the year, the beneficiary will be required to include some of the distribution in gross income and will be required to pay a 10 percent penalty tax on the amount included in gross income unless one of several exceptions applies. In addition to this favorable treatment for federal income tax purposes, some states offer income tax breaks as well, often only for residents of the state.

## Quick Quiz 4.7

**Highlight the answer to these questions:**

1. Distributions from Roth IRAs are normally included in gross income.
   a. True
   b. False

2. For the purpose of redeeming a Series EE savings bond, qualified educational expenses do not include expenses for room and board.
   a. True
   b. False

3. 529 plans may be either prepaid tuition programs or college savings plans.
   a. True
   b. False

4. Up to $12,000 per year may be contributed to a Coverdell Education Savings Account.
   a. True
   b. False

False, True, True, False.

Transfers to Section 529 plans are considered gifts for federal gift tax purposes. The federal gift tax exclusion of $13,000 (for 2009 and 2010) per donee per year is allowed for a gift to a qualified tuition program. A special rule allows a taxpayer to transfer up to $65,000 (for 2009 and 2010) to a qualified tuition program in one year without paying gift taxes if the taxpayer elects to treat the gift as an annual exclusion gift for the year of the gift and for each of the next four years.

The definition of qualified education expenses for a 529 plan is very broad. These eligible expenses include tuition, fees, books, supplies, equipment required for enrollment at an eligible institution, and the reasonable costs of room and board for a designated beneficiary who is at least a half-time student. When determining the amount of qualified education expenses for the year, the total must be reduced for any scholarships, Pell Grants, other tax-free payments received as educational assistance, and for expenses used to generate either of the education tax credits discussed in Chapter 9.

College savings plans are operated primarily by states or agencies of state governments. Although each plan may have some unique provisions, all of the plans allow the donor to enjoy significant control over an account even though any gross income is normally taxed to the designated beneficiary rather than the donor. Each plan may specify limits on contributions, but the basic limitation is that contributions on behalf of a beneficiary cannot exceed the amount necessary to provide for the beneficiary's qualified education expenses. The donor may contribute a lump-sum payment or make regular periodic payments to the plan. Donors are not allowed to actively manage the investments in an account, but they are normally allowed to change to another available portfolio or move the account to another 529 plan once per year. The donor decides when distributions will be made and the donor is allowed to change the beneficiary to another family member at any time. Taxpayers may make contributions to both a qualified tuition program and a Coverdell Education Savings Account in the same year for the same beneficiary. Finally, and importantly, there are no income limitations on the right to contribute to a 529 plan. Donors may make withdrawals from 529 plans for purposes other than paying qualified education expenses, but they must include any income distributed to them in gross income and must also pay a 10 percent penalty on any earnings included in gross income.

### Coverdell Education Savings Account

As with a college savings plan, distributions from a **Coverdell Education Savings Account** are excluded from the gross income of the beneficiary if they are less than or equal to the qualified educational expenses of the beneficiary for the year. If the distributions for the year exceed the qualified educational expenses, some of the distribution will be recognized as gross income by the beneficiary.

In many other respects, a Coverdell Education Savings Account is similar to a college savings plan. Some of the features of a Coverdell Education Savings Account that are different are:

- The maximum contribution per year per beneficiary is $2,000.
- The definition of qualified educational expenses includes (1) qualified elementary and secondary school expenses, (2) certain special needs services, and (3) contributions to a qualified tuition program (529 plan).
- Contributions must be completed by the time the beneficiary reaches age 18.
- Distributions from the account must be completed by the time the beneficiary reaches age 30.
- More investment options are available for a Coverdell Education Savings Account than for a Section 529 plan.
- The ability of the donor to contribute is phased out based on the modified adjusted gross income (MAGI) of the donor.

The following exhibit shows the beginning and ending phaseout thresholds for taxpayers contributing to a Coverdell Education Savings Account.

**EXHIBIT 4.12**   **COVERDELL EDUCATION SAVINGS ACCOUNT PHASEOUTS**

| Married Filing Jointly, Surviving Spouse | $190,000 - $220,000 |
|---|---|
| All Other | $95,000 - $110,000 |

When the taxpayer's MAGI exceeds the beginning of the phaseout range, the maximum allowable contribution is reduced ratably using the following formula:

$$\$2,000\,(\text{Maximum Contribution}) \times \frac{\text{AGI - Beginning Phaseout}}{\text{Ending Phaseout - Beginning Phaseout}} = \text{Reduction}$$

EXAMPLE 4.20

Tony and his wife Kate would like to make a contribution to a Coverdell Education Savings Account for their son, Jethro. Tony and Kate are married filing jointly and their AGI is $200,500. Because they are in the phaseout range, Tony and Kate will not be able to make the maximum contribution of $2,000. Instead, their contribution limit will be reduced by $700. The contribution limit is $1,300 ($2,000 - $700).

$$\$2,000 \times \frac{\$200,500 - \$190,000}{\$220,000 - \$190,000} = \$700 \ (\text{Reduction})$$

## Improvements by Tenant to Landlord's Property

A lessee of real estate may build buildings on or make other improvements to the real property that is rented from the lessor. At the end of the lease term, the tenant gives up all rights to the leased buildings and other improvements. Therefore, the landlord or lessor may receive valuable property in the form of buildings or other improvements upon the termination of the lease. The landlord may exclude the value of these improvements from gross income. The reason that an improvement would not be taxable is that if there is any improvement of significance it will result in either higher rent or a higher sales price. Either way, the IRS will ultimately receive its share.

# INCOME FROM PERSONAL ACTIVITIES

## ITEMS INCLUDED IN GROSS INCOME

### Prizes and Awards

In most cases, prizes and awards received by a taxpayer must be included in gross income. Two exceptions to the general rule exist in the case that the prize, such as a Nobel Prize, is received and it is paid directly to a qualified charity or if the exclusion qualifies under IRC Section 74(c). In the first case, if at the request of the recipient, the prize is paid directly to the qualified charity, the recipient is allowed to exclude the prize from gross income if three requirements are met: (1) the prize or award must be given primarily in recognition of religious, charitable, scientific, educational, artistic, literary, or civic achievement; (2) the recipient must not apply for the award; and (3) the recipient must not be required to render substantial future services to receive the prize or award.

In the second exception, IRC Section 74(c) excludes from gross income the value of an employee achievement award received by the taxpayer, unless the cost to the employer exceeds the amount that can be deducted by the employer for the cost of the employee achievement award. Two limitations apply to the employer's deduction for the cost of an employee achievement award made to a particular employee: (1) awards to a single employee which are not qualified plan awards cannot exceed $400 during a year and (2) the total awards to a single employee, under all plans, cannot exceed $1,600 for the year. Qualified plan awards are employee achievement awards granted as part of an established written plan or program of the employer. The plan cannot discriminate in favor of highly compensated employees.

### *Alimony and Separate Maintenance Payments*

**Alimony** (sometimes referred to as separate maintenance payments) must be included in the gross income of the recipient, and is deducted for AGI (above the line) by the payor. It is intended to replace income lost by one spouse as the result of the divorce and is usually paid by the spouse with higher income. Alimony shifts both income and tax liability from one former spouse to the other when paid.

It is sometimes difficult to determine when a payment incident to divorce is alimony, as opposed to child support or a property settlement. The difference is significant because different tax treatments apply to these three types of payments.

**Key Concepts**

Underline/highlight the answers to these questions as you read:

1. Identify the types of income from personal activities that are included in gross income.

2. Describe the imputed interest rules for below-market loans.

3. Identify personal activity income that is excluded from gross income.

### ALIMONY PAID

Generally, alimony is deducted from income (as an adjustment to income, or an above-the-line deduction) by the individual making the payment (payor), and included in the income of the individual receiving the payment (payee). Therefore, alimony generally receives pass-through tax treatment – the person who winds up with the cash has to pay the tax.

To achieve pass-through tax treatment, however, the payments must actually constitute alimony. IRC Section 71(b) sets forth the requirements necessary to classify payments as alimony. These requirements include:
1. the payments must be in cash or a cash equivalent (such as a check or money order);
2. the payments must be required by a court decree;
3. the court decree must not specify that the payments are "not alimony;"
4. the payments must cease at the death of the recipient;
5. the payments may not be disguised child support payments;
6. the former spouses may not be members of the same household; and
7. the parties may not file a joint income tax return (married filing jointly).

Note that the word alimony need not appear in the written instrument for the payment to be alimony. Child support may or may not be called child support in the written instrument. If any amount in the written instrument will be reduced on the happening of a contingency related to a child, the amount is deemed to be child support.

EXAMPLE 4.21

Under a provision of a divorce decree, Thomas is to pay his former spouse, Sheila, $5,000 per month. Sheila has custody of their only child, Alex. When Alex reaches age 18, the payments are to be reduced to $3,000 per month. The remaining $3,000 is to be paid to Sheila for as long as she lives or until she remarries. $2,000 of the $5,000 is child support because the payment is reduced when Alex reaches age 18 (a contingency related to a child). The remaining $3,000 is alimony.

A property settlement involves the division of marital assets between the spouses. At times, it may appear that the payor of alimony is seeking to take tax deductions for a payment that is really part of a property settlement. If the amount of alimony paid is over $15,000 per year and the payments decrease significantly from year one to years two and three, a front-loading formula is used to determine the amount of excess alimony that must be recaptured. This recaptured amount must be added to the gross income of the payor and deducted from the gross income of the payee for the third year that such payments are made. The amount of alimony recaptured in Year 3 (R3) is equal to the amount of Year 2 (R2) recapture plus Year 1 (R1) recapture.

$$R3 = R2 + R1$$

The alimony recapture in Year 2 (R2) is calculated as follows:

$$R2 = P2 - (P3 + \$15,000)$$

The alimony recapture in Year 1 (R1) is calculated as follows:

$$R1 = P1 - \left(\frac{P2 - R2 + P3}{2} + \$15,000\right)$$

In the above calculations, P1 is the alimony payment in Year 1, P2 is the payment in Year 2 and P3 is the payment in Year 3.

EXAMPLE 4.22

Brent pays alimony to his former spouse, Susan, in the following amounts: $120,000 in year 1; $30,000 in year 2; and $12,000 in year 3. It appears that part of the payments for the first and second years is actually part of a property settlement. In the third year, Brent will be required to include in gross income and Susan will be allowed to deduct $88,500 for excess alimony reported in years 1 and 2. "P" = payment in the calculations shown below.

$$R2 = P2 - (P3 + \$15,000)$$
$$R2 = \$30,000 - (\$12,000 + \$15,000)$$
$$R2 = \$3,000$$

$$R1 = P1 - \left(\frac{P2 - R2 + P3}{2} + \$15,000\right)$$

$$R1 = \$120,000 - \left( \frac{\$30,000 - \$3,000 + \$12,000}{2} + \$15,000 \right)$$

$$R1 = \$120,000 - \$34,500$$

$$R1 = \$85,500$$

$$R3 = R2 + R1$$
$$R3 = \$3,000 + \$85,500$$
$$R3 = \$88,500$$

The amount of alimony recaptured in Year 3 may also be calculated by using the following formula if alimony payments decreased by more than $15,000 per year over the first three years. The formula is:

$$R3 = P1 + P2 - 2P3 - \$37,500$$

where:
R3 = Recapture in year 3
P1 = Alimony payment in year 1
P2 = Alimony payment in year 2
P3 = Alimony payment in year 3

Please note that this shortcut formula will not work unless the alimony payments decline by $15,000 or more each year during the first three years of payments.

For instance, Example 4.18 could have been calculated as follows:
$$R3 = \$120,000 + \$30,000 - (2 \times \$12,000) - \$37,500 = \$88,500$$

This formula was derived from the regulations and the $37,500 is a fixed amount to determine the total to recapture in Year 3. It is a shortcut when compared to the two previous formulas.

### *Income from Discharge of Indebtedness*
When a taxpayer's debt is discharged or forgiven by a lender, the taxpayer must normally include the amount of the discharge of indebtedness in gross income. However, the amount of debt forgiven need not be included in gross income in certain circumstances, including the following:
- Certain forgiven student loans,
- Debts forgiven in bankruptcy,
- Debts forgiven when a taxpayer is insolvent (up to the amount of a taxpayer's insolvency),
- Debt cancelled as a result of Hurricane Katrina,
- Forgiveness of qualified farm indebtedness,
- Forgiveness of qualified real property business indebtedness,
- Forgiveness by a seller of a buyer's debt, and
- Forgiveness of debt as a gift.

Although current gross income recognition is not required in these situations, the taxpayer is usually required to reduce specified "tax attributes" (such as net operating losses, the general business tax credit carryforward, the minimum tax credit, net capital losses, and the income tax basis of assets) in the amount of the debt forgiveness that is excluded from gross income.

EXAMPLE 4.23

Joe owes $100,000 to Billy Bob Inc. Billy Bob Inc. agrees to discharge the debt in exchange for a cash value life insurance policy with a fair market value of $40,000. Joe has imputed income of $60,000 from the discharge of indebtedness.

## Imputed Interest on Loans with Below-Market Interest Rates

When an interest-free or below-market rate loan is made to an individual, interest will be imputed to the lender for income tax purposes. The amount of **imputed interest** will equal the difference between the interest rate charged on the loan and the applicable federal rate, which is set by the IRS on a monthly basis. In addition to the phantom income from imputed interest that is included in the lender's gross income, the lender is deemed to make a gift of the imputed interest back to the borrower. If the imputed interest is less than $13,000 (2009 and 2010), the gift may be shielded by the gift tax annual exclusion. This treatment must be applied to a variety of loans, including gift loans, compensation-related loans, and corporation to shareholder loans.

EXAMPLE 4.24

Bill Jensen (lender) loans $300,000 to his daughter, Heather (borrower) and does not charge any interest. The applicable federal rate is 5%. There are two consequences of this transaction. First, the imputed interest rules will apply, and Bill will be deemed to receive interest from Heather on the loan each year. The imputed interest payment of $15,000 (5% of $300,000) is phantom income for Bill and must be included on his income tax return. Heather may be able to deduct the imputed interest payment if it is considered deductible interest (such as home mortgage or investment interest). Second, because Heather is not making the interest payment to Bill, Bill will be deemed to make a gift to Heather of the imputed interest. Since Heather has use of the property, the gift would be considered a present interest gift and would qualify for the gift tax annual exclusion of $13,000 (in 2009 and 2010). Therefore, Bill will have made a taxable gift of $2,000 ($15,000 imputed interest, $13,000 annual exclusion) to Heather, which will reduce his applicable credit for gift and estate tax purposes, or, if Bill has already fully used his applicable credit, will result in the payment of a gift tax on $2,000.

**EXHIBIT 4.13**  IMPUTED INTEREST DIAGRAM

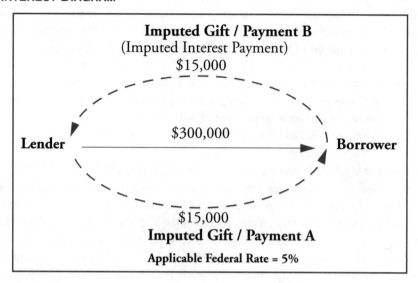

**Imputed Gift / Payment B**
(Imputed Interest Payment)
$15,000

Lender — $300,000 → Borrower

$15,000
**Imputed Gift / Payment A**

**Applicable Federal Rate = 5%**

**EXAMPLE 4.25**

Crandle Corporation (lender) loans $300,000 to an employee (borrower) and does not charge interest. The applicable federal rate is 5%. The employee is deemed to pay $15,000 (5% x $300,000) in annual interest to Crandle Corporation. This interest may be deductible by the employee if it otherwise meets the requirements for deductible interest. Crandle Corporation will report $15,000 of phantom interest income on it's tax return. In addition, Crandle Corporation will be deemed to pay compensation equal to the imputed interest amount to the employee. Crandle Corporation will be able to deduct this payment (provided that total compensation is deemed to be reasonable), and the employee will have to include the payment in his or her gross income as salary/wages (which is subject to both income and Social Security/Medicare taxes). When a below market loan is made from a corporation to an employee, both the corporation and the taxpayer will incur additional tax liability. Even though the corporation reports the imputed interest in income, and receives a deduction for the compensation payment made, it will have to pay ½ of the Social Security and Medicare taxes on the compensation payment. Even if the employee is able to deduct the imputed interest, he or she must pay Social Security tax on the deemed compensation payment received.

**EXAMPLE 4.26**

Highland Corporation (lender in the diagram above) loans $300,000 to a shareholder (borrower) of Highland Corporation and doesn't charge any interest. The applicable federal rate is 5%. Highland Corporation is deemed to pay the shareholder dividends in the amount of $15,000 (payment A). Highland Corporation is not allowed a tax deduction for the deemed dividend payment, but the shareholder must include the payment in gross income. The shareholder is then deemed to pay interest in the amount of $15,000 to Highland Corporation (payment B). Highland Corporation must include the deemed interest payment in gross income and the shareholder may be allowed to take a tax deduction for the deemed interest paid.

## Limitations on Imputed Interest

While the imputed interest rules are designed to limit the planning opportunities associated with gift loans, compensation related loans, and shareholder loans, there are exceptions. First, there is a de minimis amount of $10,000 that applies. If the outstanding loan balance is $10,000 or less, no interest will be imputed on the loan.

A special exception applies to gift loans. The imputed interest rules will not apply if the total outstanding balance of the loan is $100,000 or less and the borrower has less than $1,000 in net investment income for the year. If the outstanding loan balance is $100,000 or less and the borrower's net investment income exceeds $1,000 per year, the interest imputed on the loan will be the lesser of (1) the borrower's net investment income, or (2) the amount necessary to match the percentage interest paid on the loan with the applicable federal rate.

Angee loans her daughter $30,000 for a down payment on a house. If her daughter has only $200 of investment income for the year and no investment deductions, no interest will be imputed. If the daughter has net investment income of $1,100 for the year, the amount of imputed interest will not exceed $1,100.

**EXAMPLE 4.27**

| | | |
|---|---|---|
| **EXHIBIT 4.14** | **SUMMARY OF IMPUTED INTEREST RULES FOR LOANS** | |

| Loan Value | Imputed Interest |
|---|---|
| $0 ≤ $10,000 | $0 |
| $10,001 ≤ $100,000 | The lesser of:<br><br>•   Net investment income, or<br>•   Interest calculated using AFR less interest calculated using stated rate of the loan<br><br>If borrower's net investment income ≤ $1,000, $0 imputed interest |
| > $100,000 | Interest calculated using AFR less interest calculated using stated rate of the loan. |

### Tax Benefit Rule

If a taxpayer takes a tax deduction for an expenditure in one year and recovers (i.e., receives a refund) part or all of the expenditure in a later year, the recovered amount should be included in gross income in that later year. If he receives a limited or no tax benefit for his deduction; however, only part or none of the recovered amount must be included in gross income.

Todd itemizes his deductions in year one. His total itemized deductions, including a deduction for state income taxes in the amount of $3,000, exceed his standard deduction by $2,000. If he receives an $800 state income tax refund in year two for overpayment of his year one taxes, he must include the $800 in his gross income for year two. If Todd's itemized deductions for year one had exceeded his standard deduction by only $200, Todd would be required to include only $200 of the refund in his gross income because he received a tax benefit of only $200 for itemizing and deducting his state income taxes. If Todd had taken the standard deduction in year one, none of the refund would be includible in gross income because he received no tax benefit from deducting state income taxes in year one.

### Other Income

Some other income items that must be included in gross income are:

• Gambling winnings,

• Fees for jury duty,

• Fees for being an executor, administrator, or personal representative of an estate (unless you are a professional), and

• Income from a hobby.

# ITEMS EXCLUDED FROM GROSS INCOME

## Gifts

The value of property received as a gift is excludable from gross income by the recipient (the donee). This exclusion applies whether the gift is a birthday gift with a small value or a gift of a stock portfolio worth several million dollars. The value is irrelevant. The gift can be in cash, property, or even services. In order to qualify for the income tax exclusion, the transfer must be a gift, not a disguised form of compensation.

Income generated by gifted property must be included in gross income of the donee. A gift from an employer to an employee is not normally excludable from the employee's gross income, but there are exceptions (see the discussion of employee achievement awards and certain de minimis fringe benefits in Chapter 5).

## Inheritances

The value of property received by bequest, devise, or inheritance is excludable from gross income by the recipient, regardless of the value of the inherited property.

Any income generated by inherited property must be included in the gross income of the heir. Generally, the receipt of property from a decedent's estate in lieu of compensation or fees receivable from the decedent or the decedent's estate must be included in gross income. The executor of an estate, however, may elect to waive the right to collect fees for the services performed, and therefore avoid a gross income inclusion.

## Scholarships

The value of a scholarship or fellowship can be excluded from gross income by an individual who is a candidate for a degree at an eligible educational institution if the proceeds are used for qualified tuition and related expenses. An eligible educational institution must maintain a regular faculty and curriculum and have a regularly enrolled student body at the place where it carries on its educational activities. Most colleges and universities, as well as other schools, qualify as eligible educational institutions.

Qualified tuition and related expenses include required tuition and fees and course-related expenses such as required books, supplies, and equipment.

Scholarship proceeds used for purposes other than qualified tuition and related expenses must be included in gross income. Therefore, amounts used for room, board, research, travel, clerical help, equipment not required for the course of study, and other purposes are subject to income taxes. In addition, amounts received that represent payment for teaching, research, or other services by the student that are required as a condition for receiving the scholarship, fellowship, or tuition reduction must be included in gross income, even if used to pay tuition.

Qualified tuition reductions and need-based educational grants, such as Pell Grants, can also be excluded from gross income. A qualified tuition reduction allows the taxpayer to study at an eligible educational institution for free or for a reduced rate of tuition.

## Compensation for Injuries and Sickness

When one person (or entity) injures another person or damages another person's property, the injured party may seek and receive compensatory damages (compensation) for the losses and injuries suffered. The **compensatory damages** may be intended to compensate for damage to property, for recovery of expenses incurred, for income lost, or for personal injury. The injured person may also receive **punitive damages** (payments intended to punish the offending party). The tax treatment for the receipt of such payments, as addressed below, is the same whether the payments are received as a result of court action or not. The treatment is also the same whether the payment is received from the injuring party or from an insurance company.

### Destruction of Property

If compensatory damages are received for the destruction of the taxpayer's property, the recipient normally treats the payments received as payment received for the sale of the property. Therefore, a gain may need to be recognized. However, the gain may be deferred until a later date if the taxpayer meets the criteria for an involuntary conversion under IRC Section 1033 (discussed in more detail in Chapter 13).

### Recovery of Expenses Incurred

Compensatory damage payments intended to reimburse the injured person for expenses incurred are excluded from gross income unless the taxpayer receives a tax benefit from the deduction of the expenses in a prior year.

**EXAMPLE 4.29**

Joe is injured in 2005 by Hurricane Katrina. On his 2005 tax return, Joe claimed and deducted medical expenses related to the injury. He was later reimbursed by his health care insurer. He must include the reimbursement in gross income to the extent he received a tax benefit for the prior deduction.

### Lost Income

If compensatory damage payments are received to compensate the injured person for lost income, the payments must normally be included in gross income because the income replaced would have been taxable if it had actually been earned. A major exception to this rule exists (see the discussion of physical personal injury below).

**EXAMPLE 4.30**

A driver loses control of his truck and damages the front of Janet's business building. She is required to shut down her business for two weeks while the building is repaired. She receives $12,000 from the driver's insurance company to compensate her for the lost income. She must include the $12,000 in gross income.

## Punitive Damages

Punitive damage payments to the injured party must be included in gross income.

## Physical Personal Injury

If a person suffers physical personal injuries or physical sickness as a result of the actions of someone else, any compensatory damages received can be excluded from gross income. The compensatory payments are fully excludable even if the payments are intended to replace lost income. If punitive damages are received; however, they must be included in gross income.

John's car was hit by another driver who was intoxicated and John was seriously injured. In addition to payment for the damage to his car, John received compensatory payments of $30,000 to reimburse him for medical expenses, $2,000,000 for lost future income, and $100,000 for pain and suffering. He also received $300,000 in punitive damages. John must include the punitive damages in gross income. The remaining $2,130,000 can be excluded from gross income.

Compensatory damages for physical injuries are intended to make the recipient "whole" and are therefore not taxable. In contrast, punitive damages are intended to "punish" and are fully taxable.

## Other Personal Injuries

Compensatory damages can be received for personal injuries that are not due to physical injuries or sickness. Examples include damages for age discrimination and damage to the reputation of the injured party. Compensatory damage payments for non-physical personal injuries must be included in gross income.

## INCLUSION/EXCLUSION OF COMPENSATION FOR DAMAGES FROM INJURIES

| Injury Type | Compensatory Damages | Punitive Damages |
|---|---|---|
| Bodily injury | Excluded | Included |
| Personal injuries not including bodily injury | Included | Included |
| Lost income | Included | Included |
| Any other type of injury | Included | Included |

## Child Support and Property Settlements

When a divorce occurs, three different types of payments can be made by one former spouse to the other: alimony, child support, and property settlements. All of these topics were briefly covered under the discussion of alimony, above. As indicated in that discussion, alimony must be included in the gross income of the payee and is deductible (for AGI) by the payor. Child support payments are excluded from the gross income of the payee and are not deductible by the payor since these payments simply satisfy the legal obligation of the payor to support the children. Property settlements do not result in any immediate tax consequences for either party, but the recipient of any property has an income tax basis in the property equal to the basis of the property before the divorce. IRC Section 1041 requires all transfers between spouses during marriage or incident to a divorce to be treated as a gift for income tax purposes, resulting in a carryover basis (basis adjustments for losses, as discussed in the capital assets chapter, do not apply). Other tax attributes of the property may also influence the tax impact when the property is sold in subsequent years.

<table>
<tr><td>**EXAMPLE 4.32**</td><td>Allison and Hector recently divorced. As part of a property settlement incident to that divorce, Allison received the personal residence that she had shared with Hector. The personal residence has a basis of $150,000 and a value of $250,000. Hector received a stock portfolio with a basis of $150,000 and a value of $250,000. Both properties had been owned for more than two years as joint tenants with rights of survivorship. At the time of the property settlement, neither party reports any gross income or deductions. If each property is sold shortly after the divorce for $250,000, Allison will be able to exclude all of the $100,000 gain on the sale of the principal residence under Section 121, but Hector will be required to recognize $100,000 of long-term capital gain on the sale of the stock.</td></tr>
</table>

### Gain on the Sale of Residence (Section 121)

As explained in Chapter 13, a realized gain of up to $250,000 ($500,000 on a joint return) can be excluded from gross income on the sale of a residence that has been owned and occupied as the taxpayer's principal residence during two of the preceding five years.

### Amounts Received Under Insurance Contracts for Certain Living Expenses

As a result of a fire, storm, or some other type of casualty, a taxpayer may be unable to occupy his residence. If these events seem imminent, government officials may not allow people to occupy their residences. Payments received from insurance companies to pay for additional temporary housing costs as a result of these events may be excluded from gross income.

### Qualified Foster Care Payments

Certain qualified care payments received by a foster care provider can be excluded from gross income.

## Disaster Relief Payments

Qualified disaster relief payments received by a taxpayer can be excluded from gross income. A qualified disaster relief payment must be received for one of the following reasons:

- To pay for reasonable and necessary personal, family, living, or funeral expenses incurred as a result of a qualified disaster;

- To pay reasonable and necessary expenses to repair or rehabilitate a personal residence or its contents as a result of a qualified disaster;

- To promote the general welfare in connection with a qualified disaster and paid by a federal, state, or local government, or government agency; or

- It is paid by a person engaged in the furnishing or sale of transportation as a common carrier by reason of the death or personal physical injuries incurred as a result of a qualified disaster.

A qualified disaster includes a disaster resulting from a terrorist attack or military action, a Presidentially declared disaster, a disaster that results from an accident involving a common carrier, a disaster from any other event, which is determined by the Secretary of the Treasury to be of a catastrophic nature, or a disaster which is determined by an applicable federal, state, or local authority to warrant assistance from a federal, state, or local government, or government agency.

Most of the disaster relief payments received by taxpayers as a result of hurricanes Katrina, Rita, Gustav, and Ike would qualify for this exclusion. Under the tax benefit rule, however, disaster payments may be taxable if the recipient had previously deducted losses associated with the same disaster (at least to the extent of the deduction, according to the tax benefit rule).

# Key Terms

*Accrual Method* - An accounting method under which income is reported when it is earned rather than when it is received in cash, and expenses are reported when they are incurred rather than when they are paid.

*Alimony* - A separate maintenance payment that is intended to replace income lost by one spouse as the result of a divorce and must be included in the gross income of the payee.

*Annuitized* - When regular periodic payments on an annuity contract begin for life or for a specified period of time in excess of one year.

*Bartering* - An exchange of property and/or services for other property and/or services.

*Cash Receipts and Disbursements Method* - An accounting method under which income items are reported for the tax year in which they are received in cash and expenses are deducted in the year in which they are paid with cash.

*Community Property* - A regime in which married individuals own an equal, undivided interest in all of the property accumulated, using either spouse's earnings, during the marriage.

*Compensatory Damages* - Monetary award intended to compensate for damage to property, for recovery of expenses incurred, for income lost, or for personal injury.

*Coverdell Education Savings Account* - Plan similar to a college savings plan that allows taxpayers to contribute up to $2,000 per beneficiary per year to an account.

*Dividend Income* - A distribution of corporate earnings to shareholders, usually in cash.

*Endowment Contract* - A type of insurance contract that pays a specified death benefit to a beneficiary upon the death of the insured owner, but also pays a specified benefit (in lieu of the death benefit) to the owner of the policy if the insured person lives to a specified age or date.

*Gross Income* - All income from whatever source derived unless it is specifically excluded by some provision of the Internal Revenue Code.

*Imputed Interest* - A payment deemed to be made by the borrower to the lender when the interest rate on a loan is less than the applicable federal rate.

*Interest Income* - Gross income generated by a variety of debt instruments, including bank accounts, money market instruments, and bonds. This is income to the lender and a gift to the borrower.

*Municipal Bonds* - Debt instruments issued by states and their political subdivisions, the interest income from which is generally excluded from federal gross income.

# Key Terms

**Original Issue Discount** - The difference between the redemption price at maturity and the purchase price for debt instruments issued at a discount.

**Punitive Damages** - Payments intended to punish the offending party.

**Qualified Dividends** - Dividends subject to favorable tax rates.

**Qualified Education Expenses** - Educational expenses that receive favorable tax treatment. Such expenses may vary depending on the type of program or tax benefit.

**Qualified Tuition Programs** - Also known as 529 Plans, permit taxpayers to save for post-secondary education of family members in a tax-favored manner through either a prepaid tuition program or a college savings plan.

## DISCUSSION QUESTIONS

1. What is a barter transaction and how is income associated with such a transaction reported?

2. To whom is investment income normally taxable?

3. How do community property regimes affect the reporting of income?

4. What are the three types of relief provided by Section 66 to spouses?

5. Give several examples of income generated by investment activities that are included in gross income.

6. What types of investments generate interest income and how is interest income reported?

7. What are the requirements for a dividend to be a qualified dividend?

8. How is an annuity contract annuitized?

9. What are the tax consequences of taking distributions from an annuity without annuitizing?

10. What are the tax consequences of surrendering a life insurance contract?

11. Under what circumstances are life insurance proceeds excluded from gross income?

12. What are the requirements for a qualified savings bond?

13. Compare and contrast prepaid tuition programs and college savings plans.

14. Describe the characteristics of a Coverdell Educational Savings Account that make it different from a college savings plan.

15. Under what circumstances can a prize or award be excluded from the recipient's gross income?

16. What are the requirements for treating a payment made between divorcing spouses as alimony?

17. Summarize the imputed interest rules.

18. Compare and contrast compensatory damages and punitive damages.

19. Discuss the tax treatment of child support payments.

20. When is the amount of debt forgiven not included in gross income?

1. Gibbs has an account at First Maryland Bank. $10,000 of his account balance is invested in a certificate of deposit (CD). When must interest paid on the CD be included in Jonas' income?

   a. Interest on a CD is never included in income.

   b. The interest is included in Gibbs' income when it is added to his account balance.

   c. The interest is included in Gibbs' income when he withdraws it from the account.

   d. The interest is included in Gibbs' income when he spends it.

2. Patrick owns 100 shares of Darling Company stock. On December 29, 2009, Darling Company prepared the dividend checks for its shareholders. On December 31, 2009, Darling Company mailed dividend checks to all of its shareholders. Patrick did not receive his dividend check until January 3, 2010. On what date must Patrick include the dividends in his income?

   a. Patrick is not required to include the dividends in his income.

   b. Patrick must include the dividends in his income on December 29, 2009.

   c. Patrick must include the dividends in his income on December 31, 2009.

   d. Patrick must include the dividends in his income on January 3, 2010.

3. Trip loans $11,000 to his sister, Tish, and does not charge her interest. Should interest be imputed on this loan?

   a. Interest would not be imputed because the loan is less than the amount of the gift tax annual exclusion.

   b. Interest would be imputed because loans of $100,000 or less are always exempt from both income tax and gift tax consequences.

   c. Interest would be imputed if Tish has unearned income of $1,100.

   d. Interest would not be imputed if Tish's earned income is less than $1,000.

4. George is awarded $55,000 in compensatory damages for harm to his reputation and $30,000 in compensatory damages for bodily injury. In addition, he was awarded $275,000 in punitive damages. How much of these awards must George recognize in income?

   a. $85,000.

   b. $275,000.

   c. $330,000.

   d. $360,000.

5. Brian had the following items of income this year.

- Salary - $22,000
- Child support received - $6,000
- Alimony received - $10,000
- Personal Injury award from an auto accident. He lost the use of his left hand and was awarded compensatory damages of $200,000. He also received $50,000 in punitive damages.

Calculate Brian's gross income for the current year.

    a. $32,000.

    b. $38,000.

    c. $82,000.

    d. $288,000.

6. Jeremy and Juliet were recently divorced. Jeremy has been ordered by the court to pay alimony to Juliet. In the first year after the divorce, Jeremy pays Juliet $100,000. In the second year after the divorce, he pays her $50,000. In the third year, Jeremy pays Juliet $20,000. How much alimony recapture must Juliet report in the third year?

    a. Juliet is not subject to alimony recapture.

    b. Juliet must report $43,333 in alimony recapture for the over payment in the first year.

    c. Juliet must report $72,500 in alimony recapture.

    d. Juliet must report $110,000 in alimony recapture.

7. Which of the following statements regarding community property is not correct?

    a. If two married taxpayers file married filing separately, the community property income is divided equally, but the separate property income is reported by the spouse owning the separate property.

    b. In community property states, half of the income earned (wages, salaries, etc.) by a spouse is deemed to be earned by each spouse and half of the income earned from community property is deemed to be the income of each spouse.

    c. The community property regime survives divorce with regard to property.

    d. Property acquired before marriage or acquired by gift or inheritance before or after marriage is normally considered to be the separate property of the spouse.

8. Which of the following must be included in Pete's income?

    1. Short-term capital gains of $10,000 from the sale of stock.
    2. Long-term capital gains of $80,000 from the sale of real property.
    3. Interest income from Pete's savings account.
    4. A gift from Pete's brother of $15,000.
        a. 1 and 2.
        b. 3 and 4.
        c. 1, 2, and 3.
        d. 1, 2, 3, and 4.

9. Addison pays $15,000 for an annuity that will pay $1,000 a year, starting this year. If the annuity is for a term of 20 years, how much taxable income will Addison have from the annuity each year?
        a. Addison will not ever have taxable income from the annuity.
        b. Addison will have $250 of taxable income from the annuity each year.
        c. Addison will have $750 of taxable income from the annuity each year.
        d. Addison will have $1,000 of taxable income from the annuity each year.

10. Which of the following is true regarding the proceeds of a life insurance policy?
        a. Proceeds paid by reason of the death of the insured are always included in the income of the recipient.
        b. When the owner of a life insurance policy surrenders a life insurance policy to the issuing insurance company in exchange for the cash surrender value of the policy, the owner of the policy is not required to recognize any gross income.
        c. Life insurance proceeds are not included in gross income of the new owner if the life insurance policy is sold ("transferred for value") by the original owner of the policy.
        d. Accelerated death benefits paid by an insurance company under a life insurance policy before the death of the insured are excluded from gross income if the insured person is terminally ill.

11. After 1989, Patty purchased series EE savings bonds for $5,000 at the age of 25. This year she redeemed the bonds for $10,000 and paid qualified higher educational expenses in the amount of $7,000 for her daughter. For 2009, Patty is a single taxpayer with a MAGI of $73,100. What are the tax consequences of this transaction?

   a. All $10,000 of the proceeds of the EE savings bonds must be included in Patty's gross income.

   b. Only $5,000 of the proceeds of the EE savings bonds must be included in Patty's gross income.

   c. Only $2,900 of the proceeds of the EE savings bonds must be included in Patty's gross income.

   d. Only $1,500 of the proceeds of the EE savings bonds must be included in Patty's gross income.

12. Which of the following can be excluded from Ellen's gross income?

   1. The value of a diamond ring that Ellen received as a gift from David.
   2. The value of a mansion that Ellen inherited from her parents.
   3. The value of concert tickets that Ellen won in a radio contest.
   4. The value of a scholarship for room and board that Ellen received to her state university.

   a. 1 only.

   b. 1 and 2.

   c. 1, 2, and 3.

   d. 2, 3, and 4.

13. Which of the following payments would not qualify as a qualified disaster relief payment?

   a. Payments for unlimited funeral expenses incurred as a result of a qualified disaster.

   b. Payments for reasonable and necessary expenses to repair a personal residence as a result of a qualified disaster.

   c. Payments to promote the general welfare in connection with a qualified disaster and paid by the federal government.

   d. Payments made by a person engaged in the furnishing or sale of transportation as a common carrier by reason of personal physical injuries incurred as a result of a qualified disaster.

4. Sean owns stock in the McNamara Corporation. Sean has a basis in his stock of $100. Which of the following would <u>not</u> be included in Sean's income?

    a. Qualified dividends received from McNamara Corporation.

    b. A distribution by McNamara Corporation to its shareholders in excess of earnings and profits, of which Sean's share of the distribution is $50.

    c. Dividends paid by the McNamara Corporation of less than $10.

    d. Dividends paid by the McNamara Corporation, assuming that it is not a U.S. corporation.

5. Twenty-five years ago, Derek paid $11,000 for an annuity that paid $625 a year for life. At the time he purchased the annuity, Derek's life expectancy was 22 years. How much taxable income will Derek have from the annuity this year?

    a. Derek will have no taxable income from the annuity.

    b. Derek will have $125 of taxable income from the annuity this year.

    c. Derek will have $500 of taxable income from the annuity this year.

    d. Derek will have $625 of taxable income from the annuity this year.

# Quick Quiz Explanations

## Quick Quiz 4.1

1. True.
2. False. When barter transactions are made through a barter exchange, an organization established to facilitate the trading of goods and services, the transaction must be reported to the taxpayer and the Internal Revenue service by the barter exchange.

## Quick Quiz 4.2

1. True.
2. False. There are three types of relief available under Section 66: separated spouse relief, innocent spouse relief, and equitable relief.

## Quick Quiz 4.3

1. False. Interest income of $10 or more per year is normally reported to a taxpayer on Form 1099-INT by the payor of the interest, but the interest must be recognized by the taxpayer even when this form is not received or when the interest income is less than $10.
2. True.

## Quick Quiz 4.4

1. False. In addition to being paid by a U.S. corporation (or qualified foreign corporation), qualified dividends must also meet the following requirements: (1) the dividend must not be a type of dividend excluded by law from the definition of a qualified dividend; and (2) the shareholder must meet a holding period requirement.
2. True.
3. True.

## Quick Quiz 4.5

1. True.
2. True.

## Quick Quiz 4.6

1. False. Municipal bonds are generally more appropriate for taxpayers with high marginal tax rates than for those with lower marginal rates.
2. True.

# Quick Quiz Explanations

### Quick Quiz 4.7

1. False. Distributions from Roth IRAs are normally excluded from gross income while distributions from traditional IRAs are normally included in gross income.
2. True.
3. True.
4. False. The maximum contribution per year per beneficiary to a Coverdell Education Savings Account is $2,000.

### Quick Quiz 4.8

1. True.
2. True.

### Quick Quiz 4.9

1. False. Any income generated by inherited property must be included in the gross income of the heir.
2. True.
3. False. Child support payments are excluded from the gross income of the payee and are not deductible by the payor since these payments simply satisfy the legal obligation of the payor to support the children.

# Gross Income from Employment

## INTRODUCTION

The primary source of income for most people is employment, where an individual provides services to an employer in exchange for **compensation** in the form of salary or wages and various fringe benefits. Compensation received by an employee as salary or wages is normally includible in gross income. Fringe benefits are compensation for services, and therefore, meet the definition of income. They must be included in gross income unless they are excluded by some provision of the Internal Revenue Code (IRC). Fortunately for employees, many fringe benefits are excluded from gross income if certain requirements are met.

Some individuals are compensated for their services through self-employment rather than through working for a business owned by someone else. Although the self-employed may enjoy more freedom to control their work environment and work activities, they are required to pay taxes on their net earnings, bear the burden of various payroll taxes, and have more difficulty enjoying tax-free treatment of some fringe benefits than do regular employees.

This chapter discusses gross income and exclusions related to employment and self-employment.

## GROSS INCOME RELATED TO EMPLOYMENT

Compensation for services must be included in gross income, regardless of the type of compensation received. Therefore, salary, wages, commissions, fees, tips, or any other type of compensation earned by an employee is subject to income taxation.

Although compensation is normally received in cash, it may be received in some other form. As discussed in Chapter 4, compensation may be received in the form of cash or a cash equivalent, including non-cash property, services, and benefits. If non-cash compensation is a substitute for salary, wages, and other familiar forms of compensation, it must nevertheless be included in gross income unless it is specifically excluded by the Code.

Gross income received for services provided to an employer is normally taxable to the person who performs the services. This rule is an application of the fruit and the tree doctrine. For example, income earned by a child actor is taxable to the child rather than to the parent of the child. Gross income cannot normally be assigned by the person who earns it to anyone else. In community property states, however, half of the income earned (wages, salaries, etc.) by a spouse is deemed to be earned by each spouse. See Chapter 4 for a discussion of community-property laws.

Gross income from compensation and taxable fringe benefits are treated as ordinary income and must be reported to the employee by the employer on Form W-2.

## Key Concepts

Underline/highlight the answers to these questions as you read:

1. Identify the various sources of gross income from employment.

2. Describe the tax consequences of self-employment income.

3. Explain the tax consequences of foreign-earned income.

Income generated by an employer as a result of the services of an employee is included in the gross income of the employer. Only the compensation paid by the employer to the employee (or the employee's designee) must be included in the employee's gross income.

Income generated through self-employment in a sole proprietorship or in certain other forms of business is normally taxable to the self-employed person, but in some cases, the income is taxable to the business itself. The taxation of business income is discussed more fully in Chapter 16.

Compensation received by an independent contractor (a self-employed person) must normally be reported to that contractor as nonemployee compensation on Form 1099-MISC by a business that receives services from the independent contractor. All income (or revenue) received by an independent contractor, including revenue reported on Forms 1099-MISC, must normally be reported as income on Schedule C (Profit or Loss from Business) if the business is conducted in the form of a sole proprietorship. If payments received by a self-employed person relate to an agricultural business of that taxpayer, the revenues must be reported on Schedule F, Profit or Loss from Farming. In addition, statutory employees (those determined to be employees by statute) have their compensation reported on Form W-2 even though they report their income on Schedule C.

A limited liability company (LLC) usually has more than one owner and file as a partnership, but most states permit an LLC to have just one owner. The owner of an LLC that has only one owner will normally report the income and deductions of the LLC on Schedule C in the same manner as a sole proprietor. (Note: An LLC owner could elect S or C Corp status, although such an election is unusual.)

A partner receives a Schedule K-1 from a partnership each year. The Schedule K-1 allocates to the partner his distributive share of the partnership's income, deductions, and tax credits. Some of a general partner's income from a partnership may be classified as self-employment income

See line 14 of the Schedule K-1). General partnerships, limited partnerships, limited liability companies, and limited liability partnerships are normally taxed as partnerships for federal income tax purposes. If an LLC is treated as a partnership for income tax purposes, any active member (sometimes referred to as a managing member) is taxed as a general partner.

Gross income from self-employment does not necessarily equal gross receipts or gross sales if inventories are involved. Gross income from the sale of inventory is equal to gross profit, which equals revenues from sales less the cost of goods sold. Gross income from self-employment also includes a variety of other types of income including revenues generated by providing services.

The owner of a proprietorship is not usually considered to be an employee of the entity for fringe benefit purposes. A partner in an entity taxed as a partnership is treated as an employee for some fringe benefit purposes, but not for others. A more than two percent owner of an S corporation is normally not considered to be an employee of the S corporation for fringe benefit purposes. See Chapter 16 for a more detailed discussion of fringe benefits and other matters related to business owners.

While unemployment compensation, as the name indicates, is not employment related income, it is income that is meant to replace employment income when a taxpayer is out of work. Unlike workers' compensation, which is designed to compensate a worker for physical injuries received at work (and is therefore not included in income), unemployment income is included in gross income. If, however, an employee made after-tax contributions to a government or private unemployment compensation fund, the benefits would be excluded from income. This treatment is consistent with the tax treatment of private disability insurance benefits, which are included in income if premiums are paid with pre-tax dollars or by the employer, but are excluded from income if the premium payments are made with after-tax dollars by the employee.

## FOREIGN EARNED INCOME

Since the United States taxes its citizens on their global income, citizens and certain other residents of the United States who work in foreign countries may be subject to income tax on both their U.S. sources and foreign sources of income. In certain circumstances, taxpayers may be able to exclude some or all of their income earned in foreign countries from U.S. taxation (foreign earned income exclusion). They may also be able to exclude a portion of their housing costs incurred in foreign countries.

Income earned by employees of the U.S. government and its agencies while they serve in foreign countries does not qualify for the foreign earned income exclusion.

For 2009, a qualifying citizen or resident of the United States may exclude from U.S. gross income up to $91,400 (less any foreign housing exclusion taken for the year) of income earned from personal services performed in foreign countries ($91,500 for 2010). To exclude **foreign earned income**, a qualified individual must have a tax home in a foreign country and must either (1) qualify as a bona fide resident of a foreign country or countries for an uninterrupted period that includes an entire taxable year (bona fide resident test) or (2) qualify by being present in a foreign country or countries for at least 330 full days during any period of twelve consecutive months (physical presence test).

A taxpayer's tax home is normally the general area of the taxpayer's business (for self-employed persons) or employment, regardless of the location of the taxpayer's home or principal residence. The tax home of an employee is the place where the employee is permanently or indefinitely engaged to work. An employee who is "temporarily" assigned to work in a foreign country would not be eligible for the foreign earned income exclusion.

To be considered a bona fide resident of a foreign country (or countries), an individual must generally intend to work there for an indefinite or extended period and must establish permanent quarters in the foreign country for himself and his family. The individual's intentions, purpose for travel, and length of stay in the foreign country are important variables in determining bona fide residency. The Internal Revenue Service must determine whether a person meets the bona fide residence test based on information submitted on Form 2555 (to view the form, see www.irs.gov).

Treaties and agreements with specific foreign countries may impact a taxpayer's ability to be considered a bona fide resident of that country. Occasional trips back to the United States for vacation or other purposes will not usually prevent a taxpayer from meeting the bona fide resident test. If a bona fide resident of a foreign country fails to meet the full tax year requirement only because he must leave the country due to war or civil unrest, he will normally be deemed to have met the full tax year requirement. Once an individual has met the **bona fide resident test**, the taxpayer is considered to be a bona fide resident until he abandons his residence in that country, even for a year in which he is not a bona fide resident for the entire tax year.

In order to meet the **physical presence test**, an individual must be present in a foreign country or countries for at least 330 full days during any period of 12 consecutive months. The twelve month period can begin on any day of any month. The 330 days do not have to be consecutive and days spent in foreign countries for any purpose can be included. A person who is present in foreign countries for only 329 days completely fails the test unless the early departure is due to war or civil unrest.

## Quick Quiz 5.1

**Highlight the answer to these questions:**

1. A person may assign the gross income that he earns to any other person for tax purposes.
   a. True
   b. False

2. In 2009, a qualifying citizen or resident of the U.S. may exclude up to $91,400 of foreign-earned income from their U.S. gross income.
   a. True
   b. False

False, True.

| EXAMPLE 5.1 | Sonya is a U.S. citizen who works for a U.S. corporation in London. During 2009, she earned $70,000 and was present in London for the entire year. Even though the income was paid by a U.S. corporation, her income is considered to be foreign earned income and can be fully excluded from her U.S. gross income. |
|---|---|

A person who meets the physical presence test, but is not present in foreign countries during every day of the year, is allowed to exclude only a prorated portion of the maximum exclusion amount.

Bill lives and works in France during 340 days out of the 365 days during the 2009 calendar year. He meets the physical presence test. The maximum amount of foreign earned income that he can exclude from his gross income is $85,140 [(340/365) x $91,400]. Assuming the same facts for 2010, the maximum amount of foreign earned income Bill can exclude from his gross income is $85,233 [(340/365) x $91,500].

When a taxpayer qualifies for the exclusion for only part of a tax year, the maximum amount that can be excluded is determined using the following formula:

$$\frac{\text{Qualifying Days in the Tax Year}}{\text{Total Days in Tax Year}} \times \text{Maximum Annual Exclusion Amount} = \text{Exclusion}$$

Aleisha earned $40,000 from her employment in Singapore during 2009. She met the physical presence test during a period beginning in 2009 and ending in 2010. She lived and worked in Singapore for 80 days during 2009 and has not returned to the United States since she first arrived in Singapore in 2009. She will be allowed to exclude a maximum of $20,033 [(80/365) x $91,400] of foreign earned income for 2009.

An exclusion for foreign housing costs is available to employees for housing costs considered to be paid by an employer. The amount of the exclusion is limited to total housing expenses of the employee's family less a base housing amount (16 percent of the maximum annual exclusion). Any housing amount excluded cannot exceed 30 percent of the maximum foreign earned income exclusion amount for the year and it reduces the maximum amount available for the foreign earned income exclusion. Therefore, the housing exclusion must be calculated before the foreign earned income exclusion.

An eligible taxpayer must elect (choose) to use the foreign earned income exclusion. Once the election is made, it remains in effect until it is revoked. If the election is made but foreign earned income exceeds the maximum exclusion amount or if the election is not made, the taxpayer may take a foreign tax credit (Chapter 9) or an itemized deduction (Chapter 7) for foreign taxes paid on foreign source income not excluded from gross income. However, the most beneficial treatment is generally the exclusion of foreign earned income.

## EXHIBIT 5.1  FOREIGN INCOME OPTIONS FOR U.S. TAXATION PURPOSES

| OPTIONS | Foreign Earned Income Exclusion | Tax Credit for Foreign Taxes Paid | Deduction for Foreign Taxes Paid |
|---|---|---|---|
| BENEFIT | Taxpayer can exclude up to $91,400 for 2009 ($91,500 for 2010) of foreign earned income from gross income. | Taxpayer can claim a credit for some or all of the taxes paid to the foreign country, including taxes on foreign earned income that *exceeds* the amount ($91,400) of foreign earned income exclusion taken. | Taxpayer's foreign taxes paid may be deducted as an itemized deduction on Schedule A to reduce adjusted gross income. |

## MAJOR EMPLOYER-PROVIDED FRINGE BENEFITS

### INTRODUCTION TO FRINGE BENEFITS

When an employee provides services to an employer in return for compensation, the employee often receives **fringe benefits** in addition to wages or salary. Most employees value these fringe benefits, especially insurance benefits such as medical, life, and disability insurance, and consider them to be part of their overall compensation package. With a large number of employees, employers may be able to negotiate lower group insurance rates and better coverage than an individual employee would be able to negotiate in the open market. Thus, where insurance coverage is desired by a large number of employees, the employer may adopt an insurance plan as part of an overall compensation package. Providing insurance and other fringe benefits may make employers more attractive to potential employees while providing valuable tax-advantaged benefits to employees and their family members.

### TAXATION OF FRINGE BENEFITS

Salary and wages paid to employees are income tax deductible by the employer and must be included in the gross income of the employees. Employers are also allowed to take income tax deductions for fringe benefits provided to employees. Under the general gross income provisions of IRC Section 61, all fringe benefits provided to an employee must be included in gross income as wages unless a specific provision of the IRC excludes the benefit from taxation or unless the employee pays fair value for the fringe benefit. Although a fringe benefit may not be specifically excluded, the value of the fringe benefit is not taxable if it is paid for by the employee.

Recall that, generally, when someone (such as the employer) claims an income tax deduction, there must be a corresponding income inclusion somewhere in the tax system.

Fortunately for employees, Congress has chosen to promote certain fringe benefits by allowing employers to deduct the cost of the benefits while allowing employees to exclude the value of the benefits from gross income. Through this favorable tax treatment for selected fringe benefits, Congress seeks to promote a variety of social, economic, health, fitness, child welfare, educational, and other purposes. For example, if employers provide medical insurance for employees, the citizens of the United States may enjoy better health care and the government may have less of a financial burden to provide health care to its citizenry. By allowing favorable ncome tax treatment to employees, the government is foregoing tax revenues and is indirectly 'unding part of the cost of employer-provided medical insurance.

The employer reports taxable fringe benefits as compensation on each employee's Form W-2. Taxable fringe benefits are also subject to Social Security, Medicare, and federal unemployment taxes. Excludable fringe benefits are not reported as taxable compensation on an employee's Form W-2 nor are they usually subject to the payroll taxes itemized above.

In order to receive favorable income tax benefits for both the employer and the employee, each type of excludable fringe benefit has specific requirements.

## NONDISCRIMINATION OF FRINGE BENEFITS

To achieve favorable income tax treatment, most, but not all, fringe benefits require the employer not to discriminate against different classes of employees, especially the employees who are not highly compensated. If nondiscrimination requirements apply and the fringe benefit is provided primarily to **highly compensated employees** (or **key employees**), and the benefit is not available on substantially the same terms to non-highly compensated (or non-key) employees, then the fringe benefit is deemed to be discriminatory. Highly compensated employees are those employees who (1) hold a greater than five percent ownership interest or (2) have compensation in excess of $110,000 for 2009 and 2010. A key employee is an employee who is (1) a greater than five percent owner, (2) a greater than one percent owner with compensation in excess of $150,000 (not indexed), or (3) an officer with compensation in excess of $160,000 for 2009 and 2010. If a fringe benefit is discriminatory, then the exclusion may be lost by all employees (or by the favored group of employees), resulting in the value of the fringe benefit being included in the recipient employee's gross income. As discussed below, some fringe benefits have nondiscrimination requirements while others do not.

## INDIVIDUALS WHO MAY ENJOY BENEFITS

An employee performing services in return for a fringe benefit need not be the person who actually uses or enjoys the fringe benefit. For instance, the spouse and children of an employee normally receive benefits from employer-provided medical insurance. Retired employees, spouses of employees, dependent children of employees, spouses of deceased employees, partners, directors, and even independent contractors may be able to enjoy excludable fringe benefits. The provisions related to each fringe benefit normally indicate who is eligible to enjoy the benefit without inclusion in taxable income.

## HEALTH INSURANCE

There are several ways that an employer can provide an employee with benefits for medical care. The employer may (1) establish and pay part or all of the premiums for group medical insurance, (2) pay part or all of the premiums for private medical insurance policies, (3) contribute to a separate trust or fund that provides medical benefits to employees, or (4) directly pay or reimburse employee medical expenses. Medical insurance plans are normally written, but they need not be written to enjoy favorable tax benefits.

Employer payments of insurance premiums or contributions to medical benefit trusts or funds under these plans are income tax deductible by the employer and excludable from the gross income of employees. Medical benefits received by employees, their spouses, and dependents are excludable from the gross income of employees.

Medical plans normally cover hospital expenses, physician expenses, prescription medications, and other medical costs. These medical plans may or may not provide for vision and dental benefits. Eligible medical benefits include the payment or reimbursement of expenses for medical care due to personal injury or sickness and payments for (1) the permanent loss or loss of use of a member or function of the body, or (2) for permanent disfigurement.

| EXAMPLE 5.4 | Arnold was seriously injured in a motorcycle accident. His employer's group medical insurance plan paid approximately $85,000 for his hospital expenses, physician expenses, and prescription medications. It also paid him $10,000 for the loss of his left hand and $5,000 for permanent disfigurement. All $100,000 of these payments from the insurance company are excluded from Arnold's gross income. |
|---|---|

A group accident or health plan is an arrangement that provides benefits for employees, their spouses, and their dependents in the event of personal injury or sickness. The plan may be insured by an outside company or self-insured by the employer and does not need to be in writing. The premiums paid by the employer for health insurance are not includible in the gross income of employees, but they are deductible as business expenses for the employer under IRC Section 162.

If an employee pays part or all of the insurance premiums through a payroll withholding arrangement, it is possible to exclude the amount of such premiums from the employee's gross income under the provisions of IRC Section 125 (See the discussion of cafeteria plans that follows).

**Health reimbursement arrangements (HRAs)** are employer-funded plans that reimburse employees for medical expenses and allow employees to carry any unused balances forward to be used in future years. The taxation of employer contributions and employee benefits is the same as for other employer-sponsored medical plans.

| Medical Fringe Benefits | Employer | Employee |
|---|---|---|
| Health insurance premiums paid by employer | Deduct | Exclude |
| Employer contributions to a fund that provides medical benefits to employees | Deduct | Exclude |
| **Payment of employee medical expenses:** | | |
| By the employer | Deduct | Exclude |
| By an insurance company | No Impact | Exclude |
| By a separate fund or trust | No Impact | Exclude |
| **Reimbursement of employee medical expenses in the year paid by the employee:** | | |
| Reimbursed by the employer | Deduct | Exclude |
| Reimbursed by an insurance company | No Impact | Exclude |
| Reimbursed by a separate fund or trust | No Impact | Exclude |
| **Reimbursement of employee medical expenses after the year paid by the employee\*** | | |
| Reimbursed by the employer | Deduct | Tax Benefit Rule |
| Reimbursed by an insurance company | No Impact | Tax Benefit Rule |
| Reimbursed by a separate fund or trust | No Impact | Tax Benefit Rule |

\*If the employee used the standard deduction in the year paid, the reimbursement is excluded. If the employee itemizes deductions in the year paid, some or all of the reimbursement may be included in gross income based on the tax benefit rule. The tax benefit rule is discussed in Chapter 4.

Employees who do not enjoy the benefits of an employer-provided medical plan often purchase private medical insurance coverage. Under these circumstances, the employees must pay for insurance premiums and out-of-pocket medical costs with after-tax dollars unless they establish Health Savings Accounts (discussed below) or qualify to deduct some of their medical expenses as itemized deductions (discussed in Chapter 7).

## ARCHER MEDICAL SAVINGS ACCOUNTS

The Health Insurance Portability and Accountability Act of 1996 (HIPAA) established tax-favored savings accounts for medical expenses called **Archer Medical Savings Accounts (MSAs)**. MSAs could be established for eligible employees after 1996 and before 2006 for employers with fifty or fewer employees and for self-employed individuals. Employees could not establish MSAs but could contribute (subject to the limitations discussed below) to such accounts if the employer established MSAs for their benefit. After 2005, an MSA cannot be established and has been replaced by the Health Savings Account (HSA), which is discussed below. However, many of the MSAs that were established prior to 2006 are still in existence, may still be maintained, and retain their tax-favored status.

For MSAs to be established, the employer must have provided its employees with a high deductible health plan with a maximum out-of-pocket cost for employees. A high deductible plan for purposes of meeting the requirements of the MSA is a major medical health insurance plan with a deductible between $2,000 and $3,000 for 2009 (and 2010) for individual coverage and between $4,000 and $6,050 for 2009 (between $4,050 and $6,050 for 2010) for family coverage. The maximum out-of-pocket cost for the plan is $4,000 for 2009 ($4,050 for 2010) for individual coverage and $7,350 for 2009 ($7,400 for 2010) for family coverage. These same limitations apply for self-employed individuals.

Contributions can be made to an MSA by the employee or the employer, subject to limits. Employee contributions are deductible for adjusted gross income. Contributions to MSAs are reported on Form 8853, which should be filed with Form 1040. The MSA deduction is reported on line 36 of the 1040 (2009). Employer contributions are tax deductible by the employer, are not subject to payroll taxes, and are excludable from gross income by the employee. The aggregate contributions to the plan by the employee and the employer cannot exceed 65 percent of the deductible for individual coverage and 75 percent of the deductible for family coverage.

The earnings on the assets within an MSA are tax deferred until a distribution is taken from the account. If a distribution is for qualified medical expenses, the distribution, including any earnings, is not taxable. If the distribution is not for qualified medical expenses, the entire distribution is taxable as ordinary income. In addition, if a taxable distribution is taken before the owner of the account is age 65, the distribution is subject to an additional 15 percent excise penalty tax.

## HEALTH SAVINGS ACCOUNTS

The Medicare Act of 2003 created **Health Savings Accounts (HSAs)**, which are very similar to MSAs but less restrictive. In comparison with an MSA, an HSA can be established by an eligible individual with a high deductible health insurance plan (as explained below), allow a higher contribution amount, and reduce the penalty for non-medical distributions. With a few exceptions, an individual and spouse (if the insurance covers the family) cannot have any medical coverage other than a high deductible health plan.

An HSA may be independently established by an employee, or it may be facilitated by an employer. An employee who does not enjoy the benefits of any type of medical plan through an employer may obtain a private high-deductible health plan and establish an HSA with a qualified HSA trustee. Qualified HSA trustees include banks, insurance companies or any other entity already approved to serve as trustee of an IRA or Archer MSA.

The money in an HSA can be invested in a variety of instruments, including bank accounts, money market instruments, mutual funds, or even individual stocks.

To qualify for an HSA, an individual must have a health or medical insurance plan with a deductible of at least $1,150 for 2009 ($1,200 for 2010) for single coverage and the annual out-of-pocket costs cannot exceed $5,800 for 2009 ($5,950 for 2010). For family coverage under an HSA, the health insurance plan deductible must be at least $2,300 for 2009 ($2,400 for 2010) and the annual out-of-pocket costs cannot exceed $11,600 for 2009 ($11,900 for 2010). The t-of-pocket costs include deductibles, co-payments, and other payments for medical benefits, it they do not include insurance premiums paid by the individual.

ontributions to the HSA can be made by the individual or by the individual's employer. In her case, the aggregate annual contributions cannot exceed $3,000 for individuals and $5,950 r families for 2009 ($3,050 and $6,150 for 2010). However, individuals who are at least 55 ars of age and younger than 65 years of age can make additional catch-up contributions of ,000 over these limits for 2009 and 2010. In addition to these amounts, rollovers into the count are allowed from an existing Archer MSA and from other HSAs of the individual. It ould also be noted that family members or any other person can make contributions to an SA on behalf of the owner.

ontributions to an employee's HSA by an nployer are deductible by the employer and cludable by the employee. Contributions by an nployee or any other person (other than the nployer) to an HSA are deductible for AGI on e employee's individual income tax return. All ontributions to HSAs are reported on Form 389, which should be filed with Form 1040. he deduction for HSA contributions is reported n line 25 of Form 1040 2009.

arnings within the HSA are tax deferred (not irrently taxable), and amounts distributed from HSA are excludable from the owner's gross icome provided the distributions are used to ay for qualified medical expenses. If a istribution is not for qualified medical expenses, e entire distribution is taxable as ordinary icome. If a distribution is taken before the wner of the account is 65 years old and it is not sed to pay for qualified medical expenses, the istribution is includible in gross income and it is so subject to an additional 10 percent excise enalty tax.

**Quick Quiz 5.2**

**Highlight the answer to these questions:**

1. Fringe benefits are valuable to employees because they are always nontaxable.
   a. True
   b. False

2. Some fringe benefits have nondiscrimination requirements, while others do not.
   a. True
   b. False

3. An HSA must be established by an employer.
   a. True
   b. False

False, True, False.

EXHIBIT 5.3    SIGNIFICANT TAX CHANGES TO HSAs (BEGINNING IN 2007)

| |
|---|
| 1. Annual contributions to an HSA are no longer limited to the high deductible health plan's deductible amount. |
| 2. An individual who is an eligible individual during the last month of the tax year is considered to be an eligible individual for the entire year. Therefore, in most cases, the annual contribution limit no longer needs to be prorated on a monthly basis for the first year of participation in an HSA. |
| 3. An individual may make a one-time, tax-free IRA distribution to fund an HSA, as long as the HSA owner remains eligible for the HSA for 12 months following the IRA distribution. |
| 4. An employee may be able to have the employer make a one-time transfer of the employee's balance in a health reimbursement arrangement (HRA) or flexible spending plan (discussed below) to the employee's HSA. |

## LIFE INSURANCE

If an employer provides group permanent (not term) life insurance coverage for employees, the employees must normally include in gross income the insurance premiums paid by the employer. Permanent life insurance generally provides a permanent death benefit by building a cash value inside the policy. If group term life insurance is provided to employees, however, a limited amount of coverage can be provided to an employee without any inclusion of the premiums in the employee's gross income.

### Group Term Life Insurance

An employer can deduct the cost of up to $50,000 (face or death benefit amount) of group term life insurance for each employee, and the employee can exclude the premiums paid by the employer from gross income if certain requirements discussed below are met.

**Key Concepts**

Underline/highlight the answers to these questions as you read:

1. Identify the amount of group term life insurance that can be provided to employees as a fringe benefit.

2. Explain the consequences of providing life insurance in excess $50,000.

3. Explain the tax consequences of employer-provided disability insurance.

4. Describe the purpose of and rules associated with cafeteria plans.

The cost, as determined under the Uniform Premium Table provided by the IRS, of any death benefit coverage in excess of $50,000 is taxable to the employee. The monthly cost of the insurance to include in the employee's gross income is determined by multiplying the number of thousands of dollars of insurance coverage over $50,000 (figured to the nearest $100) by the cost shown in the following table. The table corresponds with the employee's age as of the last day of the tax year and the includible amount is reduced by any contribution payments made by the employee.

EXHIBIT 5.4

| AGE | COST |
|---|---|
| Under 25 | 0.05 |
| 25 through 29 | 0.06 |
| 30 through 34 | 0.08 |
| 35 through 39 | 0.09 |
| 40 through 44 | 0.10 |
| 45 through 49 | 0.15 |
| 50 through 54 | 0.23 |
| 55 through 59 | 0.43 |
| 60 through 64 | 0.66 |
| 65 through 69 | 1.27 |
| 70 and older | 2.06 |

**EXAMPLE 5.5**

Edward's employer provides him with $80,000 of group term life insurance for which Edward pays none of the premiums. Edward is 56 years old at the end of the year. He can exclude the cost of the first $50,000 of coverage. He must include $154.80 (30 thousand x $0.43 per thousand per month x 12 months) in his gross income. This amount is generally reported as part of the employee's W-2 income. If Edward pays any amount toward the cost of the insurance coverage, the taxable amount will be reduced by the amount of the payment.

If the plan is considered to discriminate in favor of key employees, each key employee must include in gross income the cost of all of the group term life insurance provided to that key employee. The cost to be included in gross income is the greater of the cost determined using the Uniform Premium Table above or the actual cost of the life insurance coverage to the employer. Under these circumstances, key employees are not allowed to exclude the cost of any group term life insurance. Employees other than the key employees are taxed the same as they would be taxed if the plan were not discriminatory.

**EXAMPLE 5.6**

Janice is provided with $100,000 of group term life insurance by her employer. Her employer's plan is deemed to discriminate in favor of key employees and Janice is a key employee. Janice is 46 years old at the end of the year and the company actually paid $250 for her life insurance coverage. The cost of Janice's coverage is $180 (100 x 0.15 x 12) according to the Uniform Premium Table. Janice will be required to include $250 in her gross income as a result of her life insurance coverage. Employees who are not key employees will still be able to exclude the cost of up to $50,000 of coverage for the year.

The cost of up to $2,000 of group term life insurance coverage paid for by the employer for the spouse or a dependent of an employee may be excludable from an employee's gross income as a de minimis fringe benefit (discussed below).

### *Employee Death Benefits*

Employers sometimes pay death benefits to the spouse or family of a deceased employee. The Internal Revenue Service generally considers such payments to be compensation for past services rendered by the deceased employee. Under certain circumstances, however, some courts have held that such payments are in the nature of gifts and can be excluded from the recipient's gross income. For example, when there is clearly no obligation on the part of the employer to pay and the facts and circumstances clearly imply a gratuitous payment to the surviving spouse and children following the death of an employee, the payment would be **excluded** from the recipient's gross income.

## DISABILITY INSURANCE

**Disability insurance** provides benefits in the form of periodic payments to a person who is unable to work due to sickness or accidental injury. The cost of disability insurance varies depending on occupation, age, and gender of the insured, as well as the benefit term, the amount of coverage, and the length of the waiting period (elimination period) provided under the policy.

Disability insurance can be provided under a group or individual plan and as either short-term (up to two years) or long-term coverage (over two years). In any case, the *premiums* paid by the employer are deductible by the employer as a business expense and are excluded from the employee's gross income. However, when an employer pays the premium and the premium is excluded from the employee's gross income, any *disability income benefit* received by the employee is taxable and must be included in the employee's gross income. If the employee pays the entire premium with after-tax income or the employer pays the premium and the employee includes the premium payment in gross income, any benefits received can be excluded from the employee's gross income. This exclusion of disability income benefits also applies if a person purchases a private disability insurance policy rather than obtaining it through his employer. If the employer and employee each pay part of the premium, the prorated part of the benefits associated with the employer's contribution is taxable to the employee.

| EXAMPLE 5.7 | Joyce pays 20% of the premiums for disability insurance and her employer pays the remainder. Joyce became disabled and received disability income benefits under the policy for several years. Joyce must include 80% of any disability income benefits in gross income. The remaining 20%, the portion for which she paid the premiums, is excluded from her gross income. The premiums paid by Joyce's employer can also be excluded from her gross income. If Joyce's employer had paid all of the premiums, 100% of the disability income benefits |

would be taxable to her. If Joyce had paid 100% of the premiums with after-tax income, none of the income benefits would have been taxable to her.

The reason for the inclusion of benefits in gross income is that the disability benefits received are in lieu of wages that would have been taxable. If an individual buys a private disability insurance policy, however, the premiums paid are not deductible, but any disability income benefits received are excluded from gross income.

## CAFETERIA PLANS

A **cafeteria plan** is a written plan under which the employee may choose to receive either cash or taxable benefits as compensation or qualified fringe benefits that are excludable from wages. Provided the cafeteria plan meets the requirements explained below, the value of any qualified tax-free fringe benefit, if chosen by the employee, will generate a deductible expense for the employer and will be excludable from gross income by the employee. An employee who chooses cash or taxable benefits rather than excludable fringe benefits will be required to include the cash or taxable benefit in gross income as taxable compensation.

These plans are referred to as Section 125 plans because they are permitted by IRC Section 125, which requires a cafeteria plan to offer at least one taxable benefit, usually cash, and one qualified nontaxable benefit. Commonly included qualified benefits are group term life insurance, medical reimbursement or insurance plans, disability benefits, and dependent care assistance.

## Quick Quiz 5.3

**Highlight the answer to these questions:**

1. Any group life insurance benefit in excess of $50,000 is taxable to the employer.
   a. True
   b. False

2. Disability insurance premiums paid by the employer are deductible by the employer and are excluded from the employee's gross income.
   a. True
   b. False

3. A cafeteria plan is most appropriate when all of the employees need the same benefits.
   a. True
   b. False

False, True, False.

A cafeteria plan is appropriate when employee benefit needs vary within the employee group. The employee mix includes young, unmarried people with minimal life insurance and medical benefits needs, as well as older employees with families who need maximum medical and life insurance benefits. A cafeteria plan is also appropriate when employees want to choose the benefit package most suited to their individual needs.

A cafeteria plan is a way of managing fringe benefit costs to the employer by individually pricing each benefit. Such plans help give employees an appreciation of the value of their benefit package by allowing them to choose the cash or purchase the benefit. Cafeteria plans can also help control employer costs of providing benefit packages because the employer does not pay for benefits that are not used by the employees. These plans can be complex and expensive to design and administer.

IRC Section 125 provides an exception to the constructive receipt rule, which would otherwise require an employee to include the value of qualified excludable benefits in gross income simply because the employee had an unrestricted right to receive cash. Therefore, the cafeteria plan must meet all of the requirements of Section 125 to obtain exclusion treatment for employees who choose to receive the excludable fringe benefits.

A cafeteria plan meets the qualifications of the IRC if the benefits provided under the plan are qualified (as discussed above), the plan does not favor the highly compensated employees, and the nontaxable benefits provided to key employees is less than 25 percent of the total nontaxable benefits provided under the plan to all employees.

If the plan provides a benefit that is not qualified, the value of that benefit will be included in the employee's gross income. If the plan is deemed discriminatory by favoring the highly compensated or by providing more than 25 percent of the benefits to the key employees, the value of the nontaxable benefits chosen by the highly compensated or key employees will be included in their gross income.

## FSAs

A **flexible spending account (FSA)** is a type of cafeteria plan that is funded through employee salary reductions. The employee can elect to have a portion of his salary or wages retained by the employer to fund an FSA. Any amount so retained by the employer is excludable from the salary or wages of the employee. The money in the FSA account can then be used to pay for or reimburse the employee for deductibles, co-payments, and medical expenses (including vision and dental expenses) that are not covered by the employer's medical plan. The end result of this arrangement is that certain expenses can be paid with pre-tax rather than after-tax dollars.

### Key Concepts

**Underline/highlight the answers to these questions as you read:**

1. Identify the advantages and disadvantages of FSAs.

2. Explain the tax consequences of employer-provided long-term care insurance.

The type of FSA introduced above is called a health or medical FSA. It is also possible to set up an FSA to pay for child care.

The employee must elect the amount of compensation to be retained and placed in the FSA before each plan year begins. One disadvantage of an FSA is that amounts remaining in the account at the end of the year are forfeited back to the employer (a use it or lose it arrangement). However, the employer can allow employees to use the money in an FSA to pay for qualified expenses incurred up to two and one-half-months after the end of the year of the plan. In addition, the employer can allow the employee a 90-day period at the beginning of the year to seek reimbursement for qualified expenses incurred in the previous year of the plan. Since it is difficult to estimate the optimal amount to put into an FSA, many employees choose not to participate at all or to participate only modestly.

One advantage of an FSA to an employee (and a disadvantage to the employer) is that the entire annual amount that an employee elects to pay into an FSA is available for the employee's use at the beginning of the plan year. This is true even though the employee contributions to the FSA will take place throughout the year. The employer is therefore at risk for the total annual amount an employee elects to allocate to health benefits under an FSA even if the employee terminates employment before funding the amount used from the plan.

Tanya elects to pay $400 per month into an FSA for the plan year. During the first month of the year, Tanya has elective lasik eye surgery at a cost of $4,000. Since this type of surgery is not covered by her employer's medical plan, Tanya pays for her surgery with money from her FSA. After three months of the plan year have passed, she leaves her job to take other employment. Through the FSA, the employer must pay $4,000 for the surgery even though Tanya only paid $1,200 into the FSA for the year. The employer will not be allowed to recover the $2,800 shortfall from Tanya's last paycheck or through any other means.

A flexible spending account is appropriate in any of the following situations:
- An employer wants to expand employee benefit choices without significant employer out-of-pocket costs (or possibly realize some actual dollar savings);
- Many employees have employed spouses with duplicate medical coverage;
- An employer wants employees to contribute to health insurance costs;
- The employer's medical plans have large deductibles or coinsurance (co-pay) provisions;
- There is a need for benefits that are difficult to provide on a group basis, such as dependent care; and/or
- The costs of employee benefit plans, such as health insurance, have increased and the employer must impose additional employee cost sharing in the form of increased employee contributions and deductibles.

The FSA approach provides many potential advantages. It minimizes employee outlay since the FSA converts what would have been after-tax employee expenditures for the benefits selected to pre-tax expenditures. It provides employees a degree of choice to receive either cash as compensation or the cash to pay for the costs of certain benefits. Since an FSA is normally funded entirely through employee salary reductions, an employer is only required to bear the administrative costs. The administrative costs of the employer may be more than offset by payroll tax savings, since salary reductions elected by employees are not subject to payroll taxes.

Using a flexible spending account to pay for dependent care expenses (if provided) may provide more tax savings than using the Child and Dependent Care Credit discussed in Chapter 9.

An FSA must meet the nondiscrimination requirements as previously discussed for cafeteria plans. Although the Internal Revenue Code does not specify the maximum amount that an employee may contribute to an FSA, the plan must specify a maximum dollar amount or maximum percentage of compensation that can be contributed.

Qualified medical expenses do not include amounts paid for health insurance premiums, amounts paid for long-term care insurance or expenses, and amounts that are covered under another health plan of the employee. Qualified expenses do include most non-prescription medications, but not health food supplements.

## LONG-TERM CARE

**Long-term care insurance** pays benefits when the insured person is unable to perform some of the activities of daily living. Long-term care policies normally identify five or six **activities of daily living** (ADLs), including eating, bathing, dressing, toileting, transferring (walking), and continence. If the insured cannot perform two or more of these activities of daily living, the policy normally pays benefits.

Premiums paid by an employer for qualified group long-term care insurance are tax deductible to the employer and excludable from gross income by the covered employee. Benefits received from a qualified long-term care insurance plan are excludable by the employee to the extent that they do not exceed the greater of $280 per day for 2009 ($290 for 2010) or the actual cost of the care.

Premiums paid by an employee for group coverage or for private coverage provide a tax benefit to the employee only if the individual itemizes deductions and has enough medical expenses to generate a medical expense deduction (see Chapter 7). In addition, there is a limit on the amount of premiums that can be deducted for long-term care insurance depending on the age of the insured individual. Benefits received under such policies are excludable subject to the limits in the preceding paragraph. Long-term care premiums cannot be paid for through a cafeteria plan or flexible spending account.

To be a qualified long-term care insurance plan, the plan must meet the following requirements:
- Does not duplicate benefits paid by Medicare,
- Must be guaranteed renewable,
- Does not have a cash surrender value,

*Quick Quiz 5.4*

**Highlight the answer to these questions:**

1. Any funds remaining in an FSA are rolled over for use in future years.
   a. True
   b. False

2. FSAs must meet nondiscrimination requirements.
   a. True
   b. False

3. When long-term care premiums are paid by the employer, benefits received by the employee (up to $280/day for 2009 or the actual cost of the care) are excluded from gross income.
   a. True
   b. False

False, True, True.

- Only provides qualified long-term care insurance coverage, and
- Only pays benefits when the employee or beneficiary of the plan is certified by a licensed health care practitioner as chronically ill.

In addition to the tax advantages, group long-term care insurance generally also provides the following other advantages:

- Lower rates than individual policies (generally 30% - 60% less),
- Guaranteed coverage for all employees, even those who might not be insurable under an individual policy,
- Increased eligibility for extended family members, including parents, grandparents, and in-laws, and
- Must be guaranteed renewable.

## OTHER EMPLOYEE FRINGE BENEFITS

In addition to the major employer-provided fringe benefits discussed above, a variety of other tax-favored fringe benefits can be provided by employers to employees.

### MEALS AND LODGING

The provisions of IRC Section 119 permit an employee to exclude the value of meals and lodging provided by the employer if certain requirements are met. If the requirements are not met, the value of the meals and lodging must be included in the employee's gross income unless the meals can be excluded as a de minimis fringe benefit (discussed later in this chapter).

In general, an employee can exclude from gross income the value of meals provided in-kind (not as cash reimbursement) to the employee as long as the meals are furnished, (1) on the employer's business premises, and (2) for the convenience of the employer.

**Key Concepts**

**Underline/highlight the answers to these questions as you read:**

1. Describe the rules regarding the provision of meals and lodging as a fringe benefit.

2. Define no-additional-cost services.

3. Identify the requirements for qualified employee discounts.

The business premises of the employer is the place of employment of the employee. For example, meals provided in the employer's home to a domestic servant would constitute meals furnished on the business premises of the employer. Similarly, meals furnished to cowhands while herding their employer's cattle on leased land would be regarded as furnished on the business premises of the employer.

Meals furnished by an employer without charge to the employee will be regarded as furnished for the convenience of the employer if the meals are furnished for a substantial business reason of the employer, not just as a means of providing additional compensation to the employee. The determination of "for the convenience of the employer" is made based on the surrounding facts and circumstances.

<table>
<tr><td>EXAMPLE 5.9</td><td>Kristin works as a waitress in a restaurant. She has only thirty minutes for a lunch break. She is provided with lunch at no charge by her employer because of the short lunch break and so that she will be readily available if the restaurant becomes busy. Since the meals are provided at the business premises and are clearly provided for the convenience of the employer, Kristin is allowed to exclude the value of the meals from her gross income. The owner of the restaurant will be able to deduct the cost of providing the meals to Kristin and the other employees.</td></tr>
</table>

An employee is allowed to exclude from gross income the value of lodging furnished by an employer to the employee if the lodging is furnished (1) on the employer's business premises, (2) for the convenience of the employer, and (3) the employee is required to accept the lodging as a condition of employment. The first two requirements are the same as for meals. The third requirement applies only to lodging.

The third requirement is normally met if the employee is required to accept the lodging in order to properly perform the duties of his employment. If an employee is required to be readily available at all times, this requirement is met.

<table>
<tr><td>EXAMPLE 5.10</td><td>Todd and Barbara Johnson manage apartments and they are required to live in apartment 101, the managers' apartment, as a condition of their employment. If they had refused to live in the managers' apartment, they would not have been hired. The lodging meets all three requirements, and Todd and Barbara will be able to exclude the value of the lodging from gross income. Even if Todd and Barbara were paid a housing allowance and then required to pay it back to the employer for rent, they would be able to exclude the housing allowance from gross income.</td></tr>
</table>

As indicated in the preceding example, if all three requirements are satisfied, the exclusion applies regardless of whether the employee is charged a fee for the lodging.

A construction worker is employed at a construction project at a remote job site in Alaska. Due to the inaccessibility of facilities for the employees who are working at the job site to obtain food and lodging in the prevailing weather conditions, the employer is required to furnish meals and lodging to the employee at the camp site in order to carry on the construction project. The employee is required to pay $40 a week for the meals and lodging. The weekly charge of $40 is not part of the compensation includible in the gross income of the employee, and the value of the meals and lodging is excludable from his gross income.

EXAMPLE 5.11

If an employee is given the choice of accepting the lodging or receiving additional pay instead, the employee is not allowed to exclude the value of the lodging if the lodging is accepted.

An employee of an institution is given the choice of residing at the institution free of charge or of residing elsewhere and receiving a cash allowance in addition to his regular salary. If he elects to reside at the institution, the value to the employee of the lodging furnished by the employer will be includible in the employee's gross income because his residence at the institution is not required as a condition of employment.

EXAMPLE 5.12

There has been significant litigation concerning what constitutes the business premises of the employer. The courts have been somewhat flexible on this issue.

## NO-ADDITIONAL-COST SERVICES

An employee can exclude the value of any service provided to the employee by the employer if (1) the service is offered for sale to customers, (2) in the line of business in which the employee works, and (3) the employer incurs no substantial additional costs (including foregone revenue) in providing the service to the employee. Examples of **no-additional-cost services** include providing airline tickets, bus tickets, train tickets, hotel accommodations, or telephone services at no cost or at reduced prices to employees who work in those lines of business.

John, a parking lot attendant, is allowed to park in the employer's parking lot for free. The cost of parking can be excluded from John's gross income for days when the parking lot has excess capacity. On days when the parking lot is full and customers must be turned away, the employer loses revenue in order to provide free parking for John; therefore one of the three requirements is not met and John must include the value of the free parking in his gross income for those days.

EXAMPLE 5.13

A service provided to an employee's spouse or dependent child is viewed as being provided to the employee individually. Use of air transportation by an employee's parents is considered to be use by the employee. Former employees and other specified individuals can also qualify for no additional-cost services.

Services must be in the line of business in which the employee works. If an employer has several lines of business and an employee receives services from another line of business, those services must be included in the employee's gross income. If unrelated employers in the same line of business have reciprocal arrangements to provide each other's employees with services, each employee can treat any services received from the other employer as though they were provided by his own employer.

Airlines frequently provide personal flights at no charge for employees or family members of employees. Whether the no-additional-cost exclusion is available depends upon seat availability to other customers. The key issue is that the airline must not forego revenue in order to provide the excludible fringe benefit.

<table>
<tr><td>

**EXAMPLE 5.14**

</td><td>

Commercial Airline permits its employees to enjoy personal travel on its scheduled flights at no charge and receive reserved seating. Because Commercial Airline foregoes potential revenue by permitting the employees to reserve seats, employees receiving free flights are not eligible for the no-additional-cost exclusion and must include the value of the flight in their gross income. However, if the employees are not allowed to reserve seats and only board the flight if there is available capacity, then employees receiving those flights are eligible for the no-additional-costs exclusion and may exclude the value of the flight from their gross income.

</td></tr>
</table>

If a no-additional-cost service discriminates in favor of highly-compensated employees, the highly-compensated employees must include the value of the service in gross income.

## QUALIFIED EMPLOYEE DISCOUNTS

**Qualified employee discounts** on qualified property and services can be excluded from an employee's gross income. Qualified employee discounts on property cannot exceed the employer's gross profit percentage of the price at which the employer offers the property for sale to customers. Qualified employee discounts on services cannot exceed 20 percent of the price at which the employer offers the services for sale to customers. Qualified property means any property other than real property or personal property of a kind that is held for investment (such as stocks or bonds) which is offered for sale to customers in the line of business in which the employee works. Qualified services means any services offered by the employer to customers in the line of business in which the employee provides services.

**EXAMPLE 5.15**

During the prior year, Don's employer sold property to customers at a gross profit percentage of 40%. For example, an item purchased for $60 was sold for $100, and the gross profit of $40 was 40% of the sales price. During the current year, Don paid $65 for a sleeping bag that was priced at $100 by his employer. His employee discount was 35% of the normal price. Since Don's discount of 35% is less than his employer's normal gross profit percentage of 40%, Don can exclude the discount from his gross income.

**EXAMPLE 5.16**

Tatiana worked for a carpet cleaning company. Her employer cleaned her carpets and charged only $140 for services that would cost $200 for regular customers. Her discount on the service is $60 or 30%. She will be able to exclude $40 or 20% from her gross income, but the remaining $20 must be included in her gross income as compensation.

In addition to current employees, certain individuals (such as spouses and dependents) are permitted to exclude qualified employee discounts.

As with no-additional-cost services, if qualified employee discounts discriminate in favor of highly-compensated employees, the highly-compensated employees must include the discounts in gross income.

## WORKING CONDITION FRINGE BENEFITS

A **working condition fringe benefit** provided by an employer to an employee to help the employee perform his job better can be excluded from the employee's gross income. A working condition fringe benefit is defined as any property or service for which the employee could have taken a tax deduction as a business expense or as depreciation expense if the employee had personally paid for the benefit. Working condition fringe benefits might include such things as employer-paid subscriptions to professional journals, dues for professional organization memberships, payment or reimbursement for employment-related professional education, or business use of a company car.

The use of a company car is a common working condition fringe benefit. If the employee uses the car for both personal and business purposes, the business-use value is considered to be a working condition fringe benefit, but the personal use value of the car must normally be included in the employee's gross income. Use of a demonstration car by full-time automobile salespersons qualifies as a working condition fringe benefit if the demonstration car is predominately used to facilitate the services the sales person provided to the employer and there are restrictions on personal use of the automobile.

All of an employee's use of a qualified non-personal use vehicle, such as a police car, fire vehicle, ambulance, hearse, farm tractor, or school bus, is treated as a qualified working condition fringe benefit.

In addition to employees, eligible recipients of excludable working condition fringe benefits might include a partner who performs services for a partnership, a member of the employer's board of directors, or an independent contractor who performs services for the employer.

Working condition fringe benefits are not subject to nondiscrimination requirements; therefore, they **can** be used by any employee **even** if the benefits favor highly compensated employees.

## DE MINIMIS FRINGE BENEFITS

An employee can exclude the value of de minimis fringe benefits from gross income. A **de minimis fringe benefit** is defined in Internal Revenue Code as "any property or service the value of which is (after taking into account the frequency with which similar fringes are provided by the employer to the employer's employees) so small as to make accounting for it unreasonable or administratively impracticable." De minimis fringes are considered to be minimal or small. A partial list of de minimis fringe benefits is presented in Exhibit 5.5.

- Occasional personal use of an employer's copy machine,

- Occasional typing of a personal letter by a secretary hired by an employer,

- Occasional cocktail parties, group meals, or picnics for employees and guests,

- Birthday or holiday gifts (not cash) with a low value,

- Occasional theater or sporting event tickets,

- Coffee, donuts, or soft drinks, and

- Flowers, fruit, books and similar items provided to an employee because of illness or a family crisis.

A cash de minimis fringe benefit is not usually excludable unless the cash is for reasonable, occasional meal money or local transportation fare. The furnishing of meal money or local transportation fare on a regular or routine basis is not considered to be "occasional." Further, the meal money (or actual meals) or local transportation fare must be provided due to overtime work necessitating an extension of the employee's normal work schedule.

Employer-operated eating facilities for employees qualify for this exclusion if the facility is located on or near the business premises of the employer and the annual revenue of the facility is equal to or greater than the direct operating costs of the facility.

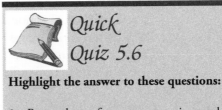

**Quick Quiz 5.6**

**Highlight the answer to these questions:**

1. Personal use of a company car is a working condition fringe benefit.
   a. True
   b. False

2. There is no limit on qualified transportation fringe benefits.
   a. True
   b. False

False, False.

Nondiscrimination rules do not normally apply in determining the amount of a de minimis fringe benefit. However, nondiscrimination rules do apply to employer-operated eating facilities. If access to such facilities discriminates in favor of highly compensated employees, highly compensated employees who use the facilities must include the value of meals received in gross income.

## QUALIFIED TRANSPORTATION FRINGE BENEFITS

The value of **qualified transportation fringe benefits** provided by an employer can be excluded from the gross income of employees if certain requirements and limitations are met. Qualified transportation fringe benefits include (1) transportation between an employee's residence and the place of employment in a commuter highway vehicle, (2) any transit pass, and (3) qualified parking.

The amounts that can be excluded from gross income are limited to $230[1] per month for 2009 and 2010 for commuter highway vehicle use (item 1) and transit passes (item 2) combined. The monthly limit for qualified parking is $230 for 2009 and 2010. Any benefits received in excess of these amounts, less any amount paid by the employee for the benefits, must be included in an employee's gross income.

**EXAMPLE 5.17**

Emily was provided with free parking at her employer's workplace beginning in March, 2009. The value of the parking was $300 per month during 2009. Emily paid $50 of the cost each month. The monthly parking benefit provided by the employer is $250 ($300 - $50). Emily can exclude $230 per month as qualified parking; she must report the remaining $20 per month in her gross income ($20 ($250-$230) for 2009 and 2010)). The $20 excess cannot be excluded as a de minimis fringe benefit.

**EXAMPLE 5.18**

For 2010, George's employer provides him with a bus pass at a cost of $160 per month for work purposes. George can exclude the entire monthly amount since it doesn't exceed $230 per month for 2010. He could also exclude the transit pass if it were for rail or ferry transportation.

After 2008, an employee who does not receive any of the transportation fringe benefits explained above, may exclude up to $20 per month of qualified bicycle commuting reimbursements from an employer. Qualified bicycle commuting reimbursements are employer reimbursements for the purchase, improvement, repair, or storage of a bicycle that is regularly used for travel between the employee's residence and place of employment. The $20 per month limit is not adjusted for inflation.

Qualified transportation fringe benefits can be provided in a discriminatory manner. Both current employees and leased employees are eligible.

Under appropriate circumstances, some transportation-related benefits may be excludable as de minimis or working condition fringe benefits.

## QUALIFIED MOVING EXPENSE REIMBURSEMENTS

Qualified moving expense reimbursements from an employer can be excluded from gross income by employees. A **qualified moving expense reimbursement** includes direct or indirect payment by the employer to pay for the cost of moving an employee's family and belongings. In order to qualify for exclusion by the employee, the reimbursement must be for expenses that would be deductible by the employee as moving expenses under IRC Section 217 if paid by the employee. Expenses such as house hunting expenses and meals are not eligible to be deducted as moving expenses. The requirements for deducting moving expenses are discussed more fully in Chapter 6.

---

1. Note that for January and February 2009, the amount that can be excluded from gross income for transit passes and commuter highway vehicle use is $120 per month.

Monica paid $3,800 to move her family and belongings to her new work location with the same company. All $3,800 would be deductible under IRC Section 217. Her employer paid her $3,800 as reimbursement for her moving expenses. She can exclude the $3,800 from gross income. If Monica had deducted the moving expenses in one year and received the reimbursement in the next year, she would not be allowed to exclude the reimbursement from gross income. If the employer had reimbursed Monica for nondeductible expenses, such reimbursement would have to be included in Monica's gross income as well.

EXAMPLE 5.19

Both employees and leased employees qualify for the exclusion of qualified moving expense reimbursements. Such reimbursements can discriminate in favor of highly compensated employees.

## QUALIFIED RETIREMENT PLANNING SERVICES

Qualified retirement planning services provided by an employer can be excluded from an employee's gross income. As defined in IRC Section 132(m)(1), **qualified retirement planning services** include "any retirement planning advice or information provided to an employee and his spouse by an employer maintaining a qualified employer plan." Qualified employer plan refers to an employer-sponsored retirement plan.

*Key Concepts*

**Underline/highlight the answers to these questions as you read:**

1. Explain how employers can assist employees with educational costs, dependent care costs, and adoption costs.

2. Identify the rules for qualified moving expense reimbursements.

3. Describe qualified retirement planning services.

Excludable services may include advice and information about the employer's retirement plan as well as general advice and information on retirement. The exclusion does not apply to the value of services for tax preparation, accounting, legal, or brokerage services.

If qualified retirement planning services discriminate in favor of highly compensated employees, the highly compensated employees must include the value of such services in gross income.

## ATHLETIC FACILITIES

The value of the use of on-premises gyms and other athletic facilities can be excluded from an employee's income if (1) the facilities are located on the premises of the employer, (2) the employer operates the facilities, and (3) substantially all the use of the facilities is by employees of the employer, their spouses, and their dependent children. The facilities have to be on premises owned or leased by the employer; the facilities do not have to be on the business premises of the employer.

<table>
<tr><td>

**EXAMPLE 5.20**

</td><td>

Troy uses tennis courts and other athletic facilities provided by his employer on their business property on a daily basis. He can exclude the value of such use from his gross income if the facilities are used almost exclusively by employees and their immediate family members. If Troy's employer had paid for his membership to a private gym, the cost of the membership would be includible in Troy's gross income.

</td></tr>
</table>

The athletic facilities fringe benefit can discriminate in favor of certain employees or groups of employees without jeopardizing the exclusion for any employees. A variety of individuals other than current employees are eligible to receive this benefit.

## EDUCATIONAL ASSISTANCE PROGRAMS

The value of educational assistance provided by an employer through an **educational assistance program** to an employee can be excluded from the employee's gross income up to $5,250 per year. The program must be a separate written plan of the employer set forth in a separate document, must only provide educational assistance, and must meet several other requirements specified in IRC Section 127.

Qualifying educational assistance can be provided for tuition, fees, books, supplies, and equipment, but it cannot pay for lodging, meals, transportation, nor tools and supplies that are retained by the employee after the course of instruction. Qualifying assistance can pay for either undergraduate or graduate education, but it cannot pay for courses related to sports, games, or hobbies unless those courses are either required for the employee's degree program or have a reasonable relationship to the employer's business.

Nondiscrimination rules apply to educational assistance programs. Once again, individuals other than current employees may be eligible for participation.

If an educational assistance program provides an employee with assistance in excess of $5,250 in a given year, the excess may or may not be excludable as a working condition fringe benefit.

## DEPENDENT CARE ASSISTANCE

Dependent care assistance provided or paid for by an employer through a dependent care assistance program can be excluded from the benefited employee's gross income up to $5,000 per year ($2,500 for a married employee filing separately). The amount excluded cannot exceed the earned income of the employee or the earned income of the employee's spouse (if less than the employee's earned income). A spouse is deemed to earn income ($250 with one qualifying person or $500 for two or more) for each month that the spouse is a full-time student or is incapable of caring for himself. Any amount paid by the employer in excess of the above limits must be included in the gross income of the employee.

Household or dependent care assistance must be paid for the care of a qualifying person and must be paid to allow the employee to work. A qualifying person can be (1) a dependent of the employee who has not attained the age of 13, (2) a dependent of the employee who is physically or mentally incapable of caring for himself and who has the same principal place of abode as the employee for more than one-half of the year, or (3) the employee's spouse who is physically or mentally incapable of caring for himself and who has the same principal place of abode as the employee for more than one-half of the year.

To qualify for exclusion treatment, the employer's dependent care assistance plan must be a separate written plan for the exclusive benefit of employees and must normally meet a variety of other requirements.

Nondiscrimination requirements apply to the dependent care assistance exclusion. If the plan discriminates in favor of highly compensated employees, the highly compensated employees are not allowed to exclude the benefits.

## TUITION REDUCTIONS GRANTED TO EMPLOYEES OF EDUCATIONAL INSTITUTIONS

An employee of an educational institution can exclude from gross income the value of a qualified tuition reduction for himself, his spouse, or his dependent child. This exclusion normally applies to education below the graduate level. However, a tuition reduction for graduate education can be excluded if the graduate student performs teaching or research activities for the educational institution. For education below the graduate level, the educational institution can be an elementary school, a secondary school, a college, or a university.

Individuals other than current employees may also be eligible for this exclusion. If tuition reductions discriminate in favor of highly compensated employees, the highly compensated employees must include the tuition reduction in gross income.

## ADOPTION ASSISTANCE PROGRAMS

Normally, the gross income of an employee does not include amounts paid by the employer for qualified adoption expenses in connection with the adoption of a child by the employee if such amounts are furnished pursuant to a written adoption assistance program of the employer. A maximum exclusion of $12,150 for 2009 ($12,170 for 2010) applies to the adoption of a child with special needs, regardless of the actual qualified adoption expenses. For other children, the maximum exclusion is equal to the amount of qualified adoption expenses up to $12,150 for 2009 ($12,170 for 2010).

**EXAMPLE 5.21**

Samantha's employer pays for her qualifying adoption expenses in 2009 through its adoption assistance program. Her actual qualifying expenses in 2009 are $9,000. If the adopted child is a child with special needs, Samantha will be able to exclude up to $12,150 of adoption assistance payments from her employer. If the child is not a child with special needs, she will be able to exclude up to a maximum of $9,000 of adoption assistance payments from her employer.

There is a phaseout of the amount excludable by an employee when the employee's modified adjusted gross income exceeds $182,180 for 2009 ($182,520 for 2010). The phaseout is complete when the employee's modified adjusted gross income reaches $222,180 for 2009 ($222,520 for 2010).

The employer's **adoption assistance program** must meet a variety of requirements, and nondiscrimination rules apply. Qualified adoption expenses include reasonable and necessary adoption fees, court costs, attorney fees, and other expenses for the legal adoption of an eligible child. An eligible child is a child under 18 or a child who is physically or mentally incapable of caring for himself. Qualified adoption expenses do not include the costs of adopting a child of the employee's spouse.

## EMPLOYEE ACHIEVEMENT AWARDS

Awards and prizes are normally includible in an individual's gross income. Certain employee achievement awards, however, can be excluded from an employee's gross income. The exclusion is allowed for the value of tangible personal property (such as a watch) given to an employee for length of service or safety achievement. Eligible tangible personal property does not include cash, vacations, meals, lodging, tickets to theater and sporting events, and stocks, bonds, and other securities.

The maximum amount that an employee can exclude from gross income is $1,600 ($400 for awards that are not "qualified plan awards"). Amounts in excess of the limits must be included in the employee's gross income.

Excludable awards must be made based on an employer's written plan that meets a variety of requirements. Nondiscrimination rules apply to employee achievement awards.

*Quick Quiz 5.7*

**Highlight the answer to these questions:**

1. The qualified retirement planning services exclusion does not apply to the value of tax preparation services.
   a. True
   b. False

2. The athletic facilities fringe benefit can discriminate without jeopardizing the exclusion.
   a. True
   b. False

3. Combat zone pay received by military personnel is included in gross income.
   a. True
   b. False

True, True, False.

## COMBAT PAY AND OTHER BENEFITS OF MILITARY PERSONNEL

Military personnel can exclude combat zone pay from gross income. They can also exclude a variety of other fringe benefits and allowances, including basic allowances for housing, cost-of-living allowances abroad, overseas housing allowances, military base realignment and closure benefits (subject to limits), death gratuity payments to eligible survivors, and many others. IRS Publication 3, Armed Forces Tax Guide, contains a list of excludable items.

## RENTAL VALUE OF PARSONAGE

The rental value of a home furnished to a minister can be excluded from the minister's gross income. Alternatively, a rental allowance paid to a minister can be excluded from the minister's gross income to the extent that it is used to rent or provide a home.

## FREQUENT FLYER MILES

The Internal Revenue Code does not contain a provision that specifically allows an employee to exclude from gross income the value of frequent flyer miles earned through employment activities. In Announcement 2002-18, however, the Internal Revenue Service announced that it will not assert that any taxpayer has understated his . . . federal tax liability by reason of the receipt or personal use of airline frequent flyer miles or other in-kind promotional benefits attributable to the taxpayer's business or official travel." In other words, the value of the frequent flyer miles can be excluded from gross income. The Announcement also indicates that any change in this policy will not be applied retroactively. This exclusion may be allowed by the IRS because of the associated enforcement challenges of including such amounts in gross income.

# EMPLOYER-SPONSORED RETIREMENT PLAN CONTRIBUTIONS AND DISTRIBUTIONS

## EMPLOYEE DEFERRALS

When an employee elects to make contributions (salary deferrals) to an employer-sponsored retirement plan, those contributions can be excluded from the employee's gross income (but not from payroll taxes).

## EMPLOYER CONTRIBUTIONS

When an employer makes contributions to an employer-sponsored retirement plan, the employee can exclude the employer's contribution from gross income.

## RETIREMENT PLAN EARNINGS

Any earnings (including interest, dividends and capital gains) on the amounts contributed to the plan are tax deferred until the employee receives distributions from the plan. This means that no one pays income taxes on the earnings until they are distributed to the employee.

*Key Concepts*

**Underline/highlight the answers to these questions as you read:**

1. Identify the tax consequences of employer-sponsored retirement plan contributions and distributions.

2. Describe the tax consequences of employee stock options.

## RETIREMENT PLAN DISTRIBUTIONS

When distributions are made from a retirement plan to an employee, the employee must report the distributions as ordinary income, but not as compensation subject to payroll taxes.

If after-tax contributions are made to a plan by the employee, then part of each periodic distribution from the plan is normally treated as a nontaxable return of investment (basis) and the remainder is included in gross income as ordinary income.

If a taxable distribution is made from a retirement plan before the employee reaches the age of 59½, a 10 percent penalty tax is also imposed (in addition to the income tax) on the taxable amount unless the distribution meets one of the exceptions provided in the Internal Revenue Code.

## INCOME FROM ROTH 401(k) AND 403(b) ACCOUNTS

Beginning in 2006, employees have been allowed to designate part or all of their contribution (elective deferrals) to a 401(k) or 403(b) retirement account as after-tax Roth contributions. The contributed amounts are included in gross income and the earnings are tax deferred. The real benefit of making such after-tax contributions is that amounts distributed from the retirement plan can be fully excluded from gross income if (1) the account remains open for at least five years from the beginning of the year for which the first contribution is made to the account and (2) the distributions are made after the employee reaches age 59½, becomes disabled, or dies. A distribution from a designated Roth account can be rolled over to another designated Roth account or to a Roth IRA.

## EMPLOYEE STOCK OPTIONS: ISOs & NQSOs

An **incentive stock option (ISO)** is an option granted by a corporation (or a parent or subsidiary corporation) to an employee (or certain other individuals) to purchase the stock of that corporation (or a parent or subsidiary corporation) if numerous requirements are met by the ISO plan. Two of the most important plan requirements are that (1) the option must be exercisable within 10 years of the date it is granted and (2) the exercise price of the option (the purchase price of the stock) must not be less than the fair market value of the stock at the time the option is granted.

A **nonqualified stock option (NQSO)** is a type of stock option that does not meet the statutory requirements applicable to incentive stock options. If, at the date of grant of the option, the exercise price of the NQSO is greater than or equal to the fair market value of the stock, there is no income to the employee at that time. If the fair market value is less than the exercise price at the grant date, the employee has income as of the date of the grant for the difference.

**Quick Quiz 5.8**

**Highlight the answer to these questions:**

1. Employer contributions to employer-sponsored retirement plans are generally excluded from the employee's gross income.
   a. True
   b. False

2. No gross income is recognized by the employee on the date an ISO is granted nor on the date an ISO is exercised.
   a. True
   b. False

True, True.

The ordinary tax treatment of nonqualified stock options is relatively straightforward and follows the general rules of income taxation. At the date of exercise, if the fair market value of the stock exceeds the exercise price, however, the employee will have W-2 income to the extent of the difference. In addition, the employee will have a basis in the stock equal to the fair market value of the stock on the date of exercise. If the stock is later sold, any gain or loss will depend on the sale price of the stock.

The exercise of an incentive stock option (ISO), however, generally has much more favorable tax consequences because the simple exercise of the ISO does not ordinarily result in regular income. In addition, if certain requirements are met, more favorable capital gains rates will apply to a subsequent sale of the stock after exercise of the ISO. No gross income is recognized by the employee on the date the ISO is granted nor on the date the ISO is exercised. However, the exercise of an ISO will cause a positive adjustment in the calculation of alternative minimum taxable income (AMTI) and may result in the taxpayer having to pay alternative minimum tax (AMT). The AMT is discussed in Chapter 15. When stock acquired through the exercise of an ISO is sold, any gain or loss on the sale is normally treated as a capital gain or loss unless the employee sells the stock within two years from the day the ISO was granted or within one year from the day the ISO was exercised. If either holding period requirement is not met, any gain or loss on the sale is treated as an ordinary gain to the extent of the difference between the value of the stock and the option price on the day the option is exercised; any remaining gain is a capital gain. Any loss on the sale is a capital loss.

## TAX CONSEQUENCES OF STOCK OPTIONS

EXHIBIT 5.6

|  | NQSO | ISO |
|---|---|---|
| At Grant Date | If Strike Price ≥ FMV<br>No Income Tax Consequence | No Income Tax Consequence |
| At Exercise Date | Ordinary (W-2) Income*<br>= FMV - Exercise Price | No Ordinary Income<br>AMT Preference = FMV - Strike Price |
| At Sale Date | Long-Term or Short-Term Capital Gain/ Loss Depending on Holding Period<br><br>Basis = FMV at Date of Exercise | If stock was held for 2 years from date of grant and 1 year from date of exercise: Gain = LTCG.<br><br>If holding period not met, gain is treated as ordinary (W-2) income. |

*This result can be changed if the taxpayer makes an election under IRC Section 83(b).*

EXAMPLE 5.22

On June 20, 2008, Samantha was granted an ISO to purchase 100 shares of her employer's stock at $10 per share, the value of the stock on the day the option was granted. When the stock had a value of $14 per share on February 20, 2009, Samantha exercised the option and purchased 100 shares for $1,000. On July 25, 2010, Samantha sold the shares for $1,700. She is not required to recognize any gross income on June 20, 2008 (the grant date) nor on February 20, 2009 (the exercise date). Since she met both of the holding period requirements, she can report her entire gain of $700 as a long-term capital gain. If she had sold the stock before both of the holding period requirements had been met, she would have reported $400 (the difference between the value of the stock and the exercise price on the exercise date) of the gain as ordinary wages and the remaining $300 of the gain as a capital gain in the year of the sale.

## GOVERNMENT-REQUIRED BENEFITS

### UNEMPLOYMENT COMPENSATION

Unemployment compensation must be included in gross income unless the employee made after-tax contributions to a government or private unemployment compensation fund. Since unemployment compensation benefits are normally funded by employer contributions to government programs, benefits received by an employee are normally taxable. Any unemployment taxes paid by the employer to fund the program can be deducted by the employer and excluded from gross income by the employee. Because of a provision in the American Recovery and Reinvestment Act of 2009, gross income does not include unemployment compensation received by an individual in an amount up to $2,400 for any tax year beginning in 2009 (IRC Section 85(c)).

**Key Concepts**

Underline/highlight the answers to these questions as you read:

1. Explain the taxation of unemployment compensation.

2. Describe how Social Security is funded by employers and employees.

3. Explain how Social Security benefits may be taxable.

### WORKERS' COMPENSATION

An employee may receive workers' compensation benefits to pay for medical expenses, rehabilitation expenses, or lost income due to work-related injuries and sickness. Workers' compensation insurance premiums paid by an employer and any benefits received under workers' compensation insurance are excludable from an employee's gross income. Workers' compensation is intended to alleviate the conflict between employers and employees and attempts to make the employee whole.

### SOCIAL SECURITY

The employer and the employee contribute equally to the funding of old age, survivors, and disability income (OASDI) benefits under the Social Security system of the United States. The employer pays a payroll tax of 6.2 percent of compensation up to an annual contribution base limit ($106,800 for 2009 and 2010) for each employee. In addition, the employer pays 1.45 percent (no limit on compensation) for each employee for the Medicare portion of the Social Security tax. The employer is allowed to deduct this payroll tax, and the employee is allowed to exclude the employer paid portion from gross income. The employer withholds an identical 6.2 percent amount (up to $106,800 of compensation for 2009 and 2010) and 1.45 percent amount (no limit on compensation) from each employee's compensation and remits it to the federal government. This half is included in the employee's gross income as taxable compensation and is withheld (along with federal income taxes) from the employee's gross pay and remitted to the federal government. The amount withheld from an employee's pay for OASDI and Medicare benefits is often referred to as **FICA (Federal Insurance Contributions Act)** on the employee's pay stub.

When an employee receives Social Security retirement or other benefits, up to 85 percent of the benefits may be included in the employee's gross income, depending on the employee's modified adjusted gross income (MAGI) for the year. If a retired taxpayer's only income is from Social Security retirement benefits, the benefits will be completely excludable. If a taxpayer receives Social Security benefits and has significant amounts of other income for the year as well, a portion of the Social Security benefits, up to a maximum of 85 percent of benefits received, must be included in gross income for the year.

If a taxpayer's MAGI plus one-half of the Social Security benefits received during the year does not exceed the base amount below, none of the Social Security benefits are includible in gross income.

## SOCIAL SECURITY BASE AMOUNTS

EXHIBIT 5.7

|  | Married Filing Jointly | All Others (Except MFJ=0) |
| --- | --- | --- |
| Base Amount | $32,000 | $25,000 |
| Adjusted Base Amount | $44,000 | $34,000 |

**EXAMPLE 5.23**

JoAnn, an unmarried taxpayer using the single filing status, received $15,000 of Social Security retirement benefits this year. She also received $5,000 of interest income during the year. Since the total of JoAnn's MAGI ($5,000) and one-half of her Social Security benefits (0.50 x $15,000 = $7,500) is less than her base amount ($25,000), none of her Social Security benefits are included in gross income.

If a taxpayer's MAGI plus one-half of Social Security benefits exceeds the relevant base amount but not the adjusted base amount, the amount of Social Security benefits that must be included in gross income is equal to the lesser of:

1. 50% of Social Security benefits,
   OR

2. 50% x [MAGI + (50% x Social Security Benefits) - Base Amount]

**EXAMPLE 5.24**

JoAnn, an unmarried taxpayer using the single filing status, received $15,000 of Social Security retirement benefits this year. She also received $5,000 of interest income, $3,000 of dividend income, and $18,000 of income from her retirement plan during the year. Since her MAGI ($26,000) plus one-half of her Social Security benefits (0.5 x $15,000 = $7,500) exceeds her base amount ($25,000) but not her adjusted base amount ($34,000), she must calculate her includible Social Security benefits using the formulas above. Half of her Social Security benefits is $7,500. The second formula yields an inclusion amount of $4,250 [0.5 x

($26,000 + $7,500 - $25,000)]. She must include the lesser of the two amounts ($4,250) in her gross income.

If a taxpayer's MAGI plus one-half of Social Security benefits exceeds the adjusted base amount, the amount of Social Security benefits that must be included in gross income is equal to the lesser of:

3.  85% of Social Security benefits,

    OR

4.  85% x [MAGI + (50% x Social Security Benefits) - Adjusted Base Amount]
    PLUS

    Lesser of: Amount included from formulas 1 and 2 OR $4,500 ($6,000 for married filing jointly; $0 for married filing separately)

| EXAMPLE 5.25 |
| --- |

JoAnn, an unmarried taxpayer using the single filing status, received $15,000 of Social Security retirement benefits this year. She also received $5,000 of interest income and $48,000 of income from her retirement plan during the year. Since her MAGI ($53,000) plus one-half of her Social Security benefits (0.5 x $15,000 = $7,500) exceeds her adjusted base amount ($34,000), she must calculate her includible Social Security benefits using the formula 3 or 4 above.

3.  0.85 x $15,000 = $12,750

4.  0.85 x [$53,000 + (0.50 x $15,000) - $34,000] = $22,525 plus the lesser of the amount calculated using 1 and 2 above:

1.  0.50 x $15,000 = $7,500

2.  0.50 x [$53,000 + (0.50 x $15,000) - $25,000] = $17,750

The lesser amount is $7,500

The formula 4 total is $30,025 ($22,525 + $7,500) OR $27,025 ($22,525 + $4,500)

The lesser of the formula 3 or 4 amounts is $12,750. Therefore, $12,750 of the Social Security benefits must be included in JoAnn's gross income.

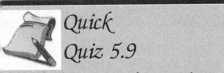
## MODIFIED ADJUSTED GROSS INCOME (MAGI) FOR SOCIAL SECURITY INCOME INCLUSION

Modified adjusted gross income is equal to adjusted gross income before any Social Security benefits plus excluded municipal bond interest, excluded foreign earned income and housing allowances, excluded U.S. Savings Bond interest, excluded adoption assistance benefits, deducted student loan interest expense, excluded income from Guam, American Samoa, the Northern Marianna Islands, and Puerto Rico, and the deduction for domestic production activities.

## BASE AMOUNT AND ADJUSTED BASE AMOUNT

EXHIBIT 5.8

| BASE AMOUNT | |
|---|---|
| $32,000 | Married taxpayers filing jointly |
| $0 | Married taxpayers filing separately who do not live apart for the entire tax year |
| $25,000 | All others |
| **ADJUSTED BASE AMOUNT** | |
| $44,000 | Married taxpayers filing jointly |
| $0 | Married taxpayers filing separately who do not live apart for the entire tax year |
| $34,000 | All others |

The rules above also apply to tier 1 railroad retirement benefits, which serve as a substitute for Social Security retirement benefits.

# CHAPTER SUMMARY

The following two tables contain summary information about employment-related income and fringe benefit items that are commonly (1) included in gross income and (2) excluded from gross income, respectively.

EXHIBIT 5.9  **SUMMARY OF GROSS INCOME ITEMS**

| Item | IRC Section | Category | Reported on Form | IRS Publication |
|------|-------------|----------|------------------|-----------------|
| Wages, Salaries, Tips, Commissions, Fees, Etc. | 61(a)(1) | Employment | 1040 | 17 |
| Fringe Benefits (Unless Specifically Excluded) | 61 | Employment | 1040 | 15 |
| Self-Employment Income | 61(a)(2) | Self-Employment | Sch. C or F | 334 |
| Disability Income Insurance Benefits (If Employer Pays Premiums) | 105 | Employment | 1040 | 17 |
| Retirement Plan Distributions | 61(a)(11) | Employment | 1040 | 575 |
| Nonqualified Stock Options (NQSO) | 422/83 | Employment | 1040 | 525/15 |
| Unemployment Compensation | 85 | Employment | 1040 | 525 |
| Social Security Benefits (0% to 85% Included in Gross Income) | 86 | Employment | 1040 | 915 |

EXHIBIT 5.10

| Item | IRC Section | Category | IRS Publication |
|---|---|---|---|
| Foreign Earned Income Exclusion | 911 | Employment | 54 |
| Health Insurance Premiums and Benefits | 105/106 | Employment | 15B |
| Medical Reimbursement Plans | 105/106 | Employment | 15B |
| Loss or Loss of Use of a Member or Function of the Body | 105/106 | Employment | 15B |
| Archer Medical Savings Accounts | 106(b)/220 | Employment | 969 |
| Health Savings Accounts | 106(d)/223 | Employment | 15B |
| Group Term Life Insurance | 79 | Employment | 15B |
| Employee Death Benefits | 102 | Employment | * |
| Survivor Benefits for Public Safety Officer Killed in the Line of Duty | 101(h) | Employment | 17 |
| Disability Insurance Premiums and Benefits | 105/106 | Employment | 17 |
| Cafeteria Plans | 125 | Employment | 15B |
| Flexible Spending Plans | 125 | Employment | 969 |
| Long-term Care Premiums and Benefits | 7702B | Employment | 525 |
| Meals and Lodging | 119 | Employment | 15B |
| No-additional-cost Services | 132 | Employment | 15B |
| Qualified Discounts on Goods and Services | 132 | Employment | 15B |
| Working Condition Fringe Benefits | 132 | Employment | 15B |
| De minimis Fringe Benefits | 132 | Employment | 15B |
| Qualified Transportation Fringe Benefits | 132 | Employment | 15B |
| Qualified Moving Expense Reimbursements | 132 | Employment | 15B |
| Qualified Retirement Planning Services | 132 | Employment | 15B |
| Athletic Facilities Provided to Employees | 132 | Employment | 15B |
| Educational Assistance Programs | 127 | Employment | 15B |
| Dependent Care Assistance Programs | 129 | Employment | 15B |
| Tuition Reductions Granted to Employees of Educational Institutions | 117 | Employment | 15B |
| Adoption Assistance Program Payments | 137 | Employment | 15B |
| Employee Achievement Awards | 74 | Employment | 15B |
| Combat Pay | 112 | Employment | 3 |
| Other Specified Military Fringe Benefits | 134/132 | Employment | 3 |
| Rental Value of Parsonage | 107 | Employment | 517 |
| Frequent Flyer Miles | An. 2002-18 | Employment | ** |
| Other Fringe Benefits | | Employment | 15B |
| Retirement Plan Contributions and Earnings | 401/402 | Employment | 560 |
| Incentive Stock Options | 422 | Employment | 15B/525 |
| Workers' Compensation Premiums & Benefits | 104 | Employment | 907/525 |
| Social Security Benefits (0% to 85% Included in Gross Income) | 86 | Employment | 915 |

* Estate of Sydney J. Carter v. Comm, 29 AFTR2d 332
** Announcement 2002-18

# Key Terms

*Activities of Daily Living* - Eating, bathing, dressing, toileting, transferring (walking), and continence.

*Adoption Assistance Program* - An employer plan that assists employees with the cost of adoption and may not discriminate in favor of highly compensated or key employees.

*Archer Medical Savings Accounts (MSAs)* - Tax-favored savings accounts for medical expenses that were established by HIPAA in 1996, but cannot be established after 2005.

*Bona Fide Resident Test* - Requirement for the Foreign Earned Income exclusion that requires the taxpayer to generally intend to work and reside in the foreign country for an indefinite period of time.

*Cafeteria Plan* - A written plan under which an employee may choose to receive either cash or taxable benefits as compensation or qualified fringe benefits that are excludable from wages.

*Compensation* - Salary, wages, and fringe benefits received in exchange for providing services to an employer.

*De Minimis Fringe Benefit* - Fringe benefits that are so small or insignificant that accounting for them would be unreasonable or administratively impracticable.

*Disability Insurance* - Provides benefits in the form of periodic payments to a person who is unable to work due to sickness or accidental injury.

*Educational Assistance Program* - A separate written plan that establishes a program through which an employer provides educational assistance to employees.

*Federal Insurance Contributions Act (FICA)* - The amount withheld from an employee's pay for OASDI benefits.

*Flexible Spending Account (FSA)* - A type of cafeteria plan that is funded through employee salary reductions.

*Foreign Earned Income* - Income earned by a qualifying citizen or resident of the United States in exchange for personal services rendered in a foreign country.

*Fringe Benefits* - Non-cash benefits provided to an employee by an employer in addition to wages and salary.

*Health Reimbursement Arrangements (HRAs)* - Employer-funded plans that reimburse employees for medical expenses and allow employees to carry any unused balance forward to be used in future years.

*Health Savings Accounts (HSAs)* - Accounts that allow individuals who have high deductible health insurance plans to save on a tax-free basis to fund their medical expenses.

# Key Terms

**Highly Compensated Employees** - Those employees that are either a greater than five percent owner or have compensation in excess of $110,000 (2009 and 2010).

**Incentive Stock Option (ISO)** - A stock option that meets certain requirements and is granted by a corporation to an employee to purchase the stock of that corporation.

**Key Employee** - An employee who is (1) a greater than five percent owner, (2) a greater than one percent owner with compensation in excess of $150,000, or (3) an officer with compensation in excess of $160,000 (2009 and 2010).

**Long-Term Care Insurance** - Provides benefits when the insured is unable to perform some of the activities of daily living.

**No-Additional-Cost Services** - A fringe benefit provided by employers that may be excluded from the employee's gross income if the service is (1) offered for sale to customers, (2) in the line of business in which the employee works, and (3) does not cause the employer to incur any substantial costs (including foregone revenue) in providing the service to the employee.

**Nonqualified Stock Option (NQSO)** – A right to purchase shares of company stock at a given strike price (generally set at the market price of the stock on the day the option is granted).

**Physical Presence Test** - Requirement for the Foreign Earned Income exclusion that requires the taxpayer to be present in a foreign country or countries for at least 330 full days during any period of 12 consecutive months.

**Qualified Employee Discounts** - Employer-provided discounts on qualified property and services that can be excluded from an employee's gross income.

**Qualified Moving Expense Reimbursement** - Direct or indirect payments by an employer to pay the cost of moving an employee's family and belongings.

**Qualified Retirement Planning Services** - Any retirement planning advice or information provided to an employee and his spouse by an employer maintaining a qualified employer-sponsored retirement plan.

**Qualified Transportation Fringe Benefits** - Benefits in the form of (1) transportation between an employee's residence and the place of employment in a commuter highway vehicle, (2) any transit pass, or (3) qualified parking.

**Working Condition Fringe Benefit** - Any property or service provided to an employee to help the employee perform his job better.

1. Discuss the various types of compensation and whether they must be included in gross income.

2. How is compensation received by an independent contractor reported?

3. Under what circumstances can foreign earned income be excluded from gross income?

4. Explain the bona fide resident test and the physical presence test.

5. When are fringe benefits included in the gross income of employees?

6. How do nondiscrimination requirements affect the taxation of fringe benefits?

7. List the various ways that an employer can provide an employee with benefits for medical care.

8. How much group term life insurance can be provided to employees without causing inclusion in gross income?

9. Describe the circumstances under which disability insurance benefits are excludible from gross income.

10. How do cafeteria plans help manage the costs of fringe benefits?

11. In what situation would a flexible spending account be appropriate?

12. Under what circumstances are meals provided by an employer excludable from the employee's gross income?

13. Under what circumstances can the value of lodging furnished by an employer be excluded from the employee's gross income?

14. What are no-additional-cost services?

15. Describe the rules regarding qualified employee discounts.

16. What are de minimis fringe benefits?

17. Under what circumstances can the value of athletic facilities be excluded from an employee's income?

18. Describe the taxation of ISOs.

19. Describe the taxation of unemployment compensation.

20. What percentage of Social Security benefits are taxable?

. Regis and Kelly, a married couple, have income of $50,000 and Social Security benefits of $20,000. What amount of their Social Security benefits must be included in their taxable income?

    a. $13,600.

    b. $14,000.

    c. $17,000.

    d. $19,600.

. Freddie and Karen are married and had the following income and expenses for 2009:

    1. Freddie's salary of $60,000.

    2. Freddie's employer provides him with a group term life insurance policy for 2 times his salary. The policy premium paid by the employer is $150 per year. The Uniform Premium Table amount is $0.10.

    3. Karen had salary of $10,000 and unemployment compensation of $9,000.

    4. Karen won $1,500 on a game show.

What is Freddie and Karen's joint gross income?

    a. $71,584.

    b. $78,184.

    c. $78,250.

    d. $80,584.

. Piper, age 68, had $50,000 in salary for the current year. She also received Social Security benefits of $10,000 and workers' compensation of $25,000. Which of the following is true?

    a. The salary, 100% of the Social Security benefits, and 100% of the workers' compensation will be taxable to Piper.

    b. The salary, 75% of the Social Security benefits, and 50% of the workers' compensation will be taxable to Piper.

    c. The salary, 50% of the Social Security benefits, and 100% of the workers' compensation will be taxable to Piper.

    d. The salary and 85% of the Social Security benefits will be taxable to Piper.

4.  Suri recently entered an assisted living facility. She is unable to feed or dress herself although she can still walk and go to the bathroom unassisted. She had a life insurance policy with a death payout of $100,000. She sold the policy to a viatical company for $60,000 and used the money to pay for her long-term care at the assisted living facility. Which of the following statements is true?

    a.  The policy proceeds will be excluded from Suri's income.

    b.  85% of the policy proceeds will be taxed.

    c.  The policy will be included in Suri's income at $100,000.

    d.  The policy will be included in Suri's income at $60,000.

5.  Tyler has lived and worked in Florida for 30 years. He was divorced recently and decided he needed a change of scenery. He applied for and was offered a job in California. Tyler has the following expenses related to the move:

    1.  House hunting expenses - $5,000

    2.  Moving truck service - $12,000

    3.  Lodging en route - $600

    4.  Meals en route - $250

    5.  New driver's license in California - $35

    6.  Ticket for speeding en route - $250

    Tyler's new employer reimbursed him for $8,000 in moving expenses. Tyler's salary for the year was $100,000. What is Tyler's AGI?

    a.  $87,400.

    b.  $95,400.

    c.  $100,000.

    d.  $108,000.

6.  Which of the following fringe benefits provided by Oceanside Company would be taxable to its employee, Violet?

    a.  Flowers sent to Violet when her mother was ill.

    b.  The value of doughnuts provided by Oceanside on a weekly basis for the enjoyment of all employees.

    c.  Monthly dues to the local health club paid by Oceanside for Violet and all other employees.

    d.  A 10% employee discount on merchandise sold by Oceanside.

7. Which of the following requirements must be satisfied in order for a U.S. citizen to exclude foreign earned income from U.S. taxation?

    a. Both the bona fide resident test and the physical presence test must be satisfied.

    b. The income must be earned by employees of the U.S. government.

    c. The taxpayer must also elect to take the foreign tax credit.

    d. Either the bona fide resident test or the physical presence test must be satisfied.

8. Which of the following statements is correct regarding the taxation of fringe benefits?

    1. The value of the fringe benefit is included in the employee's gross income unless the Code specifically excludes it from taxation.

    2. The value of the fringe benefit is excluded in the employee's gross income unless the Code specifies otherwise.

    3. The value of the fringe benefit is taxable if the benefit is only provided to employees owning more than 5% of the company and the fringe benefit has a nondiscrimination requirement.

    4. The value of the fringe benefit is always taxable if someone other than the employee (e.g., the employee's spouse) benefits from the fringe benefit provided by the employer.

    a. 1 and 2.

    b. 1 and 3.

    c. 2 and 4.

    d. 3 and 4.

9. Which of the following can make contributions to Heidi's HSA?

    a. Heidi's employer.

    b. Heidi's aunt.

    c. Heidi's ex-husband.

    d. All of the above.

10. Henrietta is unmarried, as a high-deductible medical plan, and recently set up an HSA. Under what circumstances are contributions to Henrietta's HSA deductible for 2010?

    a. Contributions to Henrietta's HSA by her employer are deductible by Henrietta.

    b. Contributions made by Henrietta are only deductible to the extent that her contributions exceed the deductible on her high-deductible plan.

    c. Contributions made by Henrietta up to $3,050 are deductible.

    d. Contributions are only deductible to the extent of qualified medical expenses.

11. Which of the following is not a qualifying person for the purpose of employer-provided dependent care assistance?

    a. A child of the employee regardless of whether the child can be claimed as a dependent on the employee's tax return.

    b. A dependent of the employee who has not attained the age of 13.

    c. A dependent of the employee who is physically or mentally incapable of caring for himself and who has the same principal place of abode as the employee for more than one-half of the year.

    d. The employee's spouse who is physically or mentally incapable of caring for himself and who has the same principal place of abode as the employee for more than one-half of the year.

12. Mike, a short order cook at the Bull's Corner restaurant, works from 12 p.m. to 10 p.m. five days a week. Each workday, he is furnished two meals without charge. The manager of the restaurant encourages Mike to eat lunch in the employee break room each day before 12 p.m., but does not expressly require him to do so. The manager does, however, require Mike to eat dinner in the employee break room. The cost to the restaurant is $5 per lunch and $7 per dinner. Assuming that Mike eats both lunch and dinner at the restaurant, what amount of this fringe benefit should be included in Mike's income?

    a. Neither the cost of the lunches nor the cost of the dinners should be included in Mike's income.

    b. Only the cost of the lunches should be included in Mike's income, because he is not required to eat them.

    c. Only the cost of the dinners should be included in Mike's income, because is he required to eat them as part of his job.

    d. Both the cost of the lunches and the dinners should be included in Mike's income.

13. Anne recently decided to adopt a special needs child named Ford. Anne was excited to find out that her employer has an adoption assistance program that reimburses the maximum possible amount to employees who adopt children. Anne incurs the following expenses in 2009 associated with her adoption of Ford:

    1. Legal fees of $5,000.
    2. Court costs of 2,000.
    3. Renovation costs of $4,000 (to make her home more accessible to Ford).

    How much can Anne receive as a reimbursement from her employer and how much of that payment can she exclude from her income?

    a. Anne can receive $11,000 from her employer and can exclude all of it from her income.

    b. Anne can receive $12,150 from her employer and can exclude all of it from her income.

    c. Anne can receive $7,000 from her employer, but can exclude $11,000 from her income.

    d. Anne can receive $7,000 from her employer, but can exclude $12,150 from her income.

14. Ralph receives stock options (ISOs) with an exercise price of $16 when the stock is trading at $16. Ralph exercises these options two years after the date of the grant when the stock price is $37 per share. Which of the following statements is correct?

    a. Upon exercise Ralph will have no income for regular tax purposes.
    b. Ralph will have W-2 income of $21 per share upon exercise.
    c. Ralph will have $16 of AMT income upon exercise.
    d. Ralph's adjusted basis for regular income tax will be $37 at exercise.

15. George is single and received $28,000 of dividend income during the year. He also received $18,000 of Social Security benefits. What portion of his Social Security benefits are taxable?

    a. $0.
    b. $7,050.
    c. $9,000.
    d. $15,300.

# Quick Quiz Explanations

## Quick Quiz 5.1

1. False. Gross income cannot normally be assigned by the person who earns it to anyone else.
2. True.

## Quick Quiz 5.2

1. False. Fringe benefits are not always nontaxable. However, fringe benefits may still be valuable to employees even if they are taxable. For example, with a large number of employees, employers can negotiate lower group insurance rates and better coverage than an individual employee would be able to negotiate in the open market.
2. True.
3. False. An HSA may be independently established by an employee, or it may be facilitated by an employer.

## Quick Quiz 5.3

1. False. The cost, as determined under the Uniform Premium Table provided by the IRS, of any death benefit coverage in excess of $50,000 is taxable to the employee, not the employer.
2. True.
3. False. A cafeteria plan is appropriate when employee benefit needs vary within the employee group; the employee mix includes young, unmarried people with minimal life insurance and medical benefits needs, as well as older employees with families who need maximum medical and life insurance benefits.

## Quick Quiz 5.4

1. False. One disadvantage of an FSA is that amounts remaining in the account at the end of the year are forfeited back to the employer (a use it or lose it arrangement).
2. True.
3. True.

## Quick Quiz 5.5

1. False. In general, an employee can exclude from gross income the value of meals provided in-kind (not as cash reimbursement) to the employee as long as the meals are furnished (1) on the employer's business premises (2) for the convenience of the employer.
2. False. Guaranteed seats are not a no-additional-cost service because guaranteeing seats for an employee might cause the employer to forego revenue. Only standby seats, which depend on availability, are a no-additional cost service.
3. True.

# Quick Quiz Explanations

## Quick Quiz 5.6

1. False. If the employee uses the car for both personal and business purposes, the business-use value is considered to be a working condition fringe benefit, but the personal use value of the car must normally be included in the employee's gross income.

2. False. The amounts that can be excluded from gross income are limited to $230[1] per month for 2009 and 2010 for commuter highway vehicle use (item 1) and transit passes (item 2) combined. The monthly limit for qualified parking is $230 for 2009 and 2010. Any benefits received in excess of these amounts, less any amount paid by the employee for the benefits, must be included in an employee's gross income.

## Quick Quiz 5.7

1. True.
2. True.
3. False. Military personnel can exclude combat zone pay from gross income.

## Quick Quiz 5.8

1. True.
2. True.

## Quick Quiz 5.9

1. True.
2. True.

---

1. Note that for January and February 2009, the amount that can be excluded from gross income for transit passes and commuter highway vehicle use is $120 per month.

# Introduction to Deductions

## INTRODUCTION

The 16th Amendment to the U.S. Constitution gives Congress the power to tax income. Congress could, presumably, assess an income tax on gross income without taking into consideration any deductions, but for fairness and public policy reasons, several deductions from income are made available to taxpayers. Deductions are not entitlements for taxpayers – they are based on legislative grace. Legitimate deductions from income must be permitted by statute (the Internal Revenue Code).

In our tax system, the taxpayer, not the IRS, has responsibility for substantiating deductions. To justify deductions taken for income tax purposes, taxpayers should maintain adequate records of their expenses. Receipts or proof of expenditures should be kept by taxpayers at least until the statute of limitations expires for the tax year in question. For some deductions, such as those for meals and entertainment expenses, more extensive recordkeeping is required, and these rules will be discussed in this chapter with the deductions to which they apply.

## CLASSIFICATION OF DEDUCTIBLE EXPENSES

Income tax deductions fall into two basic categories: **above-the-line deductions** (or deductions for AGI) which are sometimes referred to as adjustments, and **below-the-line deductions** (deductions from AGI) which are often referred to as Itemized Deductions. (Note that the "line," for income tax purposes, is adjusted gross income (AGI).) AGI sets many of the phase-outs and thresholds that will have to be met to take advantage of certain deductions and tax planning tools. Understanding where deductions are taken in the tax formula, therefore, is important when considering tax planning alternatives for clients.

When considering income tax deductions and their planning implications for clients, it is helpful to recall the income tax formula.

> **Gross Income**
> - Exclusions
> - Adjustments (Above-the-line deductions)
> = **Adjusted Gross Income (AGI)**
> - The greater of the Standard Deduction or Itemized Deductions (Below-the-line deductions)
> - Personal and Dependency Exemptions
> = **Taxable Income**

As the tax formula illustrates, above-the-line deductions are subtracted from gross income to arrive at AGI, while below-the-line deductions are subtracted from AGI and are not taken into account until after AGI is computed.

| EXHIBIT 6.1 | **FORM 1040 ADJUSTMENTS SECTION** |

| Adjusted Gross Income | | | | |
|---|---|---|---|---|
| | 23 | Educator expenses (see page 29) . . . . . . . | 23 | |
| | 24 | Certain business expenses of reservists, performing artists, and fee-basis government officials. Attach Form 2106 or 2106-EZ | 24 | |
| | 25 | Health savings account deduction. Attach Form 8889 . | 25 | |
| | 26 | Moving expenses. Attach Form 3903 . . . . . . | 26 | |
| | 27 | One-half of self-employment tax. Attach Schedule SE . | 27 | |
| | 28 | Self-employed SEP, SIMPLE, and qualified plans . . | 28 | |
| | 29 | Self-employed health insurance deduction (see page 30) | 29 | |
| | 30 | Penalty on early withdrawal of savings . . . . . . | 30 | |
| | 31a | Alimony paid  **b** Recipient's SSN ▶ _____ | 31a | |
| | 32 | IRA deduction (see page 31) . . . . . . . . | 32 | |
| | 33 | Student loan interest deduction (see page 34) . . . | 33 | |
| | 34 | Tuition and fees deduction. Attach Form 8917 . . . | 34 | |
| | 35 | Domestic production activities deduction. Attach Form 8903 | 35 | |
| | 36 | Add lines 23 through 31a and 32 through 35 . . . . . . . . . | 36 | |
| | 37 | Subtract line 36 from line 22. This is your **adjusted gross income** . . . . . ▶ | 37 | |

## Key Concepts

**Underline/highlight the answers to these questions as you read:**

1. Name the two categories of income tax deductions.

2. Describe an above-the-line deduction.

3. Describe a below-the-line deduction.

4. Explain which type of deduction is generally considered to be most favorable to taxpayers.

## DEDUCTIONS FOR AGI (ABOVE THE LINE)

Adjustments, or above-the-line deductions, reduce a taxpayer's adjusted gross income (AGI). Most above-the-line deductions relate to expenses for business and production of income activities (from investment activities) by taxpayers, but there are some deductions permitted for individual taxpayers as well (such as IRA deductions, student loan interest, and educator expenses, to name a few). Above-the-line deductions are listed in IRC Section 62, and they can be claimed by the taxpayer even if the taxpayer does not itemize deductions. See Exhibit 6.1.

Whenever expenses are associated with a business activity, they are above-the-line deductions. Only the net income of the business (gross receipts from the business less expenses incurred in producing that income) is included in the taxpayer's gross income for the year. For example, if a taxpayer operates a sole proprietorship, the financial results will be reported on Schedule C of the taxpayer's individual tax return. If, instead of operating a business, a taxpayer engages in rental real estate activities, the gross receipts from the rental activity less expenses associated with the rental activity will be reported on Schedule E of the income tax return, and only the net income from the activity will be reported in the taxpayer's gross income for the year. Schedules C and E are essentially income statements for the business and production of income activities, detailing the gross receipts and expenditures incurred in the activity. Since business related and production of income related expenses directly reduce gross income, they are effectively treated as above-the-line deductions.

All other above-the-line deductions are found in the adjustments section (Exhibit 6.1) on the front page of Form 1040 and are discussed below.

## ITEMIZED DEDUCTIONS (BELOW THE LINE)

When most taxpayers think of deductions, they usually think of itemized deductions. Itemized, or below-the-line, deductions are deductions that are allowed for personal expenses and losses that are not typically associated with the conduct of a business or with production of income activities. While there are fewer itemized deductions (there are only six categories of itemized deductions) than above-the line deductions, itemized deductions are sometimes more important when planning for individual clients.

Taxpayers may take the greater of their itemized deductions or the standard deduction in determining taxable income. In order to achieve a tax benefit, the taxpayer will need his total itemized deductions to be greater than the standard deduction.

The types of itemized deductions, and their associated limitations, are discussed below.

## WHICH TYPE OF DEDUCTION IS BETTER – ABOVE OR BELOW-THE-LINE DEDUCTIONS?

Due to the limitation imposed on itemized deductions by the standard deduction (a taxpayer can only take the greater of the two), various deduction floors and ceilings, as well as phase-outs associated with below-the-line deductions,

### Quick Quiz 6.1

**Highlight the answer to these questions:**

1. Above-the-line deductions are also known as adjustments to income.
   a. True
   b. False

2. Whenever expenses are associated with a business activity, they are below-the-line deductions.
   a. True
   b. False

3. Taxpayers may deduct the lesser of their itemized deductions or the standard deduction.
   a. True
   b. False

4. Above-the-line deductions are usually considered to be more favorable to the taxpayer on a dollar-for-dollar basis.
   a. True
   b. False

True, False, False, True.

above-the-line deductions are usually considered to be more favorable to the taxpayer on a dollar-for-dollar basis.

EXAMPLE 6.1

Erin and Brian are single, and each of them has gross income of $50,000 and deductions of $8,000. Erin's deductions, however, can be taken above-the-line, while Brian will have to report his deductions as itemized deductions. Erin and Brian's taxable income for 2009 is calculated as follows:

|  | Erin | Brian | Difference |
|---|---|---|---|
| Gross Income | $50,000 | $50,000 | $0 |
| - Adjustments (for AGI ded) | $8,000 | $0 | $8,000 |
| = Adjusted Gross Income (AGI) | $42,000 | $50,000 | $8,000 |
| - Standard/Itemized Deductions | $5,700 | $8,000 | $2,300 |
| - Personal Exemption | $3,650 | $3,650 | $0 |
| = Taxable Income | $32,650 | $38,350 | $5,700 |

While both Erin and Brian have exactly the same gross income and the same out of pocket deductions, Erin's taxable income is less than Brian's. The difference between their incomes equals the standard deduction. Erin was able to take both the standard deduction and her above-the-line deductions, while Brian was only able to benefit from his below-the-line deductions and then only to the extent that they exceeded the standard deduction. Erin will pay a much lower tax than Brian, even though their income and out-of-pocket expenses were the same. For 2010, the calculation remains the same.

In the example above, Erin and Brian had modest income, and would not have been subject to phase-outs, floors, and ceilings that apply to some itemized deductions. If their income was higher, or their expenses were subject to the limitations imposed on itemized deductions, the difference in tax liability between the two parties would be even greater.

## ABOVE-THE-LINE DEDUCTIONS FOR INDIVIDUALS

### TRADE OR BUSINESS EXPENSES

Trade or business expenses are, by their very nature, above-the-line tax deductions. If a taxpayer has a C corporation, S corporation or Partnership (including general and limited partnerships, LLCs, and LLPs), business expenses are deducted from income on the entity tax return, and only the net profit (in the case of S corporations and partnerships), or dividends distributed (in the case of C corporations) are included on an individual taxpayer's income tax return. If the taxpayer conducts business as a sole proprietorship, business income and expenses are reported on Schedule C, and only the net income of the business (gross receipts less expenditures) is included in gross income on the front page of the taxpayer's income tax return.

For sole proprietors and partners, there are three additional above-the-line deductions that may be available. These include: (1) one-half self-employment tax paid; (2) self-employed pension contributions (to Simplified Employee Pensions (SEPs), SIMPLEs, and other qualified pension plans); and (3) the self-employed health insurance deduction.

Self-employed individuals must pay Social Security taxes, just like employees. Employees, however, have an advantage in this area in that one-half of their Social Security taxes are paid by their employer. An employee pays 7.65 percent on income up to the Social Security wage base for Social Security and Medicare taxes, and 1.45 percent (the Medicare component) on income above the Social Security wage base ($106,800 for 2009 and 2010). The employer matches these contributions. Self-employed individuals have a dual role – they are both the employer and the employee, so they must pay both the employer and employee portion of the tax. Employers who pay Social Security and Medicare taxes on behalf of an employee deduct their payment from business income in arriving at a net profit amount, so a self-employed person should be able to do the same. A deduction is not allowed on Schedule C for employment taxes paid, but an adjustment to income (an above-the-line deduction) is permitted for one-half of the self-employment taxes paid. Allowing this deduction above the line ensures that it will not be subject to the limitations and phase-outs that apply to below-the-line (itemized) deductions.

Self-employed individuals are also permitted to set up qualified and non-qualified tax advantaged retirement plans, and are permitted to deduct contributions to those plans up to a specified amount. The deduction allowed depends on the type of plan established, as well as the coverage rules that apply to the plan. Allowable deductions are treated as adjustments to income and are deducted above-the-line.

Self-employed individuals are also permitted to deduct 100 percent of health insurance premiums paid on behalf of themselves and their dependents. The deduction for their own insurance is not permitted on Schedule C, but can be taken as an adjustment to income (above-the-line). Health care premiums paid on behalf of employees by the self-employed individual are deducted on Schedule C. These rules apply to self-employed individuals who file a Schedule C, partners, and more than two percent owners of S corporations.

One type of health insurance often overlooked is long-term care insurance. Self-employed individuals may deduct the cost of long-term care insurance on their lives, up to specified amounts based on their age (see Exhibit 6.2) as an adjustment to income (above-the-line). Long-term care can be provided as an employee benefit on a discriminatory basis, so business owners who wish to purchase long-term care coverage for themselves may do so without creating an obligation to purchase similar coverage for their employees.

In order to get the deduction, however, the contract must be a qualified long-term care contract. Most contracts currently being sold are qualified contracts. Qualified contracts cover only qualified long-term care expenses, are guaranteed renewable, do not provide cash surrender value, and do not reimburse expenses recovered under Medicare. Long-term care policies that have life insurance features and cash values will not generally meet the definition of a qualified long-term care contract.

EXHIBIT 6.2 **DEDUCTION LIMITATION ON LONG-TERM CARE INSURANCE PREMIUMS**

| Age | 2009 Deduction Limit | 2010 Deduction Limit |
|---|---|---|
| 40 or less | $320 | $330 |
| 41-50 | $600 | $620 |
| 51-60 | $1,190 | $1,230 |
| 61-70 | $3,180 | $3,290 |
| 71 and over | $3,980 | $4,110 |

## MEDICAL SAVINGS ACCOUNTS (MSAs) AND HEALTH SAVINGS ACCOUNTS (HSAs)

As part of the Health Insurance Portability and Accountability Act (HIPAA) passed in 1996, Congress created **Medical Savings Accounts**. These accounts were available to self-employed individuals and small corporations, and allowed participants to contribute part of the annual deductible amount on their health insurance policies to the MSA, which could grow on a tax-free basis if funds distributed from the account were used to pay for medical expenses. MSAs were available on a pilot basis, and few are created now due to new legislation in 2003 authorizing the creation of **Health Savings Accounts** (HSAs). MSAs that were in existence at the time of the HSA legislation may still be used, and are referred to as "Archer MSAs" in honor of their sponsor, Congressman Bill Archer of Texas. Subject to certain limits, contributions to an HSA or MSA allow the taxpayer to take an above-the-line deduction on their income tax returns.

**Key Concepts**

Underline/highlight the answers to these questions as you read:

1. List those who qualify to participate in MSAs and HSAs.

2. Discuss the contribution rules for MSAs and HSAs.

3. Describe the deduction for contributions to an HSA or MSA.

4. Explain the circumstances under which long-term care insurance premiums are deductible.

Unlike MSAs, which were primarily for the self-employed, HSAs allow individuals to save on a tax-free basis to fund their medical expenses. To qualify for an HSA, a taxpayer must:

1. be covered by a high deductible health insurance plan (sometimes referred to as an HDHP);
2. have no other health insurance coverage except the HDHP;
3. not be enrolled in Medicare; and
4. not be claimed as a dependent on someone else's tax return.

A High Deductible Health Plan (HDHP) is any plan that had a deductible falling between the minimum and maximum annual amounts, shown in Exhibit 6.3.

EXHIBIT 6.3

**DEDUCTIBLE LIMITS FOR HDHPS, 2009 AND 2010**

| | Minimum Deductible | | Maximum Deductible and Out of Pocket Expenses | |
|---|---|---|---|---|
| | 2009 | 2010 | 2009 | 2010 |
| Individual | $1,150 | $1,200 | $5,800 | $5,950 |
| Family | $2,300 | $2,400 | $11,600 | $11,900 |

HSA contributions can be made at any time during the tax year and up to the due date of the tax return, plus extensions. Contributions may not be made in advance, however. If the HSA is offered through an employer, contributions may be made through the employer's cafeteria plan. For taxable years beginning after December 31, 2006, the maximum allowable contribution to an HSA is an indexed amount provided by the IRS. In addition, individuals over 55 are entitled to a catch-up contribution. Under previous law, the maximum contribution was the lesser of (1) the annual deductible amount under the policy, or (2) if age 55 or older, the annual deductible amount under the policy plus an indexed catch-up amount, or (3) an indexed amount provided by the IRS.

EXHIBIT 6.4

**MAXIMUM HSA CONTRIBUTIONS, 2009 AND 2010**

| | Maximum Contribution | | Age 55 or older Catch-Up | |
|---|---|---|---|---|
| | 2009 | 2010 | 2009 | 2010 |
| Individual | $3,000 | $3,050 | $1,000 | $1,000 |
| Family | $5,950 | $6,150 | $1,000 | $1,000 |

The maximum allowable contribution to a HSA is reduced by any contributions made to an MSA. Under previous law, to the extent that the taxpayer was covered by a HDHP for only part of the year, the maximum allowable contribution is reduced by 1/12 for every month that the taxpayer was not covered under the plan. As a result of the Health Opportunity Empowerment Act of 2006, however, proration is no longer necessary for plan years beginning after December 31, 2006.

If contributions exceed the allowable amount, they are not deductible if made by the individual, and are included in the gross income of employees who receive funding through a cafeteria plan at work. In addition, if the excess contribution is not distributed prior to the due date of the income tax return including extensions, a six percent penalty applies to the excess contribution (which is similar to the excess contribution penalty that applies to retirement plans).

If a self-employed individual makes a contribution to his own HSA, that contribution is not taken into account when calculating net earnings from self employment. Consequently, the contribution to the HSA is subject to employment tax, but will not reduce self-employment earnings for purposes of calculating the maximum self-employed pension contribution for the individual.

Once in the HSA, contributions are placed in available investment vehicles to generate a return on investment. Unlike Flexible Spending Accounts offered by employers, which allow employees to make an election to allocate part of their income on a pre-tax basis each year to the account but required the funds to be used or forfeited by the end of the calendar year, contributions to HSAs are not required to be spent or forfeited at the end of each year, allowing taxpayers to accumulate an emergency fund for future health care purposes.

Distributions from HSAs used to cover qualified medical expenses for the taxpayer, taxpayer's spouse, or taxpayer's dependent are excluded from income. "Qualified medical expenses" are the same as medical expenses eligible for deduction if a taxpayer itemizes deductions, with the exception of medical insurance premiums. Interestingly, distribution of amounts to cover long-term care insurance premiums, and health insurance premiums under COBRA are also excluded from income. Any distributions from an HSA that are not used to pay for qualified medical expenses are subject to income tax plus a 10 percent penalty. Note that if a medical expense is reimbursed from an HSA, it is not a deductible qualified medical expense. See IRS Publication 502 for more information on this topic.

Once the taxpayer reaches age 65, he is eligible to receive Medicare health coverage from the government. Amounts in the HSA may continue to be used to cover medical expenses after age 65 (and will therefore be excluded from income), but if distributions are made for other purposes, the 10 percent penalty rule will not apply. Other exceptions to the 10 percent penalty rule include distributions caused by the account owner's death or disability. In the event the account owner dies when there are still funds in the HSA, the account is transferred to the person who is named as beneficiary, which is often the surviving spouse. A spouse beneficiary may treat the account as his own HSA, but a nonspouse beneficiary must treat the HSA as ordinary income.

HSAs are particularly valuable tools for younger individuals. Since young individuals tend to have few health problems, using a HDHP will help lower their annual insurance costs. If contributions are made to HSAs on an annual basis, but are not used each year (during the taxpayer's younger years) to fund health care expenses, the funds inside the HSA are permitted to grow, creating an emergency fund for medical expenses. This emergency fund can be drawn down without income tax consequences when needed, allowing the taxpayer to continue to use high deductible health plans when they are older since the funds needed to cover increased medical expenses incurred as the taxpayer ages can be drawn from the HSA. HSAs are tools that can be used to help minimize an individual's health insurance premiums over their lifetime by creating a tax-advantaged reserve of funds to pay health care expenses when necessary.

## INDIVIDUAL RETIREMENT ACCOUNTS

### *Traditional IRAs*

In addition to the use of company-sponsored retirement plans, taxpayers can also save for retirement by making contributions to Individual Retirement Accounts. Some taxpayers can make tax deductible contributions to traditional IRAs, while others may not. All taxpayers making traditional IRA contributions, however, receive the benefit of tax-deferred growth. The earnings generated on traditional IRA investments are not subject to income taxation until they are withdrawn from the account, which will presumably occur on or after the date of the taxpayer's retirement. Penalty free distributions may be made after the age of 59½. Furthermore, distributions must begin by April 1 of the year following the year the taxpayer attains age 70½, or a penalty tax will be assessed. Note that under the Worker, Retiree, and Employer Recovery Act of 2008, the 2009 required minimum distribution has been suspended that is generally applicable to retirement plans, with respect to defined contribution arrangements, including IRAs. An individual may still withdraw

**Key Concepts**

Underline/highlight the answers to these questions as you read:

1. Describe the circumstances under which an individual can make a contribution to a traditional and Roth IRA.

2. Explain the limits on the deductibility of a contribution to a traditional IRA.

3. Discuss the active participant rules for contributions made to a deductible traditional IRA.

4. Explain under what circumstances a non-active participant spouse can contribute to a deductible traditional IRA.

needed funds from his or her retirement plan or IRA, however he or she is not required to do so for 2009. The 2008 Act did not suspend the requirements that a taxpayer who turned 70½ in 2008 must make a required minimum distribution no later than April 1, 2009.

### Contributions

Those taxpayers who qualify for an income tax deduction on contributions to a traditional IRA, take that deduction as an above-the line deduction. The maximum allowable contribution to a traditional IRA is $5,000 for 2009 and 2010. Taxpayers over age 50 can make an additional $1,000 catch-up contribution. If the taxpayer has both a traditional and a Roth IRA, the maximum contributed to both accounts is aggregated and may not exceed these limits.

To make a contribution to a traditional IRA, the taxpayer must have earned income. The maximum allowable contribution to a traditional IRA in any one tax year is the lesser of the taxpayer's earned income or the contribution limit (including the catch-up amount) set forth by law. If a taxpayer is married and has a non-working spouse, a spousal IRA can be set up and the same amounts can be contributed to the spousal IRA even if the spouse does not have any earned income and the working spouse has sufficient earned income to cover both contributions.

Contributions to traditional IRAs that are in excess of the allowable amount are subject to a six percent penalty. In addition, contributions must be made by the tax-filing deadline for the year usually April 15, (not including extensions).

### Deductibility of Contributions

Traditional IRA contributions are fully deductible each year for all individuals who are not active participants in qualified retirement plans. This rule is modified, however, when a spousal traditional IRA is created, and one spouse is an active participant while the other is not.

Active participants in retirement plans may still be able to make tax-deductible contributions to an IRA provided that their adjusted gross income does not exceed specified limits. An "active participant" in a defined contribution pension plan is any person who contributes to the plan (in a cash or deferred arrangement) or who receives an allocation from the employer for the plan year (including forfeitures). Any employee eligible to participate in a defined benefit plan is also considered to be an active participant, even if he or she declines to be covered by the plan.

Once an individual is considered an active participant in a retirement plan, deductible traditional IRA contributions are phased out over specified AGI ranges. The AGI ranges for 2009 and 2010 are shown in Exhibit 6.5.

The deductibility threshold for a traditional IRA is increased for a non-active participant spouse. For purposes of determining the non-active participant spouse's IRA deduction, the AGI phase-out range is $166,000 - $176,000 (2009). To qualify for this increased phase-out range, the spouses must be filing their income tax return jointly.

Those with an AGI below the lower limit can make a fully deductible traditional IRA contribution. The deductibility of the contribution is phased out for AGI between the noted limits. Once the taxpayer has income equal to or in excess of the upper limit, no deductible IRA contribution can be made.

EXHIBIT 6.5

| Taxpayer is not an active participant | Taxpayer(s) is an active participant | | One spouse is an active participant, while the other spouse is not |
|---|---|---|---|
| No AGI Limit | Single | **AGI Phaseout** | The spouse who is not an active participant may have a deductible traditional IRA contribution as long as their joint AGI does not exceed $176,000. The deductible IRA contribution is phased out between $166,000 - $176,000 for 2009 and between $167,000 - $177,000 for 2010. |
| | | $55,000 - $65,000 (2009) $56,000 - $66,000 (2010) | |
| | MFJ | **AGI Phaseout** | |
| | | $89,000 - $109,000 (2009) $89,000 - $109,000 (2010) | |

Ryan, a recent college graduate, had AGI this year of $45,000. Ryan is single, and has no dependents. If Ryan made a contribution of $5,000 to a traditional IRA this year, he would be able to deduct the entire contribution, since his AGI is below the phaseout threshold.

EXAMPLE 6.2

Liam, a single individual, has AGI of $60,000. If Liam makes a contribution to a traditional IRA in 2009, he will be able to deduct $2,500 (since Liam's AGI is exactly half way through the phaseout range, he can only deduct 50% of the otherwise allowable amount, or $2,500). The first $2,500 of the IRA contribution could be made to a traditional IRA, but if Liam wishes to make additional contributions, the additional amounts (up to another $2,500) should be made to a Roth IRA.

EXAMPLE 6.3

$$\text{Reduction} = \text{Contribution Limit} \times \frac{\text{AGI} - \text{Lower Limit}}{\text{Phaseout Range}}$$

$$\text{2009 Reduction} = \$5,000 \times \frac{(\$60,000 - \$55,000)}{\$10,000} = \$2,500$$

$$\text{2010 Reduction} = \$5,000 \times \frac{(\$60,000 - \$56,000)}{\$10,000} = \$2,000$$

The phaseout range for tax deductibility of IRA contributions for married filing jointly taxpayers is twice the phaseout range for single individuals. Therefore, the phaseout reduction calculation for married filing jointly is as follows:

$$\text{MFJ Reduction} = \text{Contribution Limit} \times \frac{\text{AGI} - \text{Lower Limit}}{\$20,000}$$

**EXAMPLE 6.4**

Chris and Kelly, both age 35, are married and filed a joint return for 2009. Chris earned a salary of $110,000 in 2009 and is covered by his employer's 401(k) plan. Chris and Kelly earned interest of $15,000 in 2009 from a joint savings account. Kelly is not employed, and the couple had no other income. On April 15, 2010, Chris contributed $5,000 to an IRA for himself and $5,000 to an IRA for Kelly. The maximum allowable IRA deduction on the 2009 joint return is $5,000. Chris will not be permitted to make a tax deductible IRA contribution for the year, since he is an active participant in his employer's plan and the couple's AGI for the year exceeds the phaseout threshold. Kelly, however, will be permitted to make a tax-deductible traditional IRA contribution since she is not an active participant in a qualified plan, and the couple's AGI fell below the increased threshold (that applies to non-participant spouses) of $166,000 ($167,000 for 2010). Since Chris cannot make a tax-deductible traditional IRA contribution, and the AGI on his tax return this year falls below $166,000 (the lower end of the Roth IRA phaseout range and $167,000 for 2010), Chris should place his IRA contribution in a Roth IRA because he will get tax-free compounding and tax-free distributions in the Roth. He cannot get a deduction with the Roth. Kelly should consider whether Kelly's IRA should be a Roth, but if they want the current income tax deduction they will have to use the traditional IRA.

Taxpayers who cannot make income tax-deductible contributions to a traditional IRA may still make nondeductible contributions to nondeductible IRAs to achieve the tax benefits of income tax deferral on the earnings growth. Those electing to do this should file Form 8606 each year to keep track of their adjusted basis in the IRA so that the basis can be distributed to them tax-free when distributions begin.

### Roth IRAs

A better alternative than a nondeductible IRA for many taxpayers above the traditional IRA phaseout range but below the Roth IRA phaseout range (see Exhibit 6.6) is to make IRA contributions to a Roth IRA. Contributions made to a Roth IRA are not deductible, but the growth and withdrawals are tax-free for qualified distributions made after the age of 59½. Roth

IRAs do not have required mandatory distributions, therefore unlike traditional IRAs, there is no penalty tax on insufficient withdrawals after age 70½.

## Contributions

The maximum allowable contribution to a Roth IRA is $5,000 for 2009 and 2010. Taxpayers over age 50 can make an additional $1,000 catch-up contribution. As stated previously, if the taxpayer has both a traditional and a Roth IRA, the maximum contributed to both accounts is aggregated and may not exceed these limits.

## Quick Quiz 6.3

**Highlight the answer to these questions:**

1. An unmarried taxpayer can make a contribution to an IRA, even if he does not have earned income.
   a. True
   b. False

2. Active participation in a retirement plan does not affect the deductibility of a traditional IRA.
   a. True
   b. False

3. The deductibility threshold for a traditional IRA is increased for a non-active participant spouse.
   a. True
   b. False

4. Contributions to traditional and Roth IRAs that are in excess of the allowable amount are subject to a 4% penalty.
   a. True
   b. False

False, False, True, False.

To make a contribution to a Roth IRA, the taxpayer must have earned income. The maximum allowable contribution to a Roth IRA in any one tax year is the lesser of the taxpayer's earned income or the contribution limit (including catch-up amount) set forth by law. If a taxpayer is married and has a non-working spouse, a spousal IRA can be set up and the same amounts can be contributed to the spousal IRA even if the spouse does not have any earned income as long as the working spouse has sufficient earned income.

Contributions to Roth IRAs that are in excess of the allowable amount are subject to a six percent penalty. In addition, contributions must be made by the tax-filing deadline for the year (not including extensions).

The 2009 and 2010 AGI phaseout ranges for Roth IRAs are identified in Exhibit 6.6.

The phaseout ranges for single taxpayers and for married taxpayers filing jointly are increasing each year, but the phaseout range for those married filing separately is static. Distributions from Roth IRAs will be tax-free if the account has been open for at least five years and the distribution occurs after the taxpayer reaches age 59½.

EXHIBIT 6.6 **ROTH IRA PHASEOUTS**

| Filing Status | 2009 | 2010 |
| --- | --- | --- |
| Single | $105,000 - $120,000 | $105,000 - $120,000 |
| Married Filing Jointly | $166,000 - $176,000 | $167,000 - $177,000 |
| Married Filing Separately | $0 - $10,000 | $0 - $10,000 |

## MOVING EXPENSES

One of the few business related deductions that employees can take as above-the-line deductions is the moving expense deduction. Most employee-incurred business expenses that are not reimbursed by an employer are deducted as miscellaneous itemized deductions subject to a two percent floor. However, moving expenses are treated as an above-the-line deduction.

Many employees will not be able to deduct moving expenses; if an employer reimburses moving expenses through use of an accountable expense reimbursement plan, or when the employer pays for moving expenses directly. There is no out-of-pocket cost for the employee in these situations, and hence, no deduction is available to the employee (since the company's expenditure will qualify for a business expense deduction). An **accountable expense reimbursement plan** is one that only reimburses employees for the actual expenses incurred, and requires the employee to substantiate the expenditures by producing receipts.

 *Key Concepts*

Underline/highlight the answers to these questions as you read:

1. Name the expenses that are deductible as moving expenses.

2. Explain who is entitled to deduct student loan interest incurred on qualified student loans.

3. Describe the requirements for classifying a payment as alimony.

4. Explain the consequences of alimony recapture.

If an employer does not have an accountable expense reimbursement plan, moving expense deductions may need to be claimed on the tax return. This situation normally arises when an employer provides the employee with an allowance for moving expenses, but does not require substantiation of expenditures. In this instance, the allowance will be included in the employee's W-2 income and the employee can offset this income by claiming the moving expense deduction. Note that even if the employee spends all of the allowance on moving expenses, this will not necessarily result in a deduction that completely offsets the recognizable income. Since the allowance is included in W-2 income, it is subject to payroll taxes, increasing the tax liability for the employee, and some expenses allowed for, may not be deductible.

EXAMPLE 6.5

John was recently transferred from the California office of his company to the Boston office. His company gave him a $12,000 allowance for his move, and did not require him to substantiate his expenses. Since the expense reimbursement plan was not accountable, the $12,000 was included in John's W-2 income. The actual deductible expenses that John incurred in the move were $10,500, which he took as a moving expense above-the-line deduction on his personal tax return. The difference between the allowance and the actual expenses John incurred will be subject to income tax, and the entire amount of the moving expenses included in his W-2 income is subject to payroll taxes.

Sometimes when an employer provides an expense allowance or limits the total amount of reimbursement available under a qualified expense reimbursement plan, the actual expenses exceed the inclusion in income. In this case, the employee will have a net reduction in gross income, resulting in some tax savings.

EXAMPLE 6.6

Continuing our example above, assume that John's actual deductible moving expenses were $14,000. While $12,000 will be included in John's income, he will be able to take an above-the-line deduction for $14,000, thereby reducing his gross income by $2,000. John will be subject to payroll taxes on the $12,000 included in his W-2 income.

EXAMPLE 6.7

Instead of having a moving expense allowance, John's company has a qualified expense reimbursement plan, but limits the reimbursable moving expense to $12,000. John incurred $14,000 in actual deductible moving expenses, and his employer reimbursed $12,000 of those costs. John can still deduct the additional $2,000 of expenses as a moving expense deduction, and will not have to pay any payroll tax on the $12,000 reimbursement, since it was made through a qualified expense reimbursement plan. John will have to file Form 3903 with his tax return, which details non-reimbursed employee moving expenses.

Moving expenses that can be deducted include costs associated with moving household goods and personal effects, storage of these items while in transit, and travel expenses for one trip by the taxpayer and members of the household. Expenses that cannot be deducted include meals during travel (these are considered personal expenses), the expenses of buying or selling a home (these expenses are either added to basis or subtracted from the amount realized in a transaction), temporary living expenses, and house-hunting expenses. The deduction is available to those moving for an existing or new employer, but in either case, it must involve full-time employment at the new location.

To qualify for a moving expense deduction, a **distance test** must be met. The distance between the old home and the new job location must be at least 50 miles greater than the distance between the old home and the old job location. Recognize that it is not important where taxpayer moves to, only that the distance test is met.

**EXAMPLE 6.8**

John and Patty have lived in their current home for the past 10 years. John used to commute to Boston, a distance of 25 miles, for work each day, and recently received and accepted a job offer at another company located 90 miles from their current home. The value of John and Patty's home has increased by about $500,000 and they would like to stay in the same community so that their children can continue to go to school there. They have been looking at a home a few streets away from theirs which would give the family a bit more room, and give them a private backyard. If John and Patty sell their current home and move a few streets away, their moving expenses will be deductible, since the distance test is met (the distance between their old home and the new job location is 90 miles, which is more than 50 miles greater than the distance between their old home and the old job location).

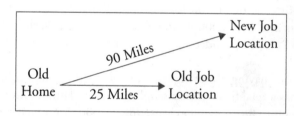

In addition to the distance test, a time test must also be met. The time test requires a full time employee to work at the new location for 39 weeks out of the 12 month period following the work location change. Self-employed individuals must work in the new community for 78 weeks during the 24 month period following the change in work location. The time test is imposed to ensure that the move is work related, and was not primarily for personal reasons.

## PENALTY ON EARLY WITHDRAWAL OF SAVINGS

Penalties paid on early withdrawal of savings are deductible as an adjustment to income. Typically, penalties are imposed when an individual who has a Certificate of Deposit with a bank cashes in that certificate early. The penalty constitutes a forfeiture of interest. Under the doctrine of constructive receipt, money set aside for a taxpayer is taxable to the taxpayer in the year it is credited to their account, not the year the taxpayer receives the interest payment. Often, a CD can be purchased for a greater than one year maturity, in which case the bank will send the taxpayer a Form 1099 at the end of each year indicating the amount of interest that has been credited to the taxpayer's account, and the taxpayer must include that amount in their income tax return for that year, and pay tax on the interest. The allowance of a deduction for a penalty on the early withdrawal of savings simply reverses the inclusion of interest income on the CD when it is cashed in early. The penalty must be reported as an adjustment to income, however, and cannot be used to directly offset interest income in the gross income section of the tax return (including the interest reported by the bank on a CD that was cashed in early).

## EDUCATOR EXPENSES

Teachers in elementary and secondary schools (grades Kindergarten through 12th grade), principals, aides, and counselors may deduct up to $250 of out-of-pocket expenses paid as an adjustment to gross income (on line 23 of Form 1040). Expenses that can be deducted include items such as books, supplies, computers, computer equipment, and materials used in the classroom. To qualify for the deduction, an individual must have spent more than 900 hours during a school year as a K-12 educator. Expenses in excess of the $250 above-the-line maximum may be deducted below-the-line, as an unreimbursed employee business expense (a miscellaneous itemized deduction subject to the two percent floor, which will be discussed in the next chapter).

## STUDENT LOAN INTEREST

Up to $2,500 of student loan interest incurred on qualified student loans may be deducted as an adjustment to gross income. The deduction is available for interest on loans for the benefit of the taxpayer, the taxpayer's spouse, or the taxpayer's dependent that were incurred while the student was either the taxpayer, a spouse, or a dependent. To be eligible for the deduction, the taxpayer must have a primary obligation to repay the debt, and must actually make interest payments during the year (deferred interest payments are not deductible until they are paid, since all individuals are cash-basis taxpayers).

## DEDUCTIBILITY OF STUDENT LOAN INTEREST

EXHIBIT 6.7

| LOAN MADE BY | LOAN REPAID BY | IS IT DEDUCTIBLE? |
|---|---|---|
| Parent | Parent | Yes |
| | Student | No |
| Student | Parent | No |
| | Student | Yes |

The ability to deduct student loan interest is phased-out for higher income taxpayers, and the phaseout range is indexed for inflation. Individuals with modified adjusted gross income (MAGI) below the lower limit may take a deduction for student loan interest up to $2,500. The deduction is phased out ratably over the phaseout range, and once MAGI reaches the upper limit, no deduction for student loan interest is permitted. Modified adjusted gross income (MAGI) for purposes of determining the student loan interest deduction phaseout is calculated by taking the taxpayers AGI and adding back the foreign earned income exclusion plus the income exclusion for certain U.S. Possessions and Puerto Rico, as well as the deductions taken for tuition and fees and for qualified U.S. production activities. Qualified production activities include manufacturing, producing, growing, and extracting tangible personal property, computer software, and sound recordings, and the construction and substantial renovation of real property including infrastructure.

EXHIBIT 6.8

## STUDENT LOAN INTEREST DEDUCTIBLE PHASEOUT

| Filing Status | 2009 | 2010 |
|---|---|---|
| Single | $60,000 - $75,000 | $60,000 - $75,000 |
| Married Filing Jointly | $120,000 - $150,000 | $120,000 - $150,000 |
| Married Filing Separately | $0 | $0 |

Married individuals filing separately and dependents are not eligible to take the student loan interest deduction.

In order to be deductible, the interest must have been incurred on a qualified education loan. A qualified education loan is one that is taken out to cover qualified education expenses, which include tuition, fees, books, equipment, transportation and room and board incurred to attend a post-secondary school or college eligible to participate in the Department of Education student loan programs.

To the extent that educational expenses are paid with pre-tax or tax-free benefits, such as with distributions from Section 529 plans, series EE Savings Bonds, or employer provided and veterans educational benefits, qualified education expenses must first be reduced by these amounts before determining the amount of interest that is deductible under the Student Loan interest deduction.

Furthermore, the loan must have been incurred for an individual who was at least a half-time student (a student who maintained a credit load of at least one-half of the normal full-time credit load).

### ALIMONY PAID

Generally, alimony is deducted from income (as an adjustment to income, or an above-the-line deduction) by the individual making the payment (payor), and included in the income of the individual receiving the payment (payee). Therefore, alimony generally receives pass-through tax treatment – the person who winds up with the cash has to pay the tax.

To achieve pass-through tax treatment, however, the payments must actually constitute alimony. IRC Section 71(b) sets forth the requirements necessary to classify payments as alimony. These requirements include:
1. the payments must be in cash or cash equivalent (such as a check or money order);
2. the payments must be required by a court decree;
3. the court decree must not specify that the payments are "not alimony;"
4. the payments must cease at the death of the recipient;
5. the payments may not be disguised child support payments;
6. the former spouses may not be members of the same household; and
7. the parties may not file a joint income tax return (married filing jointly).

Child support payments are not alimony – they are a right of the child to receive support from the parent, and are therefore not deductible as alimony even though the payments are typically made to the former spouse. If alimony payments are structured to decline when a child reaches he age of majority, the decline in payments will be assumed to be child-support and not eductible alimony, even if the court decree refers to the payment as alimony. Technically, if the ayments are reduced within six months before or after the child attains the age of majority, that ortion of the payment will be presumed to be child support and will not be treated as eductible alimony (see Treasury Regulation 1.71-1T(c)Q-A18 for more information).

EXAMPLE 6.9

Charlie and Jane recently divorced. They had been married for 15 years, and had two children, Erin (14 years old) and Brian (12 years old). Under the terms of the divorce decree, Charlie is required to pay Jane $2,000 per month in alimony for four years, $1,500 for the next two years, and $1,000 per month for the following two years. Charlie's alimony deduction each month will be $1,000. Even though the divorce decree classified the payment as alimony, the payment was reduced by $500 when each child reached the age of 18, so $1,000 of the payment ($500 x 2) will be reclassified as child support for income tax purposes.

RC Section 1041 states that all property transfers between spouses and incident to a divorce are onsidered to be nontaxable exchanges for income tax purposes, and therefore result in a carry-ver basis. Property settlements of divorcing spouses fit into this rule, and do not result in ncome tax benefits. Due to the pass-through nature of alimony payments, some individuals may e encouraged to re-characterize property settlements related to divorce as alimony payments. This is especially true when one spouse (payor) is in a high income tax bracket (and can use the ax deduction), and the other spouse (payee) is in a low income tax bracket. Characterizing a roperty settlement as deductible alimony would permit the divorcing spouses to achieve a tax-rbitrage due to the different tax rates paid by each spouse.

While the temporary regulations covering alimony payments have indicated that it is possible to lassify a single payment from one divorcing spouse to another as alimony, several tax court decisions have come to the conclusion that a single alimony payment is "in the nature of a property settlement," and have denied an alimony deduction in such cases.

The **alimony recapture** rules are designed to prevent taxpayers from transforming more complex property settlements into deductible alimony. Under the alimony recapture rules, the first three post-separation years are examined to determine if the alimony payments claimed as deductions on the payor's tax return are really disguised property settlements. A mathematical test is employed to make this determination. Alimony recapture will only be an issue if (1) alimony payments decline during the first three post-separation years, and (2) the alimony payment in years two and three decrease by more than $15,000 per year. The mathematical test will determine the amount of excess alimony in the first and second post-separation years. Any excess alimony is added to the payor's income in the third post-separation year, and is deducted from the payee's income in the third post-secondary year. Prior year tax returns are not amended and refiled to take excess alimony into account.

An amount for excess alimony is determined for the first and second post-separation years (the third post-separation year serves as the base for the calculation). The sum of these amounts is added to the payor's income in the third post-separation year, and subtracted from the payee's income for the third post-separation year. The calculation of excess alimony is determined as follows:

## Quick Quiz 6.4

**Highlight the answer to these questions:**

1. If an employer reimburses an employee for moving expenses, the employee may not claim a deduction based on the same expenses.
   a. True
   b. False

2. Temporary living expenses may be deducted as moving expenses.
   a. True
   b. False

3. Educator expenses in excess of $250 may be deducted below-the-line, as an unreimbursed employee business expense.
   a. True
   b. False

4. Alimony recapture is only an issue if alimony payments increase during the first three post-separation years.
   a. True
   b. False

True, False, True, False.

1. For the second post-separation year, excess alimony (R2) equals the amount in excess of year 3 alimony (P3) plus $15,000 over the year 2 alimony (P2). If the result is zero or negative, it is not taken into account in determining the total amount of excess alimony. Stated mathematically, the formula is:

$$R2 = P2 - (P3 + 15{,}000)$$

2. For the first-post separation year, excess alimony (R1) takes into account the alimony payments in years 1 and 2, as well as the excess alimony from year 2. If the result is zero or negative, it is not taken into account in determining the total amount of excess alimony. Stated mathematically, the formula is:

$$R1 = P1 - \left( \frac{P2 - R2 + P3}{2} + \$15{,}000 \right)$$

3. Add the results from steps 1 and 2. This equals the total amount of excess alimony.

EXAMPLE 6.10

Karen and Cory were recently divorced. In the first year after their divorce, Cory pays Karen $80,000; in the second year, he pays her $50,000; and in the third year, he pays her $20,000. The excess alimony in Year 2 (R2) is equal to $15,000.

$50,000 – ($20,000 + $15,000) = $15,000.

The excess alimony in Year 1 (R1) is equal to $37,500.

$$\$80,000 - \left( \frac{\$50,000 - \$15,000 + \$20,000}{2} + \$15,000 \right) = \$37,500$$

The total excess alimony is $52,500.

Remember, the purpose of alimony is to provide support. It probably should not decrease substantially in future years and cannot be paid to the payee or the payee's estate after the payee's death.

If alimony payments decreased by more than $15,000 per year over the first three years of payments, a shortcut formula can be used. The formula is:

$$R3 \ = \ P1 + P2 - 2P3 - \$37{,}500$$

where:
R3 = Recapture in year 3
P1 = Alimony payment in year 1
P2 = Alimony payment in year 2
P3 = Alimony payment in year 3

Please note that this shortcut formula will not work unless the alimony payments decline by $15,000 or more each year during the first three years of payments.

EXAMPLE 6.11

Using the same facts as presented in Example 6.10 along with the formula presented above, excess alimony is calculated as:

R3 = $80,000 + $50,000 - 2($20,000) - $37,500
R3 = $52,500

Note that this answer is the same as the answer derived using the long-method since the alimony payments declined by more than $15,000 per year.

EXHIBIT 6.9

## SUMMARY OF ABOVE-THE-LINE DEDUCTIONS FOR INDIVIDUALS

- MSAs
- HSAs
- Trade or Business Expenses
- IRAs
- Moving Expenses

- Penalty or Early Withdrawal
- Educator Expenses
- Student Loan Interest
- Alimony Paid

# DEDUCTION ISSUES FOR EMPLOYERS AND EMPLOYEES

## TYPES OF BUSINESSES AND GENERAL DEDUCTION RULES

For federal income tax purposes, there are only three types of businesses: Corporations, Partnerships, and Sole Proprietorships. Regardless of what state law calls a particular business organization, it must fit into one of these categories for federal income tax purposes.

Corporations are created under state law, and give the business owner the advantage of limited liability protection. The creation of a corporation involves a formal process, and, once in existence, a corporation is treated as a person in the eyes of the law. Regular corporations are taxed under Subchapter C of the Internal Revenue Code, and are therefore referred to as C corporations. Since a C corporation is separate and distinct from its owners (it is treated as a separate entity), it is subject to tax on its income, and must file its own income tax return (a form 1120). When a C corporation distributes some of its earnings to its shareholders (the owners of the corporation), the distribution is referred to as a dividend. Dividends are taxable to the shareholder when received. Under current law, qualified dividends are taxed at a flat 15 percent rate, and non-qualified dividends are taxed at ordinary income tax rates.

C corporations, as separate taxable entities, will deduct all ordinary, necessary, and reasonable expenses incurred in the production of income for the company on its own income tax return. The deductions for these expenses do not pass through to the owners of the corporation.

Once organized, the owners of a corporation can make an election under Subchapter S of the Internal Revenue Code to have the corporation taxed as a pass-through entity. When this election has been made, the corporation is referred to as an S corporation. S corporations are corporations, and are treated as entities distinct and separate from their owners, and must still file a separate income tax return (a Form 1120S), but the incidence of federal income tax changes. Instead of having the corporation pay tax on its operating income, the operating income is "passed through" to the owners the year it is earned, and the shareholders will report their proportionate share of corporate operating income on their individual income tax returns. This does not mean that the owners actually receive a cash distribution from the corporation – whether or not the corporation distributes anything to the owners, the owners must pay tax on their pro-rata share of the corporate income in the year it is earned.

The advantage of S corporation status is that corporate income is taxed only once – on the individual tax returns of the owners. Distributions issued from S corporations are not subject to tax, since the owners paid tax on the corporate operating income when it was earned (whether or not the operating income was distributed). From an operating standpoint, S corporations look a lot like partnerships, which pass through all of their income to their owners, but some attributes of corporate taxation still apply to S corporations.

Like C corporations, S corporations deduct all the ordinary, necessary, and reasonable expenses incurred in generating corporate income on the S corporation tax return. Only the net profit or loss flows through to the owners to report on their individual income tax return. There is one major exception to this rule, however. An S corporation cannot deduct medical insurance costs or pension contributions for greater than two percent owners of the corporation. These amounts are passed through to the individual shareholder and are deducted as adjustments to income (above-the-line deductions) on the individual shareholder's personal income tax return. Medical insurance costs and pension plan contributions for employees and less than two percent shareholders are deducted on the S corporation income tax return.

Any organization created under state law that is not a corporation or a trust, and that has two or more owners, is classified as a partnership for federal income tax purposes. The term partnership as used in federal income tax implies general partnerships, limited partnerships (LPs), family limited partnerships (FLPs), limited liability partnerships (LLPs), limited liability companies (LLCs), Limited Liability Limited Partnerships (LLLPs), and any other organization that meets the above criteria. Partnerships must file informational tax returns (Form 1065), but are not responsible for paying any federal income tax. All of the ordinary, necessary, and reasonable expenses of partnerships are deducted on the partnership tax return, and it is only the net income of the partnership that flows through to, and is subject to tax in the hands of, the owner. Partners may not be treated as employees of the company, however. Similar to the treatment of more than two percent owners of S corporations, medical insurance costs and pension contributions cannot be deducted as business expenses on the partnership's income tax return, but are separately reported to the partners, who may deduct them as an adjustment to income (above-the-line). Furthermore, partners are not classified as employees of the business, so payments for their services are not deducted on the partnership tax return. Instead, they are classified as guaranteed payments and are passed through to the owners to be individually reported on the owner's tax return.

Any organization created under state law that is not a corporation or a trust, and that has only one owner, is classified as a sole-proprietorship for federal income tax purposes. Sole proprietorships include traditional sole proprietorships, and single-member LLCs. A sole proprietor files Schedule C with his personal income tax return to report the net income associated with business operations. All necessary, reasonable, and ordinary business expenses incurred in the production of the sole proprietorship's income are deducted on Schedule C, and only the net income or loss from the activity is included in the gross income on the owner's personal income tax return. As is the case with all other business entities, business expense deductions for sole proprietors are above-the-line deductions, since they directly offset the income generated through the conduct of the trade or business activity. Sole proprietors are not permitted, however, to deduct medical insurance costs or pension contributions against business income, but must report those amounts separately as adjustments to income (above-the-line deductions).

## COMMON DEDUCTIONS FOR EMPLOYERS AND THE SELF-EMPLOYED

As a threshold matter, to qualify as deductions for federal income tax purposes, a business related expense must be ordinary, necessary, and reasonable. If the expenditure fails to meet all three of these requirements, it will be disallowed by the IRS.

An **ordinary expense** is one that is typically incurred in the normal, usual, or customary conduct of businesses in the same line of operations. As discussed in other areas of this textbook, expenses usually cannot be capital in nature. Capital expenditures generally must be capitalized, and can be deducted (through the use of cost recovery methods, such as depreciation, depletion, or amortization) over the useful life of the asset, although there are some provisions that enable a small business owner to deduct an expense that would otherwise be capitalized. Only expenses that are ordinarily incurred in the conduct of the given trade or business will qualify as a current deduction.

Assuming that an expense is considered to be ordinarily incurred in the conduct of a trade or business, the taxpayer must demonstrate that the expense is necessary. A **necessary expense** is one that a prudent business person would incur in the conduct of business. For example, lavish travel and entertainment expenses are rarely considered to be necessary expenses associated with the conduct of business. Only those travel and entertainment expenses that are both ordinary and necessary will qualify for a deduction.

both the ordinary and necessary requirements have been met, the taxpayer must still demonstrate that the expense in question is reasonable. Reasonableness is a question of fact, and overlaps with the ordinary and necessary requirements. An expense that may be ordinary and necessary in the conduct of business may not be reasonable if it does not contribute to the goal of generating income for the business activity.

## Fringe Benefits

**Fringe benefits** include non-cash compensation provided by an employer to an employee. An employer can deduct the costs of providing qualified fringe benefits to employees without causing the value received by the employee to be included in the employee's income.

Perhaps the most well-known fringe benefit provided by employers is insurance coverage for the employees, including accident and health plans, Health Savings Accounts and Medical Savings Accounts, most long-term care plans, and life insurance.

For health insurance and long-term care plans, the employer can pay the premium on behalf of the employee, and the employee will not have to include the benefit received in his taxable income. Recall that, generally, when someone takes a tax deduction, someone else must include the same amount in income. This rule does not apply to employer provided health insurance. Furthermore, the Economic Benefit doctrine, which requires economic benefits conferred on an employee to be included in taxable income, does not apply to medical insurance. Congress has provided a specific exemption for the inclusion of the economic benefit received by an employee from employer payments of health insurance premiums in Code Section 106. Furthermore, benefits received under these plans by employees are not included in taxable income provided that the benefit received does not exceed the cost of the health services provided.

When group term insurance is provided to employees, the employer can deduct the premium paid for the coverage. The first $50,000 of coverage will not be taxable to the employee provided that the benefit is nondiscriminatory, but any coverage in excess of $50,000 will be considered an economic benefit received by the employee and the imputed premium cost will be included in the employee's income. This exception only applies to employees and is not available to partners.

Other examples of fringe benefits that can be provided by an employer without requiring the employees to recognize income include qualified transportation expenses (as discussed in Chapter 5), meals and lodging furnished on the employer's premises for the convenience of the employer, qualified educational assistance plans (providing benefits of up to $5,250 per year), qualified adoption assistance and retirement planning services.

## Self-Employed Retirement Contributions and Health Insurance Costs

Sole proprietors, partners, and more than two percent owners of S corporations are considered to be self-employed individuals. As noted earlier, the costs of providing retirement planning benefits or medical insurance cannot be deducted from business income for the self-employed. Instead, retirement plan contributions are deducted as an adjustment to income (above-the-line) on the personal tax return of the self-employed individual.

Self-employed retirement contributions made to qualified defined benefit or defined contribution pension plans, or simplified employee pension plans (SEPs) and Simplified

Incentive Match Plans for Employees (SIMPLE plans) are deductible as an adjustment income on the self-employed individual's personal income tax return.

Medical insurance premiums are likewise deducted as an adjustment to income on the self employed individual's personal tax return. Under current law, the deduction for medic insurance premiums is not limited, but long-term care insurance premium deductions a limited based on the age of the individual as of the end of the tax year.

### Social Security and Self-Employment Tax Costs

Self-employed individuals, like all employees, must pay Social Security taxes. Unlike employee who only pay half of the applicable Social Security and Medicare taxes (the other half is paid k the employer), a self-employed individual must pay both the employee and the employ portions of Social Security and Medicare taxes. The tax equals 15.3 percent (12.4 percent fe Social Security, and 2.9 percent for Medicare) of income up to the Social Security wage ba ($106,800 for 2009 and 2010), and 2.9 percent on income over the Social Security wage base.

When a business pays half of the Social Security taxes on behalf of an employee, the business entitled to deduct that expense since it constitutes an ordinary, necessary, and reasonable expens in the conduct of the trade or business. To give equal treatment to self-employed individuals, th Code allows self-employed individuals to deduct one half of self-employment taxes paid as a adjustment to income (above the line) on their personal income tax return.

### Investigation of Business Expenditures

An often overlooked business deduction is the ability to deduct the costs of investigating th purchase of a new business line. The amount of the deduction depends on two factors: (1 whether the expenses are incurred in the investigation of purchasing a business in the same lir of business, and (2) whether the new business is actually acquired.

If the new business is not acquired, no deduction is permissible.

If the new business is acquired, the deduction depends on whether or not the business acquired in the same line of business as the current trade or business operation. If a new, similar type c business is acquired, all of the investigation of business expenses are fully deductible. If a nev but different line of business is acquired, the expenses are subject to the same capitalization rule as a new line of business. In the case of a new (and unrelated) line of business, up to $5,000 c start up costs (reduced (but not below zero) by the amount the start up expenditures excee $50,000) can be deducted in the year that the new active trade or business begins its operation Start up organizational costs in excess of $5,000 are amortized for 180 months beginning wit the month the new business begins its operations.

## Home Office Deduction for Business Owners

In some cases, a taxpayer who uses part of his home for the conduct of a trade or business is entitled to take a deduction for costs associated with business use of the home. Expenses must be prorated between personal and business use based on the percentage of the home that qualifies for the home office deduction, and only those expenses allocated to the business use of the home are deductible as a business expense. Some of the expenses that can be claimed for the home office include mortgage interest, real estate taxes, utilities (such as electric, oil or gas, and security costs), homeowners insurance, casualty losses, maintenance and repairs, and depreciation. Any expenses incurred by a taxpayer that benefit only the portion of the home used for business purposes are deductible in full (they do not have to be prorated between business and personal use).

The ability to take a home office deduction depends on whether the taxpayer is a business owner or an employee. If the taxpayer owns a business, a portion of the home must be used regularly and exclusively as a principal place of business, as a place to meet clients in the normal course of business, or in connection with the business if the home office is not included in a separate structure that is detached from the taxpayer's principal residence. If one of these use tests is met, a self-employed business owner may deduct home office expenses against income generated by the business, but the deduction of home office expenses cannot cause the business to show a loss for the tax year.

If the taxpayer is an employee rather than a business owner, the taxpayer must meet an additional use test to take a deduction for a home office. The use of the home office must be for the "convenience of the employer," not just helpful and appropriate for the taxpayer.

A key to the availability of the home office deduction is use of a portion of the home *exclusively* for business purposes. If the space is used for both business and personal purposes, no deduction is permitted. There are two exceptions to the exclusivity requirement. The first exception deals with storage of inventory or product samples. Provided that storage space or inventory is used regularly for business purposes, and the home is the only fixed location for a retail or wholesale business, a deduction is permitted as long as the space used is identifiable as space separate from areas used for personal use. The second exception deals with day care facilities run from the home of a taxpayer. Taxpayers who run day care facilities may deduct costs associated with the

### Quick Quiz 6.5

**Highlight the answer to these questions:**

1. An S corporation cannot deduct medical insurance costs or pension contributions for greater than 2% owners of the corporation.
   a. True
   b. False

2. An ordinary expense is one that is typically incurred in the normal conduct of businesses in the same line of operations.
   a. True
   b. False

3. The costs of investigating the purchase of a new business line are deductible regardless of whether the new line of business is actually acquired.
   a. True
   b. False

True, True, False.

business use of the home even if the same space is used for personal purposes during nonbusiness hours.

When a taxpayer claims a home office deduction, depreciation is taken on the portion of the home used for business purposes. The depreciation method that must be used is 39 year straight line depreciation (since that portion of the home is being used for commercial purposes). As depreciation deductions are taken, the taxpayer's basis in their home decreases, and, upon sale, gain on the home to the extent of depreciation taken is considered to be unrecaptured Section 1250 depreciation subject to a special tax rate of 25 percent. The Section 121 exclusion on the sale of a principal residence cannot be used to offset the portion of the gain that is classified as Unrecaptured Section 1250 gain. Gain in excess of depreciation taken will be capital gain, and may be offset by the Section 121 exclusion on the sale of a principal residence (allowing a taxpayer to exclude up to $250,000 in gain, if single, or $500,000 in gain, if married on the sale of the home, provided some additional requirements are met).

## DEDUCTIONS AND TAX PLANNING

In order to deduct an expense for income tax purposes, the expense must be incurred in the conduct of an individual's trade or business, or in a transaction entered into for profit. Personal expenses are generally not deductible (although some exceptions have been made for public policy reasons, such as the mortgage interest deduction, deduction for taxes paid to state and local governments, medical expenses, and casualty losses).

### Key Concepts

**Underline/highlight the answers to these questions as you read:**

1. Explain why it is more advantageous to classify expenses as business expenses rather than employee-related business expenses.

2. Describe the deductibility of investor expenses.

### FOR EMPLOYEES

As a review of this chapter indicates, deductions available to those workers classified as employees are relatively limited. An employee is permitted to take an above-the-line deduction for unreimbursed moving expenses and educator expenses up to $250, but other unreimbursed business expenses are deducted as a miscellaneous itemized deduction subject to the two percent floor.

The timing of some of these business related expenses can be controlled by an employee taking advantage of the cash basis reporting requirements imposed by the IRS. From a planning perspective, assuming that expenses will be incurred for business related purposes, an employee should attempt to incur those expenses in one tax year if possible, since it will be more likely that he or she will exceed the two percent of AGI floor that applies to miscellaneous itemized deductions.

EXAMPLE 6.12

Kasey is an employee at JarvCo, Inc. and he regularly incurs business related expenses that are not fully reimbursed by his employer. His AGI for this year is $100,000. This year, his employer did not reimburse him for $800 in travel expenses, $500 in professional dues and fees, and $500 for periodicals and books relating to Kasey's business activities, for a total of $1,800 in unreimbursed employee business expenses. If Kasey does not incur additional expenses, he will not receive any deduction since this amount does not exceed $2,000 (two percent of his AGI).

Beginning in January of next year, Kasey plans on taking three classes toward his MBA, at a cost of $6,000 (for all three classes). In addition, he can prepay his professional dues and fees, and renew his periodical and book subscriptions early if he would like to. If Kasey pays the tuition by December 31 (instead of January 20, the due date for tuition for the next term), and prepays $1,000 in professional dues, fees, and periodical and book subscriptions, he will increase his business related expense deduction to $8,800. Kasey will be able to take a Tier II miscellaneous itemized deduction for business related expenses of $6,800 this year (the portion that exceed two percent of his AGI). He should attempt to defer costs next year to the following tax year, so he can bunch expenses again in that year and potentially receive a higher overall business expense deduction.

## FOR BUSINESS OWNERS

Business owners have the advantage of being able to classify expenses related to the trade or business as above-the-line deductions. All ordinary, necessary, and reasonable expenses associated with the active conduct of a trade or business directly offset the income generated from that activity.

To the extent possible, individuals who own businesses should classify as many of their expenses as they can as business expenses instead of as employee related business expenses. This achieves two things: (1) it avoids the two percent floor on miscellaneous itemized deductions – there is no floor imposed on the business expenses incurred by owners of businesses, and (2) the expenses directly offset income from business operations, which has the impact of reducing AGI.

EXAMPLE 6.13

Rennie is principal of his Town's middle school, but also has a consulting practice in which he confers with boards of education and schools within the state on educational programs and functions. His consulting business is set up as a single-member LLC filing a Form 1040 Schedule C. Rennie subscribes to several journals, and purchases several timely books covering topics that apply to both his job as a principal and his consulting practice. Each year, he spends approximately

$1,500 on these materials. Assuming that Rennie's AGI is $100,000 for the current year, if he tried to take a deduction for these materials as an employee related unreimbursed business expense, he would receive no tax benefit (assuming he had no other miscellaneous itemized deductions). To get a tax benefit, he would have had to spend more than $2,000 (two percent of his AGI). Since these expenditures represent ordinary, necessary, and reasonable expenses for the conduct of his consulting practice, however, Rennie can deduct the cost against his consulting income. This deduction directly offsets income, and is therefore an above-the-line deduction that reduces Rennie's AGI. Furthermore, there is no floor that applies to business expense deductions, so Rennie can deduct the full $1,500 from his income this year on his Schedule C.

Remember that only those expenses that are ordinary, necessary, and reasonable may be deducted as business expenses. To the extent that a business owner can satisfy these requirements for an expenditure, he or she should deduct those expenses from the income of the business, and should not deduct them as an itemized deduction on his tax return.

| EXHIBIT 6.10 | SUMMARY OF ABOVE-THE-LINE BUSINESS DEDUCTIONS |
|---|---|

| | |
|---|---|
| • Ordinary | • Self-Employed Retirement and Health Costs |
| • Necessary | • Social Security Costs |
| • Reasonable | • Investigation of a Business |
| • Fringe Benefits | • Home Office Deduction |

## FOR INVESTORS

Like business owners, investors may deduct expenses that are necessary to generate profits. When the expenses are directly related to the production of income, such as when a taxpayer operates a rental real estate activity, those expenses are claimed directly against the income generated by the activity and therefore are above-the-line deductions that reduce the taxpayer's gross income.

As noted earlier, some investment expenses, such as those associated with ownership of a portfolio of intangible investment assets (such as stocks and bonds) are miscellaneous itemized deductions. Expenses in this category include investment advisory and custodial fees, the cost of preparing income tax returns, safe deposit rental fees, and the cost of receiving investment and tax advice. Itemized deductions are only advantageous, however, if the total deductions exceed the standard deduction. Furthermore, through the end of 2009 there is an indirect limitation on itemized deductions when the taxpayer's AGI exceeds the itemized deduction phaseout limitation (see our discussion on the overall limitation on itemized deductions).

To the extent possible, investors should keep track of their investment expenses and claim them as expenses on their tax returns. This is an area that is often overlooked by individual taxpayers.

## Quick Quiz 6.6

**Highlight the answer to these questions:**

1. Businesses owners should classify as many of their expenses as they can as business expenses in order to avoid the 2% floor on itemized deductions.
   a. True
   b. False

2. Investor expenses such as investment advisory and custodial fees and tax advice are subject to the 2% floor.
   a. True
   b. False

True, True.

# Key Terms

***Above-the-Line Deductions*** – Deduction for adjusted gross income, also known as adjustments to income.

***Accountable Expense Reimbursement Plan*** – A plan under which an employer reimburses employees for certain actually incurred expenses and requires the employee to substantiate the expenditures by producing receipts.

***Alimony Recapture*** – Rules designed to prevent taxpayers from transforming property settlements into deductible alimony payments.

***Below-the-Line Deductions*** – Deductions from adjusted gross income, also known as itemized deductions.

***Distance Test*** – In order to qualify for a moving expense deduction, the distance between the taxpayer's old home and new job location must be at least 50 miles greater than the distance between the old home and the old job location.

***Fringe Benefits*** – Non-cash benefits provided to an employee by an employer in addition to wages and salary.

***Health Savings Account (HSA)*** – Accounts that allow individuals who have high deductible health insurance plans to save on a tax-free basis to fund their medical expenses.

***Medical Savings Account (MSA)*** – Accounts authorized by HIPAA 1996 which allowed contributions to the account to grow tax-free if funds distributed from the account were used to pay for medical expenses.

***Necessary Expense*** – An expense that a prudent business person would incur in the conduct of business.

***Ordinary Expense*** – An expense that is typically incurred in the normal, usual, or customary conduct of businesses in the same line of operations.

1. Who is responsible for substantiating income tax deductions and how are income tax deductions substantiated?

2. Name and describe the two basic categories of deductions.

3. Explain why taxpayers generally prefer above-the-line deductions to below-the-line deductions.

4. Describe the consequences of contributing too much to an HSA.

5. In addition to general business expenses, what above-the-line deductions may be available to sole proprietors, partners, and greater than two percent owners of S corporations?

6. What are the requirements for making a deductible contribution to a traditional IRA?

7. Describe what does and does not qualify as a deductible moving expense.

8. Explain the distance test and the time test.

9. Describe how the deduction for a penalty on the early withdrawal of savings would affect a taxpayer who cashed in a CD before its maturity.

10. Explain the above-the-line deduction for educator expenses.

11. What are the requirements for deducting student loan interest?

12. Why do some divorcing spouses try to characterize property settlements as alimony?

13. What is the purpose of alimony recapture and how does it work?

14. Under what circumstances is a business-related expense considered "ordinary?"

15. Under what circumstances is a business-related expense considered "necessary?"

16. Under what circumstances will a business-related expense be considered "reasonable?"

17. Describe the deduction for the cost of investigating the purchase of a new business line.

18. If a taxpayer owns a business, what are the three circumstances under which expenses related to a home office can be deducted?

19. Describe the exceptions to the exclusivity requirements.

20. How does timing affect the deduction of business-related expenses by an employee?

1. Last year, James, a single individual, received a salary of $85,000 after making contribution to his 401(k) plan. James incurred the following deductions last year:

| | |
|---|---|
| Moving expenses (due to change in employment) | $5,000 |
| Individual Retirement Account Contribution | $5,000 |
| Mortgage Interest | $6,500 |
| Charitable gifts | $2,000 |

   What is James' adjusted gross income?

   a. $68,500.

   b. $75,000.

   c. $80,000.

   d. $85,000.

2. Which of the following expenses can a taxpayer deduct as an adjustment to gross incom (above-the-line)?

   a. Expenses incurred in conducting a sole proprietorship.

   b. Real estate taxes paid on the taxpayer's principal residence.

   c. Charitable gifts made to the taxpayer's church.

   d. Employee business expenses that are not reimbursed by the taxpayer's employe

3. Brian recently moved due to a change in employment. Before his move, Brian only had a 2( mile commute to work, but after his move, he had to commute 25 miles to his new job. I he had stayed in his old home, however, he would have had to commute 75 miles to his new job. If Brian incurred $5,000 of moving expenses, and $4,000 were reimbursed by hi employer under an accountable expense reimbursement plan, how much can Brian take as tax deduction?

   a. $1,000 as an employee business expense.

   b. $1,000 as an adjustment to income.

   c. $5,000 as an employee business expense.

   d. $5,000 as an adjustment to income.

4. All of the following requirements must be met for a payment to be treated as alimon EXCEPT:

   a. The payment must be required by a court decree.

   b. The payment must cease at the death of the payor.

   c. The parties may not live in the same household.

   d. The payment must not be a form of disguised child support.

5.  On January 1 of this year, Henry and Sandra were divorced. Under the terms of the divorce decree, Sandra was given custody of their only child, Jennifer, who is 16 years old. The court decree also requires Henry to pay Sandra $1,000 a month in alimony for two years, followed by $800 a month for the next four years. Which of the following statements concerning the payments that Henry makes to Sandra is correct?

    a.  Henry will be able to reduce his AGI by the $12,000 in alimony payments he makes to Sandra this year.

    b.  Sandra will not be required to report any of the payments that Henry makes to her as income on her tax return.

    c.  Henry will not be able to take a deduction for the alimony payments made due to the alimony recapture rule.

    d.  Henry's tax deduction will be limited to $9,600 per year during the six year period.

6.  Marty Smith, a vocalist, has frequently undergone cosmetic surgery. Marty claims that the reason for his surgery is to maintain the air passages from his nose through his throat so he can have a consistent singing voice. Several other vocalists have claimed deductions for this type of surgery. This year, Marty spent $25,000 on cosmetic surgery, and his AGI for the year was $200,000. How much of the cosmetic surgery expenses will Marty be able to deduct as an itemized deduction?

    a.  $0.

    b.  $10,000.

    c.  $15,000.

    d.  $25,000.

7.  Brian is a single individual who works for Dutch Enterprises, Inc., and is a participant in their qualified defined benefit plan and profit sharing plan. His adjusted gross income this year was $90,000. While watching the television show of a financial planner who claims to have all the answers for everyone, Brian decides to make a contribution to a traditional IRA of $5,000. How will the contribution be reflected on his income tax return for the year?

    a.  Brian may not deduct any portion of the IRA contribution.

    b.  Brian may deduct $2,000 of the contribution as an adjustment to income (above the line).

    c.  Brian may deduct $5,000 of the contribution as an itemized deduction.

    d.  Brian may deduct $5,000 of the contribution as an adjustment to income (above the line).

8. Which of the following statements concerning Medical Savings Accounts (MSAs) and Health Savings Accounts (HSAs), is correct?

   a. MSAs can be created by anyone who has a high deductible health insurance plan.

   b. Taxpayers who use MSAs and HSAs convert below the line deductions into above the line deductions.

   c. Retired taxpayers enrolled in Medicare can use HSAs to generate tax benefit for out of pocket medical costs.

   d. MSA and HSA contributions are permitted to be claimed as a medical expense on the taxpayer's Schedule A (Itemized Deductions).

9. All of the following statements concerning Health Savings Accounts (HSAs) are correct EXCEPT:

   a. Excess contributions to HSAs are subject to a 6% penalty tax.

   b. When a self-employed individual makes a contribution to an HSA, the contribution is disregarded when calculating self-employment (Social Security) taxes.

   c. Contributions to HSAs must be distributed to cover health care costs by the end of the taxable year, or they are forfeited.

   d. Distributions from HSAs that are not used to cover medical expenses are subject to a 10% penalty until the taxpayer reaches age 65.

10. All of the following individuals are considered to be self-employed individuals except:

    a. Sole Proprietors.

    b. Partners.

    c. Greater than 2% owners of S corporations.

    d. Greater than 5% owners of C corporations.

11. Ryan is a 20% owner in Beverly Farms, Inc., an S corporation. All of the following expenses incurred by or on behalf of Ryan by the corporation are deductible on the corporation's tax return, EXCEPT:

    a. Travel expenses associated with a corporate business trip.

    b. Contributions to Ryan's account in the company profit sharing plan.

    c. Subscriptions to business research services used for business purposes.

    d. Salary costs for Ryan's executive assistant.

12. Kasey is the three year old son of Randy. Since he was born, Kasey has received large gifts from family members, which have been invested for his benefit, and are now beginning to generate some investment income even though a majority of the funds are invested in growth-type investments. This year, Kasey will earn $2,000 in investment income, but due to his age, he does not have any earnings from employment. Randy recently attended a financial planning seminar sponsored by Fly-By-Nite Financial Services, and based on advice he received at the seminar, has decided to take Kasey's income and contribute it to an IRA for Kasey's benefit. Randy feels that the additional deferral of tax on the income would be beneficial from an income tax standpoint. How much can Kasey contribute to his IRA this year?

    a.  $0.

    b.  $2,000.

    c.  $4,000.

    d.  $5,000.

13. Orion works for Mad Hatter Chemical Company, Inc. as an engineer. He has been employed there for the past 5 years, and earns a salary of $100,000. Earlier this year, acting on advice given to him by his financial planner, Orion purchased a qualified long-term care insurance policy, and paid a premium of $800. All of his other medical expenses are covered by his employer sponsored health insurance plan. Which of the following statements concerning the long-term care policy is correct?

    a.  Orion is not permitted to deduct the cost of long-term care insurance that he purchased, since it is treated as a disability policy for income tax purposes.

    b.  Orion can deduct the cost of the long-term care insurance as an adjustment to income.

    c.  Orion can receive a tax benefit by claiming the cost of the long-term care insurance as a medical expense deduction.

    d.  Mad Hatter Chemical Company could have provided the long-term care policy to Orion as an employee benefit even if they did not provide similar coverage for other employees.

14. Mark owns a security consulting firm. He gained experience in security issues through his tenure in the Marine Corps. The security business was established 10 years ago, and now practically runs itself. Aside from helping with occasional projects, Mark has found himself in the enviable position of collecting a large residual cash flow from the business while expending minimal effort in running it. To fill up the empty hours in his day, Mark decides to investigate new lines of business, and has been looking into purchasing a retail Army-Navy store chain. He has taken several trips to inspect the properties, and has retained accountants and lawyers to review the financial and business operations. Which of the following statements concerning these business investigation expenses is correct?

    a. Mark may deduct the costs incurred regardless of whether he purchases the Army-Navy retail business.

    b. Mark may immediately deduct the costs incurred in the tax year that he acquires the Army-Navy retail business.

    c. Mark may deduct the costs incurred up to $5,000 of start up expenses in the year the start up begins operations.

    d. Investigation of business expenses are not deductible for federal income tax purposes.

15. Richard is preparing his personal tax return for the year. He is a sales representative for a major pharmaceutical firm, and operates his sales business as a sole proprietorship. This year was not the best for Richard, and he net earnings of $2,000. Since the pharmaceutical companies he works for do not provide him with office space, Richard has a room in his home that he uses exclusively and regularly for the conduct of his business. The expenses Richard incurred that could be properly allocated to the home office were $5,000. How much can Richard take as a home office deduction this year?

    a. $0.

    b. $2,000.

    c. $2,500.

    d. $5,000.

# Quick Quiz Explanations

### Quick Quiz 6.1

1. True.
2. False. Whenever expenses are associated with a business activity, they are above-the-line deductions.
3. False. Taxpayers may deduct the greater of their itemized deductions or the standard deduction.
4. True.

### Quick Quiz 6.2

1. False. Individuals who are enrolled in Medicare do not qualify for an HSA.
2. True.
3. True.
4. True.

### Quick Quiz 6.3

1. False. To make a contribution to an IRA, the taxpayer must have earned income.
2. False. Deductible traditional IRA contributions are phased out over specified AGI ranges for active participants.
3. True.
4. False. Contributions to traditional and Roth IRAs that are in excess of the allowable amount are subject to a 6% penalty.

### Quick Quiz 6.4

1. True.
2. False. Temporary living expenses cannot be deducted as moving expenses.
3. True.
4. False. Alimony recapture is only an issue if alimony payments decrease during the first three post-separation years.

### Quick Quiz 6.5

1. True.
2. True.
3. False. The cost of investigating the purchase of a new business line are only deductible if the new line of business is actually acquired.

### Quick Quiz 6.6

1. True.
2. True.

# *Itemized Deductions*

## INTRODUCTION

Recall from the previous chapter that itemized deductions can provide a significant tax benefit to taxpayers. Although above-the-line deductions are usually considered to be more favorable to the taxpayer on a dollar-for-dollar basis, itemized deductions can allow the taxpayer to take a below-the-line deduction in excess of the standard deduction.

## GENERAL CLASSIFICATION OF EXPENSES

Expenses related to the conduct of a trade or business or those related to the production of income are allowed to be deducted "above the line" and are often obtained by offsetting gross income from the business or production of income activity. Since the taxpayer is generating income that can be shared with the government through the tax system, the costs of producing that income can be directly offset against income.

Personal expenses are generally not deductible. Congress does, however, allow deductions for personal expenses when it desires to encourage certain behavior or wishes to encourage investment in specific types of property. Some personal deductions are adjustments to income (above-the-line deductions), such as contributions to HSAs (Health Care Savings Accounts), IRAs, alimony, educator expenses, and student loan interest. Most personal deductions that can be taken by taxpayers are taken "below-the-line" and are referred to as itemized deductions. These deductions reduce adjusted gross income in arriving at taxable income. Itemized deductions are reported on Schedule A of the tax return, and include:

- Medical Expenses
- Taxes
- Interest
- Charitable Contributions
- Casualty Losses
- Miscellaneous Itemized Deductions

EXHIBIT 7.1 FORM 1040 SCHEDULE A

**SCHEDULE A
(Form 1040)**

Department of the Treasury
Internal Revenue Service (99)

**Itemized Deductions**

▶ **Attach to Form 1040.**     ▶ **See Instructions for Schedule A (Form 1040).**

OMB No. 1545-0074

20**09**

Attachment
Sequence No. **07**

Name(s) shown on Form 1040

Your social security number

| | | | |
|---|---|---|---|
| **Medical and Dental Expenses** | **Caution.** Do not include expenses reimbursed or paid by others. | | |
| | 1 Medical and dental expenses (see page A-1) . . . . . | 1 | |
| | 2 Enter amount from Form 1040, line 38  2 | | |
| | 3 Multiply line 2 by 7.5% (.075) . . . . . . . . | 3 | |
| | 4 Subtract line 3 from line 1. If line 3 is more than line 1, enter -0- . . . . . . . . | | 4 |
| **Taxes You Paid** (See page A-2.) | 5 State and local **(check only one box):** a ☐ Income taxes, **or** b ☐ General sales taxes | 5 | |
| | 6 Real estate taxes (see page A-5) . . . . . . . . | 6 | |
| | 7 New motor vehicle taxes from line 11 of the worksheet on back. Skip this line if you checked box 5b . . . . . | 7 | |
| | 8 Other taxes. List type and amount ▶ _____ | 8 | |
| | 9 Add lines 5 through 8 . . . . . . . . . . . | | 9 |
| **Interest You Paid** (See page A-6.) **Note.** Personal interest is not deductible. | 10 Home mortgage interest and points reported to you on Form 1098 | 10 | |
| | 11 Home mortgage interest not reported to you on Form 1098. If paid to the person from whom you bought the home, see page A-7 and show that person's name, identifying no., and address ▶ _____ _____ | 11 | |
| | 12 Points not reported to you on Form 1098. See page A-7 for special rules . . . . . . . . . . . . . | 12 | |
| | 13 Qualified mortgage insurance premiums (see page A-7) . | 13 | |
| | 14 Investment interest. Attach Form 4952 if required. (See page A-8.) | 14 | |
| | 15 Add lines 10 through 14 . . . . . . . . . . . | | 15 |
| **Gifts to Charity** If you made a gift and got a benefit for it, see page A-8. | 16 Gifts by cash or check. If you made any gift of $250 or more, see page A-8 . . . . . . . . . | 16 | |
| | 17 Other than by cash or check. If any gift of $250 or more, see page A-8. You **must** attach Form 8283 if over $500 . . . | 17 | |
| | 18 Carryover from prior year . . . . . . . . . | 18 | |
| | 19 Add lines 16 through 18 . . . . . . . . . . . | | 19 |
| **Casualty and Theft Losses** | 20 Casualty or theft loss(es). Attach Form 4684. (See page A-10.) . . . . . . . | | 20 |
| **Job Expenses and Certain Miscellaneous Deductions** (See page A-10.) | 21 Unreimbursed employee expenses—job travel, union dues, job education, etc. Attach Form 2106 or 2106-EZ if required. (See page A-10.) ▶ _____ | 21 | |
| | 22 Tax preparation fees . . . . . . . . . . . | 22 | |
| | 23 Other expenses—investment, safe deposit box, etc. List type and amount ▶ _____ _____ | 23 | |
| | 24 Add lines 21 through 23 . . . . . . . . . | 24 | |
| | 25 Enter amount from Form 1040, line 38  25 | | |
| | 26 Multiply line 25 by 2% (.02) . . . . . . . . | 26 | |
| | 27 Subtract line 26 from line 24. If line 26 is more than line 24, enter -0- . . . . . . | | 27 |
| **Other Miscellaneous Deductions** | 28 Other—from list on page A-11. List type and amount ▶ _____ _____ | | 28 |
| **Total Itemized Deductions** | 29 Is Form 1040, line 38, over $166,800 (over $83,400 if married filing separately)? ☐ **No.** Your deduction is not limited. Add the amounts in the far right column for lines 4 through 28. Also, enter this amount on Form 1040, line 40a. ☐ **Yes.** Your deduction may be limited. See page A-11 for the amount to enter. ▶ | | 29 |
| | 30 If you elect to itemize deductions even though they are less than your standard deduction, check here . . . . . . . . . . . . . . . . . ▶ ☐ | | |

For Paperwork Reduction Act Notice, see Form 1040 instructions.     Cat. No. 17145C     Schedule A (Form 1040) 2009

Recall that a taxpayer can take the greater of itemized deductions or the standard deduction. A tax benefit is only achieved by itemizing if the taxpayer's total itemized deductions exceed the standard deduction. As the example at the beginning of the last chapter illustrates, below-the-line itemized deductions are not as beneficial to the taxpayer as above-the-line adjustments to income.

Keep in mind that itemized deductions such as interest on a home mortgage and property taxes are reported to the IRS by the recipient institution, but medical expenses, charitable contributions, casualty losses, and miscellaneous itemized deductions are only verifiable by the IRS by using an audit. Therefore, it should be obvious that the IRS has a vested interest in reducing the number of itemizers, reducing the number of audits, and making the IRS audit process more effective. Because the standard deduction is inflation-adjusted, it helps to reduce the number of taxpayers who would otherwise itemize.

## Key Concepts

**Underline/highlight the answers to these questions as you read:**

1. Describe the function of below-the-line deductions.

2. Explain the IRS' interest in reducing the number of individuals who itemize their deductions.

3. Explain the circumstances under which medical expenditures are deductible.

4. Describe the circumstances under which a medical expenditure might be an above-the-line deduction.

From a personal financial planning standpoint, itemized deductions are important for a planner to know about because they impact a large number of clients. Some itemized deductions will be routinely used in the planning process (such as the deduction for taxes, interest, and charitable contributions), while other itemized deductions are best avoided through the use of insurance products (such as the medical expense deduction and the casualty loss deduction). In either case, a working knowledge of itemized deductions and their limitations is important for anyone advising a financial planning client.

## MEDICAL EXPENSES

In general, amounts spent for the diagnosis, cure, treatment or prevention of disease or for treatment of conditions affecting any structure or function of the body are deductible if incurred by the taxpayer, the taxpayer's spouse, or the taxpayer's dependent. These items are not deductible if the taxpayer has been reimbursed through insurance or other means, since this would provide a double benefit to the taxpayer.

### TIMING OF DEDUCTION

Medical expenditures are deductible in the year paid, since individuals are cash-basis taxpayers. To receive a tax benefit for medical expenses, medical expenses must exceed 7.5 percent of the taxpayer's AGI and only those expenses in excess of this threshold are deductible. This type of limitation is referred to as a "floor," since no deduction is allowed until the allowable expenses exceed the threshold. Medical expenses within the first 7.5 percent of AGI are nondeductible.

| EXAMPLE 7.1 | Ryan has an AGI of $40,000 and medical expenses of $4,000. Ryan's medial expense deduction will equal $1,000 [$4,000 - 0.075($40,000)]. The first $3,000 of medical expenses are not deductible. |
|---|---|

## ITEMIZED DEDUCTIBLE MEDICAL EXPENSES OVERVIEW

Medical expenses that are deductible include, among others, prescription drugs and insulin, acupuncture, treatment for alcoholism, artificial limbs and teeth, diagnostic fees, drug addiction treatment, hearing aids and batteries, health insurance premiums (including Medicare and long-term care insurance premiums), laser eye surgery, nursing care, medical aids, and x-ray services. Deductible medical expenses generally require doctor's orders.

## CAPITAL EXPENSES

Capital expenses incurred to improve the taxpayer's home are deductible in an amount equal to the difference between the cost of the improvements and the increase in the value of the taxpayer's home provided that the expenditures are made primarily to provide medical benefits (Treas. Reg. Sec. 1.213-1(e)(1)(iii)). To be deductible, capital medical expenses must be medically necessary, advised by a physician, used primarily by the patient, and reasonable given the health status of the patient. Examples of capital improvements to homes that are deductible include installation of air conditioning for taxpayers who have respiratory ailments, installation and maintenance of a swimming pool for taxpayers with severe arthritis or asthma, and elevators to allow individuals to access all floors of their home. Improvements made for accessibility are fully deductible, and include handicapped entrance and exit ramps, and modifications to bathrooms and kitchens for the physically handicapped.

## NURSING HOMES AND SPECIAL SCHOOLS

Nursing home and special school expenses are also deductible as medical expenses if the primary purpose of the service is to provide medical treatment. If the primary purpose is personal (for example, custodial care or attainment of educational degrees), only those costs specifically allocable to medical treatment are deductible.

## TRAVEL AND LODGING EXPENSES

Travel and lodging expenses incurred to acquire medical care are also deductible up to specified limits. The mileage allowance is $0.24 per mile (2009) and the maximum deductible lodging expense is $50 per night per person. If it would be prudent to have another individual accompany the patient while the patient is receiving care (such as a parent accompanying a child receiving care in a specialized medical facility), that person's travel and lodging expenses (up to the specified maximums) are also considered to be deductible medical expenses.

## NONDEDUCTIBLE MEDICAL EXPENSES

Medical expenses that do not qualify for a deduction include elective cosmetic surgery (including face lifts, hair transplants, hair removal, teeth whitening even when performed by a dentist) (Rev. Rul. 2003-57), dancing lessons even if recommended by a doctor, funeral expenses (these are deductible on the decedent's estate tax return), health club dues (unless related to a specific medical condition), marijuana (even if prescribed legally by a physician in the state of the taxpayer's domicile) (Treas. Reg. Sec. 1.213-1(e)(2); Rev. Rul. 97-9), over-the counter drug purchases without a prescription (although these can be reimbursed through a flexible-spending arrangement sponsored by an employer), and general health items.

## ABOVE-THE-LINE MEDICAL EXPENSES

Not all medical expenses must be deducted as a below-the-line deduction and some medical expenses that are disallowed below the line may be permitted to be deducted elsewhere. For example, consider an actress who undergoes elective cosmetic surgery to reverse signs of aging, thereby allowing her to star in more movies or television shows. In this case, the cosmetic surgery will be considered a trade or business related expense and may be deducted above-the-line (the expenses can be deducted on the taxpayer's Schedule C to offset income received from the acting trade or business). If given a choice of taking the medical expenses as a trade or business expense or as an itemized deduction, a taxpayer should deduct the expenses as a trade or business expenses. Trade or business expenses result in a reduction of AGI and are not subject to the 7.5 percent floor that applies to itemized medical expenses. Above-the-line deductions also reduce the floor associated with other itemized deductions.

## SUMMARY OF DEDUCTIBLE AND NONDEDUCTIBLE MEDICAL EXPENSES

EXHIBIT 7.2

| DEDUCTIBLE | NONDEDUCTIBLE |
|---|---|
| • Prescription Drugs | • Elective Cosmetic Surgery |
| • Expenses Related to Diagnosis, Cure, & Treatment | • Dance Lessons |
| • Health Insurance Premiums | • Health Club Dues |
| • Capital Expenditures | • Marijuana |
| • Nursing Home and Special Schools | • Over-the-Counter Drugs |
| • Travel and Lodging | • General Health Items (e.g., vitamins) |

## TAXES

Taxes paid to state, local, and foreign governments are deductible as an itemized deduction. Excise taxes, gift taxes, and estate taxes are not deductible.

### TIMING OF DEDUCTION

State and local income taxes are deducted in the year paid. A deduction is available, therefore, for all amounts withheld, made as estimated payments, and paid to satisfy a prior year income tax liability. When a taxpayer receives a state income tax refund in a subsequent year, the tax benefit rule applies and requires the taxpayer to include the state income tax refund in his or her taxable income to the extent that a deduction was taken for state income taxes paid in a prior tax year.

**Key Concepts**

Underline/highlight the answers to these questions as you read:

1. Describe how the tax benefit rule affects the deduction of taxes paid to state, local, and foreign governments.

2. Explain the general rule concerning the deductibility of interest for income tax purposes.

3. List the limitations on deducting qualified personal residence interest.

4. Describe the extent to which investment interest is deductible.

**EXAMPLE 7.2**

In 2009, Keegan had withholding for Connecticut Income Tax of $4,000 and had made estimated tax payments to Connecticut totaling $2,000. Keegan itemizes deductions on his tax return, and includes all $6,000 as a deduction on his 2009 Federal Income Tax Return. When he completed his 2009 State Income Tax Return (which he filed on April 15, 2010), Keegan found out that he had overpaid state income taxes for the year, and was entitled to a $500 state income tax refund, which he received in June of 2010. Note that when Keegan files his 2010 income tax return, he must include the $500 state income tax refund in his income (due to the imposition of the tax-benefit rule, which states that when a deduction has been taken, and the amount deducted was later refunded, the refund must be included in income).

**EXAMPLE 7.3**

Assume the same facts as the prior example, except that Keegan did not itemize deductions on his 2009 Federal Income Tax Return. In this case, since Keegan took the standard deduction and did not deduct his state income tax, he will not have to include the $500 state income tax refund in his taxable income for the year.

As an alternative to deducting state income taxes, a taxpayer may deduct state sales taxes. Those taxpayers who live in states with no income tax, or those taxpayers who have made large urchases during the year and whose sales taxes exceed their state income taxes will benefit by sing the sales tax deduction. A taxpayer may deduct either state sales taxes or state income taxes, ut not both. The deduction for sales taxes can be either the actual sales taxes paid (which equires the taxpayer to keep records showing the total sales taxes paid throughout the year), or a redetermined deduction amount provided by the IRS that is based on the taxpayer's AGI plus ontaxable income for the year.

oreign income taxes may be deducted as an itemized deduction on Schedule A or may be laimed as a Foreign Tax Credit. Generally, the foreign tax credit will give the taxpayer a greater ax benefit since a credit is a dollar for dollar reduction in tax liability while a deduction simply educes the amount subject to income tax. In determining whether to claim foreign taxes as a leduction or as a credit, the taxpayer should calculate the benefit he or she will receive using each pproach and use the method that will result in the lowest tax liability.

roperty taxes paid to state and local governments are also deductible, provided that the taxes are ased on the value of the property (referred to as an *ad valorem* tax). While the federal overnment is constitutionally prohibited from taxing property, state and local governments may ax property, and these taxes often provide a significant source of revenue for the operation of ocal governments. Property taxes are deducted in the year paid to the taxing authority. If a axpayer makes monthly payments into an escrow account with a mortgage lender, no deduction s permitted until the funds are disbursed from the escrow account to the taxing authority.

There is no limitation on the amount that can be claimed as a deduction for property taxes; if the axpayer has multiple properties, he may claim all of the property taxes paid.

When property is sold, the taxes will be prorated between the buyer and seller of the property ased on the date ownership of the property changed hands. Adjustments can be found on the closing statements of the property that is sold, and should be reflected on the taxpayer's Schedule A. One special rule applies when the seller of real estate pays property taxes that are considered to be the obligation of the purchaser. The purchaser is deemed to have paid the property taxes and can take an income tax deduction for the taxes paid, which results in a reduction in basis in the property. The seller is treated as receiving a reduced price for the real estate, thereby reducing the amount realized, and the gain or loss, on the transaction.

## NONDEDUCTIBLE FINES AND FEES

Taxes do not include fines and fees, even if paid to the state or local government. Fines and fees are intended to be punitive in nature and are therefore nondeductible.

Larry has an appointment with an important client at the client's home in Manhattan, and is having a difficult time finding a parking spot. Believing that his time is valuable, he parks in a no-parking zone and visits the client. When he returns, he finds a $200 parking ticket on his windshield. Larry will not be able to deduct the parking ticket as a local tax, since it was a fine for violating local law.

**EXAMPLE 7.4**

EXHIBIT 7.3 **SUMMARY OF DEDUCTIBLE AND NONDEDUCTIBLE TAXES**

| DEDUCTIBLE | NONDEDUCTIBLE |
|---|---|
| • State and Local Income Taxes | • Fines or Fees |
| • State Sales Tax (Alternative Income) | • Excise Taxes |
| • Foreign Income Taxes | • Gift Taxes |
| • Property Taxes | • Estate Taxes |

## INTEREST

The general tax rule concerning the deductibility of interest for income tax purposes may com
as a surprise to most people. It states that all interest paid or accrued within the taxable year o
indebtedness is deductible. Of course, many exceptions apply, resulting in interest bein
deductible only when it is (1) qualified residence interest; (2) interest incurred in a trade o
business; or (3) interest incurred for the production of income (investment interest).

Interest incurred in the conduct of an active trade or business is deductible against busines
income above-the-line. It is not treated as a Schedule A itemized deduction.

Personal interest, which includes all interest other than qualified residence interest, investmen
interest, and trade or business interest, is not deductible for income tax purposes. Examples o
personal interest include interest incurred on personal credit cards, personal car loans, interes
paid on personal obligations and bills, and finance charges for personal transactions.

For interest to be deductible, it must be incurred on a valid obligation to pay a fixed o
determinable sum of money in return for the use of money. The amount of interest must b
within limits set by the state. If interest is charged on an obligation at a rate higher than th
maximum rate permitted by law, collection of the interest is not legally permissible, and i
therefore not deductible for income tax purposes, even if paid.

Another requirement necessary for the interest deduction to apply is that the obligation to pay
the interest must be the taxpayer's obligation. Payment of the interest obligation of anothe
person does not give rise to an interest expense deduction.

**EXAMPLE 7.5**

Years ago, Randy set up a business called Sports Fanatic, Inc.,
a C corporation. The business had been successful, but has
recently fallen on hard times and does not have the cash flow
necessary to make the required interest payments on its outstanding loans. Since Randy anticipates that the business
problems are temporary and he does not want to jeopardize
the company's credit rating, he personally makes the payments on the loans. While Randy has paid the interest, he
may not deduct those payments as an interest expense on his
personal tax return since he was not obligated to make the

loan payments – the corporation had the obligation. Instead, Randy will treat the payments as a capital contribution to the corporation, which will increase his basis in his interest in the corporation. The corporation will be permitted to take an interest expense deduction, which may increase its tax loss, but will be permitted to carry-back that loss to generate an immediate tax deduction, or carry that loss forward to offset future income generated by the company.

## QUALIFIED RESIDENCE INTEREST DEDUCTION

Perhaps one of the most frequently used income tax deductions by individuals is the home mortgage interest deduction, referred to in tax parlance as the **qualified residence interest deduction**. Taxpayers are permitted to deduct interest on up to $1 million of home indebtedness (referred to as acquisition indebtedness), as well as the interest on up to $100,000 of home equity indebtedness. Interest expense incurred on amounts in excess of $1 million of acquisition indebtedness and in excess of $100,000 of home equity indebtedness is not deductible.

### *Acquisition Indebtedness*

**Acquisition indebtedness** is indebtedness used to acquire, construct, or improve the taxpayer's primary residence and one additional residence (third, fourth, and fifth residences do not qualify for the interest deduction). To meet the definition of qualified residence interest, the indebtedness must be secured by the home. The interest expense on the first $1 million of acquisition indebtedness (a combined limit for both the primary and secondary residence - not $1 million of indebtedness for each residence) is deductible as an itemized deduction. Since most home loans are amortized, acquisition indebtedness is reduced as payments of principal are made and the acquisition indebtedness cannot be increased (e.g., by refinancing) unless a new home is acquired. Interest-only loans do not result in amortization of acquisition indebtedness.

### *Home Equity Indebtedness*

**Home equity indebtedness** is additional debt secured by the home that exceeds the amount of acquisition indebtedness. The interest on up to $100,000 of home equity indebtedness is deductible as qualified residence interest without regard for what purpose the funds were used. Interest on home equity indebtedness in excess of $100,000 is not deductible.

> Five years ago, Roger purchased a home for $400,000, paying $80,000 in cash and taking out a $320,000 mortgage. The outstanding balance of the mortgage is now $270,000, but the value of the home as risen to $800,000. Roger needs some additional cash to pay for his children's education and to cover some personal expenditures, so he refinances the home, taking out an additional $210,000. His mortgage balance is now $480,000. Roger will be able to deduct the interest on $370,000 ($270,000 + $100,000) of the mortgage, but will not be permitted to deduct the interest on the remaining $110,000. $270,000 of the refinanced amount continues to be treated as acquisition indebtedness and an

**EXAMPLE 7.6**

additional $100,000 will be considered home equity indebtedness. The interest on the additional $110,000 is not deductible since it exceeds the permissible home equity interest expense deduction.

**EXAMPLE 7.7**

Five years ago, Larry purchased a home for $400,000 paying $80,000 in cash and taking out a $320,000 mortgage. Larry recently was appointed CEO of The Amazing Company, and is drawing a salary far in excess of what he thought he would make. About six months ago, Larry was watching television when Susie, a nationally known self-proclaimed expert on personal finance, gave advice to pay off existing home mortgages. Larry took Susie's advice and paid off his mortgage, which used up most of his available cash. Last week, Larry was presented with a business opportunity that would require a $300,000 investment on his part, and he would like to participate. Since he does not have any spare cash, he takes out a $300,000 home equity loan on his home. Larry will only be able to deduct the interest on the first $100,000 of the loan. When he paid off his mortgage, he retired his acquisition indebtedness, which means he can only deduct the interest on home equity indebtedness up to $100,000. The interest on the remaining $200,000 refinanced will not be considered qualified residence interest. If Larry had not taken Susie's advice, and did not pay off the mortgage, he would have been able to deduct all of the interest on his loan as qualified residence interest and use his cash to make the investment.

When taxpayers acquire or refinance homes, they often pay "points" (a form of pre-paid interest) to get a lower rate on the mortgage loan. When points are paid to acquire a new personal residence or vacation home, or to improve a personal residence or vacation home, the points paid are fully deductible as qualified residence interest expense in the current tax year provided that they are clearly identified, that they represent a percentage of the principal amount of the mortgage, and they are paid from the taxpayers' own funds (Rev. Proc. 94-27). Only the points paid on the first $1 million of acquisition indebtedness qualify for a tax deduction. Points paid to refinance an existing loan are amortized over the life of the loan.

Late payment fees on mortgage loans are also deductible as mortgage interest, since they represent an additional interest charge on the loan. If the late payment fees are reimbursements for specific services such as collection of the amount due, then they are not deductible.

For purpose of the qualified residence interest deduction, a "home" includes not only a traditional residence, but also mobile homes, trailers, boats, and timeshares. Provided that the "residence" has cooking, toileting, and sleeping facilities, it can be considered a residence for purposes of the qualified residence interest deduction.

One limitation on qualified residence interest that sometimes becomes important concerns homes that have declined in value. Interest that otherwise meets the requirements of acquisition indebtedness is deductible even if the loan balance exceeds the fair market value of the home. Under the home equity loan rules, however, a deduction is not allowed for interest on debt that exceeds the fair market value of the home.[1]

<table>
<tr><td>

Pat buys a house on the Gulf Coast for $800,000 during a very high period in the market. She pays $40,000 down (5%) and takes out a jumbo mortgage for $760,000. Subsequently, she decides to make improvements to the home and takes out a home equity loan for $60,000. Shortly after two hurricanes, the house is appraised at $550,000. Technically Pat can only deduct the mortgage interest related to the acquisition debt because the home equity mortgage interest is only deductible up to the fair market value of the home. Here, the acquisition debt on the home exceeds the fair market value of the property, so there is no home equity available for the deductibility of the home equity loan interest.

</td><td>

**EXAMPLE 7.8**

</td></tr>
</table>

## INVESTMENT INTEREST DEDUCTION

An itemized deduction is also allowed for investment interest expense, which is interest incurred to purchase or hold securities and income-producing instruments. Investment interest is typically associated with margin accounts used to purchase stocks, bonds, and mutual funds.

Investment interest is deductible but only to the extent of net investment income. Net investment income equals investment income less investment expenses other than investment interest expense. Investment expenses include any expenses that were directly connected with the production of investment income without regard to any disallowance caused by the two percent floor on miscellaneous itemized deductions. Investment income includes gross income from property held for investment (interest and dividends) and gains on the sale of property in excess of net capital gain (i.e., gains on the sale of property that are taxed at ordinary income tax rates due to the imposition of the depreciation recapture rules). Investment income can include short-term capital gains and non-qualified dividends, however, qualified dividends and net long-term capital gains are excluded unless elected as discussed below.

Any investment interest expense not used in the current year due to the net investment income limitation may be carried forward indefinitely.

Investors with growth-oriented portfolios may have little investment income to offset their investment interest expenses due to the exclusion of capital gains from the definition of net investment income. Taxpayers may elect to include qualified dividends and net capital gains in their net investment income, but there is a cost to making the election – the taxpayer will lose the preferential capital gains tax rate (currently 15%) that applies to qualified dividends and long-term capital gains. This election would most likely be made by a taxpayer who has a significant amount of investment interest expense which would offset tax liability on the identical amount

---

1. IRC Sections 163(h)(3)(B) and 163(h)(3)(c)(i)(1).

of net investment income. A taxpayer can make the election to include capital gains in net investment income on Form 4952.

Two additional issues need to be addressed – one deals with interest paid on the acquisition of investments that generate tax-free income, and the second deals with interest paid on the acquisition of passive investments. The deduction of investment interest is allowed because the taxpayer is purchasing assets that will generate taxable income in the future, which will be shared with the government through the tax system. Loans used to acquire assets that will generate tax-free income will not qualify for the investment interest deduction and interest paid on loans to acquire passive investments will be subject to the passive loss limitation rules.

When interest is paid on a loan used to purchase assets that will not generate taxable income in the future, such as a portfolio of municipal bonds, the investment interest itemized deduction will not be permitted. If, however, the taxpayer purchases municipal bonds that are not public purpose municipal bonds, and the taxpayer becomes an AMT taxpayer, the interest on those bonds will become taxable in the AMT tax system (even though the interest is exempt for regular tax purposes), and the taxpayer will receive an investment interest expense deduction in the AMT tax system (but not the regular tax system). Special rules apply to income subject to the alternative minimum tax and will be addressed in more detail in Chapter 15.

**Quick Quiz 7.2**

**Highlight the answer to these questions:**

1. Taxpayers must include state income tax refunds in taxable income to the extent that a deduction was previously taken for state income taxes paid in a prior tax year.
   a. True
   b. False

2. Only property taxes paid on the taxpayer's primary residence are deductible.
   a. True
   b. False

3. Interest is only deductible if it is incurred on a valid obligation to pay a fixed or determinable sum of money in return for the use of the money.
   a. True
   b. False

4. Taxpayers are permitted to deduct the interest on an unlimited amount of home indebtedness.
   a. True
   b. False

True, False, True, False.

When interest is paid on loans used to acquire passive assets, such as investment real estate and limited partnership interests, the interest will be deductible to the extent that the passive investment generates investment income. The interest deduction is suspended and will be carried forward in the passive income bucket until passive income is generated to deduct the loss generated by the interest charges. In this respect, the passive activity loss rules are similar to the investment interest deduction rules. Investment interest expense used to acquire either portfolio assets or passive investments may only be deducted to the extent that the taxpayer has either net investment income (in the case of portfolio investment interest expense) or passive income (in the case of passive investment interest expense).

EXHIBIT 7.4

# SUMMARY OF DEDUCTIBLE AND NONDEDUCTIBLE INTEREST EXPENSE AS ITEMIZED DEDUCTION

| DEDUCTIBLE | NONDEDUCTIBLE |
|---|---|
| • Qualified Residence Interest (Limit 2 houses and $1,000,000 debt) <br> • Home Equity Line of Credit ($100,000 limit) <br> • Investment Interest Expense (to extent of investment interest income) | • Personal Interest Including Credit Cards, Bank Loans, etc. <br> • Interest Used to Buy Tax-Free Municipal Bonds |

# CHARITABLE CONTRIBUTIONS AND DEDUCTIONS

Americans are the most charitably inclined individuals in the world. Studies consistently show that Americans, as a whole, give a greater percentage of their income to charitable causes than citizens of other countries. In the United States, individuals who give to qualified charitable organizations qualify for an income tax charitable deduction. The charitable deduction is an itemized deduction taken on Schedule A of Form 1040.

## QUALIFIED CHARITABLE ORGANIZATIONS

Not all donations made for charitable purposes are deductible on the donor's income tax return, however. Only contributions made to qualified charitable organizations qualify for an income tax deduction. A **qualified charitable organization** is operated exclusively for religious, charitable, scientific, literary, or educational purposes, or for the prevention of cruelty to animals or children (the charitable purposes listed here are sometimes referred to as the charitable purpose test). Qualified charitable organizations may not allow any part of the earnings of the charity to be used for the private benefit of an individual, an event called "private inurement" in tax parlance, and are prohibited from engaging in propaganda or lobbying at the federal level, although they are allowed to influence state and local legislation. To ensure that deductions to a charitable organization are deductible for income tax purposes, a taxpayer should make sure that the charity has received an exempt determination letter from the IRS. A list of charities that have received exempt determination letters may be obtained from the Internal Revenue Service, or may be accessed on the IRS website at www.irs.gov.

**Key Concepts**

**Underline/highlight the answers to these questions as you read:**

1. List the requirements that must be met in order to qualify a charitable contribution for an income tax charitable deduction.

2. Name the exceptions to the partial interest rule.

3. Describe how the type of charity and type of property donated impact the limits on charitable contribution deductions.

4. Explain how the special election impacts the charitable contribution deduction.

For income tax purposes, only gifts to U.S. based charities are eligible for a charitable income tax deduction; gifts to foreign charities do not qualify. When an individual dies and makes charitable gifts through his or her estate, the estate tax charitable deduction applies to both U.S. based and foreign charities, provided that the charitable purpose test is met.

There are two primary ways a taxpayer can avoid the income tax rule limiting the income tax charitable deduction for donations to domestic charities. The first method involves a transfer from the taxpayer to a U.S. based charity that will subsequently transfer the funds oversees for the use of a foreign charity. Common examples of this approach include Save the Children type funds (which sponsor economically disadvantaged children in third world countries), or "friend of organizations," such as The Friends of Oxford University (a U.S. based charity that transfers donated funds from the United States to Oxford University in England). The second method taxpayer could use to obtain an income tax deduction for foreign charitable gifts is to form private foundation in the United States and make tax-deductible contributions to the foundation. The private foundation may then transfer the funds to a foreign charity or charitable cause.

## ADDITIONAL REQUIREMENTS FOR DEDUCTION

Three additional requirements must be met to qualify for an income tax charitable deduction.
1. The subject of the charitable gift must be property, not services.
2. The deductible portion of the gift must not exceed the value received by the charity.
3. The charitable gift must be paid in cash or property by the close of the taxable year.

## GIFTS THAT QUALIFY FOR THE DEDUCTION

Only gifts of cash or property will qualify for a charitable income tax deduction. Volunteering time for a charity by donating services is a great way to make a charitable gift, but the value of the time donated will not qualify for the income tax charitable deduction. This rule is consistent with the matching principal of income taxation, which states that for every deduction, there must be an inclusion. Since the value of the taxpayers services have never been brought into income and the charity will not report income due to receipt of the gift, the value of service cannot be deducted as a charitable gift. A taxpayer could elect to include the value of services in income to generate a charitable deduction, but for reasons that will be discussed in detail later this will rarely be beneficial for the taxpayer (due to the limitation imposed on charitable deductions). Consequently, only gifts of cash or property will be eligible for the income tax charitable deduction.

Individuals who volunteer time for charitable causes often incur expenses in completing their charitable service. To the extent that these expenses are not reimbursed, they qualify as a charitable income tax deduction. Examples may include mileage (at $0.14 per mile) and travel expenses, parking costs, and incidental expenses (for supplies and materials) incurred when performing charitable services.

EXAMPLE 7.9

Ryan, a tax attorney, volunteered to create a private operating foundation for a local group that was forming a new charitable organization. Usually, Ryan charges $5,000 to draft the documents and obtain the IRS exempt determination letter for the operating foundation. Ryan may not deduct the value of his services as a charitable deduction, since he never recognized the $5,000 as income. Ryan will be able to deduct the actual costs he incurred in setting up the operating foundation, such as the cost of obtaining the exempt determination letter for the organization.

Likewise, giving a charity the right to use property will generally not qualify the donor for an income tax charitable deduction. To be deductible for income tax purposes, a gift of property must be a gift of the donor's entire interest in the property. Since the donor does not transfer control of the asset to a charity when he or she gives the charity the right to use the asset, no tax deduction is available.

EXAMPLE 7.10

Craig is a board member of Friends of Foley, a charitable organization dedicated to prevention of cruelty to animals. Friends of Foley is embarking on a fundraising campaign to expand their animal shelter facilities and Craig has an office building with vacant office space. Craig allows Friends of Foley to use the vacant office space to run their fundraising campaign. While Craig has made a significant contribution to the charity, he may not take an income tax charitable deduction for the value of the rental use of the office since he did not donate his entire interest in the property (the entire building) to the charity. Similar to the donation of services to charitable organizations, this donation is a variation on the matching principal of income taxation. Since Craig never included the rental income value of the office in his income, he may not take a charitable deduction for the value given to charity.

EXAMPLE 7.11

Scott owns an original sculpture created by the late artist, Frederick Hart. The Wadsworth Athenaeum, a local art museum, is sponsoring a special exhibit on the work of Frederick Hart and Scott allowed the museum to display his sculpture at the museum during the exhibit. While the donation of the use of the sculpture made the exhibit more complete and attracted more patrons to visit the exhibit and pay the entrance fee to the museum, Scott may not deduct the value of the use of the sculpture by the museum as an income tax charitable deduction, since he did not give his entire interest in the property (a fee simple ownership interest) to the museum.

There are some exceptions to the partial interest rule. As noted above, a gift of a partial interest in property (something less than the donor's entire interest) is not deductible for income tax purposes unless an exception applies. The primary exceptions (which will be covered later in this section) include:

- A gift of an undivided portion of the donor's entire interest in the property;
- A gift of a remainder interest in a personal residence or farm;
- A gift of a partial interest if transferred in trust (a charitable remainder trust, a charitable lead trust, or a pooled income fund); and
- Purchase of a charitable gift annuity.

When a donor makes a charitable gift, the charitable income tax deduction must not exceed the value received by the charitable organization. When a taxpayer makes a gift and receives something from the charity in return, the value of the charitable deduction is reduced by the fair market value of the property received by the donor. Small gifts, however, do not reduce the value of the income tax deduction.

**EXAMPLE 7.12**

Pat, a fan of the Britcom Keeping Up Appearances, donated $100 to her local public television station (a qualified charity) to encourage them to keep the show on the air. In return for her donation, the television station sent her a coffee mug with the name of the station and its logo prominently displayed on the mug. Pat's charitable deduction is $100, since the mug is a de-minimus item (a small gift).

**EXAMPLE 7.13**

Randy, a fan of the Britcom Father Ted (which details the life of a Catholic priest serving in a remote area of Ireland) makes a $500 donation to his public television station. In return for the donation, the public television station gives Randy front-row tickets to the Irish Tenors concert coming up later in the month, as well as a backstage pass and reception, and a CD of the performance. The fair market value of this package is $250. Randy is entitled to take a charitable deduction for the difference between what he donated to the charity, and what he received from the charity or a total of $250.

The final general requirement for the income tax charitable deduction is that the gift must be made in cash or property by the close of the taxable year. As cash basis taxpayers, individuals must make the charitable gift prior to the close of the taxable year in order for the gift to be deductible. Gifts made on or before December 31 may be deducted by the taxpayer.

ssuming that the requirements for the charitable deduction have been met, our attention turns ɔ the amount of the charitable deduction that may be taken. The amount of the deduction epends on:

1. The type of property given away;
2. The identity of the donee/charity;
3. The identity of the contributor; and
4. The amount of property given away.

he starting point for determining the amount of the charitable deduction allowed in any one ear is the amount of cash given or the fair market value of property that is transferred to charity.

## ITEMIZED DEDUCTION LIMITATIONS

Unlike other itemized deductions, which are limited by the imposition of "floors" that must be xceeded by the taxpayer in order to receive a deduction, the charitable deduction is limited by a ceiling." The maximum amount that may be deducted in any one year equals 50 percent of the axpayer's contribution base. Contribution base is the taxpayer's adjusted gross income not taking nto account any net operating loss carry-backs. Since most individual taxpayers do not have net perating loss carrybacks, AGI can generally be used as the taxpayer's contribution base. By mposing a ceiling limitation on charitable gifts, Congress has made it impossible to wipe out axable income by making contributions to charity.

he first characteristic that determines the amount of the allowable charitable deduction is the ype of property given away. There are two classifications of property:

1. Gifts of cash and non-long-term gain property; and
2. Gifts of long-term capital gain property.

When a taxpayer makes a gift of cash, the amount of cash given is the value of the charitable gift. f non-long-term capital gain property is given instead of cash, the taxpayer is only permitted to leduct his or her cost basis in the property. When a taxpayer makes a gift of long-term capital ain property to a charity, however, the value for charitable deduction purposes is the fair market alue of the property on the date of the gift.

Gifts of long-term capital gain property offer the taxpayer a significant planning opportunity. If he property was sold and the proceeds were given to charity, the taxpayer would have to ecognize gain on the sale of the asset and subject that gain to capital gains tax. When the property is given directly to the charity, however, the taxpayer can deduct the entire fair market alue of the property even though he or she did not bring the gain into taxable income. This is a najor exception to the matching principal of income taxation. When making gifts of long-term apital gains property to a charitable organization, the taxpayer can avoid paying tax on the gain, ut get a fair market value deduction for the gift. Further information about making an election ɔn contributions of long-term capital gain property is available under the Special Election ection in this chapter.

The second characteristic that determines the amount of the allowable charitable deduction is he type of charity that receives the donation. For income tax purposes, all charities are classified is either public charities or private charities. **Public charities** are organizations that receive upport from a wide cross-section of the population. Public charities include organizations such as the Red Cross, universities, hospitals, animal shelters, and the YMCA. **Private charities** are corporations or trusts structured to further the charitable intentions of a donor or the donor's family. Private charities include private foundations and charitable lead trusts.

The deduction limitations for charitable gifts are determined based on the type of charity receiving the contribution and the type of property contributed. The deduction limitations are described in the following table.

**EXHIBIT 7.5** **CHARITABLE CONTRIBUTION DEDUCTIONS (PERCENT OF TAXPAYER'S AGI)**

| Type of Property Donated | Valuation for Purposes of Charitable Deduction | Ceiling for Public Charities, Private Operating Foundations and Certain Private Nonoperating Foundations* | Ceiling for Other Private Nonoperating Foundations (PNOF) | |
|---|---|---|---|---|
| Cash | Fair market value | 50% | 30% | |
| Ordinary Income Property and Short-term Capital Gain Property | Lesser of the adjusted basis or the fair market value | 50% | 30% | |
| **Long-term Capital Gain property:**<br>- Intangible | Fair market value | 30%* | | 20%** |
| - Tangible Personalty | Fair market value --<br>(a) related use<br>Adjusted basis --<br>(b) unrelated use | 30%*<br><br><br>50% | Adjusted Basis | 20% |
| - Real Property | Fair market value | 30%* | | 20% |

*Taxpayer has the option to use the adjusted basis and the 50% of AGI ceiling for Regular Charities.
**Certain contributions of Qualified Appreciated Stock may use the fair market value.

Gifts of cash and non-long-term capital gains property to a public charity are deductible to the extent that they do not exceed 50 percent of the taxpayer's contribution base (referred to as 50 percent gifts). Recall that the value of gifts of non-long-term capital gains property for income tax purposes is the donor's cost basis in the property.

Long-term capital gains property donated to a charity may only be deducted to the extent of 30 percent of the donor's contribution base (referred to as 30 percent gifts). Recall, however, that the donor will not be required to recognize gain on the asset donated, even though the value of the deduction is the fair market value of the property. The lower percentage limitation reflects the benefit of avoiding income inclusion on the gain.

Private foundations do not receive funding from the general public, but instead receive funding through private contributions, investments, and endowments. There are two types of private foundations: operating and nonoperating. An operating foundation spends substantially all of its income each year in fulfillment of its charitable mission (i.e., its tax exempt purpose).

Nonoperating foundations typically make grants to other organizations and can receive operating foundation treatment (the same as public charity treatments) if the nonoperating foundation distributes its income by the 15th day of the 3rd month after the close of its tax year.

When gifts are made to private foundations or charitable lead trusts (CLT), the deduction limitations are further reduced to 30 percent for gifts of cash and non-long-term capital gain property (referred to as 30 percent gifts) and to 20 percent for gifts of long-term capital gain property (referred to as 20 percent gifts). The lower deduction limitations in this instance are a reflection of the increased control that the donor has over the private foundation or CLT as compared to a public charity.

If an individual makes a contribution that exceeds the allowable contribution, the excess amount can be carried forward for up to five years. In each of those carryforward years, however, the taxpayer must otherwise be able to deduct the charitable gift based in the limitations on charitable deductions calculated for those years.

Brian has AGI of $100,000 for the current tax year, and has no net operating loss carry-backs. He made a cash gift of $60,000 to his university to assist in the construction of a new building on campus. Brian is permitted to deduct up to 50% of his contribution base as a charitable contribution. Since he made a charitable gift of cash to a public charity, the 50% limit applies and he will be able to deduct $50,000 in the current year. The remaining $10,000 will be carried forward for up to five years and deducted against future income, subject to the limitations on charitable gifts imposed in those years.

**EXAMPLE 7.14**

Assume the same facts as the prior example, except that Brian's gift was stock with a fair market value of $60,000. He paid $40,000 for the stock 3 years ago. Brian will be able to deduct $30,000 this year (30% of his contribution base) and will be able to carry over the remaining $30,000 for use over the next five tax years. By making the gift with appreciated long-term gain property, Brian will not be required to recognize the gain on the stock in his income.

**EXAMPLE 7.15**

## Special Election

A special election is available for taxpayers who wish to make contributions of long-term capital gain property. Instead of subjecting the gift to the 30 percent (for public charities) or 20 percent (for private charities) contribution limitations, the taxpayer can elect to treat the gift as a 50 percent contribution, thereby allowing a greater portion of the gift to be deducted as a charitable deduction in the current year. However, there is a cost to making this election. Instead of taking a deduction for the fair market value of the property donated, the deduction is limited to the donor's cost basis.

| **EXAMPLE 7.16** | Continuing our example above, concerning Brian's gift of $60,000 of long-term capital gain stock to his university, if Brian elects to treat the contribution as a 50% contribution, Brian's charitable deduction for the current year will be $40,000, his cost basis in the property. By making the election, Brian is able to deduct $10,000 more this year, but loses the ability to deduct the appreciation in the stock of $20,000. |
|---|---|

The overall limitation on charitable contributions for a given tax year is 50 percent of the taxpayer's contribution base. When applying the overall limitation, allowable deductions first come from 50 percent gifts, then from 30 percent gifts, and finally from 20 percent gifts.

| **EXAMPLE 7.17** | Ryan has AGI this year of $200,000. He contributed $80,000 of cash, and $70,000 of long-term capital gain property (stock with a basis of $20,000) to the Irish Heritage Museum, a qualified charity. Under the 50% limit, Ryan's maximum contribution is $100,000, and under the 30% limit, his maximum contribution is $60,000. An overall limit of 50% of contribution base applies. For the current year, Ryan will be able to deduct the full amount of his cash contribution ($80,000), plus $20,000 of his property contribution, for a total of $100,000 (which equals 50% of his adjusted gross income). The remaining $50,000 of the property contribution will be carried forward for up to five tax years. |
|---|---|

### Special Rule for Tangible Personalty

Another special rule applies to donations of tangible personal property to charitable organizations. Normally when charitable contributions are made they are either paid in cash or marketable securities that can be easily transformed into cash. Securities and cash equivalents are intangible forms of property interests. Sometimes a donor may wish to give tangible personal property to a charity. When tangible personal property is donated to a charity, the amount and type of deduction that applies will depend on whether or not the charity uses the tangible personal property in its tax exempt function.

If tangible personal property donated to a charity is used by the charity to carry out its tax exempt purpose, the donor may take a deduction equal to the fair market value of the property on the date of the gift and the donation will be subject to the 30 percent limitation as long as the property had a long-term holding period in the hands of the donor. If the tangible property donated did not have a long-term holding period, the donor would be required to reduce the fair market value by 100 percent of the gain, resulting in a cost basis deduction, subject to the 50 percent limitation.

When tangible personal property donated to a charity will not be used by the charity to carry out its tax-exempt purpose, the deduction available to the donor is the fair market value of the property reduced by 100 percent of the gain (a cost basis deduction) and will be subject to the 50 percent limitation.

William is redecorating his manor house and decides to donate to his local YMCA an original Rembrant sketch that had been purchased 20 years ago and was hanging in his study. Since the YMCA does not display fine art in fulfilling its tax exempt function, the YMCA will sell the painting and use the proceeds to support their activities. William will be able to take a charitable income tax deduction for the cost basis of the sketch, and the donation will be subject to the 50% limit.

EXAMPLE 7.18

Assume the same facts as the previous example except that William donates the Rembrant sketch to the Smithsonian Museum of Fine Art in Washington, D.C. Since one of the charitable purposes of the Smithsonian is to acquire and display fine art, William will be entitled to take a charitable income tax deduction equal to the fair market value of the sketch at the time of the gift. The contribution will be subject to the 30% limitation because it was a gift of long-term capital gain property to a public charity.

EXAMPLE 7.19

Brendan donates a painting of a religious theme that he has owned for several years to his church. The church will include the painting in a silent auction coming up later in the year and the proceeds of the auction will be dedicated to restoration of the church. Since the church will sell the property (in this case, by silent charitable auction) and will not use it in its tax-exempt purpose, Brendan is entitled to receive a cost basis deduction for the gift.

EXAMPLE 7.20

## Ordinary Income Property

When a taxpayer donates ordinary income property to a charity, the donation will be valued at cost basis and will be subject to the 50 percent limitation. As discussed later in the property transactions section of this text, there are only three types of assets in the tax world – capital assets, ordinary income assets, and Section 1231 assets. Ordinary income assets include accounts/notes receivable, inventory, and copyrights or creative works held by the creator. Ordinary income assets, when sold, generate income subject to ordinary tax rates; they do not qualify for capital gains tax rates. As a result, ordinary income assets will always be subject to the 50 percent limitation (or 30 percent limitation for private charities) and will generate a cost basis tax deduction for the donor. Ordinary income assets receive the same tax treatment as short-term capital gains assets for purposes of the income tax charitable deduction.

One of the most common types of ordinary income assets donated to charity is a creative work in the hands of the author. Works of art, books and writings, letters, musical compositions and other creative works donated by the creator of the work to charity will qualify for a cost basis deduction. In most cases, the cost basis will be very low if it is a creative work. The tax treatment should make sense in that if the work was sold, the creator would recognize the sale price as ordinary income. Remember that if a creative work is held by someone other than the author, it may be classified as a capital asset and may qualify for a full fair market value deduction if the asset is held for a long-term holding period.

<table>
<tr><td>EXAMPLE 7.21</td><td>Kelly, a renowned author of children's novels and professor of literature, wrote all of her manuscripts by hand. Kelly's novels have been widely acclaimed as the best children's literature of the era. She kept the original drafts of each of her novels for her own purposes, but recently decided to get rid of the growing mass of paper in her home. Kelly donated all of the original manuscripts to the museum/archive of her university. Kelly's charitable deduction is limited to her cost basis in the property – the cost of the paper and the ink that was used to write the novels.</td></tr>
</table>

From a financial planning perspective, authors of creative works should consider holding those works until death, and leaving those items to family members. At death, the basis of the asset in the hands of the beneficiary will be the fair market value of the asset as of the date of the decedent's death and a subsequent transfer of the property to a charity by the family member will qualify for a full fair market value deduction. The fair market value deduction applies since all property transferred through the estate of a decedent is deemed to have a long-term holding period.

<table>
<tr><td>EXAMPLE 7.22</td><td>In our example above, if Kelly held the drafts of her literary works until her death, and left them to her children, the papers would have a basis equal to their fair market value at the date of her death, significantly more than the cost of the paper and the ink. When her children donate the documents to the university museum, they will be entitled to a full fair market value charitable deduction on their income tax returns.</td></tr>
</table>

One special exception to the charitable deduction rules covering ordinary income property involves a contribution of tangible personal property for scientific research. The charitable deduction for such property is the lesser of (1) the cost of the property plus half of the gain; or (2) two times the cost basis of the property. To receive this increased deduction for scientific research property, two additional requirements must be met: (1) the property must be new inventory-type scientific equipment manufactured by the donor, and (2) the property must be donated to the charity within two years of its purchase, or, in the case of a manufacturer, when the equipment was fully constructed.

## Financial Planning Applications

Three final charitable deduction rules are important for financial planning purposes:

1. charitable deductions by corporations;
2. contributions made to purchase sporting tickets from universities; and
3. raffle tickets sold by charitable organizations.

### Charitable Deductions by Corporations

Unlike individuals, who can deduct up to 50 percent of their contribution base for gifts made to charitable organizations, regular corporations (C corporations) are only permitted to deduct up to 10 percent of their income for charitable gifts. Subchapter S corporations must pass through the charitable gifts to the owners on Form K-1 and the owners will include their portion of the charitable contribution on their personal income tax return as an itemized deduction (below-the-line deduction).

Closely held and family business owners who have business interests in corporate form (C corporations, not S corporations) may wish to use the corporation as a means of achieving an above-the-line charitable deduction. While C corporation charitable deductions are limited to 10 percent of their income, gifts of corporate income to charity avoid tax at both the corporate and owner levels. Normally, corporate earnings are taxed to the corporation and are again taxed to the owners when they are distributed in the form of dividends. An owner who receives a dividend distribution could use the distribution to make a charitable gift, but that gift will be a below-the-line itemized deduction subject to limitations (based on the contribution base test). A more efficient way of making the transfer to charity is to have the corporation, to the extent it can achieve a charitable income tax deduction, make the gift directly to the charity. This planning tool can be particularly useful as a method of funding a private foundation.

| | |
|---|---|
| Reilly is the 100% shareholder of RKLJ, Inc., a C corporation. Reilly is also charitably inclined, and created the Jarvis Foundation earlier this year. RKLJ, Inc. expects to have net profits of $200,000 for the year, and Reilly would like to take some money out of the corporation to begin to fund his foundation. The corporation will have to pay tax on its income for the year, and any amount remaining will be available for distribution as a dividend. Assume, for purposes of this example, that the corporation's combined federal and state income tax is $40,000. This leaves $160,000 of income available for distribution this year. If Reilly distributes $20,000 to himself in the form of a dividend, he will have to pay tax on the dividend (which will most likely be classified as a qualified dividend and be subject to tax at the 15% rate) of $3,000. The tax on the dividend will be offset by Reilly's charitable deduction, but if Reilly is in a high personal income tax bracket, or if he has made other significant charitable gifts for the current tax year, the limitations that apply to charitable deductions may limit his ability to deduct those charitable gifts for income tax purposes. | **EXAMPLE 7.23** |

**EXAMPLE 7.24**

Continuing with the same facts from the prior example, assume that instead of distributing a dividend to himself and making a charitable gift, Reilly has his corporation make a gift of $20,000 directly to the Jarvis Foundation. In this case, the corporation's income will be reduced from $200,000 to $180,000, lowering corporate income tax liability from $40,000 to $36,000 (a $4,000 corporate tax savings). Since the gift was made directly to the Foundation, there is no need for Reilly to declare a $20,000 dividend to make the charitable gift, further saving $3,000 in income taxes on Reilly's personal income tax return. Reilly will not be able to deduct the charitable gift on his own tax return, but he does not have to include income in his return in order to make the charitable gift, either. In a sense, Reilly has taken an above-the-line charitable deduction for the $20,000 contribution to the Foundation since he did not include any incremental income in his tax return. Avoiding inclusion of incremental income in his tax return lowers Reilly's AGI, which has a positive effect on other personal tax planning options that are phased-out as AGI increases. Furthermore, corporate taxes were reduced, allowing Reilly to donate pre-tax income to the Foundation as opposed to after-tax income. Since the charitable gift is not being deducted as an itemized deduction on Reilly's personal tax return, the percentage limitations on charitable gifts are not an issue, although the overall deductibility limit for corporate donations does impose a limitation on the total amount that can be given to charity using this technique.

**EXHIBIT 7.6** **SUMMARY OF EXAMPLES 7.23 AND 7.24**

| Dividend by C Corporation | | Charitable Donation by C Corporation | |
|---|---|---|---|
| C Corporation Income | $200,000 | C Corporation Income | $200,000 |
| Less: Tax | <$40,000> | Less: Charitable Deduction | <$20,000> |
| Less: Dividend Paid | <$20,000> | Taxable Income | $180,000 |
| Net Income | $140,000* | Tax @ 20% | <$36,000> |
| | | Net Income | $144,000 |
| *Note that the $20,000 dividend is offset by the $20,000 charitable contribution. | | | |

Particularly for high income taxpayers who wish to make large charitable gifts as a percentage of their income, using corporate earnings to make all or some of those charitable gifts may be a very effective planning technique.

## Contributions to Universities for Sporting Tickets

When reviewing the general rules for charitable deductions, we noted that a taxpayer can only get a charitable deduction for the difference between the amount that he or she gives to the charity and the fair market value of what the taxpayer receives in return. In some cases, however, the value of what the taxpayer receives in return for a charitable gift is difficult to determine. One example is a charitable gift made to a university so that the donor can be placed on a waiting list to purchase basketball or football tickets. Due to the popularity of collegiate sports, and, in particular, basketball and football, some colleges and universities have conditioned purchase of game tickets on a donation to the school. Once the donation is made, the donor may then purchase tickets to the sporting event. It is clear that the purchase of the game tickets is not a charitable gift, but what about the original donation to the charity? Was the entire donation a charitable gift, or did the taxpayer receive something in return that reduces the value of that charitable gift?

The answer to this question is that the gift to the school was really part charitable gift and part purchase of an option to buy sporting event tickets. In these situations, Congress has resolved the valuation issue associated with the option contract. When a donation made to a school is a precondition to purchase event tickets, 80 percent of the donation is deductible as a charitable gift, and 20 percent is deemed to be the nondeductible option cost. Of course, if a taxpayer wishes to receive a 100 percent deduction, the taxpayer could make the gift to the university while specifically electing out of receiving the option to purchase event tickets.

## Raffle Tickets Sold by Charitable Organizations

Purchase of raffle tickets from a charitable organization is not a tax-deductible donation – it is the purchase of a chance to win the prize offered in the raffle. Taxpayers who wish to generate a charitable deduction for purchasing raffle tickets from a charity may do so by agreeing in advance that if they win the prize, it will be donated back to the charity.

## PARTIAL INTEREST GIFTS

One of the general rules for charitable giving states that a donor must give his or her entire interest in the property to qualify for an income tax charitable deduction (known as the partial interest rule). As noted earlier in the chapter, there are several exceptions to the partial interest rule, including:

- A gift of an undivided portion of the donor's entire interest in the property;
- A gift of a remainder interest in a personal residence or farm;
- A gift of a partial interest if transferred in trust (a charitable remainder trust, a charitable lead trust, or a pooled income fund); and
- Purchase of a charitable gift annuity.

When a donor owns only a portion of a property, a charitable income tax deduction is available provided that the donor gives away his or her entire interest in the property. These types of charitable gifts are often seen when a taxpayer holds property jointly with another taxpayer.

**EXAMPLE 7.25**

Ken, Rob, and Kyle own Greenacre as tenants in common. Each has a 1/3 interest in the property. A tenancy in common interest is an undivided interest in property. Ken no longer wants to deal with his co-tenants, and would like to make a charitable gift. He gives his 1/3 tenancy in common interest to his private foundation, which will then sell the interest (probably to Rob and Kyle). Since Ken gave away his entire interest in the property to a charitable entity, he will be entitled to a charitable income tax deduction. In this case, Ken's charitable income tax deduction will be limited to his cost basis in the asset, since it was donated to his private foundation.

Another method of making a partial gift in property to a charitable organization in a way that will qualify for the income tax charitable deduction is to give a remainder interest in a personal residence or farm. This technique can be useful when a taxpayer has a residence or farm that he or she would like to use until death, but the taxpayers heirs do not want to use the property and would likely sell it shortly after the taxpayer dies. Administering unwanted real property in the estate of a decedent increases costs and lengthens the estate settlement process. Assuming that the taxpayer is interested in making a charitable gift, donating a remainder interest in the property to a charitable organization would achieve two objectives: (1) the present value of the remainder interest will qualify for an income tax charitable deduction; and (2) at death, title immediately vests in the charity, removing the expense and hassle of dealing with unwanted real property in the decedent's estate.

A charitable gift annuity is an arrangement where a taxpayer transfers an asset to charity in return for annuity payments over the taxpayer's lifetime. Charitable gift annuities are typically structured so that 50 percent of the transaction involves purchase of an annuity contract and 50 percent represents a charitable gift. Consequently, 50 percent of the value of the property transferred will qualify for the charitable income tax deduction. If the asset transferred has a value in excess of basis, there may be additional income tax consequences, but these are beyond the scope of this book.

# CASUALTY LOSSES

One of the few tax deductions allowed for personal expenses is the **casualty loss deduction**. Generally, personal expenses are not deductible. By allowing a deduction for casualty losses, Congress has made an exception in extreme cases where a taxpayer has suffered a large loss.

As a threshold matter, only personal casualty losses will be deducted as an itemized deduction on the taxpayer's Schedule A. If the casualty loss is associated with a trade or business, the loss will be deducted above-the-line as a business expense. If personal risks are properly insured, it is unlikely that the taxpayer will be able to generate a tax deduction for casualty losses, since the insurance proceeds received offset the taxpayer's loss. In a financial planning context, a client's

**Key Concepts**

Underline/highlight the answers to these questions as you read:

1. Describe the types of casualty losses that may be deducted as an itemized deduction.

2. Explain the restrictions on the deduction of personal casualty and theft losses.

ability to take a casualty loss deduction is probably evidence of a failure to identify and properly insure the risks that were facing the taxpayer. As you will see when we review the limitations on the casualty loss deduction, the tax deduction is not a good substitute for insurance coverage.

A casualty loss deduction is available for losses or damages to a taxpayer's property resulting from sudden or unexpected events, such as fire, storm, shipwreck, or theft. To qualify for the deduction, the event causing the loss must be identifiable. Losses resulting from events that are not sudden or unexpected, such as insect damage to a home, are not eligible for an income tax deduction. Any allowable deduction is taken in the year the loss is sustained (in the case of a casualty), or in the year that the loss was discovered (in the case of theft).

## CASUALTY LOSS LIMITATIONS

For personal casualty and theft losses, the amount of the loss is the lower of (1) the difference between the fair market value of the property before the event and the fair market value of the property after the event, less insurance proceeds received or (2) the taxpayer's adjusted basis in the property less insurance proceeds received. This valuation rule prevents a taxpayer from taking a casualty loss on the gain attached to property that had not been brought into the taxpayer's income.

> Beau owned a home in New Orleans that was severely damaged by a hurricane. Beau had purchased the home for $200,000, and the fair market value of the home prior to the

**EXAMPLE 7.26**

hurricane was $400,000. His homeowners insurance policy had lapsed one month before the hurricane hit and Beau had not obtained any other insurance. After the hurricane, the property had a fair market value of $90,000. Beau's casualty loss is valued at $200,000 which is his adjusted basis less insurance proceeds received (insurance proceeds in this case are zero). The decline in the fair market value of the property is equal to $310,000, but Beau's casualty loss is limited to his adjusted basis because his adjusted basis is less than the decline in the fair market value of the property.

The limitations on the deduction for personal casualty and theft losses do not end there. Two additional restrictions apply. First, $100 must be deducted from each occurrence. An occurrence is treated as one event, such as a hurricane. If a hurricane caused damage to a taxpayer's house and car, $100 in total would be deducted from both losses (not $200, or $100 for each separate loss). Second, to be deductible, the taxpayer's aggregate casualty and theft losses must exceed 10 percent of the taxpayer's adjusted gross income.

<table>
<tr><td>**EXAMPLE 7.27**</td><td>Using the facts from the prior example, assume that Beau's AGI for the year is $100,000. Beau's casualty loss of $200,000 must be reduced by $100 and the result is only deductible to the extent it exceeds 10% of AGI. The deductible portion of Beau's casualty loss is $189,900 ($200,000 - $100 - $10,000[10% of AGI]).</td></tr>
</table>

There is one further limitation that applies to personal casualty and theft losses. To the extent that the taxpayer has a casualty gain, that casualty gain offsets any casualty losses suffered in the same year. For example, assume a taxpayer experienced two events causing complete losses to two assets and one of the assets was insured. Also assume the insurance company paid the taxpayer more than his or her basis in the property (which could happen when the property is insured for its fair market value), and the property for which the insurance proceeds were received will not be replaced. In this situation, the casualty gain on the insured asset will offset the casualty loss on the uninsured asset, and the net loss will then be subject to the $100 and 10 percent of AGI limitations.

## BUSINESS CASUALTY LOSSES

As mentioned earlier, business casualty losses are deducted above the line against the income from the business activity. The amount of the business casualty loss is the lower of (1) the difference between the fair market value of the property before the loss and the fair market value of the property after the loss, or (2) the adjusted basis of the property in the case of a partial loss. If a casualty causes a complete loss of the property, the amount of the casualty loss is the taxpayer's adjusted basis in the property. A casualty loss is reduced by insurance or any other type of reimbursement.

<table>
<tr><td>**EXAMPLE 7.28**</td><td>In a fire that swept through his factory recently, Nero lost several pieces of business property. One item, a machine that made Roman Widgets, had an adjusted basis of $3,000 and</td></tr>
</table>

was completely worthless after the fire. The fair market value of the machine at the time of the loss was $1,300. Nero's business casualty loss deduction is $3,000. Since the machine was used in a trade or business, Nero is entitled to recoup his entire basis in the property even though the fair market value of the machine was lower at the time of the loss. The entire loss will be deductible against the income of Nero's business, and no limitations or phaseouts apply since the loss was incurred on a business asset.

Note that this result differs substantially from a personal loss situation. If the property was not a business machine, but rather a personal use asset that had an adjusted basis of $3,000 and a fair market value of $1,300, only $1,300 (the lower of the difference in fair market value before and after the casualty event, or the taxpayer's adjusted basis) would be deductible (before the imposition of limitations and phaseouts). Since the remaining part of the property ($1,700 = $3,000 - $1,300) was used for personal purposes (not in a trade or business or for the production of income), it does not qualify for a deduction.

## Quick Quiz 7.4

**Highlight the answer to these questions:**

1. Casualty losses are only deductible if they result for sudden or unexpected events.
   a. True
   b. False

2. Casualty losses must exceed the lesser of $100 or 10% of the taxpayer's AGI in order to be deductible.
   a. True
   b. False

True, False.

**EXAMPLE 7.29**

The fire that swept through Nero's factory also damaged the factory building. The fair market value of the building was $800,000 before the fire, and $650,000 after the fire. Nero's basis in the factory is $500,000. In this case, the deductible casualty loss is $150,000 (the difference in value before and after the loss). This was not a complete loss, so Nero can still use the remaining property and recoup the remaining capital investment over the property's useful life. Since the loss was sustained on a business asset, the entire loss is deductible against business income, and no limitations or phase-outs apply.

# MISCELLANEOUS ITEMIZED DEDUCTIONS

Miscellaneous itemized deductions include all of the remaining deductions that individual taxpayers can take on their income tax return. Miscellaneous itemized deductions fall into two categories: (1) those that are deductible without limitation, and (2) those that are subject to the two percent floor. Almost all of the miscellaneous itemized deductions are subject to the two percent floor.

## DEDUCTIONS NOT SUBJECT TO THE TWO PERCENT FLOOR (TIER I)

The deductions not subject to the two percent floor generally involve transactions where Congress deems it unfair to subject taxpayers to taxation on transactions where income is required to be included above the line, while deductions are taken below the line. The most important miscellaneous itemized deductions not subject to the two percent floor for financial planning purposes are:

1. Gambling losses (to the extent of gambling income),
2. Credit for estate taxes imposed on IRD (income in respect of a decedent's assets),
3. Loss on the disposition of an annuity contract,
4. Repayments of income (such as repayments of Social Security income when the taxpayer fails the earnings test).

Each of these instances requires income inclusion. Gambling winnings must be included in gross income, but losses to the extent of winnings can be used to offset the income. When IRD assets (such as pension plans, IRAs, and annuity contracts) are taxed in the estate of a decedent, the additional estate tax paid by reason of including the IRD asset becomes an income tax deduction for the person who receives the asset. Like the case with gambling winnings, distributions from inherited IRD assets must be included in income, so offsetting deductions should be allowed without being subject to the two percent floor. If a taxpayer purchased an annuity, and later surrenders the annuity suffering a loss, a full deduction should likewise be afforded to allow the taxpayer to recoup his or her full investment in the contract. Finally, if an individual under normal retirement age is receiving Social Security and has wage income above specified thresholds, the worker must pay back part of the Social Security benefit. The full amount received is included in income, so the taxpayer should be able to deduct the amount paid back without being subject to the two percent floor.

The final miscellaneous itemized deduction not subject to the two percent floor applies to job related expenses for handicapped workers. Specified expenses, such as the cost of purchasing readers or retaining aids to help the handicapped person perform his or her job function will not be limited by the two percent floor.

While these expenses may be deducted without regard to the two percent floor, recall that some limitations still apply. These deductions are itemized deductions (below-the-line), so they are only taken into account after adjusted gross income (AGI) has been determined. All else equal, the higher a person's AGI, the more likely he or she is liable to be subject to deduction limitations.

## DEDUCTIONS SUBJECT TO THE TWO PERCENT FLOOR (TIER II)

The remaining expenses that are classified as miscellaneous itemized deductions are subject to the two percent floor. There are many items that fall into this category. The major categories of miscellaneous itemized deductions subject to the two percent floor that affect financial planning decisions are:

- Employee business expenses.
- Hobby expenses (to the extent of hobby income).
- Investment expenses and tax advice.
- Losses on IRAs (when the IRA has been terminated).

Hobby expenses will be considered in the next chapter, and therefore will not be covered here.

### Employee Business Expenses

Unreimbursed employee business expenses are deductible as a miscellaneous itemized deduction subject to the two percent floor. **Employee business expenses** include professional and union dues of employees, travel, supplies and services, professional books and journals, job related educational expenses, work clothes and uniforms, and job hunting expenses in the same line of work.

Professional fees (such as licensing fees for lawyers, physicians, and accountants) or union dues are deductible as an employee business expense if they are not reimbursed by the employer. Recall that self-employed individuals will deduct these costs against business income (above the line) such as the Schedule C. Only professionals and union members who are employees will claim professional and union dues as below-the-line itemized deductions.

Travel expenses include costs for transportation, lodging, incidental expenses and 50 percent of meals when a taxpayer is away from his or her tax home. The taxpayer's tax home is the general area where the taxpayer regularly conducts business. To be deductible as travel expenses, the expenses must be incurred when the taxpayer must be away from their tax home for work related reasons and it is reasonable for the taxpayer to require rest and lodging away from their tax home. Generally, domestic transportation expenses are fully deductible if the primary purpose of the trip is business related. The cost of lodging, dry cleaning and laundry, telephone, tips, and local transportation are fully deductible for the days that the taxpayer is conducting business. Meals for those days are deductible, but are limited to 50 percent of the cost incurred. Expenses incurred (with the exception of transportation expenses when the primary purpose of the trip is business-related) on days when the taxpayer is not conducting business are not deductible.

<table>
<tr><td>

**EXAMPLE 7.30**

</td><td>

Michael normally works in Connecticut. He traveled to San Diego, California for a business conference, and was not reimbursed by his employer. Since he enjoys sailing, Michael decided to stay an extra two days to sail around San Diego Bay after the 3-day conference ended. Since the primary purpose of the trip was business related (he spent 2 days on personal matters, and 3 days on business matters), Michael will be able to deduct the full cost of the airfare to and from San Diego. For the three days that Michael is attending the conference, he can also deduct the cost of lodging, dry cleaning, telephone, local transportation, incidental expenses, and 50% of the cost of his meals. The travel expenses for the two days that Michael spends sailing on San Diego Bay, however, are not deductible since they are personal expenses.

</td></tr>
</table>

For travel outside the United States, the rule is a bit different. Expenses associated with trips purely for business will be fully deductible. When the trip is primarily for business, the travel expenses must be prorated between the personal and business days, and only the expense associated with the business days may be deducted. If the trip is primarily for personal purposes, none of the transportation expenses are deductible. Some exceptions do apply. A trip outside the United States will be considered to be purely business related when one of the following conditions exists:

1. The taxpayer does not have control over the timing or arrangements for the trip.
2. The trip outside the United States lasted for less than seven days.
3. Less than 25 percent of the time spent on the trip was for personal activities.
4. Vacation was not a primary consideration for the trip.

When counting days used for personal and business travel while on a foreign trip, all of the following are considered to be business days:

- Days during which business is conducted.
- Travel days to and from the location.
- Weekends and holidays provided that they fall between business days.

<table>
<tr><td>

**EXAMPLE 7.31**

</td><td>

Thomas traveled to London for a business meeting. He left on Wednesday evening, and returned the following Saturday. The meeting began on Thursday, broke for the long weekend (Monday was Queen Elizabeth's official birthday), and

</td></tr>
</table>

resumed on Tuesday. On the weekend, Thomas spent time touring Southern England. The business meetings were concluded on Thursday, and Thomas resumed his tour of Southern England until his departure flight on Saturday evening. In this case, the travel covered a period of 11 days. The two travel days were business days, as were the 5 days actually spent at the business meeting. The three day weekend (including the holiday) were also business days, since business was conducted both before and after the holiday weekend. Out of the 11 day trip, 10 days were classified as business days, and one day was classified as a personal day. Since Thomas spent less than 25% of the trip on personal travel, the trip is deemed to be solely for business, and the full cost of the airfare is a deductible travel expense. The cost of lodging, incidentals, and 50% of meals on the one day that Thomas was not deemed to be conducting business will not be deductible, but those costs for the three-day weekend that were presumed to be business days are deductible.

There are also limitations imposed on water travel and conventions due to taxpayer abuse in the past. A deduction of up to $2,000 is permitted for conventions on cruise ships provided that the following conditions are met:

1. The convention is directly related to the taxpayer's trade or business;
2. The cruise ship is registered in the United States (has a U.S. Flag); and
3. During the convention cruise, the ship only docks at ports within the United States or its possessions.

If any of these conditions are not met, no deduction for cruise-ship conventions is permissible. For conventions on land within the United States, travel expenses are deductible provided that the convention is directly related to the taxpayer's trade or business. For a convention outside of the United States, travel expenses are deductible provided that the meeting is directly related to the taxpayer's trade or business, and it is as reasonable to hold the meeting outside of North America as inside North America.

**EXAMPLE 7.32**

John paid $3,500 for a convention on board a cruise ship. The convention was directly related to his trade or business. The ship left San Diego and sailed north, stopping in San Francisco, Seattle, one or two Canadian ports and finally arriving in Alaska. John will not be permitted to deduct any portion of the cost of this trip, since the cruise ship docked in a foreign port.

**EXAMPLE 7.33**

Randy, a neurosurgeon, decided he needed to learn how to invest all of the money that he had been making in his capacity as a surgeon. He paid $4,000 to attend an Investment Convention in Palm Springs this year. Randy will not be able to deduct any of the cost associated with the convention as a business expense, since the convention is not directly related to Randy's trade or business activity (medicine).

Travel related expenses are deductible only if the taxpayer's absence from their work-home is temporary. Temporary means that the work assignment is for one year or less. If the assignment exceeds one year, then none of the travel expenses are deductible, since the taxpayer is deemed to have changed his or her tax home. For taxpayers who have long work assignments away from their tax home, travel between their tax home and the work location (provided that they do not exceed the one year limitation) is deductible to the extent that the travel does not exceed the cost of remaining at the temporary workplace.

**EXAMPLE 7.34**

Christopher has spent the last three months working on a contract in Arizona. His regular tax home is Connecticut. On weekends, Christopher flies home to spend time with his wife and children. The cost of the flight home (round-trip) is $350. If Christopher had remained at his work location, he would have incurred three additional nights of hotel bills per week (at $125 per night), plus meal and incidental costs. Since the cost to return home is less than the cost of remaining in the temporary work location, Christopher may deduct the full cost of the travel between his tax-home and temporary work location.

The cost of supplies and services incurred for work purposes while working at home are also deductible as work related expenses. If a home phone is used for both personal and work purposes, however, a special limitation applies. The cost of the first phone line into the home is not deductible as a business expense. Additional costs, such as long-distance calls for business, a second phone line installed for business use, a dedicated fax line, or telephone features such as call forwarding are deductible provided that those expenses are work related.

Likewise, the cost of professional books and journals necessary for the taxpayer to maintain his or her skills in a current trade or profession are deducted as employee related business expenses.

Educational expenses are deductible as employee business expenses provided that the purpose of the expense is to maintain or expand the taxpayer's competency in his or her current trade or profession. Tuition costs, books, supplies, transportation to and from class, meals and lodging while attending school away from home, and fees are deductible. Educational expenses incurred to meet the minimal requirements for a trade or business, to qualify the taxpayer for a new trade or business, or to help the taxpayer return to a former trade or business are not deductible.

**EXAMPLE 7.35**

Ginny worked as a law librarian for Hogwarts University School of Law. In performing her duties as law librarian, Ginny assisted law professors with legal research and oversaw the administration of the library. While serving as Law Librarian, Ginny began to take law school classes and ultimately received a law degree. Despite the fact that the law school classes maintained or further expanded her skills in her current trade or profession (as law librarian), the classes qualified her to enter a new trade or profession (the practice of law) and are therefore nondeductible (Gilligan, T.C.M. 2002-150).

EXAMPLE 7.36

Ron, a financial planner, began taking classes to prepare him for the CFP® Certification Examination at a prestigious east-coast university. The classes were conducted every other weekend on Friday nights and Saturdays. Every other week, Ron flew in to take the course and stayed at a hotel on Friday and Saturday night (there were no flights that could get Ron back home on Saturday night). Since Ron is taking classes that further expand and enhance his knowledge in his current trade or profession, the tuition and fees for the program are deductible. Likewise, the cost of airfare, hotel, incidentals, and half of the cost of meals are also deductible as a business related education expense. Since completing the program (and the CFP® Exam) does not qualify Ron to enter a new trade or profession, all of the costs are deductible.

Work clothes and uniforms are also deductible as a business related expense provided that they are purchased as a condition of employment and they are not items that could be worn outside of work. The cost of items that are suitable for wear outside of work will not qualify for a deduction.

EXAMPLE 7.37

Ted, an employee of The Amazing Company, makes most of his money performing as a clown at childrens' birthday parties and corporate events. The cost of clown clothing is deductible as an employee related business expense, since it is not suitable to be worn outside of a work setting.

An often overlooked group of work-related expenses that may be deducted as a business expense are job-hunting expenses. To be deductible, the expenses must be incurred in finding a new job in the taxpayer's current trade or profession. Provided that this condition is met, the expenses are deductible even if the taxpayer does not find, or is not selected, to fill a new job. Deductible expenses include travel costs, costs of printing resumes and assembling portfolios of work, phone calls, and fees paid to employment agencies or recruiters. Generally, the IRS will disallow a deduction if the primary purpose of a trip is personal as opposed to job-related, so it is wise to keep a log of job-hunting activities if the taxpayer would like to claim the costs as a deduction.

EXAMPLE 7.38

Laura just graduated from law school, and passed the bar exam. She would like to try to find a job in California, so she flew to San Diego and San Francisco for a series of interviews with law firms. The primary purpose of the trip was to find a job, and her activities were substantiated with a detailed log that was kept by Laura. Laura will not be able to claim any deduction for job hunting expenses, since she is not already in the trade or business of practicing law. She is seeking admission to practice, not seeking a new job in her current trade or profession, so no deduction will be allowed.

The discussion relating to business-related expenses above applies to unreimbursed employee business expenses. If an employer reimburses an employee for business related expenses, the tax result will be dictated by whether or not the employer has an accountable expense reimbursement plan.

An accountable plan is a reimbursement plan that reimburses employees only for actual expenses incurred, and requires the employees to provide proof of, or "account for" their expenditures (usually, receipts are sufficient). When an employer has an accountable plan in place, there will be no tax impact for the employee. The reimbursement will not be included in the employee's income and the employee will not be entitled to take a deduction for the expenses incurred, since he or she has been fully reimbursed for those payments.

Some employers have **non-accountable reimbursement plans**. In this type of plan, the employer gives the employee a specified sum of money out of which the employee will cover all of the business related expenses. If the employee spends more than the amount given, he or she will be out of pocket for that amount. If the employee spends less, the excess does not have to be returned to the employer. When this type of plan is in place, the entire amount given to the employee will be included in the employee's W-2 income, thereby increasing AGI. The employee can claim an employee business expense deduction for amounts actually spent in the employee's itemized deductions to offset the income in the W-2. This treatment hurts the employee in two ways. First, the inclusion of the entire amount paid to the employee is included in income thereby increasing AGI and subjecting the employee to higher expense deduction floors and possible phaseouts. Second, only miscellaneous itemized deductions in excess of the two percent floor are deductible, so if the employee does not have any other miscellaneous itemized deductions, the business expenses up to two percent of the employees AGI are out of pocket expenses that are not deductible. An accountable plan, which would exclude reimbursements from taxable income, would have put the employee in a much better tax position by reducing AGI and eliminating the need to claim an employee business expense deduction.

Employees can claim a home office deduction if a portion of the home is being used regularly and exclusively (1) as a principal place of business, (2) as a place to meet clients in the normal course of business, or (3) in connection with the business if the home office is not included in a separate structure that is detached from the taxpayer's principal residence. In addition, the home office must be for the convenience of the employee's employer. In other words, an employee must be required by the employer to maintain a home office in order to claim the deduction. Employees deduct home office expenses as a miscellaneous itemized deduction (an employee business expense), which is subject to the two percent floor.

### Investment Expenses and Tax Advice

Taxpayers are also permitted to deduct investment expenses as a miscellaneous itemized deduction subject to the two percent floor. Allowing investment expense deductions is consistent with the partnership concept discussed earlier in the text – when a taxpayer engages in trade or business or investment activity, he or she is in partnership with the government, since the government will share in the gains through the tax system. Consequently, it is only fair to allow investment expenses incurred in producing that income to be deducted for income tax purposes. Under IRC Section 212, any ordinary and necessary expenses incurred for the production of income or for the management of assets held for the production of income are deductible. Examples of deductible investment expenses include:

- Custodial fees paid on Retirement Plans or IRAs with funds outside of the plan.
- Cost of investment and tax advice (including legal fees and the cost of preparing tax returns).
- Cost of materials for researching investments (books, magazines, periodicals).
- Investment expenses allocated from partnerships and S corporation.
- Safe deposit box fees.

### Losses on IRAs

An investment related deduction often overlooked by taxpayers and planners is the ability to claim a loss on IRAs that have been surrendered. This loss may only be claimed when all amounts have been withdrawn from the IRA and the taxpayer's basis in the IRA exceeded his or her recovery. To meet the "all amounts withdrawn" test, all funds in IRAs of the same type must be withdrawn. For example, to claim the deduction for traditional IRAs/Roth IRAs, the taxpayer must distribute all of the funds remaining in all of his or her traditional IRAs/Roth IRAs. Note that for this provision to apply, the taxpayer must have basis in the IRA. Usually, this means that he or she has made non-tax-deductible contributions to the IRA in previous years. Like any other investor, a taxpayer who loses money on a retirement account (i.e., receives less than his or her basis in the contract) should be permitted to recoup his or her capital through a loss deduction. Note that in the case of an IRA, though, the deduction is subject to the two percent floor. Unless the taxpayer has already met the two percent floor with his or her other deductions, the taxpayer will not be able to recoup all of his/her capital. This requirement is somewhat bizarre, especially considering the fact that a loss associated with an annuity contract (another type of retirement savings vehicle) can be deducted as a miscellaneous itemized deduction without regard to the two percent floor.

**EXHIBIT 7.7** **DEDUCTIBLE MISCELLANEOUS ITEMIZED DEDUCTIONS**

| FULLY DEDUCTIBLE (TIER I)<br>(NOT SUBJECT TO 2% HURDLE) | DEDUCTIBLE (TIER II)<br>(SUBJECT TO 2% HURDLE) |
|---|---|
| • Gambling Losses to Extent of Gains<br>• Credit for Estate Tax on IRA Assets<br>• Loss on Disposition of Annuity Contract<br>• Repayment of Income | • Unreimbursed Employee Business Expenses (Travel, Journals, Uniforms, Union Dues)<br>• Hobby Expenses to Extent of Hobby Income<br>• Investment Expenses (e.g., Fees)<br>• Tax Advice and Preparation<br>• Losses on Terminated IRAs<br>• Educational Expenses to Maintain or Improve Taxpayer Competency<br>• Home Office Deduction |

# OVERALL LIMITATION ON ITEMIZED DEDUCTIONS

In addition to all of the floors, ceilings, and special rules that apply to the deductibility of itemized deductions, a further overall limitation is imposed. To the extent that a taxpayer has AGI greater than a threshold amount, IRC Section 68 states that the taxpayer's itemized deductions are reduced by the lesser of (1) three percent of AGI in excess of the threshold, or (2) 80 percent of the taxpayer's total itemized deductions. For tax year 2009, the AGI threshold for purposes of this test is $166,800.

The Economic Growth and Tax Reform Reconciliation Act of 2001 (EGTRRA 2001) phased out the phaseout of the itemized deductions over the years 2006-2009. In 2010, there will be no phaseout of itemized deductions based on AGI, but for tax years beginning after January 1, 2011 the old rule of IRC Section 68 applies (unless Congress takes steps to make the phaseout permanent).

Under the provisions of EGTTRA 2001, for tax year 2009, the itemized deduction is reduced by the lesser of (1) three percent of AGI in excess of the threshold, then further reduced to a 1/3, or (2) 80 percent of the taxpayer's total itemized deductions, then further reduced to a 1/3. For tax year 2010, there will be no phaseout of a taxpayer's itemized deductions.

EXAMPLE 7.39

In 2009, Charles had AGI of $259,950. Charles' total itemized deductions for 2009 were $24,000. Charles will only be able to claim $23,068.50 of his itemized deductions. Charles' income exceeds the AGI threshold of $166,800, by $93,150. He will have to reduce his itemized deductions by $931.50 ($93,150 x 0.03 = $2,794.50; $2,794.50 x 2/3 (to reduce to a third) = $1,863; $2794.50 - $1,863 = $931.50; $24,000 - $931.50 = $23,068.50).

# Key Terms

***Acquisition Indebtedness*** – Indebtedness that is secured by the home and is used to acquire, construct, or improve the taxpayer's primary residence and one additional residence.

***Casualty Loss Deduction*** – Deduction allowed for losses or damages to a taxpayer's property resulting from a sudden or unexpected event, such as fire, storm, shipwreck, or theft.

***Employee Business Expenses*** – Expenses that include professional and union dues of employees, travel, supplies and services, professional books and journals, job related educational expenses, work clothes and uniforms, and job hunting expenses in the same line of work, which may be deductible as a miscellaneous itemized deduction subject to the two percent floor if they are not reimbursed by the employer.

***Home Equity Indebtedness*** – Additional debt secured by the home that exceeds the amount of acquisition indebtedness.

***Non-accountable Reimbursement Plans*** – Plans in which the employer gives the employee a specified sum of money out of which the employee will cover all of the business related expenses.

***Private Charities*** – Corporations or trusts structured to further the charitable intentions of a donor or the donor's family.

***Public Charities*** – Charitable organizations that receive support from a wide cross-section of the population, such as the Red Cross or the YMCA.

***Qualified Charitable Organization*** – An organization that is operated exclusively for religious, charitable, scientific, literary, or educational purposes, or for the prevention of cruelty to animals or children.

***Qualified Residence Interest Deduction*** – Tax deduction that permits taxpayers to deduct the interest on up to $1 million of home indebtedness and the interest on up to $100,000 of home equity indebtedness.

# DISCUSSION QUESTIONS

1. Why does Congress sometimes allow deductions for personal expenses?

2. How can a taxpayer achieve a tax benefit by itemizing his deductions?

3. Under what circumstances are capital expenses a deductible medical expense?

4. How does the tax benefit rule affect the deduction of state and local taxes?

5. Describe the deduction for state sales tax.

6. Under what circumstances is interest deductible?

7. What are the limits on the qualified residence interest deduction?

8. To what extent is investment interest deductible?

9. Describe the rules regarding interest paid on the acquisition of investments that generate tax-free income.

10. What is a qualified charitable organization?

11. What are the requirements for an income tax charitable deduction?

12. What is the partial interest rule and what are the exceptions to this rule?

13. Name the factors that affect the amount of an income tax charitable deduction.

14. What are the limits on the charitable contribution deduction?

15. Describe the special election available to taxpayers making contributions of long-term capital gain property.

16. What are the limits on charitable deductions by corporations?

17. What are the limits on deducting personal casualty losses?

18. Name several miscellaneous Tier I itemized deductions that are not subject to the two percent floor.

19. What are the major categories of Tier II miscellaneous itemized deductions that are subject to the two percent floor?

20. Describe how a taxpayer can deduct job-hunting expenses.

1. Ryan has a severe asthmatic condition, and his physician recommended that he install a lap pool in his home so that he can swim regularly, which should help control his condition. Ryan has a friend who is a real estate agent, and strongly advised him not to install the pool since pools depress the market value of homes in the area. If Ryan's AGI for the year is $100,000 how much of the cost of the lap pool can Ryan actually deduct as a medical expense if it cost him $12,000 to install the pool and all of his other health insurance costs were covered by his health insurance policy?

    a. $0.

    b. $900 as an itemized deduction.

    c. $4,500 as an itemized deduction.

    d. $12,000 as an adjustment to income.

2. Last year, Randy incurred the following tax expenses and related items:

    | | |
    |---|---|
    | Federal income tax due with return | $2,150 |
    | State income tax withheld this year | $4,500 |
    | State income tax paid with return this year | $600 |
    | Real estate taxes paid on residence | $6,500 |
    | Sewer and water tax | $600 |
    | Car tax (flat rate for all car owners) | $300 |
    | State income tax refund from prior year | $400 |

    How much can Randy claim as a deductible tax expense for his itemized deductions this year?

    a. $11,600.

    b. $11,800.

    c. $12,200.

    d. $13,750.

3. Rennie purchased a new car this year, and paid $3,600 in sales taxes. Rennie's state income tax for the year was $2,000. The property taxes on Rennie's home this year were $6,000, and he made approximately $12,000 in charitable deductions. How much should Rennie deduct for taxes as an itemized deduction?

    a. $3,600.

    b. $6,000.

    c. $8,000.

    d. $9,600.

In June of this year, Kelly purchased her first home. The price of the house was $260,000, and she financed the purchase with a 30-year, $200,000 mortgage. Since she plans on staying in the home for quite a while, and she expects interest rates to rise in the future, she paid $4,000 in points to receive a lower interest rate on the loan. As of the end of the year, Kelly had paid $7,614 in interest on the loan by making her monthly installment payments. How much should she claim as mortgage interest on her itemized deductions this year?

    a.  $7,614.

    b.  $7,747.

    c.  $9,614.

    d.  $11,614.

Keegan is in a high tax bracket, and decided to add some public purpose municipal bonds to his portfolio. He did not want to liquidate any of his current positions to acquire the bonds, however, so he took out a margin loan to make the purchase. Keegan incurred $800 of margin interest on the loan used to purchase the bonds, and received $600 of coupon payments from the bonds this year. Assuming that Keegan had no other margin interest or other investment income this year, which of the following statements is correct?

    a.  Keegan cannot deduct any of the margin interest incurred this year.

    b.  Keegan can deduct $600 of the margin interest.

    c.  Keegan can deduct $800 of the margin interest.

    d.  If Keegan becomes an AMT taxpayer, he can deduct $600 of the margin interest.

Patrick, a small business owner who is worn out from years of work without a vacation, decides he needs a break and wants to go on a 3-month cruise around the world. The cost of the cruise is $45,000, and Patrick does not have the liquid funds to pay for the extravagant vacation. Patrick does not want to liquidate investments to cover the expenses, and does not want to incur high-interest credit card debt. His only debt outstanding is the remaining balance on his mortgage of $60,000, so he decides to take out a home equity loan for $45,000 to pay for the trip. Which of the following statements concerning this situation is correct?

    a.  Since the proceeds will not be reinvested in his home, he cannot deduct the interest incurred on the home equity loan.

    b.  Taking the home equity loan out for this purpose would not increase his acquisition indebtedness; therefore, none of the interest is deductible.

    c.  Patrick should consider having the business pay for the vacation, since the expense will be deductible as an above-the-line business expense.

    d.  Even though the loan proceeds will be used for vacation purposes, the entire amount of interest paid on the loan is deductible for income tax purposes.

7. Kasey has been an avid investor since his teenage years, when his uncle taught him the basics of investing. This year, Kasey incurred investment interest expenses of $800. Kasey had $200 of dividend income and $100 of interest income this year since he has a growth focus in his portfolio. Kasey also realized $600 of capital gains for the current year. Applying the default rules for the deductibility of investment interest expenses, which of the following statements is correct?

    a. Kasey can deduct the full $800 in investment interest expense this year.

    b. Kasey's investment income (for purposes of the investment interest expense deduction) for the year is $800.

    c. Kasey will be able to carryover $500 of investment interest expense to deduct against future investment income in subsequent tax years.

    d. Kasey can deduct the allowable portion of his investment expenses this year subject to the two percent floor that applies to miscellaneous itemized deductions.

8. Ryan's AGI this year was $100,000. He inherited a large amount of money from the estate of his grandfather, and is very charitably inclined. A recent earthquake devastated several cities on the West Coast, and Ryan wanted to assist in getting the people affected back on their feet. He gave a $75,000 donation to the Red Cross, which is spearheading relief efforts in the region. How much of the contribution can Ryan deduct on his income tax return this year?

    a. $20,000.

    b. $30,000.

    c. $50,000.

    d. $75,000.

9. Brendan is a tax attorney who specializes in intergenerational wealth transfer planning. He is also very charitably inclined, and sits on several boards. A local animal shelter and Friends of Animals group recently decided to work together on joint goals, and decided to form a new charitable organization, which meets the definition of a public charity. Brendan created the organization and received exempt determination status from the IRS. He usually charges $5,000 to perform this service, plus the exempt determination letter fee charged by the IRS of $500, but he volunteered for this activity since his wife will be on the board. Brendan was not reimbursed for the expenses he incurred. Assuming that his AGI and contribution base is $150,000, how much can Brendan deduct for income tax purposes?

    a. $0.

    b. $500.

    c. $2,750.

    d. $5,500.

0.  Edward, a US Citizen, has always felt drawn to the town in Ireland that his family came from. The local church in that town is in dire need of repair, and Edward would like to make a contribution to the restoration fund which is managed by the Archdiocese of Laois, Ireland. If Edward makes a contribution, which of the following statements is correct?

    a.  If Edward makes the contribution directly to the Archdiocese, he qualifies for an income tax deduction, since the money will be used for one of the classic charitable purposes – support of a religious organization.

    b.  Edward's deduction will be subject to the 50% limit if he makes the contribution to a church in Ireland.

    c.  If Edward donates the funds to his parish in the United States, and the parish sends the fund to the church in Ireland, Edward will qualify for an income tax charitable deduction.

    d.  If Edward wants to get a charitable deduction for the gift, he must make the gift through his will when he dies, or no charitable deduction will be allowed.

1.  John is the 100 percent owner, president, and CEO of FadCo, Inc. His salary is approximately $1 million per year, and he has substantial income from investments and other business interests. FadCo's net income each year is $10 million. Due to his high level of income, his itemized deductions are in the phaseout range. John would like to make a $1.8 million contribution to the local opera company to renovate the concert hall and stage, but does not feel that he can get significant tax benefits if he makes them himself. Instead, he has his company make the contribution on December 31, and he reduces his salary to $100,000 per year for the next two years so that the contribution does not deprive the company of cash flow needed for expansion. Which of the following statements concerning this situation is correct?

    a.  FadCo will be able to take a charitable deduction of $1 million on its tax return this year.

    b.  The reduction in salary will constitute a charitable gift that John can deduct as an itemized deduction.

    c.  FadCo will qualify for a $1.8 million charitable deduction, some of which must be carried forward to future tax years.

    d.  Both John and FadCo will qualify for a charitable deduction.

12. Bertie is an avid fan of his alma-mater's football team. The team has had such a good record in the last 6 years that getting tickets to the games has proven difficult. Recently the school announced that those wishing to purchase football tickets could have their name placed on a waiting list once they made a $5,000 contribution to the University. Since Bertie did not want to miss any of the games, he made the contribution, and also paid $1,000 for the season tickets. How much can Bertie deduct as a charitable contribution on his income tax return?

    a.  $2,500.

    b.  $4,000.

    c.  $5,000.

    d.  $6,000.

13. Jennifer, a college student, had her car recently broken into. The perpetrators caused $800 in damage to her car, and stole a camera with a fair market value of $700 that was originally purchased for $1,500. Jennifer's AGI for the year is $8,000. How much can Jennifer claim as a casualty loss deduction on her income tax return this year?

    a.  $500.

    b.  $600.

    c.  $700.

    d.  $1,400.

14. Which of the following miscellaneous itemized deductions is not subject to the 2 percent floor?

    a.  Gambling losses.

    b.  Investment expenses.

    c.  Hobby activity expenses.

    d.  Unreimbursed employee business expenses.

15. In which of the following situations would educational expenses be deductible for income tax purposes?

    a.  A physician's assistant who works the night shift is attending medical school during the day.

    b.  A paralegal attends law school at night, hoping to obtain a law degree.

    c.  A retired business executive begins a Ph.D. program in business to help relieve him of the boredom of retirement.

    d.  A financial planner takes classes necessary to sit for the CFP® Certification Examination.

# Quick Quiz Explanations

## Quick Quiz 7.1

1. False. Personal expenses are generally not deductible.
2. False. The standard deduction is adjusted annually for inflation.
3. True.
4. True.

## Quick Quiz 7.2

1. True.
2. False. There is no limitation on the amount that can be claimed as a deduction for property taxes; if the taxpayer has multiple residences, he or she may claim all of the property taxes paid.
3. True.
4. False. Taxpayers are permitted to deduct the interest on up to $1 million of home indebtedness, as well as the interest on up to $100,000 of home equity indebtedness.

## Quick Quiz 7.3

1. False. Only gifts of cash or property will qualify for a charitable income tax deduction.
2. True.
3. False. Gifts of cash and non-long-term capital gains property to a public charity are deductible to the extent that they do not exceed 50% of the taxpayer's AGI.
4. True.

## Quick Quiz 7.4

1. True.
2. False. The first step in calculating a casualty loss is to deduct $100 from each occurrence. Second, a taxpayer's aggregate casualty and theft losses must exceed 10% of the taxpayer's AGI in order to be deductible.

## Quick Quiz 7.5

1. False. Gambling losses, to the extent of gambling income, are a miscellaneous itemized deduction not subject to the 2% floor.
2. True.
3. True.

# Other Deductions, Penalties, & Loss Disallowance

## INTRODUCTION

In the two previous chapters, we reviewed deductions that directly reduce gross income (deductions associated with a trade or business or with the production of income), adjustments to income (above-the-line deductions), and itemized deductions (below-the-line deductions). This chapter discusses some special rules and circumstances that apply to income tax deductions, penalties associated with income and deductions, and circumstances that result in loss disallowance.

## GENERAL RULES & ISSUES RELATED TO DEDUCTIONS AND LOSS DISALLOWANCE

For a variety of reasons, Congress has chosen to place certain limitations on the ability of taxpayers to take certain deductions and losses. Some of the most common of these limitations will be discussed in this chapter and include:

- Public policy limitations,
- Political contributions,
- Excessive compensation,
- Hobby losses,
- Rental of vacation homes, and
- Personal expenditures.

### PUBLIC POLICY LIMITATIONS

Public policy concerns impose some limitations on taxpayers' ability to take deductions. Deductions for activities that violate public policy are not permitted for income tax purposes. Some examples of items which are not deductible due to public policy considerations include penalties, fines, illegal bribes, and kickbacks.

Penalties and fines are intended to be a form of punishment for legal violations. Allowing taxpayer to deduct penalties or fines assessed, even those incurred when in the conduct of a trade or business, would provide individuals with an incentive to engage in the action the penalty was designed to discourage. It does not make sense from a public policy standpoint to discourage behavior by imposing a penalty while creating tax rules that reward individuals who engage in the prohibited behavior.

<table>
<tr><td>

**EXAMPLE 8.1**

</td><td>

When Brian left his office to go to visit a client at the client's home, he was already running late. To make matters worse, he ran into a traffic jam caused by an accident, and by the time he arrived at the client's home he was approximately one hour late. There was no room in the client's driveway, and despite the presence of no parking signs all along the street, Brian parked in front of the client's house and ran to the door to apologize for his tardiness. After the meeting, and upon return to his car, Brian was greeted by a parking ticket prominently displayed on his windshield. Despite the fact that Brian was conducting business at the time he incurred the parking fine, he cannot deduct the cost of the ticket as a business expense, since this would violate public policy.

</td></tr>
</table>

## Key Concepts

**Underline/highlight the answers to these questions as you read:**

1. Explain why penalties and fines are not deductible.

2. Describe the circumstances under which an illegal activity may give rise to an income tax deduction.

3. Explain the rules regarding the deductibility of political contributions and money spent monitoring legislation.

4. Describe the limits on the ability of publicly held corporations to deduct executive compensation.

Bribes and kickbacks are illegal acts in themselves, and are never deductible for income tax purposes. This rule applies even when it is customary to provide bribes to facilitate the conduct of business. Individuals engaged in international business transactions in some part of the world may be faced with such a situation. Giving or receiving a bribe, even in those jurisdictions, is an illegal act in the United States (and may also be a violation of the Foreign Corrupt Practices Act). These payments may never be deducted on a taxpayer's tax return.

There are some illegal activities that will generate tax deductions, however. If a taxpayer is involved in the operation of an illegal trade or business, the taxpayer is permitted to take all ordinary, necessary, and reasonable expenses associated with the production of that income as if the business activity was a legal business. As noted above, fines, penalties, bribes, and kickbacks may not be deducted, and are not considered to be ordinary, necessary, or reasonable business expenses. This appears to be a strange rule, but remember that the 16th Amendment grants

Congress the power to collect tax on income from whatever source derived. "Income" constitutes the gross receipts of a business enterprise reduced by all ordinary, reasonable, and necessary expenses to generate that income.

Tony runs an illegal gambling operation in the back room of his meat packing firm. This year, Tony received $750,000 in gross receipts from the gambling operation. The pro-rata portion of rent Tony paid for the space used for the gambling operation was $40,000. He paid his employees $250,000 to run the operation, and incurred $20,000 in product costs (cards, chips, dice, etc.). Tony's income from the gambling operation is $440,000 ($750,000 in gross receipts less $250,000 in salaries, $40,000 for rent, and $20,000 for product costs).

It may seem odd to calculate the income from an illegal operation, since it seems that no smart criminal would be careless enough to tell the government that he was running an illegal business by reporting the income on his tax return. In reality, however, smart criminals do report their illegal source income as "other income" on their tax return. Failure to do so would constitute fraud, which would allow the IRS to reopen the tax return for that year at will. By declaring the income, the statute of limitations begins to run, and, as discussed earlier, the IRS generally has three years to challenge the income and expenses reported on the return. Furthermore, due to the imposition of privacy rules on the IRS, the IRS cannot inform the Department of Justice, or other law enforcement agencies, that the taxpayer is conducting an illegal business activity. If the IRS provides this information to law enforcement, it may be possible for the criminal to have all evidence obtained from that tip classified as inadmissible for trial. This gives a fair degree of protection to the criminal, and encourages reporting of illegal source income. By structuring the system in this way, Congress is clearly indicating that it wants to tax ALL income from whatever source derived, even if that income is generated by illegal activities.

All tax rules have exceptions, and the rules governing illegal source income do not deviate from this rule. If the illegal activity generating income involves trafficking in controlled substances (drugs), the only deduction the taxpayer is permitted to take is the cost of goods sold (the cost of the drugs).

Ted supplements his income by running an illegal drug procurement and distribution business. This year, Ted received $750,000 in gross receipts from the illegal drug business. Ted paid $40,000 in rent for the space used to store and package the drugs. He also paid his employees and street pushers $250,000 to run the operation, and incurred $150,000 in product costs (costs of drugs sold) plus incidental expenses of $20,000. Ted's taxable income from the drug operation is $600,000 ($750,000 in gross receipts less $150,000 cost of goods sold).

## POLITICAL CONTRIBUTIONS

As a general rule, neither businesses nor individuals can deduct political contributions or lobbying expenses, however, expenses incurred to influence local legislation are deductible.

Businesses can also deduct expenses associated with the monitoring of legislation. Many large businesses may be affected by pending legislation, and need to know if that legislation becomes law due to the added compliance responsibilities that must be performed. These types of expenditures do not attempt to influence legislation, and are considered ordinary, necessary, and reasonable business expenses.

Finally, businesses may deduct de minimis in-house expenses associated with lobbying, provided that the total expenses incurred do not exceed $2,000. If the expenses do exceed $2,000, none of the expenses are deductible.

## EXCESSIVE COMPENSATION

Publicly held corporations are subject to a deduction limitation on executive compensation. The maximum deduction that can be taken for compensation paid to the chief executive officer and the four highest compensated executives is $1 million each. Regular compensation in excess of $1 million is not deductible by the corporation.

The $1 million compensation limitation does not apply, however, to performance-based compensation and commissions, payments to qualified retirement plans, or payments that are otherwise excludible from gross income.

While the purpose of this expense limitation is to encourage limitations on executive compensation, due to the exception for performance-based compensation, it has had minimal effect. After this limitation became law, corporations restructured executive pay to consist primarily of performance-based, as opposed to salaried, compensation.

## HOBBY LOSSES

All ordinary, necessary, and reasonable business expenses are deductible against income. To be classified as a business activity, the taxpayer must have a profit motive. Some individuals attempt to classify their hobbies as business activities so that they can deduct the expenses incurred in engaging in the activity.

Under IRC Section 183, a **hobby activity** is any activity that the taxpayer engages in without a profit motive. Hobby activities are usually activities that involve personal pleasure, such as raising horses, gardening, racing sailboats, and collecting and/or trading stamps or coins.

Often, it is difficult to determine whether an activity is a hobby or a trade or business. The distinction between the two centers on the presence or absence of a profit motive. Profit motive does not imply that the activity must generate a profit each year. Most profit-motivated business activities generate losses in the early years of operation, turning profits as the business matures. Treasury Regulation 1.183-2(a) defines **profit motive** as "an actual and honest, even though unreasonable or unrealistic, profit objective in engaging in the activity."

Treasury Regulation 1.183-2(b) provides nine factors that should be considered in determining whether or not a taxpayer has a profit motive, including:

1. The manner in which the taxpayer manages the activity;
2. The time and effort spent in running the activity;
3. The expertise of the taxpayer and the taxpayer's advisors;
4. The taxpayer's success in similar activities;
5. The taxpayer's history of profit/loss associated with the activity;
6. The amount of occasional profits generated by the activity;
7. The expectation that assets used in the business will increase in value;
8. The financial status of the taxpayer; and
9. The extent to which personal pleasure or recreation dictates the taxpayer's involvement in the activity.

IRC Section 183 sets forth a rebuttable presumption that an activity is engaged in for profit if the activity has generated a profit in three out of the last five years (two out of seven years for horse breeding, racing, or training). If the activity generates a profit for the required number of years, the burden of proof shifts to the IRS to show that the taxpayer did not have a profit motive. If the activity does not generate a profit for the required number of years, the taxpayer has the burden of proving that he or she has a profit motive for the activity.

## Quick Quiz 8.1

**Highlight the answer to these questions:**

1. Penalties and fines are intended to be a form of punishment for legal violations, and are therefore not deductible.
   a. True
   b. False

2. The IRS can inform a law enforcement agency if a taxpayer is conducting an illegal business activity.
   a. True
   b. False

3. Lobbying expenses for influencing legislation at both the federal and state level are deductible.
   a. True
   b. False

4. The $1 million limit on deductible executive compensation does not apply to performance-based compensation.
   a. True
   b. False

True, False, False, True.

**EXAMPLE 8.4**

Randy, an avid baseball fan, started a baseball card trading activity. Randy's profit or loss for the activity for the past seven years is shown in the following table. Using the three out of five year "for profit activity" presumption, the third column indicates whether or not the burden of proof has shifted to the IRS to show the taxpayer does not have a profit motive.

| Year | Income (loss) | Profit Motive Presumed |
|:---:|:---:|:---:|
| 1 | $500 | No |
| 2 | (1,500) | No |
| 3 | 700 | No |
| 4 | (1,000) | No |
| 5 | 900 | Yes, profit 3 of 5 years |
| 6 | (500) | No, profit only 2 of 5 years |
| 7 | 1,200 | Yes, profit 3 of 5 years |

In Years 5 and 7, there is a rebuttable presumption that the activity has a profit motive. If the IRS can prove that Randy does not have a profit motive despite the presence of a profit in three out of the last five years, the activity will be classified as a hobby activity for Years 5 and 7.

When a taxpayer operating an activity has a profit motive, the activity is classified as a trade or business. Business expenses are deductible against the income of the business (above the line) even if the expenses exceed the income from the business (generating a loss). If the business is a passive activity, however, the loss may be suspended under the at-risk or passive activity loss rules, as discussed in Chapter 14.

When there is no profit motive and the activity is classified as a hobby, all of the hobby income must be included in gross income, but expenses associated with the activity may only be deducted to the extent of the income from the activity. In other words, hobby activities cannot generate losses.

Unlike business activities, which allow expenses to be deducted above the line, hobby activity expenses are deducted as a miscellaneous itemized deduction (below the line), subject to the two percent floor. Some expenses associated with the hobby, such as mortgage interest or property taxes associated with use of part of the home for the hobby activity, are not subject to the two percent floor.

## Key Concepts

**Underline/highlight the answers to these questions as you read:**

1. Name the factors to be considered in determining whether a taxpayer has a profit motive.

2. Describe the rules for deducting expenses related to a hobby activity.

3. Explain the three ways that a rental real estate activity can be classified for income tax purposes.

4. Describe the tax rules for each category of rental real estate activities.

Alternatively stated, if hobby expenses exceed hobby income, the expenses are only deductible to the extent of income, and the expenses are deducted in the following order:

1. Expenses that are otherwise deductible, such as mortgage interest, property taxes, and casualty losses;
2. Non-depreciation expenses not deducted under (1) above; and
3. Cost-recovery (depreciation, depletion, amortization).

The ordering rule for hobby expenses generates favorable results for the taxpayer. To the extent that cost recovery deductions (depreciation, amortization, or depletion) are claimed, sale of the asset that generated the cost recovery deductions would be subject to depreciation recapture. By requiring depreciation expenses to be deducted last, the Code minimizes the taxpayer's potential exposure to the depreciation recapture rules.

**EXAMPLE 8.5**

Pat raises and sells toy poodles. This activity is motivated primarily by Pat's love of dogs, and has been classified as a hobby activity for income tax purposes. This year, the gross income from the activity was $20,000. Pat incurred the following expenses:

| | |
|---|---|
| Interest | $6,000 |
| Taxes | $3,000 |
| Vet Bills | $6,000 |
| Food & Treats | $5,000 |
| Advertising | $2,000 |
| Depreciation | $1,000 |
| **Total Expenses** | **$23,000** |

Since the activity has been classified as a hobby activity, Pat will only be able to deduct $20,000 of the $23,000 in expenses, and this deduction will be below-the-line. The first tier of expenses that can be deducted are those that would otherwise be deductible, including the interest and taxes, for a total of $9,000. The second tier of expenses that can be deducted are non-depreciation related expenses, which would include the Vet bills, food and treats, and advertising. These expenses total $13,000. Adding the tier 2 expenses to the tier 1 expenses, the grand total would be $22,000. Since only a total of $20,000 can be deducted against the income from the hobby activity, $11,000 of the tier 2 expenses ($13,000) will be deductible. None of the depreciation expenses will be deductible, which will avoid potential depreciation recapture if Pat sells those assets at a later time.

## RENTAL OF VACATION HOMES

Many individuals accumulate wealth by investing in rental real estate. While the investment often does not produce immediate cash returns, the use of rent received to reduce mortgage balances, plus appreciation on the real estate over time, assists in the wealth accumulation process.

Almost all rental real estate activities are passive activities, and are subject to the passive activity loss rules covered in Chapter 14. There are three general ways that a rental real estate activity can be classified for income tax purposes: (1) as a nontaxable rental activity, (2) as a "primarily rental use" activity, and (3) as a mixed-use rental activity.

To determine whether a rental activity will be treated as primarily rental use or as mixed-use, a two part test is applied. The first question that must be answered is whether the real estate was rented for less than 15 days. If the property is rented for 14 days or less, the activity will be a **nontaxable rental activity** for income tax purposes. None of the income received from the rental activity will be included in income, and none of the expenses associated with the rental may be deducted. Note that this rule follows the general principal that deductions are only permitted for items that have already been brought into a taxpayer's income. If no income is reported, no deductions should be allowed.

**EXAMPLE 8.6**

Laurence owns a vacation home on a famous golf course where a national tournament is played each year. The prize for winning is so large that the tournament attracts all of the big-name golfers on an annual basis. The tournament is sponsored by corporations, which use their sponsorship as a way to advertise their product or service and entertain potentially large clients. Each year, Laurence rents his home on the golf course to Monopoly, Inc. for a 10-day period, and the rest of the time uses the house as a personal vacation residence. Monopoly, Inc. pays Laurence $120,000 in rent for the use of the home. Since Laurence rents the home for less than 15 days each year, he is not required to report the $120,000 in rental income received, but is not permitted to claim any expenses associated with the rental.

If real estate is rented for 15 days or more, a second question must be answered to determine the classification of the activity for federal income tax purposes. This question focuses on the personal use of the property by the owner. If the owner's personal use of the property is not more than the greater of 14 days or 10 percent of the rental days, the activity will be classified as a **primarily rental use activity**. If the owner's personal use exceeds this threshold, then the activity is considered to be a **mixed-use rental activity**.

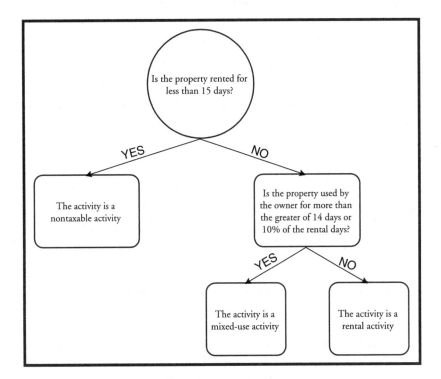

EXAMPLE 8.7

Ari has a beach home that he rents for 180 days a year. Whether the activity is classified as a primarily rental activity, or a mixed-use activity, will depend on Ari's personal use. To be classified as a primarily rental activity, Ari's personal use of the property cannot exceed the greater of 14 days, or 10 percent of the rental days. Ten percent of the rental days in this example would be 18 days.

If Ari uses the property personally for 10 days during the year, the activity will be classified as primarily rental.

If Ari uses the property personally for 18 days during the year, the activity is still classified primarily as a rental activity. While Ari's use exceeds the 14 day mark, it does not exceed 10 percent of the rental days, or 18 days.

If Ari uses the property personally for 25 days during the year, the activity will be classified as a mixed-use activity.

If the activity is classified as a nontaxable activity, the income is not reported but expenses may not be claimed. To the extent that the taxpayer makes mortgage interest or property tax payments on the property, however, those amounts can be claimed as personal expenses as itemized deductions. The taxpayer is not required to prorate mortgage interest and taxes betwee personal use and nondeductible rental use when the activity is classified as a nontaxable activity

| EXAMPLE 8.8 | James owns a condo at the beach that is classified as a nontaxable activity. James has mortgage interest of $15,000 and property taxes of $7,000 on the property this year. James can deduct the $15,000 as qualified mortgage interest, provided that he otherwise meets the requirements to deduct mortgage interest, and he will be allowed to deduct the full $7,000 of property taxes paid. |
|---|---|

If the activity is classified as a primarily rental use activity, the taxpayer must report all of th income generated from the activity, but is permitted to deduct all ordinary, necessary, an reasonable expenses associated with the operation of the activity even if the activity produces loss. The expenses for primarily rental use activities are above-the-line deductions, and directl offset the income from the activity. Typically (for individual taxpayers) the profit or loss from this type of rental activity is reported on Schedule E of Form 1040, and only the net profit or lo enters the taxpayer's gross income. While losses can be generated on a primarily rental us activity, they may not be currently deductible by the taxpayer due to the application of the at-ris and passive activity loss rules (covered in Chapter 14).

If the activity is classified as a mixed-use activity, the tax rules that apply are similar to the hobb loss rules. All of the income of the activity must be reported, but the taxpayer can only clair expenses in the current year to the extent of the income from the activity (i.e., the activity cannc generate a loss). The order in which deductions are taken matches the rules that apply to hobb losses. Expenses that are otherwise deductible ("tier 1 expenses" such as mortgage interest an taxes) are claimed first, followed by other non-depreciation expenses ("tier 2 expenses"), an finally depreciation or cost-recovery expenses ("tier 3 expenses"). While the taxpayer may not b able to claim all of the expenses associated with the activity, mixed-use property is never subjec to the passive loss limitations or the at-risk rules because it cannot generate a loss.

Mixed-use rental real estate activities differ from hobby losses in two ways. First, any disallowe rental expenses can be carried forward and deducted against income in future years (to the exten that the deduction of those expenses will not cause the activity to show a loss). Second, th expenses that are deductible are deducted directly against the income of the property, and ar therefore above-the-line deductions. Recall that hobby loss deductions can only be taken as miscellaneous itemized deduction, in most cases, subject to the two percent floor.

Expenses incurred in the operation of both mixed-use activities and primarily rental use activitie must be allocated between personal and rental expenses. Only the rental expense portion i deductible.

The method of allocating mortgage interest and taxes is currently in dispute. The IRS requires the allocation of expenses to be based on the total days the property is used. For example, if the property is rented for 60 days, and personally used by the owner for 30 days, two thirds of mortgage interest and taxes must be allocated to the rental portion of the activity, and one third is allocated to the personal portion of the activity. By requiring this treatment, the IRS is attempting to skew the expenses into the rental portion which may not give the taxpayer a current tax benefit, since expenses can only be deducted to the extent of the income from the property. The courts, however, have allowed taxpayers to allocate certain expenses (real estate taxes and mortgage interest expenses) based on 365 days in the year. This approach tends to skew the expenses toward the personal use portion of the activity, which potentially allows the taxpayer to deduct any remainder of those expenses as itemized deductions.

All other expenses (other than mortgage interest and taxes) associated with the mixed-use activity are allocated based on the total number of days that the property was used (the IRS approach). To the extent that expenses other than mortgage interest and taxes are allocated to the personal use portion of the activity, they are not deductible by the taxpayer.

## Quick Quiz 8.2

**Highlight the answer to these questions:**

1. Raising horses is not generally considered to be a hobby activity.
   a. True
   b. False

2. Hobby expenses are only deductible to the extent of hobby income.
   a. True
   b. False

3. Real estate that is rented for 15 days per year is always a nontaxable activity.
   a. True
   b. False

4. Mixed-use rental activities are not subject to the passive loss limitations or the at-risk rules.
   a. True
   b. False

False, True, False, True.

**EXAMPLE 8.9**

Mike rents his beach condo for 60 days and uses the condo for personal use for 30 days. The income and expenses are as follows:

| | |
|---|---|
| Rental Income | $8,000 |
| Mortgage Interest | $5,000 |
| Taxes | $10,000 |
| Utilities | $1,200 |
| Condo Association Fees | $6,000 |
| Depreciation | $2,000 |

## The IRS Position on Mixed-Use Property

| FORM 1040 SCHEDULE E FOR RENTAL PROPERTY | | |
|---|---|---|
| **RENTAL INCOME & EXPENSES*** | | |
| Rental Income | $8,000 | |
| Expenses | | |
| Mortgage Interest | $3,333 | (60/90) x $5,000 |
| Taxes | $6,666 | (60/90) x $10,000 |
| Utilities | $800 | (60/90) x $1,200 |
| Association Fees | $4,000 | (60/90) x $6,000 |

* Interest and taxes would be limited to $8,000, the total income. Utilities and Association fees would not be deductible, nor would any depreciation. Mortgage interest and tax may be deductible if itemized.

| PERSONAL EXPENSES DEDUCTIBLE AS ITEMIZED DEDUCTIONS | | |
|---|---|---|
| Mortgage Interest | $1,667 | Possible Deduction as Itemized Deduction |
| Taxes | $3,333 | Possible Deduction as Itemized Deduction |
| Utilities | $1,003 | Not Deductible |
| Condo Association Fees | $4,014 | Not Deductible |

* * *

## The Current (Courts) Position on Mixed-Use Property

| RENTAL INCOME & EXPENSES | | |
|---|---|---|
| Rental Income | $8,000 | |
| Expenses | | |
| Mortgage Interest | $822 | 60/365 x $5,000 |
| Taxes | $1,644 | 60/365 x $10,000 |
| Utilities | $800 | 60/90 x $1,200 |
| Association Fees | $4,000 | 60/90 x $6,000 |
| Depreciation | $1,333 | 60/90 x $2,000 |
| **Net Income** | **($599)*** | |

* Expenses would be limited to $8,000. Therefore, $599 of depreciation expenses would not be deductible.

| PERSONAL EXPENSES DEDUCTIBLE AS ITEMIZED DEDUCTIONS | | |
|---|---|---|
| Mortgage Interest (Balance) | $4,178 | Possible Deduction as Itemized Deduction |
| Taxes (Balance) | $8,356 | Possible Deduction as Itemized Deduction |
| Utilities | | Not Deductible |
| Condo Association Fees | | Not Deductible |

Comparing the IRS method and the courts' method of allowing rental real estate income and expenses, the IRS method results in the taxpayer having no net rental income.

In addition, the IRS method results in personal itemized deductions of $5,000.

Using the courts' method, the taxpayer has no net rental income and personal itemized deductions of $12,534.

Clearly, the court position is more favorable to the taxpayer in many instances.

## TYPES OF HOMES

EXHIBIT 8.2

- Personal residence
- Second home
- Vacation home (rental less than 15 days)
- Mixed-use vacation home (>14 days of rental; personal use more than the greater of 14 days or 10% of rental days)
- Rental homes (>14 days of rental; personal use less than the greater of 14 days or 10% rental days)

## PERSONAL EXPENDITURES

Unless otherwise provided in the Code, personal expenses are not deductible. Most itemized deductions, and some adjustments to income (such as the tuition and fees deduction and student loan interest), are personal expenses that Congress has permitted taxpayers to deduct to further policy goals. For example, Congress considers home ownership to be a worthy goal, so it allows taxpayers to deduct mortgage interest and real estate taxes paid on their personal residence and one vacation home. Ownership of a personal residence is not active conduct of a trade or business or an activity entered into for profit, so without the special exception in the Code, expenses associated with home ownership would not be deductible.

## SPECIFIC DEDUCTIONS

This section of the chapter will address limitations on the following specific deductions:
- Bad debts,
- Worthless securities,
- Section 1244 stock,
- Losses of individuals,
- Research and experimental expenditures,
- Net operating losses, and
- Depreciation.

## BAD DEBTS

The tax benefits and classification of bad debts depends on whether the bad debt is a business or personal bad debt.

Business bad debts are only deducted if the taxpayer uses the accrual method of accounting. If the business is a cash-basis taxpayer, income would not have been reported if it was not received. One of the general rules of income taxation is that deductions can only be taken for amounts brought into income, so if the taxpayer is a cash-basis taxpayer, no income would have been reported and no deduction will be permitted.

**EXAMPLE 8.10**

Bruce is a CPA. He prepared Cindy's tax return and sent her a $2,000 bill for the work. Cindy refused to pay because it took Bruce 8 months to complete the return. Cindy has since disappeared. If Bruce is an accrual-basis taxpayer, he includes the $2,000 in income upon the completion of the tax return then writes it off when he discovers that he cannot collect. If Bruce is a cash-basis taxpayer, he does nothing because he has not taken the $2,000 into income.

**EXAMPLE 8.11**

MedCare Clinic is an accrual basis taxpayer and has a $10,000 receivable from a drug company. The drug company files for bankruptcy and the clinic now expects to recover only $1,000 of the outstanding balance ($0.10 on the dollar) next year. The clinic can deduct $9,000 this year. If they only collect $500 next year instead of the expected $1,000 then they can deduct the additional $500 next year.

Businesses that use the accrual method of accounting report income when it is earned (when all events necessary to earn the income have been performed), not when it is received. Accrual method taxpayers may deduct bad debts to offset income reported but not received.

Most businesses are required to use the specific charge-off method, which allows the business to deduct the bad debt as an ordinary loss in the year in which the debt becomes partially or wholly worthless. An ordinary loss deduction is allowed, since accrual accounting subjected the income earned but not received to ordinary income tax in the year in which the income was reported. The only way to offset this ordinary income inclusion is to allow an ordinary loss deduction.

Some businesses (such as financial institutions) are permitted to use the **reserve method** of bad debt deductions, allowing them to take a bad debt deduction based on a percentage of accounts receivable representing the historical percentage of accounts that go bad.

If the bad debt is classified as a nonbusiness bad debt, the **specific charge-off method** must be used. A bad debt deduction is allowed only when the debt becomes wholly worthless, and is treated as a short-term capital loss. No deduction is permitted for partial worthlessness when the debt is a nonbusiness bad debt.

## WORTHLESS SECURITIES

On occasion, an investor will unfortunately purchase a security that will later become worthless. These taxpayers are entitled to take a loss on a security that becomes worthless during the taxable year. IRC Section 165 creates an artificial sale date on the last day of the taxable year in which the security becomes worthless. For most taxpayers, since they are cash basis taxpayers, the artificial sale date will be December 31. Fiscal year taxpayers may have a different artificial sale date.

The impact of the artificial sale date is to classify the loss as a long-term loss unless the taxpayer either purchased the investment in the same year that it became worthless, or purchased it on the last day of the tax year preceding the security becoming worthless (a holding period of exactly one year is not considered long-term).

Kelly, an avid reader, purchased common stock in Jane Austin Industries, Inc. on February 1 of this year. On August 30 of this year, the company announces that it is filing Chapter 7 bankruptcy and that the common shareholders should not expect to receive anything on liquidation of the corporation. Since the stock became worthless during the year, there will be a constructive sale of the stock on December 31, and Kelly will be able to claim the amount she invested (her basis) as a loss deduction this year. The loss will be a short-term capital loss, since she held the stock for less than a year as of the artificial sale date.

**EXAMPLE 8.12**

John purchased common stock in Satellite Television, Inc. on December 31 of last year. On August 30 of this year, the stock became worthless. A constructive sale will occur on December 31 of this year, and John will be able to claim the amount he invested (his basis) as a loss deduction this year. The loss will be a short-term capital loss, since he held the stock for exactly one year (not more than one year) on the date of the artificial sale.

**EXAMPLE 8.13**

**EXAMPLE 8.14**

Randy purchased 100 shares of Yankees Inc. on October 1 of last year. Unfortunately, Yankees Inc. has had some trouble, and became worthless on March 1 of this year. A constructive sale will occur on December 31 of this year, and Randy will be able to claim the amount he invested (his basis) as a loss deduction this year. The loss will be a long-term capital loss, since he is deemed to have held the stock for more than one year as of the artificial valuation date. If Randy was able to take the loss based on the day that Yankees Inc. shares became worthless, he would have been able to classify the loss as a short-term capital loss, which would potentially offset higher taxed income (recall that short-term capital gains are taxed at ordinary income tax rates, while long-term capital gains are generally taxed at the 15% rate).

In the Yankees, Inc. example, above, we can see that the tax benefits of the transaction may be affected by the creation of an artificial sales date. As a practical matter, some brokers will allow clients to sell worthless securities for a penny to book the transaction as a sale. While the client will not receive any cash from the transaction, the sale occurs on the actual trade date instead of on the artificial trade date presumed under IRC Section 165. Selling the worthless security in a book transaction can, in certain circumstances, allow the taxpayer to categorize the loss as a short-term capital loss.

**EXAMPLE 8.15**

Use the same facts as the prior example, with the exception that, on September 15, Randy sold the shares of Yankees, Inc. for a penny through his broker. When Randy completes his tax return, he will show a short-term capital loss for Yankees, Inc. since he did not hold the shares for more than one year as of the sale date, September 15 of this year. If Randy had other short-term capital gains this year, the loss of Yankees, Inc. would offset those short-term capital gains taxed at ordinary tax rates, generating a larger tax benefit for Randy compared to using the loss to offset long-term capital gains taxed at the 15% rate.

## SECTION 1244 STOCK

Much of the economic growth we experience in the United States is due to the operation of small businesses. Small businesses are riskier from an investment perspective, since they are often subject to strict competition and have an unproven business track record.

To encourage investment in small business enterprises, Congress enacted Section 1244 of the Code, which allows the first $50,000 of losses ($100,000 for taxpayers who are married filing jointly), per year, on Section 1244 stock to be classified as an ordinary instead of as a capital loss. Any additional loss incurred on the stock would still qualify as a capital loss. Section 1244 only applies to losses, not gains, so any gains on the sale of the stock will still be taxed at the favorable capital gains tax rate.

To qualify for this special tax treatment, the loss must be incurred by one of the original purchasers of the company (i.e., the shareholder provided some of the initial capitalization for start-up of the company), and, upon organization the company must have had $1 million or less in initial capitalization. While, in this discussion, we have focused on corporate structures, it is also possible to apply the principles of Section 1244 to individuals (sole proprietorships) and partnerships.

Christopher purchased a 20% interest in Advertising Specialty Products, Inc. (ASP) for $150,000 when the company was first formed, which was held in a joint account with his wife. Christopher is married to Kelly, and they file a joint income tax return. Things have not been going well for ASP, and Christopher decides to sell his stock. He is able to find a buyer who pays him $25,000 for the stock. Upon sale of the stock, Christopher realizes a $125,000 loss. $100,000 of this loss can be deducted directly against ordinary income, and the remaining $25,000 will be treated as a capital loss. Assuming that Christopher has no other capital gains or losses in the current year, his AGI is reduced by $103,000 (comprised of the $100,000 deduction from ordinary income, plus the $3,000 loss deduction from the capital loss). The remaining $22,000 of capital loss must be carried forward and deducted against future year income.

## LOSSES OF INDIVIDUALS

As a general rule, the only losses that an individual can deduct are those incurred in a trade or business, incurred in a transaction entered into for profit, or specifically allowed by the Code (i.e., casualty losses).

Personal losses are generally not deductible. Since personal losses are incurred in a transaction where the government is not intended to be a partner (due to the revenue sharing that occurs through the income tax system), those losses are generally disallowed (the exception is casualty losses, which are itemized deductions). Generally losses are allowed only when a taxpayer engages in an activity designed to generate taxable income.

At the peak of the real estate market, Rupert purchased a large personal residence with a jumbo mortgage. To afford the home, he took out a variable interest-only loan, with a balloon payment due in seven years (he had planned to refinance the loan at that time). Unfortunately, real estate prices have dropped, mortgage interest rates have climbed, and Rupert can no longer afford to make the mortgage payments. The bank foreclosed on the home, and Rupert suffered a $200,000 loss. Despite the loss of $200,000 in capital, Rupert is not entitled to a tax deduction, since the loss was incurred on the sale (or, in this case, other disposition) of a personal asset.

## RESEARCH AND EXPERIMENTAL EXPENDITURES

Businesses often incur costs for the development of products, processes, and formulas that can be used to generate a profit. These expenses are incurred to increase future profit or produce income, and are generally considered to be ordinary, necessary, and reasonable business expenses.

There are three methods that can be used to deduct research and experimental costs. First, the expenses can be deducted in the year paid or incurred. Often, this is the most favorable choice since it gives the company an immediate tax deduction for research costs. Second, the expenses can be amortized over a five year (60 month) period. Finally, the expenses can be capitalized (added to basis), and can be deducted when the project is abandoned or becomes worthless.

A tax credit of up to 20 percent of certain research and experimental costs may also be available.

## NET OPERATING LOSSES

When trade or business activities generate higher expenses than income in a given year, a **net operating loss** (NOL) results. A taxpayer can trigger NOLs by generating deductions for their trade or business or production of income activities (such as rental real estate), employee-related business expenses, personal casualty or theft losses, moving expenses, or foreign government confiscations of property.

NOLs for one taxable year can be taken as a deduction (for AGI, or above-the-line) against income from prior and future tax years. Under current law, the NOL can be carried back two years, and carried forward 20 years. The carry-back provision is extended to three years for small businesses if the NOLs results from casualty or theft losses, or are associated with presidentially declared disaster areas. Farm losses qualify for a five year carry-back provision.

NOLs must first be carried back and applied against prior income, and to the extent that there are additional NOLs remaining, carried forward and applied against future income. Generally, a taxpayer would want to carry the losses back first, since this will generate an immediate income tax refund for prior tax years. To claim the loss against prior year income, the taxpayer would file an amended income tax return for that year, recomputing taxable income.

When losses are carried back to prior tax years, there is a change in the taxpayer's AGI for those years. Any tax deductions or credits based on AGI will be affected. Examples include (among others), the IRA deduction, student loan interest deduction, tuition and fees deduction, excludable savings bond interest for bonds used to pay for educational expenses, medical expenses, casualty losses, and miscellaneous itemized deductions. Charitable deductions are not affected by the NOL carryback, since the contribution base for determining the ceiling for charitable deductions in any one year is equal to the taxpayer's AGI not taking into account any NOL carry-backs. Furthermore, a NOL carryback does not impact the self-employment tax of the individual for the carryback years.

Some taxpayers may not want to go through the hassle of amending prior year income tax returns, or may anticipate a greater tax benefit if the losses are carried forward instead of carried back. These taxpayers can make an irrevocable election to waive the carry-back period. To make the election, the taxpayer simply attaches a statement to their income tax return which states "The taxpayer elects to waive the NOL carry-back period under Section 172(b)(3) of the Code."

## DEPRECIATION

Depreciation represents the portion of an asset placed in service in a trade or business that is used up in the conduct of business for that year. When assets are purchased for business or production of income purposes, the taxpayer is entitled to recoup the cost of that asset over its useful life, so that the cost can presumably be reinvested in replacement assets that will generate more income for the company. Depreciation, therefore, is a form of cost recovery.

The method of depreciation used depends on the type of asset purchased, as well as elections that the taxpayer is entitled to make. When a depreciable asset is sold, the depreciation deductions taken may be subject to recapture to the extent that the asset was depreciated for tax

## Quick Quiz 8.3

**Highlight the answer to these questions:**

1. If a debt is a nonbusiness debt, a bad debt deduction will only be allowed when the debt becomes wholly worthless.
   a. True
   b. False

2. IRC Section 165 creates an artificial sale date for worthless securities.
   a. True
   b. False

3. Section 1244 is intended to discourage investment in small businesses.
   a. True
   b. False

4. Net operating losses can be carried forward, but cannot be carried back.
   a. True
   b. False

True, True, False, False.

purposes at a rate greater than the actual decline in the value of the asset. More detailed information on depreciation and depreciation recapture is covered in Chapters 10 and 12.

## SUMMARY OF SPECIFIC DEDUCTIONS

EXHIBIT 8.3

| | |
|---|---|
| **Bad debts** | If business debt and accrual method taxpayer, ordinary loss<br>If personal, specific write off and short-term capital loss |
| **Worthless securities** | Assumed worthless at year-end of realization |
| **Section 1244 stock** | $100,000 ordinary loss for married filing jointly, excess is capital loss ($50,000 for single filers) |
| **Losses of individuals** | Not deductible except as casualty loss |
| **Research and experimental expenditures** | In year paid, amortized over 60 months, or capitalized |
| **Net operating losses** | Back 2 and forward 20 years, can elect forward only |
| **Depreciation** | Ratably written off |

# PENALTIES

In addition to the penalties that may be incurred for failure to file an income tax return, failure to pay the tax due, and taking unreasonable positions on returns or in tax court actions, three additional penalties apply directly to pension plan and IRA contributions and accumulations: the excess contributions penalty, the early distribution penalty, and the late distribution penalty.

| EXHIBIT 8.4 | RETIREMENT PLAN PENALTIES |
| --- | --- |

- Excess Contributions
- Early Distributions
- Late Distributions

## EXCESS CONTRIBUTIONS PENALTY

While Congress views saving for retirement as a worthy goal, contributing too much to retirement plans can generate a tax penalty. Retirement plans and IRAs give the taxpayer the ability to make tax-deductible contributions to the plan that directly reduces the taxpayer's taxable income in the current tax year. To prevent taxpayers from contributing excessive amounts to pension plans and IRAs in an effort to avoid current tax liability, Congress has set contribution limits that vary based on the type of pension plan or IRA being used. Under IRC Section 4973(a), excess contributions made to pension plans or IRAs will be subject to a six percent excise tax, and the excess contribution must be distributed from the plan. Typically, the excess contribution amount is applied to the subsequent year contribution instead of forcing a distribution from the plan. To avoid the imposition of the six percent excise tax, the taxpayer should withdraw the excess (or allocate it to the contribution for the next tax year) by the due date of their income tax return, including extensions. Any withdrawal to reverse out an excess contribution must include the income earned on the excess contribution while inside of the retirement account or IRA, so taxpayers should take action quickly to avoid potential income taxation on additional growth.

### Key Concepts

Underline/highlight the answers to these questions as you read:

1. Describe the penalties applicable to pension plan and IRA contributions and distributions.

2. Describe the two types of temporary loss disallowance.

3. Describe the three types of permanent loss disallowance.

Employers sponsoring certain types of retirement plans, such as SEPs, SIMPLEs 401(k)s, defined contribution profit sharing plans and defined benefit plans, are subject to a ten percent excess contributions penalty unless exceptions apply.

# EARLY DISTRIBUTION PENALTY

Due to the tax benefits (a tax deduction and tax-deferral) received for contributions to pension plans and IRAs, Congress wants to encourage taxpayers to use the plan for its intended purpose - funding retirement. If the taxpayer takes a distribution from a qualified retirement plan or IRA prior to age 59½, a 10 percent excise tax applies to the distribution. The 10 percent excise tax is imposed in addition to any tax incurred due to the inclusion of the distribution in the taxable income of the taxpayer. A special early distribution penalty applies to SIMPLE plans. If an early distribution is taken from a SIMPLE plan within two years of the date the taxpayer first participated in the plan, a 25 percent penalty applies to the distribution in addition to the regular income tax liability incurred as a result of the distribution.

There are several exceptions to the 10 percent early distribution penalty. Whether or not a particular exception applies depends on the type of plan from which the distribution is made. Some exceptions apply to qualified plans only, some to qualified plans and IRAs, and some to IRAs only.

## Quick Quiz 8.4

**Highlight the answer to these questions:**

1. If a taxpayer takes a distribution from a qualified retirement plan or IRA prior to age 59½, a 25% excise tax applies to the distribution.
   a. True
   b. False

2. Losses related to wash sales are temporarily disallowed.
   a. True
   b. False

3. Losses incurred in related party transactions are permanently disallowed.
   a. True
   b. False

False, True, True.

There are three exceptions to the early distribution penalty that apply only to qualified plans:
1. Distributions to an employee who separates from service and has attained the age of 55;
2. Public safety employee separated from service after age 50 as in Exhibit 8.5; and
3. Distributions made in accordance with a Qualified Domestic Relations Order (QDRO) or state order distribution under divorce (which splits plan benefits in the event of a divorce).

Qualified plan participants who take advantage of early retirement can begin to take distributions from the plan (on separation from service) at 55 without fear of the early distributions penalty.

Three exceptions to the early distribution penalty apply only to IRAs. These include:
1. Distributions to pay for health insurance for unemployed taxpayers;
2. Distributions to pay for qualified higher education expenses of the taxpayer, spouse, or dependents; and
3. Distributions of up to $10,000 (lifetime maximum) for the first-time purchase of a home. A first-time home buyer is defined as a person who had not owned a home in the prior two tax years.

The remaining exceptions apply to both qualified plans or IRAs. These exceptions include:
1. Substantially equal periodic distributions under IRC Section 72(t);
2. Distributions made as a result of the disability of the taxpayer;
3. Distributions made by reason of the death of the taxpayer;
4. Distributions necessary to cover unreimbursed medical expenses that exceed 7.5 percent of the taxpayer's AGI; and
5. Distributions due to an IRS levy to collect taxes due.

**EXHIBIT 8.5** **SUMMARY OF 10 PERCENT PENALTY EXCEPTIONS FOR QUALIFIED PLANS AND IRAs**

| Applies to Distributions from: | Exception to 10% Early Withdrawal Penalty |
| --- | --- |
| Both Qualified Plans & IRAs | Death |
| Both Qualified Plans & IRAs | Attainment of age 59½ |
| Both Qualified Plans & IRAs | Disability |
| Both Qualified Plans & IRAs | Substantially equal periodic payments (Section 72(t)) |
| Both Qualified Plans & IRAs | Medical expenses that exceed 7.5% of AGI |
| Both Qualified Plans & IRAs | Tax levy |
| Only Qualified Plans | QDRO or state order under divorce* |
| Only Qualified Plans | Attainment of age 55 and separation from service |
| Only Qualified Plans | Public safety employee separated from service after age 50 |
| Only IRAs | Higher education expenses |
| Only IRAs | First time home purchase (up to $10,000) |
| Only IRAs | Health insurance for unemployed |

*Where there is a distribution at divorce and the payee is under 59½, the use of a QDRO directed distribution will result in a taxable event but will not incur the 10% early withdrawal penalty. Under the same circumstances, except that the distribution is from an IRA, the result is both a taxable event and the application of the 10% early withdrawal penalty. However, the payee in any case can choose to rollover the distribution in which case, the rollover rules would apply or the payee can take substantially equal periodic payments under Section 72(t).

## LATE DISTRIBUTION PENALTY

Congress views late distributions from pension plans and IRAs as a more serious problem than early distributions or excess contributions to plans, since late distributions defer the taxation of plan benefits. Individuals who are required to take distributions from retirement plans and IRAs (due to the imposition of the required minimum distribution rules) but fail to do so are subject to a 50 percent excess accumulation penalty. The required minimum distribution rules (RMDs) are found in Treasury Regulations 1.401(a)(9) and 1.408-8. Additional information on RMDs may also be obtained in IRS Publication 590, available at www.irs.gov. Minimum distributions are generally required by April 1 of the year following the year in which the taxpayer reaches age 70½. The excess accumulation penalty may be waived if the taxpayer received erroneous advice from an advisor to the pension plan, or if the taxpayer can demonstrate that he or she acted in good faith when attempting to apply the RMD rules.

# OTHER LOSS DISALLOWANCES – TEMPORARY AND PERMANENT

There are a number of other types of losses that may be either temporarily or permanently disallowed. Each of the following types of losses is discussed more extensively later in this text, but it is appropriate to mention them briefly in this chapter. The following chart references the chapter in which a full discussion of each of these topics can be found.

## LOSS DISALLOWANCE CROSS REFERENCES

EXHIBIT 8.6

| Section 1031 Exchanges | Chapter 13 |
| --- | --- |
| Wash Sales | Chapter 11 |
| Related Party Transactions | Chapter 11 |
| Gifts Below FMV | Chapter 11 |
| Sale of Personal Assets | Chapter 11 |

## SECTION 1031 EXCHANGES RESULTING IN A LOSS ARE NOT IMMEDIATELY DEDUCTIBLE

When like-kind assets are exchanged under Section 1031, no gain or loss is recognized in the transaction. The loss is not permanently disallowed; it is deferred and increases the basis of the new asset.

EXAMPLE 8.18

John and Jeff exchange like-kind machines in a transaction that qualifies for nonrecognition under Section 1031. John's machine is worth $17,000 and he has an adjusted basis of $18,000. Jeff's machine has a fair market value of $14,000 and he pays John cash of $3,000 in the exchange. John's realized loss is $1,000 ($17,000 amount realized - $18,000 adjusted basis). The loss is not deductible but John's new basis in Jeff's old machine is $15,000 ($18,000 - $3,000 cash = $15,000) and the fair market value of the new asset is $14,000. If John sells the new asset immediately he will have a $1,000 loss.

## WASH SALES

When a taxpayer sells stock at a loss, and purchases substantially identical securities within 30 days before or after the sale, the taxpayer has participated in a wash sale and cannot recognize any loss from the sale of the stock. Note that this loss disallowance is temporary and the full benefit of the loss may still be recognized at a future date.

EXAMPLE 8.19

Five years ago, Jay bought 80 shares of Bicycle Corp. at $50 per share. The stock has declined to $30, and Jay decides to sell it to take the loss deduction. Soon after, Jay sees some good news on Bicycle Corp. and buys it back for $32 approximately two weeks after he sold his original stock. Jay cannot deduct his loss of $20 per share. However, Jay does add $20 per share to the basis of his replacement shares. Those shares have a basis of $52 per share: the $32 Jay paid, plus the $20 wash sale adjustment. In other words, Jay is treated as if he bought the shares for $52. If Jay ends up selling the shares for $55, he will only report $3 per share of gain. In the alternative, if Jay later sells the shares for $32 (the same price he paid to buy them), he will report a loss of $20 per share.

## RELATED PARTY TRANSACTIONS

Unlike the losses from Section 1031 exchanges and wash sales, losses incurred in related party transactions are permanently disallowed. When property is sold at a loss to a related party, the seller may not recognize any loss on the sale.

**EXAMPLE 8.20**

Laura owns 100 shares of CityCo stock, which have a fair market value of $20 per share. Laura sells all 100 shares to her sister Jill for $15 per share. Although Laura has realized a loss of $5 per share, she is not allowed to recognize this loss and it is permanently disallowed.

The **double basis rule** is also applied to the transferee. The double basis rule applies to certain related party transactions and to certain gift transactions. The purpose of the rule is to discourage the transfer by sale or gift to related parties or those to whom the taxpayer would make gifts of property which at the time of the transfer has a fair market value less than the transferor adjusted taxable basis.

In the above example, Jill will have a basis of $15 for future losses but a second (thus, double) basis of $20 for gains. If Jill later sells the stock for $21, she will have a gain of $1. If instead, she were to sell the stock for $13, she would have a $2 loss. If she sold between the gain basis and the loss basis, she would have no gain or loss. In addition, the double basis rule applies to gifts where the fair market value of the gift is below the donor's (transferor) adjusted taxable basis. The holding period will be discussed in Chapter 11.

## GIFTS BELOW FAIR MARKET VALUE

Like related party transactions, certain gifts will result in the permanent disallowance of a loss. When gifted property has a fair market value that is less than the donor's adjusted basis, the double basis rule applies, meaning that the donee has one basis for gains (the donor's original basis) and another basis for losses (the value of the property on the date of the gift). If the gifted property is subsequently sold by the donee for less than the fair market value on the date of the gift, part of the loss is permanently disallowed.

EXAMPLE 8.21

Susan purchased CatCo stock several years ago for $40 per share. When the stock price fell to $30 per share, Susan decided to gift the stock to her friend Marshall. Under the double basis rule, Marshall's basis will be $30 for losses and $40 for gains. If Marshall subsequently sells the stock for $25 per share, he will recognize a loss of $5 per share. However, the loss that occurred while Susan owned the stock ($40 - $30 = $10 per share) will be permanently disallowed.

## SALE OF PERSONAL ASSETS FOR LOSS

When personal assets are sold at a loss, that loss may not be recognized. Rather, in order for a loss on the sale of an asset to be recognizable, that asset must be used for the production of income in a trade or business. If a loss is disallowed because the asset is a personal asset, the loss is permanently disallowed and the taxpayer may not recognize it at any point in the future.

## SUMMARY OF DISALLOWED LOSSES

EXHIBIT 8.7

| Temporarily Disallowed | Permanently Disallowed |
|---|---|
| • Section 1031 exchanges<br>• Wash sales | • Related party transactions<br>• Gifts below fair market value<br>• Sale of personal assets at a loss |

# Key Terms

***Double Basis Rule*** - A rule that applies to gifts and related party transactions where the transferee has a basis of the fair market value for losses and the transferor's basis for gains. The rule applies when the asset that is transferred has a fair market value less than the transferor's basis at the time of the transfer. This rule does not apply to arms-length unrelated party transactions. This rule may also be referred to as the split basis rule, dual basis rule, or bifurcated basis rule.

***Hobby Activity*** - Any activity that a taxpayer engages in without a profit motive.

***Mixed-Use Rental Activity*** - Rental activity in which the real estate is rented for 15 days or more per year and the owner's personal use of the property is more than the greater of 14 days per year or 10 percent of the rental days.

***Net Operating Loss*** - Occurs when trade or business activities generate higher expenses than income in a given year.

***Nontaxable Rental Activity*** - Rental activity in which the real estate is rented for less than 15 days per year.

***Primarily Rental Use Activity*** - Rental activity in which the real estate is rented for 15 days or more per year and the owner's personal use of the property is less than the greater of 14 days per year or 10 percent of the rental days.

***Profit Motive*** - An actual and honest, even though unreasonable or unrealistic, profit objective in engaging in an activity.

***Reserve Method*** - A method of deducting bad debts used by some businesses in which bad debt deductions are taken based on a percentage of accounts receivable representing the historical percentage of accounts that go bad.

***Specific Charge-Off Method*** - Allows businesses to deduct bad debts as an ordinary loss in the year in which the debt becomes partially or wholly worthless.

. Explain why penalties and fines are not deductible.

. Under what circumstances do illegal activities give rise to income tax deductions?

. Why are businesses allowed to deduct the costs of monitoring legislation?

. What are the limits on deducting executive compensation?

. How does the IRS determine whether an activity is a hobby or a trade or business?

. What presumption regarding hobby activities is provided for under IRC Section 183?

. What are the consequences of an activity being classified as a hobby instead of a trade or business?

. What are the three ways that a rental activity can be classified for income tax purposes?

. What are the requirements for the different ways that a rental activity can be classified?

0. How does the taxation of mixed-use rental activities differ from hobby activities?

1. Describe the specific charge-off method used to deduct bad debts.

2. When can a taxpayer take a deduction for worthless stock?

3. How does Section 1244 encourage investment in small businesses?

4. What are the three methods for deducting research and experimental costs?

5. For how many years can a net operating loss be carried back or forward?

6. Under what circumstances can a taxpayer choose not to carryback a net operating loss?

7. What is the excess contribution penalty?

8. What is the early distribution penalty?

19. What is the late distribution penalty?

20. List two types of temporarily disallowed losses and three types of permanently disallowed losses.

## MULTIPLE CHOICE PROBLEMS

1. All of the following expenses incurred when an individual travels from his office to a client place of business to discuss business matters will qualify as a business deduction, EXCEPT

    a. A $6 toll to cross the commerce bridge.

    b. Mileage expense for the round trip to visit the client.

    c. A $30 parking ticket for parking in a no-parking zone since no other parking spaces were available.

    d. Cost of printing material for the client meeting.

2. Christopher runs an extortion racket in his home neighborhood. He paid Bobby $100,000 to run the street operations, and incurred $30,000 for secretarial support and $20,000 in miscellaneous expenses, such as rent for his office and supplies. Christopher had gross income from the extortion ring of $400,000. How much of the income is subject to income tax this year?

    a. $250,000.

    b. $270,000.

    c. $300,000.

    d. $400,000.

3. Happy Harry not only uses drugs, he also sells them to a circle of friends and associates. This year, Harry grossed $650,000 from drug sales. He paid $125,000 to his street pushers to compensate them for their services, $200,000 for the raw drugs, $30,000 for rent for the drug processing and packaging plant, and $30,000 in supplies and equipment leasing costs. How much income will be subject to tax on Harry's income tax return?

    a. $275,000.

    b. $325,000.

    c. $450,000.

    d. $650,000.

4. Which of the following statements concerning the tax deductibility of executive compensation is correct?

    a. Publicly traded companies may not deduct compensation payments made to any employees to the extent that the employee's compensation exceeds $1 million.

    b. The compensation cap applies to all compensation (cash and non-cash) received by the executive in the taxable year.

    c. Performance based compensation and payments to qualified retirement plans are not considered to be compensation subject to the $1 million deduction cap.

    d. Private companies may elect to apply the deductibility cap for compensation to only the top 5 officers of the company.

. John is an avid coin collector. To raise some money to support his hobby, John began to occasionally buy and sell coins about 10 years ago, incurring business-related expenses in those transactions. John does not consider himself to be in the business of dealing in coins, and over the time he has been selling coins, he has never made a profit. This year, John grossed $4,000 in sales, and had $4,500 in expenses associated with the activity. John's AGI for the year (including any inclusion due to the coin trading activity) is $50,000, and aside from the coin trading loss, his only other permissible itemized deductions are mortgage interest of $8,000 and real estate taxes of $2,500. Which of the following statements concerning this situation is correct?

    a.  John will take the $500 loss from the coin business into his gross income.

    b.  Since he has never made money from the activity, he is not required to report the purchase and sale transactions on his return.

    c.  John can offset the $4,000 in income with $4,000 of his expenses, so the coin trading activity will have no impact on his AGI.

    d.  The increase in John's taxable income as a result of the coin trading activity is $1,000 ($4,000 - $3,000 deduction).

5. Charles owns a mansion on a cliff on a large island overlooking the Atlantic ocean. Each year, an international sailing race takes place around the Island, and large corporations descend on the town, inviting clients and business associates to entertain them. Carman Corporation, a custom designer of racing sailboats, is particularly interested in this event each year, and for the week and a half of the race, they rent Charles' mansion, paying him $200,000. At first, Charles was hesitant to rent the home, but decided that since it would only be a week and a half, he could go on vacation himself at that time. Charles incurs some costs associated with the rental, including storage charges for his valuables of $10,000, cleaning expenses before and after the rental of $8,000 and he estimates that the pro-rata portion of real estate taxes for the period of the rental is $1,000. How much income from this rental activity will be included in Charles' AGI?

    a.  $0.

    b.  $181,000.

    c.  $190,000.

    d.  $200,000.

7. Michael owns a beach home, which is his second home, in a national resort area. Since this home is only a vacation home, and he can generate substantial cash flow by renting the property, Michael lists the property with a real estate agent who successfully rents the property for 12 weeks a year. Michael and his family use the home for the entire month of September, for two weeks in January, and for two weeks in May each year. If Michael's gross rental income from the property is $60,000, and he has $75,000 of expenses (mortgage interest, real estate taxes, brokerage fees, and miscellaneous expenses) associated with the rental activity, which of the following statements is correct?

    a. Michael will be able to take a deduction for expenses limited to $60,000.

    b. Michael will report a $15,000 loss on the property for tax purposes this year.

    c. The $15,000 loss on the property is suspended under the passive activity rules.

    d. By increasing Michael's AGI, the inclusion of the income could result in the loss of some of Michael's otherwise allowable itemized deductions.

8. Keegan owns and operates an engineering consulting business as a sole proprietorship. For tax reporting, Keegan uses the cash method. Last year, he provided services to a local builder, and upon completing the task he was asked to do, he sent an invoice to the builder for $5,000. The builder never paid the bill, and recently filed for bankruptcy, so Keegan will not be able to collect the amount due. How should this bad debt be treated for income tax purposes?

    a. No bad debt deduction is permitted.

    b. Keegan may deduct $5,000 from his business income.

    c. Keegan may deduct $5,000 as a short-term capital loss.

    d. Keegan may deduct $5,000 as a long-term capital loss.

9. Ten years ago, Fernando loaned his son, Salvatore, $20,000 to start a business. The note required the payment of interest at a rate of nine percent for ten years, with a balloon payment of the principal at the end of the note term. Salvatore has been making interest payments on the note for the past six years, but this year his business took a turn for the worse and he was not able to make the annual interest payment of $1,800. The business was closed down, and Salvatore owed an amount greater than his net worth to secured creditors, so he informed his father that he would not be able to make the interest or principal payments on the note. How should Fernando treat the default for income tax purposes?

    a. Fernando may deduct $20,000 as a short-term capital loss.

    b. Fernando may deduct $21,800 as a short-term capital loss.

    c. Fernando may deduct $20,800 as a long-term capital loss.

    d. Fernando may deduct $21,800 as a long-term capital loss.

0. On December 1 of last year, Bertie purchased 100 shares of Wooster Enterprises, Inc. (a large, publicly held company established 80 years ago that is traded on the New York Stock Exchange) common stock for $5,000. On March 1 of this year, Wooster Enterprises declared that it was bankrupt, that it will wind up operations and that all of its assets will be used to satisfy secured creditor claims so there will be no residual equity left for the stockholders. Which of the following statements describes the tax treatment of this transaction?

    a.  Bertie may deduct the $5,000 as an ordinary loss.

    b.  Bertie may deduct the $5,000 investment as a short-term capital loss.

    c.  Bertie may deduct the $5,000 investment as a long-term capital loss.

    d.  Bertie is not permitted to take a loss deduction.

1. Harry, a married individual who files jointly with his wife, is one of the founders and original shareholders of Brittania Yacht Charters, Inc., a company that charters yachts for corporate events. The company was initially capitalized with $200,000, and Harry was a 50 percent owner. The company was structured as a C corporation, and all filing requirements and permissible tax elections that could benefit the taxpayers were made at the time the company was created. After several years of successful operations, Brittania Yacht Charters, Inc. lost market share to large national firms, and eventually closed down operations. Since it had no assets other than the goodwill of the business after all secured creditors were paid, there was nothing left to distribute to the shareholders. Assuming that there were no changes to Harry's ownership interest in Brittania Yacht Charters, Inc. over his period of ownership, and that Harry had no other capital transactions in the current tax year, what portion of Harry's loss on his investment in Brittania Yacht Charters can he deduct against ordinary income this year?

    a.  $0.
    b.  $3,000.
    c.  $50,000.
    d.  $100,000.

2. Two years ago, Roger purchased his dream home, paying $800,000 for the house. Unfortunately, the real estate market was at its height when he purchased the home, and has since "corrected" as interest rates began to climb. Roger was transferred by his employer to an office across the country, and he put his home on the market, eventually selling it for $720,000. Assuming Roger had no other capital transactions this year, which of the following statements correctly describes the income tax consequences of this transaction?

    a.  Roger can reduce his adjusted gross income by the amount of his loss, $80,000.

    b.  Roger can reduce his adjusted gross income by $3,000 this year.

    c.  Roger will carryforward a $77,000 short-term capital loss.

    d.  Roger's AGI will not be affected in any way by the loss.

13. Which of the following statements concerning Net Operating Losses (NOL) is correct?

    a. NOLs must be used in the current tax year to offset other income; they canno be applied to other tax years.

    b. NOLs can be carried back up to 6 years to offset income from those prior ta years.

    c. Unused NOLs can be carried forward for 20 years.

    d. Prior to carrying forward NOLs, a taxpayer is required to apply the NOL against prior-year income for at least 2 years.

14. Wally, a 45 year old professor, was speaking with his good friend, Larry, who is 53 years old The topic of retirement savings came up, and Larry told Wally that individuals age 50 and over could contribute $6,000 to an IRA. Wally did not review the laws for those younger than 50 which indicates the deduction limit to be $5,000, but instead contributed $6,00 also. Assuming that Wally does not correct his error, what is the amount of the tax penalty that Wally must pay for making the $6,000 contribution for 2009 to the IRA?

    a. $0.

    b. $60.

    c. $100.

    d. $500.

15. One year ago, David, age 55, changed jobs and now works for a company that offers SIMPLE plan to its employees. Each year, the company makes a non-contributory contribution of two percent of an employee's salary to the account of each participant David's daughter is getting married this year, and he needed some extra funds to help pay the expenses associated with the wedding. David took a $4,000 distribution from the SIMPLE Plan. What is the amount of the tax penalty that David must pay for taking the distribution from the SIMPLE plan?

    a. $0.

    b. $360.

    c. $400.

    d. $1,000.

# Quick Quiz Explanations

### Quick Quiz 8.1

1. True.
2. False. Due to privacy laws, the IRS cannot inform a law enforcement agency if a taxpayer is conducting an illegal business activity.
3. False. Expenses incurred to influence local legislation are deductible, but expenses incurred to influence federal legislation are not.
4. True.

### Quick Quiz 8.2

1. False. Raising horses is generally considered to be a hobby activity.
2. True.
3. False. Real estate that is rented for 15 days per year may or may not be a nontaxable activity, depending on the personal use of the property by the owner.
4. True.

### Quick Quiz 8.3

1. True.
2. True.
3. False. Section 1244 is intended to encourage investment in small businesses.
4. False. Net operating losses can be carried back for two years and forward for 20 years.

### Quick Quiz 8.4

1. False. If a taxpayer takes a distribution from a qualified retirement plan or IRA prior to age 59½, a 10% excise tax applies to the distribution, unless the taxpayer is covered by one of the exceptions to the 10% penalty.
2. True.
3. True.

# *Tax Credits*

## INTRODUCTION

Tax deductions (discussed in prior chapters) reduce the amount of income tax that is subject to tax. In contrast, a **tax credit** reduces the calculated tax liability of the taxpayer. Income tax credits are subtracted from the tax on taxable income. As explained in Chapter 3, a taxpayer's income tax is determined by multiplying taxable income by the appropriate income tax rates (or by using the appropriate tax table).

Taxable Income x Tax Rate(s) = Tax on Taxable Income

As illustrated by the following formula, tax credits reduce the tax on taxable income.

Tax on Taxable Income – Credits = Tax Due

Tax credits come in two forms; nonrefundable or refundable. Nonrefundable credits may only apply to the current year or, in some cases, they may be carried back to an earlier year, carried forward to future years, or both. Refundable tax credits can be used to reduce or eliminate the current year's tax, but can also generate a refund.

### NONREFUNDABLE TAX CREDITS

**Nonrefundable tax credits** can reduce the tax on taxable income to zero, but they cannot generate a tax refund, an excess withholding, estimated payments, amounts applied from prior years tax refunds to this year's tax liability, and excess Social Security tax contributions. Nonrefundable tax credits include:

*Key Concepts*

**Underline/highlight the answers to these questions as you read:**

1.  Define "tax credit."

2.  Compare refundable and nonrefundable tax credits.

3.  Describe the difference between a tax credit and a tax deduction.

4.  List the general requirements for claiming a tax credit.

- Foreign Tax Credit
- Credit for Child and Dependent Care
- Credit for the Elderly or Disabled
- Education Credits: Lifetime Learning, and part or all of the American Opportunity Tax Credit
- Retirement Savings Contributions Credit
- Child Tax Credit
- Qualified Adoption Expenses Credit
- Residential Energy Efficient Property Credit
- Nonbusiness Alternative Motor Vehicle Credit
- Nonbusiness Alternative Fuel Vehicle Refueling Property Credit
- General Business Credit

**EXAMPLE 9.1**

Julie's tax on taxable income is $600. She is eligible for a nonrefundable tax credit of $700. Julie is allowed to use the credit to reduce her tax to $0 for the year, but she is not allowed to use the remaining $100 of the credit to generate a refund.

### Carryback or Carryforward of a Credit

If a nonrefundable credit exceeds the tax on taxable income for a tax year, the excess credit i normally lost. With certain credits, however, the excess can be carried back and/or carrie forward to be offset against the tax on taxable income for the years to which the excess credit i carried (see Exhibit 9.1).

**EXAMPLE 9.2**

Keith's tax on taxable income for the year is $1,200. He is eligible to claim a nonrefundable tax credit of $1,500. Keith is allowed to offset his tax with $1,200 of the credit to reduce his tax for the current year to $0. Since the credit is of a type that can be carried back to the preceding year, he is allowed to carryback the remaining $300 of the credit to be offset against his tax for that year. He will carry the credit back by filing an amended income tax return and claiming a $300 refund of taxes for the preceding year. If he owed no tax for the preceding year, the excess credit for the current year may be lost.

**EXAMPLE 9.3**

Use the facts from the preceding example, but assume that the credit is of a type that can be carried forward to the following five years (but not carried back). Keith can claim the $300 excess credit from the current year (Year 1) on the following year's tax return. If he is only able to use $200 of the excess on the tax return for the following year (Year 2), he will be able to use the remainder of $100 as a credit on his tax return for Year 3. If he is unable to use the excess in the five years following the current year, the unused credit will be lost.

## Sequence of Nonrefundable Credits

Nonrefundable credits must be used in a specified sequence. All of the first credit in the sequence must be used up before the second credit can be considered. A partial list of nonrefundable credits, including sequence numbers, is presented in Exhibit 9.1. All of the credits in Exhibit 9.1 are personal credits except for the last one (General Business Credit) and the first one (Foreign Tax Credit). The foreign tax credit can be generated by foreign source income from investment, employment, self-employment, or other business activity.

## NONREFUNDABLE TAX CREDITS

EXHIBIT 9.1

| Item | Nonrefundable Credit Sequence | IRC § | IRS Publication | Reported on Form | Category | Additional Information |
|------|---------|-------|-----------------|------------------|----------|------------------------|
| Foreign Tax Credit | 1 | 27/901 | 514 | 1116 | Various | Carryback 1/Carryforward 10 |
| Credit for Child and Dependent Care | 2 | 21 | 503 | 1040 | Personal | |
| Credit for the Elderly or Disabled | 3 | 22 | 524 | Schedule R | Personal | |
| Education Credits: American Opportunity and Lifetime Learning | 4 | 25A | 970 | 8863 | Personal | |
| Retirement Savings Contributions Credit | 5 | 25B | 17/590 | 8880 | Investing | |
| Child Tax Credit | 7 | 24 | 972 | 1040 | Personal | See Additional Child Tax Credit |
| Qualified Adoption Expenses Credit | 9 | 23 | 17 | 8839 | Personal | Carryforward 5 years |
| Residential Energy Efficient Property Credit | 11 | 25D | 17/523 | 5695 | Personal | Carryforward to next year |
| Non-business Alternative Motor Vehicle Credit | 13 | 30B | 17/334 | 8910 | Various | |
| Non-business Alternative Fuel Vehicle Refueling | 14 | 30C | 17/334 | 8911 | Various | |
| General Business Credit | 15 | 38 | 334 | 3800 | Business | Carryback 1/Carryforward 20 |

Notice the Additional Information column in Exhibit 9.1. For many of these credits, there is no carryback or carryforward of the unused portion of the credit; any portion of the credit that cannot be used in the current year is lost. For the foreign tax credit and the general business credit, however, any portion of the credit that cannot be used in the current year can be carried back to the preceding year to generate a tax refund for that year. Any remaining credit after the carryback is then carried forward to be used in future years. A residential energy efficient property credit that cannot be used in the current year can be carried forward only to the following year. Any unused adoption expenses credit can be carried forward for up to five years. If a taxpayer is unable to use all of the available child tax credit in the current year, some or all of the unused child tax credit can be used to generate a refundable credit called the additional child tax credit.

## REFUNDABLE TAX CREDITS

**Refundable tax credits** can be used not only to reduce or eliminate the current year's tax, but also to generate a tax refund in excess of tax pre-payment.

$$\text{Tax on Taxable Income} - \text{Refundable Credits} = \text{Tax Due (or Refund Due)}$$

For federal income tax purposes, nonrefundable credits are used before refundable credits. A more complete presentation of the use of tax credits is presented by the following formula:

$$\text{Tax on Taxable Income} - \text{Nonrefundable Credits} - \text{Refundable Credits} = \text{Tax Due (or Refund Due)}$$

**EXAMPLE 9.4**

The tax calculated on the taxable income of Jeremy and Sally Johnson is $3,000. They are eligible to claim a $1,000 non-refundable credit and a refundable credit of $2,800. They can claim a tax refund of $800 ($3,000 - $1,000 - $2,800) even if they had no withholding or other tax prepayments for the year.

**EXAMPLE 9.5**

Continuing with the previous example, assume that the Johnson's calculated tax for the year is only $600. They can claim a refund of $2,800 ($600 - $600 - $2,800). Only $600 of the nonrefundable credit can be used, but all $2,800 of the refundable credit can be used. Unless the remaining $400 of the nonrefundable credit can be carried back or forward, it will be lost. Note that all of the nonrefundable credit would have been lost if refundable credits had to be used before nonrefundable credits [$600 - $2,800 - $0 = -$2,200 (refund)].

A list of refundable credits is presented in Exhibit 9.2. Refundable credits are far fewer in number than nonrefundable credits. After all available nonrefundable credits have been used to the extent possible to reduce the income tax calculated for the year, the refundable credits can be subtracted to reduce the remaining tax or to generate a tax refund. It is not necessary to carry refundable credits back or forward because they are usable in the current year.

Note that the American Opportunity Tax Credit shown in Exhibit 9.2 is refundable up to 40 percent unless the taxpayer claiming the credit is a child (1) under the age of 18 (or a student up to age 24) whose earned income does not exceed one-half of his own support, (2) who has at least one living parent, and (3) who does not file a joint return.

EXHIBIT 9.2

| Item | IRC § | IRS Publication | Reported on Form |
|---|---|---|---|
| American Opportunity Tax Credit (formerly the Hope Scholarship Credit) | 25A(i)(6) | 970 | 1040 |
| Federal Income Tax Withheld from Forms W-2 & 1099 | 31 | 17/505 | 1040 |
| First Time Homebuyers Tax Credit | 36 | 530 | 1040 |
| Estimated Tax Payments | 6402 | 17/505 | 1040 |
| Federal Income Tax Refunds Applied from Prior Years | 6402 | 17 | 1040 |
| Excess Social Security Taxes Withheld | 31(b) | 17/505 | 1040 |
| Earned Income Credit | 32 | 17/596 | Sched. EIC |
| Additional Child Tax Credit | 24(d) | 17/972 | 8812 |
| Credit for Tax on Undistributed Capital Gain From: | | | |
|   A Mutual Fund | 852(b)(3)(D)(ii) | 17/564/550 | 2439 |
|   A Real Estate Investment Trust (REIT) | 857(b)(3)(D)(ii) | 17/550 | 2439 |
| Health Coverage Tax Credit | 35 | 17/502 | 8885 |
| Credit for Excise Taxes on Gasoline and Special Fuels | 34 | 510 | 4136 |

## TAX CREDITS VS. TAX DEDUCTIONS

The benefit received by a taxpayer from a tax credit is not dependent on the taxpayer's marginal tax rate (tax bracket). A tax credit of $1,000 provides the same $1,000 tax reduction for a taxpayer in the 15 percent tax bracket or the 35 percent tax bracket. On the other hand, the tax reduction received by a taxpayer for a tax deduction is entirely dependent on the marginal tax rate of the taxpayer. A tax deduction of $1,000 generates a tax reduction of $150 ($1,000 x 0.15) for a taxpayer in the 15 percent bracket and a tax reduction of $350 ($1,000 x 0.35) for a taxpayer in the 35 percent tax bracket.

## TAX POLICY ISSUES

The equal tax benefit generated by tax credits for taxpayers with different marginal tax rates is one of the reasons for the increasing number of tax credits. Congress has created a variety of tax credits for social, economic, fairness (equity), environmental, and other purposes. For example, the earned income credit was enacted to encourage low-income taxpayers to seek gainful employment and to reward them for doing so (social, economic, and perhaps equity purposes). Residential energy credits were provided to encourage taxpayers to make energy-saving improvements to their homes (environmental and economic purposes).

## TAX CREDIT REQUIREMENTS

In order to claim a tax credit, a taxpayer must normally do the following:
- Meet eligibility requirements;
- Determine the amount of the credit by multiplying a base by an applicable rate(s);
- Apply any specified limitations to the credit;
- Subtract the allowable credits from the tax in the proper sequence; and
- Carryback or carryforward any amounts disallowed for the current tax year, if permitted.

## NONBUSINESS AND BUSINESS TAX CREDITS

Tax credits can be conveniently divided into those that relate to business activities and those that do not. This chapter will present a discussion of a few of the many available tax credits in the following order:

- Nonrefundable credits that may not relate to business,
- Refundable credits, and
- The general business credit.

The foreign tax credit is included in this section of the chapter even though this credit may relate to foreign source *business* income.

Most of the credits available to businesses are built into the nonrefundable general business credit.

A few of the most common credits will be discussed in some detail, some less common credits will be described only briefly, and some are beyond the scope of this text.

## NONREFUNDABLE CREDITS NOT RELATED TO BUSINESS

### FOREIGN TAX CREDIT

A taxpayer who pays income and similar taxes to a foreign country (or a possession of the United States) on foreign source income, and also pays U.S. income taxes on the same income, is usually eligible to claim a **foreign tax credit** for some or all of the taxes paid to the foreign country. Alternatively, the taxpayer can claim an itemized deduction for the taxes paid as discussed in Chapter 7. Each year, the taxpayer must choose to take either a credit or a deduction for all of the qualifying foreign taxes for the year. The foreign tax credit is usually more beneficial to the taxpayer than a deduction for foreign taxes paid. If there is a question about whether the credit or the deduction is better, the taxpayer should calculate his federal income tax both ways and then choose the one that is more favorable.

An individual is not allowed to claim a foreign tax credit for foreign taxes paid on income that is excluded from U.S. gross income. However, if foreign earned income exceeds the amount of the foreign earned income (and housing) exclusion, a foreign tax credit can be claimed for the excess. The foreign earned income exclusion is discussed in Chapter 5.

*Key Concepts*

**Underline/highlight the answers to these questions as you read:**

1. Describe the requirements for claiming the foreign tax credit.

2. Explain the purpose and requirements of the credit for child and dependent care expenses.

3. Define employment-related dependent care expenses.

4. Describe the requirements for the credit for the elderly or disabled.

The amount of the foreign tax credit that can be offset against the U.S. federal income tax is typically 100 percent of the qualifying taxes paid to the foreign country on foreign source income, subject to limitations.

The foreign tax credit is intended to avoid double taxation of foreign source income, but it is not intended to reduce U.S. taxes on U.S. source income. Therefore, all of the foreign taxes paid on foreign source income can offset U.S. taxes if the foreign jurisdiction imposes taxes at the same rate as (or at a lower rate than) the United States. If the foreign country imposes taxes at a higher rate than the United States, however, not all of the foreign taxes will be allowed as a credit against the U.S. income tax. Otherwise, the foreign tax credit would reduce the U.S. tax on U.S. source income. This limitation on the foreign tax credit is calculated using the following formula:

$$\frac{\text{Taxable Income from Sources Outside the U.S.}}{\text{Worldwide Taxable Income}} \times \frac{\text{Pre-credit U.S. Tax}}{\text{on Worldwide Income}} = \text{Maximum Credit}$$

**EXAMPLE 9.6**

John earns taxable income of $100,000 in France. He has no other income for the year. His U.S. tax on that income is $25,000 (25%). France imposes an income tax of $35,000 (35%) on the same income. John will be allowed to claim a foreign tax credit of only $25,000 on his U.S. income tax return [($100,000/$100,000) x $25,000 = $25,000]. If he were allowed to claim a foreign tax credit of $35,000, the credit would reduce the U.S. income tax on some of his income earned in the United States.

**EXAMPLE 9.7**

Use the facts from Example 9.6 and assume that France imposes an income tax of only $2,000 on the $100,000 of income that John earns in France. John will be allowed to claim a $2,000 foreign tax credit on his U.S. income tax return.

**EXAMPLE 9.8**

Use the facts from Example 9.6 (John earns France income of $100,000 and pays $35,000 in France income tax) and assume that John earned $25,000 of taxable income in the U.S. in addition to his income from France. John's U.S. tax on $125,000 of income is $35,000 (28%). John will be allowed to claim a foreign tax credit of $28,000 [($100,000/ $125,000) x $35,000 = $28,000].

Although the foreign tax credit is a nonrefundable credit, any unused credit for the current year can be carried back to the preceding year and carried forward for up to ten years.

As indicated earlier, most taxpayers find it more beneficial to take the foreign tax credit rather than an itemized deduction for foreign income taxes. The reasons for the greater benefit provided by the credit include: (1) a tax credit reduces tax liability dollar for dollar, while a tax deduction reduces tax liability by the amount of the deduction multiplied by the marginal tax rate; (2) many taxpayers do not itemize deductions, and (3) an unused foreign tax credit can be carried back and carried forward to be used in other tax years.

| EXAMPLE 9.9 | Mary Ann pays foreign income taxes of $3,000 for the current year. Her U.S. income tax for the year is $8,000. Her total itemized deductions other than the allowable deduction for foreign income taxes are $2,000 less than her standard deduction. If she takes an itemized deduction for foreign income taxes, only $1,000 of the $3,000 of foreign taxes paid will produce a tax benefit. The tax benefit will be equal to $1,000 multiplied by her marginal tax rate. Any tax benefit for the remaining $2,000 of foreign taxes will be lost. Alternatively, if she takes a foreign tax credit, she will reduce her U.S. income tax by the full $3,000 of foreign taxes paid. Finally, if she can't use the entire foreign tax credit in the current year, she may be able to carry it back to the preceding year and forward to future tax years, as needed. |
|---|---|

The foreign tax credit is normally calculated on Form 1116. An individual taxpayer with less than $300 ($600 on a joint return) of investment income (1) is not normally required to file a Form 1116 and (2) is exempt from the foreign tax credit limitation (the limitation formula). In such circumstances, foreign taxes withheld from dividends and other types of investment income earned outside the United States can be claimed as a foreign tax credit (without the limitation) directly on the Form 1040. It should be noted that a foreign tax credit is also available for business.

## CREDIT FOR CHILD AND DEPENDENT CARE EXPENSES

The **credit for child and dependent care expenses** is intended to provide some financial relief to individuals who incur employment-related expenses for the care of one or more qualifying individuals. The amount of the credit is equal to employment-related expenses of up to $3,000 for one qualifying individual ($6,000 for two or more qualifying individuals) multiplied by the applicable percentage explained below. The dollar limits above must be reduced by any excludable benefits received from an employer as dependent care assistance under IRC Section 129.

## Qualifying Individual

A qualifying individual includes any of the following:

1. A dependent who is a qualifying child* under the age of 13;
2. A dependent of the taxpayer who (1) is physically or mentally incapable of caring for himself, and (2) has the same principal place of abode as the taxpayer for more than half the year; or
3. The spouse of the taxpayer who (1) is physically or mentally incapable of caring for himself, and (2) has the same principal place of abode as the taxpayer for more than half the year.

* The requirements for a qualifying child are the same as those explained in Chapter 3.

## Employment-Related Expenses

Employment-related expenses are expenses incurred for the care of qualifying individuals that enable the taxpayer to be employed.

## Eligible Expenses

Eligible expenses include expenses for household services and expenses for the care of a qualifying individual.

## Employment-Related

To qualify as employment-related expenses, the child and dependent care expenses must be incurred to enable the taxpayer to work or to actively look for work. The work can be as an employee or in the taxpayer's own proprietorship or partnership and can be either full-time or part-time.

## Earned Income Limit

In order to claim the credit for child and dependent care expenses, the taxpayer (and spouse if married) must have earned income such as wages, salary, tips, net earnings from self-employment, and certain nontaxable fringe benefits. Although the credit is based on up to $3,000 of employment-related expenses for one qualifying individual ($6,000 for two or more), the eligible employment-related expenses cannot exceed the earned income of the taxpayer, or for married taxpayers, the earned income of the spouse with the lesser amount of earned income.

> Clint and Anna have earned income of $30,000 and $2,000 respectively. Even though they pay $3,600 for child care expenses for their three-year-old daughter during the year, their eligible employment-related expenses amount for the year is limited to $2,000 (Anna's earned income). If Anna earns $3,000 or more for the year, $3,000 of the child care expenses will qualify for the child and dependent care credit.

**EXAMPLE 9.10**

For each month that an unemployed spouse who lives with the taxpayer for more than half the year is (1) a full-time student, or (2) is physically or mentally unable to care for himself, then the unemployed spouse is deemed to earn $250 monthly if the married couple pays for the care of one qualifying individual ($500 for two or more). This treatment can only apply to one spouse in a given month. If both spouses are unemployed and are full-time students for a given month, only one of them can be treated as though he had earned income for the month. To be considered a student, an individual must be a full-time student during five months of the tax year.

**EXAMPLE 9.11**

David earned $32,000 during the year. His wife, Pamela, was unemployed but she was a full-time student during five months of the year. They paid $200 per month for the care of their young son, Jake, who is their only child. Even though they paid $2,400 for child care during the year, their employment-related expenses for the child and dependent care credit will be limited to $1,250 ($250 x 5 months), the amount of income that Pamela is deemed to have earned during the year.

### Payments to Relatives or Dependents

Payments for employment-related care, that are made to relatives of the taxpayer, may qualify for the dependent care credit even if the relatives live with the taxpayer.

### Joint Return

Married taxpayers must normally file a joint return to claim the child and dependent care credit.

### Amount of the Credit

The amount of the credit is the total of the qualifying employment-related expenses multiplied by the applicable rate in the exhibit below. The rate ranges from 20 percent to 35 percent and declines as the taxpayer's adjusted gross income (AGI) increases.

**EXHIBIT 9.3**  **APPLICABLE PERCENTAGE FOR CHILD AND DEPENDENT CARE EXPENSES CREDIT**

| If AGI is Over | But Not Over | Then the Percentage is |
|---|---|---|
| $0 | $15,000 | 35% |
| $15,000 | $17,000 | 34% |
| $17,000 | $19,000 | 33% |
| $19,000 | $21,000 | 32% |
| $21,000 | $23,000 | 31% |
| $23,000 | $25,000 | 30% |
| $25,000 | $27,000 | 29% |
| $27,000 | $29,000 | 28% |
| $29,000 | $31,000 | 27% |
| $31,000 | $33,000 | 26% |
| $33,000 | $35,000 | 25% |
| $35,000 | $37,000 | 24% |
| $37,000 | $39,000 | 23% |
| $39,000 | $41,000 | 22% |
| $41,000 | $43,000 | 21% |
| $43,000 | No limit | 20% |

The maximum credit is $2,100 ($6,000 x 35%). Any credit that cannot be used in the current year is lost.

## SUMMARY OF ELIGIBILITY RULES FOR THE CREDIT FOR CHILD AND DEPENDENT CARE EXPENSES (EXCERPT FROM IRS PUBLICATION 503)

EXHIBIT 9.4

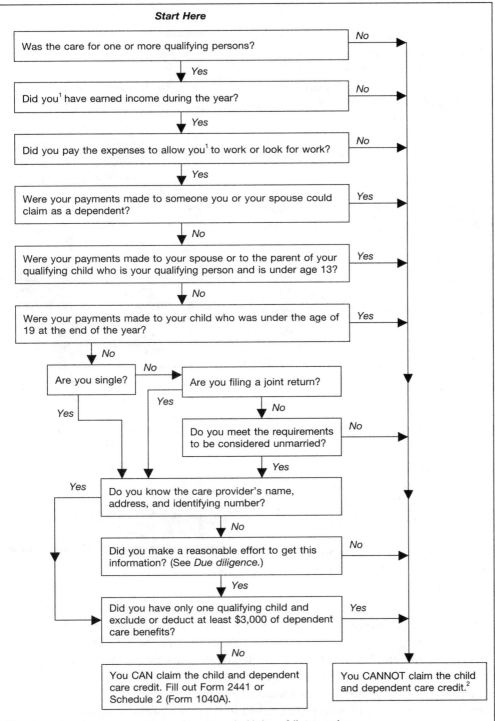

**Start Here**

Was the care for one or more qualifying persons? — No →

↓ Yes

Did you[1] have earned income during the year? — No →

↓ Yes

Did you pay the expenses to allow you[1] to work or look for work? — No →

↓ Yes

Were your payments made to someone you or your spouse could claim as a dependent? — Yes →

↓ No

Were your payments made to your spouse or to the parent of your qualifying child who is your qualifying person and is under age 13? — Yes →

↓ No

Were your payments made to your child who was under the age of 19 at the end of the year? — Yes →

↓ No

Are you single? — No → Are you filing a joint return?

↓ Yes (Are you single)

Are you filing a joint return? — Yes → / No ↓

Do you meet the requirements to be considered unmarried? — No →

↓ Yes

Do you know the care provider's name, address, and identifying number? — Yes →

↓ No

Did you make a reasonable effort to get this information? (See *Due diligence*.) — No →

↓ Yes

Did you have only one qualifying child and exclude or deduct at least $3,000 of dependent care benefits? — Yes →

↓ No

**You CAN claim the child and dependent care credit. Fill out Form 2441 or Schedule 2 (Form 1040A).**

**You CANNOT claim the child and dependent care credit.[2]**

1. This also applies to your spouse, unless your spouse was disabled or a full-time student.
2. If you had expenses that met the requirements for the current year, except that you did not pay them until the next year, you may be able to claim those expenses in the later year.

## CREDIT FOR THE ELDERLY OR DISABLED

The **credit for the elderly or disabled** is intended to provide financial assistance to elderly or disabled individuals with modest incomes.

The credit for the elderly or disabled is available to a U.S. citizen or resident who is a qualified individual and has income below specified limits. A qualified individual must normally be 65 or older at the end of the tax year. Certain disabled individuals under the age of 65 are also eligible for the credit. The maximum credit is $750 ($5,000 x 15%) per year for an unmarried taxpayer.

The maximum credit for two qualified individuals who are married and file jointly is $1,125 ($7,500 x 15%) per year.

**EXAMPLE 9.12**

Paul (age 69) and Beth (age 67) are married and file jointly. Their adjusted gross income for the year is $9,500 and they receive no Social Security benefits. Their credit for the elderly or disabled for the year is $1,125 ($7,500 initial amount x 15%).

If they had received nontaxable Social Security benefits or if their AGI had exceeded $10,000, the initial amount of $7,500 would have been reduced or perhaps completely eliminated.

## EDUCATION CREDITS (AMERICAN OPPORTUNITY TAX AND LIFETIME LEARNING CREDITS)

Two nonrefundable education tax credits are available under IRC Section 25A to an individual taxpayer who pays qualified tuition and related expenses to an eligible educational institution for the taxpayer, the spouse of the taxpayer, or a dependent for whom the taxpayer claims a dependency exemption. The two credits, the American Opportunity Tax Credit (formerly the Hope Scholarship Credit) and the Lifetime Learning Credit, are calculated for the tax year, added together, and then subjected to a limit based on the taxpayer's income (discussed under "Income Limitation"). A detailed explanation of these credits is provided below.

## Qualified Tuition and Related Expenses

Qualified tuition and related expenses consist of tuition and academic fees that are required for enrollment. Nonacademic fees such as student activity fees, athletic fees, insurance expenses, or other fees that are unrelated to a student's academic course of instruction are not eligible for the credit. Expenses for courses or education involving sports, games, or hobbies are not eligible for the credit unless the courses or education are part of the student's degree program. If activity fees and expenses for course-related books, supplies, and equipment must be paid to the educational institution as a condition of enrollment or attendance, they may qualify. If required textbooks must be purchased from an educational institution, the cost of the textbooks may qualify. For tax years beginning in 2009, "course materials" (including books, supplies, and equipment needed for a course of study) count as "qualified related expenses" whether or not the materials purchased from an educational institution is a condition of enrollment or attendance.

## Key Concepts

**Underline/highlight the answers to these questions as you read:**

1. Explain the "no double benefit" rule.

2. Describe who can claim an education credit.

3. Explain the "eligible student" requirement of the American Opportunity Tax Credit.

4. Define the amount of credit available under the American Opportunity Tax Credit and the Lifetime Learning Credit.

Qualified education expenses for a tax year must be paid during the year or for an academic period that begins during the first three months of the following tax year.

## No Double Benefit

A double benefit for the same expenses is not allowed. Qualified tuition and related expenses that are paid with scholarships, Pell grants, excludable employer-provided educational assistance, veterans' educational assistance, and similar sources of funding that are excluded from gross income are not eligible for the credit. Therefore, total qualified tuition and related expenses must be reduced by such funding sources before the credits are calculated. However, qualified expenses do include tuition and related expenses paid with borrowed money or with money received as a gift or inheritance.

Other prohibitions against a double benefit from the same expenditures include the following:

A taxpayer is not allowed to:
- Deduct qualifying expenses as a business expense or otherwise and also claim an education credit based on the same expenses;
- Claim an education credit in the same year that the taxpayer takes a tuition and fees deduction for the same student;
- Claim an American Opportunity Tax Credit and a Lifetime Learning Credit based on the same qualified education expenses; or

- Claim an education credit based on the same expenses used to figure the tax-free portion of a distribution from a Coverdell Education Savings Account or qualified tuition program.

A taxpayer can claim both credits in the same year but not for the same student. If a student qualifies a taxpayer for both education credits, the taxpayer may claim either the American Opportunity Tax Credit or the Lifetime Learning Credit for that student for that year. If the qualifying expenses for a student are less than $8,250 for a student, it is generally better to choose the American Opportunity Tax Credit.

### Eligible Educational Institution

An eligible educational institution is a college, university, vocational school, or other postsecondary educational institution that is eligible to participate in a student aid program administered by the federal Department of Education. Almost all accredited postsecondary institutions meet the eligibility requirements.

### Income Limitation

Once the tentative combined total for the two credits is determined, it must be reduced ratably as the taxpayer's modified adjusted gross income (MAGI) for 2009 and 2010 ranges between $80,000 - $90,000. The phaseout range for joint returns is $160,000 - $180,000 for 2009 and 2010. The credit is phased out over a $10,000 range ($20,000 for a joint return) and the lower limit is adjusted for inflation. For purposes of these education credits, MAGI is equal to adjusted gross income plus excluded income from foreign countries, specified U.S. possessions, and Puerto Rico.

### Claiming the Credits

The education credits are normally claimed by a taxpayer who pays qualified education expenses for himself, his spouse, or his dependent for whom he claims an exemption. When the taxpayer pays qualified education expenses for a claimed dependent, any expenses paid by the dependent or even by a third party are considered to be paid by the taxpayer. If the taxpayer does not claim an exemption for a dependent (even if the taxpayer is entitled to do so), the dependent can claim the credit, but the taxpayer cannot. In this situation, any qualified education expenses paid by the taxpayer or another person are normally considered to be paid by the dependent. A person who is claimed as the dependent of another is not eligible to claim an education credit.

In order to claim the education credits, a married taxpayer must file a joint return.

| Feature | American Opportunity Tax Credit | Lifetime Learning Credit |
|---|---|---|
| Base and Rate | $2,000 @ 100% plus $2,000 @ 25% (2009 and 2010) | $10,000 @ 20% |
| Maximum Annual Credit | $2,500 per eligible student (2009 and 2010) | $2,000 per tax return |
| General Availability | For the first four years of postsecondary education | For all years of postsecondary education and for courses to acquire or improve job skills |
| Years Available | Four years per student | Unlimited number of years |
| Degree Requirement | Student must pursue an undergraduate degree or other recognized education credential | Student does not need to pursue a degree or education credential |
| Half-time Requirement | Student must be enrolled at least half-time for one academic period during the year | Student must take one or more courses |
| Drug Conviction | No felony drug conviction on student's record | Felony drug conviction rule does not apply |

## American Opportunity Tax Credit

The **American Opportunity Tax Credit** is allowed for the qualified education expenses of an eligible student during the first four years of postsecondary education, and the credit can be claimed for only four tax years. The American Opportunity Tax Credit is not allowed for a student who has completed the first four years of postsecondary education before the beginning of the tax year.

### Eligible Student

An eligible student for the American Opportunity Tax Credit must meet all of the following requirements:

- Be enrolled at least half-time for one quarter, semester, or other academic period;
- Be enrolled in a program leading to a degree, certificate, or other educational credential; and
- Be free of any federal or state felony conviction for possessing or distributing a controlled substance.

### Amount of the Credit

The amount of the American Opportunity Tax Credit is 100 percent of the first $2,000 of qualified tuition and related expenses plus 25 percent of the next $2,000 of qualified expenses for the 2009 and 2010 tax years. Therefore, the maximum credit is $2,500 for 2009 and 2010. The percentages are fixed, but the dollar amount is indexed for inflation.

**EXAMPLE 9.13**

Bradley McKay, a married taxpayer filing jointly, paid $5,000 of qualified tuition and related expenses for each of his twin daughters (a total of $10,000), Ashley and Kate, during 2009. They finished their freshman year and started their sophomore year of college during 2009. Bradley claims both of his daughters as dependents. His modified adjusted gross income for the year is $70,000. His American Opportunity Tax Credit for 2009 is $5,000 (maximum credit of $2,500 x 2). Since the American Opportunity Tax Credit is available for each student, he can claim the maximum credit for each daughter. If he uses the expenses to claim the Lifetime Learning Credit instead, his maximum credit will be $2,000 (20% x $10,000).

## Quick Quiz 9.3

**Highlight the answer to these questions:**

1. A taxpayer may claim both the American Opportunity Tax Credit and the Lifetime Learning Credit based on the same qualified education expenses.
   a. True
   b. False

2. The education credits are normally claimed by the taxpayer who pays the qualified education expenses.
   a. True
   b. False

3. The felony drug conviction rule does not apply to the American Opportunity Tax Credit.
   a. True
   b. False

4. The maximum annual Lifetime Learning Credit is $2,000.
   a. True
   b. False

False, True, False, True.

### Lifetime Learning Credit

The **Lifetime Learning Credit** is available to a taxpayer who pays qualified tuition and related expenses to an eligible institution for himself, his spouse, and his dependent for whom he claims a dependency exemption. The qualified expenses must relate to any course of instruction at an eligible educational institution to acquire or improve job skills of the individual.

### No Eligible Student Requirement

With the Lifetime Learning Credit, there is no requirement for the student to (1) seek a degree or certificate, (2) pay the expenses for the first four years of postsecondary education, or (3) be free of a felony conviction related to a controlled substance. Qualified education expenses related to class at an eligible educational institution or even a continuing professional education course offered by such an institution will qualify for this credit.

### Amount of the Credit

The amount of the Lifetime Learning Credit is 20 percent of up to $10,000 of qualified tuition and related expenses for the year. Therefore, the maximum annual credit is $2,000. Both the rate and the $10,000 are fixed (no inflation adjustments). Unlike the American Opportunity Tax Credit, the Lifetime Learning Credit limits are based on the tax return rather than the number of eligible students. With the Lifetime Learning Credit, the qualified education expenses for all family members can be combined to calculate the credit.

## RETIREMENT SAVINGS CONTRIBUTIONS CREDIT

The **retirement savings contributions credit** is intended to encourage lower-income taxpayers to save for retirement. The rate used in calculating the credit is reduced as modified adjusted gross income (MAGI) increases, until the rate reaches zero percent at MAGI of $55,500 on a joint return for 2009 and 2010, $41,625 for a head of household for 2009 and 2010, and $27,750 in all other cases for 2009 and 2010. For purposes of this credit, MAGI is defined in IRS Publication 590 as adjusted gross income less any exclusion or deduction claimed for the year for foreign earned income, foreign housing costs, income for bona fide residents of American Samoa, or income from Puerto Rico.

The retirement savings contributions credit is available to an eligible individual who makes qualified retirement savings contributions of up to $2,000 ($2,000 per spouse on a joint return) for a tax year. An eligible individual is a person who is 18 or older at the end of the tax year if that person is not allowed to be claimed as a dependent of another person for the year and is not considered to be a full-time student.

The amount of the credit is determined by multiplying a taxpayer's qualified retirement savings contributions (after the reduction for certain distributions) by the applicable percentage from Exhibit 9.6 below.

## APPLICABLE PERCENTAGE FOR QUALIFIED RETIREMENT SAVINGS CONTRIBUTIONS CREDIT

EXHIBIT 9.6

| 2009 and 2010 | | | | | | |
|---|---|---|---|---|---|---|
| Joint Return Modified AGI | | Head of a Household Modified AGI | | All Other Cases Modified AGI | | Applicable Percentage |
| Over | Not over | Over | Not over | Over | Not over | |
| $0 | $33,000 | $0 | 24,750 | $0 | 16,500 | 50% |
| 33,000 | 36,000 | 24,750 | 27,000 | 16,500 | 18,000 | 20% |
| 36,000 | 55,500 | 27,000 | 41,625 | 18,000 | 27,750 | 10% |
| 55,500 | -- | 41,625 | -- | 27,750 | -- | 0% |

The maximum credit is $1,000 per person each year, or $2,000 on a joint return. Any credit that cannot be used in the current year is lost.

Kiley contributed $4,000 to her Roth IRA for 2009. She had MAGI of $15,000 for 2009 and used the single filing status. She has never taken a distribution from a retirement plan. Her maximum credit for 2009 is $1,000 ($2,000 x 50%). If her MAGI is $18,000 for 2009, her maximum credit is $400 ($2,000 x 20%).

EXAMPLE 9.14

Assume the same facts as above, except that Kiley contributes $5,000 to her Roth IRA for 2010. Also assume that if her MAGI was $19,000 for 2010, then her maximum credit is $200 ($2,000 x 10%).

## CHILD TAX CREDIT (IRC SECTION 24)

A nonrefundable **child tax credit** of $1,000 (through 2010) is available to an individual taxpayer for each qualifying child under the age of 17. The amount of the credit is simply 100 percent of $1,000, the base for the child tax credit. In order to claim the credit, the taxpayer must provide the name and Social Security number of each child on the tax return.

### A Qualifying Child

A qualifying child is defined in a manner similar to that for a dependency exemption, as discussed in Chapter 3. A qualifying child for the child tax credit is a person who:

- Is the son, daughter, stepchild, foster child, brother, sister, stepbrother, stepsister, half brother, half sister, or a descendant of any of them (for example, grandchild);
- Was under the age of 17 at the end of the tax year;
- Did not provide over half of his own support for the tax year;
- Lived with the taxpayer for more than half the year (see exceptions below); and
- Was a U.S. citizen, a U.S. national, or a resident of the United States.

**Key Concepts**

Underline/highlight the answers to these questions as you read:

1. Describe a qualifying child.

2. Explain the child tax credit limitation on income.

3. Describe the circumstances under which the child tax credit is a refundable credit.

### Adopted Child

An adopted child is always treated as the taxpayer's own child. An adopted child includes a child who has been lawfully placed with the taxpayer for adoption.

### Exceptions to Time Lived with the Taxpayer

A child who is born or dies during the year is considered to have lived with the taxpayer for the entire year if he lived with the taxpayer for the entire time he was alive during the year. A child is also considered to have lived with the taxpayer for any period during which the child is temporarily absent for school, military service, medical care, detention in a juvenile facility, or other similar purposes.

## Limitation Based on Income

The allowable child tax credit amount is reduced $50 for each $1,000 (or fraction of $1,000) that a taxpayer's modified adjusted gross income (MAGI) exceeds the following amounts:

| | |
|---|---|
| Married filing jointly* | $110,000 |
| Married filing separately* | $55,000 |
| Any other filing status* | $75,000 |

*Not adjusted for inflation*

For the child tax credit, MAGI is equal to adjusted gross income increased by excluded income from foreign countries, specified U.S. possessions, and Puerto Rico.

After any reduction of the credit because MAGI exceeds the limits, the remaining child tax credit is allowed as a nonrefundable credit.

### Additional Child Tax Credit

For a taxpayer who is unable to use all of the nonrefundable child tax credit because the tax has been reduced to zero by nonrefundable credits, some or all of the unused child tax credit may be used as a refundable credit called the additional child tax credit. The computation of the **additional child tax credit** can be complicated. It is explained in IRC Section 24(d) and it is reported on Form 8812. The solution for the following example is presented on a completed Form 8812 in Exhibit 9.7.

**EXAMPLE 9.15**

Savanna Radison is a divorced mother. She has three children under the age of 10, has custody of the children, claims them as dependents, uses the head of household filing status, and does not itemize deductions. She earns a salary of $38,025 for 2009 and has federal income tax in the amount of $2,000 withheld from her salary. Her adjusted gross income for the year is $38,025. Her taxable income is $15,075, calculated as follows:

|            |                       |
|-----------:|-----------------------|
| $38,025    | Salary                |
| - $8,350   | Standard Deduction    |
| - $3,650   | Personal Exemption    |
| - $3,650   | Dependency Exemption  |
| - $3,650   | Dependency Exemption  |
| - $3,650   | Dependency Exemption  |
| **$15,075** | **Taxable Income**   |

Her tax before credits is $1,664. She has no nonrefundable credits other than the child tax credit. She is eligible for a child tax credit of up to $3,000. She will use a child tax credit of $1,664 to reduce her tax liability to $0, but she will lose the remaining $1,336 of the credit unless she can use it as a refundable additional child tax credit. After completing the Form 8812 shown in Exhibit 9.7, she determines that she will be allowed to claim the entire $1,336 as an additional child tax credit. When the $1,336 is added to the $2,000 of federal income taxes withheld from her salary, she will receive a tax refund of $3,336.

---

**Form 8812**

Department of the Treasury
Internal Revenue Service (99)

**Additional Child Tax Credit**

*Complete and attach to Form 1040, Form 1040A, or Form 1040NR.*

1040
1040A
1040NR
8812

OMB No. 1545-0074

20**09**

Attachment
Sequence No. **47**

Name(s) shown on return

Your social security number

### Part I    All Filers

| | | | | |
|---|---|---|---|---|
| 1 | **1040 filers:** Enter the amount from line 6 of your Child Tax Credit Worksheet (see the Instructions for Form 1040, line 51). | | | |
| | **1040A filers:** Enter the amount from line 6 of your Child Tax Credit Worksheet (see the Instructions for Form 1040A, line 33). | 1 | 3,000 | 00 |
| | **1040NR filers:** Enter the amount from line 6 of your Child Tax Credit Worksheet (see the Instructions for Form 1040NR, line 47). | | | |
| | If you used Pub. 972, enter the amount from line 8 of the worksheet on page 4 of the publication. | | | |

| | | | | | | |
|---|---|---|---|---|---|---|
| 2 | Enter the amount from Form 1040, line 51, Form 1040A, line 33, or Form 1040NR, line 47 . . . . . . | | | 2 | 1,664 | 00 |
| 3 | Subtract line 2 from line 1. If zero, **stop**; you cannot take this credit . . . . . . . . . | | | 3 | 1,336 | 00 |
| 4a | Earned income (see instructions on back) . . . . . . . . . . . | 4a | 38,025 | 00 | | |
| b | Nontaxable combat pay (see instructions on back) . . . . . . . . . . | 4b | | | | |
| 5 | Is the amount on line 4a more than $3,000? | | | | | |
| | ☐ **No.** Leave line 5 blank and enter -0- on line 6. | | | | | |
| | ☐ **Yes.** Subtract $3,000 from the amount on line 4a. Enter the result . . . | 5 | 26,275 | 00 | | |
| 6 | Multiply the amount on line 5 by 15% (.15) and enter the result . . . . . . . . . . . | | | 6 | 3,941 | 00 |

**Next.** Do you have three or more qualifying children?

☐ **No.** If line 6 is zero, stop; you cannot take this credit. Otherwise, skip Part II and enter the **smaller** of line 3 or line 6 on line 13.

☐ **Yes.** If line 6 is equal to or more than line 3, skip Part II and enter the amount from line 3 on line 13. Otherwise, go to line 7.

### Part II    Certain Filers Who Have Three or More Qualifying Children

| | | | | | |
|---|---|---|---|---|---|
| 7 | Withheld social security and Medicare taxes from Form(s) W-2, boxes 4 and 6. If married filing jointly, include your spouse's amounts with yours. If you worked for a railroad, see instructions on back . . . . . . . . . | 7 | | | |
| 8 | **1040 filers:** Enter the total of the amounts from Form 1040, lines 27 and 57, plus any taxes that you identified using code "UT" and entered on the dotted line next to line 60. | | | | |
| | **1040A filers:** Enter -0-. | 8 | | | |
| | **1040NR filers:** Enter the total of the amounts from Form 1040NR, line 53, plus any taxes that you identified using code "UT" and entered on the dotted line next to line 57. | | | | |
| 9 | Add lines 7 and 8 . . . . . . . . . . . | 9 | | | |
| 10 | **1040 filers:** Enter the total of the amounts from Form 1040, lines 64a and 69. | | | | |
| | **1040A filers:** Enter the total of the amount from Form 1040A, line 41a, plus any excess social security and tier 1 RRTA taxes withheld that you entered to the left of line 44 (see instructions on back). | 10 | | | |
| | **1040NR filers:** Enter the amount from Form 1040NR, line 63. | | | | |
| 11 | Subtract line 10 from line 9. If zero or less, enter -0- . . . . . . . . | 11 | | 0 | 00 |
| 12 | Enter the **larger** of line 6 or line 11 . . . . . . . . . . | 12 | | 3,941 | 00 |

Next, enter the **smaller** of line 3 or line 12 on line 13.

### Part III    Additional Child Tax Credit

| | | | | |
|---|---|---|---|---|
| 13 | **This is your additional child tax credit** . . . . . . . . . . . . . . | 13 | 1,336 | 00 |

1040
1040A
1040NR

*Enter this amount on Form 1040, line 65, Form 1040A, line 42, or Form 1040NR, line 61.*

---

For Paperwork Reduction Act Notice, see back of form

Cat. No. 10644E

Form **8812** (2009)

## QUALIFIED ADOPTION EXPENSES CREDIT

The **adoption expenses credit** is designed to encourage the adoption of children. More generous provisions apply if an adopted child is a U.S. citizen or resident with special needs. If a child is not a citizen or resident of the U.S. at the time the adoption process begins, no credit is allowed unless the adoption becomes final.

An adoption expenses credit is allowed for qualified adoption expenses paid by an individual to adopt an eligible child. Qualified adoption expenses include adoption fees, court costs, attorney fees, and travel expenses (including amounts spent for meals and lodging) while away from home. An eligible child is a child under 18 or a child who is physically or mentally incapable of caring for himself.

**Key Concepts**

Underline/highlight the answers to these questions as you read:

1. Define qualified adoption expenses.

2. Explain the standards for considering a child to be a special needs child.

3. Describe the phaseout range for the qualified adoption expenses credit.

Qualifying adoption expenses do not include any of the following expenses:
- Expenses that violate state or federal law;
- Expenses for carrying out any surrogate parenting arrangement;
- Expenses for the adoption of a spouse's child;
- Expenses for which the taxpayer received funds under any federal, state, or local program;
- Expenses allowed as a credit or deduction under any other federal income tax rule; or
- Expenses paid or reimbursed by the taxpayer's employer or any other person or organization.

The maximum credit (subject to income limitations) is allowed for the adoption of a child with special needs even if the adopting parent has no qualified adoption expenses. For a child to be considered a child with special needs, (1) he must be a citizen or resident of the United States (including U.S. possessions) at the time the adoption process begins, (2) the state must have determined that the child cannot or should not be returned to his parents, and (3) the state has determined that the child will not be adopted due to a physical, mental, or emotional handicap, age, or one of several other specified factors unless assistance is provided to the adopting parents.

For expenses paid or incurred in a tax year before the adoption becomes final, the credit is allowed for the following year. For expenses paid or incurred during or after the tax year the adoption becomes final, the credit is allowed for the year of the expense.

The amount of the adoption expenses credit is 100 percent of the qualified adoption expenses up to $12,150 for 2009 ($12,170 for 2010) for the adoption of each child. The amount of the credit for the adoption of a child with special needs is $12,150 for 2009 ($12,170 for 2010) regardless of the amount of the qualified adoption expenses. Portions of the credit may be claimed in different years.

Whether the adopted child is a child with special needs or not, the maximum amount of the credit is phased out if the taxpayer's modified adjusted gross income (MAGI), as defined in IRC Section 23, exceeds $182,180 for 2009 ($182,520 for 2010). The maximum credit is ratably phased out as the taxpayer's MAGI ranges between $182,180 and $222,180 for 2009 ($182,520 - $222,520 for 2010), the $40,000 phaseout range.

**EXAMPLE 9.16**

During 2009, Beth and Paul Campbell paid $14,000 of adoption expenses to adopt their new daughter, Ashley. The adoption was final in October of 2009. Their modified adjusted gross income for 2009 was $190,000. Their maximum allowable adoption expenses credit is $9,775 for 2009 ($9,894 for 2010) as calculated below.

| | | |
|---|---|---|
| 1. Maximum credit | | $12,150 |
| 2. Excess MAGI: | | |
| MAGI | $190,000 | |
| Lower MAGI limit | $182,180 | |
| Excess | $7,820 | |
| 3. Reduction of maximum credit: | | |
| $\frac{\$7,820}{\$40,000} \times \$12,150 =$ | | $2,375 |
| 4. Maximum (the difference between 1 and 3) | | $9,775 |

For 2010, the calculation is $190,000 - $182,520 = ($7,480 / $40,000) x $12,170 = $2,276. $12,170 - $2,276 = $9,894.

If the MAGI of the Campbells had been $120,000 for 2009 ($120,000 for 2010) they would have been allowed to claim an adoption expenses credit of $12,150 for 2009 ($12,170 for 2010). If their MAGI had been $120,000 and they had paid qualifying adoption expenses of only $9,000 during 2009 or 2010, their adoption expenses credit would have been $9,000. Finally, if their MAGI had been $120,000 for 2009, their qualified adoption expenses had been $9,000 during 2009, and Ashley had been a child with special needs, their adoption expenses credit would have been $12,150 ($12,170 for 2010).

Any portion of the adoption expenses credit that cannot be used in the tax year can be carried forward for up to five years using a first-in, first-out (FIFO) method. The FIFO method allows the taxpayer to use the oldest credits first.

## RESIDENTIAL ENERGY PROPERTY AND RESIDENTIAL ENERGY EFFICIENT PROPERTY CREDITS

The American Recovery and Reinvestment Act of 2009 provides energy saving incentives for taxpayers. For 2009 and 2010, the **Residential Energy Property Credit** increases the energy tax credit for energy efficient improvements made to a taxpayer's existing home. The credit rate is 30 percent of the cost of all qualifying improvements (i.e., adding insulation, energy efficient heating and air conditioning systems, and energy efficient exterior windows) with a maximum combined credit limit of $1,500 for both tax years.

The **Residential Energy Efficient Property Credit** is a nonrefundable energy tax credit that helps an individual taxpayer pay for qualified residential alternative energy equipment. Previously imposed dollar caps on the residential alternative energy equipment have been removed leaving a credit equal to 30 percent of the cost of qualified property (see Exhibit 9.8).

**EXHIBIT 9.8** RESIDENTIAL ENERGY EFFICIENT PROPERTY CREDIT

| Property Type | Rate |
|---|---|
| Qualified solar electric property | 30% |
| Qualified solar water heating property | 30% |
| Qualified fuel cell property | Lesser of: 30%, or $500 for each half kilowatt of capacity |
| Qualified wind energy property | 30% |
| Geothermal heat pump property | 30% |

The limits in the table above apply to each residence. If a taxpayer has more than one residence, the limits for qualified solar electric property and qualified solar water heating property apply to each residence. Any limits for qualified fuel cell property limits apply only to the taxpayer's principal residence.

f more than one taxpayer occupies a residence, each taxpayer may have to report his qualifying expenditures for the year on his own return and the limits for the residence in the table above may have to be allocated to the eligible taxpayers. Such an allocation is not necessary for married taxpayers filing a joint return.

The amount of the annual credit is equal to the sum of the credits for each type of qualifying expenditures. Any amount of the credit that cannot be used in the current year because the nonrefundable credits have reduced the year's income tax to zero can be carried forward to the next year.

EXAMPLE 9.17

In 2009, Angelina paid $8,000 for qualified solar electric property for her vacation home and also paid $6,000 for qualified fuel cell property with one kilowatt of capacity for her principal residence. Her maximum residential energy efficient property credit for 2009 is $3,400 [($8,000 x 30% = $2,400) + (lesser of, $6,000 x 30% = $1,800 or $500 x 2 = $1,000)]. $2,400 of the $8,000 spent for the qualified solar electric property qualifies for the credit even though the expenditures were not for her principal residence. The lesser of, $500 for each half kilowatt of capacity of the cost of the qualified fuel cell property or 30% of expenditures, qualifies for the credit. Since the property has one kilowatt of capacity, the $500 must be multiplied by two. If Angelina had installed the fuel cell property in her vacation home, it would not have qualified for the credit. If Angelina's income tax liability before this credit is $2,800, she will be allowed to carry the remaining $600 of the credit forward to be used in 2010.

# REFUNDABLE CREDITS

Once nonrefundable credits have been used to the extent possible to reduce the tax calculated on taxable income, the full amount of refundable credits can be used in the current year to further reduce the year's tax liability and/or to generate a tax refund.

## CREDITS FOR TAXES PAID

Quite appropriately, any federal income taxes paid in advance by a taxpayer will generate a refundable **credit for taxes paid** for the taxpayer. Such advance payments of taxes include (1) federal income taxes withheld by employers and others, (2) estimated federal income taxes paid by the taxpayer, (3) refunds from prior tax years that have been retained by the Internal Revenue Service at the request of the taxpayer, and (4) excess Social Security taxes (OASDI) withheld when a taxpayer has more than one employer.

For 2009 and 2010, Social Security or OASDI taxes of 6.2 percent must be withheld by the employer on the first $106,800 of salary or wages earned by an employee. This wage base is adjusted upward each year due to inflation. Each employer is required to withhold this tax and remit it to the federal government. If the combined compensation subject to Social Security taxes exceeds the wage base for the year, excess taxes may be withheld and should be repaid to the taxpayer.

**EXAMPLE 9.18**

Elizabeth earns a salary of $110,000 from Company A during 2009. Company A withholds OASDI taxes in the amount of $6,622 (0.062 x $106,800). She also earns $10,000 of wages from Company B. Company B withholds OASDI taxes in the amount of $620 (0.062 x $10,000). Elizabeth will be allowed to take a $620 refundable credit against income taxes for the excess Social Security taxes withheld from her compensation during the year.

If a taxpayer has only one employer and that employer withholds too much in Social Security taxes from his compensation for the year, he is not allowed to take a refundable credit for the excess. He must seek a reimbursement from his employer for the excess taxes withheld.

In addition to the federal income taxes withheld from compensation by employers, federal income taxes are often withheld and paid to the government by the payors of other taxable payments, such as retirement plan distributions, traditional IRA distributions, and annuities.

## EARNED INCOME CREDIT

The **earned income credit** is intended to motivate lower-income taxpayers to earn income. The credit increases as the individual's earned income increases up to a maximum level of earned income. This generous refundable credit provides a tax refund to many people who have not paid in any federal income taxes through withholding or otherwise. In one sense, it is effectively a negative or reverse income tax since money is paid out to the taxpayer by the government rather than having the taxpayer pay taxes to the government. It is slightly more generous for taxpayers who are married filing jointly than for those who are not. It is much more generous for a taxpayer who has one qualifying child than for a taxpayer who has no qualifying child, and more generous for a taxpayer who, in 2009, has two or more qualifying children (three or more qualifying children for 2010) than for a taxpayer who has only one qualifying child.

The earned income credit is available to an eligible individual who has earned income for the tax year provided his income does not exceed specified limits. As income increases beyond the maximum level of earned income, the credit remains level until a phaseout level of income is reached. The credit is then gradually decreased as higher levels of income are earned until the credit is reduced to zero. The relevant income levels, credit rates, and phaseout rates are dependent on filing status and the number of qualifying children of the taxpayer. These income levels and rates are presented in the following exhibit.

## EARNED INCOME CREDIT

EXHIBIT 9.9

| Filing Status | Married Filing Jointly | | | | Other Filing Status | | | |
|---|---|---|---|---|---|---|---|---|
| Number of Qualifying Children | 0 | 1 | 2 | 3 or more | 0 | 1 | 2 | 3 or more |
| **2009 Tax Year** | | | | | | | | |
| 1 Maximum Earned Income | $ 5,970 | $ 8,950 | $ 12,570 | | $ 5,970 | $ 8,950 | $ 12,570 | |
| 2 Credit Percentage | 7.65% | 34.00% | 40.00% | | 7.65% | 34.00% | 40.00% | |
| 3 Maximum Earned Income Credit | $ 457 | $ 3,043 | $ 5,028 | | $ 457 | $ 3,043 | $ 5,028 | |
| 4 Phaseout Amount >EI or AGI of* | $ 10,590 | $ 19,540 | $ 19,540 | | $ 7,470 | $ 16,420 | $ 16,420 | |
| 5 Phaseout Percentage on Excess | 7.65% | 15.98% | 21.06% | | 7.65% | 15.98% | 21.06% | |
| 6 Phaseout Ends > EI or AGI of* | $ 16,560 | $ 38,583 | $ 43,415 | | $ 13,440 | $ 35,463 | $ 40,295 | |
| **2010 Tax Year** | | | | | | | | |
| 7 Maximum Earned Income | $ 5,980 | $ 8,970 | $ 12,590 | $ 12,590 | $ 5,980 | $ 8,970 | $ 12,590 | $ 12,590 |
| 8 Credit Percentage | 7.65% | 34.00% | 40.00% | 45.00% | 7.65% | 34.00% | 40.00% | 45.00% |
| 9 Maximum Earned Income Credit | $ 457 | $ 3,050 | $ 5,036 | $ 5,666 | $ 457 | $ 3,050 | $ 5,036 | $ 5,666 |
| 10 Phaseout Amount >EI or AGI of* | $ 12,490 | $ 21,460 | $ 21,460 | $ 21,460 | $ 7,480 | $ 16,450 | $ 16,450 | $ 16,450 |
| 11 Phaseout Percentage on Excess | 7.65% | 15.98% | 21.06% | 21.06% | 7.65% | 15.98% | 21.06% | 21.06% |
| 12 Phaseout Ends > EI or AGI of* | $ 18,470 | $ 40,545 | $ 45,373 | $ 48,362 | $ 13,460 | $ 35,535 | $ 40,363 | $ 43,352 |

*EI = Earned Income; AGI = Adjusted Gross Income

The information in the table above for married filing jointly with two or more children is illustrated by the following graph.

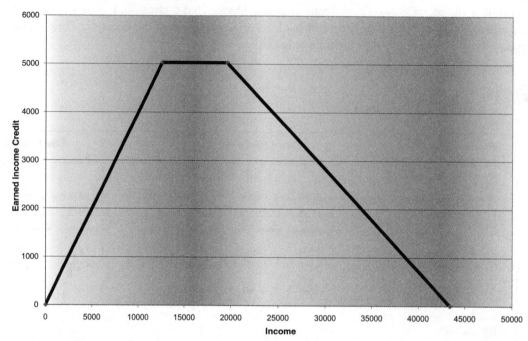

As illustrated in the graph above, the earned income credit of eligible individuals who are married filing jointly with two or more qualifying children is zero when earned income is zero. As earned income increases up to the maximum level of earned income (row 1 in Exhibit 9.9), the credit is determined by multiplying earned income by the credit percentage (row 2 in Exhibit 9.9). At the $12,570 maximum level of earned income for 2009, the maximum credit is $5,028 ($12,570 x 40%). That maximum credit is allowed until the phaseout amount of income is reached (row 4 in Exhibit 9.9). Please note that for 2010, the maximum credit rate for three or more children is 45 percent and a maximum credit of $5,666 is available at $12,590 of earned income.

The income level at which the credit phaseout begins is based upon the greater of earned income or adjusted gross income (AGI). In the graph above, the phaseout begins at $19,540 of income for two children for 2009. The phaseout amount is subtracted from the $5,028 maximum credit (for 2009). The phaseout amount is equal to the income (the greater of earned income or AGI) of the taxpayer in excess of the phaseout amount multiplied by the phaseout percentage (row 5 in Exhibit 9.9).

For the graph above, if the eligible individuals have earned income of $20,000 and adjusted gross income of $21,000, the earned income credit in this situation will be $4,721 ($5,028 - $307) and the phaseout amount will be $307 [($21,000 - $19,540) x 21.06%]. Once the income (greater of earned income or AGI) reaches $43,415, the earned income credit is entirely eliminated.

The table, graph, and explanation above are intended to illustrate the concepts behind the determination of the earned income credit. In filing a tax return, the taxpayer may determine the amount of the earned income credit by filling in the applicable worksheets and referring to a table for the amount of the credit or may simply use a computer program to calculate the credit. IRS Publication 596 contains several examples with filled-in schedules and worksheets. The 2009 and 2010 numbers are provided in Exhibit 9.9.

## Eligible Individual

All eligible individuals must meet the following requirements:
- Taxpayer (or spouse if married) must have earned income;
- Adjusted gross income cannot exceed the phaseout end amount on row 6 of Exhibit 9.9 for 2009 (row 12 of Exhibit 9.9 for 2010);
- Earned income cannot exceed the phaseout end amount on row 6 of Exhibit 9.9 for 2009 (row 12 of Exhibit 9.9 for 2010);
- Taxpayer (and spouse if married) must have a valid Social Security number;
- Filing status cannot be married filing separately;
- Taxpayer (and spouse if married) must be a U.S. citizen or resident alien all year;
- Cannot claim a foreign earned income exclusion for the year;
- Cannot be a qualifying child of another person; and
- Investment income must be $3,100 or less for 2009 and 2010.

Additional requirements for a taxpayer with a qualifying child:
- The child must meet relationship, age, and residency tests; and
- The qualifying child cannot be used by more than one person to claim the earned income credit.

Additional requirements for a taxpayer with no qualifying child:
- Taxpayer (or spouse if married) must be at least age 25 but under age 65;
- Taxpayer cannot be the dependent of another person; and
- Taxpayer must have lived in the United States more than half of the year.

## Qualifying Child

A qualifying child of an eligible individual must meet (1) relationship, (2) age, and (3) residency tests that are almost identical to those required to claim a dependency exemption for a qualifying child. These relationship, age, and residency tests are briefly summarized below. A qualifying child for the earned income credit is a person who:
- *Relationship:* Is the son, daughter, stepchild, foster child, brother, sister, stepbrother, stepsister, half brother, half sister, or a descendant of any of them;
- *Age:* Was under the age of 19 as of the end of the calendar year, a student under the age of 24 as of the end of the calendar year, or permanently and totally disabled at any time during the year; and
- *Residency:* Lived with the taxpayer in the United States for more than half the year.

### *Advance Payment of the Earned Income Credit*

Although an eligible individual normally claims the earned income credit on his tax return, he may be able to receive advance payments of the credit from his employer if he meets three requirements and files a Form W-5 with his employer. To receive advance payments, an eligible individual must (1) have a qualifying child, (2) expect to have adjusted gross income and earned income of less than $35,463 ($38,583 on a joint return) for 2009 (see row 6 of Exhibit 9.9) or less than $35,535 ($40,545 on a joint return) for 2010 (see row 12 of Exhibit 9.9), and (3) expect to be eligible for the earned income credit for the year.

## ADDITIONAL CHILD TAX CREDIT

The refundable additional child tax credit is actually based on a portion of the nonrefundable child tax credit that cannot be used by the taxpayer for the year. This refundable portion of the child tax credit is called the additional child tax credit on tax forms and in IRS publications. See the discussion of the child tax credit earlier in this chapter.

## FIRST-TIME HOMEBUYER CREDIT

For 2009, the American Recovery and Reinvestment Act extended the refundable **first-time homebuyer credit** for main home purchases made during 2009 and before December 1, 2009. Qualifying purchases can qualify for a credit up to $8,000. The credit is 10 percent of the purchase price of the main home up to $8,000 for either a single taxpayer or a married couple filing jointly (limited to $4,000 for married filing separately taxpayers). The credit is phased out for married filing jointly taxpayers at modified adjusted gross income (MAGI) of $150,000 - $170,000 (for 2009) and for other taxpayers at MAGI of $75,000 - $95,000 (for 2009).

In order to qualify for the credit, the following criteria must be met:
- The main home being purchased must be located in the United States.
- The taxpayer cannot own another main home for a period of three years prior to the date of the purchase.

Note that vacation homes and rental properties are not eligible for the credit. In addition, nonresident aliens do not qualify for the credit. The credit taken for a 2009 main home purchase must be repaid if the home ceases to be the taxpayer's main home within three years subsequent to the date of purchase.

The first-time homebuyer credit has been modified and extended in a similar version for 2010. More information is available at www.money-education.com.

## Quick Quiz 9.6

**Highlight the answer to these questions:**

1. A taxpayer who has too much OASDI tax withheld may only take a refundable credit if he has more than one employer.
   a. True
   b. False

2. The earned income credit is not a refundable credit.
   a. True
   b. False

True, False.

# GENERAL BUSINESS CREDIT

The **general business credit** is actually a combination of more than thirty different nonrefundable tax credits. These credits are intended to promote social, economic, environmental, and other objectives favored by Congress.

Like the nonbusiness credits that are nonrefundable, the components of the general business credit must be considered in sequence. Any portion of the general business credit that cannot be used in the current year can be carried back to the preceding year and then carried forward for up to twenty years if necessary.

In a given tax year, the general business credit may consist of credit amounts carried forward to the current year, the business credit generated in the current year, and credit amounts carried back to the current year. These credits are used in a first-in, first-out (FIFO) sequence. The credits are to be used in the following order:

- The business credit carryforwards to the current year;
- The amount of the current year business credit; and
- The business credit carrybacks to the current year.

## Key Concepts

**Underline/highlight the answers to these questions as you read:**

1. Describe the carryforward and carryback rules for the general business credit.

2. List the components of the general business credit.

This sequence is favorable to the taxpayer because it gives the taxpayer the best opportunity to use the general business credit carryforwards before they expire.

The general business credit may not be allowed to offset all of the income tax remaining after the application of the nonrefundable credits discussed earlier in this chapter. A limit must be calculated to determine how much of the general business credit can be used in the current year.

The components of the general business credit are listed in Exhibit 9.10.

EXHIBIT 9.10    GENERAL BUSINESS CREDIT

**General Business Credit (Nonrefundable)**
**Unused Credit: Carryback 1 Year; Carryforward 20 Years**
**See IRS Publication 334, Tax Guide for Small Business**

| Item | Credit Sequence | IRC § | Reported on Form |
|---|---|---|---|
| General Business Credit | | 38 | 3800 |
| Investment Credit | 1 | 46 | 3468 |
| Work Opportunity Credit | 2 | 51(a) | 5884 |
| Research Credit (Credit for Increasing Research Activities) | 3 | 41(a) | 6765 |
| Low-income Housing Credit | 4 | 42(a) | 8586 |
| Enhanced Oil Recovery Credit | 5 | 43(a) | Sched K-1 |
| Disabled Access Credit | 6 | 44(a) | 8826 |
| Renewable Electricity Production Credit | 7 | 45(a) | 8835 Sec. A |
| Indian Employment Credit | 8 | 45A(a) | 8845 |
| Employer Social Security Credit | 9 | 45B(a) | 8846 |
| Orphan Drug Credit | 10 | 45C(a) | 8820 |
| New Markets Credit | 11 | 45D(a) | 8874 |
| Small Employer Pension Plan Startup Costs Credit | 12 | 45E(a) | 8881 |
| Employer-Provided Child Care Credit | 13 | 45F(a) | 8882 |
| Qualified Railroad Track Maintenance Credit | 14 | 45G(a) | 8900 |
| Biodiesel and Renewable Diesel Fuels Credit | 15 | 40A(a) | 8864 |
| Low Sulfur Diesel Fuel Production Credit | 16 | 45H(a) | 8896 |
| Distilled Spirits Credit | 17 | 5011(a) | 8906 |
| Nonconventional Source Fuel Production Credit | 18 | 45K(a) | 8907 |
| Energy Efficient Home Credit | 19 | 45L(a) | 8908 |
| Energy Efficient Appliance Credit | 20 | 45M(a) | 8909 |
| Alternative Motor Vehicle Credit | 21 | 30B(g)(1) | 8910 |
| Alternative Fuel Vehicle Refueling Property Credit | 22 | 30C(d)(1) | 8911 |
| Credits for Employers Affected by Hurricane Katrina, Rita, or Wilma | 23 | 1400P/1400R | 5884-A |
| Mine Rescue Team Training Credit | 24 | 45N(a) | 8923 |
| Credit for Contributions to Selected Community Development Corps. | 25 | | 8847 |
| General Credits from an Electing Large Partnership | 26 | | Sched K-1 |
| General Business Credits Not Reported on Form 3800: | | | |
| Empowerment Zone and Renewal Community Employment Credit | | 1396(a) | 8844 |
| Alcohol Fuel Credit | | 40(a) | 6478 |
| Renewable Electricity, Refined Coal, & Indian Coal Production Credit | | 45 | 8835 Sec. B |

The general business credit is reported on Form 3800. The last three items in Exhibit 9.10 are components of the general business credit, but they are not reported on Form 3800 because each of them has special limitations that are not easily accommodated by that form.

A brief discussion of a few of the components of the general business credit follows.

## INVESTMENT CREDIT

The **investment credit** consists of the sum of four different credits, (1) the rehabilitation credit, (2) the energy credit, (3) the qualifying advanced coal project credit, and (4) the qualifying gasification project credit. Only the rehabilitation credit will be discussed here.

### Rehabilitation Credit

This rehabilitation credit is intended to promote the improvement and continued use of older buildings. The credit is allowed for qualified rehabilitation expenditures made for any qualified rehabilitated building if the building is substantially rehabilitated. A qualified building must have been placed in service before 1936 or it must be a certified historic structure.

The amount of the rehabilitation credit is 10 percent of the qualified rehabilitation expenditures made for pre-1936 buildings plus 20 percent of the qualified rehabilitation expenditures for certified historic structures. These rates are 13 percent and 26 percent if the buildings are in the Gulf Opportunity Zone which consists of certain counties and parishes affected by Hurricanes Katrina and Rita.

The total of the four components of the investment credit is calculated on Form 3468 and then carried to Form 3800, the general business credit form.

## WORK OPPORTUNITY CREDIT

The **work opportunity credit** is intended to promote the hiring of targeted groups of people who have special needs or high unemployment rates. The credit is allowed for up to $6,000 of qualified first-year wages paid to an employee in a targeted group. A targeted group employee must be certified by a state employment security agency to be a member of one of the following targeted groups:

1. Recipients of assistance under Temporary Assistance for Needy Families (TANF),
2. Veterans,
3. Ex-felons,
4. High-risk youth, age 18 to 24, who live in an empowerment zone, enterprise community, or renewal community,
5. Vocational rehabilitation referrals,
6. Summer youth employees, age 16 or 17, who live in an empowerment zone, enterprise community, or renewal community,
7. Food stamp recipients, or
8. Supplemental security income (SSI) recipients.

The amount of the credit is 40 percent of the qualified first-year wages up to $6,000 ($3,000 for a summer youth employee) paid to a targeted group employee. This 40 percent rate applies only if the employee works at least 400 hours during the year. For an employee who work at least 120 hours but less than 400 hours, the rate is 25 percent.

Wages expense for the tax year must be reduced by the amount of the work opportunity credit of the taxpayer.

## CREDIT FOR INCREASING RESEARCH ACTIVITIES

The **credit for increasing research activities** is intended to encourage businesses to conduct research and to increase their research expenditures. The credit is allowed for specified increases in qualified research expenditures.

The credit is really the sum of three components. First, the amount of the incremental research activities credit is 20 percent of a specified increase in qualified research expenditures over a base amount. Second, the amount of energy research portion is 20 percent of business expenses paid to an energy research consortium. Third, the amount of the basic research component is 20 percent of a specified increase in certain basic research payments over a base amount. The third component is available only to regular corporations (C corporations). It is not available to individuals.

Research expenses for the tax year must be reduced by the amount of the research credit determined for the tax year.

## LOW-INCOME HOUSING CREDIT

The **low-income housing credit** is intended to promote the construction of housing for low-income residents. The credit is based on the qualified basis or cost of the building and the portion of the units that are rented to low-income tenants.

The amount of the credit is the qualified basis of the building multiplied by an applicable percentage rate that is updated by the IRS on a monthly basis. The resulting credit is allocated over a ten-year period if the building continues to meet qualification requirements.

## DISABLED ACCESS CREDIT

The **disabled access credit** is intended to encourage small businesses to make their buildings accessible to persons with disabilities. The credit is available to eligible small businesses for eligible access expenditures of up to $10,250. Eligible access expenditures are expenditures made by small businesses to comply with requirements under the Americans with Disabilities Act of 1990.

The amount of the credit is 50 percent of the eligible access expenditures in excess of $250 and not in excess of $10,250. Therefore, the maximum credit is $5,000 [50% x ($10,250 - $250)].

## SMALL EMPLOYER PENSION PLAN STARTUP COSTS CREDIT

The **small employer pension plan startup costs credit** is intended to encourage small employers to set up retirement plans for employees. The credit is based on qualified startup costs paid or incurred by the employer for the first three years of the plan. Qualified startup costs include the costs of setting up and administering the plan and the cost of retirement-related education for employees with respect to the employer plan.

The amount of the credit is 50 percent of the qualified startup costs of up to $1,000 for the tax year. The maximum credit is therefore $500 per year. The credit is allowed for the first three years of the employer plan.

The taxpayer's deduction for startup costs must be reduced by the amount of the credit for the tax year.

## EMPLOYER-PROVIDED CHILD CARE CREDIT

The **employer-provided child care credit** is intended to encourage employers to help provide and promote appropriate child care for their employees.

The amount of the credit is equal to the sum of 25 percent of the qualified child care facility expenditures and 10 percent of the qualified child care resource and referral expenditures of the taxpayer for the tax year. The maximum amount of the credit allowed is $150,000 per year.

The basis of a purchased child care facility must be reduced by the amount of any related credit. The deduction for other child care expenditures must be reduced by the amount of the related credit.

# Key Terms

*Additional Child Tax Credit* – The refundable portion of the Child Tax Credit.

*Adoption Expenses Credit* – A nonrefundable credit allowed for qualified adoption expenses paid by an individual to adopt an eligible child.

*American Opportunity Tax Credit (formerly Hope Scholarship Credit)* – A credit (a portion of which is refundable) allowed for the qualified education expenses of an eligible student during the first four years of post-secondary education.

*Child Tax Credit* – A nonrefundable tax credit of $1,000, which is available to an individual taxpayer for each qualifying child under the age of 17.

*Credit for Child and Dependent Care Expenses* – A nonrefundable credit intended to provide some financial relief to individuals who incur employment-related expenses for the care of one or more qualifying individuals.

*Credit for Increasing Research Activities* – A component of the general business credit intended to encourage businesses to conduct research and increase their research expenditures.

*Credit for the Elderly or Disabled* – A nonrefundable credit intended to provide financial assistance to elderly or disabled individuals with modest incomes.

*Credits for Taxes Paid* – Refundable credits generated by federal income taxes paid in advance.

*Disabled Access Credit* – A component of the general business credit intended to encourage small businesses to make their buildings accessible to persons with disabilities.

*Earned Income Credit* – A refundable credit intended to reward lower-income taxpayers for earning income.

*Employer-Provided Child Care Credit* – A component of the general business credit intended to encourage employers to help provide and promote appropriate child care for their employees.

*First-Time Homebuyer Credit* - A refundable tax credit available for the purchase of a main home by first-time homebuyers.

*Foreign Tax Credit* – A nonrefundable tax credit available to qualifying taxpayers who pay income taxes to a foreign country on foreign source income and also pay U.S. income taxes on the same income.

*General Business Credit* – A combination of more than thirty different nonrefundable tax credits that must be considered in a specific sequence.

# Key Terms

**Investment Credit** – Part of the general business credit consisting of the sum of four different credits, (1) the rehabilitation credit, (2) the energy credit, (3) the qualifying advanced coal project credit, and (4) the qualifying gasification project credit.

**Lifetime Learning Credit** – A nonrefundable credit available to taxpayers who pay qualified tuition and related expenses to an eligible institution for themselves, their spouses, and their dependents for whom a dependency exemption is claimed.

**Low-Income Housing Credit** – A component of the general business credit intended to promote the construction of housing for low-income residents.

**Nonrefundable Tax Credits** – Tax credits that can reduce the tax on taxable income to zero, but cannot generate a tax refund.

**Refundable Tax Credits** – Tax credits that can be used not only to reduce or eliminate the current year's tax, but also to generate a tax refund.

**Residential Energy Efficient Property Credit** – A nonrefundable energy tax credit that helps an individual taxpayer pay for qualified residential alternative energy equipment.

**Residential Energy Property Credit** – A credit that increases the energy tax credit for energy efficient improvements made to a taxpayer's existing home.

**Retirement Savings Contribution Credit** – A nonrefundable credit intended to encourage lower-income taxpayers to save for retirement.

**Small Employer Pension Plan Startup Costs Credit** – A component of the general business credit intended to encourage small employers to set up retirement plans for employees.

**Tax Credit** – An amount that is subtracted from a calculated tax.

**Work Opportunity Credit** – Part of the general business credit intended to promote the hiring of targeted groups of people who have special needs or high unemployment rates.

1. Compare and contrast nonrefundable and refundable tax credits.

2. Why is a tax credit generally more beneficial than a tax deduction of the same amount?

3. What are the requirements for claiming a tax credit?

4. Can a taxpayer take both a deduction for foreign taxes paid and take the foreign tax credit?

5. What is a qualifying individual for the purpose of the credit for child and dependent care expenses?

6. Who is a qualified individual for the purpose of the credit for the elderly or disabled?

7. Define qualified tuition and related expenses.

8. Who is an eligible student for the purpose of the American Opportunity Tax Credit (formerly Hope Scholarship Credit)?

9. What is the maximum amount of the Lifetime Learning Credit?

10. What is the purpose of the retirement savings contribution credit and to whom is it available?

11. What is a qualifying child for the purpose of the child tax credit?

12. Describe the earned income credit.

13. What is the general business credit?

14. Can the general business credit offset all income?

15. What is the purpose of the work opportunity credit?

1. Which of the following is a refundable credit?

    a. Child Tax Credit.

    b. Earned Income Credit.

    c. Qualified Adoption Credit.

    d. Lifetime Learning Credit.

2. Which of the following statements is true regarding refundable tax credits?

    a. There are more refundable tax credits than nonrefundable credits.

    b. Refundable tax credits can be used only to reduce or eliminate the current year's tax.

    c. Refundable tax credits can generate a tax refund.

    d. For federal income tax purposes, refundable credits are used before nonrefundable credits.

3. Amber pays foreign income taxes of $1,200 (at the same rate as U.S. income taxes) on foreign earned income for the current year. Her U.S. income tax for the year is $22,000. Her total itemized deductions other than the allowable deduction for foreign income taxes are $500 less than her standard deduction. If she is in the 28% marginal tax bracket, which of the following should she do?

    a. She should take a credit for the foreign tax paid.

    b. She should take an itemized deduction for the foreign tax paid.

    c. She should take a deduction for a portion of the foreign tax paid and a credit for the rest.

    d. She cannot take a deduction or a credit for the foreign tax paid.

4.  Brandy is a single mom with 2 children, Zach and Wendy. Zach is 14 years old and Wend is 3 years old. Brandy has AGI of $50,000. She paid the following expenses for child car this year:

    - $300 to Zach to care for Wendy so Brandy could go out to dinner with friends.
    - $1,000 for an after-school program for Zach.
    - $3,500 to Brandy's mother for the care of Wendy during the day.

    What is Brandy's available child and dependent care credit?

    a.  $0.
    b.  $200.
    c.  $600.
    d.  $700.

5.  Which of the following is true regarding the Credit for the Elderly or Disabled?

    a.  The credit is available without regard to the individual's income if he i disabled.
    b.  A qualified individual must be over 65 at the end of the tax year or be 65 o younger and meet one of the listed exceptions.
    c.  The credit is a fixed amount for all individuals.
    d.  For purposes of this credit, the taxpayer is considered to be age 65 on the da before his actual birthday.

6.  Jim, a married filing jointly taxpayer, paid $10,000 of qualified tuition and related expense for each of his twin daughters, Stephanie and Amanda, during 2009. They started thei freshman year of college during 2009. Jim was very excited that both daughters excelled i the college environment; especially since Stephanie had a drug addiction during her senio year of high school (Jim had a friend on the college admissions board that thankfull overlooked Stephanie's felony drug conviction). Jim also paid $2,000 of qualified tuitio and related expenses for his daughter Linda's sophomore year of college and $3,000 for hi own master's degree program. Jim claims all three of his daughters as dependents. Hi modified gross income for the year is $60,000. What is the available American Opportunit Tax Credit for 2009?

    a.  $2,000.
    b.  $2,500.
    c.  $4,500.
    d.  $7,000.

7. Jim, a married filing jointly taxpayer, paid $5,000 of qualified tuition and related expenses for each of his twin daughters, Stephanie and Amanda, during 2009. They started their freshman year of college during 2009. Jim was very excited that both daughters excelled in the college environment; especially since Stephanie had a drug addiction during her senior year of high school (Jim had a friend on the college admissions board that thankfully overlooked Stephanie's felony drug conviction). Jim also paid $2,000 of qualified tuition and related expenses for his daughter Linda's sophomore year of college and $3,000 for his own master's program. Jim claims all three of his daughters as dependents. His modified gross income for the year is $60,000. What is the available Life Time Learning Credit assuming he elects to use the Lifetime Learning Credit for those expenses that do not qualify for the American Opportunity Tax Credit?

   a. $0.

   b. $1,000.

   c. $1,600.

   d. $2,000.

8. Sara contributed $5,000 to her Roth IRA for 2009. She had MAGI of $20,000 for 2009 and used the single filing status. She has never taken a distribution from a retirement plan. What is her maximum retirement savings credit for 2009?

   a. $0.

   b. $200.

   c. $400.

   d. $2,000.

9. Andy's second wife, Gina, died several years ago. Andy and Gina had two children together, Sara and Ben (twins, age 6) and they had adopted a child Andrew (age 10). Andy also had a child, Angela, age 18, with his first wife. Andy's fiancé (who also lives with Andy) gave birth to Andy's biological child, Sue Ellen, in November of the current year. All five children live with Andy and he claims all of them as dependents. Andy's AGI for the current year is $60,000 and he files head of household. What is Andy's available child tax credit?

   a. $2,000.

   b. $3,000.

   c. $4,000.

   d. $5,000.

10. Steve and Kendra have been unable to have a baby. They decided last year that adoption would the best choice for them. They believe that they can support a child that has special needs both financially and emotionally. Therefore, they adopted, Janice, a four year old special needs child this year. They paid $8,000 in qualifying adoption expense for the current year. Their MAGI for the year is $160,000 and their tax due before the application of the qualified adoption credit is $10,000. What is Steve and Kendra's available adoption credit for 2009?

    a.  $8,000.

    b.  $10,000.

    c.  $12,150.

    d.  $12,170.

11. In 2009, Ginger paid $5,000 for qualified solar electric property and $4,000 for qualified fuel cell property with one kilowatt of capacity for her vacation home. She also paid $10,000 for qualified solar water heating property for her personal residence. What is her maximum residential energy efficient property credit for 2009?

    a.  $4,500.

    b.  $5,000.

    c.  $5,500.

    d.  $6,500.

12. Kathryn earns a salary of $150,000 from Hospitals, Inc. as a hospital administrator during 2009. Hospitals, Inc. withholds OASDI taxes in the amount of $6,622. She also earns $20,000 of wages from CPR Experts where she teaches CPR. CPR Experts withholds OASDI taxes in the amount of $1,240. What is Kathryn's available credit for excess Social Security taxes withheld, assuming Kathryn's tax due before application of the credit is $800?

    a.  $0.

    b.  $440.

    c.  $800.

    d.  $1,240.

13. Which of the following is true regarding the earned income credit?

    a.  The taxpayer must have either wages or investment income.

    b.  If a married couple files married filing separately only one can claim the credit.

    c.  If the taxpayer does not have a qualifying child then the taxpayer must be at least 21 but under age 65.

    d.  If the taxpayer has a qualifying child, the child must meet a relationship, age, and residency test.

14. Which of the following is true regarding the general business credit?

    a.   Any unused credit can be carried back 5 years or forward 20 years.

    b.   The general business credit is a combination of more than 30 different nonrefundable tax credits.

    c.   The credits are used in a LIFO Sequence – carrybacks, current year, then carryforward credits.

    d.   The general business credit can offset all of the income tax remaining after the application of the other nonrefundable credits.

15. Which of the following is true regarding business credits?

    a.   The investment credit consists of the sum of two different credits, (1) the rehabilitation credit, and (2) the qualifying gasification project credit.

    b.   The amount of the rehabilitation credit is 10 percent of the qualified rehabilitation expenditures made for pre-1936 buildings plus 20 percent of the qualified rehabilitation expenditures for certified historic structures.

    c.   The work opportunity credit is a credit for employees of certain high risk jobs to provide them with an additional benefit because of the risks involved in their job (for example, police officers).

    d.   The employer-provided child care credit allows a credit for employer provided payments to 3rd party caregivers.

# Quick Quiz Explanations

### Quick Quiz 9.1

1.  False. A tax credit is an amount that is subtracted from a calculated tax.
2.  True.
3.  True.
4.  False. The benefit received by a taxpayer from a tax credit is not dependent on the taxpayer's marginal tax rate. The benefit received by a taxpayer from a tax deduction, on the other hand, is entirely dependent on the marginal tax rate of the taxpayer.

### Quick Quiz 9.2

1.  True.
2.  False. Because the child and dependent care expenses credit is intended to provide relief for employment-related expenses for the care of one or more qualifying individuals, it is intended to benefit taxpayers who are either working or who are looking for work.
3.  True.
4.  False. For the purpose of the credit for the elderly or disabled, a qualified individual must be 65 or older at the end of the tax year or under age 65 and (1) retired on total and permanent disability, (2) the recipient of taxable disability benefits, and (3) younger than the mandatory retirement age of the employer at the beginning of the tax year.

### Quick Quiz 9.3

1.  False. Under the double benefit rule, a taxpayer may not claim both the American Opportunity Tax Credit and the Lifetime Learning Credit for the same expenses.
2.  True.
3.  False. The felony drug conviction rule applies to the American Opportunity Tax Credit, but not to the Lifetime Learning Credit.
4.  True.

### Quick Quiz 9.4

1.  False. To be a qualifying child for the purposes of the child tax credit, the qualifying child must be under the age of 17 at the end of the tax year.
2.  True.

# Quick Quiz Explanations

### Quick Quiz 9.5

1. True.
2. True.
3. False. The qualified adoption expenses credit is completely phased out in 2009 for MAGI above $222,180. The phaseout range for 2009 begins at $182,180.

### Quick Quiz 9.6

1. True.
2. False. The earned income credit is a refundable credit intended to reward lower-income taxpayers for earning income.

### Quick Quiz 9.7

1. False. The components of the general business credit must be considered in a specific sequence.
2. False. While the general business credit is reported on Form 3800, certain components of the credit are reported separately due to special limitations that are not easily accommodated on Form 3800.
3. True.
4. True.

# Basis Rules, Depreciation, & Asset Categorization

## 10

## INTRODUCTION TO BASIS

In order to understand the taxation of property transactions, it is first necessary to develop a sense of the purpose of basis in the tax system and the manner in which assets are categorized. This chapter will review these rules, and will set the groundwork for several chapters to come.

### CALCULATING GAIN OR LOSS

Before we can discuss basis rules and the categorization of assets for tax purposes, a general understanding of the calculation of taxable gain or loss on an asset is important. This concept will be developed in more depth later in this textbook, but the basic rules are needed to understand the material included in this chapter.

**Key Concepts**

**Underline/highlight the answers to these questions as you read:**

1. Describe how gain or loss is calculated.

2. Define the purpose of basis.

3. Identify the uses of basis.

The formula for calculating gain or loss is set forth in Section 1001 of the Internal Revenue Code. The amount of money plus the value of property received in a sale or exchange of an asset is referred to as the **amount realized**. To calculate gain or loss, the taxpayer's adjusted basis is subtracted from the amount realized. The concept of basis is developed in this chapter. Future chapters will deal with the issue of amount realized in more depth.

EXAMPLE 10.1

Logan purchased 100 shares of XYZ stock for $10,000. Last week, he sold all 100 shares for $13,000. The amount realized in the transaction is what Logan received, $13,000. His adjusted basis is $10,000 (what he paid for the stock, in this case). Therefore, Logan's gain on the sale of the stock is $3,000, calculated as follows:

| | |
|---|---|
| Amount Realized | $13,000 |
| Less: Adjusted Basis | ($10,000) |
| Equals: Gain | $3,000 |

EXAMPLE 10.2

Logan purchased 100 Shares of ABC stock for $12,000. Last week, he sold all 100 shares for $5,000. The amount realized in the transaction is $5,000 (what Logan received). Logan's adjusted basis is $12,000 (what he paid for the stock, in this case). Therefore, Logan's loss on the sale of the stock is $7,000, calculated as follows:

| | |
|---|---|
| Amount Realized | $5,000 |
| Less: Adjusted Basis | ($12,000) |
| Equals: Loss | ($7,000) |

## PURPOSE OF BASIS

In the United States, an individual's income is subject to income tax only once. The portion of income retained after income tax is paid is referred to as capital and should never be subject to income tax again.

Perhaps the two most common ways to earn income are through employment and through ownership of investments. While the full amount received by a taxpayer as salary or wages is fully subject to income tax, only part of the amount received from the sale of an investment is subject to income tax. When an investment is sold, the investor is permitted to recoup his or her basis tax-free; only the amount received in excess of basis is subject to income tax. The purpose of basis is to keep track of after-tax dollars an individual invests so that upon the sale of an investment, income is not taxed twice.

EXAMPLE 10.3

After receiving this week's paycheck, Ryan decides to invest $100 in the S&P 500 Index fund in his mutual fund account. The $100 that Ryan invests represents after-tax income, or capital. At the end of the year, Ryan will receive a W-2 form that will include this $100 in his income, and he will report and pay income tax on that amount for this year. When Ryan sells the S&P 500 Index fund, he will be entitled to receive the $100 back income tax-free as basis, since he already paid income tax on that amount. Any remaining gain in excess of his $100 basis will be subject to income tax.

## Quick Quiz 10.1

**Highlight the answer to these questions:**

1. The taxpayer's adjusted basis is subtracted from the amount realized to calculate gain or loss.
   a. True
   b. False

2. The purpose of basis is to make sure that income is taxed twice.
   a. True
   b. False

3. Basis may be used to determine a taxpayer's depreciation deductions.
   a. True
   b. False

*True, False, True.*

**Basis** represents capital (or after-tax income) that a taxpayer uses to purchase an investment. An easy way to remember this is to think of a toll booth. Picture yourself driving along a highway with a car full of cash earned in your most recent business deal. As you drive along, you come upon a toll booth (representing the income tax system). All the cash that approaches the toll booth is income. Once you pay the toll (the tax on the income), all of the cash that comes out the other side of the toll booth is capital. You can choose to consume your capital or reinvest it in other income producing assets. If a taxpayer invested capital in income producing assets, and had to pay income tax on that same amount again when the asset is sold, the taxpayer would be paying tax on income twice – once when income was earned and again when the investment was sold. To make sure that you don't fall into this trap, taxpayers keep track of the capital that was used to purchase the investment, or basis, so that the capital can be recovered without the imposition of a second income tax.

## USES OF BASIS

Basis is the income tax system's method of keeping track of capital in an investment, and is used in several different ways. First, as we have already seen, basis is used to determine gain or loss on an investment when it is sold. An investor would subtract his or her basis from the sales proceeds of the investment to determine the taxable gain or loss. Second, basis is used to determine depreciation deductions that an investor can take on an investment. Depreciation will be discussed in more depth later in this chapter. Third, basis is used to determine the amount an investor has "at risk" which limits loss deductions for income tax purposes under the at risk and passive activity loss rules. The at risk and passive activity rules will be discussed in more depth in Chapter 14.

## DETERMINING BASIS

### COST BASIS

**Cost basis** is the initial basis an investor acquires in an asset by using capital to purchase an investment. As explained above, it represents the amount of after-tax dollars that the investor has dedicated to purchasing an investment. For most investments, the initial basis in an investment is the cost basis.

| **EXAMPLE 10.4** | Nina believes that the real estate market will be strong for the next several years, and purchases an apartment building for $400,000 in cash. Nina's initial basis in the apartment building is $400,000. |

Cost basis includes not only the cash paid by the taxpayer to purchase the investment, but also the amount of recourse debt that the investor incurs to purchase the investment. **Recourse debt** is debt that the taxpayer is personally liable to repay regardless of whether or not the investment produces a return for the investor. Creditors holding recourse debt may receive payment on the debt from the personal resources of the taxpayer if the investment did not provide a sufficient return to cover the outstanding liability. Whenever a taxpayer incurs recourse debt, that debt must be paid back with after-tax dollars. The taxpayer must earn money, pay tax on those earnings, and use the after-tax earnings to make debt payments. As a result, recourse debt assumed by the taxpayer is added to the cash invested to determine the taxpayer's cost basis in an investment.

**Key Concepts**

Underline/highlight the answers to these questions as you read:

1. Define the cost basis of an asset.

2. Identify items that increase basis.

3. Identify items that decrease basis.

| **EXAMPLE 10.5** | In our previous example, Nina purchased an apartment building for $400,000 in cash. Assume that instead of paying the full purchase price, she decides to obtain a recourse loan from Jarvis Savings Bank. Nina pays $80,000 in cash, and Jarvis Savings Bank gives her a mortgage for $320,000. Nina will have to pay back the $320,000 loan with after-tax dollars, so her initial basis in the apartment building is still $400,000. |

Unlike recourse debt, **nonrecourse debt** cannot be recovered tax-free by the taxpayer Nonrecourse debt is a debt secured only by the investment itself; in the event of a default the creditor may not seek to receive payments from the personal assets of the investor. Since a nonrecourse debt places the investment, not the investor at risk, the amount of nonrecourse debt assumed to obtain the property does not result in a tax-free return of capital unless actually paid by the investor.

| **EXAMPLE 10.6** | Continuing our example above, assume that instead of a recourse note, Nina obtains a nonrecourse note from Jarvis Savings Bank. If the real estate market declines, and the value of the apartment building drops dramatically causing Nina to default on the note, Jarvis Savings Bank's only recourse is to foreclose on the apartment building and use the sales proceeds to satisfy the note. The bank cannot seek repayment from Nina's personal assets. In this circumstance, since the |

bank, not Nina, is taking the risk of loss for the amount of the nonrecourse loan, Nina will not be able to take a loss in excess of what she actually paid for the property. Furthermore, Nina can only take the loss when she transfers the property to the bank in satisfaction of the debt. Nina's basis in this scenario is $80,000.

The amount paid for an asset includes not only its purchase price, but also any amounts paid for sales tax, freight, installation and testing of the asset and any other costs necessary to acquire the asset and get it into operations. All of the items below are included in the cost basis of the asset.

| Items Included in Basis |
|---|
| Purchase Price |
| Sales Tax |
| Freight |
| Installation and Testing Costs |
| "All costs to get the asset into operations" |

If the investor engages in certain types of transactions, such as a Section 1031 like-kind exchange, the investor's basis in the property may not equal the economic cost of the property acquired in the exchange. When a Section 1031 exchange is used, any gain that the taxpayer had in the property that was given up in the exchange would be deferred into the new property and would not be taxed until the property received in the exchange is subsequently sold. Section 1031 exchanges will be discussed in more detail in Chapter 13.

## ADJUSTMENTS TO BASIS

Once an asset is acquired and it's initial cost basis is established, that basis may be adjusted over the holding period of the asset, resulting in an adjusted basis for income tax purposes.

### Increases in Basis

The first and most frequently encountered adjustment to basis is an upward adjustment to cost basis for additions to the investment. If additional capital is added to the investment, the cost basis must be increased to reflect this so that upon sale, the investor receives all of his or her capital back income tax-free. Examples of capital infusions that increase a taxpayer's basis in an investment include subsequent investments in the same vehicle, additions to the investment, or changes to the investment.

> **EXAMPLE 10.7**
>
> Five years ago, Randy and Kelly built their first house. At the time they designed and constructed the house they had one child, with another child on the way, so they built a house with three bedrooms. Recently, Kelly found out that she will be having another child. Randy, in anticipation of the new arrival, has finished plans for an addition to the house to add a new bedroom for their third child. The costs Randy incurs

in adding the new bedroom to the house will increase his basis in the house by the amount the new addition costs.

Donald was trained well by his Uncle Scrooge, and he has made prudent investments throughout his life. Instead of taking dividend distributions from stocks and mutual funds that he owns, he reinvests those dividends by purchasing additional shares of the investments. In December of this year, a mutual fund that Donald owns made a long-term capital gains distribution of $450, which was automatically reinvested for him on the day of distribution into additional shares of the same fund. Early next year, the mutual fund company will send an IRS Form 1099 to Donald showing that he had a $450 capital gains distribution, and Donald will report that capital gain on his tax return. Since the $450 distribution went through the tax toll booth (Donald paid tax on the distribution even though he did not receive it in cash), Donald's basis in his interest in the mutual fund will increase by $450.

Another item that can cause an increase in basis is amortization of the discount on bond purchased below face value. Due to fluctuations in interest rates, a bond may sell for more or less than its face value. If the bond sells for less than its face value, the investor's return will consist of two components: (1) the periodic interest payments on the bond; and (2) the difference between the face amount (maturity value) of the bond and the bonds purchase price, or discount. While individuals are cash-basis taxpayers and generally pay tax on income when it is received, the income tax rules include a special exception to that general rule which requires the discount on bonds to be amortized over the remaining life of the security. When this happens, the taxpayer will have phantom income (i.e., income without a corresponding cash receipt) subject to income tax each year until the bond matures, but will not receive the actual payment until the bond matures. Since the amount amortized each year passes through the tax toll booth and is subject to income tax, the investor's basis in the bond is increased by the amount of the discount subject to tax. For income tax purposes, bonds (other than U.S. savings bonds) sold at a discount are called "**Original Issue Discount (OID)" bonds**, and the rules governing the tax treatment of these bonds are referred to as the OID rules.

James purchased a $1,000 face value bond this year for $939.43 with a coupon rate of 9% when the prevailing interest rate was 11.5%. The bond will mature in 3 years. The coupon rate of the bond James purchased was lower than the current market rate, causing the price discount of $60.57. This year, James will report Original Issue Discount (OID) interest (the amortizable discount for the current year) of $18.04 on his tax return. Because James paid tax on $18.04 of the bond discount, his basis in the bond will increase from $939.43 to $957.47 (rounded). The increase in basis will prevent James from paying income tax on the $18.04 twice –

once in the current year when he has phantom income due to the imposition of the OID rules, and once in the year the bond matures and he receives payment. The interest in this example is calculated using an interest method not straight-line amortization.

The profit (or loss) of pass-through entities will also result in an increase (or decrease) in the basis that each owner has in his or her interest. **Pass-through entities** are not treated as separate taxable entities for income tax purposes, and the income that the entity earns is generally taxed to each of the owners in proportion to their ownership interest. The owner of the entity pays tax on the business earnings. Consequently, the earnings have passed through the tax toll booth, and the owner's basis in the business interest must be increased by a like amount. Pass-through entities include general partnerships, limited partnerships, LLCs, LLPs, and all unincorporated entities (other than trusts) that have two or more owners.

EXAMPLE 10.10

Brian was an original investor in, and owns a 20% interest in LuckyHeart, LLC, an internet dating service. To acquire his interest, he paid $100,000. The owners agreed that no distributions would be made from the business during the first two years since the funds would be necessary to finance business expansion. In its first year of operation, Lucky Heart, LLC earned $50,000 and Brian's share of the profits was $10,000 (20% of $50,000). This amount was reported to Brian on Form K-1 and Brian paid income tax on these earnings when he filed his personal income tax return. Brian's basis in LuckyHeart, LLC, therefore, increased to $110,000 ($100,000 + $10,000) at the end of year one. In year two, Brian's share of the profits was $25,000. Consequently, his basis at the end of year two increased to $135,000 ($110,000 + $25,000) assuming he took no distributions.

## Decreases in Basis

If an individual's basis in an investment increases when capital is added to the investment, the opposite will happen when capital is removed from an investment. When capital is removed from an investment, a basis reduction must occur because the taxpayer has received a refund of some of his or her capital. Capital can be taken out of an investment in several ways. Two of the most common methods of removing capital from an investment are (1) distributions from business entities that have pass-through tax treatment (such as partnerships, LLCs, and S corporations), and (2) claiming depreciation deductions.

EXAMPLE 10.11

Brian owns a 20% interest in LuckyHeart, LLC, an internet dating service. His cost basis was $100,000 and while the company has been operating, it has never made a cash distribution to owners. Each year as the company earned money, Brian paid tax on his portion (20%) of the earnings even though he did not receive any distributions from the LLC. As a result, Brian's basis in the LLC increased each year in an amount equal to his share of the company earnings, and his adjusted basis in his LLC interest is currently $135,000. This year, the owners decided that they needed to enjoy some of their profits, so they made a distribution, and Brian's share of the distribution was $25,000. The distribution from the partnership is not taxable, since the partners previously paid tax on the partnership income as it was being earned. Therefore, the $25,000 distribution to Brian reflects a return of capital (after-tax income), and his basis in the LLC will be reduced by a like amount to $110,000 ($135,000 - $25,000). After the distribution, Brian still has capital worth $135,000, but the character of the capital has changed. He has $110,000 of the capital in the LLC, and the remaining $25,000 of capital in cash, for a total of $135,000.

When an asset is used in a trade or business, or for the production of income, the owner of the asset is permitted to take depreciation deductions. **Depreciation** is a form of cost recovery designed to return capital to a business, presumably so that it can be reinvested in additional equipment for the business. The depreciation deduction causes a basis reduction in the asset for which depreciation is claimed. In the context of this discussion, the term "depreciation" encompasses not only the classic form of depreciation, but also amortization, depletion, and other "cost recovery" methods. Since the cost of these items is recovered through depreciation, the adjusted basis of the asset is decreased by the depreciation claimed each year. A more detailed discussion of depreciation occurs later in this chapter.

Just as bond discounts cause an upward adjustment in basis, bond premiums may cause a downward adjustment in basis. If an investor pays a premium upon the purchase of a bond (most likely due to a decline in interest rates compared to the coupon rate since the bond was issued), the investor may elect to amortize the bond premium over the lifetime of the bond. One difference between taxable bond premium and discount is that the discount on a bond must be amortized (with a few rare exceptions, such as U.S. savings bonds), the premium paid to acquire a bond is amortized only if the investor elects to do so (pursuant to IRC Section 1016). When a tax-exempt bond is purchased at a premium, Section 171(c) requires the premium to be amortized.

## Quick Quiz 10.2

**Highlight the answer to these questions:**

1. A taxpayer's cost basis does not include any nonrecourse debt.
   a. True
   b. False

2. The earnings of a pass-through entity may increase the basis of the owner of the entity.
   a. True
   b. False

3. Depreciation deductions increase the basis of an asset.
   a. True
   b. False

True, True, False.

f the investor elects to amortize the premium paid on a taxable bond, the amount amortized is treated as an interest deduction, which can be used to offset other income taxed at ordinary income tax rates. Generally, making the election is favorable to the taxpayer, since the capital loss that will be generated by the bond upon maturity (equal to the difference between the purchase price and the maturity value of the bond) will offset capital gains which may be taxed at a lower rate. If the election is made, and the taxpayer amortizes the bond premium, the amount amortized each year will reduce the taxpayer's basis in the bond.

Donna purchased a bond with a $1,000 face value for $1,040 (a premium of $40). The bond will mature in two years. If Donna elects to do so, she may amortize the premium over the two-year period, and, in year one, take an interest expense deduction of $20. Assuming Donna makes the election, at the end of year one her basis in the bond will be $1,020 (equal to the cost basis of $1,040 minus the amortization deducted for income tax purposes of $20). Since Donna recouped $20 of her capital through the deduction, she only has $1,020 left to recoup in the future.

**EXAMPLE 10.12**

# BASIS RULES FOR PERSONAL USE ASSETS

When an asset is purchased for personal use, its initial basis equals its cost. If the taxpayer adds any capital into the asset (such as building an addition on a personal residence), the taxpayer's basis in the asset will be increased by a like amount. This treatment allows the taxpayer to receive their capital back tax-free at a later point in time. Upward adjustments to cost basis are often observed for personal use assets.

Personal use assets, such as a personal residence, personal automobiles, furniture, and the like do not qualify for depreciation deductions because they are not employed for use in a trade or business or for the production of income. Taxpayers who hold personal use assets typically get their capital back only when they sell or dispose of the asset. Therefore, downward adjustments in basis are not typically observed with personal use assets.

There are exceptions, however. Perhaps the most common downward adjustment for basis in a personal use asset involves the use of part of a personal residence for business purposes. An individual who meets certain requirements can deduct costs associated with the use of his or her home for business purposes (the rules for the home office deduction are covered elsewhere in the text). Among the costs that may be deducted is depreciation. If the owner of a personal residence claims the home office deduction, a downward adjustment to basis in the home will be necessary to account for the partial return of capital.

John is an executive with a major pharmaceutical company, and as a condition of his employment he is required to maintain an office in his home. Earlier this year, John purchased his current principal residence for $350,000. John's expenses directly associated with his home office are $2,650 this year,

**EXAMPLE 10.13**

of which $400 represents depreciation. John's adjusted basis in his home will be $349,600 (Cost basis of $350,000 less $400 of depreciation) since he recovered $400 of his capital through the depreciation deduction.

## SPECIAL BASIS RULES

In addition to the general rules governing the basis of assets discussed above, some special rule apply when property is gifted or inherited, and when property is sold to a related party.

### BASIS OF INHERITED PROPERTY

The basis of property that passes through a decedent's estate is stepped to the fair market value of the asset on the date of the decedent's death, or, if elected by the executor of the decedent's estate, to the fair market value of the asset on the alternate valuation date. This **step-to fair market value** may result in an increase (step-up) or decrease (step-down) in the basis of the asset, depending on the asset's value at the decedent's date of death (or the alternate valuation date). Section 1014 simply states that the basis in the hands of the recipient of inherited property is the value at which it was included in the gross estate.

*Key Concepts*

**Underline/highlight the answers to these questions as you read:**

1. Define how the basis of inherited property is determined.

2. Describe how the basis of gifted property is determined.

3. Identify the basis of property transferred between spouses.

4. Identify the effect of related party transactions on asset basis.

**EXAMPLE 10.14**

Gerald recently received an inheritance from his Uncle Frank. The inheritance consisted of a 40% ownership interest in Dunn's Funeral Home, a family business started by Gerald's father, William, and his Uncle Frank. Uncle Frank paid $10,000 for his 40% ownership interest in the business, and it was worth $250,000 at the time of his death. Gerald's basis in the 40% inherited business interest he receives through Uncle Frank's estate is $250,000. Gerald's step-to fair market value resulted in an increase in basis of $240,000 ($250,000 - $10,000).

**EXAMPLE 10.15**

Wally, a self-proclaimed expert on investments and finance, died last month. At the height of the last bull market, Wally made a significant investment in Fly-By-Nite WebCo. (FBN), an internet based company. Wally's basis in his FBN interest is $250,000. Wally left his entire portfolio to his son, Wally Jr. The value of the FBN interest held by Wally's estate as of the date of his death was $10,000. Wally Jr.'s basis in the FBN interest he receives through his father's estate is $10,000. Wally Jr.'s step-to fair market value resulted in a decrease in basis of $240,000 ($250,000 - $10,000).

The rationale for the Section 1014 "step-to fair market value" basis provision is two pronged. First, since the asset is included in the estate of a decedent, and is subject to estate tax (which is generally assessed at a rate higher than income tax rates), it is fair to match the basis to the estate tax value, since taxes are being paid on that amount. Second, the provision is one of convenience. It is difficult and, in many cases, impossible, to track basis when assets are passed through an estate. Very few individuals keep detailed records of the cost of the assets they acquire, and assets held for the longest holding periods are not often transferred with complete basis information. By setting the basis equal to the value in the estate, the need for detailed records spanning several generations simply to compute taxable gain or loss on the sale of an asset is diminished, and eases the administrative burden on both the taxpayer and the government.

The basis of IRD (income in respect of a decedent) assets do not receive a step-to fair market value at the death of the transferor. IRD assets were not subject to ordinary income tax during the life of the transferor. To prevent these assets from escaping income taxation, they do not receive a step-to fair market value basis at death, rather the decedent's basis carries over to the beneficiary. Some examples of IRD assets are IRAs, annuities, installment notes, and back wages payable to the decedent.

### Death Bed Gifts - Modification to Step-to Fair Market Value at Death

Another exception to the step-to fair market value basis provision occurs when a donor (transferor) makes a gift of appreciated property to a donee who later dies and leaves the property to the original transferor or the spouse of the transferor, and the death occurs within one year of the gift. When this type of death-bed gift is made, the step-to fair market value rule will not apply and the beneficiary's basis will be the original basis of the transferor.

The basis rules for inherited property are expected to change in 2010 if the estate tax is phased out. This issue is discussed in more detail in an estate planning course.

## BASIS OF GIFTED PROPERTY

When an individual (donor) gives property to another person (donee), the donor's basis typically carries over to the donee. No gain or loss is recognized at the time of the gift, but when the donee sells the gifted property, recognition will occur and income tax will be paid on the gain. There are some situations, however, when the basis of property in the hands of the donee will differ from the donor's basis. This may occur when (1) the donor pays gift tax on the transfer; or (2) when the donor gifts property that has a fair market value less than the donor's adjusted basis as of the date of the gift.

The gift tax is a type of transfer tax. When a transfer is made at the death of a decedent, like the estate tax, the "step-to fair market value" basis rule applies. Likewise, if appreciated property is transferred during lifetime and a gift tax must be paid on the transfer, an adjustment in the basis of the property should be made since the gift and estate tax are designed to serve similar functions. When a donor is required to pay gift tax, the portion of the gift tax paid that represents appreciation in the value of the property that occurred while in the hands of the donor may be added to the donor's original basis when determining the basis in the hands of the donee. The formula that is used to calculate this increase in basis is:

$$\frac{\text{Appreciation in the Property}}{\text{FMV of Property at Date of Gift}} \times \text{Gift Tax Paid} = \text{Increase in Basis for Donee}^{[1]}$$

**EXAMPLE 10.16**

Charlie gives ABC Stock to his daughter, Erin. Charlie's basis in the stock is $5,000 and the stock is worth $8,000 on the date he transfers it to Erin. Charlie made no other gifts to Erin this year. Since the transfer qualifies for the gift tax annual exclusion (it is a present interest gift of less than $13,000), Charlie did not have to pay any gift tax on the transfer. Erin's basis in the ABC stock is $5,000.

**EXAMPLE 10.17**

John, a successful attorney and security consultant, wants to transfer $100,000 of XYZ stock to his son, Ryan. John's basis in the stock is $60,000 and he thinks that it has substantial appreciation potential over the next few years. John has already used his lifetime exemption for gift tax purposes ($1,000,000) and has already made gifts to Ryan this year that qualify for the full annual exclusion of $13,000. Assume John pays $40,000 in gift taxes to transfer the XYZ stock to Ryan. Ryan's basis will equal $76,000, which is John's original basis of $60,000 plus $16,000 due to the payment of gift tax, calculated as follows:

$$\frac{\text{Appreciation of \$40,000}}{\text{FMV of \$100,000}} \times \text{Gift Tax Paid of \$40,000} = \$16,000 \text{ (increase in basis for donee)}$$

The second circumstance causing the basis of gifted property to differ from the donor's basis occurs when gifted property has a fair market value that is lower than the donor's basis. When this occurs, the **double basis rule**, which states that the asset owner will have one basis for loss purposes and another basis for gain purposes, applies. The double basis rule is sometimes referred to as the split basis rule, dual basis rule, or bifurcated basis rule. When gifted property has a fair market value that is less than the donor's basis, the donee's basis for gain purposes equals the donor's original basis, and the donee's basis for loss purposes equals the fair market value of the property on the date of the gift. If the property is later sold by the donee at a price between the donor's original basis and the value on the date of the gift, there is no gain or loss to the donee.

---

1. The "FMV of Property at Date of Gift" is the amount of taxable gift which includes a deduction for any gift exclusion taken for the particular gifted property.

| If the donee's sale price is... | less than FMV | between the original basis and FMV | greater than the original basis |
|---|---|---|---|
| Then the donee's basis used is ... | the loss basis, which is the FMV at the date of the gift | no gain or loss | the gain basis, which is the donor's original basis |

EXAMPLE 10.18

Wally purchased 100 shares of Hyde, Inc. five years ago for $5,000. He just gave those shares to his son, Junior, and the value of the 100 shares of stock on the date of the gift was $1,000. Wally's son will have a double basis in the stock, determined as follows:

| If the donee's sale price is... | less than FMV | between the original basis and FMV | greater than the original basis |
|---|---|---|---|
| Then the donee's basis used is ... | $1,000 (Loss Basis) | no gain or loss | $5,000 (Gain Basis) |

If Junior sells the stock for $5,500 he can use the gain basis of $5,000 (Wally's original basis), for purposes of calculating gain or loss. In this case, Junior will have to pay tax on a $500 gain ($5,500 amount realized less $5,000 adjusted gain basis).

If Junior sells the shares for $750, his loss is $250. In this case, since the stock was sold for less than the value on the date of the gift, the loss basis must be used for purposes of calculating loss. The $750 amount realized, less his loss basis of $1,000 yields a loss of $250.

If Junior sells the shares for $3,000 he will have no gain or loss to report, since the sales price was between the gain and loss basis.

Note that the gift of property in a loss position followed by a subsequent sale at less than the donor's adjusted basis in the property results in a loss of capital, since nobody will be able to take a loss deduction for the difference between the amount realized and the gain basis of the gift. In the last part of this example, for instance, the $2,000 difference between the donor's cost basis of $5,000 and the sale price of $3,000 will never be recovered. A better way of handling this scenario would be for the donor to sell the property and recognize a $4,000 taxable loss, and subsequently transfer the $1,000 in sale proceeds to the donee. The donee could then buy the stock on the market for $1,000. If this was done, all of the capital (after-tax dollars) would be recovered through the loss deduction plus the proceeds received at the sale. The holding period for assets acquired by gift is discussed more fully in Chapter 11.

## BASIS OF PROPERTY TRANSFERRED BETWEEN SPOUSES AND INCIDENT TO DIVORCE

A special rule, found under Section 1041 of the Code, governs the treatment of basis for all asset transferred between spouses or incident to a divorce. Section 1041 states that, regardless of whether property is sold or given to a spouse, the basis of the original owner spouse will carry over to the new owner spouse. This treatment is mandatory; it is not an election of the taxpayer.

**EXAMPLE 10.19**

John and Patty have been married for 10 years. In celebration of their 10th anniversary, John gives Patty a diamond ring valued at $20,000. The ring belonged to John's grandmother, and he inherited it from her estate. At the time his grandmother died, the ring had a fair market value of $15,000. John's basis, which is $15,000, will carry over to Patty. If Patty sells the ring for $20,000 she will have to recognize a $5,000 gain. When a gift is made from one spouse to another, Section 1041 does not require different treatment from the normal rule covering the basis of gifted property – both rules require a carry-over basis.

**EXAMPLE 10.20**

Randy and Kelly have been married for 10 years. Kelly decides to sell a beach house that she owns to Randy. Kelly purchased the beach house 15 years ago for $400,000. The current fair market value of the beach house is $1,500,000. Randy transfers $1,500,000 in cash to Kelly's account, and Kelly signs over the deed to the beach house to Randy. If Randy sells the beach house for $1,500,000 he will recognize a $1,100,000 gain on the property. Randy's basis in the beach house is $400,000 and this amount subtracted from the amount realized yields a gain of $1,100,000. Even though the property was sold, and Randy paid full and fair consideration for the property, he only receives a carry-over basis because he was married to Kelly on the date of the sale.

Example 10.20 illustrates that a husband and wife are treated as a single economic unit for tax planning purposes. Randy receives a carry-over basis at the time of sale because Kelly does not pay any tax on the gain inherent in the property at that time. It is only when the property is sold to a non-spouse that recognition occurs.

**EXAMPLE 10.21**

Lauren and Rob, who jointly own a house in Maryland, are in the process of getting divorced. Lauren and Rob each own 50% of the house, which has a basis of $100,000 and a FMV of $175,000. As part of their divorce settlement, Lauren will receive sole ownership of the house in Maryland. Lauren's basis in the house will be $100,000 (her $50,000 basis plus $50,000 of carryover basis from Rob).

# Related Party Transactions (Sales, Gifts and Basis-IRC Section 267)

When property is sold to a related party (other than the seller's spouse), and the sale will result in a gain to the selling party, the normal basis rules apply. That is, the selling party will recognize gain and the purchasing party will acquire a basis in the property equal to the price he or she paid for the property. Related parties include a taxpayer's lineal ascendants (e.g., parents and grandparents), lineal descendants (e.g., children and grandchildren), and brothers and sisters (of whole or half blood). The definition of a related party also includes certain business entities and trusts, although this information is beyond the scope of this textbook. Collateral relatives (aunts, uncles, nephews, nieces, cousins, stepchildren, step-parents, or in-laws) are not considered to be related parties.

EXAMPLE 10.22

Randy sells stock in Baseball Enterprises, Inc. to his son, Kasey. Randy purchased the stock 5 years ago for $1,500 and the current fair market value of the stock is $2,000. Since Randy believes that the stock will experience significant growth (and he does not want that growth to increase his taxable estate), he sells the stock to Kasey for its current fair market value. Randy will recognize a gain of $500 ($2,000 amount realized minus the $1,500 basis), and Kasey's basis in the stock will be $2,000, which equals the amount he paid to acquire it.

If property is sold to a related party (other than the seller's spouse) at a loss, however, the seller is not permitted to deduct the loss and the double basis rule applies. As a result, the purchaser will have one basis for purposes of calculating gain and another basis for purposes of calculating loss, and the seller will not be permitted to recognize the loss for tax purposes. The gain basis will equal the seller's original basis in the property, and the loss basis will equal the fair market value of the property at the time of the sale. The holding period used to determine whether gains or losses are short-term or long-term are based on the purchaser's holding period. The significance of holding period will be discussed in the next chapter.

EXAMPLE 10.23

Randy sells stock in Baseball Enterprises, Inc. to his son, Kasey. Randy purchased the stock five years ago for $2,000 and the current fair market value of the stock is $1,500. On the date of sale, Randy will not be permitted to recognize a $500 loss on his tax return (the difference between his purchase price of $2,000 and the sale price of $1,500). Kasey's gain or loss on subsequent disposition of the stock will be dependent on the selling price of the stock, and there are three possible outcomes from a related party sale.

If Kasey sells the stock to Bill (an unrelated party) for $2,500, he uses his gain basis for purposes of determining gain. Recall that Kasey's gain basis is the same as Randy's basis. As long as the property is ultimately sold for more than the original purchaser's basis, the result is the same as the normal carry-over basis rule. Upon the sale to Bill, Kasey will realize and recognize a $500 gain ($2,500 amount realized less $2,000 gain basis).

If Kasey sells the stock to Bill for $900, he uses his loss basis for purposes of determining loss. Kasey's loss basis equals the fair market value on the date of the original sale from Randy to Kasey, or in this case, $1,500. Upon the sale to Bill, Kasey will realize a $600 loss on the stock ($900 amount realized less $1,500 loss basis). This is a bad result for the family, because the $500 loss incurred during Randy's holding period is never deductible – Randy is not permitted to deduct the $500 when he sells the property to Kasey (a related party), and Kasey is not permitted to deduct that loss on the sale to Bill because Kasey is required to use his loss basis to determine the amount of his loss.

If Kasey sells the stock for $1,750, or, in fact, for any amount between his gain and loss basis, there will be no gain or loss recognition on the sale. In this instance, the sale is said to occur within the "no gain/no loss corridor." This is still a bad result for the family, since the actual loss suffered by the family as a whole is still not deductible (calculated by subtracting the sale price in the "no gain/no loss corridor" from the basis of the original seller).

The purpose of applying the double basis rule to related party transactions is to prevent families from allocating losses to the family member with the best ability to use them. If, using the above example, Randy had $750,000 of carry-forward losses, triggering a loss on the sale of the stock will not give him an additional tax benefit, since he can only take a maximum of $3,000 of losses against ordinary income in any one year. If the double basis rule did not apply, he might be encouraged to sell the stock to his son and let his son take the loss, which would generate an immediate income tax benefit for his son, and, therefore, be better for the family unit as a whole.

Assuming that a taxpayer does not have a large carry-forward loss position for income tax purposes, a better course of action is to sell the property, recognize the loss, and give the proceeds to the related party. This course of action will allow loss recognition, and, therefore, recovery of capital for the losses generated during the first owner's holding period.

Recall that the double basis rule may also apply to gifts. One significant difference between the double basis rule for sales and gifts is that for sale transactions, the holding period for determining the nature of the gain or loss starts anew on the date of sale. If loss property is gifted to a related party, the holding period only starts anew if, on disposition of the property, the loss basis is used to determine the donee's loss.

**EXAMPLE 10.24**

John purchased 100 Shares of International Security, Inc. for $2,000 five years ago. He gives the stock to his son, Ryan when the fair market value of the stock is $1,750. Since this is a gift transaction, a carry-over basis generally applies, but in this case, John is gifting loss property to Ryan, so Ryan will have a different basis for purposes of gain and loss.

If Ryan sells the stock for $2,500 he will use his gain basis to calculate gain. Ryan's gain basis would equal John's basis in the stock, or $2,000. Therefore, upon sale, Ryan would recognize a $500 gain (the $2,500 amount realized less the $2,000 gain basis). The character of the gain would be long-term gain regardless of Ryan's holding period. Since gifted property was sold at a gain, the donor's holding period tacks on to the donee's holding period. In this case, John held the stock for 5 years, so the character of the gain would be long-term capital gain. Note that this is no different than if John gifted the property to Ryan at a time when the stock was in a gain position – both the donor's basis and holding period carry over to the donee.

If Ryan sells the stock for $1,500 he will use his loss basis to calculate loss. Ryan's loss will be $250 ($1,500 amount realized less his loss basis of $1,750).

## Quick Quiz 10.3

**Highlight the answer to these questions:**

1. A taxpayer's basis in inherited property is the same as the decedent's basis in the property.
   a. True
   b. False

2. Gift tax paid does not affect the donee's basis in gifted property.
   a. True
   b. False

3. Property transferred between spouses has a carryover basis.
   a. True
   b. False

4. If property is sold to a related party at a loss, the double basis rule applies.
   a. True
   b. False

False, False, True, True.

The character of the loss, however, will be dependent on Ryan's holding period. If Ryan held the stock for at least a year and a day from the date of the gift, he will recognize a long-term capital loss. If, however, he sold the stock within a year from the date of the gift, the character of the loss will be short-term.

As the above example illustrates, the use of the double basis rule works the same way for both sales and gifts with one major exception: If gifted property is subsequently sold at a gain, the holding period of the donor tacks onto the holding period of the donee for purposes of determining the character of the gain, and in a sale it does not.

## BASIS OF JOINTLY HELD PROPERTY

If property is held jointly (joint tenants with rights of survivorship, tenants in common, or community property), each owner's basis usually follows the actual contribution rule. Each owner's basis equals their original contribution when purchasing the property. However, if the joint owners are married and the property is titled in joint tenancy with right of survivorship, tenancy by the entirety, or community property, the basis of each spouse equals one half of the total basis regardless of their actual contribution. If the interest in joint tenancy was acquired by gift, then we follow the gift basis rules.

# DEPRECIATION

## INTRODUCTION

Depreciation is a method of capital recovery that allows a taxpayer to receive his or her capital back over the useful life of the asset. We have already seen that assets purchased for personal use are not entitled to depreciation deductions. Assets held for productive use in a trade or business, or held for the production of income, however, generate depreciation deductions for their owner. As we have seen in our discussion of basis, depreciation deductions cause a downward adjustment in basis, since the taxpayer receives his or her capital back over the lifetime of the asset through the depreciation deductions.

 *Key Concepts*

**Underline/highlight the answers to these questions as you read:**

1. Identify the purpose of depreciation.

2. Identify the methods of depreciation.

3. Identify the various asset classes.

## PURPOSE

When a taxpayer employs an asset in productive use in a trade or business or for the production of income, he or she becomes a partner of Uncle Sam. As that asset is used to generate income (and, hopefully, profit), some of the profits go to the taxpayer, and some go to Uncle Sam through the income tax system.

Keeping machinery and equipment, or assets used to produce income, up to date and in working order is in the interest of both the taxpayer and the government. Both parties profit from the employment of the asset in a profit seeking venture. Since the asset is being used to generate income subject to tax, the government permits the taxpayer to recoup his capital earlier than the date the asset is sold or discarded. As depreciation deductions are taken, the taxpayer can use the recovered capital to reinvest in other assets that can be employed in a trade or business or for the production of income, thereby increasing the income potential of the activity. Depreciating the asset over its useful life is also consistent with Generally Accepted Accounting Principles (GAAP), since it ties the expenses incurred in acquiring the asset to the income produced by the use of the asset.

## METHODS OF DEPRECIATION

The **Modified Accelerated Cost Recovery System (MACRS)** applies to most types of depreciable property placed in service after 1986. Among the classes of property that are excluded from MACRS are:

- Intangible Property (such as goodwill, copyrights, and patents)
- Public utility property
- Motion pictures and sound recordings

Several depreciation methods are allowed under MACRS. The depreciation methods vary depending upon the type of asset employed in productive use in a trade or business, and the life expectancy of the asset.

### *Real Estate*

For real estate, depreciation for federal tax purposes depends on the use of the property. Under current law, if the real estate is used for residential rental purposes, the property is depreciated according to the **straight-line depreciation** method over 27½ years. If the real estate is used for commercial purposes, depreciation occurs on a straight-line basis over 39 years. Of course, the value of land cannot be depreciated; only the value of improvements to land qualify for depreciation.

| | |
|---|---|
| Kasey purchases an 8-unit rental apartment unit for $900,000. The value of the land is determined to be $60,000. Since the property is used for residential rental purposes, Kasey will be able to depreciate the building (at a value of $840,000, which equals the purchase price of $900,000 less the land value of $60,000) over a 27.5 year period. Therefore Kasey's annual depreciation deduction will be $30,545. | **EXAMPLE 10.25** |

| | |
|---|---|
| Ryan purchases an office building that he plans to rent out. The building cost $1.4 million, and $200,000 of the purchase price is attributed to the land. Since the property is used for commercial rental purposes, Ryan can depreciate the building (at a value of $1.2 million, which equals the purchase price of $1.4 million less the land value of $200,000) on a straight-line basis over a 39 year period. Therefore, Ryan's annual depreciation deduction will be $30,769.23. | **EXAMPLE 10.26** |

### *Personalty*

To calculate depreciation for personalty, defined as any property other than real property, under MACRS, the property must first be assigned to a class life or recovery period. The following exhibit lists the various asset classes and examples of assets included in each class.

EXHIBIT 10.2    **MACRS ASSET CLASSES**

| 3-Year Class Life Assets | Automobiles used as taxis, hogs used for breeding, racehorses, qualified rent to own property, tractors and some manufacturing tools. |
|---|---|
| 5-Year Class Life Assets | Most cars, trucks and airplanes, heavy construction equipment, assets used for the manufacturing of apparel and other finished products, timber cutting equipment, electronic office equipment (such as computers, calculators, adding machines, typewriters, and copiers), information systems, alternative energy equipment (solar and wind), cattle used for breeding and dairy purposes, and sheep and goats used for breeding. |
| 7-Year Class Life Assets | Office furniture, fixtures, and equipment; agricultural machinery and equipment; cotton ginning assets; breeding and work horses under 12 years old; equipment used for mining, quarrying, and milling; assets used in the manufacturing of furniture and wood products, assets used in printing and publishing industries; assets used for the manufacture of jewelry and athletic goods; recreational assets. |
| 10-Year Class Life Assets | Vessels, barges, tugs and water transportation equipment; single purpose agricultural or horticultural structures; property used in petroleum refining. |
| 15-Year Class Life Assets | Improvements to land (such as sidewalks, roads, canals, waterways, docks, fences, shrubbery); pipelines; billboards. |
| 20-Year Class Life Assets | Farm buildings; municipal sewers. |

While it is not necessary for a financial planner to commit the various class life categories to memory, it is important to note that the law attempts to assign a class life to an asset that is roughly the same as its useful life. The use of class lives is for both the taxpayer's and the government's convenience. Without standard classifications, it would be necessary to value each asset used by a business at the end of each year, compare it to the value at the beginning of the year, and take a tax deduction for the actual decline in value of the asset. While this system would certainly make some appraisers happy, it is not a practical way to administer either a business or the tax system. Once an asset is classified into a particular class life, the depreciation deduction for that asset each year is fixed, which eases the administrative burden for both the business and the government. When an asset is sold, an accounting must be made for the difference between the depreciation taken on the asset for tax purposes, and the actual depreciation of the asset determined by the difference between the purchase price and adjusted basis. The depreciation recapture rules are designed to take care of this issue when an asset is sold. These rules will be covered in Chapter 12.

The depreciation method for personalty used under MACRS is an accelerated depreciation system unlike the straight-line depreciation used for real property. Assets that have a 3, 5, 7, or 10 year class life are depreciated under a depreciation method known as the **double declining balance** (or "200 percent") **method**, but switch to straight-line depreciation when the straight-line method would produce a greater deduction than the double declining balance method. Property in the 15 and 20 year class lives are depreciated under the **150 percent declining balance method**, but also switch to straight-line depreciation when the straight-line method would produce a greater deduction for the current tax year. One notable exception from these rules is the depreciation of software, which is depreciated on a straight-line basis over 3 years.

Accelerated depreciation is generally more favorable for a taxpayer than straight-line depreciation. If given the choice, a taxpayer would typically choose to use the accelerated method available under MACRS. If the taxpayer is subject to AMT (alternative minimum tax), however, much of the benefit of accelerated depreciation is lost, and the taxpayer may wish to consider alternative methods of depreciation. Furthermore, a taxpayer may choose an alternative method of depreciation so that the depreciation system used for tax purposes matches the system used for financial reporting purposes. If a taxpayer so chooses, he or she can elect out of MACRS and can depreciate the assets used in his or her trade or business in one of the following ways:

1. The taxpayer can elect straight-line depreciation for property that is otherwise eligible for the declining-balance method of depreciation. If a taxpayer chooses to use straight-line depreciation, depreciation will not cause any potential problems with the alternative minimum tax (discussed in Chapter 15).
2. The taxpayer can elect the alternative depreciation system (ADS). Under ADS:
   - Property that would have been depreciated under the 200 percent double declining balance method under MACRS will be depreciated using the 150 percent declining balance method, over the MACRS class life (for property placed in service after December 31, 1998).
   - Property that would have been depreciated under the 150 percent declining balance method under MACRS will be depreciated on a straight-line basis.
   - Real estate will be depreciated over a 40 year period on a straight-line basis.

## *Conventions*

When depreciable assets are placed in service, certain **conventions** govern the amount of the depreciation deduction available for the first year. For personalty (assets with a class life of 20 years or less), a "half-year" convention is used. The half-year convention assumes that the asset was placed in service half-way through the year regardless of the date it was actually employed, and therefore a half-year of depreciation deduction is allowed in the year in which the asset is placed in service. To prevent businesses from engaging in too much tax planning (by purchasing all of their assets in December and claiming a half-year of depreciation deductions up front), a special rule applies for a year when more than 40 percent of all depreciable property is placed in service in the last three months of the taxable year. When this occurs, a "mid-quarter" convention is used, which states that the first-year depreciation deduction for the property will be calculated as if each asset purchased during that year was placed in service in the middle of the quarter in which it was actually placed in service.

For real property (property subject to 27½ and 39 year class lives), a mid-month convention is used. For purposes of calculating the depreciation deduction for real property placed in service, it is considered to be placed in service in the middle of the month it is actually employed. For real estate, therefore, depreciation can only be taken if the asset is actively being used in the trade or business – it is not possible to get additional depreciation deductions in the first year simply by delaying purchase of the asset until later in the year and using a mid-year or mid-quarter convention.

## AMORTIZATION OF INTANGIBLE ASSETS

Intangible assets, such as the goodwill of a business, patents and copyrights acquired with the acquisition of a business interest, covenants not to compete and franchises, trademarks, and tradenames acquired in connection with the acquisition of a business, may be amortized on a straight-line basis over a 15 year (180 month) period. The term "**amortization**" is typically used to signify that cost recovery deductions are being taken for intangible assets.

## SPECIAL DEPRECIATION ISSUES

The general rules for depreciation discussed above apply in most circumstances, but there are a few special situations that are important for a planner to know. The first issue deals with "listed" property, and the second is an election available for small businesses known as the Section 179 election.

## Key Concepts

**Underline/highlight the answers to these questions as you read:**

1. Define amortization.

2. Define listed property and describe its treatment.

3. Describe the Section 179 election.

"**Listed Property**" can more accurately be described as suspect property, at least from the perspective of the IRS. Listed property includes automobiles weighing less than 6,000 pounds, cellular telephones, and computers. Listed property is considered suspect because it is easily used for both business and personal purposes, and taxpayers will be tempted to take a deduction for

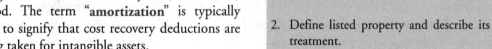

their personal use of the asset. Since only the business use of the asset qualifies for depreciation deductions, those taking deductions for such property will merit special review.

If listed property is used more than 50 percent for business purposes, the normal MACRS rules will apply, and the deduction will equal the allowable depreciation for the asset multiplied by its percentage of business use. If listed property is not used more than 50 percent for business purposes, depreciation must be computed under the alternative depreciation system (ADS) of MACRS. Furthermore, if use of listed property that was being depreciated under MACRS falls to 50 percent or less for any year, excess depreciation is recaptured. Excess depreciation, for this purpose, equals the depreciation actually claimed in prior years, less the amount of depreciation that would have been allowed under ADS.

In addition to the limitations placed on listed property, further limitations apply to the deductibility of automobiles that weigh less than 6,000 pounds. The additional limitations apply to both the depreciation deductions allowable and to first-year expensing under Section 179 (discussed later). The maximum depreciation deduction (based on 100 percent business use) that can be taken on an automobile is shown in the following exhibit (Rev. Proc. 2009-24).

**2009 MAXIMUM DEPRECIATION DEDUCTIONS FOR AUTOMOBILES**                    EXHIBIT 10.3

| Year | Passenger Auto Deduction | Truck & Van Deduction |
|------|--------------------------|-----------------------|
| 1    | $2,960                   | $3,060                |
| 2    | $4,800                   | $4,900                |
| 3    | $2,850                   | $2,950                |
| 4    | $1,775                   | $1,775                |
| 5    | $1,775                   | $1,775                |
| 6    | $1,775                   | $1,775                |

Of course, the normal rule that limits the deduction to the percentage of business use applies, so, for example, if the car was used 60 percent for business purposes, only 60 percent of the above limit would be permitted as a depreciation deduction. Furthermore, if a taxpayer has unrecovered basis in a vehicle after the five year period has expired, the amount allowed in the 4$^{th}$ year for depreciation is allowed as a deduction in subsequent years until the vehicle is fully depreciated.

Section 179 provides business owners with an option to elect to expense property placed in service during the year instead of capitalizing the assets and depreciating them over their MACRS class life, provided that certain requirements are met. To qualify for expensing under Section 179, an asset must be used more than 50 percent of the time in a trade or business (if the asset is used less than 100 percent of the time in a trade or business, only the percentage of business use may be expensed under Section 179). A business owner may elect to immediately expense up to $250,000 for 2009 ($134,000 for 2010) of assets placed in service during the year, unless the phaseout limit has been met. The amount that can be immediately expensed is subject to a phaseout, and is reduced dollar for dollar for depreciable property placed in service during the year that exceeds $800,000 for 2009 ($530,000 for 2010).

**EXAMPLE 10.27**

James owns and operates a printing company. As the end of the year approaches, he reviews the financial results for the company operations for the year, and decides to purchase some new printing equipment. Since he anticipates a large increase in demand for his products, he decides to purchase a printing press at a cost of $664,000, which is the only depreciable property he places in service for the year. James will not be able to make a Section 179 election for the printing press due to the phaseout. The Section 179 deduction is reduced, dollar for dollar, by the amount of depreciable property placed in service during the year exceeding $530,000 (2010). James purchased a printing press for $664,000, which exceeds the limit of $530,000 by $134,000 (2010), which exceeds the amount of the otherwise allowable Section 179 deduction. James could take regular depreciation based on the entire value of the asset.

## Quick Quiz 10.5

**Highlight the answer to these questions:**

1. Amortization is cost recovery for intangible assets.
   a. True
   b. False

2. The Section 179 election allows business owners to expense property placed in service during the year instead of capitalizing it.
   a. True
   b. False

True, True.

**EXAMPLE 10.28**

Continuing with the previous example, assume that James decides to purchase a less expensive printing press for $580,000. Again, this is the only depreciable property that he will place in service for the year. The $580,000 press exceeds the $530,000 limit by $50,000. Therefore, James' Section 179 deduction will be limited to $84,000 ($134,000 - $50,000). He can then take regular depreciation on the rest of the asset. ($580,000 - $84,000 = $496,000 is the depreciable basis.)

In addition, electing Section 179 treatment cannot result in a loss for the business, so the maximum Section 179 deduction that can be taken in any year will be further limited by the income of the business. To the extent that a business owner makes an otherwise allowable Section 179 expense election that is limited in the current year by the income of the business, the elected expenses over the business income may be carried forward to future tax years, and applied against future income of the business.

EXAMPLE 10.29

Allison recently opened a new business, and it is off to a good start. She anticipates that her profit at the end of the year will be $100,000. Looking forward, she knows she will have to invest in additional machinery and equipment to meet the growing demand for her products, so she purchases $250,000 (2009) of equipment this year. Allison has heard that she can elect to expense up to $250,000 (2009) of equipment placed in service, and asks you for confirmation of this fact. Since the profit of Allison's business is only $100,000 she can only take a $100,000 Section 179 deduction for the current year. If she makes an election to expense the full amount, however, the remaining $150,000 of her $250,000 equipment purchase will be carried forward to a future year when she has profits to offset the additional expense deduction. Assuming the above facts, except that Allison purchased the equipment in 2010, she would be limited to $134,000 of Section 179 expense and would still be limited by a Section 179 deduction of $100,000 with a $34,000 carry forward.

There is an additional limitation on the Section 179 expense election that applies to the purchase of automobiles. If a vehicle weighing over 6,000 pounds but less than 14,000 pounds is purchased, the maximum Section 179 expense that can be elected with respect to that vehicle is limited to $25,000. This limitation was enacted as part of the 2004 tax legislation to close a perceived loophole allowing businesses owners to purchase SUVs and expense them immediately under Section 179.

EXAMPLE 10.30

Brian, owner of Lucy Heart, LLC, has always wanted a school-bus yellow Hummer. Brian recently purchased one, to be used solely in his business, paying $80,000. Brian can elect to expense up to $25,000 of the cost immediately under Section 179 if he meets all of the other requirements for application of that section.

# CATEGORIZING ASSETS FOR INCOME TAX PURPOSES

Thus far we have reviewed the purpose of basis and the uses of depreciation in the income tax system, but to determine what the income tax consequences of a particular transaction are, we must categorize the asset that is being transferred. In the U.S. income tax system, there are only three types of assets: capital assets, ordinary income assets, and Section 1231 assets. Categorizing the asset is essential because the tax consequences resulting from the transfer of each of the three types of assets differs. In this chapter, we introduce the concept of categorizing the assets for income tax purposes and give a brief overview of the tax characteristics that apply to that asset.

## CAPITAL ASSETS

Most assets are **capital assets**. This category is the catch-all category – capital assets are all assets that are not ordinary income assets or Section 1231 assets. Specifically, capital assets are defined in Section 1221 as everything in the world other than:

1. Accounts and Notes Receivable from a trade or business;
2. Copyrights, literary[2], musical, and artistic creations and similar assets in the hands of the creator;
3. Inventory or stock in trade held for sale to customers in the ordinary course of business;
4. Depreciable property or real property used in a trade or business;
5. Publications of the United States Government;
6. Supplies used in the ordinary conduct of a trade or business;
7. Derivative instruments for commodities held by a dealer (subject to various restrictions); and
8. Hedging transactions entered into in the normal course of business.

**Key Concepts**

Underline/highlight the answers to these questions as you read:

1. Identify the various categories of assets for income tax purposes.

2. Describe a capital asset.

3. Identify ordinary income assets.

4. Define Section 1231 assets.

From an introductory tax and financial planning standpoint, the first four items in the list are the most important. The last four on the list other than supplies used in business apply to specialized situations that are beyond the scope of this textbook. An easy way to remember the definition of a capital asset is "everything in the world is a capital asset except ACID." ACID is constructed using the first letter of the items 1-4 on the list above.

---

2. Effective May 17, 2006, through February 8, 2011, there is a temporary regulation that allows an election by musicians for musical compositions or copyrights. The taxpayer may elect for tax treatment of the composition or copyright as a capital gain or loss instead of inventory subject to ordinary income.

EXAMPLE 10.31

Reilly recently purchased a painting by Worthington, an aspiring artist, to hang in his dining room. Reilly is not an art dealer, but rather a collector. The painting is a capital asset in Reilly's hands, since it was not created by Reilly, it is not being held as inventory for sale to Reilly's customers, and is not depreciable property used in a trade or a business.

If a capital asset is transferred or sold, the gain or loss recognized for tax purposes will depend on three items: (1) the holding period of the asset; (2) the type of asset; and (3) the use of the asset. If a taxpayer disposes of a capital asset at a gain, and has held that asset for more than a year, he or she will qualify for a special capital gains tax rate that, under current law, is lower than the tax rate that applies to ordinary income. Capital gains tax rates range from zero percent to 28 percent. The specifics of capital transactions are covered in Chapter 11. While gains on personal capital assets are fully taxable, losses on personal capital assets are not fully deductible.

The benefit to having a capital asset with a long-term holding period (held for more than one year) disposed of at a gain is that a lower tax rate applies. While the lower tax rate also applies to losses (which is not such a good thing, since the taxpayer receives less of a tax benefit in this case), the deductibility of losses is limited. Capital losses in any year are fully deductible against capital gains in the same year. If a capital loss exceeds gains for the year, however, the maximum loss that may be deducted against other forms of income is $3,000. Losses in excess of this amount may be carried forward indefinitely.

The bottom line for capital assets is that gains are good, (they typically result in paying tax at a lower rate) but losses are bad (losses are either limited, or result in a decreased tax benefit for the taxpayer when compared to other types of assets).

If capital assets include all assets other than those on the list above, the assets on the list are ordinary income assets or Section 1231 assets. These are covered in detail below.

## ORDINARY INCOME ASSETS

Ordinary Income Assets are, simply, assets that will generate tax at ordinary income rates when transferred. We know from our prior discussion that most assets are capital assets. Out of the universe of assets that we have left to discuss, the only ones left are:

| |
|---|
| Accounts and Notes Receivable from a trade or business |
| Copyrights, literary, and artistic creations and similar assets in the hands of the creator |
| Inventory or stock in trade held for sale to customers in the ordinary course of business |
| Depreciable property or real property used in a trade or business |

The first three items in this list are the ordinary income assets. The last item (depreciable property or real property used in a trade or business) is a 1231 asset.

First, consider inventory. Inventory is purchased by a business or business person for sale to customers. When the inventory is sold, there is (hopefully) a gain for the business that will be subject to tax at the end of the tax year. All earnings from business operations are taxed at ordinary income tax rates. Therefore, inventory must be an ordinary income asset because it generates ordinary income when sold.

Copyrights, literary compositions, and artistic creations in the hands of the author are really a form of inventory. A writer who composes a novel does so for sale to customers. That sale is in the ordinary course of business, and therefore results in ordinary income tax on the gain. The same is true for an artist who paints a painting. By creating a work available for sale to a customer, the author of the work is creating his or her inventory.

Accounts and notes receivable are items of inventory that have been sold in return for a customer's promise to pay for that item at some point in the future. They represent delayed payment for the sale of inventory, and the gain on the sale will be subject to ordinary income tax rates. Think of the tax planning that could occur if accounts and notes receivable were treated as capital assets – businesspeople would have an incentive to sell on account, meet the requisite holding period, and pay tax on the gain at capital, rather than ordinary tax rates. Because Congress does not want business people to be able to transform their ordinary income taxed at a higher rate to capital gains taxed at a lower rate, accounts and notes receivable are treated as ordinary income assets.

| **EXAMPLE 10.32** | Catherine is a renowned artist in New England, and her work is sought after by the rich and famous. Catherine has recently painted her newest masterpiece. The painting in Catherine's hands is inventory, and is therefore an ordinary income asset. |

| **EXAMPLE 10.33** | George is an art dealer, and has galleries in New Orleans, New York, and San Diego. George recently purchased a painting by Wentworth, and places it in his New Orleans studio for sale to his customers. Because the painting is being held for sale to customers in the ordinary course of business, it is inventory, and, therefore, is an ordinary income asset. |

Since we began our discussion of asset categorization, all of the examples have dealt with one type of property – a painting. As the above examples illustrate, it is important to remember that asset categorization does not depend on the asset, but rather, the use to which that asset is put. In Example 10.31, when Reilly purchased a painting for use in his home, the painting was a capital asset. When Catherine creates a painting for sale to her patrons (Example 10.32), or when George purchases a painting for sale to customers of his art gallery (Example 10.33), the paintings are ordinary income assets, and the tax consequences are different.

The consequence of classifying an asset as an ordinary income asset depends on whether the asset is transferred at a gain or at a loss. If the asset is transferred for a gain, ordinary income tax rates will apply. Ordinary income tax rates are the highest tax rates in our tax system, implying that ordinary income assets carry a higher tax burden when sold for a gain. If, however, an ordinary asset is sold for a loss, there is no decrease in the tax rate (as would occur, for example, if the asset was a capital asset and was held for a long-term holding period), so the loss will generate a higher tax benefit for the taxpayer. Furthermore, ordinary losses, unlike capital losses are not subject to deduction limitations.

The bottom line for ordinary income assets is this: gains are bad (from a tax perspective, not an economic perspective), but losses are good (no rate reductions or limitations apply).

If a taxpayer had a crystal ball and could tell which assets would generate gains and which would generate losses, the taxpayer would hold all of the assets that would generate gains as capital assets (to get the tax-rate break that long-term capital assets offer), and hold all of the assets that would generate a loss as ordinary income assets (since the losses would generate a bigger tax benefit and would not be limited, as is the case with capital losses). Unfortunately, this is a difficult planning feat to achieve.

## SECTION 1231 ASSETS

The final type of asset in our income tax system is known as a **Section 1231 asset**, obviously named after the Code section that defines it. Since capital assets consist of everything other than ordinary income assets and Section 1231 assets, and ordinary income assets include three of the four items in our list, there is only one item left to constitute a Section 1231 asset - depreciable property or real property used for productive use in a trade or business or for the production of income.

Technically, Section 1231 assets include:
1.  Depreciable property or real property used for productive use in a trade or business or for the production of income;
2.  Timber, coal, and iron to which Section 631 applies;
3.  Livestock held for draft, breeding, dairy or sporting purposes;
4.  Unharvested crops on land used in business; and
5.  Purchased intangible assets eligible for amortization (such as Goodwill).

Items 2-5 apply to very specific situations, and are therefore beyond the scope of this textbook. From a planning perspective, the most important Section 1231 asset is item number 1: depreciable property or real property used for productive use in a trade or business or for the production of income.

You may recall from our discussion above that in order to be depreciable, the property must be used in a trade or business or for the production of income. Personal property (such as a personal residence) is not eligible for depreciation deductions.

> Homer Headshrinker, a prominent psychiatrist, purchases new furniture for his office. Since the furniture is being used in Homer's trade or business, the furniture is categorized as a Section 1231 asset.

**EXAMPLE 10.34**

In addition to meeting the definition of a Section 1231 asset, to qualify for the tax advantages Section 1231 confers, the asset must have been held for a long-term holding period. The only exception to the long-term holding period requirement deals with un-harvested crops (a special exception that is beyond the scope of this textbook).

When engaging in tax planning, it is important to recognize that if you are dealing with depreciable property or land used in a trade or business, that such property will be treated as a Section 1231 asset. If the property is not real or depreciable property used in a trade or business, it is not a Section 1231 asset.

Once an asset has been categorized as a Section 1231 asset, it is afforded special tax treatment. Gains on Section 1231 assets are treated as capital gains, and losses on Section 1231 assets are treated as ordinary losses. Section 1231 gives the taxpayer the best of Capital and Ordinary Income Asset treatment. Since gains are treated as capital gains, and, by definition, Section 1231 requires a long-term holding period, the long-term capital gains rates will apply, reducing the tax burden on the asset when compared to an ordinary income asset. If a Section 1231 asset is sold at a loss, ordinary loss treatment applies, granting the taxpayer a greater tax benefit (due to the higher tax rate that applies to ordinary income assets) and removing the limitation on losses that are associated with capital assets.

While Section 1231 grants the best of both worlds treatment (gains are capital; losses are ordinary), there are some limitations. Whenever an asset is categorized as a Section 1231 asset, there is the potential for depreciation recapture. Depreciation recapture will be discussed in Chapter 12.

## Quick Quiz 10.6

**Highlight the answer to these questions:**

1. A copyright in the hands of the creator is a capital asset.
   a. True
   b. False

2. Inventory is an ordinary income asset.
   a. True
   b. False

3. Section 1231 assets are afforded special tax treatment.
   a. True
   b. False

False, True, True.

| EXHIBIT 10.4 | ASSET CATEGORIES |
| --- | --- |

| | CAPITAL ASSETS | ORDINARY ASSETS | 1231 ASSETS |
| --- | --- | --- | --- |
| **Sold for Gain** | Capital Gain Treatment | Ordinary Income Treatment | Capital Gain Treatment (part or all gain may require recapture) |
| **Sold for Loss** | Capital Loss Treatment (current loss may be limited) | Ordinary Loss Treatment | Ordinary Loss Treatment |

# CHAPTER SUMMARY

This chapter reviewed the purpose of basis rules, depreciation, and asset categorization in our income tax system. Basis is simply a way of keeping track of capital that has been invested in an asset so that upon disposition of the asset, the capital can be returned income tax-free to the owner. Recall that capital represents after-tax income, and should not be subject to income tax again. Depreciation allows those who use assets in a trade or business or for production of income to receive their capital back earlier than the date the asset is sold so that capital can be reinvested in the business and, as a result, the business will continue to make money upon which taxes will be due. Depreciation is not allowed on personal use assets. Finally, the chapter reviewed the categorization of assets for federal income tax purposes. All assets are either capital assets, ordinary income assets, or Section 1231 assets. To qualify as a Section 1231 asset, the asset must either be real property or depreciable personal property used in a trade or business. Section 1231 assets have the best of both worlds tax treatment, but may be subject to depreciation recapture rules.

# Key Terms

**Amortization** - Cost recovery deductions for intangible assets.

**Amount Realized** - The amount of money plus the value of property received in the sale or exchange of an asset.

**Basis** - Represents the total capital or after-tax income used by a taxpayer to purchase an investment.

**Capital Assets** - All assets that are not specified as ordinary income assets or Section 1231 assets.

**Conventions** - Rules that govern the amount of depreciation that may be deducted during the first year that an asset is put into service.

**Cost Basis** - Initial basis an investor acquires in an asset by using capital to purchase the investment.

**Depreciation** - A return of capital to a business that results in a reduction in the basis of the asset for the amount of depreciation that is claimed.

**Double Basis Rule** - A rule that applies to gifts and related party transactions where the transferee has a basis of the fair market value for losses and the transferor's basis for gains. The rule applies when the asset that is transferred has a fair market value less than the transferor's basis at the time of the transfer. This rule does not apply to arms-length unrelated party transactions. This rule may also be referred to as the split basis rule, dual basis rule, or bifurcated basis rule.

**Double Declining Balance Method** - An accelerated depreciation method used for MACRS assets with a 3, 5, 7, or 10 year class life in which the annual depreciation percentage is twice the annual depreciation percentage under the straight-line depreciation method.

**Listed Property** - Suspect property that is easily used for both business and personal purposes.

**Modified Accelerated Cost Recovery System (MACRS)** - An accelerated depreciation system under which assets are divided into specific classes according to their useful lives.

**Nonrecourse Debt** - Debt that is secured only by the asset pledged as security and not by any personal guarantee of the debtor.

**150 Percent Declining Balance Method** - An accelerated depreciation method used for MACRS assets with a 15 or 20 year class life in which the annual depreciation percentage is 150 percent of the annual depreciation percentage under the straight-line depreciation method.

**Ordinary Income Assets** - Accounts receivable, copyrights, and inventory, all of which generate gains that will be taxed at ordinary income rates.

# Key Terms

***Original Issue Discount (OID) Bonds*** - A bond that is issued for a price that is less than its face amount or principal amount on which interest is usually paid only at maturity.

***Pass-Through Entities*** - Legal business forms that are not treated as separate taxable entities for income tax purposes. The income of a pass-through entity is taxed to each of the owners in proportion to their ownership interest.

***Recourse Debt*** - Debt that the taxpayer is personally liable to repay regardless of whether the investment produces a return for the investor.

***Section 1231 Assets*** - Depreciable property or real property used for productive use in a trade or business or for the production of income.

***Step-to Fair Market Value*** - The basis of inherited property, which is equal to the fair market value of the asset on the date of the decedent's death, or, if elected by the executor of the decedent's estate, the alternate valuation date.

***Straight-Line Depreciation*** - A depreciation method under which the purchase price of the asset, less its expected salvage value, is divided by the expected useful life of the asset to determine the annual depreciation deduction.

# DISCUSSION QUESTIONS

1. How is gain or loss calculated?

2. What is basis and what is the purpose of basis?

3. Describe three uses of basis.

4. What is cost basis?

5. What is the difference between recourse debt and nonrecourse debt?

6. Name several items that increase basis.

7. Name several items that decrease basis.

8. What is depreciation?

9. How is the basis of inherited property determined?

10. What is the rationale for the step-to fair market value of the basis for inherited property?

11. What is the general rule for determining the basis of gifted property?

12. How is the basis of gifted property affected when the donor pays gift tax on the transfer?

13. How is the basis of gifted property determined when the donor gifts property that has a fair market value less than the donor's adjusted basis on the date of the gift?

14. How is the basis of property transferred between spouses determined?

15. What is a related party?

16. What are the tax consequences of selling property to a related party at a loss?

17. How is real property depreciated?

18. What are the two methods of depreciation used with MACRS?

19. How is the cost of an intangible asset recovered?

20. What is "listed property?"

21. What is the Section 179 deduction?

. Five years ago Frederick purchased 1,000 shares of Ickingham Industries, Inc. for $10 per share. He signed an agreement with the company which allowed the company to use his dividend payments to purchase additional shares for him. Over the last 5 years, Frederick received a total of $1,200 in dividend payments, which purchased an additional 100 shares of stock. If Frederick sells his shares for $24,000, what is his taxable gain?

    a. $0.

    b. $12,800.

    c. $14,000.

    d. $24,000.

. Which of the following items is not included in the cost basis of an investment?

    a. Cash used to purchase the investment.

    b. Recourse debt incurred in purchasing the investment.

    c. Nonrecourse debt incurred in purchasing the investment.

    d. The fair market value of property transferred to acquire the investment.

. When Uncle Richard died, he left his kingdom to his ungrateful cousin, Henry. Richard's cost basis in his property was $2 million but, due to turbulent political and economic times, it was worth $1 million at his death. Richard had reinvested approximately $250,000 of dividends during his holding period, and his estate paid $500,000 in transfer taxes at his death. What is Henry's basis in the property?

    a. $1 million.

    b. $2 million.

    c. $2,250,000.

    d. $2,750,000.

4. Tanya gave her nephew Liam 100 shares of Bridge Corporation stock that she purchased 6 months ago for $10,000. At the time of the gift, the fair market value of the stock was $12,000. Which of the following statements concerning the stock is correct?

    a. If Tanya sold the stock, she would have realized a long- term capital gain.

    b. Liam's basis in the stock is $10,000.

    c. Liam's basis in the stock is $12,000.

    d. If Liam sells the stock immediately after the gift, he will realize a long-term capital gain.

5.  Two months after Tom purchased Greenacre for $30,000, he died. The fair market value of Greenacre as of the date of Tom's death was $32,000. He left Greenacre to his son, Kevin. Since Kevin was the only beneficiary of the estate and there were no estate taxes due, the title to the property was transferred to Kevin within one month of Tom's death. Two weeks after receiving title to the property, Kevin sold Greenacre for $35,000. What is the amount and type of income that Kevin will report on the sale?

    a.  $5,000 short-term capital gain.

    b.  $5,000 long-term capital gain.

    c.  $3,000 short-term capital gain.

    d.  $3,000 long-term capital gain.

6.  Mike gave his granddaughter, Jordan, stock worth $500,000 this year. He purchased the stock for $250,000 several years earlier, and felt that the value would increase substantially in the near future. Since he had already used up his lifetime gift-tax exemption in prior tax years, Mike paid $200,000 in gift taxes on the transfer. If Jordan sells the stock for $750,000 six months after the transfer, which of the following statements is correct?

    a.  Jordan will realize a $400,000 long-term capital gain.

    b.  Jordan will realize a $250,000 long-term capital gain.

    c.  Jordan will realize a $500,000 long-term capital gain.

    d.  Jordan will realize a $250,000 short-term capital gain.

7.  Two years ago, Vernon purchased 100 shares of Stairwell Refitters, Inc., a start-up company, for $12,000. Unfortunately, Stairwell Refitter's business model did not perform as expected, and the value of the shares has dropped to $8,000. Vernon's son, Dudley, recently realized a large capital gain on an investment he held, so Vernon gave his shares of Stairwell Refitters, Inc. to Dudley when they were worth $8,000. If Dudley sells the shares for $5,000 thirteen months after the transfer, what is the amount and character of his gain or loss?

    a.  $7,000 long-term capital loss.

    b.  $7,000 short-term capital loss.

    c.  $3,000 long-term capital loss.

    d.  $3,000 short-term capital loss.

8.  Two years ago, Olive purchased 100 shares of Pennsylvania Railroad, Inc. for $15,000. Unfortunately, the value of the shares has dropped to $10,000. Olive's daughter, Agnes, was heading off to college, and Olive was tired of waiting for a return on the stock. Olive gave the stock to Agnes when it was worth $10,000 to help fund Agnes' education. If Agnes sells the shares for $12,000 three months after the transfer, what is the amount and character of his gain or loss?

    a.  $0.

    b.  $2,000 short-term capital gain.

    c.  $3,000 long-term capital loss.

    d.  $3,000 short-term capital loss.

9. Two years ago, Amanda purchased 100 shares of Quick Produce, Inc. for $15,000. Unfortunately, the value of the shares has dropped to $10,000. Amanda gave the stock to her daughter, Daphna, when it was worth $10,000. If Daphna sells the shares for $17,000 three months after the transfer, what is the amount and character of his gain or loss?

    a. $2,000 short-term capital gain.

    b. $2,000 long-term capital gain.

    c. $7,000 short-term capital gain.

    d. $7,000 long-term capital gain.

10. Several years before his marriage to Marie, Patrick purchased a vacation home in a remote shoreline community for $250,000. After their marriage, Patrick needed some cash to invest in a new business opportunity, so he sold the house to his wife Marie for its current fair market value, $750,000. Nine months after purchasing the house, Marie sold it for $1 million. What is the amount and nature of Marie's taxable gain on the sale of the home?

    a. $250,000 short-term capital gain.

    b. $250,000 long-term capital gain.

    c. $750,000 short-term capital gain.

    d. $750,000 long-term capital gain.

11. All of the following statements concerning depreciation are correct EXCEPT:

    a. Depreciation is a method of cost recovery that allows a taxpayer to receive his capital back over the useful life of an asset.

    b. Assets purchased for personal use are eligible for depreciation deductions.

    c. Depreciation deductions cause a downward adjustment in the taxpayer's basis.

    d. Depreciation on real estate is taken on a straight-line basis.

12. Christopher recently purchased Quarry City Industrial Park, a commercial industrial and office community, as an investment. The complex is already rented out to tenants, and Christopher will continue to lease the property to industrial and office space tenants while he owns the property. Which of the following statements concerning the depreciation deductions that can be taken on the property is correct?

    a. Christopher cannot take depreciation deductions on real property, so the land and apartment house is not eligible for depreciation.

    b. Christopher can depreciate the cost allocable to the buildings (but not the land) over a 20 year period.

    c. Christopher can depreciate the cost allocable to the buildings (but not the land) over a 27.5 year period.

    d. Christopher can depreciate the cost allocable to the buildings (but not the land) over a 39 year period.

13. Milton, an independent consultant for Initech, Inc., purchased a new red laptop computer to match his red stapler. He plans to use the computer primarily for personal purposes, but will occasionally use it (perhaps 25% of the time) to complete assignments that he has accepted from Initech. Which of the following statements concerning the red computer is correct?

    a. If Milton purchases the computer through Initech, he will be able to depreciate the full cost of the computer.

    b. Milton will not be eligible to claim depreciation deductions for the computer.

    c. Since he purchased the computer to match the red stapler in his office, he can depreciate the full cost of the computer over the appropriate class life.

    d. Milton can depreciate 25% of the cost of the computer, since the computer is used for business purposes 25% of the time.

14. Wilson runs an oil and gas operations consulting practice, and has had a very good year. Oil prices, as well as the demand for his services, have risen. Given the windfall profits his firm received this year, in December of 2010 Wilson decided to redecorate his office and upgrade the computer system used by himself and his employees. The cost of the office equipment is $40,000 and the computer upgrade cost $20,000. Assuming Wilson has purchased no other depreciable assets in 2010, that the gross income from his consulting practice was $500,000 and Wilson would like to minimize his exposure to income taxes, how should he treat the new purchases for income tax purposes?

    a. Wilson should deduct the entire cost of the office equipment and computer upgrades against this year's business income.

    b. Wilson must use the mid-month convention in determining depreciation deductions, since he placed the upgrades in service in December.

    c. Wilson must use the mid-quarter convention in determining depreciation deductions, since he placed the upgrades in service in December.

    d. Wilson must use the mid-year convention in determining depreciation deductions, since he placed the upgrades in service in the second half of the year.

15. Which of the following assets qualifies as a Section 1231 asset?

    a. Greeting cards held by the owner of a gift shop for sale to customers.

    b. A bicycle owned by a 12 year old child.

    c. An apartment building held for rental to tenants.

    d. Artwork prominently displayed in a taxpayer's summer residence.

# Quick Quiz Explanations

### Quick Quiz 10.1

1. True.
2. False. The purpose of basis is to keep track of after-tax dollars an individual invests so that upon the sale of the investment, income is not taxed twice.
3. True.

### Quick Quiz 10.2

1. True.
2. True.
3. False. Since the cost of an asset is recovered through depreciation, the adjusted basis of the asset must be decreased by the depreciation claimed each year.

### Quick Quiz 10.3

1. False. The basis of property that passes through a decedent's estate is stepped to the fair market value of the asset on the date of the decedent's death, or, if elected by the executor of the decedent's estate, to the fair market value of the asset on the alternate valuation date.
2. False. When a donor pays gift tax, the portion of the gift tax paid that represents appreciation in the value of the property may be added to the donor's original basis to determine the basis in the hands of the donee. Therefore, gift tax paid increases the donee's basis in gifted property.
3. True.
4. True.

### Quick Quiz 10.4

1. True.
2. True.
3. False. Most cars are 5-Year Class Life Assets.

### Quick Quiz 10.5

1. True.
2. True.

### Quick Quiz 10.6

1. False. A copyright in the hands of its creator is an ordinary income asset, not a capital asset.
2. True.
3. True.

# The Taxation of Capital Assets

## 11

## INTRODUCTION

As discussed in the previous chapter, the tax characteristics of a particular asset depends upon the categorization of the asset. There are three categories of assets in our income tax system: capital assets, ordinary income assets, and Section 1231 assets. This chapter covers the income tax rules associated with capital assets.

"**Capital assets**" is the catch-all category in our income tax system; all assets that are not specified as ordinary income assets or Section 1231 assets are capital assets. IRC Section 1221 defines capital assets as all assets *other than*:

- Accounts and notes receivable;
- Copyrights, musical[1] and literary compositions, and artistic creations in the hands of the author;
- Inventory; and
- Real or depreciable personal property used in a trade or business.

While Section 1221 does specify that a few additional categories of assets are not capital assets, these categories deal with specialized transactions and as such do not have general applicability from a planning perspective. Remember the asset categorization memory aid that was introduced in the prior chapter: all assets are capital assets except ACID (Accounts Receivable, Copyrights, Inventory, and Real or Depreciable Personal Property used in a trade or business).

Once an asset has been categorized as a capital asset, the tax attributes of that asset are defined. As discussed in Chapter 10, gains on capital assets are subject to favorable income tax rates if the asset has a long-term holding period, but losses on capital assets are limited. The details of the tax rules governing capital assets are covered in this chapter.

---

1. Effective May 17, 2006 through February 8, 2011, there is a temporary regulation that allows an election by musicians for musical compositions or copyrights. The taxpayer may elect for tax treatment of the composition or copyright as a capital gain or loss upon the sale of the property instead of inventory subject to ordinary income.

## REALIZATION AND RECOGNITION

Unlike ordinary income, which is subject to income tax when earned, gains on capital assets are subject to tax only when there has been both a **realization event** (implying that the asset has been sold or exchanged) and a **recognition event** for federal income tax purposes. Recognition occurs when a realized gain is required to be included on a taxpayer's income tax return. Generally, all realized gains are recognized (that is, all realized gains are subject to current taxation) unless a provision can be found in the Code that either exempts the gain from taxation or defers the gain to a future tax period. The various types of transactions that constitute tax deferred and tax-free transfers will be discussed in Chapter 13 on nontaxable exchanges.

### SALE OR EXCHANGE REQUIREMENTS

In order for a gain to be subject to income tax, there must first be a sale or exchange of the asset. Sometimes, as in the case of a sale, the **sale or exchange requirement** is both obvious and easily met. In other cases, it may be less obvious whether the sale or exchange requirement has been met.

First, consider the sale of an asset. When the owner of an asset sells that asset in exchange for another asset (which could include cash or any other property), a realization event occurs.

### Key Concepts

Underline/highlight the answers to these questions as you read:

1. Describe a realization event and a recognition event.

2. Define the sale or exchange requirement.

3. Explain how to calculate gains and losses.

4. Define the amount realized.

5. Identify the disallowed losses.

| EXAMPLE 11.1 |
| :--- |

After conducting a thorough investment portfolio analysis, Colin decides that MNL, Inc. stock no longer fits into his asset allocation, and sells the shares of MNL that he owns on the open market. The sale constitutes a realization event. Colin will calculate gain or loss and, absent a special Code provision deferring or exempting any gain, will be required to recognize any gain on his individual income tax return.

In the case of the sale of an asset, it does not matter what type of asset is sold. It could be stocks, bonds, real estate, personal assets, business use assets, intangible assets, or antique furniture. Realization of gain or loss will occur on the sale, and recognition will occur in the same tax year unless a special provision of the Code exempts or defers it from taxation in the current year.

In some cases, it may be less obvious that the sale or exchange requirement has been met. Consider the following examples.

EXAMPLE 11.2

After finishing college, Paul moved from New England to Louisiana. Over the past several years, Paul has lost his home three times to forces of nature that have created havoc in the gulf region of the United States. When Hurricane Katrina passed through, destroying his home for the third time, Paul decided to pack up what little he had left and moved back to New England. Since he does not know where he will end up settling when he receives his insurance check for the damage to his home in Louisiana, he deposits it into his savings account and does not rebuild or replace his home. In this instance, a realization event has occurred, and Paul will be required to calculate gain or loss on his Louisiana home and may have to recognize that gain on his income tax return.

Natural disasters that destroy property cause a realization event for income tax purposes, since the gain or loss in a particular property can be calculated at that time. It is possible in this circumstance to defer recognition of the gain by following the rules of IRC Section 1033, which are discussed in Chapter 13 on nontaxable exchanges. If those rules are not followed, however, the gain or loss is recognized as well as realized, much to the surprise of some taxpayers who experience these types of losses.

Another event that could cause realization of a loss is the bankruptcy of a company. When a company and its stock become worthless, a constructive sale of the stock held in the worthless company is deemed to occur on December 31 of the year in which the stock becomes worthless, forcing loss recognition in that year.

EXAMPLE 11.3

On December 28 of last year, Kasey purchased 1,000 shares in Heidi Industries, Inc. This investment was not one of Kasey's best investments; the company declared bankruptcy on January 5 of the current year, and the security became worthless. For federal income tax purposes, when a security becomes worthless, a constructive sale occurs on December 31 of that year. Therefore, Kasey will have a recognition event due to the bankruptcy of Heidi Industries, Inc. as of December 31 of the current year.

There are special rules governing worthless securities, which were covered in Chapter 8. It is important to see, however, that an event over which the taxpayer has no control, such as the bankruptcy of a company or the occurrence of a natural disaster, will be considered a sale or exchange of an asset and may trigger a recognition event for federal income tax purposes.

## CALCULATION OF GAIN OR LOSS

When a sale or exchange occurs, gain or loss must be determined. As explained in Chapter 10, IRC Section 1001 provides the formula that is used to calculate gain or loss on the sale or exchange of an asset. The gain or loss equals the amount realized by the taxpayer on the sale or exchange of the asset, less the taxpayer's adjusted basis in the asset. Mathematically, the formula is:

Amount Realized

Less: Adjusted Basis

Equals: Gain or (Loss)

### *The Amount Realized*

The **amount realized** on a sale includes the cash received plus the fair market value of any other property received in exchange for the asset. While a sale generally involves cash, in some cases the party purchasing the asset may give cash plus other property in the sale or exchange.

| | |
|---|---|
| **EXAMPLE 11.4** | Craig owns an interest in Beverly Farms, LLC. He inherited this interest from his grandfather and does not believe that it is the most efficient asset to include in his investment portfolio given his goals and objectives. On the date of his grandfather's death, the interest was worth $90,000. One year later, Craig agrees to sell his interest in Beverly Farms, LLC to his cousin in return for $20,000 in cash plus a piece of raw land currently worth $90,000. Craig would like to hold the land as an investment, since he believes that the value will increase substantially over the next 5 years. The amount that Craig realized in this transaction is $110,000 (equal to the $20,000 in cash that he received, plus the fair market value of the land received, $90,000). To calculate his gain or loss, Craig would have to subtract his adjusted basis from the amount realized in the transaction. |

In the above example, an asset was transferred for cash plus other property, so the amount realized equals the cash plus the fair market value of the property received. Sometimes, instead of transferring property in exchange for assets, the parties to a transaction transfer debt. This can occur when, for example, the property being transferred has an assumable mortgage or has a liability attached to the property that will not be released until paid. In these circumstances, the transfer of debt is treated as the transfer of "other property" in the exchange and is included in the amount realized for the transaction. The party that is giving up, or "shedding" the debt will be deemed to have an additional amount realized and the party assuming the debt will be deemed to be paying that amount in the exchange.

| | |
|---|---|
| **EXAMPLE 11.5** | Continuing with our previous example, assume that instead of receiving Beverly Farms, LLC from his grandfather's estate, Craig purchased the interest many years ago for $90,000. He paid $20,000 in cash, and obtained an assum- |

able loan for the balance of $70,000. Currently, the balance of the note is $50,000. Craig is no longer interested in the business. His cousin, Steve, who also owns an interest in the company, agrees to purchase Craig's interest for $60,000 in cash, and he will assume the note with a balance of $50,000. The amount realized in this transaction by Craig is $110,000 (equal to the cash received, $60,000 plus the value of the "liability shed" by Craig, $50,000, for a total of $110,000).

## Sample Calculation of Gain or Loss

Basis represents capital that is invested in an asset, which is returned tax-free to the investor when he or she sells the asset. Basis must be subtracted from the amount realized to determine the amount of the gain or loss on the transaction. Issues associated with the determination of basis were discussed at length in the prior chapter.

Continuing with the example above, Craig's basis in Beverly Farms, LLC is $90,000 regardless of whether he received it from his grandfather's estate (Example 11.4), or he purchased the interest for $90,000 ($20,000 in cash plus the $70,000 note) (Example 11.5).

If Craig received the interest from his grandfather's estate, his basis in the interest was stepped to the fair market value of the property on the date of the decedent's death.

If Craig purchased the interest for $90,000 by paying $20,000 in cash and financing the rest of the acquisition, his basis is also $90,000. Since Craig must pay back the note with after-tax dollars (he must earn money, pay taxes on those earnings, and use what is left to make payments on the note), the amount borrowed is included in his basis.

Therefore, since Craig's basis is $90,000 in either case, he is entitled to recoup his capital of $90,000 tax-free when he sells the asset.

As discussed in the previous section, the amount realized from either transaction is $110,000. Craig's gain in both cases is $20,000, calculated as follows:

| | |
|---|---|
| Amount Realized | $110,000 |
| Less: Adjusted Basis | - 90,000 |
| Equals: Gain or (Loss) | $20,000 |

Assuming that Craig cannot find a provision in the Code that allows him to defer or avoid the gain, he will have to recognize the gain in the current tax year.

What is Craig's basis in his replacement asset?

In the first scenario (Example 11.4), when Craig transferred the property in return for cash plus raw land worth $90,000, his basis in the cash is the face value of the cash, $20,000. His basis in the land is the fair market value of the land, or $90,000. When property is received in an exchange, and the entire gain realized on the exchange is recognized, the basis of the replacement property will be its fair market value on the date of the exchange. Therefore, Craig recognizes $20,000 in gain and has a basis of $90,000 in the land received.

## RECOGNITION RULES

As you already know, the default rule for income taxation is that all gains realized are recognized unless a special provision of the Code exempts or defers the gain from taxation. If a gain is realized upon transfer, the use of the asset (for personal or business purposes) will not prevent the gain from being recognized.

<table>
<tr><td>**EXAMPLE 11.6**</td><td>Brendan purchased a Ferrari 10 years ago for $80,000. He used the car for personal purposes and sold it earlier this year. Because the model he purchased was a limited edition, he was able to sell the car for $90,000 even though he used it for over 10 years. Brendan's gain is calculated as follows:</td></tr>
</table>

| | |
|---|---|
| Amount Realized | $90,000 |
| Less: Adjusted Basis | - 80,000 |
| Equals: Gain or (Loss) | $10,000 |

The realized gain of $10,000 must be recognized on his income tax return this year.

The same is not true for losses on personal use assets, however. In most cases, the general rule applies to losses as well, but there are circumstances where losses that are realized are disallowed on either a permanent or temporary basis. The rules covering the disallowance of losses stem from Congress' desire to prevent taxpayers from being able to manipulate their own taxable income by incurring losses and to prevent taxpayers from allocating losses to family members who may be in a better position to take advantage of them.

### Disallowed Losses

Losses that are realized, but are not permitted to be recognized (**disallowed losses**) include:
- Losses on the sale of personal use assets;
- Losses on the subsequent sale of property gifted or sold to a related party when its fair market value is less than the original owner's adjusted basis; and
- Wash sales.

The first type of loss that is disallowed for income tax purposes is a loss generated on property that is used for personal purposes. In order for a loss to be deductible for income tax purposes, the asset generating the loss must have been used in a trade or business or for the production of income. If the taxpayer is attempting to generate gains with the property, it is only fair that losses should be allowed to be deducted if gains are subject to tax.

When an asset is used for personal purposes, however, any loss incurred during the period of personal use is considered a personal loss, and is not permitted as a tax deduction. In fact, a loss incurred while an asset is used for personal purposes will *never* be deductible and results in a permanent loss of capital for the taxpayer. This is one of the fundamental rules of income taxation – only losses incurred when the taxpayer is trying to make money may be deducted. Note that casualty losses, which were covered in more detail in Chapter 7, are an exception to this rule.

**EXAMPLE 11.7**

Bertie purchased a personal residence six months ago for $325,000 even though he knew he would be transferred by his employer to another state in less than a year. Since Bertie purchased the home, the market has slumped and prices have begun to fall. Wooster Enterprises, LLC has just informed Bertie that his presence will be required on a permanent basis in an office on the other side of the country beginning in three months. Bertie puts the house up for sale, but cannot sell it for what he paid. As the impending moving date approaches, he panics and agrees to sell the home for $310,000. Bertie's economic loss is calculated as follows:

| Amount Realized | $310,000 |
|---|---|
| Less: Adjusted Basis | - 325,000 |
| Equals: Gain or (Loss) | ($15,000) |

> Bertie will not be permitted to recognize the $15,000 loss for income tax purposes, since the asset was a personal use asset and personal use losses are not tax deductible.

Recall that most assets used in a trade or business or for the production of income are depreciable, which allows the owner to recoup his or her investment in the property before disposition so that the capital can be reinvested in the business to make more money (the only exception to this rule for trade or business or production of income assets is land). When property is put into use in a trade or business or for production of income, the amount that can be depreciated is the lesser of the taxpayer's cost basis or the fair market value of the property at the time it was converted to business use.

**EXAMPLE 11.8**

> Using the facts above, assume that Bertie does not want to realize a loss so he begins to rent out the house after he moves across the country. Assuming that none of the purchase price was allocable to land, which is not depreciable, Bertie's depreciable basis in the property will be $310,000 or the fair market value of the property at the time it was converted to business use. The $15,000 loss that Bertie incurred while he used the property for personal purposes will not be considered when calculating Bertie's depreciation deductions since that loss was personal, and was not related to a trade or business or to the production of income.

A second situation where realized losses will not be currently recognized involves the gift of property to anyone or the sale of property to a related party (other than a spouse) when the property has a fair market value less than the adjusted basis of the original owner. Related party transactions were discussed in the prior chapter. It is important to understand that the double basis rule results in the disallowance of a realized loss when the new owner disposes of the asset at a value less than the original owner's adjusted basis. In this instance, the loss will *never* be deductible, resulting in a permanent loss of capital for the taxpayer. In the event of a transfer by sale to a related party where the fair market value of the property is less than the adjusted basis of the transferor, the loss realized by transferor is disallowed. However, if the transferee later sells or disposes of the property at a value above the purchase price paid by the transferee, the transferee will use the gain basis (under the double basis rule), which will allow the transferee to benefit from the previously disallowed loss.

**EXAMPLE 11.9**

> Clarence has all the losses he will ever need. In fact, he has over $1 million in carryforward capital losses. Clarence would like to dispose of one stock in his investment portfolio, Blandings, Inc., but he currently has a loss position in the company (he purchased the stock for $50 per share, and it is currently worth $40 a share). Clarence's son, Bosham, has realized several gains on his portfolio this year, so Clarence gives the stock to Bosham thinking that Bosham could sell the stock and offset some of his gains with the loss on the stock. Upon receiving the stock, Bosham quickly sells it at a

price of $42 per share. Bosham's loss basis was $40 (the fair market value of the stock on the date of the gift) and his gain basis is $50 (adjusted basis of transfer), which means that his economic gain is $2 (calculated by subtracting his loss basis of $40 from the amount realized of $42). His taxable gain is zero because the sale occurs between the gain and loss basis. The $10 loss that occurred during Clarence's holding period (calculated by subtracting Clarence's basis of $50 from the fair market value on the date of the gift, or $40) will never be recognized but Bosham benefited by not having to recognize his $2 economic gain.

A third situation where a realized loss is not recognized is a **wash sale**. A wash sale occurs when a taxpayer sells a stock or security, and purchases (or enters into an agreement to purchase) substantially identical stock or security within a 30 day period before or after the sale. Including the day of sale, there is actually a 61 day window during which a wash sale can occur. If a wash sale transaction results in gain realization, the gain must be recognized. If, however, the wash sale results in realization of a loss, the loss is not recognized and is temporarily disallowed. The unrecognized loss will be added to the basis of the replacement securities, so that recognition will occur on the subsequent sale of the replacement securities. Unlike the situation described above with respect to personal assets and related party sales and gifts, the realized loss is permitted to be recognized, but only when the replacement securities are eventually sold.

EXAMPLE 11.10

On December 28, 2010, Erin reviews her investment portfolio and finds out that she has had a very profitable year. To offset some of her gains, Erin sells 100 shares of Orion Industries, Inc. for $10,000. She purchased those shares for $15,000 two years earlier. On January 24, 2011, Erin learns that Orion Industries, Inc. is expected to patent a new synthetic that will be in great demand if available, and that the announcement of the new product may be made soon. If the patent is in fact issued, the value of Orion Industries, Inc. stock will increase substantially. Second-guessing the wisdom of selling the company shares, she purchases 100 shares of Orion Industries, Inc. for $8,000. Since Erin purchased and sold substantially identical securities within 30 days, a wash sale has occurred. Her realized loss on the December 28 transaction is calculated as follows:

| | |
|---|---|
| Amount Realized | $10,000 |
| Less: Adjusted Basis | - 15,000 |
| Equals: Gain or (Loss) | ($5,000) |

Due to the wash sale transaction, however, Erin will not be permitted to recognize the loss in the year it was incurred. Instead, the realized but unrecognized loss of $5,000 will be added to the basis of the replacement securities. Erin purchased the replacement securities for $8,000 so adding the unrecognized loss increases her basis to $13,000. By increasing basis in the amount of the unrecognized loss, Erin will receive both the $8,000 cost and the $5,000 unrecognized loss as a tax-free return of her investment when she ultimately sells the stock.

In Example 11.10, Erin's original basis in the stock was $15,000. After she engaged in the wash sale, her basis is $13,000. What happened to the $2,000 difference? The $2,000 is in her pocket. Erin made a somewhat wise investment choice if the stock goes up later – she sold the stock when it was worth $10,000 and repurchased it when it was worth $8,000. By doing so, Erin avoided incurring $2,000 of losses. If the $2,000 avoided loss is added to the basis of the replacement securities, we see that Erin still has the same amount of capital that she originally had, but it is now spread between two assets – Orion Industries, Inc. stock, and cash.

## CAPITAL GAIN HOLDING PERIODS AND TAX RATES

 *Key Concepts*

**Underline/highlight the answers to these questions as you read:**

1. Define long and short-term holding periods.

2. Identify the various capital gain tax rates.

3. Explain the Section 1250 rules.

4. Describe the treatment of capital gains under AMT.

One of the benefits of categorizing an asset as a capital asset is that if a gain is realized, it is potentially subject to a lower income tax rate than the taxpayer's ordinary marginal income tax rate. The taxpayer's holding period for the asset will determine whether or not the lower tax rate applies. In this section, we will review the holding period rules, followed by a discussion of the tax rates that apply to sales of capital assets.

### HOLDING PERIODS

The **holding period** for an asset can be either short-term or long-term.

If a taxpayer holds an asset for a year or less, the taxpayer has a short-term holding period for that asset. If the holding period is more than one year, it is said to be a long-term holding period.

| EXHIBIT 11.1 | HOLDING PERIOD SUMMARY |
| --- | --- |

| Capital Gain/Loss | Holding Period |
| --- | --- |
| Long-Term Capital Gain/Loss | > 1 Year |
| Short-Term Capital Gain/Loss | ≤ 1 Year |

Brian purchased 100 shares of Lucky Electric, Inc. stock on March 17 for $5,000. Fearing that the stock market would experience a downturn due to recent political events, Brian sold the stock for $5,150 on September 30 of the same year. Since Brian held the stock for less than a year, his $150 gain on the stock ($5,150 amount realized less $5,000 adjusted basis) will be considered a short-term capital gain.

EXAMPLE 11.11

Erin purchased 100 shares of CivEnCo, Inc. stock on March 17 for $8,000. She sold the stock for $8,500 on March 17 of the following year. Erin's gain of $500 ($8,500 amount realized less $8,000 adjusted basis) will be considered a short-term capital gain, since she did not hold the stock for *more than* one year.

EXAMPLE 11.12

Note that in the prior example, holding an asset for exactly one year does not characterize the gain or loss as a long-term capital gain or loss. To achieve long-term capital treatment, the asset must be held for *more than* one year. As a practical matter, this means that a **long-term holding period** begins if the asset is held for a year and one day. If the asset is sold in the current year on the same day it was purchased in the prior year, the result is a **short-term holding period**.

Chris purchased 100 shares of Dowling Novelties, Inc. stock on March 17 for $10,000. On March 18 of the following year, he sold the stock for $12,000. Chris' $2,000 gain on the stock ($12,000 amount realized less $10,000 adjusted basis) will be treated as a long-term capital gain, since Chris held the stock for *more than* one year.

EXAMPLE 11.13

## Property Acquired by Inheritance

There are a few special rules concerning holding periods that are worth noting. First, whenever property is received from a decedent's estate, it is deemed to have a long-term holding period, regardless of when the asset was acquired by the decedent. An easy way to remember this rule is to recall that "death is long-term."

William died two months ago and left his entire estate to his only son, Gerald. A week before William died, he purchased a new building for $300,000 that he planned to lease to his business. William held the title to the building personally, and it was included in his estate when he died. The appraiser valued the building at $310,000 on the date of William's death. The deed to the building was just transferred to Gerald by the executor of the estate, and Gerald decides that another building would be more appropriate for use by the business. Gerald sells the building for $325,000 one week after he received title. Gerald's gain on the building is calculated as follows:

EXAMPLE 11.14

| | |
|---|---|
| Amount Realized | $325,000 |
| Less: Adjusted Basis | - 310,000  (value at date of death) |
| Equals: Gain or (Loss) | $15,000 |

The character of the gain will be long-term capital gain, despite the fact that the building was purchased by William only three months before Gerald sold it. The reason, of course, is that all property acquired by inheritance has a deemed long-term holding period.

### Gifted Property

The second special rule concerning holding periods applies to gifted property. When gifted property has a fair market value in excess of the donor's basis in the property on the date of the gift, the donee's holding period will tack on to the donor's holding period. In other words, the donee's holding period begins on the date the donor acquired the property.

EXAMPLE 11.15

Elizabeth purchases 100 shares of Texco stock on January 1, 2010 for $1,000, or $10 per share. On June 1, 2010, the price of the Texco stock has risen to $12 per share and Elizabeth decides to gift all 100 shares to her sister Lauren. If Lauren sells the Texco stock on August 1, 2010, any gain from the sale of the stock will be a short-term capital gain.

EXAMPLE 11.16

Continuing with the above example, if instead of selling the stock on August 1, 2010, Lauren decided to sell the stock on February 1, 2011, any gain from the sale of the stock will be a long-term capital gain. Even though Lauren had personally owned the stock for less than one year, her holding period began on January 1, 2010 (the date that Elizabeth, the donor, acquired the stock).

If the gifted property has a fair market value on the date of the gift that is less than the donor's basis in the property, the donee's holding period will not necessarily tack on to the donor's holding period. As discussed in prior chapters, the double basis rule would apply. If the donee subsequently disposes of the property at a gain, then the donee's holding period tacks on to the donor's holding period, resulting in the same outcome illustrated in Examples 11.15 and 11.16 above. However, if the donee subsequently disposes of the property at a loss, the donee's holding period begins on the date of the gift.

EXAMPLE 11.17

John purchased 50 shares of Clark Co. five years ago for $2,000. He just gave those shares to his daughter, Catherine, and the value of the 50 shares of stock on the date of the gift was $500. Catherine will have a double basis in the stock, determined as follows:

| If the donee's sale price is... | less than FMV | between the original basis and FMV | greater than the original basis |
|---|---|---|---|
| Then the donee's basis used is ... | $500 (Loss Basis) | no gain or loss | $2,000 (Gain Basis) |

If Catherine sells the stock one month later for $3,000 she can use the gain basis of $2,000 (John's original basis), for purposes of calculating gain or loss. In this case, Catherine will have a long-term gain of $1,000 because her holding period tacks to John's holding period.

If Catherine sells the shares one month later for $300, her loss is $200. In this case, since the stock was sold for less than the value on the date of the gift, the loss basis must be used for purposes of calculating loss. In addition, Catherine's loss will be treated as a short-term capital loss because her holding period for loss purposes began on the date of the gift (one month ago).

If Catherine sells the shares for $1,000 she will have no gain or loss to report, since the sales price was within the no gain/no loss corridor.

## Property Acquired in a Related Party Transaction

The third special holding period rule applies to property acquired in a related party transaction. When property is sold to a related party (other than the seller's spouse), the holding period used to determine whether any subsequent gains or losses are short-term or long-term is based solely on the purchaser's holding period. In other words, when property is sold to a related party, the holding period of the seller does not tack on to the holding period of the purchaser. This rule applies without regard to whether the property is subsequently sold by the purchaser at a gain or a loss.

Stacy sells stock in Baseball Enterprises, Inc. to her son, Ethan for $2,000. Stacy purchased the stock three years ago for $3,000 and the current fair market value of the stock is $2,000. If Ethan sells the stock six months later for $3,500, he uses his gain basis for purposes of determining gain. Upon sale, Ethan will realize and recognize a $500 gain ($3,500 amount realized less $3,000 gain basis) that will be classified as a short-term capital gain because Ethan has only held the stock for six months.

If Ethan sells the stock six months after the date of his purchase from Stacy for $1,200, he uses his loss basis for purposes of determining loss. Ethan's loss basis equals the fair

**EXAMPLE 11.18**

market value on the date of sale, or in this case, $2,000. Upon sale, Ethan will realize a $800 loss on the stock ($1,200 amount realized less $2,000 loss basis). In addition, the loss will be characterized as a short-term capital loss because Ethan only held the stock for six months.

If Ethan sells the stock 14 months after the date of his purchase from Stacy for $3,700, he will have a long-term capital gain of $700. Ethan's gain is long-term because he held the property for more than one year. Note that in all of these scenarios, the fact that Stacy previously held the property for three years does not impact Ethan's holding period. From a planning point of view, Stacy should not have sold the property to a related party when the fair market value was less than her basis because she would be denied the benefit of the tax loss. Stacy would have been better off selling the stock in an arm's-length transaction and taking the tax loss.

### Nonbusiness Bad Debts

A fourth special rule dealing with holding periods applies to nonbusiness bad debts. A nonbusiness bad debt is any debt created by a person who is not in the business of loaning money or who has not created the debt in the conduct of his or her trade or business. All nonbusiness bad debts are treated as short-term capital losses, regardless of how long the debt was outstanding. Nonbusiness bad debts are only deductible when they become completely worthless – a deduction for partial worthlessness is not allowed.

| **EXAMPLE 11.19** | Uncle Fred loaned money to his nephew, Bertie, two years ago. Bertie was having trouble meeting the payroll for his household staff, and when his butler threatened to leave his employment, Bertie turned to his Uncle Fred for help. Unfortunately, over the last few years, the situation has not improved for Bertie. Uncle Fred is beginning to realize that Bertie will not repay the loan, and Uncle Fred determines that the loan is worthless. Uncle Fred writes off the loan to Bertie as a capital loss. Capital treatment is required since Uncle Fred is not in the business of making loans (if he was, the loan would be treated as an ordinary asset), and the loan is not depreciable (precluding Section 1231 treatment). Despite the fact that the loan has been outstanding for two years, it is treated as a short-term capital loss. |
| --- | --- |

EXHIBIT 11.2

| Property Acquired By.... | Will have the following holding period... |
|---|---|
| Inheritance | Long-term holding period. |
| Gift | Holding period will tack to donor's holding period if gain basis is used. If loss basis is used, the donee's holding period begins on the date of the gift. |
| Related Party Transaction | Holding period starts on sale date. |
| Nonbusiness Bad Debts | Short-term capital losses. |

## CAPITAL GAINS TAX RATES

The capital gains tax rate that applies to a particular transaction is a function of the holding period of the asset.

Short-term gains and losses are subject to tax at the taxpayer's ordinary marginal income tax rate. There is no tax benefit afforded to assets held for a short-term holding period.

If the asset sold was held for a long-term holding period, the gain or loss will be subject to long-term capital gains tax rates, which are lower than the taxpayer's ordinary marginal income tax rate. Generally speaking, if the transaction results in a gain, this is a good result since the taxpayer will pay less tax on the gain. If the transaction results in a loss, however, the taxpayer will receive less of a tax benefit. As discussed in our review of asset categorization, capital gains are good, but capital losses are bad for the taxpayer.

The maximum long-term capital gains tax rate is 15 percent. This rate applies for anyone in the 25 percent or higher ordinary marginal income tax brackets. For those taxpayers in the 10 percent or 15 percent ordinary marginal income tax bracket, the normal capital gains tax rate is lowered to five percent. However, for tax years after 2007, taxpayers in the 10 or 15 percent ordinary marginal income tax brackets will pay no capital gains tax. If lower capital gains rates were not available to taxpayers in these tax brackets, there would be no benefit to long-term capital gains for those in the 15 percent tax bracket, and those in the 10 percent marginal ordinary income tax bracket would have to pay a higher tax rate on their capital gains than on their ordinary income. To ensure that all taxpayers would receive a tax break for long-term capital gains, Congress lowered the long-term capital gains tax rate for lower income taxpayers.

There are exceptions to the special tax rate that applies to long-term capital gains. These exceptions are designed to minimize tax planning opportunities for taxpayers. The two exceptions to the 15 percent maximum capital gains tax rate are (1) a 25 percent capital gains tax rate for unrecaptured Section 1250 depreciation, and (2) a 28 percent capital gains tax rate for the sale of collectibles.

### Unrecaptured Section 1250 Depreciation

The rules concerning depreciation recapture will be covered in detail in Chapter 12 on property transactions with business assets. A brief discussion of this issue is provided here to describe the purpose of the special 25 percent tax rate.

One of the tax benefits of purchasing real estate for use in a business or for the production of income (rental real estate) is the ability to take depreciation deductions for the cost basis of the property (less the portion of cost basis allocated to land) over the useful life of the asset. Because real estate used for these purposes is depreciable, it is not considered to be a capital asset, but rather a Section 1231 asset. Under Section 1231, gains are treated as capital gains, and losses are treated as ordinary losses – the "best of both worlds" treatment is obtained. Under current law, all depreciation taken on real estate is taken on a straight-line basis. When a depreciation deduction is taken, it offsets what would otherwise be ordinary income taxed at ordinary rates. That is, business income is reduced by depreciation deductions if a business owns real estate, or the profit on a rental activity is reduced when depreciation deductions are taken on "production of income" property. In both cases, the income of these activities would be subject to ordinary income tax rates. Despite the fact that depreciation is allowed on real estate used for these purposes, the value of real estate tends to increase, not decrease. By taking depreciation deductions, a real estate investor could reduce his or her ordinary income but would not really suffer an economic loss provided that the value of real property increases over time. When the value of the property is increasing, not decreasing, depreciation deductions allow a real estate investor to transform income that would otherwise be treated as ordinary income into capital gains. Congress believed that this result would be unfair, especially in light of the ordinary loss treatment that is accorded to such real estate investments if the property does not increase in value due to the imposition of Section 1231, and imposed a special capital gains tax rate on straight-line depreciation taken on real estate. That special tax rate is 25 percent.

The terminology in this area is sometimes confusing, but can be explained in the following manner. Straight-line depreciation is *not* recaptured under IRC Section 1250. The special 25 percent capital gains rate only applies to the straight-line depreciation taken on a real estate investment. Therefore, the 25 percent capital gains tax rate applies to "**unrecaptured Section 1250 depreciation**."

| | |
|---|---|
| **EXAMPLE 11.20** | Mark supplements his income by making strategic real estate investments. He purchases properties, improves them, and rents them out to generate additional cash flow for himself and his family. He is in the 35% marginal income tax bracket. Mark purchased one of his properties for $200,000 and spent approximately $50,000 on improvements. Over the years, he has taken $40,000 of straight-line depreciation deductions on the property. He has accepted an offer to sell the property to a national franchise for $450,000, a price Mark believes exceeds the fair market value of the property. |
| | Mark's adjusted basis in the property is $210,000 (equal to his cost basis of $200,000 plus the improvements of $50,000 less the depreciation deductions of $40,000). His gain on the sale may be calculated as follows: |

| | |
|---|---|
| Amount Realized | $450,000 |
| Less: Adjusted Basis | - 210,000 |
| Equals: Gain or (Loss) | $240,000 |

Mark's gain will be split into two pieces for tax purposes. First, the straight-line depreciation that Mark claimed for tax purposes will be taxed at 25%. In this case, Mark took straight-line depreciation deductions of $40,000 so the first $40,000 of the gain will be taxed at 25%. The remaining portion of the gain, $200,000 will be taxed at Mark's long-term capital gains rate of 15%.

A few issues illustrated by the previous example are worth noting. First, when real estate is sold, the straight-line depreciation will be taxed at 25 percent *before* the remaining portion of the gain qualifies for the special long-term capital gains tax rate. If the gain is less than the straight-line depreciation taken, all of the gain will be taxed at 25 percent (assuming, for the sake of simplicity that there is no recapture under IRC Section 1250).

Second, note that the actual increase in the value of the property qualifies for the long-term capital gains tax rate. In the above example, the actual increase in the value of Mark's property is the difference between what he sold the property for, and what he paid for the property without taking into consideration the depreciation deductions. This can be calculated as follows:

| | |
|---|---|
| Sale Price | $450,000 |
| Less: Cost of Building Plus Improvements | - $250,000 |
| Equals: Gain or (Loss) | $200,000 |

Out of Mark's $240,000 gain, the only portion that is taxed at a higher rate is the portion of the gain that resulted from taking depreciation deductions. By crafting the "Unrecaptured Section 1250 Depreciation" rule in this way, Congress is preserving an investor's right to receive a special tax rate on actual increases in value, but captures part of the tax benefit received from the depreciation deductions upon sale of the property.

While the "Unrecaptured Section 1250 Depreciation" rule appears to subject a taxpayer to additional tax, if the taxpayer is in a marginal tax bracket that exceeds 25 percent, the taxpayer still wins. Recall that depreciation deductions are claimed against ordinary income. In the example above, Mark is in the 35 percent marginal income tax bracket. When he claimed depreciation deductions on his property, Mark offset income that would have been taxed at 35 percent. When Mark sells the property, he only has to pay a 25 percent tax on the portion of the gain which results from those depreciation deductions. Therefore, Mark has achieved a tax arbitrage of 10 percent. Each year when he takes depreciation deductions, Mark gets a tax benefit of 35 percent, and he pays only part of that tax benefit back (due to the lower tax rate of 25 percent on the unrecaptured Section 1250 depreciation) when he ultimately sells the property. Mark has saved 10 percent in taxes and has the benefit of time value on the other 25 percent that he has to pay back when he sells the property.

As is the case with regular long-term capital gains, if a taxpayer is in a marginal ordinary income tax bracket of less than 25 percent, instead of imposing a 25 percent rate on the unrecaptured Section 1250 depreciation, the taxpayer's regular ordinary tax rate applies to that portion of the gain.

**EXAMPLE 11.21**

Violet is proud of her only nephew, Sheridan. Sheridan is currently attending University, and to provide him with a source of funds to cover his social and living expenses, Violet transfers an apartment house that she owns that is located next to the University to Sheridan. She paid $400,000 for the apartment house, and over her period of ownership she took $10,000 in straight-line depreciation deductions. Sheridan has no other source of income, and even with the profits earned from his new rental activity, Sheridan is in the 15% tax bracket. During his time at University, Sheridan claimed another $10,000 in depreciation deductions. Since Sheridan will be completing his schooling within the next six months, Aunt Violet encourages him to sell the property, and Sheridan does so on January 1. Aside from the gain on the property, Sheridan will have no other income in the year of sale. The selling price was $405,000 and Sheridan plans to use those funds to establish himself both socially and in his new career. Sheridan's gain on the apartment house is calculated as follows:

| | |
|---|---|
| Amount Realized | $405,000 |
| Less: Adjusted Basis | - 380,000 |
| Equals: Gain or (Loss) | $25,000 |

Sheridan's adjusted basis equals the original purchase price of $400,000 less the depreciation that Aunt Violet claimed ($10,000) and the depreciation that he claimed ($10,000).

In this case, $20,000 of the gain will be taxed at 15%, and $5,000 of the gain will be taxed at 5%. Because Sheridan is in the 15% ordinary income tax bracket, and the special rate that applies to unrecaptured Section 1250 depreciation cannot exceed the ordinary tax rate, the straight-line depreciation claimed is taxed at 15%. Sheridan qualifies for the special 5% capital gains tax rate on the remaining portion of the gain since he is in the 15% marginal income tax bracket.

The concept of depreciation recapture will be discussed again in Chapter 12. Remember that the form of depreciation recapture covered in this chapter – "unrecaptured Section 1250 depreciation" – only applies to straight-line depreciation taken on real estate. If depreciation on real estate was taken on an accelerated basis (which was only available for property placed in service between 1981-1986), the accelerated portion of the depreciation will be recaptured under Section 1250, and a different tax result occurs for that portion of the depreciation.

## *Capital Gains Tax Rates on Collectibles*

A second exception to the lower 15 percent tax rate on long-term capital gains applies when collectibles are sold at a gain. The capital gains tax rate that applies to the sale of collectibles is 28 percent. As with unrecaptured Section 1250 depreciation, however, if a taxpayer is in a marginal ordinary income tax bracket of less than 28 percent, instead of imposing a 28 percent rate on the entire collectible gain, the taxpayer's regular ordinary tax rate applies to that portion of the gain.

Collectibles include items such as coins, stamps, Hummels, antique furniture, oriental rugs, and similar assets. Usually, these assets are held for personal use and are rarely held by the taxpayer for use in a trade or business or for production of income. If a collectible is held for personal use and is sold at a loss, the taxpayer may not recognize the loss for income tax purposes because the loss was personal in nature. If the asset is sold at a gain, however, the realized gain must be recognized.

Before 1997, the special capital gains tax rate that applied to any long-term capital gain was 28 percent. In the Taxpayer Relief Act of 1997, Congress lowered the long-term capital gains tax rates for most assets to 15 percent, but did not extend the 15 percent rate to collectibles. In excluding collectibles from the new, lower rate, Congress was recognizing that these assets are typically used for personal purposes and did not want to give gains on personal assets the same tax treatment as gains on assets purchased for use in a trade or business or for the production of income. Consequently, the pre-TRA '97 capital gains rates continue to apply to collectibles. Whenever a collectible is sold at a gain, the capital gains tax rate that applies is 28 percent.

In some circumstances, collectibles are used in a trade or business, or for production of income. Examples might include the oriental rug in the CEO's office or a portfolio of investment grade rare coins held by an investment manager with the objective of making a profit. Gains on the disposition of these assets, even though the assets are used in a trade or business or for the production of income, are still subject to the 28 percent collectibles capital gains tax rate.

## CAPITAL GAINS AND THE AMT

The alternative minimum tax (AMT) system was created in 1986 to prevent wealthy taxpayers from eliminating their current income tax through use of tax planning devices. The AMT will be covered in depth in Chapter 15, but a brief introduction and discussion of the AMT and capital gains tax rates is warranted here. Under the AMT tax system, income is taxed at a flat 26 percent or 28 percent rate depending upon the income of the taxpayer. Since capital gains are currently subject to tax at a rate lower than the AMT tax rate, it would be possible, absent a special exception, for a taxpayer with large capital gains to be subject to the AMT tax rate. Generally, whenever a taxpayer has too much income taxed at a rate lower than the taxpayer's AMT tax rate, imposition of the AMT may be possible.

Due to the tax policy reasons for subjecting capital gains to a lower tax rate, however, Congress has applied the special capital gains tax rates for both regular and AMT tax purposes. Therefore, most capital gains will be taxed at the 15 percent rate (or zero percent for those in the 10 percent and 15 percent marginal tax brackets).

---

**EXHIBIT 11.3**  **CAPITAL GAINS TAX RATES SUMMARY**

| | |
|---|---|
| 15%/5%* | * For individuals in the 15% or less income tax bracket (Reduced to 0% beginning in 2008) |
| 25% | Rate for unrecaptured gain on 1250 assets (Straight-line depreciation taken) |
| 28% | Collectibles |

# DETERMINING NET CAPITAL GAINS AND LOSSES

Capital gains and losses must be systematically combined to determine their net income tax consequences.

As a threshold matter, all capital gains and losses are categorized as short-term or long-term. Recall that a long-term gain or loss results from holding an asset for more than one year. Short-term losses are offset against short-term gains, and long-term losses are offset against long-term gains.

**Key Concepts**

Underline/highlight the answers to these questions as you read:

1. Describe the netting procedures for short and long-term capital gains and losses.

EXAMPLE 11.22

John has been adjusting his portfolio to meet his target asset allocation and has realized several capital gains and losses this year. He categorized the capital gains and losses into short-term and long-term and added each type of gain/loss together. The net results are as follows:

|        | Short-Term | Long-Term |
|--------|-----------|-----------|
| Gains  | $15,000   | $3,000    |
| Losses | <$10,000> | <$5,000>  |
| Net    | $5,000  NSTCG | <$2,000>  NLTCL |

| | |
|---|---|
| NSTCG | $5,000 |
| NLTCL | <$2,000> |
| NSTCG | $3,000 |

The first step in the netting process is to calculate the net short-term and long-term gain or loss. In the previous example, John has a net short-term capital gain of $5,000 ($15,000 in gains less $10,000 in losses) and a net long-term capital loss of $2,000 ($3,000 in gains less $5,000 in losses).

Once net short-term and long-term gains or losses are calculated, a comparison of the short-term and long-term results must be made. If both the net short-term and long-term results are gains, or both are losses, no further action is necessary. As discussed above, short-term gains and losses are subject to ordinary tax rates, and long-term gains and losses are subject to a special capital gains tax rate. If short-term and long-term gains or losses were added together to find a total gain/loss, the tax result would be distorted.

If, however, the net results are of different signs (gain for one and loss for other), the net short-term gain/loss can be combined with the net long-term gain or loss. This can only occur in two circumstances: (1) when there is a net short-term capital gain and a net long-term capital loss; or (2) when there is a net short-term capital loss and a net long-term capital gain. The character (short-term or long-term) of the resulting gain or loss is determined by the larger net number, not taking into account whether it was a gain or loss.

**EXAMPLE 11.23** Continuing with our example above, John had a net short-term capital gain of $5,000 and a net long-term capital loss of $2,000. Since the net results are of different signs (one is a gain and one is a loss), they are netted against each other. John's result is a $3,000 net short-term capital gain.

To illustrate the characterization process, assume instead that John had a $5,000 short-term capital loss and a $2,000 long-term capital gain. The net result would be a $3,000 short-term capital loss ($5,000 is bigger than $2,000 and the $5,000 amount applied to short-term losses).

In summary, when netting capital gains and losses, if net short-term and long-term results are either both gains or both losses, no further action is required. If the net results are of different signs, however (one is a gain and the other is a loss), the net short-term and long-term results are netted together.

## LIMITATIONS ON RECOGNITION OF CAPITAL LOSSES

The netting process does not end the inquiry for taxation of capital assets. There are further limitations that must be applied to determine how much of a gain or loss is taxable (is recognized) in a given tax year.

*Key Concepts*

**Underline/highlight the answers to these questions as you read:**

1. Describe the annual limits on loss deductions for individual taxpayers.

2. Identify the loss rules associated with small business stock.

If a series of transactions results in a net capital gain, the net capital gain is recognized in the current tax year regardless of its size. In this instance, the taxpayer has received income, and the amount and character of the income could be precisely calculated, so recognition is required.

If a series of transactions results in a net capital loss, however, the amount of that loss that may be recognized in the current tax year is limited. Under current law, up to $3,000 of net capital losses (either short or long-term) may be recognized against other forms of income in any one tax year.

This limitation is a liberalization of the general rule of taxation that says that losses in one income category can only be offset against gains in that income category. If the general rule applied, no loss deduction would be allowed in the current tax year if a taxpayer had a net loss on capital transactions. The $3,000 net capital loss limitation rule is a special exception to the general rule and allows taxpayers to take up to $3,000 of losses currently against other income. If losses exceed $3,000 and the taxpayer has both short-term and long-term losses, then the short-term losses are used up first. The balance of any losses, short or long-term, carry over indefinitely and may be used in a subsequent year.

Recall that in our tax system there are three types of income: (1) ordinary (active) income; (2) portfolio income; and (3) passive income. Capital gains and losses fall into the portfolio "bucket." The general rule limits loss deductions to the income within that bucket, but the special rule allows a portion of that loss to be deducted against other income. This concept is illustrated graphically in Exhibit 11.4.

**TYPES OF INCOME**

EXHIBIT 11.4

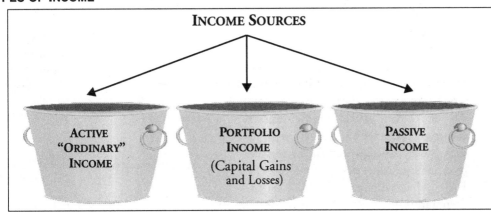

If a capital loss is realized in a given tax year, but is not recognized due to the imposition of the loss limitation rule, the remaining loss is carried forward indefinitely and may be used to offset future capital gains, or, alternatively, generate a $3,000 loss deduction against other income until the loss is eventually used up.

**EXAMPLE 11.24**

Jolly Roger, upon being hired as Executive Vice President of The Amazing Company, Inc. purchases $2 million of The Amazing Company stock without researching the viability of the business. The Amazing Company, despite its name, goes bankrupt, and Jolly Roger loses his entire investment. Jolly Roger has no other capital gains or losses in the current year. He will be able to write-off $3,000 of the $2 million loss this year and will carryforward the remaining $1,997,000 loss to future years. In the unlikely event that Jolly Roger has gains in future years, he can offset those gains dollar for dollar with the carry-forward loss. Alternatively, he could continue to deduct $3,000 per year until he dies, or the remaining loss is completely written off.

In addition to the special rule that allows up to $3,000 of capital losses to be offset against other income, another rule re-categorizes capital losses on small business stock into ordinary losses if certain requirements are met. Under Code Section 1244, a single taxpayer can deduct up to $50,000 ($100,000 for married individuals filing jointly) of the loss on small business stock as an ordinary loss in any given year if the following requirements are met:

1. The stock represents ownership in a domestic corporation.
2. The corporation was a small business corporation (less than $1 million in total capital contributions plus paid-in capital) at the time the stock was issued.
3. The company was incorporated after November 6, 1978.
4. The loss was sustained by the original owner of the stock (the person to whom the stock was issued by the corporation), who is not a corporation, trust, or estate.
5. The stock was issued to the original owner in exchange for money or property. Stock issued in return for services or other stock does not qualify.
6. For the five years prior to the loss, the corporation must have earned more than 50 percent of it's gross receipts from sources other than royalties, rents, dividends, interest, annuities, and capital gains.

**Quick Quiz 11.3**

**Highlight the answer to these questions:**

1. A taxpayer with a $20,000 long-term capital gain and a $5,000 short-term capital loss has a net $15,000 short-term capital gain.
   a. True
   b. False

2. $3,000 of capital losses may be recognized against other income each year.
   a. True
   b. False

3. A single taxpayer can deduct up to $50,000 of the loss on small business stock as an ordinary loss if certain requirements are met.
   a. True
   b. False

False, True, True.

**EXAMPLE 11.25**

Christopher, a single individual, was an original investor in Monarch, Inc. When the company was formed, it had $500,000 in initial capitalization. While the company did well for a few years, its performance has slipped, and earlier this year it declared bankruptcy. Christopher's ownership interest in the company was 20%. All of the other requirements for Section 1244 treatment have been met.

Since Christopher owned 20% of the company, his initial contribution was $100,000 (20% of $500,000). This year, the company became worthless, so a constructive sale will occur on December 31. Christopher's loss will be $100,000. Out of the $100,000 loss, Christopher can treat $50,000 as an ordinary loss, leaving the other $50,000 to be treated as a capital loss. There is no loss limitation on ordinary losses, so the entire $50,000 ordinary loss will be deductible in the current year. In addition, assuming he has no other capital losses in the current year, or carry-forward losses from prior years, Christopher will be able to deduct $3,000 of the capital loss against his other income. The remaining $47,000 capital loss will be carried forward to future tax years.

## CHAPTER SUMMARY

This chapter has introduced the tax principles associated with capital assets. In particular, the calculation of gain or loss, holding period requirements, tax rates, and special rules were reviewed. The overriding principal of taxation in the capital asset arena is that all realized gains will be recognized, but may be taxed at different rates depending on the character of the gain. The rules introduced in this chapter will apply to most capital transactions, but there are some additional rules that may alter the results illustrated here. These additional rules deal with deferral of gain, or in some instances, nonrecognition of gain, and will be discussed in detail in Chapter 12.

# Key Terms

**Amount Realized** - The amount of money plus the value of property received in the sale or exchange of an asset.

**Capital Asset** - All assets that are not specified as ordinary income assets or Section 1231 assets.

**Disallowed Losses** - Losses that are realized, but are not permitted to be recognized, including losses on the sale of personal use assets (except for casualty losses), losses on the subsequent sale of property gifted or sold to a related party when its FMV is less than the original owner's adjusted basis, and losses associated with a wash sale.

**Holding Period** - The period for which a taxpayer owns an asset.

**Long-Term Holding Period** - Occurs when an asset is owned by a taxpayer for more than one year.

**Realization Event** - Generally occurs when an asset has been sold or exchanged. Gains on capital assets are subject to tax only when there has been both a realization event and a recognition event.

**Recognition Event** - Occurs when a realized gain is included on a taxpayer's income tax return. All realized gains are generally recognized unless a provision in the Code provides otherwise.

**Sale or Exchange Requirement** - One of the requirements for a gain to be subject to income tax.

**Short-Term Holding Period** - Occurs when an asset is owned by a taxpayer for one year or less.

**Unrecaptured Section 1250 Depreciation** - The portion of gain that is attributable to non-recaptured depreciation (up to the amount of straight-line depreciation deductions taken) for depreciable real estate that is taxed at 25 percent upon the sale or exchange of the property.

**Wash Sale** - Occurs when a taxpayer sells a stock or security at a loss and purchases substantially identical stock or securities within a 30 day period before or after the sale.

1. What is a capital asset?

2. When are gains on capital assets subject to tax?

3. Give several examples of events that satisfy the sale or exchange requirement of a realization event.

4. How is the gain or loss on the sale of a capital asset calculated?

5. What is the amount realized?

6. How is the amount realized affected when the parties transfer debt in addition to cash or other property?

7. What is the default recognition rule?

8. Define a disallowed loss and give several examples of a disallowed loss.

9. Why are losses on the sale of personal use assets disallowed?

10. How is a realized loss affected when the property is sold or gifted to a related party?

11. What is a wash sale and what are the tax consequences of a wash sale?

12. What is the difference between a short-term and long-term holding period?

13. How is the holding period determined for property received from a decedent's estate?

14. How is the holding period determined for nonbusiness bad debts?

15. What is the difference between the tax rate for short-term capital gains and long-term capital gains?

16. What are the two exceptions to the 15% maximum capital gains tax rate?

17. What items generally qualify as collectibles and what is the tax treatment of these items?

18. How do capital gains affect the AMT?

19. How are net capital gains determined?

20. What is the limitation on the recognition of capital losses?

1. Which of the following statements concerning the taxation of assets is correct?

    a. Ordinary income may qualify for a special 15% rate.

    b. Capital gains are always taxed at the taxpayers marginal tax rate.

    c. Gains on Section 1231 assets are taxed at ordinary rates, and losses are taxed a capital rates.

    d. Gains on Section 1231 assets are taxed at long-term capital gains tax rates, and losses are taxed at ordinary income tax rates.

2. Which of the following statements correctly identifies when income is subject to tax?

    a. Capital gains must be realized before they can be recognized on a tax return.

    b. Realization occurs when the gain on an asset is reflected on the taxpayer' return.

    c. As a general rule, realized gains are not recognized unless a provision in the IRC requires recognition.

    d. Recognition occurs when an asset has been sold or exchanged.

3. All of the following are included in the amount realized upon disposition of an asse EXCEPT:

    a. The cash received.

    b. The fair market value of property received in the exchange.

    c. A transfer of obligation to pay debt from the seller to the buyer.

    d. The taxpayer's adjusted basis.

4. John sold a farm with an adjusted basis of $200,000 to Isaac for $500,000. In addition Isaac agreed to assume the note on the farm, which had a remaining balance of $50,000 Not taking into consideration any potential depreciation recapture, what is the amoun realized in the transaction from John's perspective?

    a. $200,000.

    b. $350,000.

    c. $500,000.

    d. $550,000.

5. Christopher purchased a home in Connecticut three years ago for $300,000. He had been working in Connecticut for the past 10 years. Yesterday, his employer decided to transfer him to the San Diego, California branch, effective next month. Unfortunately, the real estate market has weakened over the past few years, and Christopher is only able to sell his home for $270,000. Which of the following statements correctly identifies his tax consequences of the sale?

    a. Christopher is not permitted to deduct the loss on his income tax return.

    b. Christopher's loss will be reflected as a long-term capital loss on his tax return.

    c. Christopher's loss will be reflected as a short-term capital loss on his tax return.

    d. Christopher will recognize an ordinary loss of $30,000.

6. Harold purchased a home for $300,000 three years ago, and was recently transferred by his employer to an office located across the country. He made $20,000 of improvements to the residence, but if he sold the home today, he would only be able to receive $260,000 for the house due to a weak real estate market. Instead of selling the home and realizing a loss, Harold rents the home to a tenant. What is Harold's basis for depreciation purposes?

    a. $260,000.

    b. $270,000.

    c. $300,000.

    d. $320,000.

7. Andy gave 1,000 shares of Meade Productions, Inc. to his son, John. Andy paid $15,000 for the shares, and they were worth $12,000 at the time he transferred them to John. If John sells the shares for $13,000, how much capital has the family lost on a permanent basis?

    a. $1,000.

    b. $2,000.

    c. $13,000.

    d. $15,000.

8. As the end of the year was approaching, Edward reviewed his stock portfolio and decided to sell his holdings in Windsor Industries on December 28th of Year 1. The shares were purchased two years ago. His basis in the shares was $20,000 and the market value of the shares was $18,000. Edward wanted to use the $2,000 loss to help him minimize taxes for Year 1. On January 10th, Year 2, Windsor Industries announced new initiatives, and Edward has second guessed his decision to sell the shares in the company. He buys back the 1,000 shares for $17,000 on January 11th. Assuming that Edward had no other capital transactions for Year 1, what is the impact of this transaction on Edward's Year 1 income tax return?

    a. The sale of Windsor Enterprises will not impact Edward's AGI for Year 1.

    b. The sale will generate a $2,000 short-term capital loss that will reduce Edward's AGI.

    c. The sale will generate a $2,000 long-term capital loss that will reduce Edward's AGI.

    d. The sale will trigger an ordinary loss deduction for $2,000.

9. As the end of the year was approaching, Edward reviewed his stock portfolio and decided to sell his holdings in Windsor Industries on December 28th of Year 1. The shares were purchased two years ago. His basis in the shares was $20,000 and the market value of the shares was $18,000. Edward wanted to use the $2,000 loss to help him minimize taxes for Year 1. On January 10th, Year 2 Windsor Industries announced new initiatives, and Edward has second guessed his decision to sell the shares in the company. He buys back the 1,000 shares for $17,000 on January 11th. What is Edward's basis in the shares after he buys them back on January 11th?

    a. $0.

    b. $17,000.

    c. $19,000.

    d. $20,000.

10. On September 20 of Year 1, Henry purchased 1,000 shares of Tudor Enterprises, Inc. common stock for $25,000. He sold the shares for $35,000 on September 20 of Year 2. Which of the following statements correctly identifies the tax consequences of this transaction?

    a. Henry will recognize a $10,000 ordinary gain on the sale.

    b. Henry will recognize a $10,000 short-term capital gain on the sale.

    c. Henry will recognize a $10,000 long-term capital gain on the sale.

    d. Henry will not be required to recognize the gain on the transaction.

11. Jacob loaned $10,000 to his close friend and business associate, Luke, so that Luke could start up a home-based business. Jacob is not in the business of money lending. Luke paid interest on the loan annually at a rate of 6 percent, and the principal was due in a lump sum on maturity 10 years later. After 4 years of making payments, Luke informs Jacob in year 5 that he has filed for bankruptcy and will not be able to make any future interest ($500 per year) or principal payment, causing the debt to become wholly worthless. What is the income tax consequence for Jacob?

    a. Jacob will recognize an ordinary income tax loss of $10,000 for Year 5.

    b. Jacob will recognize an ordinary income tax loss of $10,500 for Year 5.

    c. Jacob will recognize a short-term capital loss of $10,000 for Year 5.

    d. Jacob will recognize a long-term capital loss of $10,000 for Year 5.

12. Ken is in the 33% marginal tax bracket. He recently sold a coin for $110,000 that he had purchased eight years earlier for $10,000. How much federal income tax will Ken pay on this transaction?

    a. $15,000.

    b. $25,000.

    c. $28,000.

    d. $33,000.

13. Michael is in the 33% marginal tax bracket. He recently sold a gold coin for $12,000 that he purchased six months ago for $2,000. How much federal income tax will Michael pay on this transaction?

    a. $1,500.

    b. $2,500.

    c. $2,800.

    d. $3,300.

14. Kevin engaged in several capital transactions this year. He had a short-term capital gain of $400; a short-term capital loss of $600; a long-term capital gain of $800 and a long-term capital loss of $500. How will Kevin report these items on his income tax return?

    a. Kevin will report a net short-term capital gain of $100.

    b. Kevin will report a net long-term capital gain of $100.

    c. Kevin will report a net short-term capital loss of $200 and a net long-term capital gain of $300.

    d. Kevin will report ordinary income of $100.

15. Ajamu, a single individual, was an investor in a company that became worthless this year and suffered an $80,000 capital loss. He initially invested in the company five years ago when it was starting up, and the company had $500,000 in initial capitalization. Assuming that Ajamu had no other capital transactions this year and has $100,000 of ordinary income, how much will his AGI for this year decline as a result of this loss?

   a.  $3,000.

   b.  $50,000.

   c.  $53,000.

   d.  $80,000.

# Quick Quiz Explanations

### Quick Quiz 11.1

1. False. Capital gains are subject to tax when there has been both a realization event and a recognition event.
2. True.
3. True.
4. False. If a wash sale results in realization of a loss, the loss is not currently recognized and is temporarily disallowed. The unrecognized loss will be added to the basis of the replacement securities, so that on sale of the replacement securities, recognition will occur. Therefore, losses associated with a wash sale are not permanently disallowed.

### Quick Quiz 11.2

1. False. To achieve long-term treatment, the asset must be held for *more than* one year. As a practical matter, this means that a long-term holding period begins if the asset is held for a year and one day. If the asset is sold in the current year on the same day it was purchased in the prior year, the result is a short-term holding period.
2. False. The maximum long-term capital gains tax rate is 15 percent. This rate applies for anyone in the 25 percent or higher ordinary marginal income tax bracket. For those taxpayers in the 10 percent or 15 percent ordinary marginal income tax bracket, the capital gains tax rate is lowered to five percent.
3. False. Unrecaptured Section 1250 depreciation applies to depreciable real estate used in a trade or business or for the production of income.
4. True.

### Quick Quiz 11.3

1. False. The taxpayer has a net $15,000 long-term capital gain. The character (short-term or long-term) of a net gain or loss is determined by the larger net number, not taking into account whether it was a gain or loss.
2. True.
3. True.

# Business Assets

## INTRODUCTION

In prior chapters, we examined the general rules governing the taxation of property transactions and how the sale of capital assets is treated within the income tax system. In that discussion, we learned that there are three types of assets in our tax system – ordinary income assets, capital assets, and Section 1231 assets. The prior chapter dealt with capital assets, which is the catch-all asset category. For income tax purposes, everything in the world is a capital asset except the items detailed in Section 1221. For financial planning purposes, remember that everything in the world is a capital asset except "ACID" (accounts receivable, copyrights, inventory, and depreciable property or real property used in a trade or business). This chapter deals with the taxation of the other two asset categories for income tax purposes – ordinary income assets and Section 1231 assets.

## ORDINARY INCOME ASSETS

**Ordinary income assets** generate gains that will be taxed at ordinary income tax rates. If an individual engages in business by selling goods or services, for example, the income generated from that business activity will be taxed at ordinary income tax rates.

Out of the items that are not defined as capital assets under IRC Section 1221 (ACID), the first three items (accounts receivable, copyrights, and inventory) are ordinary income assets. These items simply represent future or earned ordinary income and the Code will not allow taxpayers to change the characterization of that income simply by changing the nature of the asset.

*Key Concepts*

**Underline/highlight the answers to these questions as you read:**

1. Identify ordinary income assets.

2. Define what kind of income is generated by the sale or exchange of an ordinary income asset.

You may recall that accounts and notes receivable, the first type of ordinary income asset, represent ordinary income receipts that are deferred into the future. The sale of a good or service in the ordinary course of business generates ordinary income. Transforming that transaction from cash to an account or note receivable does not change the ordinary income nature of the transaction.

**Inventory** is held for resale to customers in the normal course of business and therefore generates ordinary income upon sale. Consequently, any inventory held by a business is considered an ordinary income asset. Copyrights, musical compositions[1], and artistic creations in the hands of the author are ordinary income assets because they are a form of inventory. An artist creates a masterpiece with the intent of selling it and is therefore creating inventory for his business, which is the creation and sale of pieces of art. Recall from our discussion in earlier chapters, however, that copyrights, musical compositions, and artistic creations in the hands of someone other than the creator may not be considered ordinary income assets. Rather, they may be considered collectibles or capital assets.

When a taxpayer generates ordinary income, it is taxed at ordinary income tax rates, which, under current law, are the highest tax rates in our income tax system. If a loss is incurred in the conduct of business, the loss may be deducted as an ordinary loss and will be available to reduce ordinary income without limitation. In some cases, the ordinary loss may be carried back to prior tax years to generate an income tax refund for those years or may be used to offset future income. While the generation of losses is not the objective of a well-run business, if a loss does occur, a taxpayer would prefer to have that loss treated as an ordinary loss so that he or she can make full, current use of that loss to offset other income. In the realm of ordinary income assets, speaking strictly from an income tax perspective, ordinary losses are good and ordinary gains are bad. Ordinary gains are subject to income tax at the taxpayer's highest marginal rate.

## Quick Quiz 12.1

**Highlight the answer to these questions:**

1. Notes receivable are ordinary income assets.
   a. True
   b. False

2. The deductibility of ordinary losses is limited to $3,000 per year.
   a. True
   b. False

True, False.

## SECTION 1231 ASSETS

Since the first three exceptions to the definition of a capital asset are defined as ordinary income assets, the only asset left, depreciable property or real property used in a trade or business, is a **Section 1231 asset**. One additional requirement is necessary for an asset to be classified as a Section 1231 asset. In addition to being depreciable property or real property used in a trade or

---

1. Effective May 17, 2006 through February 8, 2011, there is a temporary regulation that allows an election by musicians for musical compositions or copyrights. The taxpayer may elect for tax treatment of the composition or copyright as a capital gain or loss upon the sale of the property instead of inventory subject to ordinary income.

business, the owner of the asset must have a long-term holding period for the asset (the owner must have held the asset for more than one year).

There are two types of property that receive 1231 treatment - personal property and real property. Depreciable tangible personalty used in a trade or business or held for production of income purposes is sometimes referred to as Section 1245 property. Section 1250 property is depreciable real property used in a trade or business or held for the production of income.

From our discussion of basis rules, we know that any asset used in a trade or business that is expected to decline in value qualifies for depreciation deductions. Stated differently, for depreciation to apply, the asset must be a trade or business asset or an asset used for production of income. Personal assets cannot be depreciated. Trade or business assets and production of income assets subject to depreciation are Section 1231 assets.

## BENEFITS OF SECTION 1231

The significance of Section 1231 is that once an asset is categorized as a Section 1231 asset, gains generated from the sale of the asset are treated as capital gains for income tax purposes, and losses generated from the sale of the asset are treated as ordinary losses for income tax purposes. Therefore, gains will qualify for favorable long-term capital gains tax rate, and losses will not be subject to the limitations that typically apply to capital assets.

**Key Concepts**

Underline/highlight the answers to these questions as you read:

1. Identify Section 1231 assets.

2. Explain the advantages of Section 1231.

3. Describe the disadvantages of Section 1231.

Gains on Section 1231 assets will qualify for the long-term capital gains tax rate because the owner of the asset held the asset for more than one year (recall that a long-term holding period is required for an asset to be categorized as a Section 1231 asset). Losses, however, will be treated as ordinary losses and will therefore not be subject to the net $3,000 loss limitation that applies to capital losses.

Section 1231 gives the taxpayer the best of both worlds tax treatment. Given a choice, taxpayers would characterize all of their losses as ordinary losses (because no limitation applies and the higher ordinary tax rate generates a greater tax benefit from the loss), and all of their gains as capital gains (to take advantage of the lower capital gains tax rates). Section 1231 gives the appearance of tax nirvana, but further considerations, discussed below, will explain why Congress has given taxpayers what appears to be the best of both worlds tax treatment.

The tax treatment also differs depending on whether an individual (acting as a sole proprietor, partner, S-corporation shareholder, or member of an LLC) or a C corporation generates the Section 1231 gain or loss.

If an individual generates a Section 1231 gain, the favorable, lower capital gains rate (currently 15 percent) will apply. If the taxpayer is in the 15 percent ordinary income tax bracket or lower, the zero percent capital gains tax rate will apply. Conversely, if a loss is generated, the taxpayer can write off that loss as an ordinary loss, without limitation, against other forms of income for the current, and possibly, past tax years (due to the imposition of the look-back provision). Had the loss been categorized as a capital loss and not a Section 1231 loss, the net $3,000 loss limitation rule would have applied, and the loss may not be fully utilized by the taxpayer in the current tax year.

C corporations do not qualify for the lower, favorable tax rate on capital gains. Therefore, the generation of a Section 1231 gain will not result in a tax benefit for the corporation, since it pays the same tax rates on its ordinary income and capital gains. If a corporation generates a Section 1231 loss, however, the loss will be considered an ordinary loss and may be deducted in full against other income (or carried back if the carryback rule is invoked). For corporations, capital losses may not be deducted against other forms of income – capital losses can only be used to offset capital gains. Categorizing an asset as a Section 1231 asset, therefore, allows the corporation to recognize losses without having to generate capital gains to offset them.

Entities that are taxed as pass-through vehicles, such as partnerships, limited liability companies, limited liability partnerships, and S corporations "pass-through" their tax results to their owners, so the individual, not the corporate rules, apply. Owners of these entities qualify for the special 15 percent capital gains tax rate on their Section 1231 gains and can deduct the losses from ordinary income.

## THE CATCH – DEPRECIATION RECAPTURE

Section 1231 looks almost too good to be true, and it would be if the analysis ended at asset categorization. Once the taxpayer has categorized the asset as a Section 1231 asset, however, an additional consideration must be addressed – **depreciation recapture**. Depreciation recapture is the inclusion of a portion or all of the previously taken depreciation deductions in the current year's income as ordinary income, if a gain is associated with the sale or exchange of property. For example, if tangible property is purchased for $20,000, depreciated by $12,000 to a book value of $8,000, and later sold for $10,000, then $2,000 of the $12,000 depreciation will be recaptured as ordinary income.

In order to be classified as a Section 1231 asset, the asset must be "depreciable property or real property used in a trade or business." When an asset that was subject to depreciation is sold, depreciation recapture may apply. In order to understand depreciation recapture, it is first necessary to review the purposes and uses of depreciation.

The purpose of depreciation is to allow individuals and businesses who use property in productive use or in a trade or business to recoup their capital investment in the asset over the useful life of that asset. This is accomplished by reducing ordinary income with depreciation deductions, representing a return of capital, so that capital can be reinvested to generate more income.

In an ideal world, the depreciation expense deduction that would be claimed by the taxpayer each year would be the actual decline in value of the asset, representing the portion of the asset that was used up in that tax year. Doing this, however, would be impractical – it would require every asset to be appraised each year, followed by a comparison of the end-of-year value to the beginning-of-year value simply to ascertain the current year depreciation deduction.

Recognizing that it would be unreasonable to require taxpayers to do this for each asset they own to justify their depreciation deductions, Congress came up with a statutory scheme for depreciation. In this statutory scheme, each asset acquired is classified into a specific class life based on the rules set forth in the Code. The class lives of various types of assets were discussed in Chapter 10. Once the class life is determined, a statutorily defined deduction is taken for depreciation of the asset, regardless of the actual decline in value of the asset from year to year. Since the depreciation deduction is not based on the actual decline in the value of the asset, it could be thought of as an estimate based on averages calculated by the IRS. This real world approach that generates an estimated depreciation value is convenient and relatively easy to apply, but generates tax results that do not directly correspond to the ideal world, where depreciation deductions would be based on the actual decline in the value of each asset each year.

Many assets purchased for use in a trade or business are completely used up in that trade or business and are disposed of when their useful life expires. Often, upon disposal, the taxpayer receives nothing in return for the asset. When this happens, the taxpayer has recouped his or her capital investment in that asset over the useful life of that asset, and there is nothing to be concerned about for income tax purposes.

## Quick Quiz 12.2

**Highlight the answer to these questions:**

1. Depreciable personal property used in a trade or business is Section 1231 property.
   a. True
   b. False

2. Gains from the sale of Section 1231 property are always taxed as ordinary income.
   a. True
   b. False

3. Losses on Section 1231 property are treated as ordinary losses.
   a. True
   b. False

4. Depreciation recapture applies upon the sale or exchange of a capital asset.
   a. True
   b. False

True, False, True, False.

**EXAMPLE 12.1**

Randy, a highly sought after financial planner in his community, opened a new office several years ago. He purchased computers for use by his staff, and the computers were classified as 5-year class life property. Over the next 6 years, Randy and his staff used the computers, at which time they were replaced with new machines. The old machines were disposed of at no value. Randy was able to recover his capital investment in the computers over the 5-year class life through the depreciation expense deductions, which reduced ordinary income. He received nothing upon disposition of the computers. Consequently, the disposal of the computers does not trigger any income tax consequences.

When an asset is sold, a realization event occurs for income tax purposes and the gain or loss must be calculated. When the asset sold is a Section 1231 asset, the taxpayer may breathe a sigh of relief, since he or she knows that the optimal tax treatment will be afforded. Before that can happen, however, depreciation recapture must be taken into consideration. Section 1231 treatment only applies to the economic (i.e., ideal world) results of the transaction. To get to the economic result to which we apply Section 1231, we must first make sure that the depreciation deduction taken in the real world (by using the estimated value based on the class life of the asset) equals the depreciation deduction that would have been taken in the ideal world (where the deduction equals the actual decline in value each year).

From a planning standpoint, whenever a Section 1231 asset is sold, the taxpayer must first consider the possibility of depreciation recapture before the "best of both worlds" tax treatment can apply. The ONLY time that depreciation recapture is an issue is when the asset has been categorized as a Section 1231 asset. If the asset is a capital asset or an ordinary income asset, depreciation recapture does not apply.

## RECAPTURING DEPRECIATION ON PERSONAL PROPERTY (SECTION 1245)

 *Key Concepts*

**Underline/highlight the answers to these questions as you read:**

1. Explain depreciation recapture for personal property.

2. Identify the four possible results of Section 1245.

The sole purpose of depreciation recapture is to ensure that, when an asset is sold, the taxpayer receives his or her capital back tax-free – no more, and no less. The rules for depreciation recapture differ depending upon the type of property sold.

If personal property used in a trade or business is sold, IRC Section 1245 sets forth the rules for depreciation recapture.

Personal property, as used in Section 1245, means anything that is not real property. The depreciation recapture provisions of the Code (Sections 1245 and 1250) use the legal definition of property. **Real property** is land and anything permanently attached to the land (such as buildings, trees, and swimming pools). **Personal property** is everything else in the world (i.e., anything other than land or things permanently attached to the land). Used in this context, personal property does not imply that the property is used for personal, as opposed to business, purposes. As described in Chapter 3, both real and personal property can be used in one of three ways for income tax purposes: (1) personal use (for example, your personal residence and furnishings); (2) production of income use (for example, the residential rental building and furnishings that you own); or (3) trade or business use (for example, the office building and furniture used in your trade or business). Note that one exception to this rule includes silos and greenhouses, which are real property, but are also Section 1245 property.

When personal property is used in a trade or business or for the production of income, it is depreciable and therefore becomes a Section 1231 asset. When that property is sold, Section

1245 governs the depreciation recapture rules. Simply put, Section 1245 states that when personal Section 1231 property is sold, depreciation is recaptured as ordinary income to the extent of the gain. This means that before capital gains treatment can result under Section 1231, all of the depreciation which was previously deducted from ordinary income must be recaptured or subjected to ordinary income tax. Since depreciation was taken as a deduction against ordinary income, when depreciation is recaptured, it will be treated as an addition to ordinary income.

There are only four potential outcomes under Section 1245. While the numbers in each example or problem will change, if you can identify which of the four scenarios applies, you will be able to quickly ascertain the tax consequences. The best way to describe the application and purpose of Section 1245 is by example.

## RESULTS OF SECTION 1245

EXHIBIT 12.1

| If Sale Price: | AR = AB* | AR < AB* | AR > AB* and Gain < Depreciation | AR > AB* and Gain > Depreciation |
|---|---|---|---|---|
| Tax Consequences | No gain or loss, no depreciation recapture, **no tax consequences.** | Resulting loss is always treated as an **ordinary loss**. | Section 1245 treats the gain as **ordinary gain**. | **Gain up to amount of depreciation** taken is treated as **ordinary gain** under Section 1245. **Gain in excess of depreciation** taken is treated as **capital gain** under Section 1231. |
| Resulting from Economics | Accounting estimate of depreciation equals economic reality | Not enough depreciation was taken | Too much depreciation was taken. | Too much depreciation was taken and the asset appreciated. |
| Illustrated By | Example 12.3 | Example 12.4 | Example 12.5 | Example 12.6 |
| *AR = Amount Realized; AB = Adjusted Basis | | | | |

When faced with a property transaction question, the first step is to ascertain what type of asset you are dealing with.

EXAMPLE 12.2

Kasey, a high school student, decided to apply some of the principles of entrepreneurship that have been taught to him by his uncle and opened the KB Lawnmowing Service, LLC. Kasey purchased several pieces of equipment and hired his high school friends to help him provide lawn mowing services. One of the items Kasey purchased when he opened the business two years ago was a riding mower. He paid $1,500 for the mower and has since taken $400 in depreciation deductions. Due to the popularity of the company's service, Kasey now needs a heavy-duty mower and has decided to sell his existing riding mower to purchase the heavy-duty equipment. Kasey would like to know what the tax consequences of such an action would be and has asked you, his financial advisor, for advice.

In this case, Kasey purchased a lawnmower for use in his trade or business and has been taking depreciation deductions on that asset. Consequently, the asset is a Section 1231 asset. The asset Kasey proposes to sell is a lawnmower, which is a personal asset (it is not land or anything permanently attached to the land), so the depreciation recapture rule that applies will be found in Section 1245.

The next step is to calculate the gain or loss on the sale of the asset.

EXAMPLE 12.3 Continuing with the previous example, what is the tax result if Kasey sells the riding lawnmower for $1,100?

In this example, the amount realized will be $1,100. To calculate gain or loss, we must subtract Kasey's adjusted basis in the asset from the amount realized in the transaction. Kasey's adjusted basis is his cost basis of $1,500 reduced by his depreciation deductions (or return of capital) of $400. Kasey's adjusted basis, therefore, is $1,100.

Using the formula for calculating gain or loss found in IRC Section 1001, we find the following:

| | |
|---|---|
| Amount Realized | $1,100 |
| Less: Adjusted Basis | $1,100 |
| Equals: Gain or (Loss) | $0 |

Since there is no gain or loss, there is no depreciation recapture, and no tax consequence.

For obvious reasons, out of the four possible outcomes for the sale of personal Section 123 property, Example 12.3 illustrates the simplest result – the example where there are no ta consequences. This result will rarely occur in real life, but it does illustrate an important point This example shows what happens when the "ideal world" and the "real world" meet. Despite th fact that the depreciation deductions taken by Kasey were formula amounts based on averages se forth in the Internal Revenue Code, the actual depreciation in the asset equaled the amount o depreciation claimed for income tax purposes. Kasey purchased the asset for $1,500. He receivec his entire investment back through depreciation deductions ($400) and proceeds from the sale o the asset ($1,100). Since there is no gain or loss, there is no tax consequence. Example 12.:

illustrates the rare occurrence where the conventions used in the Code to calculate depreciation deductions match the actual decline in the value of an asset perfectly.

Since the convergence of the "ideal" and "real" world is rare, it is in the other three situations (as illustrated by Examples 12.4, 12.5, and 12.6) that the impact of the depreciation recapture rule for personal property is demonstrated. Note that the preliminary steps of categorizing the asset and identifying the potential type of depreciation recapture is presumed in each of the following three examples.

**EXAMPLE 12.4**

What is the tax result if Kasey sells the riding lawnmower for $1,000? Using the formula for calculating gain or loss found in IRC Section 1001, we find the following:

| | |
|---|---|
| Amount Realized | $1,000 |
| Less: Adjusted Basis | $1,100 |
| Equals: Gain or (Loss) | ($100) |

Kasey's adjusted basis is the same as in Example 12.3, and equals his cost basis reduced by the actual depreciation deductions he claimed on the asset. In this instance, Kasey has realized a $100 loss on the sale. Consequently, there is no depreciation recapture, since Section 1245 requires recapture of the depreciation to the extent of the *gain*. Strictly applying the language of Section 1245, no recapture occurs, but the lawnmower was a Section 1231 asset. Section 1231 states that losses on the sale of Section 1231 assets are treated as ordinary losses, so Kasey's $100 loss will be treated as an ordinary loss. The loss will not be reported as a capital transaction and will most likely be used to offset other ordinary income.

The application of the Code in this instance simply allows Kasey to recoup all of his capital investment tax-free. Capital is income that was already subject to tax, so it should be returned to the owner without assessing an additional tax. Depreciation is supposed to permit a taxpayer who uses an asset in productive use in a trade or business or for the production of income to receive his or her capital back, tax-free, as the value of the asset is used up in the activity. In this circumstance, the actual decline in value of the asset while it was being used in Kasey's trade or business was:

| | |
|---|---|
| Cost Basis | $1,500 |
| Less: Amount Realized | $1,000 |
| Decline in Value | $500 |

Although the actual decline in value was $500, Kasey was only allowed to deduct $400 of depreciation on the asset due to the asset-life rules set forth in the Code. Therefore, Kasey was not permitted to deduct the actual decline in value. If he would have been allowed a deduction based on the actual decline in the value of the asset, his depreciation deduction would have equaled $500, but the deduction contrived by application of the Code was only $400. If Kasey had taken the full decline in value as a depreciation deduction, it would have offset ordinary income from his business operations. Therefore the only fair thing to do in this instance is to allow Kasey to take an ordinary loss deduction of $100 for the additional amount of depreciation he experienced but could not take due to IRC conventions. This is why Section 1231 treats losses on the sale of Section 1231 assets as ordinary losses. If a Section 1231 asset is sold at a loss, the taxpayer did not take enough depreciation over the holding period of the asset, and, upon sale, the additional depreciation (represented by the loss on the sale) may be taken as an ordinary deduction so that the ideal and real worlds meet. After the application of Section 1231, Kasey has received all of his capital back tax-free: $400 through depreciation deductions, $1,000 upon sale of the asset, and $100 of Section 1231 loss, which is really a catch-up depreciation deduction. Example 12.4 is summarized in Exhibit 12.2.

| EXHIBIT 12.2 | SUMMARY OF EXAMPLE 12.4 |
|---|---|

| | IDEAL WORLD | REAL WORLD | NOTES FOR REAL WORLD |
|---|---|---|---|
| Cost Basis | $1,500 | $1,500 | |
| Amount Realized | $1,000 | $1,000 | |
| Actual Decline | $500 | $500 | |
| Depreciation Deduction | $500 | $400 | Specified by IRC |
| | | | |
| Amount Realized from Sale | $1,000 | $1,000 | |
| Adjusted Basis | $1,000* | $1,100 | $1,500 cost basis less $400 depreciation |
| Gain/Loss | $0 | ($100) | Ordinary Loss |
| Totals After 1231 Treatment: | | | |
| Depreciation | $500 | $500 | $400 per tax code plus $100 per Section 1231 |
| * The adjusted basis of the asset in the "Ideal World" example is calculated as follows: Cost Basis $1,500 – Depreciation Deduction $500 = $1,000. | | | |

Example 12.4 demonstrates the following rule: If a Section 1231 asset is sold at a loss, the resulting loss will ALWAYS be treated as an ordinary loss. Section 1231 allows this treatment so that the taxpayer can deduct the actual depreciation in the value of the asset from his or her ordinary business income.

| EXAMPLE 12.5 | What is the tax result if Kasey sells the riding lawnmower for $1,200? Using the formula for calculating gain or loss found in IRC Section 1001, we find the following: |
|---|---|

| Amount Realized | $1,200 |
|---|---|
| Less: Adjusted Basis | $1,100 |
| Gain/(Loss) | $100 |

In Example 12.5, Kasey has a gain on the sale of the lawnmower, which is personal property and a Section 1231 asset. Section 1231 states that all gains on the sale of Section 1231 assets are capital gains, but before we can apply that rule we have to consider depreciation recapture under Section 1245. Section 1245 states that depreciation is recaptured as ordinary income to the extent of the gain. In this example, the depreciation Kasey took on the lawnmower was $400. His gain on the sale was $100. Since the gain of $100 is less than the depreciation taken, the gain is treated as an ordinary gain. Kasey would not be able to get capital gains treatment on any of the gain until all of the depreciation was recaptured.

In Example 12.3, we saw the rare occurrence of the real world and ideal world merging. In Example 12.4, the sale of a personal Section 1231 asset resulted in a loss because not enough depreciation was taken on the asset during the holding period. Example 12.5 illustrates what happens when too much depreciation is taken on the asset for tax purposes.

In Example 12.5, the real decline in the value of the asset can be calculated as follows:

| Cost Basis | $1,500 |
|---|---|
| Less: Amount Realized | $1,200 |
| Decline in Value | $300 |

Nevertheless, Kasey claimed $400 in depreciation deductions as specified in the Code. Recall that the purpose of the depreciation recapture rules is to ensure that the appropriate amount of depreciation is taken at the time that the asset is sold. If too much depreciation was allowed under the Code, the "excess depreciation" must be added back to ordinary income so that the depreciation deduction in the real world equals the depreciation deduction in the ideal world. Example 12.5 is summarized in Exhibit 12.3.

EXHIBIT 12.3 **SUMMARY OF EXAMPLE 12.5**

| | IDEAL WORLD | REAL WORLD | NOTES FOR REAL WORLD |
|---|---|---|---|
| **Cost Basis** | $1,500 | $1,500 | |
| **Amount Realized** | $1,200 | $1,200 | |
| **Actual Decline** | $300 | $300 | |
| **Depreciation Deduction** | $300 | $400 | Specified by IRC |
| | | | |
| **Amount Realized from Sale** | $1,200 | $1,200 | |
| **Adjusted Basis** | $1,200* | $1,100 | $1,500 cost basis less $400 depreciation |
| **Gain/Loss** | $0 | $100 | Ordinary Income |
| **Totals After 1231 Treatment:** | | | |
| **Depreciation** | $300 | $300 | $400 per tax code less $100 "recaptured" per Section 1231 |

\* The adjusted basis of the asset in the "Ideal World" example is calculated as follows:
Cost Basis $1,500 – Depreciation Deduction $300 = $1,200.

As Example 12.5 illustrates, when a personal Section 1231 asset is sold at a gain, the gain (to the extent of the prior depreciation deduction taken) is treated as ordinary income to offset the excess depreciation taken over the holding period. The excess depreciation in Example 12.5 is $100 ($400 depreciation taken - $300 actual decline in value of the asset). The only way to reflect the actual amount of depreciation on the asset for income tax purposes is to reverse out $100 of the depreciation deduction by adding it to ordinary income. Once this is done, a $300 depreciation deduction results, and Kasey recoups the remaining portion of his capital, $1,200, from the amount realized in the sale.

Example 12.5 illustrates the application of the following rule: Whenever a personal Section 1231 asset is sold at a gain, compare the gain to the depreciation taken over the life of the asset. If the gain is equal to or less than the depreciation taken, Section 1245 treats the gain as ordinary income (and it is sometimes referred to as a Section 1245 gain).

**EXAMPLE 12.6**

What is the income tax result if Kasey sells the riding lawn-mower for $1,700? Using the formula for calculating gain or loss found in IRC Section 1001, we find the following:

| | |
|---|---|
| Amount Realized | $1,700 |
| Less: Adjusted Basis | $1,100 |
| Gain/(Loss) | $600 |

## Quick
## Quiz 12.3

**Highlight the answer to these questions:**

1. If a Section 1231 asset is sold at a loss, the resulting loss is always a capital loss.
   a. True
   b. False

2. When a personal Section 1231 asset is sold at a gain, the gain is always ordinary income.
   a. True
   b. False

False, False.

In Example 12.6, Kasey has a gain on the sale of the lawnmower, which is personal property and a Section 1231 asset. Section 1231 states that all gains on the sale of Section 1231 assets are capital gains, but before we can claim that for tax purposes we have to consider depreciation recapture under Section 1245. Section 1245 states that depreciation is recaptured as ordinary income to the extent of the gain. In this example, the depreciation Kasey took on the lawnmower was $400. His gain on the sale was $600. Since the gain of $600 is greater than the depreciation taken, the gain is split into two pieces. Under Section 1245, the gain to the extent of depreciation taken is ordinary income. Kasey took $400 of depreciation on the lawnmower, so the first $400 of the gain is treated as ordinary income. The remaining portion of the gain, $200, qualifies for capital gains tax treatment because the lawnmower is a Section 1231 asset. In this case, since Kasey recaptured all of the depreciation deductions that he had taken, the remaining gain is taxed as a capital gain under Section 1231.

In real life, it is rare to come across a situation like that illustrated in Example 12.6. Most assets that are purchased for productive use in a trade or business or for production of income are wasting assets – they tend to wear out as we use them to generate income. The very fact that they wear out is what justifies the depreciation deduction, which allows the taxpayer to recoup his capital as the asset is being used up to generate income. In some instances, this gain situation may occur, however. Using the facts of the current case, assume that the manufacturer of the lawnmower Kasey purchased made such good mowers that they eventually drove themselves out of business because nobody ever needed to purchase a replacement mower. Eventually, the company could not sell enough to justify continued operations, so it closed. Nevertheless, the reputation of the company's product persists, and people in the market for mowers will now pay a premium for one produced by that company, since they anticipate that it will be the last mower they will have to purchase in their lifetime. In fact, Kasey was able to sell the mower for more than he paid for it, despite the fact that he had claimed depreciation deductions. A more realistic example of this phenomenon is real estate. Depreciation deductions are allowed on the structures purchased, even though, over time, those structures may tend to appreciate in value.

In Example 12.6, observe that there is no decline in the value of the asset, so in the ideal world, no depreciation deductions should have been taken. The IRC, however, allowed Kasey to take depreciation deductions on the mower totaling $400. Since Kasey took those depreciation deductions against ordinary income, when he sells the mower for more than the amount he paid for it he will have to recapture the depreciation deductions by treating the first $400 of the gain as ordinary income. The remaining portion of the gain is capital gain, since the mower is a Section 1231 asset. Example 12.6 is summarized in Exhibit 12.4.

| EXHIBIT 12.4 | SUMMARY OF EXAMPLE 12.6 |
|---|---|

| | IDEAL WORLD | REAL WORLD | NOTES FOR REAL WORLD |
|---|---|---|---|
| Cost Basis | $1,500 | $1,500 | |
| Amount Realized | $1,700 | $1,700 | |
| Actual Decline | $0 | $0 | |
| Depreciation Deduction | $0 | $400 | Specified by IRC |
| | | | |
| Amount Realized from Sale | $1,700 | $1,700 | |
| Adjusted Basis | $1,500* | $1,100 | $1,500 cost basis less $400 depreciation |
| Gain/Loss | $200 | $600 | $400 depreciation recapture plus $200 capital gain |
| Totals After 1231 Treatment: | | | |
| Depreciation | $0 | $0 | $400 per tax code less $400 "recaptured" per Section 1231/1245 |
| * The adjusted basis of the asset in the "Ideal World" example is calculated as follows: Cost Basis $1,500 – Depreciation Deduction $0 = $1,500. | | | |

Another way of viewing the application of Section 1245 in this case is to compare the original cost basis (purchase price) of the asset to the sale price of the asset. If the sale price exceeds the purchase price, the difference between the sale price and purchase price will be treated as capital gain, and all of the depreciation will be recaptured as ordinary income under IRC Section 1245.

In fact, the only time that part of the gain on a Section 1231 asset will achieve capital gains treatment under Section 1245 is when the sales price exceeds the cost basis.

Example 12.6 illustrates the following rule: Whenever a personal Section 1231 asset is sold at a gain, compare the gain to the depreciation taken on the asset. If the gain exceeds the depreciation taken, Section 1245 treats the depreciation taken as ordinary income (and it is sometimes referred to as a Section 1245 gain), and Section 1231 treats the remaining gain as capital gain.

The examples above illustrate why asset categorization is important and should always be the first step you consider when looking at the taxation of property transactions. If you characterize the asset as a personal Section 1231 asset (personal asset used in a trade or business or for the production of income), there are four possible tax results, three of which are likely to occur in the real world that differ from the results that would apply if the asset was categorized as a capital asset or ordinary income asset. While the numbers can change, every transaction resulting from the sale of Section 1231 personal property must fall into one of these four categories. Examples 12.3 - 12.6 are summarized in Exhibit 12.5.

**SUMMARY OF EXAMPLES 12.3 - 12.6**                                    EXHIBIT 12.5

|  | EXAMPLE 12.3 | EXAMPLE 12.4 | EXAMPLE 12.5 | EXAMPLE 12.6 |
|---|---|---|---|---|
| **Amount Realized** | $1,100 | $1,000 | $1,200 | $1,700 |
| **Adjusted Basis** | $1,100 | $1,100 | $1,100 | $1,100 |
| **Gain/(Loss)** | $0 | ($100) | $100 | $600 |
| **Tax Impact** | None | Ordinary loss | Ordinary gain (Gain is less than depreciation taken) | Part ordinary gain ($400), part capital gain ($200) (Gain is more than depreciation taken) |
| **Economic Reality** | Depreciation estimate was perfect. | Taxpayer took too little depreciation. | Taxpayer took too much depreciation. | Taxpayer took too much depreciation and asset appreciated. |

# RECAPTURING DEPRECIATION TAKEN ON REAL ESTATE (SECTION 1250)

## Key Concepts

**Underline/highlight the answers to these questions as you read:**

1. Identify the property affected by Section 1250.

2. Define "unrecaptured Section 1250 depreciation."

If real property used as a Section 1231 asset is sold, the recapture rules are a bit different. IRC Section 1250 governs recapture of depreciation on real property that is a Section 1231 asset. Under Section 1250, depreciation taken on real estate that exceeds straight-line depreciation is recaptured at ordinary income tax rates.

Under current law, all depreciation on real estate is taken on a straight-line basis. If the real estate is used for residential purposes, the recovery period is 27½ years, and if the real estate is used as commercial property, the recovery period is 39 years. Real estate that was purchased and placed in service for production of income or business use before 1981 or after 1986 must be depreciated on a straight-line basis. From 1981 to 1986, depreciation was taken under the accelerated methods (not straight-line) over a 15 to 19 year period. Unlike accelerated depreciation, **straight-line depreciation** allows the owner to take a constant, monthly allowance for depreciation during the recovery period. Since Section 1250 requires only the depreciation taken in excess of straight-line depreciation to be recaptured at ordinary income rates, real property placed in service before 1981 or after 1986 will not be affected by Section 1250.

Between 1981 and 1986, real estate placed in service for business or production of income use qualified for accelerated depreciation. **Accelerated depreciation** allowed the owner of the property to front-load the depreciation deductions so that more of the depreciation deduction was taken in the early years, and less was taken in later years. When real property that was depreciated on an accelerated basis is sold, Section 1250 requires the excess depreciation, calculated by subtracting straight-line depreciation from accelerated depreciation, to be recaptured at ordinary income tax rates.

Section 1250 is quickly becoming a non-issue for income tax planning purposes. First, only real property that could have been depreciated on an accelerated basis will be affected by the provisions of Section 1250. Since 1986, real estate does not qualify for accelerated depreciation. Second, as time goes by, the total depreciation taken on an accelerated basis approaches the total depreciation taken on a straight-line basis, so that at the end of the recovery period, the total cumulative depreciation deductions taken by the taxpayer under either system are the same. By 2016, the recovery period for almost all pieces of real property for which accelerated depreciation could have been claimed will have expired, at which time the imposition of Section 1250 will not result in additional tax revenue. It is a rare occurrence where a planner will have to deal with Section 1250 for planning purposes, but it can still be an issue for compliance purposes. Section 1250 recapture applies to real property that has been owned for more than one year. If real property is held for one year or less, all depreciation taken (whether straight-line or accelerated) is subject to recapture rules.

Nevertheless, if a planner has a client who is planning to sell a piece of real estate that was used in a trade or business or for the production of income (a Section 1231 asset), and that real estate was depreciated on an accelerated basis, the gain to the extent that accelerated depreciation exceeds straight-line depreciation will be recovered at ordinary income rates.

Prior to the Taxpayer Relief Act of 1997 (TRA 97), all capital gains were taxed at 28 percent. TRA 97 lowered the maximum capital gains tax rate to 20 percent (now 15 percent as a result of EGTRRA 2001) for most assets (zero percent for those taxpayers in the 15 percent or lower marginal tax bracket), but imposed a higher capital gains tax rate in two situations. The first exception to the current 15 percent rate, covered in Chapter 11, imposed a 28 percent capital gains tax rate on collectibles. The second exception was a 25 percent capital gains tax rate on "unrecaptured Section 1250 depreciation."

Based on our discussion above, it is clear that depreciation in excess of straight-line depreciation is recaptured at ordinary income rates due to the imposition of Section 1250. Consequently, the depreciation that is not recaptured under Section 1250, otherwise known as the "unrecaptured Section 1250 depreciation," is straight-line depreciation. The recapture of straight-line depreciation taken after 1997 on real estate used as a Section 1231 asset is taxed at a flat 25 percent rate upon the sale or exchange of the asset.

To the extent that the gain on the sale of real Section 1231 property exceeds the total depreciation taken (both the "excess" portion from accelerated depreciation and the straight-line portion), any remaining gain is taxed at capital gains tax rates, as set forth in IRC Section 1231. An alternative way of looking at this is that capital gain tax treatment is limited to the excess of the sale price over the original purchase price.

From a planning standpoint, whenever a real Section 1231 asset is sold, the gain will be treated as shown in Exhibit 12.6.

## TREATMENT OF GAIN UNDER SECTION 1231 FOR REAL PROPERTY

EXHIBIT 12.6

| | |
|---|---|
| 1. | The lesser of the gain or the difference between depreciation taken and straight-line depreciation will be taxed as ordinary income. (This is recapture of "excess" depreciation under Section 1250). |
| 2. | If the gain exceeds the amount in (1), the lesser of the remaining gain or the straight-line depreciation taken on the property will be taxed at 25% (this is the "unrecaptured Section 1250 depreciation"). |
| 3. | Any gain in excess of (1) and (2) is taxed at capital gains tax rates (5% or 15%). |

EXAMPLE 12.7

Ryan owns a residential apartment building, and has grown weary of the constant management issues that confront him concerning the property. He purchased the property for $750,000, and took depreciation deductions of $400,000. Straight-line depreciation on the property would have been $375,000. What are the tax consequences if Ryan sells the property for $2,000,000?

As a threshold matter, we are dealing with a residential apartment building, which Ryan used for the production of income. Therefore, the asset is real property used for production of income, is depreciable, and is therefore classified as a Section 1231 asset. Since the property is real estate, the depreciation recapture rules that apply will be found under Section 1250.

Before we can apply the depreciation recapture rules, however, we must first calculate the gain or loss generated on the sale. Using the formula for calculating gain or loss found in IRC Section 1001, we find the following:

| Amount Realized | $2,000,000 |
|---|---|
| Less: Adjusted Basis | $350,000 |
| Gain/(Loss) | $1,650,000 |

Adjusted basis, in this example, equals the cost basis of $750,000 less the depreciation deductions actually taken of $400,000.

The next step is to determine if any of the gain will be taxed at ordinary rates under Section 1250. In this case, Ryan took $400,000 of depreciation deductions, and straight-line depreciation would have been $375,000. Therefore, Ryan took $25,000 in excess depreciation deductions. This amount is recaptured as ordinary income under Section 1250.

$25,000 of the $1,650,000 gain has been characterized, leaving $1,625,000. The next step is to subject the unrecaptured Section 1250 depreciation to a tax rate of 25%. Ryan took total depreciation deductions of $400,000 and $25,000 of that amount was recaptured under Section 1250. Consequently, the $375,000 of straight-line depreciation was not recaptured under Section 1250, and will be taxed at 25%.

The remaining portion of the gain, $1,250,000 will be taxed at capital gains tax rates (in this case, at 15%) due to the imposition of Section 1231. These steps can be summarized as follows:

| Sale Price $2,000,000<br>Adjusted Basis ($350,000)<br>Gain $1,650,000 | Total Gain = $1,650,000 | | |
|---|---|---|---|
| **Amount of Gain** | (1st) $25,000 | (2nd) $375,000 | (3rd) $1,250,000 |
| **Treatment of Gain** | Ordinary Income | 25% Tax Rate | Capital Gain |
| **Explanation of Calculation and Treatment** | Excess Depreciation (Total Depreciation less Straight-Line Depreciation) | Straight-Line Depreciation at 25% | Excess Gain under Section 1231 as capital gain |

| | | |
|---|---|---|
| Purchase Price | $750,000 | |
| Less Depreciation | (400,000) | (Straight-line depreciation would be $375,000) |
| **Adjusted Basis** | **$350,000** | |
| | | |
| Sales Price | $2,000,000 | |
| Less Adjusted Basis | (350,000) | |
| Gain | $1,650,000 | |
| Less OI | (25,000) | (Recapture accelerated vs. straight-line) |
| Less 25% Tax Rate | (375,000) | (For straight-line depreciation) |
| **Section 1231 Gain** | **$1,250,000** | (Note: 1231 Gain is sales price > Purchase price) |

EXAMPLE 12.8

Jody sold a residential apartment building that he owned for $800,000. He originally purchased it for $800,000. Jody had taken a total of $400,000 in depreciation deductions over the period he held the real estate. The straight-line depreciation would have been $375,000. What is the tax result of Jody's total gain of $400,000?

Jody's excess depreciation is $25,000 (total depreciation of $400,000 less straight-line depreciation of $375,000), which is subject to recapture under Section 1250 at ordinary income tax rates. The remainder of the gain ($375,000) is taxed at 25% because it represents the straight-line depreciation. There is no capital gain (1231).

**EXAMPLE 12.9**

Assume the same facts as Example 12.8, except that Jody sells the property for $850,000. What are the tax consequences?

As noted above, the first $25,000 will be recaptured under Section 1250 at ordinary income tax rates. The $375,000 of Jody's $450,000 gain will be taxed at 25%, since this amount represents unrecaptured Section 1250 depreciation. The remaining $50,000 is Section 1231 capital gain.

In Example 12.8, none of the gain qualifies for the favorable 15 percent capital gains tax rate. That rate can only apply once all of the depreciation is recaptured under Section 1250 or as an "unrecaptured Section 1250 gain."

An alternative way of approaching the taxation of real Section 1231 assets is to consider that the difference between the amount realized and the original purchase price equals the capital gain.

## Quick Quiz 12.4

**Highlight the answer to these questions:**

1. Real property placed in service after 1986 will not be subject to depreciation recapture.
   a. True
   b. False

2. Unrecaptured Section 1250 depreciation is equal to straight-line depreciation.
   a. True
   b. False

True, True.

In Example 12.7, Ryan paid $750,000 for the property and he sold it for $2,000,000. The difference of $1,250,000 is taxed as a capital gain under Section 1231.

The next step is to split the depreciation taken on the property into two pieces: the straight-line depreciation that is taxed at 25 percent and the depreciation in excess of straight-line that is taxed at ordinary income tax rates.

In Example 12.7, straight-line depreciation would have been $375,000. This amount will be taxed at 25 percent as "unrecaptured Section 1250 depreciation." Excess depreciation was $25,000 ($400,000 of depreciation taken, less straight-line depreciation of $375,000), which will be taxed at ordinary rates as recapture under Section 1250.

# THE IMPACT OF TAXATION OF BUSINESS ASSETS ON PLANNING

As we have seen, the depreciation recapture rules for business assets affect the tax rate that applies to gains on the sale of business assets. In addition, depreciation recapture must be considered when engaging in various types of tax planning. When assets subject to recapture are transferred, potential depreciation may be transferred as well. Depreciation recapture may be an issue with any of the following types of transfers, which will be discussed briefly below:

1. Gifts
2. Nontaxable exchanges
3. Transfers at death
4. Charitable contributions
5. Installment sales

## GIFTS

When property is gifted, the value of the gift is the fair market value of the property on the date of the gift, but the basis in the hands of the donee is the donor's basis, adjusted for any gift tax paid. Gifts are said to have a "carryover" basis, since the donor's basis is transferred to the donee. The same is true for depreciation recapture. If the donor held the asset for productive use in a trade or business or for the production of income, and depreciation was allowed on the asset, any recapture potential will carry over to the donee. If the gifted asset was personal property, the donee's gain, to the extent of the depreciation taken, will

*Key Concepts*

**Underline/highlight the answers to these questions as you read:**

1. Identify the types of transfers affected by depreciation recapture.

2. Explain the 5-year lookback rule.

be taxed at ordinary income tax rates. If the gifted asset was real property, the excess depreciation to the extent of the gain will be taxed at ordinary income tax rates, the straight-line depreciation will be taxed at 25 percent, and any remaining gain will be taxed at capital gains tax rates. Understanding that depreciation recapture will carry over may impact the donor's choice of the appropriate property to give to the donee.

**EXAMPLE 12.10**

Randy purchased a desk for use in his business. The desk cost $500 and Randy has taken $250 of depreciation deductions on the desk. Randy's son, Reilly, is in college and needs a desk to work on his course assignments. Randy transfers the desk to Reilly when the fair market value of the desk is $260. No gift tax was paid on the transfer. After Reilly finishes college, he sells the desk to his roommate for $300. What is Reilly's gain, and how is it taxed?

Since Randy gifted the desk to Reilly, and the desk had a fair market value in excess of Randy's basis ($250 = $500 cost basis - $250 in depreciation), Reilly has a carry-over basis in the desk of $250. Reilly also has a carry over of the potential depreciation recapture (requiring the first $250 of gain to be taxed at ordinary income tax rates). When Reilly sells the desk, the gain can be calculated as follows:

| | |
|---|---|
| Amount Realized | $300 |
| Less: Adjusted Basis | $250 |
| Gain/(Loss) | $50 |

In Reilly's hands, the desk is a capital asset, which is normally subject to capital gains tax treatment. Simply looking at this fact might lead one to conclude that the gain will be taxed as a capital gain. Despite the fact that the asset is a capital asset in Reilly's hands, he received the asset as a gift from Randy, who held the asset, at least for a time, as depreciable personal property used in a trade or business. The potential recapture, therefore, carried over with the gift. Since Reilly's gain is less than the potential recapture amount, the entire gain is taxed at ordinary income tax rates.

Given these facts, this result could be good or bad. If Reilly does not have substantial income (he was a college student and was not working full time), he may be in a low ordinary income tax bracket, perhaps 10 percent. If Randy sold the desk for $300 he would have had to pay 25 percent on the gain (his marginal ordinary income tax rate), but Reilly would only have to pay 10 percent on that same gain. From a family income tax planning perspective, gifting the desk was a wise strategy, since it reduced the income taxes that the family, as a group, has to pay. If Reilly was in the 35 percent ordinary income tax bracket (and the sale would generate tax at a higher rate), Randy may want to consider selling the desk and paying the tax himself (at the lower rate), and giving either the proceeds of the sale, or another asset, to Reilly.

## NONTAXABLE EXCHANGES

When property is exchanged for another property in a nontaxable exchange (such as a Section 1031 like-kind exchange, or a Section 1033 involuntary conversion), potential recapture on the asset carries over to the replacement property.

**EXAMPLE 12.11**

Keegan owns an office building that was destroyed by a hurricane. He purchased the office building for $450,000, had taken straight-line depreciation deductions of $150,000, and the fair market value of the property at the time it was destroyed was $800,000. Keegan received a check from his property insurance carrier for $800,000 and immediately purchased a replacement office building for $850,000. Keegan's basis in the original building was $300,000 (equal to $450,000 cost basis less $150,000 in depreciation deductions), and he had potential unrecaptured Section 1250 depreciation in the original building of $150,000 (all depreciation had been straight-line). Since Keegan meets the requirements for nonrecognition of gain for an involuntary conversion, his adjusted basis in the old building, plus the potential recapture, will carry over to the new building. In this example, Keegan also put another $50,000 into the property, which will add to his basis (he paid $850,000 for the new property, but only received $800,000 from the insurance company – the other $50,000 had to come out of his after-tax income, so this amount increases his basis). Therefore, Keegan's basis in the new property is $350,000; he has $150,000 of potential unrecaptured Section 1250 depreciation from the old office building that will be taxed at 25% when he disposes of the replacement property in a taxable exchange.

Exchanging properties in like-kind exchanges under IRC Section 1031 or in involuntary conversions under IRC Section 1033 does not extinguish the potential depreciation recapture that applies to the original property. As depicted in the prior example, it postpones the potential recapture until a taxable exchange occurs.

## TRANSFERS AT DEATH

One way for a taxpayer to eliminate potential depreciation recapture, although not something that planners would normally recommend to a client, is to die. Property transferred through the estate of a decedent receives a step to fair market value in basis under IRC Section 1014, and, by receiving the step to fair market value, depreciation recapture is extinguished. This fact can, in some planning situations, be valuable to consider. In the estate planning process, to the extent that a client will have assets included in his gross estate, holding those assets at death will eliminate the depreciation recapture. Other assets, not subject to recapture, could be used as gifts since all the gain will be taxed as capital gain. Structuring the transfer of the estate in this way may minimize the overall tax (income, estate, and gift tax combined) that is paid by a family on the transfer of their assets.

## CHARITABLE CONTRIBUTIONS

Potential depreciation recapture may also affect the size of the charitable deduction a taxpayer may take for gifts of property to qualified charitable organizations. When a gift of tangible personal property or real estate is made to a charitable organization that will use that property in their charitable function, the deduction for income tax purposes is generally the fair market value of the property on the date of the gift. When property subject to depreciation recapture is given to a charitable organization, and the deduction would otherwise be based on the fair market value of the property, the fair market value (and the resulting income tax deduction) is reduced by the potential depreciation recapture on the asset. By making this adjustment, the government is indirectly recouping the depreciation taken by limiting the donor's income tax deduction.

<table>
<tr><td></td><td>**EXAMPLE 12.12**</td></tr>
</table>

Prior to his retirement, Rennie owned and operated his own business (a sole proprietorship) for 30 years. He purchased a building for the business many years ago for $500,000. Out of the purchase price, $50,000 was allocated to land and the remaining $450,000 to the building, which was fully depreciated. When he closed the business, he kept title to the building personally. An animal rights charity has been looking for a new headquarters, and thinks that Rennie's building would be ideal. Rennie has no use for the building, and has always supported animal rights charities, so he decides to give the building to the charity. The value of the building at the time of the transfer is $1,500,000. Normally, Rennie would receive a $1,500,000 charitable deduction for such a transfer, but this building has potential depreciation recapture, so the charitable deduction is reduced by the amount of the recapture. Rennie can take a charitable deduction of $1,050,000 ($1,500,000 FMV - $450,000 depreciation taken) for the gift he made to the animal rights charity.

## INSTALLMENT SALES

Another planning device that can be affected by potential depreciation recapture on property is the installment sale (including, for our discussion here, regular installment sales, self-cancelling installment notes (SCINs), and private annuities). Note that on October 18, 2006, the Treasury and the IRS proposed regulations pertaining to the taxation of private annuities under Section 72. These regulations, which have not been finalized, state that the seller's entire gain or loss must be recognized when an annuity is acquired in exchange for a substantially appreciated asset, rather than ratably over the seller's life expectancy. If these regulations are finalized without changes, they will have a significant detrimental effect on the utility of private annuities in financial planning.

When an asset is transferred, gain is usually realized and recognized. Recognition of gain on the sale of an asset in return for an installment note can typically be deferred under the installment reporting provisions of the Code. For example, if an asset is sold today, but equal principal payments plus interest will be made over a ten year period, the seller can elect to report 10 percent ($1/10^{th}$) of the gain he realized this year in each of the next ten years instead of paying tax on all of the gain in the year that realization occurs. Installment reporting of the gain is helpful from a planning standpoint, since it allows the taxpayer to smooth his or her income, report less of a gain in each year during the installment period (possibly staying in a lower tax bracket) and defer tax. The installment reporting provisions, however, do not apply to potential ordinary income depreciation recapture on Section 1231 property sold in return for an installment note. The ordinary income depreciation recapture, to the extent of the gain, must be recognized in the year the gain is realized. The unrecaptured Section 1250 depreciation may be deferred under the installment reporting provisions, but all of the gain in each installment reporting year will be taxed at the 25 percent unrecaptured Section 1250 rate until all of the straight-line depreciation has been recaptured. Once the portion of the gain representing unrecaptured Section 1250 depreciation has been fully reported, any remaining gain will be taxed at the 15 percent or five percent rate.

EXAMPLE 12.13

After 20 years of managing his rental apartment building, John decides it is time to retire from the landlord business – he no longer enjoys the hassles of management. He purchased the apartment building for $1,500,000 and $100,000 of the purchase price was allocated to land. Total depreciation taken on the building was $1,000,000 and straight-line depreciation would have been $800,000. The apartment complex is now worth $8,100,000. John has agreed to sell the apartment complex to a young business associate, Ryan, for its current fair market value to be paid in an installment note over 20 years. The note carries an interest rate that matches the IRS published rate necessary to avoid gift-loan status. While John will be able to defer some of his gain over the 20 year period, the potential ordinary income depreciation recapture cannot be deferred. In this case, the potential ordinary income recapture is $200,000 ($1,000,000 in total depreciation less straight-line depreciation of $800,000). Despite the presence of the installment sale, John will be required to pay ordinary income tax on $200,000 in the year of sale. As John receives payments over the first several years, the gain portion of each payment will be treated as the unrecaptured Section 1250 gain ($800,000) and will be taxed at 25% until the tax on the unrecaptured Section 1250 gain has been paid in full. Any remaining gain will be taxed at the 15% (or 5%, if applicable) rate.

Observe that this could create a cash flow problem for John. If Ryan only pays 1/20$^{th}$ of the purchase price plus interest to John this year as the installment agreement requires, but John has to pay up to 35 percent on $200,000 in the year of sale, plus tax on the interest and a 25 percent tax on part of the unrecaptured Section 1250 gain received in this year's installment payment as the IRC requires. John may not have the cash flow from the sale necessary to meet the tax obligation. This could be an important consideration when recommending the structure of an installment sale to a client. For example, if a cash flow problem would occur, Ryan could make a down payment equal to (at a minimum) the tax that will be due as a result of the recapture. This would ensure that John does not have to utilize his other assets to pay the income tax on the sale.

As these examples illustrate, depreciation recapture is important in ways other than simply determining which tax rate applies. In many cases, the presence of potential depreciation recapture may change the planning options that may be optimal for the client. Understanding why this happens and the situations to be aware of allow planners to give better, more competent advice to their clients.

## THE 5-YEAR LOOKBACK RULE

The astute planner, having learned how the depreciation recapture rules work, might have spotted a potential planning opportunity. Similar to the netting process for capital gains, all Section 1231 gains for the year are added together, and all Section 1231 losses for the year are added together, and losses are offset against gains to determine the net Section 1231 gain or loss. Since gains are treated as capital gains (subject, at least for individuals, to a lower tax rate) and losses are treated as ordinary losses, it would be beneficial, from a tax planning standpoint, to generate Section 1231 losses in one year, and Section 1231 gains in another year. By separating gains and losses, all of the gains would be taxed at the lower capital gains tax rate in one year, and all of the losses will generate a tax benefit at a higher ordinary tax rate in another year instead of offsetting each other.

Unfortunately, Congress thought of this planning option as well. To help combat this form of planning, there is a **5-year lookback rule** that applies for Section 1231. The lookback rule states that a net Section 1231 gain in the current tax year (which should be taxed at capital gains tax rates) will be taxed at ordinary income tax rates to the extent of any unrecaptured Section 1231 losses claimed during the last five years. The lookback rule forces the netting process to occur over a five year period. Note that for the lookback rule to apply, (1) there must be a net Section 1231 gain in the current year, and (2) there must have been Section 1231 losses in the last five years. If there is a net Section 1231 loss in the current year, or if there are no unrecaptured Section 1231 losses in the last five tax years, the lookback rule does not apply.

### Quick Quiz 12.5

**Highlight the answer to these questions:**

1. Depreciation recapture carries over to the donee for gifted property.
   a. True
   b. False

2. Only like-kind exchanges and not involuntary conversions are affected by the carryover of depreciation recapture.
   a. True
   b. False

3. Depreciation recapture is extinguished upon death.
   a. True
   b. False

4. Under the 5-year lookback rule, net Section 1231 losses in the current tax year will be subject to ordinary loss rules to the extent of the 1231 gains of the last five years.
   a. True
   b. False

True, False, True, False.

Colin has a Section 1231 gain for the current year (2011) of
$15,000. In prior years, Colin had the following net Section
1231 transactions:

| | Year | Net Section 1231 Transaction |
|---|---|---|
| | 2010 | $4,000 Section 1231 Loss |
| 5-Year Lookback Period | 2009 | $2,000 Section 1231 Loss |
| | 2008 | No Section 1231 Transactions |
| | 2007 | No Section 1231 Transactions |
| | 2006 | No Section 1231 Transactions |
| | 2005 | $8,000 Section 1231 Gain |
| | 2004 | $2,000 Section 1231 Gain |

Colin would have to recognize $6,000 of his 2011 gain as
ordinary income since in 2010 and 2009 he had Section
1231 losses. The remaining $9,000 of Colin's Section 1231
gain ($15,000 - $6,000) would be treated as a Section 1231
capital gain.

EXAMPLE 12.14

# Key Terms

**5-Year Lookback Rule** - A net Section 1231 gain in the current tax year (which should be taxed at capital gain tax rates) will be taxed at ordinary income tax rates to the extent of any unrecaptured Section 1231 losses claimed during the last five years.

**Accelerated Depreciation** - Allows the owner of an asset to front-load the depreciation deductions so that more of the depreciation deduction is taken in the early years, and less is taken in later years.

**Depreciation Recapture** - Special tax consequences that occur when a Section 1231 asset is sold for an amount greater than its adjusted basis.

**Inventory** - Assets that are held for resale to customers in the normal course of business.

**Ordinary Income Assets** - Accounts receivable, copyrights, and inventory, all of which generate gains that will be taxed at ordinary income tax rates.

**Personal Property** - Any property that is not real property.

**Real Property** - Land and anything permanently attached to it (such as buildings, trees, and swimming pools).

**Section 1231 Asset** - Depreciable property or real property used for productive use in a trade or business or for the production of income.

**Straight-Line Depreciation** - A depreciation method under which the purchase price of the asset, less its expected salvage value, is divided by the expected useful life of the asset to determine the annual depreciation deduction.

**Unrecaptured Section 1250 Depreciation** - The portion of gain that is attributable to non-recaptured depreciation (up to the amount of straight-line depreciation deductions taken) for depreciable real estate that is taxed at 25 percent upon the sale or exchange of the property.

# DISCUSSION QUESTIONS

1. What is an ordinary income asset?

2. Describe the taxation of ordinary income assets.

3. What is a Section 1231 asset?

4. What is the advantage of being classified as a Section 1231 asset?

5. How are corporations affected by Section 1231 assets?

6. What is the purpose of depreciation recapture?

7. What is the difference between real and personal property?

8. What are the four possible results when personal property used in a trade or business or for the production of income is sold?

9. How is depreciation recaptured under Section 1250?

10. What is the difference between straight-line depreciation and accelerated depreciation?

11. Why is Section 1250 not as important to tax planning as it used to be?

12. What is unrecaptured Section 1250 depreciation and how is it taxed?

13. How is gain from the sale of a Section 1231 real property asset treated?

14. How is depreciation recapture affected when a Section 1231 asset is gifted?

15. How is depreciation recapture affected by a nontaxable exchange of a Section 1231 asset?

16. What happens to potential depreciation recapture when the owner of a Section 1231 asset dies?

17. How can a charitable contribution be affected by potential depreciation recapture?

18. What are the tax consequences when a Section 1231 asset is sold in an installment sale?

19. How can potential depreciation recapture create a cash-flow problem for the seller of an asset in an installment sale?

20. Describe the impact of the 5-year lookback rule.

1.  Rennie, a 12 year old middle school student, just agreed to take over a paper route to deliver Newsday to his extended neighborhood on a daily basis. To deliver the papers, he purchases a new bike with a specially equipped basket to transport the papers each morning. How is the bike classified for income tax purposes?

    a.  The bike is an ordinary income asset.

    b.  The bike is a capital asset.

    c.  The bike is a Section 1231 asset.

    d.  The bike is a personal asset.

2.  Which of the following statements properly describes the income tax treatment of asset sales?

    a.  The sale of classic movies on DVDs by Movie Emporia (a retail movie distributor) will generate income subject to capital gains tax.

    b.  The sale of Big Box Mart stock by an individual investor generates ordinary income.

    c.  The sale of a desk used for 10 years in a business at a loss will result in a capital loss.

    d.  The sale of a typewriter used for 10 years in a trade or business at a gain (after recapturing any depreciation) will generate a capital gain.

3.  Custom Framing, Inc., a C corporation, sold a machine used to cut wood used in their picture frames for $2,700. They originally purchased the machine for $2,000 and had taken $1,400 in depreciation deductions. When the company that made the machine went out of business, the machine became a collectors item, and the company sold the machine for more than they paid for it to purchase other equipment. Which of the following statements concerning the tax impact of the sale transaction is correct?

    a.  The company will recognize $2,100 of ordinary income.

    b.  The company will recognize $1,400 of ordinary income.

    c.  The company will recognize a capital gain of $700 that will be taxed at the favorable long-term capital gains tax rate.

    d.  The company will recognize a short-term capital gain of $700.

4. James sold a lathe that was used in his business operations (that he ran as a sole proprietor) for $5,000. The machine was originally purchased for $12,500 and James had claimed $6,000 of depreciation deductions over a span of four years. What will James include on his tax return as a result of the sale?

    a.  $1,500 capital loss.

    b.  $1,500 ordinary loss.

    c.  $7,500 long-term capital loss.

    d.  $7,500 ordinary loss.

5. Twenty years ago, William purchased a desk that he used in his law practice for $8,000. The desk has been fully depreciated and when he retired, William sold the desk to Harry for $3,000. What will William include on his tax return as a result of the sale?

    a.  $3,000 taxed at ordinary rates.

    b.  $3,000 taxed at long-term capital gains rates.

    c.  $5,000 ordinary loss.

    d.  $5,000 long-term capital loss.

6. Ten years ago, Chelsea purchased an industrial sewing machine used in her business, Froggie Dolls, LLC, for $10,000. She had taken depreciation deductions of $9,000 over this period, and sold the machine for $12,000 after she purchased a new state-of-the-art industrial sewing machine. How much ordinary income will Chelsea recognize on the sale of the machine?

    a.  $0.

    b.  $1,000.

    c.  $9,000.

    d.  $11,000.

7. Mark purchased an apartment building for $1.5 million several years ago. He has claimed depreciation deductions totaling $750,000 during the holding period, and straight-line depreciation would have been $700,000. How much ordinary income will Mark recognize for income tax purposes if he sells the building for $2 million?

    a.  $0.

    b.  $50,000.

    c.  $1,150,000.

    d.  $1,200,000.

8. Michael purchased an apartment building for $2 million several years ago. He has claimed depreciation deductions totaling $950,000 during the holding period, and straight-line depreciation would have been $900,000. What is Michael's long-term capital gain (taxed at the favorable 15% capital gains tax rate) that will be recognized for income tax purposes if he sells the building for $2.5 million?

    a.  $0.

    b.  $50,000.

    c.  $500,000.

    d.  $1,450,000.

9. Rich sold his home this year, and is preparing his income tax return. He sold the house for $650,000. It was purchased for $250,000 20 years ago after he was married to Mary Jane, and they have used it as their principal residence ever since. Rich ran a business from the home, using one room regularly and exclusively for business purposes. Over the 20 year holding period, Rich had claimed $15,000 of depreciation deductions on the home office. What portion of the gain, if any, will be subject to income tax?

    a.  $0.

    b.  $15,000.

    c.  $385,000.

    d.  $400,000.

10. John owns a building in a blighted downtown area that, until recently, served as his principal residence. He originally purchased the building for $200,000. When he moved out and converted the building to an office building, the fair market value of the building was $150,000. What is John's basis for purposes of determining his depreciation deductions on the building?

    a.  $0.

    b.  $100,000.

    c.  $150,000.

    d.  $200,000.

11. After 35 years in business for herself, Daisy retired and closed the doors of her office. She gave her desk to her niece, Molly, who recently completed her degree in a similar field and is opening up her practice. Daisy originally paid $12,000 for the desk, and it was fully depreciated by the time she gave it to Molly. Molly used the desk for two years, and then sold it (for $6,000) when she decided to redecorate her office. How will Molly treat the proceeds from the sale of the gift for income tax purposes?

    a. Since Molly received the desk as a gift, there is no need to pay taxes on the proceeds from the sale.

    b. Since the desk was given to Molly when it was fully depreciated, it is "loss property," and the $6,000 proceeds will not be taxable because it fell between Molly's gain basis and loss basis in the transaction.

    c. Molly will recognize $6,000 of ordinary income on the sale.

    d. Molly will recognize $6,000 of long-term capital gain on the sale.

12. Earlier this month, Jennifer's apartment house in California was completely destroyed by a forest fire that found its way into the city. She had originally purchased the apartment house for $500,000, and had claimed $100,000 in straight-line depreciation deductions. At the time of the fire, the fair market value of the building was $750,000 and the insurance company gave her a check for the full value. Instead of building on the same site, about 6 months after the fire Jennifer used the insurance proceeds to purchase a new apartment building for $800,000. Within two weeks of purchasing the new building, a real estate investor offered to purchase the new building from her for $1 million. If Jennifer sells the new building to the investor, what is her long-term capital gain for income tax purposes?

    a. $0.

    b. $200,000.

    c. $450,000.

    d. $550,000.

13. During her working years, Marge ran an antique sales and appraisal service which was very successful in the local community. When she retired, she kept some of the display cases in order to display her own collections in her home. The display cases were originally purchased for the business at a cost of $15,000 and were fully depreciated by the time Marge retired. Marge died last month, and the display cases were valued in her estate at $8,000. If Marge's daughter, Kelly, inherits the display cases, and sells them for $8,500 two months after Marge's death, what is the income tax treatment on the sale?

    a. $500 ordinary income.

    b. $500 long-term capital gain.

    c. $500 short-term capital gain.

    d. $8,000 ordinary income.

14. Prior to returning to work for a Fortune 500 company, Randy ran a consulting practice. He had purchased office furniture and modern artwork for his office, and when he closed the practice to return to the corporate world, he kept the furniture and art, which was fully depreciated. One painting that he used in the business has recently gone up substantially in value. Randy purchased it for $400, depreciated it fully, and the fair market value of the painting is now $10,000. The local art museum has an exhibit dedicated to the artist that created the painting, and since he was not using the art, Randy donated the painting to the museum. What is Randy's charitable deduction (without taking into consideration any ceiling imposed by his contribution base) for income tax purposes?

    a. $0.

    b. $400.

    c. $9,600.

    d. $10,000.

15. Edward was winding down his business, and sold a machine that he used in the business to a former business associate, Philip, for $40,000. The machine originally cost $100,000 and Edward's adjusted basis in the machine was $20,000. The sale agreement requires Philip to pay for the machine in five equal annual installments, plus interest. Which of the following statements concerning this transaction is correct?

    a. Out of each installment sale payment, the gain on the sale will be treated as ordinary income until all of the depreciation recapture has been accounted for.

    b. Edward may recognize any depreciation recapture over the term of the installment note in the same proportion as recognition of gain.

    c. Edward must recognize all depreciation recapture immediately as ordinary income.

    d. The installment reporting provisions exempt Edward from ordinary income tax treatment of depreciation recapture.

# Quick Quiz Explanations

### Quick Quiz 12.1

1. True.
2. False. Unlike a capital loss, an ordinary loss may be taken against ordinary income and is not subject to limitations.

### Quick Quiz 12.2

1. True.
2. False. Gains on Section 1231 assets will qualify for the long-term capital gains tax rate because the owner of the asset held the asset for more than one year (recall that a long-term holding period is required for an asset to be categorized as a Section 1231 asset).
3. True.
4. False. Depreciation recapture applies upon the sale or exchange of a Section 1231 asset.

### Quick Quiz 12.3

1. False. If a Section 1231 asset is sold at a loss, the resulting loss is treated as an ordinary loss.
2. False. When personal property is used in a trade or business or for the production of income, it is depreciable and therefore becomes a Section 1231 asset. When that property is sold, Section 1245 governs the depreciation recapture rules. Simply put, Section 1245 states that when personal Section 1231 property is sold, depreciation is recaptured as ordinary income to the extent of the gain. Gain in excess of depreciation is then taxed at capital gain rates.

### Quick Quiz 12.4

1. True.
2. True.

### Quick Quiz 12.5

1. True.
2. False. Exchanging properties in like-kind exchanges under IRC Section 1031 or in involuntary conversions under IRC Section 1034 does not extinguish the potential depreciation recapture that applies to the original property.
3. True.
4. False. The lookback rule states that a net Section 1231 gain in the current tax year (which should be taxed at capital gains tax rates) will be taxed at ordinary income tax rates to the extent of any Section 1231 losses claimed during the last five years.

# Nontaxable Exchanges

## 13

## INTRODUCTION

The 16th Amendment to the U.S. Constitution gives Congress the power to tax all income "from whatever source derived." Generally speaking, any accretion to wealth is income. A mere increase in the value of an asset, however, does not subject the wealth accretion to current taxation. As illustrated in prior chapters, a realization event (which fixes the taxpayer's gain or loss) must occur before the income is recognized on the taxpayer's income tax return.

While Congress has the power to tax all income when realized, in some cases it has chosen to defer collection of the tax on that income. In other cases, Congress has decided not to tax the income at all. This chapter reviews those circumstances where a realized gain or loss is deferred, as well as the rare circumstances where gains are exempt from income tax. Even though gains from these realization events could be subject to current tax, Congress has chosen to defer or forgo that revenue for public policy reasons. Usually, the decision to defer or exempt taxation is an indication that Congress feels that either the activities that generate the gains should be encouraged, or it would be unfair to subject that income to tax at the current time.

### Key Concepts

**Underline/highlight the answers to these questions as you read:**

1. Identify assets for which like-kind exchange treatment is available.

2. Describe the requirements for like-kind exchange treatment.

3. Identify the tax consequences of a like-kind exchange.

## LIKE-KIND EXCHANGES (SECTION 1031)

Perhaps the best known tax deferral device is the **like-kind exchange**, permitted under Section 1031 of the Code. This deferral technique is typically associated with real estate transactions, but has much broader applicability (i.e., the trade-in of equipment). The Section 1031 exchange is embedded in one of the most popular board games of all time –

Monopoly. In Monopoly, players trade little green houses for big red hotels. In real estate markets, investors often trade real estate properties to increase or decrease their position in real estate, and, if they follow the rules of Section 1031, they can often defer part or all of their gain to a future tax period.

A like-kind exchange resulting in tax deferral provides a benefit to investors by allowing the taxpayer to keep all of the proceeds of the sale and thus reinvest the full proceeds in a new property. By not paying the tax currently, the taxpayer is indirectly borrowing at a zero percent interest rate from the U.S government, and hopefully generating greater returns on the investment.

## ASSETS SUBJECT TO LIKE-KIND EXCHANGE TREATMENT

As a threshold matter, like-kind exchange treatment is only available for assets held for productive use in a trade or business, or for the production of income. This rule is consistent with a general theme in income taxation – only those items held to produce income that the U.S. government can tax will qualify for special tax benefits. Assets held for personal use do not qualify for like-kind exchange treatment, with the exception of the exclusion of gain on the sale of a principal residence under IRC Section 121. The sale of assets held by a taxpayer for personal use resulting in a realized gain must be recognized in the year of sale. As discussed in prior chapters, losses from the sale of personal assets are not deductible by the taxpayer.

| EXHIBIT 13.1 | ASSETS THAT QUALIFY FOR LIKE-KIND EXCHANGE TREATMENT |

| |
| --- |
| • Assets held for trade or business. |
| • Assets held for production of income. |
| Note: Personal use assets (e.g., personal residences) do NOT qualify for like-kind exchange treatment. However, personal residences are afforded special tax treatment. |

In addition to personal use assets, inventory (an ordinary income type property), partnership interests (including general partnership interests, limited partnership interests, managing member LLC interests, and non-managing member LLC interests), securities (bonds, notes, stocks, etc.), and the goodwill of a business do not qualify for deferral of gain under the like-kind exchange rules.

| EXAMPLE 13.1 | Bill owns 1,000 shares of Coca-Cola common stock. He believes that Pepsi has better current marketing programs, and anticipates that Pepsi will capture part of Coke's market share. Bill sells his 1,000 shares of Coca-Cola stock and reinvests the proceeds in Pepsi. While he has purchased and sold shares of stock in a similar industry, the transaction will not qualify for like-kind exchange treatment, and Bill will be required to recognize any gain that he realized on the sale. |

## REQUIREMENTS FOR LIKE-KIND EXCHANGE TREATMENT

Like-kind exchange treatment, when available, is mandatory; the taxpayer may not choose whether to subject the transaction to current tax, or defer the gain into the future. If a taxpayer would like to increase his basis for depreciation purposes, or anticipates higher capital gains tax rates in the future, recognition in the current year may be a better choice than deferral under Section 1031. Taxpayers who wish to subject their gains to current taxation should make sure that they do not meet all of the requirements necessary to qualify for like-kind exchange treatment under Section 1031.

Randy has a large carryforward loss that he realized from a recent stock market correction. He also owns a single family rental property, and has decided to purchase an apartment complex. If Randy engages in a tax-deferred exchange under Section 1031, his basis and, therefore, his depreciation deductions, will carry over to the new property. Of course, any additional funds he invests to purchase the larger rental property unit results in an increase in basis. As an alternative, if Randy intentionally structures the transaction so that it does not qualify for tax-deferral treatment, he can offset the gain on the sale of his rental property with his carryforward loss. When he purchases the new property, the entire cost (less the portion that represents land) will be depreciable, increasing the current depreciation deductions Randy can take on the property.

**EXAMPLE 13.2**

John is considering the sale of a residential rental property that he owns, and may decide to invest the proceeds in another piece of real property. Under current law, capital gains tax rates are relatively low, and John is unsure whether they will stay at that level in the future. Instead of deferring his gain into another property and potentially subjecting the gains to tax at a higher capital gains tax rate, John would like to pay the tax on any gain he realizes on the current property now. In order to do this, John would have to violate one of the requirements necessary to trigger deferral under Section 1031.

**EXAMPLE 13.3**

## LIKE-KIND PROPERTY

To qualify as a like-kind exchange, the asset received in the exchange must be of the same nature and character as the asset given up in the exchange. Section 1031 does not require that the properties have similar uses. Generally, personal property can be exchanged for personal property, and real property can be exchanged for real property.

When real property is exchanged, the type of property given or received will not matter, provided it is used for trade or business purposes, or for the production of income. Raw land held for investment, for example, could be exchanged for an apartment building, or an apartment building could be exchanged for an industrial warehouse. As long as the property is being used to generate taxable income, it will qualify for like-kind exchange treatment. One limitation on the tax-deferred exchange of real estate involves the transfer of U.S. real estate for foreign real estate. U.S. real estate and foreign real estate are not **like-kind assets** for income tax purposes, so a gain or loss realized on the transaction must be recognized in the year of transfer. However, foreign real estate is considered a like-kind asset when exchanged for other foreign real estate.

<table>
<tr><td>**EXAMPLE 13.4**</td><td>Mark inherited a piece of raw land from his great-grandfather, and decided to convert that property to an income-producing property. Mark later traded his raw land for an apartment building of equivalent value. Since he engaged in an exchange of like-kind property (realty for realty), the gain he realized on the raw land as of the date of the sale will be deferred into the apartment building under Section 1031.</td></tr>
<tr><td>**EXAMPLE 13.5**</td><td>Reese owns a hotel in Salem, Massachusetts. She has always wanted to own real estate abroad, and an opportunity arose for her to purchase the Killarney Hotel in Ireland. Both properties are worth the same amount of money, so Reese trades her hotel in Salem for the Killarney Hotel. Despite the fact that both of the properties were used in a trade or business or for the production of income, U.S. and foreign real estate are not like-kind assets, and therefore Reese must recognize any gain she realizes on the Salem hotel in the year of the transfer.</td></tr>
</table>

There are also a few special limitations imposed on the exchange of personal property. As with real estate, personal property used predominately in the U.S. is not considered to be like-kind when exchanged for property used predominately outside of the U.S. The predominant location of the property is determined by reviewing where the property given up was used for the two-year period before the transfer occurs, and where the property received is used for the two-year period after the transfer occurs. Furthermore, if the property being transferred is tangible personal property that was subject to depreciation, the exchange will only qualify as a like-kind exchange if the properties are of the same general business asset class or the same general product class.

<table>
<tr><td>**EXAMPLE 13.6**</td><td>Cody exchanges a widget making machine for a desk that he plans to use in the same trade or business. Both assets were depreciable tangible property, so to qualify for like-kind exchange treatment, they must be of the same general asset category or product class. Machinery and office equipment are not considered to be the same class, so any gain realized on the machine must be recognized in the year of the exchange.</td></tr>
</table>

While it is possible to engage in a tax-deferred Section 1031 exchange by simultaneous swapping two properties, doing so would be almost impossible. It is unlikely that a taxpayer will be able to find an available property that he or she wants, while at the same time holding the property that the other party wants to obtain. Often, Section 1031 exchanges are completed in two transactions, separated by time, which is referred to as a non-simultaneous exchange. The requirements that must be met in order to defer the gain on the property transferred in a non-simultaneous exchange are summarized in Exhibit 13.2.

## REQUIREMENTS FOR DEFERRAL OF GAIN UNDER SECTION 1031

EXHIBIT 13.2

| |
|---|
| • The proceeds from the sale of the original property must be held by an escrow agent (the proceeds may not be received by the property owner wishing to engage in the 1031 exchange). |
| • A replacement property must be identified within 45 days of the sale of the original property. |
| • The closing on the replacement property must take place by the earlier of (1) 180 days from the sale of the original property, or (2) the due date (including extensions) of the tax return for the year the original property was sold. |

To obtain tax-deferred exchange treatment, these requirements must be strictly observed. Any deviation from the requirements will result in recognition of the realized gain.

## RELATED-PARTY TRANSACTIONS

One additional situation that may result in a change to the normal rules associated with like-kind exchanges is a related-party transaction. If a like-kind exchange of property occurs between related parties, and either related party disposes of the property received in the exchange within two years, the deferred gain is recognized in the year of disposition. The deferred gain will not be accelerated upon disposition of property received in a like-kind exchange between related parties, if the disposition is due to the death of a related party, or due to an involuntary conversion (discussed later in this chapter). A **related party** (defined under Section 267(b)), includes brothers and sisters (of the whole and half blood or adopted), ancestors, and descendants. A spouse is considered a related party as well, but all transactions between spouses result in a carryover basis (under Section 1041), so the provisions of Section 1031 do not apply to spousal transactions. In a business context, a related party also includes a controlled corporation (a corporation in which the taxpayer owns more than 50 percent of the equity interest), or, for example, two corporations who are members of the same controlled group.

David, owner of a large apartment building, engaged in a like-kind exchange with his son, Lewis, who owned a smaller rental property. Part of the gain on David's large apartment building was deferred in a like-kind exchange under 1031 into the new, smaller property. The next year, Lewis announced that he sold the apartment building he received in a like-kind exchange. Since Lewis was a related party, and he disposed of the property received in the like-kind

EXAMPLE 13.7

exchange within 2 years of the transfer, David will be required to recognize any remaining gain he realized on the transfer of the large apartment building in the same year.

EXAMPLE 13.8

Louise owns 55% of the equity interest in Cimbel Corporation. Louise and Cimbel agree to transact a like-kind exchange of a high-rise condominium owned by Cimbel for a warehouse owned by Louise. Louise subsequently sells the high-rise condominium 18 months later. Cimbel will be required to recognize the deferred gain on the transfer of the high-rise condominium since Louise is a related party (a taxpayer who owns more than 50 percent of the equity interest in the corporation) and the property received in the like-kind exchange was sold within two years of the original exchange transaction.

## TAX CONSEQUENCES OF LIKE-KIND EXCHANGES

When considering the tax consequences of Section 1031 exchanges, it is helpful to think of an investment as a single investment solution. To visualize this, picture a beaker containing a chemical solution in a laboratory. The first layer of solution in the beaker is the cost of the investment, which becomes the taxpayer's adjusted basis and is reduced over time by depreciation deductions.

EXAMPLE 13.9

Ten years ago, Keegan purchased a residential rental property for $200,000. He has taken $70,000 in depreciation deductions over his holding period, resulting in an adjusted basis of $130,000. Graphically, Keegan's investment solution would look like this:

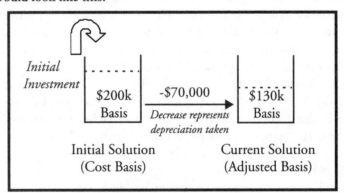

Initial Investment

$200k Basis — -$70,000 — $130k Basis

Decrease represents depreciation taken

Initial Solution (Cost Basis)  Current Solution (Adjusted Basis)

Over time, the value of some investments tends to increase, adding a second layer to the investment solution that represents the unrealized gain on the investment.

Assume that the building Keegan purchased now has a fair market value (FMV) of $450,000. Keegan's investment solution would appear as follows:

| | |
|---|---|
| FMV | $450,000 |
| Less Basis | 130,000 |
| **Potential Gain** | **$320,000** |

This text refers to deferred or unrealized gain or loss as potential gain or loss.

In deciding not to subject realized gains on assets transferred in a like-kind exchange to current taxation, Congress is recognizing that while the asset is changing, the investment solution is the same. Alternatively stated, swapping assets, as long as everything stays in the same investment solution, does not trigger gain recognition.

The tax consequences of engaging in a Section 1031 exchange will depend on the property received in the exchange. If the only thing the taxpayer receives in a like-kind exchange is like-kind property, there will be no immediate tax consequence. The taxpayer's basis in the original property, and his or her holding period, will carry over to the new property. If additional investments are made to acquire the new property, the additional amount will increase the taxpayer's basis.

Continuing with our example, assume that Keegan decides to swap his rental property for a larger rental property. The property he is interested in acquiring is worth $600,000. Keegan gives his current property, worth $450,000, plus $150,000 in cash, for the new property. Provided that Keegan meets the requirements for a tax-deferred like-kind exchange, his new investment solution will look like this:

| Before Exchange | | After Exchange | |
|---|---|---|---|
| FMV | $450,000 | FMV | $600,000 |
| Basis | 130,000 | New Basis | 280,000 |
| **Potential Gain** | **$320,000** | **Potential Gain** | **$320,000** |
| | Adds Cash to Basis ⟶ $150,000 | | |

Note that Keegan is trading up – he is adding to his investment solution. Since he qualified for like-kind exchange treatment, all of his potential gain in the old property is carried over to the new property (it stays in the investment solution), but Keegan's basis in the investment has been increased by $150,000. The basis increase results from his transfer of $150,000 of additional capital into the investment solution. Keegan's holding period will not be deter-

**EXAMPLE 13.10**

**EXAMPLE 13.11**

mined by referring to the length of time he held the asset, but rather to the length of time he held the investment solution.

Whenever a taxpayer engages in an exchange and receives only like-kind property, the tax treatment under Section 1031 defers all of the gain realized on transfer. This will occur when the taxpayer engages in an equivalent value exchange, or trades up. The only thing that will change when the taxpayer trades up is his or her basis in the investment solution increases.

### Boot

If a taxpayer receives non-like-kind property in exchange for the asset, he is not keeping all the assets in the same investment solution. Non-like-kind property received in an exchange, which usually comes in the form of cash or debt, is referred to as **boot**. The recognition rule that applies when boot is received is that the realized gain is taxable to the extent of boot received. The taxpayer has "booted" part of the investment into another investment solution, so that portion of the gain will be subject to tax. This rule applies when the taxpayer is trading down, or decreasing his investment in a particular investment solution.

**EXAMPLE 13.12**

Instead of trading his property for a $600,000 rental property, Keegan decides to engage in an exchange where he will receive a property worth $350,000 plus $100,000 in cash. Based on these facts, Keegan is trading down, which means that the gain, to the extent of boot received, is subject to income tax. The transaction could be illustrated as follows:

| Before Exchange (Old Property) | | After Exchange (New Property) | |
|---|---|---|---|
| FMV | $450,000 | FMV | $350,000 |
| Basis | 130,000 | Carryover Basis | 130,000 |
| **Potential Gain** | **$320,000** | **Potential Gain** | **$220,000** |
| | | Boot $100,000 (Cash) | |
| | | *Recognized Gain $100,000* | |

Since Keegan traded down, he has booted $100,000 out of the investment solution. When this happens, the top layer of the investment solution, the deferred gain in the property, is reduced by a like amount, and is recognized for income tax purposes. Keegan's basis in the like-kind property received is $130,000 (the basis is carried over, since the amount booted out of the solution did not dip into the basis layer), and his basis in the "boot" (cash, in this case) is $100,000 since that amount was subject to income tax.

Recall that the recognized gain may be subject to income tax at different rates. If the asset exchanged is real estate, the gain realized may be treated partly as a Section 1250 gain (for recapture of excess depreciation on real estate), partly as unrecaptured Section 1250 depreciation (taxed at a 25% rate), and partly as capital gain. If the asset is personal property, the depreciation will be recaptured at ordinary rates, and excess gain may qualify for long-term capital gains tax treatment. Refer to the rules on taxation of business assets for review of these concepts.

Note that in the above example, Keegan has still deferred part of his gain under Section 1031. The gain remaining in the investment solution was realized on the transfer, but will not be recognized. Whenever boot is received, the first thing that comes out of the investment solution is the top layer – deferred gain. If the boot received exceeds the deferred gain, the taxpayer will reduce his basis. This portion of the boot, however, would not be subject to income tax.

EXAMPLE 13.13

Instead of trading his property for a $600,000 rental property, Keegan decides to engage in an exchange where he will receive a property worth $100,000 plus $350,000 in cash. Based on these facts, Keegan is trading down, which means that the gain, to the extent of boot received, is subject to income tax.

The transaction could be illustrated as follows:

| Before Exchange (Old Property) | | After Exchange (New Property) | |
|---|---|---|---|
| FMV | $450,000 | FMV | $100,000 |
| Basis | 130,000 | New Basis | 100,000 |
| **Potential Gain** | **$320,000** | **Potential Gain** | **$0** |

Boot $350,000

*Recognized Gain $320,000 to extent of potential gain*

\* The recognized gain equals the lesser of the realized gain, or the boot received. In this case, the realized gain was $320,000 and the amount booted out of the investment solution was $350,000. Basis is reduced by $30,000.

As this example illustrates, once the top layer of the investment solution – the deferred gain – has been recognized for income tax purposes, the remaining boot received is treated as a return of basis and is not taxable.

## Assumption of Debt

One last issue concerning the taxation of like-kind-exchanges is important to review – the consequences of liability relief, or liability assumption, with the exchange. In some real estate transactions, the mortgage on the real estate is transferred with the property. When a mortgage is transferred with the property, the party transferring the mortgage is treated as having received boot equal to the amount of debt relief, and the party undertaking the mortgage obligation is treated as giving boot. The Code treats the transaction this way, since liability relief is the equivalent of receiving cash (boot) in the exchange, and using the cash to pay off the outstanding liability.

EXAMPLE 13.14

Reilly and Ryan engage in a like-kind exchange. Reilly transfers real estate with a fair market value of $400,000 and an adjusted basis of $250,000 to Ryan. Ryan transfers real estate worth $500,000 and an adjusted basis of $200,000, plus a $100,000 mortgage on the property, to Reilly. Including the mortgage, the exchange is an equivalent economic value transfer. The following illustrates the tax consequences for Reilly and Ryan:

| REILLY | | | | | |
|---|---|---|---|---|---|
| Before Exchange (Old Property) | | | After Exchange (New Property) | | |
| FMV | $400,000 | | FMV | | $500,000* |
| Basis | 250,000 | | New Basis | | 350,000 |
| **Potential Gain** | **$150,000** | | **Potential Gain** | | **$150,000** |

*$100,000 Mortgage

Boot $100,000 (Mortgage) to Ryan

*Reilly adds mortgage to old basis to get new basis*

| RYAN | | | | |
|---|---|---|---|---|
| Before Exchange (Old Property) | | After Exchange (New Property) | | |
| FMV | $500,000* | FMV | | $400,000 |
| Basis | 200,000 | Carryover Basis | | 200,000 |
| **Potential Gain** | **$300,000** | **Potential Gain** | | **$200,000** |

*Subject to Mortgage

Boot $100,000 (Mortgage) to Ryan

*Recognized Gain equal to debt relieved of $100,000*

Since Reilly was trading up, there is no recognized gain. Reilly's basis equals his basis in his original investment, plus the $100,000 in debt that he assumed in the Section 1031 exchange. Reilly will have to pay the $100,000 debt back with after-tax dollars, so the full amount of the loan will increase his basis in the investment solution. After the transaction, Reilly has a building with a fair market value of $500,000 and an adjusted basis of $350,000.

Ryan traded down in this transaction – he gave up a property with a fair market value of $500,000 and received a like-kind property with a fair market value of $400,000. Ryan's side of the transaction can be illustrated as follows:

Ryan will be able to defer part of his gain under Section 1031, but the portion of the transaction that represents liability relief will be recognized. Instead of simply transferring the liability, Ryan could have received $100,000 in cash in the transaction, and paid off the outstanding debt. If Ryan had received the $100,000 in cash, it would have been treated as boot and would be taxable to the extent of the gain. The tax result should not be different when liabilities are relieved.

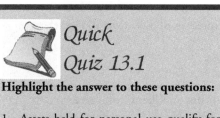

## Quick Quiz 13.1

**Highlight the answer to these questions:**

1. Assets held for personal use qualify for like-kind exchange treatment.
   a. True
   b. False

2. Section 1031 requires that exchanged properties have the same use.
   a. True
   b. False

3. If the only thing a taxpayer receives in a like-kind exchange is like-kind property, there will not be any immediate tax consequences.
   a. True
   b. False

False, False, True.

### Losses on Section 1031 Exchanges

So far, we have reviewed the rules covering the recognition/nonrecognition of gain when a transaction qualifies for like-kind exchange treatment. The rule is a little different for losses under a like-kind exchange. In this case, receiving boot does not result in recognition of a realized loss, but rather a reduction of basis.

**EXAMPLE 13.15**

Ten years ago, Keegan purchased a residential rental property for $200,000. He has taken $70,000 in depreciation deductions over his holding period, resulting in an adjusted basis of $130,000. The fair market value of the property is $120,000. Keegan engages in a Section 1031 Exchange for a new property worth $100,000, and receives cash in the amount of $20,000.

The transaction could be illustrated as follows:

| Before Exchange (Old Property) | | After Exchange (New Property) | |
|---|---|---|---|
| FMV | $120,000 | FMV | $100,000 |
| Basis | 130,000 | New Basis* | 110,000 |
| **Potential Loss** | **($10,000)** | **Potential Loss** | **($10,000)** |
| | | *Basis Reduced by Boot | |

Cash Boot $20,000

*No Gain or Loss Recognized*

Since losses on Section 1031 exchanges are not recognized, the $20,000 in boot must be taken out of the basis layer of the investment solution. After the transaction, Keegan has a property with a fair market value of $100,000 and an adjusted basis of $110,000 resulting in a deferred loss of $10,000. (An alternative way to calculate the basis on a Section 1031 exchange resulting in a realized loss is to take the fair market value of the replacement property, and add the disallowed loss. In this case, the fair market value of the replacement property is $100,000 and the disallowed loss is $10,000, resulting in a basis of $110,000). No loss can be recognized on the exchange. The loss will be recognized when the replacement property is eventually sold which is one advantage to a Section 1031 deferral of losses.

The following exhibit summarizes the income tax consequences of a Section 1031 exchange.

EXHIBIT 13.3    **TAX CONSEQUENCES OF A SECTION 1031 EXCHANGE**

| | |
|---|---|
| 1. | Determine whether your client is trading up or down. Clients who receive only like-kind property in the exchange will not have any current income tax consequences. The basis that they have in their investment solution, however, will be increased by any additional capital investment made in the investment solution. |
| 2. | The party trading down (receiving less like-kind property than given up) will be required to recognize gain to the extent of boot received. If boot exceeds gain, the amount in excess of gain is treated as a return of capital. |
| 3. | Debt relief is treated as boot, requiring gain recognition for the party no longer responsible for paying back the loan. The party assuming the debt will increase their basis in the replacement property by an equal amount. |
| 4. | Losses realized in a like-kind exchange are not recognized until the replacement property is sold. The taxpayer's basis in the replacement property equals the fair market value of the property received in the exchange plus the disallowed loss. |

## EXCHANGE OF STOCK FOR PROPERTY (SECTION 1032)

When a corporation receives money or property in return for its stock (including common, preferred, and treasury stock), no gain or loss is recognized. Sale of stock to investors is treated as an infusion of capital, and is not subject to income tax under Section 1032.

## INVOLUNTARY CONVERSIONS (SECTION 1033)

In some cases, a taxpayer may not voluntarily choose to transfer property and cause a realization event to occur for income tax purposes. Instead, either a natural disaster or a government action converts their property to cash proceeds (through insurance proceeds for the destruction of property due to a natural disaster or eminent domain payments received when the government takes the taxpayer's property). When a realization event is outside of the control of the taxpayer, the event is referred to as an **involuntary conversion**. Examples of involuntary conversions include natural disasters (e.g., hurricanes, tornadoes, or fires), theft, condemnation, seizure, or sale of property under threat of condemnation. In all of these instances, the taxpayer does not have control over the timing of the realization event. Consequently, it would be unfair to subject the taxpayer to income tax on the gain realized if the taxpayer reinvests those proceeds in a like-kind investment. Granting taxpayers time to reinvest the proceeds of such events is consistent with the general philosophy imbedded in the law of like-kind exchanges. Voluntary acts, such as destruction of the property by the taxpayer, however, will not qualify for involuntary conversion treatment.

To avoid recognition of the gain on an involuntary conversion, the taxpayer must invest the proceeds in a replacement property that has a similar use to the property that was involuntarily converted (unlike Section 1031 exchanges). Two different rules for characterizing the replacement property apply, depending on how the original property was held by the taxpayer.

If the owner of the property also used the property, the **functional use test** applies. The functional use test requires the replacement property to serve the same functional use as the original property in order for any gain realized to be deferred.

**Key Concepts**

**Underline/highlight the answers to these questions as you read:**

1. Define involuntary conversion.

2. Identify the tests for characterizing replacement property.

3. Define the reinvestment period.

**EXAMPLE 13.16**

Dylan owned a warehouse in New Orleans that he used to store his company's product for distribution to customers. A hurricane destroyed the warehouse and Dylan used the insurance proceeds to purchase a new warehouse to store his company's product for distribution to customers. Since the replacement property had the same functional use (warehouse facility for his company) as the original property, Dylan will be able to defer recognition of gain. Had Dylan invested the insurance proceeds in manufacturing facilities, in rental properties, or in any property which could be "used" in a different capacity, he would be required to recognize gain at the time of conversion.

If the owner of the property did not use the property directly, but rather held the property for investment, the **taxpayer use test** applies. The taxpayer use test requires replacement property to be used by the taxpayer in an activity which is treated the same for income tax purposes (i.e., real property held for investment) as the property that was lost, in order for any gain realized to be deferred.

**EXAMPLE 13.17**

Dylan owned a warehouse in New Orleans that he leased to several local businesses. After sustaining damage in several hurricanes in the past, it was completely destroyed by Hurricane Katrina. Dylan decided that he did not want to reinvest in New Orleans, but instead took his insurance proceeds and purchased an apartment building in Michigan. Both of the properties were rental properties. Since Dylan was an owner-investor in the old warehouse and also in the new apartment building, he will be able to defer recognition of the gain if he purchases the apartment building within the statutory period.

Under IRC Section 1033, the taxpayer must reinvest the proceeds from the involuntary conversion within a statutorily specified period in order to defer the realized gain. The **reinvestment period** varies depending upon the type of conversion the taxpayer experienced. The default rule gives the taxpayer two years from the end of the year in which the conversion occurred to replace the property with similar use property. When considering the impact of the nonrecognition rules, the date of the conversion does not matter. Instead, the last day of the year in which a conversion occurs starts the two-year time period.

| EXAMPLE 13.18 | Jordan owned a summer home in Florida, which was destroyed by a hurricane on August 1, 2009. Jordan paid $150,000 for the home, and it was insured at its full fair market value of $275,000. To avoid recognition of gain on the Florida home, Jordan must replace the property with other like-kind property by December 31, 2011. Note that Jordan will not qualify for the Section 121 exclusion of gain on the property, since she did not use the property as her principal residence. |
|---|---|

A special rule applies to involuntary conversions due to governmental action, or condemnation. When a property is condemned by the local, state, or national government through the eminent domain process, the taxpayer has one additional year to find replacement property in order to avoid recognition of gain. Therefore, instead of two years from the end of the year of conversion, the taxpayer has three years from that time to purchase the replacement property.

| EXAMPLE 13.19 | Kay owned a summer home in Florida. The State of Florida condemns the property, paying Kay the current fair market value of the property on January 5, 2009. Kay has until December 31, 2012 to reinvest the proceeds in a replacement property in order to avoid recognition of gain on the conversion. |
|---|---|

Another special rule applies to natural disasters that destroy principal residences. If the natural disaster becomes a Presidentially designated disaster, then the replacement period is four years instead of two.

When the involuntary conversion results in a replacement of the converted property with new property, nonrecognition treatment is mandatory. This type of transaction is sometimes referred to as a direct conversion. If cash is received, non-recognition treatment is available at the election of the taxpayer and this type of conversion is sometimes referred to as an indirect conversion. To avoid nonrecognition treatment in an indirect conversion, however, the taxpayer must refrain from purchasing a like-kind replacement property within the statutory period. Avoiding nonrecognition may be appropriate when a taxpayer has large carry-forward losses, or expects capital gains tax rates to increase in the future.

## Quick Quiz 13.2

**Highlight the answer to these questions:**

1. The sale of property as a result of the owner's bankruptcy is an example of an involuntary conversion.
   a. True
   b. False

2. Replacement property must only satisfy the functional use test.
   a. True
   b. False

3. Taxpayers who lose property by eminent domain have three years from the date of the conversion to replace the property.
   a. True
   b. False

False, False, False.

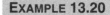

**EXAMPLE 13.20**

Kay owned a summer house in Florida. The State of Florida condemns the property, giving Kay a piece of beach-front property in a resort location that has a value of $600,000 within the statutory period. While Kay's original property was only worth $375,000, none of the gain on the conversion will be recognized, because there was a direct conversion of the property.

**EXAMPLE 13.21**

Roger, a vice president at The Amazing Company, fancied himself as an investment guru, and made large investments in trendy stocks right before the last market decline. As a result, Roger realized over $1,000,000 in capital losses. Roger is 67 years old, and has decided he has had enough with the stock market, so he will not make any future equity investments. Roger will be permitted to use $3,000 of his loss each year against his other taxable income. Recently, the State of California condemned Roger's vacation home to put in a new 12-lane highway, and paid Roger $750,000 for his property. Roger's basis in the property was $200,000. Instead of electing nonrecognition treatment, Roger could wait to replace the property for three years from the end of the year the conversion occurred, and use his carry-forward loss to offset his $550,000 of gain. When Roger purchases a new vacation property in the future, his basis will be equal to his investment in the house.

**EXAMPLE 13.22**

Rich owned a vacation home in Avalon, NJ that was destroyed by a storm surge on August 1, 2009. Rich believes that Congress will increase capital gains rates in the near future due to pressing budget concerns. Instead of buying a replacement property, Rich waits until the statutory period expires, and triggers recognition of gain. He pays capital gains tax rates at 15%. If Congress does raise capital gains rates, as Rich suspects, and capital gains tax rates increase to 25%, he may save a significant amount of money in taxes.

The bottom line with involuntary conversions is that since the taxpayer has no control over the timing of gain realization, extra time should be afforded to allow the taxpayer to replace the property and defer the gain.

## INSURANCE POLICIES (SECTION 1035)

As client needs and objectives change, it may be appropriate to change the insurance coverages that the client maintains to better serve their goals. Some insurance products have cash-value features, which permits amounts invested to grow on a tax-deferred or tax-free basis. Absent a special rule allowing deferral of gain, the surrender or sale of an insurance product would result in realization of gain or loss on the contract. IRC Section 1035 provides an opportunity to exchange insurance products for like-kind products while deferring recognition of gain.

**Key Concepts**

Underline/highlight the answers to these questions as you read:

1. Identify the three insurance products subject to Section 1035.

2. Describe which products can be exchanged without triggering recognition of gain.

There are three types of insurance products that can be exchanged in a way that will avoid gain realization. These products include life insurance contracts, modified endowment contracts, and annuities.

**Life insurance contracts** are contracts where the insurance company promises to pay a specified amount upon the death of the insured. In return for this promise, the insured pays a premium, often on an annual basis over a period of years or for his or her lifetime. One of the attractive features of a cash value life insurance policy is that lifetime and death benefits on the policy are income tax-free if the policy remains in force until the death of the insured. At certain times it may be suitable to replace a client's life insurance policies as costs may change within the policy or the client's needs may change. IRC Section 1035 permits a taxpayer to defer any gain recognition and retain the tax benefits of the old policy within the new policy.

**Modified Endowment Contracts (MECs)** are also life insurance contracts, but these life insurance contracts have taxable lifetime benefits because they were paid up too quickly. To prevent individuals from using life insurance contracts as a vehicle to temporarily defer tax on investment growth, Congress came up with a set of rules that defines MECs as life insurance policies that do not pass the 7-pay test or the corridor rule. These tests and rules are complex, and are beyond the scope of this text. As an example, if the owner of the policy takes a policy loan from a MEC, the policy loan will trigger recognition of income to the extent that there is gain on the policy. Within a non-MEC policy, this loan would have been tax-free. Death benefits on MECs, like non-MECs, are income tax-free if received by reason of the death of the insured, provided that there has not been a transfer-for-value.

**Annuity contracts** allow individuals to invest a lump sum or stream of payments with an insurance company, and defer recognition of income on the investment growth inside the contract until the owner begins to take distributions from the annuity. All distributions of growth from an annuity contract are taxed at ordinary income tax rates. Annuity contracts are Income in Respect of a Decedent (IRD) assets, and therefore do not qualify for a step-up in basis on the death of the owner. This means that any gains distributed from an annuity contract are subject to income tax. Out of the three types of insurance contracts covered under IRC Section 1035, annuity contracts are the least favorable, since all of the gains will be subject to income tax at ordinary rates.

From an income tax standpoint, of the three types of insurance contracts covered under IRC Section 1035, modified endowment contracts are not quite as good as life insurance policies (since lifetime benefits may trigger income tax), but are better than annuity contracts (since the death benefit, if received by reason of the death of the insured, is income tax-free). Exhibit 13.4 illustrates the three contracts on a ladder, with the most tax advantageous contract at the top, and the least tax advantageous contract at the bottom.

**INSURANCE PRODUCTS LADDER**                                            **EXHIBIT 13.4**

Under IRC Section 1035, the exchange of insurance contracts will achieve nonrecognition treatment if the contract is replaced with another contract of the same type, or with another type of contract that is lower on the ladder than the contract given up. A simple way to remember this rule is that the exchange is allowed if the result is neutral or better for the government, but not if it is better for the taxpayer. The following table shows how insurance contracts can be exchanged without causing recognition of gain:

**EXCHANGING INSURANCE PRODUCTS**                                        **EXHIBIT 13.5**

| This type of contract: | May be exchanged for: |
| --- | --- |
| Life Insurance | Life Insurance<br>Modified Endowment Contract<br>Annuity |
| Modified Endowment Contract | Modified Endowment Contract<br>Annuity |
| Annuity | Annuity |

As the above table illustrates, when a client exchanges something that would be tax-free for something that will create ordinary income, there is no immediate recognition of gain. However, there will be a recognition of gain if the ordinary contract in the exchange created ordinary income and the new contract has tax-free benefits.

**EXAMPLE 13.23**

Charles owns a life insurance policy that he purchased when his children were young to provide security for his family in the event of his early death (in particular, the policy was intended to pay off the mortgage, pay for children's college, and provide retirement income to his spouse). He does not need the policy for estate planning purposes, and he has paid off his mortgage, finished paying for his children's college education, and has fully funded his retirement. Charles would like to supplement his retirement income to allow him to travel a bit more frequently, and he exchanges the life insurance policy for an annuity. The exchange of the policy will not cause recognition of gain, since Charles is exchanging a tax-free contract to an ordinary income contract. If he kept the life insurance policy in force, the government would not tax the benefits, but by exchanging it for an annuity, the government is now able to subject the growth to income tax. Section 1035 will permit nonrecognition treatment in this case.

**EXAMPLE 13.24**

Early in his career, Charles purchased an annuity contract to partially fund his retirement. Charles has been very successful, and has accumulated a substantial amount of wealth both inside and outside qualified retirement plans. He does not really need the annuity contract to provide retirement income, and would like to convert the annuity contract into a life insurance policy. He paid $30,000 for the annuity, and it is currently worth $100,000. If Charles surrenders the annuity to purchase the life insurance policy, he will have to recognize the $70,000 realized gain. Charles cannot avoid gain recognition when going up the insurance ladder – it is only possible to avoid gain recognition when going down the insurance ladder.

## CORPORATE RECAPITALIZATIONS (SECTION 1036)

**Corporate recapitalizations** are often used to achieve estate planning and business succession planning goals for small and family owned businesses. Typically, the recapitalization involves a restructuring of equity interests from voting common stock to nonvoting common stock in the same corporation. IRC Section 1036 states that a shareholder does not recognize gain or loss upon recapitalization of a corporation when common stock is exchanged for other common stock in the same corporation, or when preferred stock is exchanged for other preferred stock in the same corporation.

> Scott owns 100% of Emerald Isle, Inc., and would like to begin to gift shares to his children to help facilitate his estate plan. Scott is concerned, however, about the influence that his children's spouses may have on his children, and does not want to have to worry about the in-laws creating problems for the business. Prior to gifting shares of stock to his children, Scott recapitalizes the corporation, and receives one voting share and 9 non-voting shares of common stock for every 10 shares of common stock he currently holds in the company. He gives the non-voting shares to his children, and keeps the voting shares. Scott will not be required to recognize gain on the recapitalization, since he exchanged common stock for other common stock in the same corporation.

EXAMPLE 13.25

In most cases, recapitalizations that involve an exchange of common stock for a combination of common and preferred stock usually result in recognition of gain for income tax purposes.

## REACQUISITIONS OF REAL PROPERTY (SECTION 1038)

A common way of deferring gain on the sale of appreciated property is to structure an installment sale. Under the installment reporting provisions, a taxpayer can elect to pay the tax on the realized gain over the life of the installment obligation. Installment sales are often used in family situations, and in some estate planning situations to, (1) allow the purchaser of the asset (usually a younger generation family member) to pay for the asset at least partly with the income generated by the asset, and (2) permit the senior generation to defer a large part of the gain and recognize it ratably over the life of the installment note to smooth their taxable income over the years.

One feature of an installment sale that is particularly attractive for older-generation family members is the ability to take a security interest in the property sold subject to the installment note. Particularly in situations where the seller is relying on the payments to fund or supplement their retirement income, a security interest is necessary. If the purchaser stops making the agreed-upon payments, the seller may repossess the property so that the property can be resold, or the income on the property can be used as a substitute for the installment note income.

Under IRC Section 1038, repossession of property subject to an installment note will not cause recognition of the remaining, deferred gain on the property. When the repossessed property is sold, any remaining gain will be taxed at that time.

**EXAMPLE 13.26**

Daniel, a recently retired small business owner, decided to sell his office building to his daughter, Ashley. Daniel needs to supplement his retirement income, so he sells the office building to Ashley on an installment sale basis. Daniel's gain on the building was $1,000,000, which, per the amortization schedule, will be recognized in $100,000 increments over the 10-year installment note. Three years after the office building was sold, Ashley declares bankruptcy and defaults on the note. Daniel repossesses the building in satisfaction of the note. At the time he repossessed the building, he had recognized $300,000 of the $1,000,000 gain under the installment reporting provisions, leaving $700,000 of gain that still needs to be recognized. Since Daniel repossessed the building, IRC Section 1038 will allow him to defer the remaining $700,000 gain until he sells the building.

## TRANSACTIONS BETWEEN SPOUSES INCIDENT TO DIVORCE (SECTION 1041)

Under IRC Section 1041, ALL transactions between spouses or incident to a divorce result in a carry-over basis and carry-over of holding periods.

**EXAMPLE 13.27**

Prior to getting married, Lisa owned a beach house worth $1,000,000. Her basis in the beach house was $400,000. To restructure their estates, Lisa sells the beach house to her husband, Matt, for $1,000,000. Three years later, Matt sells the home for $1,200,000, and his taxable gain is $800,000. Despite the fact that Matt paid $1,000,000 for the property, Lisa's basis was carried over to him when he purchased the home, since Lisa and Matt were married at the time.

**EXAMPLE 13.28**

Sal and Priscilla are getting divorced. As part of the divorce settlement, Priscilla receives a vacation home worth $800,000 that the couple paid $300,000 for many years earlier. Priscilla's basis in the home is $300,000. If she sells the property, she will recognize gain to the extent any sale proceeds from the home exceed this amount.

Perhaps the most widely used type of nontaxable exchange occurs when an individual sells his or her principal residence. IRC Section 121 excludes up to $500,000 of the gain from the sale of a principal residence from income tax if certain requirements are met.

The amount of the available exclusion will depend on the filing status of the individual who claims the exemption. For married couples filing jointly, up to $500,000 of the gain is excluded from income tax. All other individuals may exclude up to $250,000 of the gain from income tax. Any gain on the sale of a principal residence in excess of this amount is subject to income tax, typically long-term capital gains.

### Key Concepts

**Underline/highlight the answers to these questions as you read:**

1. Explain the requirements for an exclusion of gain under Section 121.

2. Describe the circumstances under which a reduced exclusion is available.

3. Compute the reduced exclusion.

## Qualifications

To qualify for the exclusion of gain under IRC Section 121, two requirements must be met. First, the taxpayer must have owned and used the home as his principal residence for two out of the last five years (the ownership and use test). Ownership implies that the taxpayer holds title to the home outright, or the home is owned by a grantor trust (see Ltr. Rul. 199912026). If the home is owned by a partnership, family limited partnership, or irrevocable trust, the taxpayer is not deemed to own the home for purposes of claiming the Section 121 exclusion (see Ltr. Rul. 200029046 and Ltr. Rul. 200104005). Second, to claim the exemption, the taxpayer must not have excluded gain on the sale of a principal residence within the last two years. An individual will qualify for this exclusion as often as the individual can meet these two requirements.

**EXAMPLE 13.29**

At the time of his retirement, Louis owned a principal residence and a vacation home. Needing some rest and relaxation, Louis moves into his vacation home, and, after two and a half-years, decides that he really enjoys living there and will sell his principal residence. Louis knows that he must meet the two out of five year rule in order to exclude the gain on the sale of his principal residence, so he immediately puts his old home on the market, and sells it by the close of the year. He is able to exclude all of the gain on the sale of the home under Section 121. In January of the following year, Louis and his wife decide that they are growing weary of keeping up the large vacation home that has now become their principal residence, so Louis puts that home up for sale as well, hoping to be able to move into a smaller residence. The second home sells after Louis and his wife have been in the home for three years. Even though they meet the two out of five year requirement, Louis and his wife will not be able to exclude the gain on the sale of his current residence from income tax under IRC Section 121 because they had excluded the gain from the sale of a principal residence in the prior tax year.

**EXAMPLE 13.30**

Gerald, who is single, recently retired and decided to move from New York, where he has been living for the past 15 years, to Connecticut. He immediately sells his home in New York, and realizes a $250,000 gain. Despite the fact that Gerald has a realized and recognized gain of $250,000 IRC Section 121, exempts the gain from being taxed (the Section 121 exclusion transforms the gain into a nontaxable gain) because Gerald has used the home as his principal residence for two out of the last five years. In addition, if Gerald were married, up to a $500,000 gain would be considered nontaxable. Absent a special provision in the Code exempting the gain from tax (such as Section 121), the gain on the sale of any personal asset must be recognized in the year of sale.

Married couples who wish to claim up to the $500,000 exclusion must meet conditions in addition to the two requirements set forth above. For the $500,000 exclusion to apply for a married couple, they must file a joint tax return for the year (filing status must be married filing jointly), and both spouses must have used the residence for two out of the previous five years as a principal residence (referred to as the use test). Only one of the spouses must have owned the residence for two out of the previous five years (the ownership test). Furthermore, if either spouse claimed the Section 121 exclusion within the previous two years, the gain cannot be excluded from income taxation.

If, however, a couple is getting divorced and are filing separate returns, and a principal residence is sold, both spouses can exclude up to $250,000 of gain from the sale if the ownership and use tests are otherwise met.

**EXAMPLE 13.31**

Pat and Dee recently married. About four years prior to their marriage, Pat purchased a townhouse which the couple used as their residence after they were married. Knowing that they would purchase a new residence when they started their family, Pat never added Dee's name to the title of the property. Three years after they were married, they decided to start their family and look for a new home. When the townhouse is sold, Pat and Dee may exclude up to $500,000 of the gain from the sale since Pat met the ownership test (he owned the principal residence for two years) and both Pat and Dee met the use test (they both used the residence as a principal residence for two out of the last five years).

## Proration of the Exclusion

If a principal residence is sold before the two-year ownership and use test is met, or if the exclusion was used during the last two years, it may be possible to qualify for a reduced exclusion. A reduced exclusion will be available when the sale of the principal residence is caused by (1) a change of employment, (2) a change of health, or (3) an unforeseen circumstance. When one of these exceptions apply, the amount of the exclusion is determined by dividing the number of months the taxpayer used the home as a principal residence, or the number of months since the exclusion was used last, by 24 (the number of months in a two year period), and multiplying that result by the otherwise applicable exclusion. The formula for calculating the partial exclusion may be expressed as:

$$\frac{\text{\# of months of use (or last exclusion)}}{24} \times \text{Applicable Exclusion (\$250,000 or \$500,000)}$$

## Change of Employment

The most frequently applied exception to the two-year rule is a change in employment. If the taxpayer, the taxpayer's spouse, a co-owner of the home, or a person whose principal residence is the same as the taxpayer's changes employment, and the two-year rule has not been met, a prorated exclusion is available.

After their marriage, Dee moved into Pat's home. Pat had purchased the home five years prior to the marriage, and before that did not own a residence. Six months after their marriage, Dee is offered a career opportunity that will require her to relocate across the country. Pat sells the home and seeks employment in the city where Dee will be working. Despite the fact that only Pat has met the two-year use test, a partial exclusion will be available for Dee, since the move was conditioned on a change of employment. The total exclusion would be calculated as follows:

Pat has met the ownership and use test, so he is permitted to exclude up to $250,000 of the gain.

Dee's exclusion will be:

$$\frac{6 \text{ months of use}}{24} \times \text{Applicable Exclusion (\$250,000 or \$500,000)} = \$62,500$$

Therefore, the total amount that can be excluded by them from the gain is $312,500 ($250,000 + $62,500).

If, upon sale, the gain realized was $312,500 or less, none of the gain would be taxable. Gain in excess of $312,500 would

**EXAMPLE 13.32**

be subject to tax at long-term capital gains rates (since Pat owned the home for more than one year).

To prevent abuse of the change in employment exception to the two year use rule, the law provides a safe harbor that is based on the distance of the new job from the taxpayer's current home. If the distance of the new job to the old home is 50 miles greater than the distance from the old job to the old home, the reduced exclusion will be available. Note that the safe harbor test used here matches the distance test that must be met to deduct moving expenses as an adjustment to income.

### Change of Health

For the partial exclusion to apply due to a change in health, the residence must be sold to facilitate the taxpayer's, the taxpayer's dependent, or specified family member's treatment for the diagnosis, cure, or mitigation of an illness. The sale of the home to improve the taxpayer's general health does not qualify, unless a physician recommends a change in residence due to health concerns.

### Unforeseen Circumstances

The unforeseen circumstance exception is the most difficult to apply, but the Treasury regulations do provide some guidance and safe-harbors. If any of the following situations apply, a partial exemption will be available:

1. The taxpayer, spouse, co-owner of the home or a person who also uses the home as a primary residence dies, loses their job, divorces, or separates from their spouse.
2. The government condemns the home through use of eminent domain.
3. The home is affected by a natural disaster or act of war or terrorism resulting in a casualty to the home.

Exhibit 13.6 lists some of the events that the IRS has accepted as unforeseen circumstances in the last few years.

| EXHIBIT 13.6 | **UNFORESEEN CIRCUMSTANCES** |
|---|---|

| |
|---|
| • *PLR 200702032:* Taxpayer was bothered by excessive noise from a nearby airport. |
| • *PLR 200652041:* Taxpayer/co-owner became pregnant, but was no longer in a relationship with the father/other co-owner of the house. |
| • *PLR 200613009:* Taxpayer needed a larger house in order to provide a separate bedroom for an adopted child. |
| • *PLR 200601022:* Taxpayer's new spouse's child lost ride to school when sibling graduated and taxpayer and spouse then had a baby, making house too small. |
| • *PLR 200601023:* Taxpayer needed to move out of an age-restricted community so that taxpayer's daughter (who had lost her job) and grandchild could move in with the taxpayer. |
| • *PLR 200403049:* A member of the taxpayer's family was on house arrest/probation, to which the neighbors were hostile. |
| • *PLR 200630004:* Taxpayer was accosted at gunpoint outside his residence and forced to withdraw money from ATMs. |
| • *PLR 200601009:* Taxpayers and son were assaulted in separate events in new neighborhood. |
| • *PLR 200615011:* Taxpayer's address was discovered by the associates of a drug dealer that taxpayer had arrested. |
| • *PLR 200504012:* Taxpayer was assigned to a K-9 unit, but his homeowner's association prohibited kennels. |

## Other Provisions Related to Section 121

The ability to take the Section 121 exclusion may be affected if the property was acquired in a like-kind exchange. If the home currently being used as the taxpayer's principal residence is sold within five years of acquiring the property through a like-kind exchange, the Section 121 exclusion is not available. While it is not possible to exchange personal residences and defer recognition of the gain under IRC Section 1031, conversion of a residence from rental use to personal use may invoke application of this rule.

> Four years ago, Colin engaged in a Section 1031 exchange of an apartment building for a rental house. One year after the Section 1031 exchange occurred, the tenant moved out and Colin had a difficult time finding a new tenant. Since he liked the property, he decided to move in and make it his principal residence. Colin has used the home as a principal residence for three years. Despite the fact that Colin meets both the ownership and use tests, if he sells the home he will not be able to exclude the gain under the Section 121 exclusion. To be able to exclude the gain, Colin would have to sell the home five years or more after he acquired it in the Section 1031 exchange.

**EXAMPLE 13.33**

One final issue should be addressed concerning the application of Section 121. In cases where rental property is converted to use as a principal residence, the Section 121 exclusion will permit the capital gain on the sale to be excluded from income taxation, but will not shield depreciation recapture from taxation. You may recall from the property transactions chapters that accelerated depreciation taken on real estate is recaptured at ordinary tax rates, and that straight-line depreciation (referred to as "unrecaptured Section 1250 gain") is recaptured at a 25 percent tax rate. The tax on any depreciation recapture must be paid before the Section 121 exclusion comes into effect.

> Seth purchased a home 10 years ago for $200,000 and rented it out for the first eight years. During the rental use period, Seth claimed $58,000 in straight-line depreciation deductions, and he has consistently been in the 35% marginal income tax bracket. Two years ago, the tenant moved out, and Seth converted the property to a personal residence for himself, his wife, and his two children. Seth has received an unsolicited offer to purchase the house, provided that the closing takes place within the next 6 months. The offer was for $550,000. If Seth sells the home, his gain will be calculated as follows:

**EXAMPLE 13.34**

| Amount Realized | $550,000 |
|---|---|
| Less: Adjusted Basis | $142,000 |
| Gain | $408,000 |

Note that Seth's adjusted basis is his cost basis of $200,000 reduced by the depreciation allowed or allowable of $58,000.

Both Seth and his wife have used the home for two out of the last five years as a principal residence, so they qualify to exclude up to $500,000 of the gain from income tax. However, the Section 121 exclusion applies only after depreciation has been recaptured. In this example, the first $58,000 of the gain (the "unrecaptured section 1250 depreciation" or straight-line depreciation) will be subject to tax at a flat 25 percent, requiring Seth to pay $14,500 in taxes. The remaining gain of $350,000 ($550,000 - $200,000) can be excluded from income tax under Section 121, since all of the requirements of the Section 121 exclusion have been met.

# DEATH BENEFITS AND LOANS FROM LIFE INSURANCE

## Death Benefits

Under IRC Section 101, the death benefit on a life insurance policy received by reason of the death of the insured is exempt from income tax provided that the policy has not been transferred for valuable consideration. This exception to the tax-free receipt of a life insurance death benefit is referred to as the **transfer for value rule**. If there is a transfer-for-value, the death benefit of a life insurance policy is subject to income tax. Transfers for value occur when the policy is sold, or is otherwise transferred in return for some other form of economic benefit.

The code does provide five exceptions to the transfer for value rule. The five exceptions are:
1. A transfer to the insured,
2. A transfer to a corporation in which the insured is a shareholder,
3. A transfer to a partnership in which the insured is a partner,
4. A transfer to a partner of the insured, and
5. A transfer to a transferee who takes the transferor's basis.

If a life insurance policy has been transferred for valuable consideration, but one of these exceptions apply, the death benefit will be received by the beneficiary income tax-free. The following examples give common scenarios where a transfer of a life insurance policy for valuable consideration does not cause the death benefit of the life insurance policy to be subject to income tax.

**EXAMPLE 13.35**

John is Chief Security Officer of BioTech, Inc. Because of John's unique training and skills, BioTech considers John to be a key-person for the corporation, and purchased a life insurance policy on John's life to compensate the corporation in the event John dies prior to retirement. John retired last week, and BioTech no longer has need for the life insurance policy on John's life. John, however, needs additional life insurance to support his estate plan. BioTech sells the life insurance policy to John for the value of the policy (the interpolated terminal reserve plus unearned premium). Despite the fact that a transfer-for-value has occurred, the sale of the policy was to the insured (John), so the beneficiary will receive the death benefit income tax-free.

**EXAMPLE 13.36**

Kasey is a one-third owner of KRK, Inc. As part of the company's business succession plan, KRK has entered into an entity-type buy-sell agreement, which requires the estates of deceased owners to sell their shares back to the corporation. To fund this buy-sell agreement, KRK plans on purchasing enough life insurance so that, upon the death of each owner, it will have sufficient funds to purchase the stock. Kasey happens to have an existing life insurance policy in force that he no longer needs for his other planning objectives. The death benefit on the policy is approximately the amount the company would need to purchase to fund Kasey's part of the buy-sell agreement. Kasey sells his life insurance policy to the corporation so that it can be used to fund the buy-sell agreement. Despite the fact that there has been a transfer of the policy for valuable consideration, the death benefit will be received by the corporation income tax-free, since the transfer was from a shareholder of the corporation to the corporation.

| | |
|---|---|
| **EXAMPLE 13.37** | Refer to the facts from the previous example, but assume that KRK is not a corporation, but rather a partnership. The same result would occur. While there has been a transfer-for-value, the transfer was made to a partnership in which the insured was a partner. The partnership would receive any death benefits income tax-free. |
| **EXAMPLE 13.38** | Kasey is a 50% owner of KRK, LLC. As part of the company's business succession plan, Kasey and his partner have entered into a cross-purchase type buy-sell agreement, which requires the estates of deceased owners to sell their shares back to the surviving LLC member. To fund this buy-sell agreement, Kasey and his partner plan on purchasing enough life insurance on the life of the other owner so that, upon the death of each owner, sufficient funds will be available to purchase the deceased owner's interest. Kasey happens to have an existing life insurance policy in force that he no longer needs for his other planning objectives. The death benefit on the policy matches the amount of insurance that his partner would have to purchase to fund the cross-purchase buy-sell agreement. Kasey sells his life insurance policy to his partner so that it can be used to fund the buy-sell agreement. Despite the fact that there has been a transfer of the policy for valuable consideration, the death benefit will be received by the partner income tax-free, since the transfer was to a partner of the insured. |

*Policy Loans*

While the policy is in force, the owner of the policy may borrow from the policy's cash value without triggering any income tax consequences. Borrowing from a policy, therefore, is a tax-free event, which gives the owner access to capital without any tax cost. If the policy is later surrendered, however, the amount borrowed from the cash value of a life insurance policy will be considered part of the distribution upon surrender, and will be subject to income tax. If the policy is kept in force until the death of the insured, there are no income tax consequences for policy loans.

## DISTRIBUTIONS FROM ROTH IRAS AND ROTH 401(k)/403(b)s

Roth IRAs, Roth 401(k)s and Roth 403(b)s give individuals the opportunity to accumulate money for retirement on a tax-free basis. Unlike traditional retirement savings plans, which give the taxpayer the ability to defer taxation on income until distributions are received from the retirement account, Roth savings vehicles must be funded with after-tax dollars. All of the investment growth, however, is tax-free if the account has been in existence for five years, and the distributions are made after the time the owner reaches age 59½. Roth savings accounts give taxpayers a rare opportunity to completely avoid income tax on investment gains and income.

## CONCLUSION

Tax-deferred exchanges give taxpayers the opportunity to manipulate the time when income is recognized, and tax-free exchanges exempt the taxpayer from income tax liability on certain types of income. These provisions give incentives for investment, and should be carefully considered by individuals when engaging in property transactions. Congress can, and sometimes does, change the rules governing these provisions. Tax-deferred and tax-free exchanges are matters of legislative grace; without express provisions in the Code to exempt or defer taxation, these transactions would trigger taxable income for taxpayers engaging in them.

# Key Terms

**Annuity Contract** - A contract under which an individual invests a lump sum or stream of payments with an insurance company and the income on the investment growth is deferred until the owner begins to take distributions from the annuity.

**Boot** - Non-like-kind property received in a Section 1031 exchange, usually cash or debt.

**Corporate Recapitalization** - Restructuring the equity interests of a corporation, often in an effort to achieve estate planning or business succession goals.

**Functional Use Test** - Requires the replacement property to serve the same functional use as the original property.

**Involuntary Conversion** - A realization event that occurs outside of the control of the taxpayer.

**Life Insurance Contract** - A contract under which the insurance company promises to pay a specified amount upon the death of the insured.

**Like-Kind Assets** - Property of the same nature and character that may be exchanged in a like-kind exchange.

**Like-Kind Exchange** - A tax deferral technique in which assets held for productive use in a trade or business are exchanged.

**Modified Endowment Contracts (MECs)** - Life insurance contracts that do not pass the 7-pay test or the corridor rule.

**Reinvestment Period** - Period during which the taxpayer must acquire replacement property.

**Related Party** - Anyone defined under Section 267(b) including brothers and sisters (of whole or half blood or adopted).

**Taxpayer Use Test** - Requires that the replacement property be used by the taxpayer within activities which is treated the same for tax purposes.

**Transfer for Value Rule** - An exception to the general rule that life insurance death benefits are received tax-free.

1. What is a like-kind exchange?

2. What types of assets are eligible for like-kind exchange treatment?

3. How can taxpayers avoid like-kind exchange treatment when it is available?

4. What types of assets are considered like-kind under Section 1031?

5. What are the requirements for the deferral of gain when a like-kind exchange is not accomplished by a simultaneous exchange of like-kind property?

6. How is a like-kind exchange affected by being a related party transaction?

7. What are the tax consequences of a Section 1031 exchange?

8. What happens if a taxpayer receives non-like-kind property in exchange for an asset?

9. What happens when a mortgage is part of a like-kind exchange?

10. Describe the tax consequences of exchanging property for stock.

11. What is an involuntary conversion?

12. What reinvestment period applies to involuntary conversions?

13. Name and describe the three types of insurance products that can be exchanged in a way that will avoid gain recognition.

14. How can the above types of insurance products be exchanged without realizing gain?

15. What is a corporate recapitalization and what are its tax consequences?

16. What are the tax consequences of transfers between spouses incident to divorce?

17. What are the requirements for the exclusion of gain on the sale of a personal residence?

18. Under what circumstances is a reduced exclusion available under Section 121 and how is that reduced exclusion calculated?

19. What is the transfer for value rule and what are the exceptions to this rule?

20. What are the tax consequences of distributions from Roth IRAs and Roth 401(k)/403(b)s?

1.  Which of the following could qualify as a residence, for personal residence exclusion from gain?

    1.  A condominium.
    2.  An RV.
    3.  A boat.
    4.  Vacant land adjacent to personal residence regularly used by the taxpayer.
        a.  4 only.
        b.  1 and 4.
        c.  1, 2, and 3.
        d.  1, 2, 3, and 4.

2.  Which of the following is not a like-kind exchange?

    a.  A bank building for unimproved land.
    b.  A business building in Mexico for a shopping center in Peru.
    c.  A truck in California for a computer in Oregon.
    d.  A cow for a bull.

3.  If you meet all of the requirements of a 1031 tax-free exchange, which of the following is true?

    a.  Like-kind exchange treatment is absolutely mandatory.
    b.  Like-kind exchange treatment requires an affirmative election.
    c.  Like-kind exchange treatment is completely discretionary.
    d.  None of the above are true.

4. Philip wants to sell his rental beach home and purchase rental property in the mountains. His friend Randy tells him he can do a nonsimultaneous tax-free exchange as long as the fair market value of mountain property is equal to or greater than the fair market value of the beach property. How long after selling his beach property does he have to identify and purchase the mountain property?

   a. The mountain property must be identified within 45 days of the closing of the beach property and must be closed within 180 days of the closing of the beach property.

   b. The mountain property must be identified within 30 days of the closing of the beach property and must be closed within 120 days of the closing of the beach property.

   c. The mountain property must be identified within 60 days of the closing of the beach property and must be closed within 180 days of the closing of the beach property.

   d. The mountain property must be identified within 90 days of the closing of the beach property and must be closed within 180 days of the closing of the beach property.

*Use the following information for questions 5 - 9.*

Laura has an asset used in her business. She exchanges it for a like-kind asset owned by Anne. The basis of Laura's asset is $40,000 and she gives Anne $20,000 cash plus the asset in exchange for Anne's asset, which is worth $36,000. Anne's basis in her original asset is $10,000.

5. What is Laura's gain or loss?

   a. No gain or loss.
   b. $24,000 loss realized and recognized.
   c. $24,000 loss realized, but not recognized.
   d. $44,000 loss realized and recognized.

6. What is Laura's basis in the new asset?

   a. $24,000.
   b. $40,000.
   c. $44,000.
   d. $60,000.

7. What is Anne's gain or loss?

   a. $20,000 gain recognized.
   b. $26,000 gain realized and recognized.
   c. $0 gain recognized.
   d. $0 loss recognized.

8. What is Laura's deferred gain or loss?

    a. $0.

    b. $16,000.

    c. $24,000.

    d. $40,000.

9. What is Anne's adjusted basis in the new asset?

    a. $6,000.

    b. $10,000.

    c. $16,000.

    d. $26,000.

*Use the following information for questions 10 - 13.*

Joe enters into a 1031 exchange with James. Joe's building has a basis of $300,000 and he takes James' raw land worth $800,000 with an assumable mortgage of $250,000 and a basis of $430,000. Joe also pays James $50,000 in cash.

10. What is Joe's recognized gain or loss?

    a. $0.

    b. $50,000 loss.

    c. $200,000 gain.

    d. $250,000 gain.

11. What is James' recognized gain or loss?

    a. $50,000.

    b. $250,000 gain.

    c. $300,000 gain.

    d. $300,000 loss.

12. What is Joe's basis in the new asset?

    a. $300,000.

    b. $350,000.

    c. $600,000.

    d. $700,000.

13. What is James' basis in the new asset?

     a. $200,000.

     b. $250,000.

     c. $300,000.

     d. $430,000.

14. In which of the following circumstances would a taxpayer be able to get a partial exemption for the sale of a personal residence when the taxpayer did not meet the two year ownership and use test.

     a. The taxpayer decides to move from Florida to Arizona to possibly look for a new job.

     b. The taxpayer changes jobs to a town that is 10 miles away from the former house and 10 miles away from the former job.

     c. The taxpayer sold the house in Milwaukee because the grey days were affecting her sunny disposition and general health.

     d. The taxpayer suffered anxiety attacks after a home invasion where the taxpayer was held at gunpoint for 3 days.

15. Bob, a single taxpayer, has been transferred by his company to Portland. He sold his house for $650,000 and he had an adjusted basis of $330,000. He owned and lived in the home for 18 months. What is his capital gain from the sale of the personal residence?

     a. $0.

     b. $132,500 LTCG.

     c. $187,500 LTCG.

     d. $320,000 LTCG.

# Quick Quiz Explanations

### Quick Quiz 13.1

1. False. Like-kind exchange treatment is only available for assets held for productive use in a trade or business, or for the production of income. Assets held for personal use do not qualify.
2. False. To qualify as a like-kind exchange, the asset received in the exchange must be of the same nature and character as the asset given up in the exchange. Section 1031 does not require that the properties have similar uses.
3. True.

### Quick Quiz 13.2

1. False. An involuntary conversion is a realization event that occurs outside of the control of the taxpayer. Examples of involuntary conversions include theft, condemnation, seizure, or sale of property under threat of condemnation. Bankruptcy is not an example of an involuntary conversion.
2. False. To avoid recognition of the gain on an involuntary conversion, the taxpayer must invest the proceeds in a replacement property that has a similar use to the property that was converted. Either the taxpayer use test or the functional use test must be satisfied.
3. False. Taxpayers who lose property by eminent domain have three years from the end of the year in which the conversion occurred to purchase the replacement property.

### Quick Quiz 13.3

1. True.
2. True.

### Quick Quiz 13.4

1. True.
2. False. Taxpayers who have not lived in their principal residence for two years may be entitled to a reduced exclusion if the sale of the principal residence is caused by (1) a change of employment, (2) a change of health, or (3) an unforeseen circumstance.
3. True.

### Quick Quiz 13.5

1. True.
2. False. Because Roth savings vehicles must be funded with after-tax dollars, all of the investment growth is tax-free if the account has been in existence for five years.

# Passive Activity Rules

## 14

## INTRODUCTION

The passive activity rules are a classic example of anti-abuse provisions adopted by Congress to address the planning excesses of taxpayers. They were adopted as part of the 1986 Tax Reform Act to limit the ability of high income taxpayers to manipulate their taxable income by generating losses to offset other income. While the rules appear to be complex, an appreciation of the objective of the passive activity rules makes the analysis of transactions falling under these rules much easier to understand. The impact of the passive activity rules is to restrict or limit the current deductibility of losses resulting from passive activities. The rules do not eliminate passive losses, but rather suspend them until later, making loss deductibility a timing issue.

### BACKGROUND TO THE PASSIVE ACTIVITY LOSS RULES

Prior to 1986, all income received by a taxpayer was classified as either earned income or portfolio income. **Earned income** included wages, salaries, and income from the conduct of business activities. **Portfolio income** included income generated through the investment of capital, such as dividends, interest, and capital gains.

When the passive activity rules were adopted by Congress in 1986, a new category of income was created – passive income. **Passive income** includes income generated from investments in real estate, rental activities, and income generated by businesses entities when

### Key Concepts

**Underline/highlight the answers to these questions as you read:**

1. Identify the three categories of income and losses.

2. Describe Congress' reasons for establishing the passive activity loss rules.

the owner does not materially participate (defined later in chapter) in the conduct of that business. After 1986, all income or losses received by a taxpayer must fall into one of three categories: active, portfolio, or passive.

Real estate and business investments have the potential to generate large gains over the long run, but may also generate large losses in the short run. Before 1986, wealthy taxpayers would often invest in real estate and start-up business entities that were managed by others. These investments generated taxable losses that could be used to offset their active income that otherwise would be taxed at a high marginal tax rate. By making these investments, therefore, a taxpayer could manage his or her taxable income, and also manage his or her marginal income tax rate.

In the 1980s, the sale of real estate limited partnerships and interests in start-up businesses was promoted as a way to minimize or eliminate federal income tax liability. In fact, it was possible to purchase real estate limited partnership interests that would generate a tax write-off greater than the investment made by the taxpayer. This ability to create tax write-offs that could eliminate taxable income became a major concern of Congress.

| **EXAMPLE 14.1** | In 1983, Ari anticipated his adjusted gross income to be $150,000. Ari has a high net worth, and decides that his income tax rates are too high. At the end of the tax year, he purchases a 10% interest in a real estate limited partnership interest for $100,000. The real estate limited partnership uses its initial $1 million in capital, plus a nonrecourse bank loan of $20 million to purchase an apartment building. At the time of the purchase (the early 1980s), the apartment building could be depreciated on an accelerated basis, and the first year depreciation on the apartment building is $1,500,000. The partnership has no other income for the year (since it was not created until the end of the tax year), and has no other expenses. Since Ari owns a 10% limited partnership interest, 10% of the depreciation is allocated to him, which he is able to deduct for income tax purposes. Since Ari's allocation of the depreciation expense ($150,000) equals his adjusted gross income for the year, he has completely offset his income with the loss generated on the real estate rental activity, and is not required to pay any income tax in the current year. |
| --- | --- |

While these tax planning options were certainly favorable for high income taxpayers who wanted to minimize current income taxes, most taxpayers (middle-class and low-income individuals) could not afford to purchase these types of investments, and were left paying their income tax bill. Furthermore, the Treasury, the IRS, and Congress did not like the idea that income taxes for the wealthy were essentially becoming voluntary, so they took action to limit this type of tax planning. Congress solved this problem by imposing new limitations on deductions in three ways. First, they changed the basis rules; second, at-risk rules were imposed; and third, limitations were placed on passive activity losses and the deductibility of investment interest expense. Remember that the intent of Congress was not to eliminate deductibility but rather to manage the timing of each deduction.

# APPLICATION OF THE RULES

The Passive Activity Loss Rules apply to individuals, estates and trusts, certain personal service corporations, and closely held regular corporations.

The passive activity loss rules do not apply to publicly held corporations. Purchase of an interest in a publicly held corporation will generate investment income or loss, not passive income or loss. Dividends and capital gains derived from a publicly held corporation fall into the portfolio income bucket.

## THREE TYPES OF INCOME

As you have learned in prior chapters, subsequent to the imposition of the passive activity rules in 1986, there are three types of income (or loss) that can be generated in our income tax system (active, portfolio, or passive). All income (or loss) earned by a taxpayer must fall into one of the three categories.

## Key Concepts

**Underline/highlight the answers to these questions as you read:**

1. Identify the taxpayers to whom the passive activity loss rules apply.

2. Describe the different types of income.

3. Define material participation.

4. Explain how passive activities are grouped for the purpose of imposing limits.

## TYPES OF INCOME

EXHIBIT 14.1

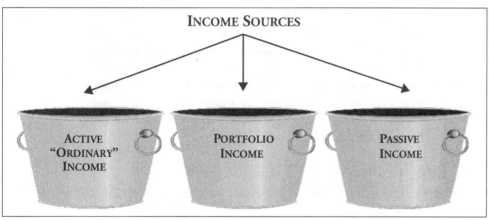

INCOME SOURCES

ACTIVE "ORDINARY" INCOME    PORTFOLIO INCOME    PASSIVE INCOME

### Active Income
Active income is income earned through the active conduct of a trade or business and earned from the provision of labor. Salaries, wages, and income from self employment, S corporations and partnerships in which the taxpayer materially participates is considered active income. Generally, active income is taxed at ordinary income tax rates.

### Portfolio Income

Portfolio income is income derived from the investment of capital. Interest, dividends, and capital gains are forms of portfolio income. Some forms of portfolio income, such as interest, annuity payments, royalties, short-term capital gains and non-qualified dividends, are subject to ordinary income tax rates. Other types of portfolio income, such as qualified dividends and long-term capital gains are taxed at favorable income tax rates.

### Passive Income

Passive income generally includes income generated from all rental and real estate activities (unless specific exceptions are met) and income generated from trade or business activities when the taxpayer receiving the income does not materially participate in the conduct of that trade or business. Distributive shares of income from S corporations and partnerships (including general partnerships, limited partnerships, limited liability companies, and limited liability partnerships) may be classified as passive income or active income depending on material participation (defined below).

The creation of the passive activity rules may result in different treatment of business income from the same business for different taxpayers. If a taxpayer regularly participates in the conduct of the business generating the income/loss, that income/loss will be allocated to the active income bucket. If the taxpayer does not regularly participate in the conduct of the business activities, the income/loss for that taxpayer is allocated to the passive bucket.

| EXAMPLE 14.2 | Reilly and Kasey are brothers, and each owns a 10% interest in JarvCo, LLC, a closely held family business. Reilly is the general manager of JarvCo's local office. Kasey decided to become a physician, and does not participate in the operation of the family business. The distributive share of the partnership income that Reilly receives is treated as active income since Reilly materially participates in the conduct of JarvCo's business. Kasey's distributive share of the partnership income will be treated as passive income/loss since Kasey is not materially participating in the conduct of the business activities. |
|---|---|

## PASSIVE ACTIVITIES

Passive income or loss is derived from the conduct of a **passive activity**. Section 469 defines a passive activity as any activity:
- In which the taxpayer does not materially participate,
- That is a limited partnership interest, or
- That is a rental activity, even if the taxpayer materially participates in the activity.

## MATERIAL PARTICIPATION

**Material participation** requires involvement in the conduct of the trade or business on a regular, continuous, and substantial basis. Mere management approval of decisions made by others does not constitute material participation. Treasury Regulation 1.469-5T sets forth seven tests to determine whether or not a person materially participates in the conduct of a trade or business.

All of these tests are designed to give taxpayers a safe harbor rule for classifying income. If one of the tests is met, material participation is presumed and the income is generally considered to be active income (there are a few exceptions, covered below). The seven tests for material participation are:

1. The taxpayer dedicates more than 500 hours of effort to the activity each year.
2. The taxpayer dedicates more than 100 hours to the activity, but no less than anyone else.
3. The taxpayer dedicates more than 100 hours to each of several activities, and more than 500 hours in total for those activities not including any activity for which he is a material participant.
4. The taxpayer is the only person substantially participating in the operation of the activity.
5. The taxpayer has materially participated in the activity for five out of the last 10 years.
6. If the activity is a personal service activity, the taxpayer has materially participated in that personal service activity for at least three years. A personal service activity includes any trade or business where capital is not a material income producing factor, and professional services (law, accountancy, medicine, engineering, performing arts, and the like).
7. The facts and circumstances surrounding the case indicate that the taxpayer has been regularly, continuously, and substantially involved in the activity.

## SUMMARY OF MATERIAL PARTICIPATION

EXHIBIT 14.2

1. >500 hours devoted to activity.
2. >100 hours devoted to activity and the most of any participant.
3. >100 hours devoted to several activities that add to more than 500 hours.

Recall that the passive activity rules, and, thus, the tests for material participation only apply to the owners of closely held businesses. Publicly traded businesses are exempt from the application of the passive activity rules. Most closely held businesses are structured as proprietorships, partnerships (general partnerships, limited partnerships, LLCs, and LLPs) or S corporations.

Special rules apply when determining whether a limited partner is materially participating in a trade or business. If the owner of the interest is a limited partner, he or she will be considered to materially participate in the operation of the business only if he or she meets the 500 hour test (number 1, above), the five of 10 years test (number 5, above); or the three year test for personal service companies (number 6 above). The other tests are not available for limited partners.

Material participation of a limited partner may be problematic if the limited partner is attempting to maintain limited liability status. To the extent that a limited partner participates in management decisions for the partnership, limited liability protection is lost. If the limited partner does not have management control, limited liability is maintained. Limited partners participating in the operation of the business need to be mindful of this distinction to maintain the asset protection features of their ownership interest. The Treasury regulations may be particularly problematic in this regard since the regulations indicate that work that is not normally performed by owners or whose principal purpose is to avoid the passive activity rules will not be considered when applying the tests for material participation. In addition, work done as an investor that does not involve direct day-to-day management of the operation (e.g., reviewing financial statements) will not be considered when applying the tests for material participation.

Proprietors, general partners, S corporation owners, and LLC members may meet any of the seven tests for material participation to qualify the income generated by the business entity as active income in their hands.

For married taxpayers, the participation of both spouses may be combined when calculating the number of hours necessary to meet the material participation tests. Unlike most other provisions in the Code, the hours of involvement by each spouse may be used to determine material participation even if the couple files separately for income tax purposes.

| **EXAMPLE 14.3** | Donna and James are married and file jointly. Donna works 300 hours in Activity A and James works 250 hours in Activity A. They are material participants in Activity A with 550 hours between them. |

## GROUPING OF PASSIVE ACTIVITIES

To make the tax rules surrounding the use of passive activities a bit more user-friendly, it is possible to group several passive activities into an "appropriate economic unit." Once grouped into an appropriate economic unit, the limitations imposed on passive activities (discussed below) will apply on a group basis, as opposed to per-unit basis. This can be useful, from a compliance and simplicity view, if the taxpayer has one activity generating passive gains that can be grouped with another activity that generates passive losses so the losses can offset the gains directly, thus decreasing the likelihood of an IRS challenge.

The factors that should be considered in grouping activities into "appropriate economic units" includes (1) the similarity and differences in the types of business; (2) the extent of common control of the business entities; (3) the extent of common ownership of the business entities; (4) geographic location; and (5) the interdependencies between the various activities. Once chosen, the activities grouped into the "appropriate economic unit" cannot be changed without IRS approval. Typically, the IRS will not give approval for a change unless the original grouping was clearly inappropriate, or there has been a material change in facts and circumstances since the activities were grouped together.

EXAMPLE 14.4

## Quick Quiz 14.1

**Highlight the answer to these questions:**

1. The passive activity loss rules do not apply to publicly held corporations.
   a. True
   b. False

2. A taxpayer who dedicates 400 hours to an activity is presumed to materially participate in that activity.
   a. True
   b. False

3. If grouped, passive activity limits apply on a group, rather than a per-unit, basis.
   a. True
   b. False

True, False, True.

Mike participates in 3 activities (A, B, and C). He dedicates 120 hours to Activity A, 150 hours to Activity B, and 270 hours to Activity C. He can group the three together to be a material participant in all (120 + 150 + 270 = 540).

There are two forms of groupings that are not appropriate: (1) groupings of rental and non-rental activities unless one activity is substantially related to the other; and (2) groupings of rental activities that involve real and personal property, unless the personal property rental activity is provided in tandem with the real estate rental activity.

The IRS has the authority to reallocate groupings if it determines that the groupings are not "appropriate economic units."

# LIMITATIONS IMPOSED ON PASSIVE LOSSES

Passive losses are subject to three primary limitations: the basis limitation, the at-risk limitation, and the passive activity loss rules. When a taxpayer generates a loss that is considered passive, each of these limitations must be applied in sequence.

## THE BASIS LIMITATION

The first limitation that is imposed on the deductibility of passive losses is the basis limitation. The **basis limitation** states that the maximum allowable loss that the taxpayer can deduct is equal to his or her basis in the investment. This limitation generally applies to all investments including those generating passive activity losses.

Basis is used to keep track of the after-tax dollars invested in an investment vehicle. In our tax

## Key Concepts

**Underline/highlight the answers to these questions as you read:**

1. Identify the three primary limitations on passive income.

2. Describe the basis limitation.

3. Explain the at-risk rules and how debt affects the amount that is considered at-risk.

4. Describe the passive activity loss rules.

system, a loss cannot be claimed in excess of basis (a notable exception to this rule is percentage depletion).

There are three ways that the basis of an investment can be increased. First, basis in an investment can be increased by adding more capital to the investment (stated differently, a taxpayer may make a further investment in the entity). Second, when a pass-through business entity earns money, each owner's basis in that business entity is increased by the owner's proportionate share of the undistributed business income because the owners pick up the income on their personal tax return. Finally, an owner's basis in a proprietorship or partnership may be increased by having the proprietorship or partnership incur debt. Since the proprietorship or partnership is not a separate legal entity, any increase in partnership debt is really an increase in the debt of each owner in proportion to his or her ownership interest in the entity. Since debt is paid back with after-tax dollars (while a deduction is allowed for interest payments, no deduction is allowed for the principal portion of debt payments) and each owner or partner is responsible for the debt, an increase in the debt of a proprietorship or partnership results in a pro-rata increase in the basis of each partner.

## AT-RISK RULES

Once the basis rule has been applied to the loss from the activity, a second test must be met in order to claim a deduction for income tax purposes – the "at-risk" rule. The **at-risk rule** states that a taxpayer may not deduct, in the current tax year, more than the amount that he/she is "at risk" for in the investment. Unlike the basis limitation, which simply states that the maximum deduction is the taxpayer's basis in the investment, the at-risk limitation only allows a deduction equal to the taxpayer's economic investment in the activity.

There are two basic forms of debt – recourse debt and nonrecourse debt. **Recourse debt** is secured by the property purchased with the loan proceeds (usually, the lender will take a secured interest in this property) and by the personal guarantee of the debtor. If the debtor defaults on a recourse loan, the lender can execute against the asset purchased and, if that is not enough to satisfy the outstanding note balance, may seek to attach the personal assets of the borrower. In contrast, **nonrecourse debt** only allows the lender to execute against the property that was the object of the loan.

Qualified nonrecourse financing is nonrecourse debt collateralized with real property that is used in the business. To determine the taxpayer's economic investment in an activity, the taxpayer's basis must be reduced by any nonrecourse debt. In the event that the activity being considered is real estate, however, the taxpayer may consider any "qualified" nonrecourse financing in determining the amount at risk.

Before 1986, a basis increase was permitted for debt assumption without regard to the type of debt that was assumed by the partnership. As illustrated in the first example in this chapter, it was common for real estate limited partnerships to solicit capital financing for use as a down payment, and then obtain a loan to purchase a large rental real estate property. Obtaining the loan resulted in a basis increase for each partner equal to the partner's proportionate share of the loan balance, since, presumably, the loan would have to be paid back with after-tax dollars. This transaction gives the investor a basis increase without any capital outlay. Typically, however, the loans were issued on a nonrecourse basis. If the investment did not work out, the investors could walk away, leaving the bank to deal with the property and any resulting loss despite the fact that the investors took depreciation deductions on the entire value of the property, including the loan balance that resulted in an increase in basis. When investors walked away from the property, they often had accumulated income tax deductions in excess of the actual capital invested in the venture.

EXAMPLE 14.5

In 1983, Keegan, a high net worth individual, invested in a real estate limited partnership. He purchased a 10% interest for $100,000. The real estate limited partnership uses its initial $1 million in capital plus a nonrecourse bank loan of $20 million to purchase an apartment building. At the time of the purchase (the early 1980s), the apartment building could be depreciated on an accelerated basis, and the losses claimed in the first several years of operation were $5,500,000. Since Keegan owns a 10% limited partnership interest, 10% of the losses were allocated to him, which he deducted for income tax purposes. In 1986, the real estate market turned sour, and the investors decide to walk away from their investment. For Keegan's $100,000 investment, he was able to generate $550,000 in tax deductions, and he was not personally liable to pay back any of the outstanding balance on the note assumed by the partnership.

To prevent wealthy taxpayers from purchasing investments to generate tax deductions, two limitations apply. First, as outlined above, the basis rule sets the maximum loss that a taxpayer can claim on a given activity within one tax year. Second, that maximum loss determined by the basis rule must be reduced by nonrecourse financing to arrive at the amount at risk under the at-risk rules. The impact of the at-risk rule is to prevent nonrecourse debt from increasing the taxpayer's maximum allowable loss for a given investment.

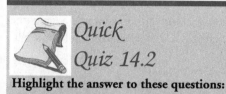

## Quick Quiz 14.2

**Highlight the answer to these questions:**

1. A taxpayer may deduct losses on an investment up to 150% of his basis in that investment.
   a. True
   b. False

2. Nonrecourse debt does not increase a taxpayer's maximum allowable loss for a given investment.
   a. True
   b. False

False, True.

EXAMPLE 14.6

In 2009, Brent, a high net worth individual, invested in a real estate limited partnership. He purchased a 10% interest for $100,000. The real estate limited partnership uses its initial $1 million in capital, plus a nonrecourse bank loan of $20 million to purchase an apartment building. While the nonrecourse loan will increase Brent's basis in the investment, it will be ignored under the at-risk limitation since Brent is not personally liable to pay back the loan. During the first year of operations the partnership incurred a $1,100,000 loss. Brent's share of this loss is $110,000. The maximum amount of loss Brent can deduct in the current tax year is limited to his basis of $100,000.

The results of the prior example may be described visually as follows:

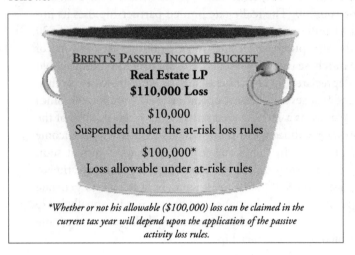

BRENT'S PASSIVE INCOME BUCKET
**Real Estate LP**
**$110,000 Loss**

$10,000
Suspended under the at-risk loss rules

$100,000*
Loss allowable under at-risk rules

*Whether or not his allowable ($100,000) loss can be claimed in the current tax year will depend upon the application of the passive activity loss rules.*

To deduct the additional $10,000 loss, Brent would have to increase his basis by making an additional capital investment. Alternatively, the partnership could either generate a gain that would be allocated to partners or incur a recourse debt, either of which would result in a basis increase for the partners.

Any losses that are disallowed are carried forward until the at-risk amount is increased, at which time they may be deductible for income tax purposes provided that they are also deductible under the passive activity loss rules.

At-risk limitations are computed separately for each passive activity owned by the taxpayer.

## PASSIVE ACTIVITY LOSS RULES

After application of the basis limitation rules and the at-risk rules, one additional test must be met before a taxpayer may deduct a passive loss for federal income tax purposes. The **passive activity loss rule** states that losses falling into the passive activity bucket from a passive activity can only be offset against gains that are in the passive activity bucket, unless special exceptions apply.

If a taxpayer's passive losses are smaller than his or her passive gains, the losses are offset by the gains, and only the net gain is included in gross income on the income tax return.

On the other hand, if the taxpayer's passive losses are larger than his or her passive gains, the excess losses are suspended under the passive activity rules, and may not be used as a deduction against active or portfolio income in the current tax year. Instead, the losses will remain in the passive activity bucket, and can be deducted in future tax years when the taxpayer's passive activities generate gains (income) or when the activity that generated the loss is disposed of or sold.

Continuing with the information from Example 14.6, now assume that real estate limited partnership is a passive activity for Brent (he does not materially participate in the operation of the business). Therefore, the activity will be placed in Brent's passive income bucket.

**EXAMPLE 14.7**

**BRENT'S INCOME SOURCES**

ACTIVE "ORDINARY" INCOME

PORTFOLIO INCOME

PASSIVE INCOME

**Real Estate LP**

Within the passive bucket, two tests will limit Brent's ability to deduct losses. The first test that applies is the basis test. The basis test will limit Brent's deduction this year to his adjusted basis in the property. The at-risk limitation, however, states that losses cannot be taken for that portion of basis that represents nonrecourse debt. Therefore, given the facts of this case, Brent's maximum allowable loss is $100,000 despite the fact that $110,000 of losses had been allocated to him on the partnership tax return. The $10,000 that Brent cannot deduct is referred to as the suspended at-risk loss. The suspended at-risk loss will be carried over to future years and to the extent that Brent's amount at risk in that investment increases, the suspended at-risk loss may be deducted. The $10,000 loss suspended by the at-risk limitation is trapped within the investment and cannot be released until additional at-risk amounts are generated. The remaining $100,000 of loss that can be deducted under the at-risk rules moves into the passive activity bucket, and will be subject to the passive activity rules. Determining the amount that can be deducted under the at-risk rule does not determine the amount of Brent's income tax deduction. Brent's income tax deduction will be determined when the third test

– the passive activity loss rule, is applied to the gains and losses in the passive bucket.

| | |
|---|---|
| Passive Activity Income | $0 |
| Passive Activity Loss | $100,000 |
| **Loss Suspended Under Passive Activity Rule** | **$100,000** |
| Loss Suspended Under the At-Risk Limitation | $10,000 |

**EXAMPLE 14.8**

Continuing our example above, Brent had a $100,000 potentially deductible loss from his Real Estate Limited Partnership that moved from the activity into the passive bucket. Since he did not have any passive gains this year, he is not permitted to deduct any of that loss and it will be suspended and remain in the passive bucket until he either generates passive income or sells (or otherwise disposes of) the Real Estate Limited Partnership.

Now assume that Brent is a 10 percent owner in HLQ, LLC in addition to his passive activity in the Real Estate Limited Partnership. Also assume Brent does not materially participate in HLQ, LLC. Brent's at-risk and loss/income for the current year is as follows:

Real Estate LP: At-risk = $100,000; Loss of $110,000

HLQ, LLC: At-risk = $250,000; Income of $70,000

Brent's actual loss deduction available for the current year is $70,000. As previously indicated, of the $110,000 loss from Real Estate LP, $100,000 is potentially deductible and $10,000 is suspended under the at risk rules. The $70,000 of passive income is available (from HLQ, LLC) in the current year to offset the current $100,000 at-risk rule loss. This allows use of the passive loss on Real Estate LP to offset the income from HLQ, LLC, with the remaining $70,000 and $30,000 suspended under the passive activity loss rule.

| | |
|---|---|
| Passive Activity Income | $70,000 |
| Passive Activity Loss | $100,000 |
| **Loss Suspended Under Passive Activity Rule** | **$30,000** |
| Loss Suspended Under the At-Risk Limitation | $10,000 |

The passive loss rules reflect the general rule discussed earlier that losses in one income category may be used to offset against gains in the same income category, but may not be used to offset other forms of income unless a special exception applies.

The planning impact of the passive activity rule is that high income taxpayers can no longer manage their income tax liability by generating losses from passive activities to offset other forms of income.

Excess passive losses may be carried forward indefinitely and may be used to offset future passive gains. Alternatively, the passive losses on an activity may be accelerated by disposing of the activity that generated the losses. Sale of the passive investment will allow passive losses generated on that investment to be used first against any gain on the sale of the passive activity. To the extent that the losses are not offset by any gain, they may be used to offset other passive income generated in the current year. If there is still a remaining loss, the remaining loss may be used to offset other active or portfolio income. Note that this ordering rule requires the taxpayer to allocate the passive losses first to income that may qualify for favorable capital gains tax rates. Only to the extent that the lower-taxed gain is eliminated can the losses be used to offset active income.

## COORDINATING PASSIVE ACTIVITY LOSS RULES WITH OTHER FINANCIAL PLANNING ISSUES

As described above, passive activity losses can be used to offset passive gains, and can be used to offset other income when the asset that generates the passive losses is sold. There are several ways of transferring an asset other than sale of the asset and an informed financial planner should be able to counsel his or her client on the application of the passive activity loss rules to those transactions.

If, when a taxpayer dies, there are remaining suspended passive activity losses that have not been used by the taxpayer, IRC Section 469(g) states that those suspended losses will be deductible on the decedent's final income tax return. The suspended losses will be deductible to the extent they exceed any step to fair market value in basis received by the passive assets under IRC Section 1014 as they pass through the estate of the decedent. If a decedent has suspended losses and the asset basis gets stepped to fair market value at death, the suspended loss is reduced by the change in basis and the remaining suspended loss is deductible. If the asset gets stepped to fair value and the decedent's basis in the asset was greater than the fair market value of the asset, the full suspended loss is deductible, but the decrease in basis is not deductible.

| EXHIBIT 14.3 | SUSPENDED LOSSES WHEN TAXPAYER DIES |

- If asset is stepped up, reduce the suspended losses by the amount stepped up.
- If asset is stepped down, deduct the full suspended loss.

| EXAMPLE 14.9 |

Joe dies when he has Asset A with a basis of $600,000 and suspended losses of $520,000. The fair value of Asset A at Joe's death is $1,000,000. The suspended loss deduction on Joe's final return is $120,000.

| FMV $1,000,000 | $520,000 | Suspended loss |
| ↑ | 400,000 | Reduction for step up |
| BASIS    $600,000 | $120,000 | Suspended loss deduction |

| EXAMPLE 14.10 |

Roger died last week. Throughout his life, he relied on the advice of his friend Larry and purchased a series of passive investments that persistently generated losses and had little prospect of increasing in value. Roger's total basis in the passive investments was $150,000. As of the date of his death, Roger had $150,000 in suspended passive losses, and the fair market value of his passive investments was $20,000. Since Section 1014 will result in a new basis of $20,000 (a step down) in the hands of the estate beneficiary who receives the investments, Roger is permitted to deduct the entire $150,000 suspended loss on his final income tax return.

When a passive activity that has generated a suspended passive activity loss is gifted to another person, the donor is not permitted to take the loss against other income. Instead, the donee's basis in the gift is increased by the suspended passive activity loss.

Sometimes, a passive asset will be sold subject to an installment note. While immediate sale of the passive activity will allow the taxpayer to trigger the suspended passive activity loss for the current tax year, an installment sale results in a deferral of the recognition of the passive activity loss over the term of the note. The portion of suspended loss deductible is the same percentage as the total gain recognized in each year the installment note is in existence.

Finally, the taxpayer may dispose of the passive activity in a nontaxable exchange. Perhaps the most frequently observed nontaxable exchange of passive activity assets is a Section 1031 exchange of real estate. Provided the requirements for a like-kind exchange are met, the suspended losses are carried over into the replacement property, and the income generated from the replacement property can be used to offset those suspended passive losses. Of course, if the requirements for a like-kind exchange are not met, the transfer of the property will result in a taxable gain/loss and the suspended passive losses may be used to offset other income.

# EXCEPTIONS TO THE PASSIVE ACTIVITY RULES

In the passive activity loss arena, as in other areas of tax planning, the best opportunities for clients are often presented in the exceptions to the general rules.

## RENTAL ACTIVITIES

In defining a passive activity, the IRC includes any activity that is a rental activity, even if a taxpayer materially participates in the activity. If this was the final word on categorizing assets into the passive category, there would be few, if any, planning options for those purchasing rental property.

The Treasury Regulations provide six exceptions to the passive categorization of tangible (real or personal) property that is used for rental purposes. If a taxpayer does **not** meet one of the exceptions, the activity is classified as a passive activity. If one of the exceptions applies, the taxpayer must still meet the material participation test to convert the asset from a passive asset to an asset used in an active trade or business.

### Key Concepts

**Underline/highlight the answers to these questions as you read:**

1. Identify the six exceptions to the passive categorization of tangible property that is used for rental purposes.

2. Identify the two circumstances where real estate activities can be classified as active businesses.

The first exception states that if the average period of customer use is seven days or less, the activity could be considered an active trade or business. This exception is necessary to allow certain industries to treat their short-term rental activities as an active trade or business.

**EXAMPLE 14.11**

Randy is the general manager and owner of The Beachcomer Hotel, a national hotel chain. Most of his customers rent rooms in his hotels for a five-day period. Because the average period of customer use is less than seven days, the activity can be considered an active trade or business, assuming that Randy materially participates in the operation of the hotel. If Randy does not materially participate in the operation of the hotel chain, any year in which the company generated a loss, that loss cannot be used to offset other forms of income since the activity will be classified as passive activity.

Under the second exception to the rental activity rule, if the average period of customer use is 30 days or less and the taxpayer provides significant personal services in concert with the rental activity, the activity may be classified as an active trade or business provided that the taxpayer materially participates in the operation of the company.

EXAMPLE 14.12

In the example above, even if the average period of customer use of The Beachcomer Hotel was 14 days, since Randy provides significant personal services as well as rents the room (such as maid service, room service, recreational facilities, and the like), he can still treat operation of the Hotel as an active trade or business provided that he materially participates in the operation of the company.

The third exception further expands the first two exceptions and states that the period of customer use is not of consequence if extraordinary personal services are provided by the company. When this exception applies, the customer's use of the property is incidental to the special services provided.

EXAMPLE 14.13

John is a part owner in a private hospital located in Long Island, NY (organized as an LLC). This year, the hospital realized a small loss and John is curious if he can use his pro-rata share to offset other income on his taxes this year. At a recent investment seminar, John found out that rental activities were classified as passive activities and he is concerned that he will not be able to recognize the loss against other income this year. While the hospital does rent beds to patients, the rental of the beds to patients is merely incidental to the personal services being provided to the patients. Therefore, provided John materially participates in the operation of the activity, he can classify it as an active trade or business and use the loss to offset other income.

The fourth exception, which is very similar to the third exception covered above, states that the activity will be considered an active trade or business if the rental of property is incidental to a non-rental activity of the taxpayer.

The fifth exception classifies a rental activity that the taxpayer customarily makes available during business hours for nonexclusive use by customers as the active conduct of a trade or business, provided that the owner materially participates in the activity.

The sixth and final regulatory exception states that if the rental property is provided for use in an activity conducted by a partnership, S corporation, or joint venture in which the taxpayer is an owner, and the taxpayer materially participates in the operation of the entity, it will be classified as an active trade or business and not as a passive activity.

EXHIBIT 14.4

1. Customer use ≤7 days.

2. Customer use ≤30 days and personal services provided.

3. Extraordinary personal services are provided.

4. Rental activities incidental to non-rental activity.

5. Rental activity available during business hours for nonexclusive use of customers.

6. Rental property used in activity conducted by partnership, etc. where taxpayer is owner and active participant.

## REAL ESTATE EXCEPTIONS

There are two circumstances where real estate activities can be classified as active businesses. The first situation involves real estate professionals and the second involves the individual investor exception.

### *Real Estate Professionals Exception*

Prior to 1993, all real estate activities were classified as passive activities regardless of whether or not the owner of the activity materially participated in the operation of the activity. Seven years after creating the passive activity rules, Congress realized that this categorization was unfair to those who spent most of their time in real estate activities and created the **real estate professionals exception**.

A real estate professional may treat a real estate activity as an active trade or business provided that the taxpayer meets the following requirements:
1. More than one-half of the taxpayer's personal services performed during the year are in real property trades or businesses in which the taxpayer materially participates, taking into consideration all of the trade and business activities engaged in by the taxpayer.
2. The taxpayer performed at least 750 hours of service in real-estate-related activities.

Closely held C corporations are also eligible if more than 50 percent of the gross receipts of the corporation are derived from real property trades or businesses in which the corporation materially participates. While this exception is available for C corporations, a special rule applies for those C corporations who wish to take advantage of it. Any excess passive activity losses generated by a C corporation that qualifies for the exception may be used to offset active, but not portfolio, income of the company. Due to the imposition of this special exception, closely held C corporations have a partial exemption from the passive activity loss rules.

### *Individual Investor Exception*

Even after the imposition of the passive activity loss rules, Congress recognized that many middle-income families used real estate investing as a way to increase their net worth. The passive activity loss rules were intended to put an end to the games that high-income taxpayers were playing to wipe out exposure to tax. Congress never really intended to discourage investment in real estate for the moderate income groups. To provide an inducement for middle-income groups to invest in real estate, Congress created the **individual investor exception** to the passive loss rules.

The individual investor exception allows individual taxpayers who actively participate in rental real estate activities to deduct up to $25,000 of losses from that activity against non-passive income for the year. Like the rule that allows taxpayers to deduct $3,000 of capital losses against other forms of income each year, this rule is a special exception to the general rule that requires losses in one income bucket to be offset only against gains in the same income bucket. The exceptions to the general rule may be illustrated as follows:

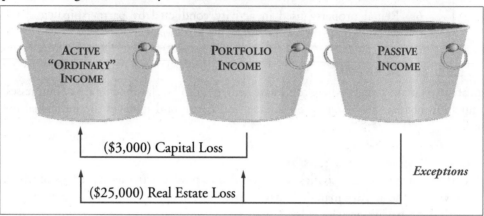

There are some limitations to the $25,000 loss deduction, however. In order to qualify, the taxpayer must:

1. Actively participate in the activity,
2. Own at least 10% of the value of the real estate, and
3. Have AGI equal to or less than $100,000 - $150,000 (including the phaseout).

For most of this chapter, we have been referring to the material participation rules. Material participation in an activity generally allows the activity to be classified as an active trade or business as opposed to a passive activity. As previously discussed, material participation requires substantial, continuous involvement in the operation of the activity.

To qualify for the individual investor exception to the passive activity loss rules, however, the taxpayer does not have to materially participate in the activity. Active participation is required. **Active participation** means that the taxpayer participates in making management decisions concerning the property, but is not substantially and continuously involved in the operation of the activity (recall that substantial and continuous involvement is the standard that applies for material participation). A taxpayer who hires a property manager to manage the property will meet the active participation standard if he or she retains the right to have the final say on all management decisions.

As you can see by the ownership requirement, the taxpayer does not have to own the entire property, but must have a minimum of a 10 percent ownership interest in the property to take advantage of the exception. This allows taxpayers to invest with others, yet still qualify for the special individual investor exception.

In the beginning of this section, we noted that Congress did not want to take away the ability of moderate income taxpayers to deduct losses by enacting the passive activity rules. Wealthy individuals were the primary target. How does Congress define a moderate income taxpayer? The answer is a taxpayer who has AGI less than $100,000. The $25,000 maximum allowable deduction is reduced by 50 cents for each dollar of adjusted gross income exceeding $100,000. Once the taxpayer reaches an AGI of $150,000, there is no remaining loss deduction available, and any losses generated by the activity will be either trapped in the activity under the at-risk limitation or trapped in the passive income bucket under the passive loss rules (unless, of course, there is other passive income that can be used to offset the passive losses).

A few items concerning the phaseout of the $25,000 loss deduction are worthy of note. First, the $100,000 - $150,000 phaseout range applies to adjusted gross income, regardless of filing status. Both single individuals, and dual-income married couples are subject to the same phaseout range. Second, the phaseout range is not inflation adjusted, so the same phaseout range has remained since 1986.

Randy, a single taxpayer, has AGI of $90,000 and has losses from a rental real estate property of $20,000. Randy can deduct the full $20,000 against his $90,000 AGI.

**EXAMPLE 14.14**

Ralph and Kaco, a married couple, have AGI of $138,000 and have a loss of $30,000 from a rental real estate property. Since they are beyond the $100,000 in AGI they can only deduct 50¢ for every dollar of loss that they are below the $150,000.

**EXAMPLE 14.15**

$150,000 - $138,000 = $12,000 / 2 = $6,000 deduction

Therefore, they can deduct $6,000 against ordinary income. The remainder of the loss is suspended under the passive activity rules.

## PASSIVE CREDITS

Some passive activities are deemed by Congress to be desirable from a public policy perspective, despite the characterization of the activity as a passive activity. To encourage individuals to engage in these types of passive activities, Congress has made **passive credits** available. Passive credits may be used to offset any tax attributed to taxable income. The passive credits are, however, non-refundable credits, so in order to get a benefit from the credit, the taxpayer must have taxable income in the year the passive credit is generated.

The passive credits currently available include the low-income housing credit, the rehabilitation credit, and the research credit. Other passive credits may be used to offset income tax only on passive activity income and are also subject to the at risk rules.

## CONCLUSION

The passive activity loss rules are anti-abuse provisions designed to prevent high-income individuals from manipulating their exposure to tax. Once an activity has been designated a passive activity, any losses generated from that activity can only be offset against gains from other activities in the passive income bucket. To determine how much of the loss can potentially be used to offset other passive income, a three-part test is employed. First, the overall loss limitation is the taxpayer's basis in the property. Second, the maximum allowable loss will be limited to the amount that the taxpayer has at-risk. Finally, the passive activity loss rule applies and states that, in most cases, passive losses may only be offset against passive gains.

The exceptions to the passive activity loss rules provide planning opportunities for individuals. Accordingly, it is important for advisors to understand the passive activity loss rules. In particular, the individual investor exception allowing deduction of up to $25,000 in real estate rental losses against other forms of income may be a valuable planning tool for clients.

# Key Terms

*Active Participation* - Requires participation in making management decisions concerning the property, but is not substantially and continuously involved in the operation of the activity (the standard that applies for material participation).

*At-Risk Rule* - Provides that a taxpayer may not deduct, in the current tax year, more than the amount that he or she has at risk.

*Basis Limitation* - Provides that the maximum allowable loss that the taxpayer can deduct is equal to his or her basis in the investment.

*Earned Income* - Income received by a taxpayer in the form of wages, salaries, and income from the conduct of business activities.

*Individual Investor Exception* - Allows individual taxpayers who actively participate in rental real estate activities to deduct up to $25,000 of losses from that activity against non-passive income for the year.

*Material Participation* - Requires involvement in the conduct of the trade or business on a regular, continuous, and substantial basis.

*Nonrecourse Debt* - Debt that is secured only by the asset pledged as security and not by any personal guarantee of the debtor.

*Passive Activity* - Any activity in which a taxpayer does not materially participate, that is a limited partnership interest, or that is a rental activity (even if the taxpayer materially participates in the activity).

*Passive Activity Loss Rule* - Provides that passive losses may only be used to offset gains from passive activities and may not be used to offset other types of income.

*Passive Credits* - Non-refundable tax credits designed to encourage individuals to engage in certain types of passive activities. Passive credits may be used to offset any tax attributed to taxable income.

*Passive Income* - Income received by a taxpayer including income generated from investments in real estate and income generated by business entities in which the owner does not materially participate.

*Portfolio Income* - Income received by a taxpayer through the investment of capital, such as dividends, interest, and capital gains.

*Real Estate Professional Exception* - Provides that if a taxpayer meets certain requirements, he is considered a real estate professional and may treat a real estate activity as an active trade or business.

*Recourse Debt* - Debt that the taxpayer is personally liable to repay regardless of whether the investment produces a return for the investor.

1. Describe the new category of income created by Congress in 1986.

2. Explain who the passive activity loss rules do and do not apply to.

3. Name and describe the three types of income.

4. How is a passive activity defined by Section 469 of the Internal Revenue Code?

5. Describe the seven tests for material participation.

6. Why are the material participation standards problematic for limited partners?

7. What factors are considered when grouping passive activities?

8. What are the ways in which it is inappropriate to group passive activities?

9. What are the three types of limits that are generally imposed on passive losses?

10. What is the basis limitation?

11. What is the at-risk rule and how is it different from the basis limitation?

12. What is the difference between recourse and nonrecourse debt?

13. What is the passive activity loss rule?

14. What happens when a taxpayer dies with suspended passive activity losses and the asset gets stepped up to fair value?

15. What happens when a passive activity that has generated a suspended passive activity loss is gifted to another person?

16. What are the six exceptions to the passive categorization of tangible (real or personal) property that is used for rental purposes?

17. What is the real estate professionals exception?

18. What is the individual investor exception?

19. What is the difference between active participation and material participation?

20. What is the purpose of a passive credit?

1.  Which of the following is not considered passive income?

    a.  Annuity payments.

    b.  Rental activities.

    c.  Real estate activities.

    d.  A limited partner's distributive share of partnership income.

2.  James and Ryann are good friends. They decide to open a sports equipment store together because of their love of the outdoors. They each own 50 percent in SportsCrazy, LLC, which is taxed as a partnership. Ryann manages the business. James has a thriving tax practice and therefore does not participate in the operation of the business. Which of the following is true?

    a.  Only the income distributed to Ryann is considered passive income.

    b.  Only the income distributed to James is considered passive income.

    c.  The income distributed to both Ryann and James is considered passive income.

    d.  The income distributed to both Ryann and James is considered active income.

3.  Paul, David, Kristina, and Rachel are partners in MovieMakers, LLC. They all participate in the business to some extent and there are no other employees. Given the following activities, which of these individuals are clearly material participants?

    *   Paul has a job outside of the business but does provide about 125 hours a year to help market the business.
    *   David devotes all of his time to the business and generally devotes 60 hours per week to the business.
    *   Kristina has materially participated in the business for the last 7 years, however she only dedicated about 50 hours this year because she had a baby in January.
    *   Rachel devotes very little time to the business and only helps on an as-needed basis. She rarely helps more than 2 or 3 hours per month.

    a.  David only.

    b.  David and Kristina.

    c.  David and Paul.

    d.  David, Kristina, Paul and Rachel.

4. Jaime and Barbara are owners in NurseStat, LLC a staffing agency for nurses. They operate the business on a part-time basis. Jaime puts in about 20 hours per week and Barbara puts in about 25 hours per week. Although they are married, they file married filing separately. Which of the following is true?

    a. Only Jaime is considered a material participant.

    b. Only Barbara is considered a material participant.

    c. Both Barbara and Jaime are considered a material participant.

    d. Neither Barbara nor Jaime are considered a material participant.

5. Cody owns a 10 percent interest in CreativeWorks, LLP. Cody originally invested $500,000 and has personally taken losses from the partnership of $200,000. The partnership took out a nonrecourse loan of $800,000. What is Cody's at-risk amount?

    a. $300,000.

    b. $500,000.

    c. $1,100,000.

    d. $1,300,000.

6. Kate is a 20 percent limited partner in DreamOn, LP a local spa. Kate invested $105,000 in DreamOn. During DreamOn's first two years of business the total losses were $300,000 in year 1 and $200,000 in year 2. If the total business loss for the current year is $100,000 what is Kate's suspended loss due to at-risk rules for the current year?

    a. $0.

    b. $5,000.

    c. $15,000.

    d. $100,000.

7. Isabel is a 10 percent owner in Bubbles, LLC a local pub that specializes in serving caviar and champagne. Which of the following will increase her basis?

    a. Isabel takes a cash distribution of income.

    b. Isabel is allocated a business loss.

    c. The business borrows nonrecourse debt.

    d. The business borrows recourse debt.

8. Kali is a 20 percent owner in CheerSquad, LLC a local gym for middle school and high school cheerleaders. The gym provides private coaches to help young cheerleaders learn stunts and improve their overall cheer performance. Kali does not materially participate. Kali contributed $200,000 initially. During the prior years she has been allocated $200,000 in income and $300,000 in losses. After a freak accident during the current year in which one of the cheerleaders was critically injured doing a stunt, the business lost many customers. The business allocated a $150,000 loss to Kali for the current year. What is Kali's suspended loss due to at-risk rules?

    a. $0.

    b. $50,000.

    c. $100,000.

    d. $150,000.

9. Lisa is a 10 percent owner in HKAccounting, LLC a review company for the CPA exam. She is also a 20 percent owner in MyPuppy, LLC a rescue organization for dogs. She does not materially participate in either company. Her at-risk and loss/income for the current year is as follows:

- HKAccounting – At-risk = $800,000; Income of $150,000
- MyPuppy – At-risk = $200,000; Loss of $350,000

Lisa also has wage income of $75,000. How much of the loss can she write off in the current year?

    a. $150,000.

    b. $200,000.

    c. $225,000.

    d. $350,000.

10. Vicky is a 15 percent owner in DesignCreative, LLC, a very successful web developing business. She is also a 15 percent owner in SafeHarbor, LLC, an internet-based virus protection service. She materially participates in DesignCreative, but does not materially participate in SafeHarbor. Her at-risk and loss/income for the current year is as follows:

- DesignCreative – At-risk = $600,000; Income of $250,000
- Safe Harbor – At-risk = $75,000; Loss of $200,000

What amount of loss is suspended because of the passive activity income rules?

    a. $0.

    b. $75,000.

    c. $125,000.

    d. $200,000.

11. Ada is a 12 percent owner in SoccerStart, LLC a coaching service for young soccer players. She is also a 15 percent owner in HandsOn, LLC a successful chain of nail salons. She does not materially participate in either business. Her at-risk and loss/income for the current year is as follows:

   - SoccerStart – At-risk = $150,000; Loss of $250,000
   - HandsOn – At-risk = $25,000; Income of $100,000

   She also has wage income of $50,000 and capital gain income of $20,000. Which of the following statements is true?

   a. The loss suspended because of the at-risk rules is $75,000 and the loss suspended because of the passive loss rules is $75,000.

   b. The loss suspended because of the at-risk rules is $75,000 and the loss suspended because of the passive loss rules is $0.

   c. The loss suspended because of the at-risk rules is $50,000 and the loss suspended because of the passive loss rules is $100,000.

   d. The loss suspended because of the at-risk rules is $100,000 and the loss suspended because of the passive loss rules is $50,000.

12. Donny died owning a 15 percent interest in EngraveIt, LLC a local trophy engraving shop. At his death his basis in the business was $800,000 and he had suspended losses of $600,000. The fair market value of the business at his death was is $950,000. What is Donny's suspended loss deduction on his final income tax return?

   a. $0.
   b. $150,000.
   c. $450,000.
   d. $600,000.

13. Darrin is the owner and manager of RUActive Bike Rental, LLC. RUActive rents bicycles to tourists at a resort that helps individuals lose weight. Most customers stay at the resort for two weeks, therefore, most bike rentals are for a period of 12 days. Darrin and his wife are the only two workers at the rental location. Which of the following is true for Darrin?

   a. The activity is passive because it is a rental activity.

   b. The activity is active because the average rental period is less than 14 days.

   c. The activity is active because the average rental period is 30 days or less and Darrin provides significant personal services.

   d. The activity is active because the rental period is inconsequential.

14. Which of the following is true regarding real estate activities?

    a. Real estate activities are always passive.

    b. An individual investor in rental real estate can always consider their real estate activities as active businesses.

    c. Closely held C corporations that participate in real estate activities will always be considered active businesses.

    d. Real estate professionals may be allowed to consider their real estate activities as active in some circumstances.

15. Ross is an individual investor in rental real estate. He actively participates in the activity. His AGI is $125,000 for the current year and the rental real estate business had a loss of $30,000. What is Ross's available loss against ordinary income assuming he has the required amount at risk?

    a. $0.

    b. $12,500.

    c. $15,000.

    d. $30,000.

# Quick Quiz Explanations

### Quick Quiz 14.1

1. True.
2. False. In terms of hours, a taxpayer must dedicate more than 500 hours of effort to an activity each year in order to be considered a material participant. In the alternative, the taxpayer may dedicate more than 100 hours to the activity, but no less than anyone else, to be considered a material participant. The question, however, does not mention that anyone else is involved in the activity, so the 500 hour rule would apply.
3. True.

### Quick Quiz 14.2

1. False. The basis limitation states that the maximum allowable loss that the taxpayer can deduct is generally equal to his or her basis in the investment.
2. True.

### Quick Quiz 14.3

1. True.
2. False. The passive activity loss rule states that losses falling into the passive bucket from a passive activity can only be offset against gains that are in the passive bucket. Excess passive losses may be carried forward indefinitely, and may be used to offset future passive gains, but may not be used to offset other income.

### Quick Quiz 14.4

1. False. The Treasury Regulations provide six exceptions to the passive categorization of tangible (real or personal) property that is used for rental purposes. If none of the exceptions are met, the property is classified as a passive activity. If one or more of the exceptions applies, the taxpayer must still meet the material participation test to convert the asset from a passive asset to an asset used in an active trade or business.
2. True.
3. False. Active participation means that the taxpayer participates in making management decisions concerning the property, but is not substantially and continuously involved in the operation of the activity (the standard that applies for material participation). Therefore, active participation is a lower standard than material participation.

# The Alternative Minimum Tax

## INTRODUCTION

The **alternative minimum tax (AMT)**, like the passive activity rules, was enacted in 1986 to curb perceived abuses by high-income taxpayers attempting to minimize their current income tax liability. The AMT is the ultimate tax oxymoron. It is neither alternative (it *must* be used to calculate tax liability), nor is it minimum (the imposition of the AMT means that the taxpayer will have to pay *more* tax than that calculated using the regular tax system). Understanding why, and how, the AMT is imposed is important for planners who are advising clients who may be caught in its snares.

As an anti-abuse technique, the AMT is designed primarily to change the timing of tax payments, although in some cases, imposition of the AMT results in a permanent increase in

## Key Concepts

**Underline/highlight the answers to these questions as you read:**

1. Describe the purpose of the alternative minimum tax.

2. Identify the taxpayers most likely to be affected by the AMT.

3. Explain how the AMT is calculated.

4. Identify the phaseout thresholds for AMT exemptions.

tax. Long ago taxpayers learned that it is generally preferable or beneficial to pay less tax now, and defer any tax liability into the future. Several planning techniques were developed to do just that, resulting in a loss of current tax revenue for Congress. Congress would rather have taxpayers pay more now, and less later, since this fills federal coffers and minimizes the need to borrow to fund government expenditures. Furthermore, Congress believed it unfair to allow wealthy taxpayers to participate in many of these activities that reduce or eliminate their current tax liability in ways that were not available to lower and middle income taxpayers. The AMT is designed to offset the timing impact of tax deductions, so that those impacted by it will have to pay more tax now, and correspondingly less in the future. Generally, those impacted by the AMT are taxpayers who take advantage of "items of tax preference."

# HOW THE AMT WORKS

The AMT is an alternative tax calculation. The AMT applies to everyone, but it does not create additional tax for everyone and therefore does not increase an unaffected taxpayer's tax payment. When a taxpayer prepares his income tax return, the taxpayer must complete two tax calculations, the regular tax and the AMT. The first calculation will use the regular tax system, and is calculated on the taxpayer's Form 1040. Prior chapters in this textbook have reviewed, in detail, the calculation of tax under the regular income tax system. The second calculation that must be completed each year is the alternative minimum tax, which is calculated separately on Form 6251. A taxpayer is liable for the greater of the regular tax liability, or the tentative minimum tax calculated for AMT on Form 6251.

To calculate the AMT, the taxpayer starts with his regular taxable income from the Form 1040. The AMT system requires that certain changes be made to regular taxable income to calculate the AMT. These changes made to regular taxable income are referred to as adjustments or preferences. **Adjustments** can either increase or reduce **alternative minimum taxable income (AMTI)**, while **preferences** always result in an addition to AMTI. Once all adjustments and preferences have been accounted for, AMTI is calculated. An exemption (discussed below) is subtracted from AMTI to arrive at the AMT tax base, to which the AMT rate is applied. For individuals, the AMT rate is 26 percent on the first $175,000 of income ($87,500 for those married filing separately), and 28 percent on the excess. The result at this point is referred to as the tentative minimum tax, which is further reduced by any foreign tax credit that the taxpayer may claim, and the taxpayer's regular tax liability from Form 1040. The above detailed AMT formula is illustrated in Exhibit 15.1.

| EXHIBIT 15.1 | ALTERNATIVE MINIMUM TAX FORMULA |

---

**Taxable Income (from regular tax system)**

Add: Adjustments that increase AMTI

Less: Adjustments that decrease AMTI

Add: Preferences

**Alternative Minimum Taxable Income (AMTI)**

Less: Exemptions

**AMT Tax Base**

Application of Appropriate AMT Rate

**Tentative Minimum Tax**

Less: Foreign Tax Credit

Less: Regular Tax Liability (Form 1040)

**Alternative Minimum Tax (AMT)**

---

The applicable exemption used within the AMT calculation depends on the taxpayer's filing status and the taxpayer's AMTI. The following exhibit contains the AMT exemption amounts.

## AMT Exemption Amounts (2009)

Exhibit 15.2

| Filing Status | AMT Exemption |
|---|---|
| Single and Head of Household | $46,700 |
| Married Filing Jointly and Surviving Spouse | $70,950 |
| Married Filing Separately | $35,475 |
| Estates and Trusts | $22,500 |

These exemptions are subject to phaseout. When the taxpayer's AMTI begins to exceed certain amounts, the phaseout rule states that the exemption amount is reduced by 25 percent of the amount by which AMTI exceeds the beginning of the phaseout range. This reduction continues until the end of the phaseout range at which point the taxpayer's AMT exemption will be reduced to zero and the taxpayer will not be entitled to any AMT exemption.

## AMT Phaseout Thresholds (2009)

Exhibit 15.3

| Filing Status | Phaseout Begins At | Phaseout Ends At |
|---|---|---|
| Single and Head of Household | $112,500 | $299,300 |
| Married Filing Jointly and Surviving Spouse | $150,000 | $433,800 |
| Married Filing Separately and Estates and Trusts | $75,000 | $216,900 |

The structure of this phaseout affects high income taxpayers, who may have their AMT exemption limited, or eliminated, in the calculation of their alternative minimum tax.

Example 15.1

Jay is a single taxpayer with an AMTI of $150,000 in 2009. Because Jay's AMTI is above the phaseout threshold for single taxpayers of $112,500, Jay's AMT exemption for 2009 must be reduced. The phaseout rule states that the exemption amount is reduced by 25% of the amount by which the taxpayer's AMTI exceed the threshold. Therefore, Jay's AMT exemption amount must be reduced by 25% of $37,500 ($150,000 - $112,500) or $9,375. Consequently, Jay's AMT exemption for 2009 is $37,325 ($46,700 - $9,375).

Example 15.2

Bradley is a married filing jointly taxpayer with an AMTI of $325,000 in 2009. Because Bradley's AMTI is above the phaseout threshold for married filing jointly taxpayers of $150,000, his AMT exemption must be reduced by $43,750 [($325,000 - $150,000) x 25%]. The maximum AMT exemption amount is $70,950 for a married filing jointly taxpayer. Therefore, Bradley's AMT exemption for 2009 is $27,200 ($70,950 - $43,750).

Now assume all the same facts except that Bradley has an AMTI of $450,000 for 2009. Bradley's AMT exemption must be reduced by $75,000 [($450,000 - $150,000) x 25%]. Because the 2009 maximum AMT exemption amount is only $70,950, Bradley is not entitled to an exemption this year. (Note: His income is greater than the limit of the phaseout.)

In some cases, triggering the AMT causes a permanent increase in tax. In other cases, the AMT merely changes the timing of the tax payment. Adjustments and preferences are classified as either exclusion items or deferral items. **Exclusion items** result in a permanent increase in tax. **Deferral items** result in a tax credit equal to the additional tax that must be paid in the current year, and this credit can be used to offset tax liability in a future year when the taxpayer is no longer subject to the AMT. There is an unlimited carryforward for the AMT credit generated from deferral items, but the credit may not be carried back and applied against regular tax liability in past years. From a planning standpoint, therefore, deferral items are better to have than exclusion items.

Additionally, capital gains are taxed at the same rate for AMT purposes as they are for regular tax purposes. As a result, even though capital gains have a lower tax rate (15%) than the AMT rates, capital gains do not have an impact on whether a taxpayer will become an AMT taxpayer.

## Quick Quiz 15.1

**Highlight the answer to these questions:**

1. The AMT was designed to curb abuses by high-income taxpayers.
   a. True
   b. False

2. The AMT is most likely to affect low-income taxpayers.
   a. True
   b. False

3. The Foreign Tax Credit increases the tentative minimum tax.
   a. True
   b. False

4. In some cases, the AMT merely changes the timing of a tax payment.
   a. True
   b. False

True, False, False, True.

## ADJUSTMENTS AND PREFERENCES

As illustrated in the AMT formula, the key planning issues surrounding the AMT involve the adjustments and preferences that are added to regular taxable income to arrive at alternative minimum taxable income (AMTI). For simplicity, we will review these adjustments and preferences in four categories: (1) exemptions and standard deduction changes; (2) itemized deduction changes; (3) investment-related changes; and (4) business-related changes.

## PERSONAL AND DEPENDENCY EXEMPTIONS AND THE STANDARD DEDUCTION

Personal and dependency exemptions are not allowed for the AMT. They are added back to the regular taxable income in computing the AMT. The standard deduction is also disallowed for taxpayers who use the standard deduction. As with personal and dependency exemptions, the standard deduction is added to the regular taxable income in calculating the AMT.

## ITEMIZED DEDUCTION CHANGES

From a personal financial planning standpoint, itemized deduction changes are perhaps the most important changes for clients. Many taxpayers itemize deductions, and it is important for the planner to understand how these deductions are treated differently under the regular tax system as compared to the AMT system.

## SUMMARY OF ITEMIZED DEDUCTIONS

EXHIBIT 15.4

|  | Deductible Regular Tax | Deductible AMT | Differences |
|---|---|---|---|
| **Home Mortgage Interest** | Regular rules | Qualified mortgage interest only | Lose tax deduction for excess refinance interest. Add back interest or refinance |
| **Medical** | Excess above 7.5% AGI | Excess above 10% AGI (Add back 2.5%) | AMT costs extra 2.5% |
| **Taxes** | Property/sales/use/ ad valorem deductible | Not deductible, except tax on qualified motor vehicles | Lose all tax deductions under AMT (Add all back except tax on qualified motor vehicles) |
| **Miscellaneous** | Subject to 2% | Not deductible | Lose all miscellaneous itemized deductions (Add back with exceptions) |
| **Charitable** | Regular rules | Same as regular | No change |
| **Casualty** | Regular rules | Same as regular | No change |

The first adjustment that must be made for itemized deductions involves home mortgage interest. Generally, qualified mortgage interest paid to acquire a primary and secondary residence is deductible for both regular and AMT tax purposes. If, however, the mortgage is refinanced in an amount in excess of the original mortgage, interest on the excess refinancing (current mortgage – amortized original mortgage), must be added back to income to calculate AMTI.

Second, medical and dental expenses are deductible for AMT purposes only if they exceed 10 percent (7.5% + 2.5%) of the taxpayer's adjusted gross income for regular tax purposes. Thus, if medical and dental expenses were claimed as a deduction for regular tax purposes, an amount equal to the lower of (1) the medical expenses claimed, or (2) 2.5% of the taxpayers adjusted gross income, must be added back to income for purposes of calculating AMTI.

Third, any state or local income, property, or sales taxes claimed as a deduction for regular tax purposes must be added back to income to determine AMTI. No deduction is allowed for state and local taxes once the taxpayer becomes an AMT taxpayer. There is only one exception to this rule. For 2009, if a taxpayer claims the standard deduction for regular tax purposes, and the standard deduction includes any state or local sales or excise tax on the purchase of a qualified motor vehicle, that tax is permitted as a deduction for AMT purposes. Taxpayers itemizing deductions on their tax return are not eligible for this special exemption.

Finally, miscellaneous itemized deductions are added back to income to determine AMTI. There are exceptions to this rule, for example, certain deductions for estate tax (the estate tax attributable to the inclusion of Income in Respect of a Decedent (IRD) assets in the decedent's estate), wagering, casualty loss, and investment interest to the extent of net investment income are allowed as a deduction for AMT purposes. All other miscellaneous itemized deductions are disallowed for AMT and must be added back, however.

Exhibit 15.5 summarizes the itemized deductions that must be added back to income to calculate AMTI.

**Key Concepts**

**Underline/highlight the answers to these questions as you read:**

1. Describe the general effect of adjustments and preferences on AMTI.

2. Identify how itemized deductions are effected by AMT.

3. Explain how the exercise of ISOs affects AMT.

4. Identify business-related items that are deferral or exclusion items for AMT.

| EXHIBIT 15.5 | DEDUCTIONS LOST USING AMT |
|---|---|

| |
|---|
| • 100% of home mortgage interest on excess refinancing (current mortgage – amortized original mortgage) |
| • An additional 2.5% of medical and dental expenses |
| • 100% of state and local income, property, and sales taxes |
| • Almost 100% of miscellaneous itemized deductions |

Note that charitable contributions and casualty losses as itemized deductions for regular tax are not impacted in any way by the AMT rules, and they do not have to be added back into income when calculating AMTI.

As discussed in Chapter 7, itemized deductions are subject to phaseout for high income taxpayers under the regular tax system. This phaseout rule does not apply when calculating AMTI. Therefore, taxpayers in the phaseout range must reduce their taxable income by the amount of the phaseout attributable to allowable itemized deductions for AMT purposes when calculating

AMTI. Beginning in 2006, the itemized deduction phaseout is itself being phased out through 2009. Until the phaseout has been eliminated, any reduction in itemized deductions caused by the phaseout rule should be subtracted from taxable income in calculating AMTI.

If an individual does not itemize deductions, the standard deduction is added back to taxable income when calculating AMTI. Only the allowable itemized deductions noted above may be used as deductions for AMT purposes.

Once the changes for itemized deductions necessary to calculate AMTI have been made, the next question that becomes important is "Are these exclusion or deferral items?" Unfortunately, all of the itemized deduction changes are classified as exclusion items. Any additional AMT generated by adding these items to calculate AMTI will not result in the creation of a credit that can be used against regular tax liability in the future, but will rather result in a permanent increase in tax liability for the taxpayer.

## INVESTMENT-RELATED CHANGES

Certain investment activities may also have an impact on AMT. The two most important considerations from a planning standpoint are (1) interest on private activity municipal bonds, and (2) exercise of incentive stock options (ISOs).

### *Private Activity Municipal Bonds*

**Private Activity Municipal Bonds** are securities issued by or on behalf of local governments that bear interest which is tax-exempt for regular tax purposes and are used to provide debt financing for private projects (as opposed to public/ governmental projects). Projects that may be financed by private activity municipal bonds include airports, residential rental projects, sports stadiums, and qualified hazardous waste facilities, just to name a few. Interest earned on private activity municipal bonds is excluded from tax for regular income tax purposes, but is potentially taxable under the AMT. This interest must be added back to regular taxable income to arrive at AMTI. Recall that if a client would like to purchase a municipal bond that will be fully exempt from income tax (both regular and AMT), he or she could purchase a public purpose municipal bond.

Quick
Quiz 15.2

**Highlight the answer to these questions:**

1. If a taxpayer's medical expenses equal 5% of their AGI, this will not affect the calculation of AMTI.
   a. True
   b. False

2. Charitable contributions must be added back to calculate AMTI.
   a. True
   b. False

3. All itemized deduction changes are deferral items.
   a. True
   b. False

True, False, False.

For tax years beginning in 2008, tax exempt interest received on the following types of municipal bonds are not considered items of tax preference and are therefore not subject to the AMT if the bonds were issued after 2008. Municipal bonds that qualify for this exemption from AMT include:

- An exempt facility bond for which 95% or more of the net proceeds are to be used to provide qualified residential rental projects,
- A qualified mortgage bond,
- A qualified veterans mortgage bond, or
- Any refunding bond of the bond being refunded (or in the case of a series of refunded bonds, the original bond) is one of the bonds listed above issued after July 30, 2008.

Furthermore, tax-exempt interest on specified private activity bonds issued in 2009 and 2010 are exempt from the AMT.

You may recall that, as a general rule, taxpayers can only deduct expenses for income tax purposes if the amount claimed had already been brought into income. Applying this general rule to municipal bonds, we learned that investment interest expense associated with acquiring a portfolio of municipal bonds is not deductible for regular tax purposes since the income generated by the bonds is exempt from tax. (Alternatively stated, since the taxpayer purchasing municipal bonds was not sharing his or her gains with the government, the government does not allow a tax deduction for the interest incurred to acquire the investment.) When municipal bond interest becomes taxable under the AMT system, however, any investment interest paid to acquire the bonds will be deductible when arriving at AMTI. This adjustment for investment interest expense used to acquire the municipal bond portfolio is in concert with the general rule that allows deductions for expenses incurred in purchasing investments where the gains from the investment will be shared with the government in the form of tax revenue.

The add-back of the interest on private activity municipal bonds (unless issued after June 30, 2008 and excluded from this treatment), and the deduction permitted for investment interest incurred to acquire those bonds, are considered to be AMT exclusion items. As a result, any increase in tax caused by the adjustments for private activity bonds will be a permanent increase in tax for the taxpayer, and no credit will be available to offset future regular tax liability.

### Incentive Stock Options (ISOs)

Another investment related activity that could have an impact on a taxpayer's AMT liability is the exercise of Incentive Stock Options (ISOs).

There are two types of stock options:
- Nonqualified Stock Options, and
- Incentive Stock Options.

A **Nonqualified Stock Option (NQSO)** is a right to purchase shares of company stock at a given strike price (generally set at the market price of the stock on the day the option is granted). The exercise of a NQSO results in ordinary income for the taxpayer equal to the difference between the value of the stock on the day of exercise and the strike price of the option. When a NQSO is granted to an employee, the employer must withhold taxes on exercise, including employment (Social Security) taxes. Since a NQSO results in ordinary income tax treatment, it is not a preference item for AMT purposes and does not have to be added back to taxable income to arrive at AMTI (it is already included in taxable income).

An **Incentive Stock Option (ISO)** has different characteristics. To qualify as an ISO, the issuing company must comply with a host of special rules. The advantage of an ISO, as compared to a nonqualified stock option, is that if the taxpayer meets the holding period requirement, the gain on the option will be taxed as capital gain instead of ordinary income. To qualify for capital gain tax treatment, the stock must be held a minimum of two years from the date of the grant of the ISO, and one year from the date of the exercise of the option. If either part of this two-pronged holding period test is not met, the taxpayer will have to report the gain as ordinary income. At the exercise of an ISO, therefore, there is no immediate regular income tax consequence since it is not possible to determine, at that time, whether the gain will be taxed as ordinary income or as a capital gain. If the taxpayer exercises the option and sells the stock within one year (referred to as a disqualifying disposition), the gain will be taxed at ordinary rates because the holding period was not met, and the ISO will be treated similarly to an NQSO.

While the exercise of an ISO does not impact the taxpayer's regular tax liability, it may result in the imposition of the AMT. The difference between the value of the stock on the date of exercise and the strike price of the option must be added to taxable income to arrive at AMTI. When a taxpayer exercises a large number of options in one tax year, and does not sell the stock (thereby triggering a disqualifying disposition and imposing ordinary income tax on the gain), there is a danger of becoming an AMT taxpayer.

**EXAMPLE 15.3**

Ryan, a single individual, who is an executive at Murphy's Consulting, Inc., was granted 1,000 ISOs on Murphy's stock two years ago when the price per share was $15. The last few years have resulted in tremendous growth for Murphy's and the stock is now trading at $75 per share. Ryan exercised the ISOs, but did not sell the stock – he plans on holding the shares for at least a year so he can pay the lower capital gains tax rate on the growth. Even though exercise of the options did not result in a taxable event for regular tax purposes this year, Ryan will have to add $60,000 to his taxable income when computing AMTI. If there are no other transactions this year that could reduce AMTI, it is likely that Ryan will become an AMT taxpayer for the year, since the tax preference item – the gain on the exercise of the ISO – is greater than his exemption for AMT purposes.

**EXAMPLE 15.4**

Assume the same facts as above, except that Ryan exercises the options and sells the shares. In this case, since there was a disqualifying disposition of the stock (Ryan did not meet the two year from date of grant/one year from date of exercise holding period), the gain will be taxed as ordinary income to Ryan this year. Since the gain is included in income, there is no adjustment to be made when calculating AMTI. In a circumstance such as this, it is unlikely that Ryan will become an AMT taxpayer in the current year.

From a planning standpoint, it may be wise to counsel clients with ISOs to exercise the ISOs in small amounts over time so that the gain is not combined into one tax year.

Unlike the itemized deduction adjustments and the preferences for private activity bonds, the adjustments to taxable income from ISOs are considered deferral items (not exclusion items), and any AMT generated by including the ISOs in AMTI will become a credit that can be used to offset future, regular tax liability.

### Other Investment-Related Changes

In addition to the AMT rules concerning private activity municipal bond interest and incentive stock options, adjustments must be made for certain transactions when the taxpayer moves to AMT status. In particular, gains or losses on the sale or disposition of property must be recalculated if the taxpayer's AMT basis in the asset is different than his or her regular basis. Likewise, loss limitations imposed by the amount at-risk limitation and the passive activity rules must be recalculated taking into account any adjustments required for AMT purposes. While calculation of these adjustments is beyond the scope of this text, you should be aware that these adjustments are often necessary due primarily to changes in allowable depreciation deductions, which will be discussed briefly below. When calculating AMTI, certain adjustments must be made to the depreciation deductions taken for regular tax purposes, and these adjustments must also be taken into account when considering gain/loss and passive limitations when calculating the alternative minimum tax.

| EXHIBIT 15.6 | SUMMARY OF AMT INVESTMENT RELATED CHANGES |

| | Regular Tax | AMT | Differences |
|---|---|---|---|
| **Private Activities Municipal Bonds** | Not taxable | Taxable | AMT preference item |
| **NQSOs** | At exercise W-2 income | Same | None |
| **ISOs** | At exercise No regular tax | At exercise AMT income to extent fair market value strike price | AMT at exercise |

### BUSINESS-RELATED CHANGES

One of the advantages of using an asset in the active conduct of a trade or business is the ability to claim depreciation deductions, which allows the taxpayer to recoup his investment over the useful life of the asset. Asset class lives and depreciation scales are provided for both real and personal property. When a taxpayer becomes an AMT taxpayer, however, the depreciation time period lengthens, requiring the taxpayer to add back some of the depreciation claimed for regular income tax purposes.

In addition to regular depreciation, the Code allows quicker expensing of asset costs, and, in some cases, immediate expensing of asset costs for certain specified expenditures. Usually, Congress allows businesses to immediately expense costs in an effort to provide an incentive for investment in that area. Expenditures that qualify for these special rules include circulation costs (for publishers), intangible drilling costs (for oil and gas investors), mining costs (for natural resource extractors) and research and experimental costs (for scientific enterprises). If a taxpayer moves from regular status to AMT status, adjustments must be made to the expenses claimed on these activities so that, usually, the taxpayer will have to add part of the expense claimed back to taxable income in arriving at AMTI.

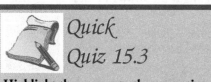

## Quick Quiz 15.3

**Highlight the answer to these questions:**

1. Interest earned on private activity bonds is added back to taxable income to calculate AMTI.
   a. True
   b. False

2. Exercising a large number of ISOs and not selling the stock in the same tax year may result in the imposition of AMT.
   a. True
   b. False

True, True.

All of the depreciation and accelerated expense adjustments mentioned above are considered to be deferral items for AMT purposes. If any AMT is generated due to the inclusion of these items in AMTI, the taxpayer will receive a credit of a like amount that can be used against future regular tax liability. These adjustments change the timing of the payment of tax (they require the taxpayer to pay more now, less later), but do not result in a permanent increase in tax burden.

Two additional business related changes are exclusion items, resulting in a permanent change in tax burden if their inclusion causes the taxpayer to be subject to the AMT. The business related exclusion items are (1) depletion, and (2) qualified small business stock (under Section 1202).

**Depletion** is a form of depreciation that applies to natural resources. As minerals are extracted from the earth, the owner of the mineral rights may claim a depletion deduction to recoup some of his capital used to acquire the mineral rights. When a taxpayer moves into AMT status, the deduction for depletion must be recalculated taking into consideration allowable AMT income and deductions from the activity. Once the taxpayer is subject to the AMT, the depletion deduction is further limited to the taxpayer's alternative minimum tax basis in the activity. Compared to the allowable depletion rules in the regular tax system, this rule severely limits the taxpayer's ability to claim deductions. As noted above, the depletion changes are exclusion items. Once the adjustment is made and the AMT applies, the taxpayer's tax burden has been permanently increased.

In an effort to encourage individuals to capitalize small corporations, Section 1202 of the Code allows investors of qualified small business stock to exclude 50 percent of the capital gain from income. If a taxpayer claiming a Section 1202 exclusion becomes an AMT taxpayer, however, seven percent of the excluded gain must be added back to taxable income in arriving at AMTI. If the gain on Section 1202 stock is large, the gain alone could cause a taxpayer to move into AMT status. Too much of a good thing can trigger the AMT – but, that is what the AMT was designed to do – minimize the ability of high income taxpayers to artificially manipulate their income tax liability down by taking advantage of tax preference items. The preference for Section 1202 stock is an exclusion item, resulting in a permanent increase in tax liability for the taxpayer.

## MISCELLANEOUS ADJUSTMENTS

In addition to the major categories of changes described above, when a person becomes an AMT taxpayer, several other adjustments must be made to the tax return as well (to calculate AMTI). While these adjustments are beyond the scope of this text, you should be aware that adjustments will be made to Section 179 depreciation deductions, expenses associated with business use of the taxpayer's home, deductions for IRAs, Keogh, SEP, and SIMPLE plans, the self-employed health insurance deduction, and distributions from IRAs.

## CORPORATIONS AND THE AMT

Corporations are also subject to the AMT. The AMT tax rate that applies at the corporate level is 20 percent. Many of the adjustment and preference items discussed above with respect to individual taxpayers also apply to corporations, and there are additional corporate AMT rules that need to be complied with. A detailed discussion of corporate AMT rules is beyond the scope of this text.

One corporate AMT rule is directly relevant to financial planners, however. Many financial planners deal with clients who have family or closely held businesses, and these businesses are often structured in corporate form. Since 1997, small corporations have been exempted from the AMT. A **small corporation** is defined as a corporation with average gross receipts of $5 million or less for the past three taxable years. Once a small corporation achieves exemption from the AMT by meeting this rule, it remains exempt as long as the corporation's three-year average gross receipts do not exceed $7.5 million. When three-year average gross receipts exceed $7.5 million, the corporation is subject to the corporate AMT.

## CONCLUSION

The AMT, like the passive activity rules, is designed to prevent abusive practices resulting in low current tax liability for wealthy individuals. While its application is complex, the idea is simple. Understanding the types of activities and events that may cause the imposition of the AMT gives financial planners an edge in counseling clients who may find themselves subject to this alternative tax system.

# Key Terms

*Adjustments* - AMT changes made to regular taxable income that either increase or decrease AMTI.

*Alternative Minimum Tax (AMT)* - An anti-abuse technique designed to change the timing of tax payments.

*Alternative Minimum Taxable Income (AMTI)* - Regular taxable income plus or minus certain adjustments and preferences.

*Deferral Items* - Adjustments and preferences that result in a tax credit that can be used in future years equal to the additional tax that must be paid in the current year.

*Depletion* - A form of depreciation that applies to natural resources.

*Exclusion Items* - Adjustments and preferences that result in a permanent increase in tax.

*Incentive Stock Option (ISO)* - A stock option that meets certain requirements and is granted by a corporation to an employee to purchase the stock of that corporation.

*Nonqualified Stock Option (NQSO)* - A right to purchase shares of company stock at a given strike price (generally set at the market price of the stock on the day the option is granted).

*Preferences* - AMT changes made to regular taxable income that increase AMTI.

*Private Activity Municipal Bonds* - Securities issued by or on behalf of local governments that bear tax-exempt interest for regular income tax and are used to provide debt financing for private projects. Private Activity Municipal Bond income is an AMT preference item.

*Small Corporation* - A corporation with average gross receipts of $7.5 million or less for the past three years.

## DISCUSSION QUESTIONS

1. Describe the purpose of the alternative minimum tax.

2. Describe, in general, how the AMT is calculated.

3. How do adjustments and preferences affect AMTI?

4. How is the AMT exemption phased out?

5. What is the difference between an exclusion item and a deferral item?

6. What itemized deduction items are lost by the application of the AMT?

7. How is qualified mortgage interest affected by the AMT?

8. What regular tax itemized deductions are not affected by AMT?

9. How are private activity municipal bonds affected by AMT?

10. How does the exercise of an ISO impact AMT?

11. Name three business-related items that can be affected by AMT.

12. Are all corporations subject to AMT?

1.  HHH Company grants Henry one incentive stock option (ISO) on January 10, 2007. The exercise price is $10. The market price on the exercise date (January 11, 2008) is $33. What is the AMT consequence when Henry exercises the ISO?

    a.  $0 AMT gain.

    b.  $10 AMT gain.

    c.  $23 AMT gain.

    d.  $33 AMT gain.

2.  Which of the following is true regarding AMT?

    a.  Interest for home acquisition indebtedness deducted for regular tax purposes must be added back.

    b.  A taxpayer who has deductible medical expenses for regular tax purposes of $10,000 will have an add-back of 2.5% of AGI for AMT purposes.

    c.  Municipal bond interest must be added back for AMT purposes.

    d.  Charitable contributions deducted for regular income tax purposes are limited to 30%.

3.  Your client, who has a taxable income of $200,000, is concerned about being subject to the alternative minimum tax (AMT). The following income and deductions were included in computing taxable income. Select the one item that may be added to (or subtracted from) regular taxable income in calculating the AMT.

    a.  A long-term capital gain of $90,000.

    b.  A cash contribution to your client's church of $18,000.

    c.  Dividend income of $80,000.

    d.  A state income tax deduction of $22,000.

4.  Gavin, a single individual who is an executive at IT Consulting, Inc. was granted 1,500 ISOs on IT's stock two years ago when the price per share was $25. The last few years have resulted in tremendous growth for IT Consulting and the stock is now trading at $55 per share. Gavin exercised the ISOs, but did not sell the stock – he plans on holding the shares for at least a year so he can pay the lower capital gains tax rate on the growth. How much will Gavin have to add to his taxable income when computing AMTI as a result of this transaction?

    a.  $0.

    b.  $37,500.

    c.  $45,000.

    d.  $82,500.

5. The alternative minimum tax (AMT) was originally designed to:

    a. Create a more user-friendly tax system.

    b. Curb abuses by high-income taxpayers.

    c. Provide additional credits to certain low-income taxpayers.

    d. Give taxpayers a choice of which tax to pay.

6. In 2009, Larry (a single taxpayer) has an AMTI of $175,000. What is Larry's AMT exemption this year?

    a. $0.

    b. $15,625.

    c. $31,075.

    d. $33,750.

7. In 2009, Elizabeth (a surviving spouse) has an AMTI of $450,000. What is Elizabeth's AMT exemption this year?

    a. $0.

    b. $45,000.

    c. $150,000.

    d. $350,000.

8. George has deductible medical expenses of $12,000 under the regular tax system and an AGI of $100,000. What are the tax consequences for computing George's AMTI?

    a. George's AMTI is not affected by his medical expenses.

    b. $300 of George's medical expenses must be added back to compute his AMTI.

    c. $2,500 of George's medical expenses must be added back to compute his AMTI.

    d. All of George's medical expenses must be deducted to compute his AMTI.

9. Which of the following deductions would be fully allowed in calculating a taxpayer's AMT?

    a. Interest on a mortgage with a principal balance of $500,000. The mortgage was originally taken out for $400,000, and was almost immediately refinanced to acquire $100,000 in home equity.

    b. Medical expenses in excess of 7.5% of AGI.

    c. Real estate taxes paid on the taxpayer's principal residence.

    d. Casualty losses in excess of 10% of AGI.

10. Which of the following would be added to a taxpayer's regular taxable income to arrive at alternative minimum taxable income?

    a. Receipt of interest on public purpose municipal bonds.

    b. Receipt of interest on private activity municipal bonds.

    c. Exercise of non-qualified stock options.

    d. Sale of the shares purchased through the exercise of incentive stock options.

11. Which of the following statements concerning the taxation of incentive stock options (ISOs) is correct?

    a. On the date of exercise, the difference between the fair market value of the stock and the exercise price is included in regular taxable income.

    b. If the taxpayer sells the stock acquired by exercising an ISO more than one year after the date the option was granted, the gain will be taxed at capital gains tax rates.

    c. The sale of stock acquired by exercising an ISO will trigger a potential AMT tax for the taxpayer.

    d. The grant of ISOs to a taxpayer does not result in a taxable event for regular or AMT tax purposes.

12. John became an AMT taxpayer last year. As a result, he had to add several items to his taxable income in arriving at alternative minimum taxable income. Which of the following items will result in an AMT credit that can be used to offset future regular tax liability?

    a. $7,000 in property taxes paid on his principal residence.

    b. $80,000 difference between the fair market value of stock and the strike price in the incentive stock option used to purchase the stock.

    c. $3,000 in interest on private activity municipal bonds.

    d. $2,000 in additional medical expenses.

13. Which of the following statements concerning the application of the AMT to C corporations is correct?

    a. As separate taxable entities, all C corporations are potentially subject to the AMT.

    b. The AMT tax rate that applies to corporations is a flat 26%.

    c. Corporations that have average gross receipts of $7.5 million or less on a rolling three-year average are exempt from the AMT.

    d. All corporations are exempt from the AMT, since the AMT applies only to individuals.

14. All of the following adjustments or preferences will result in a permanent increase in tax when a taxpayer becomes an AMT taxpayer EXCEPT:

    a. Most miscellaneous itemized deductions.

    b. Medical expenses in excess of 7.5% and less than 10% of AGI.

    c. State income taxes.

    d. The gain on stock underlying ISOs from the date of grant to the date of exercise.

15. All of the following statements about the alternative minimum tax (AMT) are correct, EXCEPT:

    a. The AMT is designed primarily to change the timing of tax payments to more current.

    b. Some adjustments made for AMT purposes result in a permanent increase in tax.

    c. As an alternative to the regular income tax system, a taxpayer may elect to pay tax based on the AMT calculation.

    d. The AMT frustrates efforts by taxpayers to participate in activities that reduce or eliminate their current tax liability.

# Quick Quiz Explanations

### Quick Quiz 15.1

1. True.
2. False. The AMT is more likely to affect wealthy taxpayers who take advantage of "items of tax preference."
3. False. The tentative minimum tax is reduced by any Foreign Tax Credit that the taxpayer may claim.
4. True.

### Quick Quiz 15.2

1. True.
2. False. Charitable contributions, like casualty losses, are itemized deductions for regular tax and are not impacted in any way by the AMT rules. In addition, they do not have to be added back into income (or, an alternative way of thinking of this is reversed out) when calculating AMTI.
3. False. All of the itemized deduction changes are classified as exclusion items, not deferral items.

### Quick Quiz 15.3

1. True.
2. True.

### Quick Quiz 15.4

1. False. Depreciation is considered to be a deferral item, not an exclusion item. for AMT purposes.
2. False. Depletion, unlike depreciation, is an exclusion item for AMT purposes.

# Business Entity Selection and Taxation

## INTRODUCTION

One of the most important decisions new business owners will make is the selection of the entity type to be used for conducting the business activities of the enterprise.

The most common legal forms of business (entity types) used in the United States are the sole proprietorship, general and limited partnerships, including limited liability partnerships (LLPs) and family limited partnerships (FLPs), the limited liability company (LLC), the regular C corporation, and the S corporation.

The selection process includes consideration of the following factors:
1. Ease and cost of formation,
2. Complexity of management and governance,
3. How transferability and dissolution are achieved,
4. Liability protection for owners' personal assets, and
5. Reporting requirements and taxation.

### EASE AND COST OF FORMATION

Proprietorships and general partnerships are less complex, inexpensive, and easy to form, while the other entity types are more complex and expensive to form. Entities are almost always formed under state law. Therefore, the state itself will dictate the requirements for formation and the formalities that must be followed to maintain the entity's status.

### COMPLEXITY OF MANAGEMENT AND GOVERNANCE

Proprietorships are the least complex in terms of management and governance. In addition, the administrative requirements and formalities dictated by state law are the least burdensome for sole proprietorships. Proprietorships and general partnerships do not typically require an initial filing registration with the state and have fewer state-imposed annual filing requirements. Furthermore, proprietorships and general partnerships have fewer state-imposed operational requirements that must be met to assure continuation of the entity's status and the benefits that the status brings.

## TRANSFERABILITY AND DISSOLUTION

Transferability of an ownership interest is easiest with a proprietorship and becomes increasingly more difficult as we move along a spectrum of business entities to the C corporation. Transferability is most difficult with a publicly traded C corporation that has stock listed on an exchange. Partnerships, limited partnerships, LLPs, FLPs, LLCs, S corporations, and smaller C corporations generally have limited or restricted transferability rights. Unlike other business forms, proprietorships can be dissolved at the election of the owner and do not require formal steps for dissolution.

### Key Concepts

**Underline/highlight the answers to these questions as you read:**

1. Name the most common legal entities.

2. Identify the factors to be considered during the entity selection process.

3. Define "piercing the veil."

## LIABILITY PROTECTION FOR OWNERS' PERSONAL ASSETS

Some business forms offer liability protection for investors. If liability protection is available, the investors in such business ventures or entities will not have their personal assets exposed to business (entity) debts or obligations. This protection, which may be the most important factor in entity choice, is not available to proprietorships or general partnerships, nor to general partners of a limited partnership and only to a limited extent for limited liability partnerships (LLP). We refer to this protection as limited liability.

There are situations in which an entity that has limited liability protection for its owners under state law can lose that protection. The state requires that for such protection to continue, the entity must alert the public to its status in a clear and identifiable manner so as to put business creditors on notice that the entity has such protection. Entities do this through markings on business correspondence such as invoices, letterhead, business cards, and through markings on vehicles (with the name and LLC or Inc. designated), which signals the limited liability status to the public. The entities receiving such protection usually are required to maintain a reasonable amount of liability insurance to protect the public (e.g., vehicle liability insurance) and are required to be vigilant in meeting any annual formalities to maintain the state-granted entity status.

### General Liability Issues

Relying on the entity as the primary source of liability protection is dependent on it maintaining a clear and consistent identity of the entity as a corporation, limited partnership, or limited liability company. Failure to maintain that identity in contracts and correspondence could result in a court **"piercing the veil"** of liability protection, which may result in personal liability for the owner(s). Piercing the veil means disregarding the status of the entity that gives the owners limited liability. A secondary source of protection is liability insurance, which must be sufficient in amount and sufficiently comprehensive in risk coverage, to cover the claims of creditors.

To avoid piercing the veil, the entity should keep its books and records separate from the personal books and records of the owners, segregate activities of business from personal affairs, follow corporate formalities such as meeting requirements and filings, and address all content in contracts and correspondence from the view point of the business entity (rather than the owners').

## REPORTING REQUIREMENTS AND TAXATION

States individually require annual filings and other types of reporting. All entities that have employees will have payroll reporting at both the state and federal level. All entities that have retail sales will have sales tax returns to prepare in states that impose sales taxes.

However, there are few, if any, other state reporting requirements for proprietorships and general partnerships. However, for all other types of entities there will be annual reporting requirements that are state-imposed to maintain the entity's status.

For federal income tax purposes, the income of a proprietorship or a single-member LLC is reported on the Schedule C of the individual owner's Form 1040. For all other types of entities, an entity-level tax return is filed. A partnership files Form 1065, an S corporation files Form 1120S, and a C corporation files Form 1120. All of the returns other than the C corporation return are informational returns because there is no tax at the entity level. The income and losses of such entities "flow through" to the individual owners. Each owner's share of the entity's income or loss is reported to the owner on a Schedule K-1.

The C corporation is a separate entity for taxation and its income is taxed at the entity level. However, it does have the advantage of being able to accumulate profits at the corporate level without the owners having to pay income taxes on those profits until they are distributed to the owners by the corporation.

## Quick Quiz 16.1

**Highlight the answer to these questions:**

1. Not all entities are separate legal entities for the purposes of taxation.
   a. True
   b. False

2. "Piercing the veil" may occur if business owners fail to keep their personal records with their business records.
   a. True
   b. False

True, False.

Choosing the correct entity type requires an understanding of each type of the entity, its advantages and disadvantages, competing considerations including each of the factors above, and business loss considerations.

In general, the most important factors in entity selection are ease of formation, liability protection, and the manner of taxation. However, serious thought should be given to all of the factors to make the right choice for the nature of the business and the objectives of the owners.

It is also important to periodically review the choice of legal form (entity) to determine whether changes in circumstances may suggest a change in entity type.

# SOLE PROPRIETORSHIPS

**Sole proprietorships** are business ventures owned and operated by a single individual. A sole proprietorship arises when an individual engages in a business for profit. A sole proprietorship can operate under the name of the owner or it can conduct business under a trade or fictitious name such as "The Corner Pocket." No filings are required with the Secretary of State and no annual filing fees are required. There is no transfer of assets to the entity because the entity is considered a legal extension of the proprietor.

## FORMATION

Formation is easy and inexpensive, although the proprietorship may be required to obtain a local business license. In addition, if the proprietorship will be collecting sales taxes, it must register with the state or local taxing authority. Operation is easy in that all decisions are made by the proprietor. Any trade names or assets are owned by the individual proprietor.

## INTEREST, DISPOSAL OF INTEREST, AND DISSOLUTION

A proprietor has a 100 percent interest in the proprietorship assets and income. It is relatively easy to sell assets of a proprietorship, but it does require finding a buyer. Dissolution is achieved by simply discontinuing business operations and paying creditors or by the death of the proprietor.

*Key Concepts*

**Underline/highlight the answers to these questions as you read:**

1. Describe the formation and operation of a sole proprietorship.

2. Describe the liability issues associated with a sole proprietorship.

3. Explain how a sole proprietorship can raise capital.

4. Explain the tax attributes of a sole proprietorship.

## CAPITAL

Capital for a proprietorship is limited to the resources of the proprietor including the proprietor's ability to borrow.

## LIABILITY

One of the major disadvantages of a sole proprietorship is the potential legal liability. The sole proprietor is personally legally liable for the debts and torts of his sole proprietorship business. There is no separate legal entity under which limited liability protection for personal assets may be claimed.

## MANAGEMENT/OPERATIONS

The proprietor has the day-to-day management and decision-making responsibilities, including the hiring and firing of employees. There is no guarantee of continuity beyond the proprietor.

## INCOME TAXATION AND PAYROLL (SOCIAL SECURITY) TAXES

The cost of tax compliance is low because the proprietor simply adds a Schedule C to his Form 1040 (See Exhibit 16.1) and generally does not even obtain a separate federal taxpayer tax identification number (unless the proprietor hires employees, in which case an Employer Identification Number (EIN) must be obtained). Rather, the proprietor conducts business under his own Social Security number. There is no ability to allocate income to other taxpayers since there is only one owner. A sole proprietor does not have to pay unemployment taxes on himself, but he must pay unemployment taxes for his employees. However, the proprietor does pay self-employment tax (up to 15.3 percent) on his own earnings (see Schedule SE, Exhibit 16.2) and one-half of Social Security taxes for his employees.

### *Taking Deductions*

The proprietor can deduct all ordinary and necessary business expenses from gross income. The business deductions are in Part II of Schedule C, lines 8-27 (2008) (Exhibit 16.1). The net profit or loss from line 31 of Schedule C is then carried over to line 12 of Form 1040 (identified by the arrow in Exhibit 16.1 and the first arrow in Exhibit 16.3). The proprietor may also make deductible contributions to a qualified or other retirement plan, but these contributions are reported on his Form 1040 as a deduction for AGI on line 28 of the 1040 (identified by the second arrow in Exhibit 16.3).

### Employer Deduction for Retirement Plans

The proprietor can usually deduct, subject to certain limitations, contributions made to a qualified plan for employees, including those made for the proprietor. The contributions (and the attributable earnings and gains) are generally not taxed to the employee until distributed by the plan. The deduction limit for contributions to a qualified plan depends on the type of plan.

The deduction for contributions to a defined contribution plan cannot exceed 25 percent of the compensation paid or accrued during the year to eligible employees participating in the plan. The proprietor must reduce this limit in figuring the deduction for contributions made to his own account. Recall that the maximum compensation that can be taken into account when calculating plan funding for each employee is the covered compensation limit, $245,000 for 2009 and 2010.

The deduction for contributions to a defined benefit plan is based on actuarial assumptions and computations. Consequently, an actuary must calculate the appropriate amount of mandatory funding.

In the case of an employer who maintains both a defined benefit plan and a defined contribution plan, the funding limit set forth is combined. The maximum deductible amount is the greater of:
* 25 percent of the aggregate covered compensation of employees; or
* The required minimum funding standard of the defined benefit plan.

This limit does not apply if the contributions to the defined contribution plan consist entirely of employee elective deferrals (elective contributions to the plan by employees). In other words, employee elective deferrals do not count against the plan limit.

**EXHIBIT 16.1** FORM 1040 SCHEDULE C

| SCHEDULE C (Form 1040) | **Profit or Loss From Business** | OMB No. 1545-0074 |
|---|---|---|
| Department of the Treasury Internal Revenue Service (99) | (Sole Proprietorship) ▶ Partnerships, joint ventures, etc., generally must file Form 1065 or 1065-B. ▶ Attach to Form 1040, 1040NR, or 1041.   ▶ See Instructions for Schedule C (Form 1040). | 20**09** Attachment Sequence No. **09** |

| Name of proprietor | | Social security number (SSN) |
|---|---|---|

| A | Principal business or profession, including product or service (see page C-2 of the instructions) | **B** Enter code from pages C-9, 10, & 11 ▶ |
|---|---|---|
| C | Business name. If no separate business name, leave blank. | **D** Employer ID number (EIN), if any |

| E | Business address (including suite or room no.) ▶ |
|---|---|
| | City, town or post office, state, and ZIP code |

**F** Accounting method: **(1)** ☐ Cash **(2)** ☐ Accrual **(3)** ☐ Other (specify) ▶

**G** Did you "materially participate" in the operation of this business during 2009? If "No," see page C-3 for limit on losses  ☐ Yes ☐ No

**H** If you started or acquired this business during 2009, check here . . . . . . . . . . . . . . . . ▶ ☐

## Part I  Income

| 1 | Gross receipts or sales. **Caution.** See page C-4 and check the box if: <br> • This income was reported to you on Form W-2 and the "Statutory employee" box on that form was checked, or <br> • You are a member of a qualified joint venture reporting only rental real estate income not subject to self-employment tax. Also see page C-3 for limit on losses. | ▶ ☐ | **1** | |
|---|---|---|---|---|
| 2 | Returns and allowances | | **2** | |
| 3 | Subtract line 2 from line 1 . . . . . . . . . . . . . . . . . . . . | | **3** | |
| 4 | Cost of goods sold (from line 42 on page 2) . . . . . . . . . . . . . . | | **4** | |
| 5 | **Gross profit.** Subtract line 4 from line 3 . . . . . . . . . . . . . . | | **5** | |
| 6 | Other income, including federal and state gasoline or fuel tax credit or refund (see page C-4) . . . . . | | **6** | |
| 7 | **Gross income.** Add lines 5 and 6 . . . . . . . . . . . . . . . . ▶ | | **7** | |

## Part II  Expenses. Enter expenses for business use of your home **only** on line 30.

| 8 | Advertising . . . . | **8** | | 18 | Office expense . . . . . | **18** | |
|---|---|---|---|---|---|---|---|
| 9 | Car and truck expenses (see page C-4) . . . . . | **9** | | 19 | Pension and profit-sharing plans . | **19** | |
| | | | | 20 | Rent or lease (see page C-6): | | |
| 10 | Commissions and fees . | **10** | | a | Vehicles, machinery, and equipment | **20a** | |
| 11 | Contract labor (see page C-4) | **11** | | b | Other business property . . . | **20b** | |
| 12 | Depletion . . . . . | **12** | | 21 | Repairs and maintenance . . . | **21** | |
| 13 | Depreciation and section 179 expense deduction (not included in Part III) (see page C-5) . . . . . . | **13** | | 22 | Supplies (not included in Part III) . | **22** | |
| | | | | 23 | Taxes and licenses . . . . . | **23** | |
| | | | | 24 | Travel, meals, and entertainment: | | |
| | | | | a | Travel . . . . . . . . . | **24a** | |
| 14 | Employee benefit programs (other than on line 19) . . | **14** | | b | Deductible meals and entertainment (see page C-6) . . | **24b** | |
| 15 | Insurance (other than health) | **15** | | 25 | Utilities . . . . . . . | **25** | |
| 16 | Interest: | | | 26 | Wages (less employment credits) . | **26** | |
| a | Mortgage (paid to banks, etc.) | **16a** | | 27 | Other expenses (from line 48 on page 2) . . . . . . . | **27** | |
| b | Other . . . . . . | **16b** | | | | | |
| 17 | Legal and professional services . . . . . . | **17** | | | | | |

| 28 | **Total expenses** before expenses for business use of home. Add lines 8 through 27 . . . . . ▶ | **28** | |
|---|---|---|---|
| 29 | Tentative profit or (loss). Subtract line 28 from line 7 . . . . . . . . . . . . . | **29** | |
| 30 | Expenses for business use of your home. Attach **Form 8829** . . . . . . . . . . | **30** | |
| 31 | **Net profit or (loss).** Subtract line 30 from line 29. <br> • If a profit, enter on both **Form 1040, line 12,** and **Schedule SE, line 2,** or on **Form 1040NR, line 13** (if you checked the box on line 1, see page C-7). Estates and trusts, enter on **Form 1041, line 3.** <br> • If a loss, you **must** go to line 32. | **31** | |
| 32 | If you have a loss, check the box that describes your investment in this activity (see page C-7). <br> • If you checked 32a, enter the loss on both **Form 1040, line 12,** and **Schedule SE, line 2,** or on **Form 1040NR, line 13** (if you checked the box on line 1, see the line 31 instructions on page C-7). Estates and trusts, enter on **Form 1041, line 3.** <br> • If you checked 32b, you **must** attach **Form 6198.** Your loss may be limited. | **32a** ☐ All investment is at risk. <br> **32b** ☐ Some investment is not at risk. | |

**For Paperwork Reduction Act Notice, see page C-9 of the instructions.**   Cat. No. 11334P   Schedule C (Form 1040) 2009

EXHIBIT 16.2

**SCHEDULE SE**
**(Form 1040)**

Department of the Treasury
Internal Revenue Service (99)

# Self-Employment Tax

► **Attach to Form 1040.**      ► **See Instructions for Schedule SE (Form 1040).**

OMB No. 1545-0074

**2009**

Attachment
Sequence No. **17**

Name of person with **self-employment** income (as shown on Form 1040)

Social security number of person
with **self-employment** income ►

## Who Must File Schedule SE

You must file Schedule SE if:

● You had net earnings from self-employment from **other than** church employee income (line 4 of Short Schedule SE or line 4c of Long Schedule SE) of $400 or more, **or**

● You had church employee income of $108.28 or more. Income from services you performed as a minister or a member of a religious order **is not** church employee income (see page SE-1).

**Note.** Even if you had a loss or a small amount of income from self-employment, it may be to your benefit to file Schedule SE and use either "optional method" in Part II of Long Schedule SE (see page SE-4).

**Exception.** If your only self-employment income was from earnings as a minister, member of a religious order, or Christian Science practitioner **and** you filed Form 4361 and received IRS approval not to be taxed on those earnings, **do not** file Schedule SE. Instead, write "Exempt—Form 4361" on Form 1040, line 56.

## May I Use Short Schedule SE or Must I Use Long Schedule SE?

**Note.** Use this flowchart **only if** you must file Schedule SE. If unsure, see *Who Must File Schedule SE,* above.

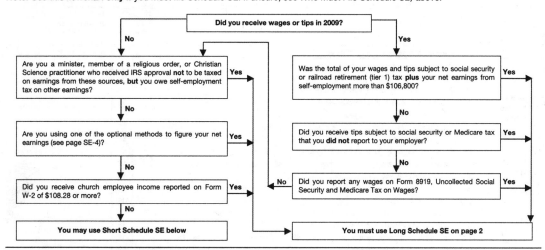

**Section A—Short Schedule SE. Caution.** Read above to see if you can use Short Schedule SE.

| | | | |
|---|---|---|---|
| **1a** | Net farm profit or (loss) from Schedule F, line 36, and farm partnerships, Schedule K-1 (Form 1065), box 14, code A . . . . . . . . . . . . . . . . . . . . . . | **1a** | |
| **b** | If you received social security retirement or disability benefits, enter the amount of Conservation Reserve Program payments included on Schedule F, line 6b, or listed on Schedule K-1 (Form 1065), box 20, code Y | **1b** ( | ) |
| **2** | Net profit or (loss) from Schedule C, line 31; Schedule C-EZ, line 3; Schedule K-1 (Form 1065), box 14, code A (other than farming); and Schedule K-1 (Form 1065-B), box 9, code J1. Ministers and members of religious orders, see page SE-1 for types of income to report on this line. See page SE-3 for other income to report . . . . . . . . . . . . . . . . | **2** | |
| **3** | Combine lines 1a, 1b, and 2 . . . . . . . . . . . . . . . . . . . . . . | **3** | |
| **4** | **Net earnings from self-employment.** Multiply line 3 by 92.35% (.9235). If less than $400, **do not** file this schedule; you do not owe self-employment tax . . . . . . . . . . . ► | **4** | |
| **5** | **Self-employment tax.** If the amount on line 4 is: ● $106,800 or less, multiply line 4 by 15.3% (.153). Enter the result here and on **Form 1040, line 56.** ● More than $106,800, multiply line 4 by 2.9% (.029). Then, add $13,243.20 to the result. Enter the total here and on **Form 1040, line 56.** . . . . . . . . . . . . . | **5** | |
| **6** | **Deduction for one-half of self-employment tax.** Multiply line 5 by 50% (.50). Enter the result here and on **Form 1040, line 27** | **6** | |

**For Paperwork Reduction Act Notice, see Form 1040 instructions.**      Cat. No. 11358Z      **Schedule SE (Form 1040) 2009**

EXHIBIT 16.3  FORM 1040

Form **1040**  Department of the Treasury—Internal Revenue Service
**U.S. Individual Income Tax Return**  20**09**  (99)  IRS Use Only—Do not write or staple in this space.

| For the year Jan. 1–Dec. 31, 2009, or other tax year beginning , 2009, ending , 20 | OMB No. 1545-0074 |
|---|---|

**Label** (See instructions on page 14.) **Use the IRS label.** Otherwise, please print or type.

L A B E L H E R E

Your first name and initial | Last name | Your social security number

If a joint return, spouse's first name and initial | Last name | Spouse's social security number

Home address (number and street). If you have a P.O. box, see page 14. | Apt. no. | ▲ You **must** enter your SSN(s) above. ▲

City, town or post office, state, and ZIP code. If you have a foreign address, see page 14. | Checking a box below will not change your tax or refund.

**Presidential Election Campaign** ► Check here if you, or your spouse if filing jointly, want $3 to go to this fund (see page 14) ►  ☐ You  ☐ Spouse

**Filing Status**
Check only one box.

1 ☐ Single
2 ☐ Married filing jointly (even if only one had income)
3 ☐ Married filing separately. Enter spouse's SSN above and full name here. ►
4 ☐ Head of household (with qualifying person). (See page 15.) If the qualifying person is a child but not your dependent, enter this child's name here. ►
5 ☐ Qualifying widow(er) with dependent child (see page 16)

**Exemptions**

6a ☐ **Yourself.** If someone can claim you as a dependent, **do not** check box 6a . . . . .
b ☐ **Spouse** . . . . . . . . . . . . . . . . . . . . . . . .
c Dependents:

| (1) First name   Last name | (2) Dependent's social security number | (3) Dependent's relationship to you | (4) ✓ if qualifying child for child tax credit (see page 17) |
|---|---|---|---|
| | | | ☐ |
| | | | ☐ |
| | | | ☐ |
| | | | ☐ |

If more than four dependents, see page 17 and check here ► ☐

Boxes checked on 6a and 6b
No. of children on 6c who:
● lived with you
● did not live with you due to divorce or separation (see page 18)
Dependents on 6c not entered above
Add numbers on lines above ►

d Total number of exemptions claimed . . . . . . . . . . . . . .

**Income**

**Attach Form(s) W-2 here. Also attach Forms W-2G and 1099-R if tax was withheld.**

If you did not get a W-2, see page 22.

Enclose, but do not attach, any payment. Also, please use Form 1040-V.

| | | |
|---|---|---|
| 7 | Wages, salaries, tips, etc. Attach Form(s) W-2 . . . . . . | 7 |
| 8a | **Taxable** interest. Attach Schedule B if required . . . . . | 8a |
| b | **Tax-exempt** interest. **Do not** include on line 8a . . . | 8b |  |
| 9a | Ordinary dividends. Attach Schedule B if required . . . . | 9a |
| b | Qualified dividends (see page 22) . . . . | 9b |  |
| 10 | Taxable refunds, credits, or offsets of state and local income taxes (see page 23) . . | 10 |
| 11 | Alimony received . . . . . . . . . . . . . . . . | 11 |
| 12 | Business income or (loss). Attach Schedule C or C-EZ . . . . . . | 12 |
| 13 | Capital gain or (loss). Attach Schedule D if required. If not required, check here ► ☐ | 13 |
| 14 | Other gains or (losses). Attach Form 4797 . . . . . . . | 14 |
| 15a | IRA distributions . | 15a | b Taxable amount (see page 24) | 15b |
| 16a | Pensions and annuities | 16a | b Taxable amount (see page 24) | 16b |
| 17 | Rental real estate, royalties, partnerships, S corporations, trusts, etc. Attach Schedule E | 17 |
| 18 | Farm income or (loss). Attach Schedule F . . . . . . . . | 18 |
| 19 | Unemployment compensation in excess of $2,400 per recipient (see page 27) . . . | 19 |
| 20a | Social security benefits | 20a | b Taxable amount (see page 27) | 20b |
| 21 | Other income. List type and amount (see page 29) _____ | 21 |
| 22 | Add the amounts in the far right column for lines 7 through 21. This is your **total income** ► | 22 |

**Adjusted Gross Income**

| | | |
|---|---|---|
| 23 | Educator expenses (see page 29) . . . . . . | 23 |  |
| 24 | Certain business expenses of reservists, performing artists, and fee-basis government officials. Attach Form 2106 or 2106-EZ | 24 |  |
| 25 | Health savings account deduction. Attach Form 8889 . | 25 |  |
| 26 | Moving expenses. Attach Form 3903 . . . . . | 26 |  |
| 27 | One-half of self-employment tax. Attach Schedule SE . | 27 |  |
| 28 | Self-employed SEP, SIMPLE, and qualified plans . . | 28 |  |
| 29 | Self-employed health insurance deduction (see page 30) | 29 |  |
| 30 | Penalty on early withdrawal of savings . . . . . | 30 |  |
| 31a | Alimony paid  b Recipient's SSN ► | 31a |  |
| 32 | IRA deduction (see page 31) . . . . | 32 |  |
| 33 | Student loan interest deduction (see page 34) . . . | 33 |  |
| 34 | Tuition and fees deduction. Attach Form 8917 . . . | 34 |  |
| 35 | Domestic production activities deduction. Attach Form 8903 | 35 |  |
| 36 | Add lines 23 through 31a and 32 through 35 . . . . . . . . . . | 36 |
| 37 | Subtract line 36 from line 22. This is your **adjusted gross income** . . . . . . ► | 37 |

For Disclosure, Privacy Act, and Paperwork Reduction Act Notice, see page 97.  Cat. No. 11320B  Form **1040** (2009)

## Deduction Limit for Self-Employed Individuals (Keogh Plans)

Sole proprietors who file a Schedule C, partners of a partnership, and members of an LLC are generally treated as self-employed individuals for tax purposes. In contrast, owners of C corporations or S corporations may also be employees of those entities. While self-employed individuals may adopt almost any qualified plan, they cannot normally choose a stock bonus plan or an employee stock ownership plan (ESOP) because there is no stock involved with sole proprietorships, partnerships, or LLCs. A qualified retirement plan selected by a self-employed individual is referred to as a **Keogh plan**. A Keogh plan is simply a qualified plan for a self-employed person usually structured as a profit sharing plan, a money purchase pension plan (MPPP), or a combination of both. (Note that self-employed individuals may also be able to establish a 401(k) plan.)An important characteristic of a Keogh plan is the reduced contribution that can be made on behalf of the self-employed individual. The employees of a firm that maintains a Keogh plan will generally be treated in the same manner as if the plan were not a Keogh plan. Employees will generally receive a benefit based on their W-2 income. The reason for the distinction is that self-employed individuals do not receive a W-2 form and will instead file a Schedule C or receive a K-1 which details the owner's earnings.

There is a special computation needed to calculate the maximum contribution and tax deduction for a Keogh plan on behalf of a self-employed individual. Since self-employed individuals do not have W-2s, the IRC uses the term "earned income" to denote the amount of compensation that is earned by the self-employed individual.

Earned income is defined as net earnings from self-employment less one-half of self-employment tax less the deduction for contributions to the qualified plan on behalf of the self-employed person. Through this process, the IRC attempts to treat self-employed individuals as if they were corporations instead of self-employed individuals. An employer and an employee each pays one-half of the employee's Social Security taxes; however, in the case of self-employed individuals, they are required to pay both halves. If the company was a corporation, then it would deduct one half of the self employment taxes paid on behalf of the individual in arriving at net income. Therefore, earned income for self-employed individuals is the self-employment income reduced by one-half of self-employment tax. Similarly, a corporation would deduct the contribution made to a qualified retirement plan in arriving at net income. Therefore, calculating earned income for a self-employed individual also requires a reduction for the amount of the contribution to the Keogh plan.

**Quick Quiz 16.2**

**Highlight the answer to these questions:**

1. Sole proprietorships are never required to register with the state in which they do business.
   a. True
   b. False

2. One of the major disadvantages of a sole proprietorship is the potential legal liability.
   a. True
   b. False

3. The ordinary and necessary expenses of a sole proprietorship are reported on Schedule C of the owner's Form 1040.
   a. True
   b. False

False, True, True.

The two primary parts of the Social Security system are OASDI (Old Age Survivor Disability Insurance) and Medicare. Both employers and employees contribute to the system through FICA payments that consist of 6.2 percent for OASDI and 1.45 percent for Medicare. The OASDI portion of 6.2 percent applies to income up to the Social Security wage base ($106,800 for 2009 and 2010) while the Medicare portion applies to all income with no limit.

The deduction for the self-employed person's own plan contribution and his net earnings are interrelated. For this reason, the self-employed person must determine the deduction for his own contributions by using simultaneous equations or a circular calculation or by using the simpler method described below that adjusts the plan contribution rate for the self-employed person.

To calculate the self-employed individual's 2009 contribution to the Keogh plan, utilize the following formulas:

1.  Calculate the self-employed individual's contribution rate:

$$\text{Self-Employed Contribution Rate} = \left( \frac{\text{Contribution Rate to Other Participants}}{1 + \text{Contribution Rate to Other Participants}} \right)$$

2.  Calculate Self-Employment Tax:

    Net Self-Employment Income

    Times: 92.35%

    **Net Earnings subject to Self Employment Tax**

    Times: 15.3% up to $106,800 + 2.9% over $106,800 (same for 2010)

    **Equals: Self-Employment Tax**

3.  Calculate the self-employed individual's contribution:

    Net Self-Employment Income

    Less: ½ of Self-Employment Taxes

    **Equals: Adjusted Net Self-Employment Income (Earned Income)**

    Times: Self-Employed Contribution Rate

    **Equals: Self-Employed Individual's Qualified Plan Contribution**

**EXAMPLE 16.1**

Alex has Schedule C net income of $200,000 and wants to know the maximum amount he can contribute to a Keogh profit sharing plan. In this instance Alex can contribute $38,140 to the plan. The contribution is calculated as follows:

1.  Calculate the self-employed individual's contribution rate:

    $$\text{Self-Employed Contribution Rate} = \left( \frac{25\%}{1 + 25\%} \right)$$

    Self-Employed Contribution Rate = 20%

2. Calculate Self-Employment Tax:

| | |
|---:|:---|
| $200,000 | Net Self-Employment Income |
| x 0.9235 | Times: 92.35% |
| $184,700 | **Net Earnings subject to Self-Employment Tax** |
| x 15.3%/2.9% | Times: 15.3% up to $106,800 + 2.9% over $106,800 (same for 2010) |
| $18,599 | **Equals: Self-Employment Tax ($16,340 + $2,259)** |

3. Calculate the self-employed individual's contribution:

| | |
|---:|:---|
| $200,000 | Net Self-Employment Income |
| $9,300 | Less: ½ of Self-Employment Taxes (50% x $18,599) |
| $190,700 | **Equals: Adjusted Net Self-Employment Income** |
| x 0.20 | Times: Self-Employed Contribution Rate |
| $38,140 | **Equals: Self-Employed Individual's Qualified Plan Contribution** |

Check figure:

$$\frac{\$38,140}{\$190,700 - \$38,140} = 25\%$$

When solving the Keogh contribution calculation, it is important to understand that while 25 percent of compensation is the limit for deductible employee contributions, the self-employed individual maximum contribution is 25 percent of the self-employed individual's earned income. The 25 percent of earned income effectively translates to 20 percent of net self-employed income less one-half of self employment tax.

In the example above, Alex's earned income is calculated as follows:

**EXAMPLE 16.2**

| | |
|---:|:---|
| $200,000 | Schedule C net income |
| - $9,300 | Less: ½ self-employment taxes |
| - $38,140 | Less: Keogh contribution |
| $152,560 | Earned income |
| X 0.25 | Times: 25% to determine Keogh contribution |
| $38,140 | **Total Keogh contribution** |

Notice that the maximum Keogh contribution is exactly 25% of the earned income.

EXAMPLE 16.3

Cargile Co., a sole proprietorship, employs B, C, D, and E as well as the sole proprietor, A, who files a Schedule C 1040 for his business.

| | Compensation | Contributions |
|---|---|---|
| A* | $150,000 | See note below |
| B | $100,000 | $15,000 |
| C | $80,000 | $12,000 |
| D | $50,000 | $7,500 |
| E | $20,000 | $3,000 |

*A's compensation is Schedule C net income

Cargile maintains a Keogh profit sharing plan with a 15% contribution to each employee (not the owner). In spite of the fact that each employee receives exactly 15%, A is limited to receiving 13.04% (0.15/1.15) of $150,000 less one-half of the self-employment taxes due on his earnings.

| | |
|---|---|
| $150,000 | Schedule C net income |
| $6,000 | Less: ½ self-employment taxes ($12,000 assumed for ease of calculation) |
| $144,000 | Self-employment income |
| X 0.1304 | Contribution rate (0.15/1.15) |
| **$18,782.61** | **Contribution on behalf of A** * |

*Rounding was not utilized when applying the contribution rate.*

The special calculation is required because Schedule C net income must be reduced by both the self-employed person's qualified plan contribution and one-half of his self-employment tax before the reduced contribution rate is applied. For all of the other employees, their contribution is calculated based upon 15% of their compensation.

| Advantages |
| --- |
| • Easy to form. |
| • Simple to operate. |
| • Easy to sell business assets. |
| • Few administrative burdens. |
| • Income is generally passed through to the owner on Schedule C of Form 1040. |

| Disadvantages |
| --- |
| • Generally have limited sources of capital. |
| • Unlimited liability. |
| • No guarantee of continuity beyond the proprietor. |
| • Business income is subject to self-employment tax. |

# GENERAL PARTNERSHIPS

Partnerships are joint business ventures among two or more persons or entities to conduct a business as co-owners under their names or under a trade or fictitious name. A partnership is automatically created when two or more individuals conduct business for a profit. There are different types of partnerships and we will examine each type, including general partnerships and limited partnerships. Typically, **general partnerships** are not required to be registered with the Secretary of State in the state of formation, but limited partnerships are required to register.

## FORMATION

Although partnerships are easy to form, state law will govern the relative rights and obligations of the partners (including equal sharing of profits and losses regardless of contributions of property or effort), unless there is a contrary agreement among the partners. Ownership of a general partnership may be in the form of partnership units, shares, or percentages.

## INTEREST, DISPOSAL OF INTEREST, AND DISSOLUTION

A partner's interest in a partnership is frequently referred to as his partnership percentage interest. The partners usually have voting power in proportion to their ownership interest. Thus, majority voting rules generally apply.

**Key Concepts**

**Underline/highlight the answers to these questions as you read:**

1. Discuss the formation and operation of a general partnership.

2. Explain why disposing of a general partnership interest may be difficult.

3. Describe the sources of liability for a general partnership.

4. Explain the tax attributes of a general partnership.

It is generally difficult to dispose of a partnership interest because any buyer will not only have to evaluate the business, but also the other partners.

In addition, partnership agreements often require the approval of non-selling partners before a partner's share can be sold to an outside party.

Partnership dissolution is either voluntary or judicial (ordered by a court). Partners usually vote for voluntary dissolution and, if affirmed, pay creditors and then distribute remaining assets to partners in accordance with either the partnership agreement or in proportion to their individual partnership interests. Judicial dissolution may be necessary when the partners cannot agree on how to conduct the business or whether to dissolve the entity. This situation is most likely to arise when partnership votes are required to be unanimous.

## CAPITAL

The amount of capital contributed usually determines the ownership interest of a partner in a partnership. However, sometimes partners allocate ownership interest differently from capital contributed. Such a situation could occur when one partner brings ideas and talent and the other brings money. Whenever partners are deviating from ownership based on capital contributed, there should be a written partnership agreement that clarifies partnership interests and each partner's distributive share of partnership profits and losses. If a partnership wants to divide profits and/or losses in a proportion that does not equal partnership interest, it will be considered a special allocation. There must be a sound business purpose for a special allocation and partners are well advised to seek the counsel of an attorney or CPA.

## LIABILITY

The co-owner partners share the risks and rewards of the business. Each partner is jointly and severally liable for partnership obligations. Like a sole proprietorship, a partner's personal assets can be seized to satisfy partnership obligations.

A principal disadvantage of the general partnership arrangement is that all general partners in a partnership are subject to joint and several liability for the debts and obligations of the partnership. These liabilities can arise from:
1. Negligence and acts of employees,
2. Negligence of other partners,
3. Commercial liabilities (e.g., loans) to the partnership, and
4. Commercial obligations to other trade creditors.

## MANAGEMENT/OPERATIONS

Partnerships are generally managed equally by all partners. It is possible to name a "**managing partner**" to have responsibilities for some specific task or day-to-day operations. Partnerships can even appoint presidents and vice presidents as officers. If so, these should be spelled out in the written partnership agreement. Partnerships are not required to have annual meetings of partners, but rather have a relatively relaxed set of rules regarding formalities.

Employees of general partnerships are eligible to receive a wide variety of tax-free fringe benefits provided by the employer such as health care. This is not so for partners since partners are not considered to be employees for most employee fringe benefit purposes. However, partners can participate in company-sponsored retirement plans, but they have the same limitations as proprietors in terms of calculations (see discussion under proprietorships).

## INCOME TAXATION AND PAYROLL (SOCIAL SECURITY) TAXATION

Partnerships are not subject to entity level taxation. Partnerships file a Form 1065 (See Exhibit 16.6), including Schedule K (Exhibit 16.7), which is the summary of all distributive items to individual partners. Income and losses are then "passed through" to the individual partners in proportion to their partnership interests on Form 1065 Schedule K-1 (see Exhibit 16.8) regardless of whether the income is distributed to partners in the form of cash. However, partnership taxation may be complex because of the tax rules related to basis. All partnership business net income is subject to self-employment tax up to 15.3 percent. Partnerships are legal entities and thus are required to obtain a Federal Employer Identification Number (FEIN). The year-end for tax purposes is usually the calendar year-end.

Partnerships can deduct all "ordinary and necessary" business expenses from their income. Partners can deduct partnership losses against other ordinary income to the extent of their investment (or their at-risk amount, as discussed in Chapter 14). However, passive partners (those not actively involved in the enterprise) may not be able to deduct losses due to passive activity rules even if they are at-risk. Limited partners may not be subject to self-employment tax.

## A SUMMARY OF ADVANTAGES AND DISADVANTAGES OF PARTNERSHIPS

EXHIBIT 16.5

| Advantages |
| --- |
| • More sources of initial capital than proprietorships. |
| • Usually have more management resources available than proprietorships. |
| • Have fewer administrative burdens than corporations. |
| • Income and losses are generally passed through to the partners for tax purposes. |

| Disadvantages |
| --- |
| • Transfer of interests is more difficult than for proprietorships. |
| • Unlimited liability - each partner is liable for partnership debts and obligations. |
| • Partnership income tax and basis adjustment rules can be complex. |
| • Business net income is subject to self-employment tax. |
| • Partners are entitled to few tax-free fringe benefits that are generally available to employees. |

EXHIBIT 16.6  FORM 1065

The 2008 forms were the latest available at the time of printing. Please visit our website at money-education.com for updates.

---

| Form **1065** | **U.S. Return of Partnership Income** | OMB No. 1545-0099 |
|---|---|---|
| Department of the Treasury<br>Internal Revenue Service | For calendar year 2008, or tax year beginning .......... , 2008, ending .......... , 20...... .<br>▶ See separate instructions. | **20 08** |

| **A** Principal business activity | Use the IRS label. Otherwise, print or type. | Name of partnership | **D** Employer identification number |
|---|---|---|---|
| **B** Principal product or service | | Number, street, and room or suite no. If a P.O. box, see the instructions. | **E** Date business started |
| **C** Business code number | | City or town, state, and ZIP code | **F** Total assets (see the instructions)<br>$ |

**G** Check applicable boxes: **(1)** ☐ Initial return  **(2)** ☐ Final return  **(3)** ☐ Name change  **(4)** ☐ Address change  **(5)** ☐ Amended return
**(6)** ☐ Technical termination - also check (1) or (2)

**H** Check accounting method: **(1)** ☐ Cash  **(2)** ☐ Accrual  **(3)** ☐ Other (specify) ▶ ------------------------

**I** Number of Schedules K-1. Attach one for each person who was a partner at any time during the tax year ▶ ------------------------

**J** Check if Schedule M-3 attached . . . . . . . . . . . . . . . . . . . . . . ☐

**Caution.** *Include **only** trade or business income and expenses on lines 1a through 22 below. See the instructions for more information.*

| | | | | |
|---|---|---|---|---|
| **Income** | **1a** Gross receipts or sales . . . . . . . . . | **1a** | | |
| | **b** Less returns and allowances . . . . . . . . . . . | **1b** | **1c** | |
| | **2** Cost of goods sold (Schedule A, line 8) . . . . . . . | | **2** | |
| | **3** Gross profit. Subtract line 2 from line 1c . . . . | | **3** | |
| | **4** Ordinary income (loss) from other partnerships, estates, and trusts *(attach statement)*. | | **4** | |
| | **5** Net farm profit (loss) *(attach Schedule F (Form 1040))* . . . . . | | **5** | |
| | **6** Net gain (loss) from Form 4797, Part II, line 17 *(attach Form 4797)* . . . . | | **6** | |
| | **7** Other income (loss) *(attach statement)* . . . . . . . . | | **7** | |
| | **8** **Total income (loss).** Combine lines 3 through 7 . . . . . . . . . | | **8** | |
| **Deductions** (see the instructions for limitations) | **9** Salaries and wages (other than to partners) (less employment credits) . . . . . . | | **9** | |
| | **10** Guaranteed payments to partners . . . . . . . . . | | **10** | |
| | **11** Repairs and maintenance . . . . . . . . . . | | **11** | |
| | **12** Bad debts . . . . . . . . . . . . . | | **12** | |
| | **13** Rent . . . . . . . . . . . . . . . | | **13** | |
| | **14** Taxes and licenses . . . . . . . . . . . . | | **14** | |
| | **15** Interest . . . . . . . . . . . . . . | | **15** | |
| | **16a** Depreciation *(if required, attach Form 4562)* . . . . . | **16a** | | |
| | **b** Less depreciation reported on Schedule A and elsewhere on return | **16b** | **16c** | |
| | **17** Depletion **(Do not deduct oil and gas depletion.)** . . . . . . | | **17** | |
| | **18** Retirement plans, etc. . . . . . . . . . . . | | **18** | |
| | **19** Employee benefit programs . . . . . . . . . . | | **19** | |
| | **20** Other deductions *(attach statement)* . . . . . . . . . . . | | **20** | |
| | **21** **Total deductions.** Add the amounts shown in the far right column for lines 9 through 20 . | | **21** | |
| | **22** **Ordinary business income (loss).** Subtract line 21 from line 8 . . . . . . | | **22** | |

| **Sign Here** | Under penalties of perjury, I declare that I have examined this return, including accompanying schedules and statements, and to the best of my knowledge and belief, it is true, correct, and complete. Declaration of preparer (other than general partner or limited liability company member manager) is based on all information of which preparer has any knowledge. | May the IRS discuss this return with the preparer shown below (see instructions)? ☐ Yes ☐ No |
|---|---|---|
| | ▶ _____<br>Signature of general partner or limited liability company member manager | ▶ _____<br>Date | |

| **Paid Preparer's Use Only** | Preparer's signature | | Date | | Check if self-employed ▶ ☐ | Preparer's SSN or PTIN |
|---|---|---|---|---|---|---|
| | Firm's name (or yours if self-employed), address, and ZIP code | ▶ | | EIN ▶ | | |
| | | | | Phone no. | ( ) | |

**For Privacy Act and Paperwork Reduction Act Notice, see separate instructions.**     Cat. No. 11390Z     Form **1065** (2008)

Form 1065 (2008)                                                                                                     Page **4**

| Schedule K | Partners' Distributive Share Items | | Total amount |
|---|---|---|---|

**Income (Loss)**

| | | | |
|---|---|---|---|
| **1** | Ordinary business income (loss) (page 1, line 22) . . . . . . . . . . . . . | **1** | |
| **2** | Net rental real estate income (loss) (attach Form 8825) . . . . . . | **2** | |
| **3a** | Other gross rental income (loss) . . . . . . . . . . **3a** | | |
| **b** | Expenses from other rental activities (attach statement). . . . **3b** | | |
| **c** | Other net rental income (loss). Subtract line 3b from line 3a . . . . . | **3c** | |
| **4** | Guaranteed payments . . . . . . . . . . . . . . . . . | **4** | |
| **5** | Interest income . . . . . . . . . . . . . . . . . | **5** | |
| **6** | Dividends: **a** Ordinary dividends . . . . . . . . . . . . | **6a** | |
| | **b** Qualified dividends . . . . . . . . **6b** | | |
| **7** | Royalties . . . . . . . . . . . . . . . . . . . . | **7** | |
| **8** | Net short-term capital gain (loss) (attach Schedule D (Form 1065)) . . . . | **8** | |
| **9a** | Net long-term capital gain (loss) (attach Schedule D (Form 1065)) . . . . | **9a** | |
| **b** | Collectibles (28%) gain (loss) . . . . . . . . . **9b** | | |
| **c** | Unrecaptured section 1250 gain (attach statement) . . . . **9c** | | |
| **10** | Net section 1231 gain (loss) (attach Form 4797) . . . . . . . . | **10** | |
| **11** | Other income (loss) (see instructions) Type ▶ _____ | **11** | |

**Deductions**

| | | | |
|---|---|---|---|
| **12** | Section 179 deduction (attach Form 4562) . . . . . . . . . . | **12** | |
| **13a** | Contributions . . . . . . . . . . . . . . . . . . | **13a** | |
| **b** | Investment interest expense . . . . . . . . . . . . . . | **13b** | |
| **c** | Section 59(e)(2) expenditures:  **(1)** Type ▶ _____  **(2)** Amount ▶ | **13c(2)** | |
| **d** | Other deductions (see instructions)  Type ▶ _____ | **13d** | |

**Self-Employment**

| | | | |
|---|---|---|---|
| **14a** | Net earnings (loss) from self-employment . . . . . . . . . . . | **14a** | |
| **b** | Gross farming or fishing income . . . . . . . . . . . . | **14b** | |
| **c** | Gross nonfarm income . . . . . . . . . . . . . . . | **14c** | |

**Credits**

| | | | |
|---|---|---|---|
| **15a** | Low-income housing credit (section 42(j)(5)) . . . . . . . . | **15a** | |
| **b** | Low-income housing credit (other) . . . . . . . . . . | **15b** | |
| **c** | Qualified rehabilitation expenditures (rental real estate) (attach Form 3468). . . . | **15c** | |
| **d** | Other rental real estate credits (see instructions)  Type ▶ _____ | **15d** | |
| **e** | Other rental credits (see instructions)  Type ▶ _____ | **15e** | |
| **f** | Other credits (see instructions)  Type ▶ _____ | **15f** | |

**Foreign Transactions**

| | | | |
|---|---|---|---|
| **16a** | Name of country or U.S. possession ▶ _____ | | |
| **b** | Gross income from all sources . . . . . . . . . . . . | **16b** | |
| **c** | Gross income sourced at partner level . . . . . . . . . | **16c** | |
| | Foreign gross income sourced at partnership level | | |
| **d** | Passive category ▶ _____  **e** General category ▶ _____  **f** Other ▶ | **16f** | |
| | Deductions allocated and apportioned at partner level | | |
| **g** | Interest expense ▶ _____  **h** Other . . . . . . . . ▶ | **16h** | |
| | Deductions allocated and apportioned at partnership level to foreign source income | | |
| **i** | Passive category ▶ _____  **j** General category ▶ _____  **k** Other ▶ | **16k** | |
| **l** | Total foreign taxes (check one): ▶ Paid ☐  Accrued ☐ . . . . . . . | **16l** | |
| **m** | Reduction in taxes available for credit (attach statement) . . . . | **16m** | |
| **n** | Other foreign tax information (attach statement) . . . . . . . . | | |

**Alternative Minimum Tax (AMT) Items**

| | | | |
|---|---|---|---|
| **17a** | Post-1986 depreciation adjustment . . . . . . . . . . . | **17a** | |
| **b** | Adjusted gain or loss . . . . . . . . . . . . . . | **17b** | |
| **c** | Depletion (other than oil and gas) . . . . . . . . . . . | **17c** | |
| **d** | Oil, gas, and geothermal properties—gross income . . . . . . | **17d** | |
| **e** | Oil, gas, and geothermal properties—deductions . . . . . . | **17e** | |
| **f** | Other AMT items (attach statement) . . . . . . . . . . | **17f** | |

**Other Information**

| | | | |
|---|---|---|---|
| **18a** | Tax-exempt interest income . . . . . . . . . . . . | **18a** | |
| **b** | Other tax-exempt income . . . . . . . . . . . . . | **18b** | |
| **c** | Nondeductible expenses . . . . . . . . . . . . . | **18c** | |
| **19a** | Distributions of cash and marketable securities . . . . . . . | **19a** | |
| **b** | Distributions of other property . . . . . . . . . . . | **19b** | |
| **20a** | Investment income . . . . . . . . . . . . . . . | **20a** | |
| **b** | Investment expenses . . . . . . . . . . . . . . | **20b** | |
| **c** | Other items and amounts (attach statement) . . . . . . . . . | | |

Form **1065** (2008)

**EXHIBIT 16.8** **FORM 1065 SCHEDULE K-1**

651108

**Schedule K-1**
**(Form 1065)**

2008

Department of the Treasury
Internal Revenue Service

**Partner's Share of Income, Deductions, Credits, etc.**

▶ See back of form and separate instructions.

☐ Final K-1    ☐ Amended K-1    OMB No. 1545-0099

For calendar year 2008, or tax

year beginning _____ , 2008

ending _____ , 20____

| **Part III** | **Partner's Share of Current Year Income, Deductions, Credits, and Other Items** | | |
|---|---|---|---|
| 1 | Ordinary business income (loss) | 15 | Credits |
| 2 | Net rental real estate income (loss) | | |
| 3 | Other net rental income (loss) | 16 | Foreign transactions |
| 4 | Guaranteed payments | | |
| 5 | Interest income | | |
| 6a | Ordinary dividends | | |
| 6b | Qualified dividends | | |
| 7 | Royalties | | |
| 8 | Net short-term capital gain (loss) | | |
| 9a | Net long-term capital gain (loss) | 17 | Alternative minimum tax (AMT) items |
| 9b | Collectibles (28%) gain (loss) | | |
| 9c | Unrecaptured section 1250 gain | | |
| 10 | Net section 1231 gain (loss) | 18 | Tax-exempt income and nondeductible expenses |
| 11 | Other income (loss) | | |
| | | 19 | Distributions |
| 12 | Section 179 deduction | | |
| 13 | Other deductions | 20 | Other information |
| 14 | Self-employment earnings (loss) | | |

| **Part I** | **Information About the Partnership** |
|---|---|
| A | Partnership's employer identification number |
| B | Partnership's name, address, city, state, and ZIP code |
| C | IRS Center where partnership filed return |
| D | ☐ Check if this is a publicly traded partnership (PTP) |

| **Part II** | **Information About the Partner** |
|---|---|
| E | Partner's identifying number |
| F | Partner's name, address, city, state, and ZIP code |

G  ☐ General partner or LLC member-manager    ☐ Limited partner or other LLC member

H  ☐ Domestic partner    ☐ Foreign partner

I  What type of entity is this partner? _____

J  Partner's share of profit, loss, and capital (see instructions):

| | Beginning | Ending |
|---|---|---|
| Profit | % | % |
| Loss | % | % |
| Capital | % | % |

K  Partner's share of liabilities at year end:

Nonrecourse . . . . . . . $_____

Qualified nonrecourse financing . . $_____

Recourse . . . . . . . . $_____

L  Partner's capital account analysis:

Beginning capital account . . . . $_____

Capital contributed during the year . $_____

Current year increase (decrease) . . $_____

Withdrawals & distributions . . . $(_____)

Ending capital account . . . . $_____

☐ Tax basis    ☐ GAAP    ☐ Section 704(b) book
☐ Other (explain)

*See attached statement for additional information.

For IRS Use Only

For Paperwork Reduction Act Notice, see Instructions for Form 1065.    Cat. No. 11394R    Schedule K-1 (Form 1065) 2008

# LIMITED PARTNERSHIPS (LP)

**Limited partnerships** are associations of two or more persons as co-owners to carry on a business for profit except that one or more of the partners have limited participation in the management of the venture and thus limited risk exposure. If the limited partners participate in the management of the enterprise, they become general partners for liability purposes. In the normal limited partnership, there is at least one general partner. Because limited partners are passive investors in the enterprise, their liability is normally limited to the amount of their investment. A limited partner's personal assets cannot normally be seized to satisfy partnership obligations.

 *Key Concepts*

**Underline/highlight the answers to these questions as you read:**

1. Describe the ways in which a limited partnership is different from a general partnership.

2. Explain the advantages and disadvantages of a limited partnership.

## FORMATION

Limited partnerships are generally required to file a partnership agreement or any other required documentation with the domiciliary state to establish the limited partnership. Those states that require initial filings also require annual filings to maintain the entity status. The written partnership agreement specifies which partners are limited partners and which partners are general partners.

## INTEREST, DISPOSAL OF INTEREST, AND DISSOLUTION

The dissolution and transfer of an interest in a limited partnership is essentially the same as for a general partnership. Although the limited liability feature might attract more buyers, the inability for limited partners to have a say in the day-to-day operations of the company is likely to make the transfer of a limited partnership share very difficult.

## CAPITAL

It is easier to raise capital in a limited partnership than in a general partnership because of the availability of the liability shield for the non-managing limited partners. However, the limited liability may negatively affect the partnership's ability to obtain outside financing. Third party lenders may desire personal guarantees from the partners (which would partially defeat the benefits associated with the limited liability feature).

## LIABILITY

Liability for limited partners is limited as long as they refrain from participating in the management of the enterprise. The general partners, who are responsible for the day-to-day operations in a limited partnership, have unlimited liability for enterprise debts and obligations.

## Quick Quiz 16.4

**Highlight the answer to these questions:**

1. Limited partnerships are generally required to register with the state.
   a. True
   b. False

2. Limited partnerships offer limited liability for all partners.
   a. True
   b. False

True, False.

## MANAGEMENT/OPERATIONS

A limited partnership is somewhat of a hybrid entity. The general partners run the business and are exposed to personal liability. The limited partners must avoid making management decisions to protect their limited liability status.

## INCOME TAXATION AND PAYROLL (SOCIAL SECURITY) TAXES

Limited partners are not usually subject to self-employment tax since they are passive investors who do not participate in management. The general partners in a limited partnership have self-employment income. As with the general partnership, the entity files a Form 1065 and issues Schedule K-1s to both its general and limited partners.

| EXHIBIT 16.9 | A SUMMARY OF ADVANTAGES AND DISADVANTAGES OF LIMITED PARTNERSHIPS |

| Advantages |
| --- |
| • Favorable pass-through partnership taxation status. |
| • Flexibility in structuring ownership interests. |
| • Limited partners are not personally liable for the debts and obligations of the limited partnership as long as they do not engage in management. |

| Disadvantages |
| --- |
| • Must file with the state to register. |
| • In most states, general partners are liable for debts and other obligations of the limited partnership. |
| • Losses for limited partners are generally passive losses (see Chapter 14). |

# LIMITED LIABILITY PARTNERSHIPS (LLP)

A **limited liability partnership (LLP)** is a hybrid entity that provides partial liability protection to its members and may be taxed as either a corporation or partnership. LLPs are similar to LLCs, but may not offer complete liability protection. The limited liability partnership is generally one comprised of licensed professionals such as accountants, attorneys, and doctors who practice together. The partners may enjoy liability protection from the acts of their other partners, but each partner remains personally liable for his own acts with respect to malpractice.

## FORMATION

Limited liability partnerships are generally required to file with the domiciliary state to establish the limited liability partnership. Those states that require initial filings also require annual filings to maintain the entity status.

## INTEREST, DISPOSAL OF INTEREST, AND DISSOLUTION

The dissolution and transfer of an interest in a limited partnership is essentially the same as for a general partnership. If the LLP is comprised of licensed professionals, however, transfer of an interest will usually be more difficult because such interest may only be transferred to another similarly licensed professional.

**Key Concepts**

Underline/highlight the answers to these questions as you read:

1. Explain who can form a limited liability partnership.

2. Explain the ways in which an LLP differs from a general partnership.

## CAPITAL

The amount of capital contributed usually determines the ownership interest in a partnership. However, sometimes partners allocate ownership interest differently from capital contributed. Such a situation could occur when one partner brings ideas and talent and the other brings money. Whenever partners are deviating from ownership, based on capital contributed, there should be a written partnership agreement that clarifies partnership interests and each partner's distributive share of the profits and losses. If a partnership divides profits and/or losses in a proportion that does not reflect partnership interests, the arrangement is considered to be a special allocation. There must be a sound business purpose for special allocations and partners are well advised to seek the counsel of an attorney or CPA.

## LIABILITY

A principal disadvantage of the general partnership arrangement is that all general partners in a partnership are subject to joint and several liability for the debts and obligations of the partnership. These liabilities can arise from:
1. liability for the negligence and acts of employees,
2. negligence of other partners,
3. commercial liabilities (e.g., loans) to the partnership, and
4. commercial obligations to other trade creditors.

However, general partners of an LLP can insulate themselves from liabilities arising from the acts of other partners. General partners of an LLP will not be personally liable for the debts and obligations arising from errors, omissions, negligence, incompetence, or acts committed by another partner or representative of the partnership who is not under the supervision or direction of the first partner. It is important to note that general partners remain personally liable for commercial and trade obligations. If the partners wish to insulate themselves from these obligations, they should consider an LLC and once formed, they should not personally guarantee commercial obligations.

## MANAGEMENT/OPERATIONS

The management of an LLP is generally the same as for any general partnership. Note that unlike a limited partnership, the LLP confers limited liability status on all partners, not just limited partners.

## INCOME TAXATION AND PAYROLL (SOCIAL SECURITY) TAXES

For federal income tax purposes, the entity may elect to file as a corporation or as a partnership. This choice is known as "**checking the box.**" Choosing to be taxed as a C corporation allows owners to take advantage of tax-free fringe benefits which may be provided by C corporations. Operating as a partnership has the disadvantages of subjecting income to employment taxes and limited fringe benefits for owners. If the entity files as a partnership it will file Form 1065. If it files as a corporation, it will file either the Form 1120S (if it elects S corporation status) or Form 1120 (if it files as a C corporation).

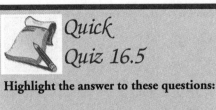

### Quick Quiz 16.5

**Highlight the answer to these questions:**

1. Limited liability partnerships are generally owned by licensed professionals.
   a. True
   b. False

2. The transferability of an interest in an LLP is the same as for any other type of partnership.
   a. True
   b. False

True, False.

---

**EXHIBIT 16.10**   **A SUMMARY OF ADVANTAGES AND DISADVANTAGES OF LIMITED LIABILITY PARTNERSHIPS**

| Advantages |
| --- |
| • Favorable pass-through partnership taxation status available. |
| • Flexibility in structuring ownership interests. |
| • Partners can insulate themselves from the acts of other partners. |

| Disadvantages |
| --- |
| • Required to file with the state to register. |
| • Unlimited liability for own acts of malpractice. |

# FAMILY LIMITED PARTNERSHIPS (FLP)

A **family limited partnership** (FLP) is a special type of limited partnership created under state law with the primary purpose of transferring assets to younger generations using annual exclusions and valuation discounts for minority interests and lack of marketability.

## FORMATION

Usually, one or more family members transfer highly appreciated property that is expected to continue to appreciate to a limited partnership in return for both a small (one percent, for example) general and a large (99 percent, for example) limited partnership interest. In a limited partnership, the general partner has unlimited liability and the sole management rights of the partnership, while the limited partners are passive interest holders with limited liability and no management rights.

### FAMILY LIMITED PARTNERSHIP

EXHIBIT 16.11

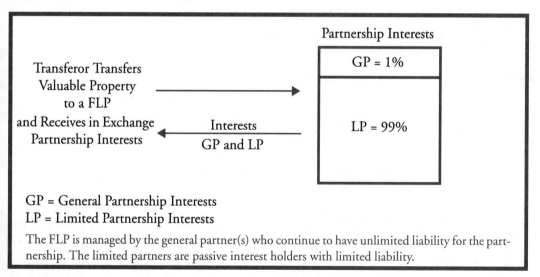

GP = General Partnership Interests
LP = Limited Partnership Interests

The FLP is managed by the general partner(s) who continue to have unlimited liability for the partnership. The limited partners are passive interest holders with limited liability.

## INTEREST, DISPOSAL OF INTEREST, AND DISSOLUTION

Upon creation of the partnership (FLP), there are neither income nor gift tax consequences because the entity created (the limited partnership and all of its interests, both general and limited) is owned by the same person, or persons, who owned it before the transfer.

Once the FLP is created, the owner of the general and limited partnership interests values the limited partnership interests. Since there are usually transferability restrictions on the limited partnership interests (lack of marketability), and since the limited partners have little control of the management of the partnership (lack of control), limited partnership interests are usually valued at a substantial discount from their fair market values. It is not uncommon for the discount of such interests to range between 20 and 40 percent for the purpose of calculating gift taxes payable by the transferor. The original transferor (grantor) then begins an annual gifting program utilizing the discounts, the gift tax annual exclusions, and gift-splitting (where applicable) to transfer limited partnership interests to younger generation family members at reduced transfer costs.

| | |
|---|---|
| **EXAMPLE 16.4** | Charles, age 52, is married to Debbie and they have three children and nine grandchildren. The three children are happily married and Charles and Debbie think of their children's spouses as their own children. Charles transfers a 100% interest in a business with a fair market value of $3,200,000 to a family limited partnership. Charles, in return, receives a general partnership interest of one percent and 162 units of limited partnership interests representing 99 percent, at $19,555 (($3,200,000 x 99%) / 162) per unit. Charles then transfers two limited partnership units to each child, the spouse of each child, and each grandchild using a 33.52 percent discount, the annual exclusion, and the gift-splitting election. |

$19,555 x 0.6648 (1.00 - 0.3352) = $13,000 x 2 = $26,000 per donee x 15 donees (three children, three spouses, nine grandchildren) = 30 units valued at $586,650 ($19,555 x 30) total but discounted to $390,000 in total and $13,000 each.

In this scenario, Charles does not pay any gift tax. It will take six years with this level of gifting for Charles to transfer his entire limited partnership interest to his children, their spouses, and his grandchildren without paying any gift taxes.

## CAPITAL

One of the unique features of the FLP, and perhaps its most important non-tax benefit, is that the original owner/transferor can maintain control of the property transferred to the limited partnership by only retaining a small general partnership interest. If the FLP is funded with a business interest, the general partner could remain president of the business, direct the company's strategic plan, receive reasonable compensation and fringe benefits, hire and fire employees, receive executive perks, and generally control the limited partners' interests. As with all limited partnerships, the limited partners have no control over any of these enumerated management decisions.

The FLP is often undertaken as a series of transfers, including an initial nontaxable contribution of property to the partnership followed by annual exclusion gifts of limited partnership interests. While a general partner has control over partnership affairs, an individual who transfers his property to an FLP needs to be financially secure without the transferred property, both from a net worth and cash flow perspective.

## LIABILITY

The use of the FLP structure can also help protect family assets. By placing the assets in the FLP and only making gifts of limited partnership interests to heirs, judgments or liens entered against a donee (limited partner) will not jeopardize the assets of the partnership. A donee's creditor would not be able to force the donee to liquidate his interest, since the donee does not have the right to force the liquidation of a limited partnership interest.

Transferring limited partnership interests to children and children's spouses can also help protect assets from divorce claims. If the child and his spouse divorce, even if the divorced spouse received a limited partnership interest, he or she could not force distributions from the partnership, participate in management, require his or her interest to be redeemed, or force a liquidation of the partnership.

## TAXATION

The creation of family limited partnerships and the use of discounts to transfer value at a lower gift tax cost has been regularly contested by the IRS. However, in several cases, the courts have ruled in favor of the taxpayer and upheld discounts on the valuation of limited partnership interests in the range of 10 percent to 40 percent, as long as the FLP was operated like a separate business. The IRS has won, and the valuation discounts have not been allowed, in cases where the family withdrew money from the business at leisure, shared checking accounts with the business, had the FLP pay medical or other ordinary living expenses for the family, and when other non-business transactions were prevalent within the FLP.

The estate planning benefits of the FLP are lost and expenses are increased (as the result of legal fees) when the IRS successfully contests the use of the FLP arrangement. To mitigate against this risk and to ensure the use of the favorable discounts, the FLP should possess economic substance by having its own checking accounts, tax identification number, payroll (including payment of reasonable compensation to the general partner if he is managing the business), and should not allow family members to withdraw funds at will, nor should the FLP pay for personal expenses of its owners.

A FLP is taxed as a partnership and, the entity files a Form 1065 and issues Schedule K-1s to both general and limited partners. The general partner may be a corporation or an individual. The treatment of payroll taxes will be determined

**Quick Quiz 16.6**

**Highlight the answer to these questions:**

1. Only a limited partner can manage a family limited partnership.
   a. True
   b. False

2. At formation of a family limited partnership, the founder is subject to gift tax on the transfer of the property interest to the family limited partnership.
   a. True
   b. False

False, False.

by whether the general partner is an individual or a corporation. The limited partners are passive and not subject to employment tax.

EXHIBIT 16.12 ADVANTAGES AND DISADVANTAGES OF FAMILY LIMITED PARTNERSHIPS

| Advantages |
|---|
| • Control retained by senior family member. |
| • Valuation discounts are available for minority interests. |
| • Annual exclusion gifts are generally used to transfer interests to family members. |
| • Some creditor protection. |
| • Restrictions can be placed on transferability of limited partnership interests of junior family members. |
| • FLP is commonly used as an estate planning strategy. |

| Disadvantages |
|---|
| • Attorney setup fees and costs. |
| • Periodic valuation costs. |
| • Operational requirements. |
| • Potential IRS challenges regarding valuations and discounts. |

# LIMITED LIABILITY COMPANIES (LLC)

**Limited Liability Companies** are separate legal entities formed by one or more individuals by meeting state statutory requirements necessary for the formation of an LLC.

## Key Concepts

**Underline/highlight the answers to these questions as you read:**

1. Discuss the formation and operation of an LLC.

2. Discuss the liability protection offered by an LLC.

3. Explain the tax attributes of an LLC.

## FORMATION

LLCs are formed in much the same way as corporations. They are chartered entities registered with the Secretary of State in the state of organization. The charter document is called **Articles of Organization** and the state requires the entity to have a resident agent. In addition, the state will require annual filings.

## INTEREST, DISPOSAL OF INTEREST, AND DISSOLUTION

Usually, owners' contributions determine the ownership percentage of an LLC. However, sometimes the organization will want to divide the ownership interests in an amount differently than the initial contributions. They can do this in a variety of ways, including revaluing assets or issuing units for some obligation.

Disposal or transferability of interests may be difficult and may be restricted to transferring only to named parties. Such restrictions are clarified in the operating agreement.

## CAPITAL

Capital is easier to raise in an LLC than in a proprietorship. Ease of raising capital in an LLC is similar to the ease of raising capital in a partnership.

### *Capital Structure*

There is no limitation on the number of members or the types of members in an LLC. Members may include foreign (nonresident aliens) individuals, estate, trusts, corporations, etc. LLCs may allocate items of income and gains in any manner agreed to by the members in the operating agreement and can also create different classes of ownership interests which have different rights.

## LIABILITY

The most important feature of an LLC is that the LLC's individual owners are protected from personal liability for the LLC's debts and obligations unless they personally guarantee such obligations.

The liability protection is not absolute. Piercing the veil and alter ego concepts give courts the power to disregard the LLC liability protection in extraordinary cases of owner/manager abuse or failure to maintain a clear and continuing identity.

## MANAGEMENT/OPERATIONS

An LLC usually is managed by virtue of an **operating agreement**. The operating agreement is similar to corporate bylaws and may be amended from time to time. The agreement specifies how and who will manage the LLC, how interests may be transferred, etc. Operating agreements are not filed with the state. Operating agreements sometimes specify simple majority rules for some decisions, super majority rules for other decisions (e.g., 2/3 or 3/4 to take on debt in excess of certain amounts) and unanimous votes for special situations (e.g., changing the operating agreement). Caution should be used with unanimous agreement provisions because they essentially give a minority owner (member) a veto power over all other members.

Note that an LLC is not legally required to have an operating agreement. If an LLC does not have an operating agreement, it will (by default) be governed by the state laws regarding LLCs. Although this might be sufficient for some LLCs, it is generally best to have a written operating agreement signed by all members that specifies the rules and regulations pertinent to the LLC.

## INCOME TAXATION AND PAYROLL (SOCIAL SECURITY) TAXES

An LLC which has a single member/owner is a disregarded entity for federal income tax purposes. The owner must file a Schedule C of Form 1040 for the LLC, the same as for a proprietorship. Such an LLC owner also has the same issues as the proprietors with regard to self-employment tax, unemployment compensation, and fringe benefits.

An LLC with two or more members can elect to be taxed for federal income tax purposes as a partnership (Form 1065 with Schedule K-1s), an S corporation (Form 1120S with Schedule K-1s), or a C corporation (Form 1120 with W-2 income to the owners).

### Taxation of Income

The LLC is not taxed at the entity level if it is boxed as a partnership. As a pass-through entity, an LLC's income is taxed to members at their personal rates. LLC losses are deductible on personal income tax returns to the extent of basis and may be limited by the passive activity rules. A unique characteristic of LLCs is that no gain or loss is recognized upon the distribution of appreciated property from an LLC to an LLC member. Gain will only be recognized to the extent that cash received exceeds the members adjusted basis.

### Fringe Benefits

LLCs are usually taxed as partnerships. Therefore, members are not generally allowed to exclude from gross income the value of fringe benefits paid on their behalf by the LLC.

### Employment Tax on Income

LLCs are usually taxed as partnerships. Income earned by the LLC is normally subject to self-employment tax on the tax returns of individual members. There are exceptions for LLC income derived from rental real estate and for LLC members who are the equivalent of limited partners.

Once elected, the tax status (partnership, S corporation, or C corporation) will dictate the handling of self-employment tax and fringe benefits.

Exhibit 16.13

| Advantages |
| --- |
| • Members have limited liability. |
| • Number of members is unlimited but a single member LLC is a disregarded entity for tax purposes (File Form 1040 Schedule C). |
| • Members may be individuals, corporations, trusts, other LLCs, and other entities. |
| • Income is passed through to the members, usually on Schedule K-1. |
| • Double taxation affecting most C corporations is avoided if partnership tax status is elected. |
| • Members can participate in managing the LLC. |
| • Distributions to members do not have to be directly proportional to the members' ownership interests as they do for S corporations. |
| • Can have multiple classes of ownership. |
| • Entity may elect to be taxed as a partnership, an S corporation, or a C corporation. |

| Disadvantages |
| --- |
| • May have limited life (often by termination on the death or bankruptcy of a member). |
| • Transfer of interests is difficult and sometimes limited by operating agreement. |
| • Some industries or professions may not be permitted to use LLC status. |
| • Laws vary from state to state regarding LLCs. |
| • Laws are relatively new for LLCs; therefore, precedent from prior court cases are limited. |
| • For tax purposes, the complex partnership rules generally apply. |
| • Members not meeting exceptions are subject to self-employment tax on all earned income if partnership status is elected. |

# C CORPORATIONS

Corporations are chartered legal entities formed by one or more individuals by meeting state statutory requirements necessary for the formation of a corporation. There are two types of corporations: the C corporation and the S corporation. For tax purposes, S corporations are simply C corporations with a special tax election and will be discussed in the next section.

## Key Concepts

**Underline/highlight the answers to these questions as you read:**

1. Describe the formation and operation of a corporation.

2. Discuss the tax attributes of a corporation.

3. Discuss the ability of a corporation to raise capital.

## FORMATION

Corporations can only be created by filing a charter document with the state of incorporation (called **articles of incorporation**). The articles of incorporation generally require a corporation to disclose its name, number of shares, and the purpose of the corporation. The corporation's purpose may be broad (e.g., to engage in any lawful activity) or specific (e.g., to sell textbooks). In addition, the corporation will be required to name a registered agent located in the state of incorporation.

## INTEREST, DISPOSAL OF INTEREST, AND DISSOLUTION

Ownership interests in a corporation are held by a shareholder and are evidenced by shares of stock certificates. Shares may be easy to transfer if there is a market, but certain small corporations restrict the transfer of shares through a shareholder agreement. The shares of stock issued by the corporation may be all one class or several classes. Different classes of stock generally have different values and/or voting rights.

## CAPITAL

Corporations can raise capital more easily than a proprietorship or partnership. The limited liability status appeals to outside non-employee owner/investors.

## LIABILITY

Liability in corporations is limited to the invested capital. Individual shareholders of the corporation have limited liability, presuming the corporation behaves in such a way as to clearly and consistently maintain its identity and complies with state-mandated requirements.

## MANAGEMENT/OPERATIONS

Corporations are managed by one or more officers appointed by the board of directors. The board of directors is the governing body of a corporation. The board of directors appoints various officers to run the corporation (usually includes president, chief financial officer, secretary, treasurer). The board of directors acts, or should act, in a very formal way and is required under the corporate charter to meet and follow certain formalities. Observing corporate formalities, and maintaining good standing with the Secretary of State in the state of incorporation, is an ongoing requirement.

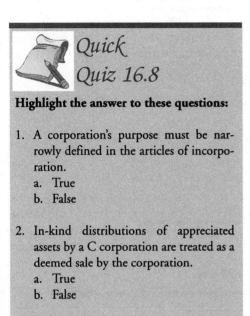

## INCOME TAXATION AND PAYROLL (SOCIAL SECURITY) TAXES

A corporation is taxed as a C corporation unless S corporation status is elected. C corporations must file Form 1120 (Exhibit 16.17) and pay taxes on their own income on a calendar or fiscal year basis. The owner/employees of both C corporations and S corporations are treated as employees for payroll tax purposes. Therefore, the entity withholds 7.65 percent of the employee's pay for Social Security taxes and matches such withholding for Social Security taxes. The owner/employee's compensation is not considered to be self-employment income.

Distributions of cash and other assets to a shareholder/employee in his capacity as a shareholder rather than as an employee are considered to be dividends. A C corporation is not allowed to take a tax deduction for dividends distributed to shareholders, but shareholders must include the dividends in gross income. Therefore, the income of a C corporation can be taxed two times, once at the corporation level and a second time at the shareholder level when dividends are distributed. In a closely-held corporation, careful tax planning can minimize or even eliminate this double taxation.

When noncash distributions of appreciated property are made to shareholder/employees, gain must be recognized at the corporate level as though the property had been sold and the cash proceeds distributed. For a C corporation, this gain must be recognized at the corporation level. For an S corporation, the gain is passed through to shareholders and taxed on their individual income tax returns based on their ownership interests in the S corporation. Unlike this corporation treatment, appreciated assets can be distributed by an LLC or by any entity taxed as a partnership without any gain recognition at the time of the distribution.

**TAX FORMULA FOR C CORPORATION**

EXHIBIT 16.14

| | |
|---|---|
| Total Income   (From Whatever Source Derived) | $XX,XXX |
| Less:  Exclusions From Gross Income | (X,XXX) |
| Gross Income | $XX,XXX |
| Less:  Deductions | (X,XXX) |
| Taxable Income | $XX,XXX |

EXHIBIT 16.15 **CORPORATION INCOME TAX RATES**

| Taxable Income | | Tax |
| --- | --- | --- |
| Over | Not Over | Rate |
| $0 | $50,000 | 15% |
| $50,000 | $75,000 | 25% |
| $75,000 | $100,000 | 34% |
| $100,000 | $335,000 | 39% |
| $335,000 | $10,000,000 | 34% |
| $10,000,000 | $15,000,000 | 35% |
| $15,000,000 | $18,333,333 | 38% |
| $18,333,333 | ....... | 35% |

EXHIBIT 16.16 **ADVANTAGES AND DISADVANTAGES OF C CORPORATIONS**

| Advantages |
| --- |

- Relative ease of raising capital.
- Limited liability of shareholders.
- Unlimited life of entity.
- Ease of transfer of ownership interests.
- Generally more management resources.
- Shareholder/employees may receive the full array of employer-provided tax-free fringe benefits.

| Disadvantages |
| --- |

- Potential for double taxation due to entity level taxation.
- Administrative burdens (e.g., filings).
- More difficult to form and dissolution can cause taxable gains.
- Borrowing may be difficult without stockholder personal guarantees, which negates part of the advantage of limited liability.
- Requires a registered agent.
- Requires a federal tax ID number.

# FORM 1120

EXHIBIT 16.17

The 2008 forms were the latest available at the time of printing. Please visit our website at money-education.com for updates.

| Form **1120** Department of the Treasury Internal Revenue Service | **U.S. Corporation Income Tax Return** For calendar year 2008 or tax year beginning _____ , 2008, ending _____ , 20 ____ ▶ See separate instructions. | OMB No. 1545-0123 **2008** |
|---|---|---|

| A Check if: | | | | |
|---|---|---|---|---|
| 1a Consolidated return (attach Form 851) ☐ | Use IRS label. Otherwise, print or type. | **Name** | | **B** Employer identification number |
| b Life/nonlife consolidated return . ☐ | | Number, street, and room or suite no. If a P.O. box, see instructions. | | **C** Date incorporated |
| 2 Personal holding co. (attach Sch. PH) . ☐ | | City or town, state, and ZIP code | | **D** Total assets (see instructions) $ |
| 3 Personal service corp. (see instructions) . ☐ | | | | |
| 4 Schedule M-3 attached ☐ | E Check if: (1) ☐ Initial return (2) ☐ Final return (3) ☐ Name change (4) ☐ Address change | | | |

### Income

| | | | |
|---|---|---|---|
| 1a | Gross receipts or sales _____ b Less returns and allowances _____ | c Bal ▶ | 1c |
| 2 | Cost of goods sold (Schedule A, line 8) . . . . . . . . . . . . | | 2 |
| 3 | Gross profit. Subtract line 2 from line 1c . . . . . . . . . . . | | 3 |
| 4 | Dividends (Schedule C, line 19) . . . . . . . . . . . . . | | 4 |
| 5 | Interest . . . . . . . . . . . . . . . . . . . . | | 5 |
| 6 | Gross rents . . . . . . . . . . . . . . . . . . | | 6 |
| 7 | Gross royalties . . . . . . . . . . . . . . . . . | | 7 |
| 8 | Capital gain net income (attach Schedule D (Form 1120)) . . . . . | | 8 |
| 9 | Net gain or (loss) from Form 4797, Part II, line 17 (attach Form 4797) . | | 9 |
| 10 | Other income (see instructions—attach schedule) . . . . . . . | | 10 |
| 11 | **Total income.** Add lines 3 through 10 . . . . . . . . . . ▶ | | 11 |

### Deductions (See instructions for limitations on deductions.)

| | | | |
|---|---|---|---|
| 12 | Compensation of officers (Schedule E, line 4) . . . . . . . . ▶ | | 12 |
| 13 | Salaries and wages (less employment credits) . . . . . . . . | | 13 |
| 14 | Repairs and maintenance . . . . . . . . . . . . . . | | 14 |
| 15 | Bad debts . . . . . . . . . . . . . . . . . . . | | 15 |
| 16 | Rents . . . . . . . . . . . . . . . . . . . . | | 16 |
| 17 | Taxes and licenses . . . . . . . . . . . . . . . . | | 17 |
| 18 | Interest . . . . . . . . . . . . . . . . . . . | | 18 |
| 19 | Charitable contributions . . . . . . . . . . . . . . . | | 19 |
| 20 | Depreciation from Form 4562 not claimed on Schedule A or elsewhere on return (attach Form 4562) . . . | | 20 |
| 21 | Depletion . . . . . . . . . . . . . . . . . . . | | 21 |
| 22 | Advertising . . . . . . . . . . . . . . . . . . | | 22 |
| 23 | Pension, profit-sharing, etc., plans . . . . . . . . . . . . | | 23 |
| 24 | Employee benefit programs . . . . . . . . . . . . . . | | 24 |
| 25 | Domestic production activities deduction (attach Form 8903) . . . . | | 25 |
| 26 | Other deductions (attach schedule) . . . . . . . . . . . | | 26 |
| 27 | **Total deductions.** Add lines 12 through 26 . . . . . . . . ▶ | | 27 |
| 28 | Taxable income before net operating loss deduction and special deductions. Subtract line 27 from line 11 . . | | 28 |
| 29 | **Less:** a Net operating loss deduction (see instructions) . . . . | 29a | |
| | b Special deductions (Schedule C, line 20) . . . . . | 29b | 29c |

### Tax, Refundable Credits, and Payments

| | | | |
|---|---|---|---|
| 30 | **Taxable income.** Subtract line 29c from line 28 (see instructions) . . . . . . . . . . . | | 30 |
| 31 | **Total tax** (Schedule J, line 10) . . . . . . . . . . . . . . . . . . . . . | | 31 |
| 32a | 2007 overpayment credited to 2008 . . | 32a | | |
| b | 2008 estimated tax payments . . . . | 32b | | |
| c | 2008 refund applied for on Form 4466 . . | 32c ( ) d Bal ▶ | 32d | |
| e | Tax deposited with Form 7004 . . . . . . . . | | 32e | |
| f | Credits: (1) Form 2439 _____ (2) Form 4136 _____ | | 32f | |
| g | Refundable credits from Form 3800, line 19c, and Form 8827, line 8c | 32g | 32h |
| 33 | Estimated tax penalty (see instructions). Check if Form 2220 is attached . . . . . . . ▶ ☐ | | 33 |
| 34 | **Amount owed.** If line 32h is smaller than the total of lines 31 and 33, enter amount owed . . . . | | 34 |
| 35 | **Overpayment.** If line 32h is larger than the total of lines 31 and 33, enter amount overpaid . . . . . . | | 35 |
| 36 | Enter amount from line 35 you want: **Credited to 2009 estimated tax** ▶ _____ Refunded ▶ | | 36 |

**Sign Here**

Under penalties of perjury, I declare that I have examined this return, including accompanying schedules and statements, and to the best of my knowledge and belief, it is true, correct, and complete. Declaration of preparer (other than taxpayer) is based on all information of which preparer has any knowledge.

| ▶ _____ | _____ | ▶ _____ | May the IRS discuss this return with the preparer shown below (see instructions)? ☐ Yes ☐ No |
|---|---|---|---|
| Signature of officer | Date | Title | |

**Paid Preparer's Use Only**

| Preparer's signature ▶ _____ | Date _____ | Check if self-employed ☐ | Preparer's SSN or PTIN _____ |
|---|---|---|---|
| Firm's name (or yours if self-employed), address, and ZIP code ▶ _____ | | EIN _____ | |
| | | Phone no. _____ | |

**For Privacy Act and Paperwork Reduction Act Notice, see separate instructions.**    Cat. No. 11450Q    Form **1120** (2008)

# S CORPORATIONS

An **S corporation** is normally created under state law by first forming a C corporation and then filing an "S" election with the IRS. The incorporation is normally the same as for a C corporation. There are, however, significant ways in which an S corporation differs from a C corporation.

## INTEREST, DISPOSAL OF INTEREST, AND DISSOLUTION

Like a C corporation, the ownership interests in an S corporation are held by shareholders and are evidenced by shares of stock. Transferability of shares may be restricted by shareholders agreement.

## CAPITAL

It is easier to raise capital in an S corporation than in a proprietorship or partnership because of the limited liability protection. However, the limited number of allowable shareholders may have a negative affect on the ability to raise capital. Recent changes in the IRC allow close family members to be treated as a single shareholder.

## LIABILITY

An S corporation offers the same limited liability protection as a C corporation or an LLC.

**Key Concepts**

**Underline/highlight the answers to these questions as you read:**

1. Explain how an S corporation differs from a C corporation.

2. Discuss the advantages and disadvantages of an S corporation.

## MANAGEMENT/OPERATIONS

Corporations are managed by one or more officers appointed by the board of directors. The board of directors is the governing body of a corporation. The board of directors appoints various officers to run the corporation. The board of directors acts, or should act, in a very formal way and is required under the corporate charter to meet and follow certain formalities. Observing corporate formalities and maintaining good standing with the Secretary of State in the state of incorporation is an ongoing requirement.

The number of shareholders of an S corporation is limited to 100 and the S corporation can only have one class of stock. LLCs, partnerships, and other corporations are prohibited from becoming S corporation shareholders. Additionally, non-resident aliens and most trusts may not be S corporation shareholders.

## INCOME TAXATION AND PAYROLL (SOCIAL SECURITY) TAXES

The income of an S corporation is passed through to shareholders and is not taxed at the corporation level. Therefore, an S corporation provides many of the benefits of a corporation without any double taxation of income earned by the corporation.

The owner/employees of S corporations are employees for payroll tax purposes. Therefore, the entity withholds 7.65 percent of the employees' pay for Social Security taxes and matches such withholding for Social Security taxes. The owner/employee compensation is not considered self-employment income. Additional distributions to shareholders beyond reasonable compensation are treated as dividends not subject to payroll tax.

Since the income of an S corporation is taxed to the shareholders for the year in which it is earned, dividend distributions to shareholders are normally not subject to income tax at the time they are distributed. Stated differently, S corporation dividends normally represent the distribution of income that has previously been taxed to the shareholder.

As indicated in the C corporation discussion, in-kind distributions of appreciated assets will be treated as a deemed sale; thus, such distributions will generate a capital gain in the case of an S corporation to all shareholders in proportion to their ownership even if the asset was only distributed to one shareholder.

Generally, S corporations file Form 1120S (Exhibit 16.19) on a calendar year basis and provide each shareholder with a Form 1120S Schedule K-1 (Exhibit 16.20).

| EXHIBIT 16.18 | ADVANTAGES AND DISADVANTAGES OF S CORPORATIONS |
| --- | --- |

| Advantages |
| --- |
| • Income is passed through to the shareholders for federal income tax purposes. |
| • Income is taxed at the individual level which may be a lower tax rate than the applicable corporate rate. |
| • Shareholders have limited liability. |
| • Distributions from S corporations are exempt from the payroll tax system, assuming the corporation provides adequate compensation to those shareholders who are employees of the corporation. |

| Disadvantages |
| --- |
| • Limited to 100 shareholders. |
| • Only one class of stock is permitted. |
| • Cannot have corporate, partnership, certain trust, or nonresident alien shareholders. |
| • Shareholder employees owning more than two percent of the company must pay taxes on a range of employee fringe benefits that would be tax-free to a shareholder/ employee of a C corporation. |
| • The tax rate of the individual shareholder may be higher than the corporate tax rate. |
| • Borrowing may be difficult without stockholder personal guarantees, which negates part of the advantage of limited liability. |

Form **1120S**

Department of the Treasury
Internal Revenue Service

## U.S. Income Tax Return for an S Corporation

▶ Do not file this form unless the corporation has filed or is attaching Form 2553 to elect to be an S corporation.

▶ See separate instructions.

OMB No. 1545-0130

**2008**

For calendar year 2008 or tax year beginning _____ , 2008, ending _____ , 20 ____

| | | |
|---|---|---|
| **A** S election effective date | **Use IRS label. Otherwise, print or type.** Name | **D** Employer identification number |
| **B** Business activity code number (see instructions) | Number, street, and room or suite no. If a P.O. box, see instructions. | **E** Date incorporated |
| **C** Check if Sch. M-3 attached ☐ | City or town, state, and ZIP code | **F** Total assets (see instructions) $ |

**G** Is the corporation electing to be an S corporation beginning with this tax year? ☐ Yes ☐ No   If "Yes," attach Form 2553 if not already filed

**H** Check if: **(1)** ☐ Final return  **(2)** ☐ Name change  **(3)** ☐ Address change  **(4)** ☐ Amended return  **(5)** ☐ S election termination or revocation

**I** Enter the number of shareholders who were shareholders during any part of the tax year . . . . . . . . . . ▶

**Caution.** *Include only trade or business income and expenses on lines 1a through 21. See the instructions for more information.*

### Income

| | | |
|---|---|---|
| **1a** | Gross receipts or sales _____ **b** Less returns and allowances _____ **c** Bal ▶ | **1c** |
| **2** | Cost of goods sold (Schedule A, line 8) . . . . . . . . | **2** |
| **3** | Gross profit. Subtract line 2 from line 1c | **3** |
| **4** | Net gain (loss) from Form 4797, Part II, line 17 (attach Form 4797) | **4** |
| **5** | Other income (loss) (see instructions—attach statement) . . . . . . . . . | **5** |
| **6** | **Total income (loss).** Add lines 3 through 5. . . . . . . . . . . . . . ▶ | **6** |

### Deductions (see instructions for limitations)

| | | |
|---|---|---|
| **7** | Compensation of officers . . . . . . . . . . . . . | **7** |
| **8** | Salaries and wages (less employment credits) . . . . . . . . | **8** |
| **9** | Repairs and maintenance . . . . . . . . . . . | **9** |
| **10** | Bad debts . . . . . . . . . . . . . . . . . | **10** |
| **11** | Rents . . . . . . . . . . . . . . . . . . | **11** |
| **12** | Taxes and licenses . . . . . . . . . . . . . . | **12** |
| **13** | Interest . . . . . . . . . . . . . . . . . . | **13** |
| **14** | Depreciation not claimed on Schedule A or elsewhere on return (attach Form 4562) . . . . | **14** |
| **15** | Depletion **(Do not deduct oil and gas depletion.)** . . . . . . | **15** |
| **16** | Advertising . . . . . . . . . . . . . . . . | **16** |
| **17** | Pension, profit-sharing, etc., plans . . . . . . . . . | **17** |
| **18** | Employee benefit programs. . . . . . . . . . . . | **18** |
| **19** | Other deductions (attach statement) . . . . . . . . . | **19** |
| **20** | **Total deductions.** Add lines 7 through 19 . . . . . . . . . . . ▶ | **20** |
| **21** | **Ordinary business income (loss).** Subtract line 20 from line 6 . . . . . . . . | **21** |

### Tax and Payments

| | | |
|---|---|---|
| **22a** | Excess net passive income or LIFO recapture tax (see instructions) **22a** _____ | |
| **b** | Tax from Schedule D (Form 1120S) . . . . . . . . . **22b** _____ | |
| **c** | Add lines 22a and 22b (see instructions for additional taxes) . . | **22c** |
| **23a** | 2008 estimated tax payments and 2007 overpayment credited to 2008 **23a** _____ | |
| **b** | Tax deposited with Form 7004. . . . . . . . **23b** _____ | |
| **c** | Credit for federal tax paid on fuels (attach Form 4136) . . . . **23c** _____ | |
| **d** | Add lines 23a through 23c . . . . . . . . . . . . . | **23d** |
| **24** | Estimated tax penalty (see instructions). Check if Form 2220 is attached . . . . . ▶ ☐ | **24** |
| **25** | **Amount owed.** If line 23d is smaller than the total of lines 22c and 24, enter amount owed . . | **25** |
| **26** | **Overpayment.** If line 23d is larger than the total of lines 22c and 24, enter amount overpaid . | **26** |
| **27** | Enter amount from line 26 **Credited to 2009 estimated tax** ▶ _____ Refunded ▶ | **27** |

**Sign Here**

Under penalties of perjury, I declare that I have examined this return, including accompanying schedules and statements, and to the best of my knowledge and belief, it is true, correct, and complete. Declaration of preparer (other than taxpayer) is based on all information of which preparer has any knowledge.

▶ _____ Signature of officer   Date   Title

May the IRS discuss this return with the preparer shown below (see instructions)? ☐ Yes ☐ No

**Paid Preparer's Use Only**

| | Date | Check if self-employed ☐ | Preparer's SSN or PTIN |
|---|---|---|---|
| Preparer's signature ▶ | | | |
| Firm's name (or yours if self-employed), address, and ZIP code ▶ | | EIN | |
| | | Phone no. ( ) | |

For Privacy Act and Paperwork Reduction Act Notice, see separate instructions.   Cat. No. 11510H   Form **1120S** (2008)

EXHIBIT 16.20 FORM 1120S SCHEDULE K-1

671108

| | | | | |
|---|---|---|---|---|
| ☐ Final K-1 | | ☐ Amended K-1 | | OMB No. 1545-0130 |

**Schedule K-1**
**(Form 1120S)**
Department of the Treasury
Internal Revenue Service

2008

For calendar year 2008, or tax
year beginning _____ , 2008
ending _____ , 20___

**Shareholder's Share of Income, Deductions, Credits, etc.**  ► See back of form and separate instructions.

| Part III | Shareholder's Share of Current Year Income, Deductions, Credits, and Other Items | | |
|---|---|---|---|
| **1** Ordinary business income (loss) | | **13** Credits | |
| **2** Net rental real estate income (loss) | | | |
| **3** Other net rental income (loss) | | | |
| **4** Interest income | | | |
| **5a** Ordinary dividends | | | |
| **5b** Qualified dividends | | **14** Foreign transactions | |
| **6** Royalties | | | |
| **7** Net short-term capital gain (loss) | | | |
| **8a** Net long-term capital gain (loss) | | | |
| **8b** Collectibles (28%) gain (loss) | | | |
| **8c** Unrecaptured section 1250 gain | | | |
| **9** Net section 1231 gain (loss) | | | |
| **10** Other income (loss) | | **15** Alternative minimum tax (AMT) items | |
| **11** Section 179 deduction | | **16** Items affecting shareholder basis | |
| **12** Other deductions | | | |
| | | **17** Other information | |

| Part I | Information About the Corporation |
|---|---|
| **A** Corporation's employer identification number | |
| **B** Corporation's name, address, city, state, and ZIP code | |
| **C** IRS Center where corporation filed return | |

| Part II | Information About the Shareholder |
|---|---|
| **D** Shareholder's identifying number | |
| **E** Shareholder's name, address, city, state, and ZIP code | |
| **F** Shareholder's percentage of stock ownership for tax year . . . . . . . . . _____ % | |

For IRS Use Only

\* See attached statement for additional information.

For Paperwork Reduction Act Notice, see Instructions for Form 1120S.     Cat. No. 11520D     Schedule K-1 (Form 1120S) 2008

## COMPARISON OF S CORPORATIONS AND LLCs

Many business owners know that they want limited liability and a flow through tax entity, but cannot distinguish between an S corporation and a LLC. Below is a side-by-side comparison of these two very important entity types.

## COMPARISON OF S CORPORATIONS AND LLCs

EXHIBIT 16.21

|  | S Corporation | LLC |
|---|---|---|
| Double taxation | No | No |
| Pass through tax losses | Yes | Yes |
| Availability of preferred return for certain investors (1 class of stock in S) | No | Yes |
| Partnerships, corporations, and trusts can be entity owners | No | Yes |
| Foreign investors | No | Yes |
| Distribute in-kind appreciated assets to owners without gain recognition | No | Yes |
| Ability to transfer interest to trust for estate planning | No | Yes |
| Low filing fees | Yes (Generally) | No |
| Self employment tax on all income for owner/employees | No | Yes (Generally) |
| Limited number of owners | Yes (100) | No |
| Owner's basis for deductibility of losses includes pro-rata share of loans to entity by third parties | No | Yes |
| The law is well settled pertaining to the entity | Yes | No |
| Filing date with extensions | October 15th | September 15th |

EXHIBIT 16.22  ENTITY COMPARISON

| | Proprietorship | General Partnership | Limited Partnership | LLP | FLP | LLC | S Corp. | C Corp. |
|---|---|---|---|---|---|---|---|---|
| Cost to create (money & time) | Low | Medium | Medium-High | High | High | High | High | High |
| Personal liability of investors for enterprise debt | Yes | Yes | No (if limited partner) | Yes | Yes | No | No | No |
| Annual state filing requirement | No | Generally Not | Yes | Yes | Yes | Yes | Yes | Yes |
| Maximum owners | One | Unlimited | Unlimited | Unlimited | Unlimited | Unlimited | 100 | Unlimited |
| Owners are known as | Owner | Partner | Partner or Limited Partner | Partner or Limited Partner | Partner or Limited Partner | Member | Shareholder | Shareholder |
| Tax filing alternatives | Schedule C 1040 | Form 1065 K-1 flows to Schedule E of Form 1040 | Form 1065 K-1 flows to Schedule E of Form 1040 | May file as corporation or partnership | Form 1065 K-1 flows to Schedule E of Form 1040 | If one member, entity is disregarded and owner files Schedule C of Form 1040. If two or more members, choice of Form 1065 (Partnership), Form 1120-S (S Corporation), or Form 1120 (C Corporation) | Form 1120S K-1 to shareholders | Form 1120 |
| Federal Tax ID required | No | Yes | Yes | Yes | Yes | No, if one member Yes, if two or more members | Yes | Yes |
| Taxation concept | Individual | Flow Through | Flow Through | Flow Through | Flow Through | Flow Through | Flow Through | Entity |
| Owners income | Self Employment | Self employment but limited partners/members are not subject to Soc. Sec. tax unless they perform personal services for the entity | Self employment but limited partners/members are not subject to Soc. Sec. tax unless they perform personal services for the entity | Self employment but limited partners/members are not subject to Soc. Sec. tax unless they perform personal services for the entity | Self employment but limited partners/members are not subject to Soc. Sec. tax unless they perform personal services for the entity | Depends on filing choice, but limited partners/members are not subject to Soc. Sec. tax unless they perform personal services for the entity | W-2 and ordinary income Excess profits distributed are not subject to Soc. Sec. tax | W-2 and dividend income |

# PROTECTING OWNERS FROM EACH OTHER

As the old saying goes "there is risk in the future." The choice of entity provides certain advantages and disadvantages to the partner, member, or shareholder. However, there are certain recurring situations where a little forethought could have prevented a bad result. Some of these situations are unexpected events like death or disability of an owner, divorce, bankruptcy, retirement, or a voluntary or involuntary disassociation with the entity.

Each owner faces the above risks. In entities where there are multiple owners, a written shareholder agreement, partnership agreement, or operating agreement addressing the listed issues and any others that are of concern should be considered.

## PROTECTING MINORITY SHAREHOLDERS/MEMBERS

A minority shareholder or member who is also an employee should have two protections from termination by having an employment agreement (rather than being an employee at will) and should also have a shareholder agreement with a buyout provision in the event of termination.

## ELEMENTS OF SHAREHOLDER/PARTNERSHIP AGREEMENTS

For each risk there should be a method provided for valuing the entity and the departing owner's interest. For example:

- For the first five years, the departing owner gets nothing.
- After five years, the departing owner is entitled to his proportional share. The company shall be valued at 1.5 times the average revenues for the three previous years.
- If the departing owner is terminated for cause, the company shall be valued at 50 percent of the average revenues for the last three years.

It is not enough to identify the risk and the valuation; a funding method must also be provided. While cross purchase or entity life insurance may work for untimely death, life insurance does not work for voluntary termination. A payout over time that will not burden the remaining owners and entity may be a solution. Whatever the solution, it needs to be clearly articulated in the shareholder agreement, the operating agreement, or partnership agreement.

## ISSUES REGARDING ADDITIONAL CAPITAL REQUIRED

In the situation where multiple owners have made a certain initial investment into a business enterprise, there is always the chance that additional capital will be needed. What happens if one of the investors refuses to pay his proportional share of such new capital? Can the partners, or shareholders compel the unwilling owner to pay? At the outset of an entity the initial owners should prepare an analysis of the risks of needing additional capital (e.g., debt service is certain). If additional capital is likely or even possibly needed, the joint owners should prepare for it. One way to do so is to have all owners put up a negotiable letter of credit for a reasonable period of time to assure cash calls will be met. Additionally, a provision should be put in the partnership agreement, shareholder agreement, or operating agreement to the effect that any owner who defaults on a cash call obligation automatically forfeits his original investment and such default makes the letter of credit immediately due and payable.

# Key Terms

**Articles of Incorporation** - The charter document for a corporation that must be filed with the Secretary of State in the state of organization.

**Articles of Organization** - The charter document of an LLC that must be filed with the Secretary of State in the state of organization.

**Checking the Box** - When an eligible entity chooses to be taxed as either a corporation or a partnership.

**Corporations** - Chartered legal entities formed by one or more individuals by meeting state statutory requirements necessary for the formation of a corporation.

**Family Limited Partnership** - A special type of limited partnership created under state law with the primary purpose of transferring assets to younger generations using annual exclusions and valuation discounts for minority interests and lack of marketability.

**General Partnership** - A joint business venture among two or more persons/entities to conduct business as co-owners in which all owners have unlimited liability with regard to the debts and obligations of the partnership.

**Keogh Plan** - A qualified plan for a self-employed person. An important distinction of Keogh plans is the reduced contribution that can be made on behalf of the self-employed individual.

**Limited Liability Company** - Separate legal entity formed by one or more individuals by meeting state statutory requirements necessary for the formation of an LLC that may be taxed as a sole proprietorship, partnership, or corporation.

**Limited Liability Partnership** - A hybrid entity generally comprised of licensed professionals that provides partial liability protection to its members and may be taxed as either a corporation or partnership.

**Limited Partnerships** - Associations of two or more persons as co-owners to carry on a business for profit except that one or more of the partners have limited participation in the management of the venture and thus limited risk exposure.

**Managing Partner** - A partner named to have responsibilities for specific tasks or for day-to-day operations.

**Operating Agreement** - A written agreement similar to corporate bylaws that specify the rules and regulations for the operation of an LLC.

**Piercing the Veil** - Occurs when a court disregards the status of the entity that gives the owners limited liability because the owners failed to maintain a clear and consistent identity for the entity.

**S Corporation** - A corporation formed under state law that elects to be taxed under Subchapter S of the Internal Revenue Code.

**Sole Proprietorship** - A business venture owned and operated by a single individual.

## DISCUSSION QUESTIONS

1.  What are the different types of legal entities from which a business owner can conduct business?

2.  How is a general partnership taxed?

3.  What are the differences between a a general and a limited partnership?

4.  How do different types of business entities differ from each other with regard to the personal liability of owners for business obligation?

5.  How is a C corporation taxed?

6.  What type of business entity should be chosen if the owners expect losses in the first few years and the owners want limited personal liability?

7.  How is a limited liability company taxed if it has one or more owners?

8.  Compare an S corporation to a limited liability company.

9.  How can an entity avoid having a court "pierce the veil?"

10. Why is it often difficult to dispose of an interest in a partnership?

11. What is the principal disadvantage of the general partnership arrangement?

12. How does the limited partnership arrangement affect an entity's ability to raise capital?

13. Define "checking the box."

14. How is a family limited partnership usually formed?

15. What are the risks associated with the taxation of an FLP?

16. What is an operating agreement and why is it important to have this document?

17. What are some of the advantages of a corporation?

18. What are some of the disadvantages of an S corporation?

1.  An architect performed services for Bill and Sue and, in lieu of her normal fee, accepted a 10 percent interest in a partnership with a fair market value of $10,000. How much income from this arrangement should the architect report on her income tax return?

    a.  The architect does not have any currently taxable income.

    b.  The architect has realized $10,000 in capital gains.

    c.  The architect must recognize $10,000 in compensation income.

    d.  The architect has realized $10,000 in compensation income, but does not have to recognize it until she sells her interest in the partnership.

2.  An S corporation has the following information for the taxable year:

    | | |
    |---|---|
    | Net Income before the items below | $90,000 |
    | Bill's Salary | ($38,000) |
    | Other Income | $29,000 |
    | Other Expenses | ($14,000) |
    | Net Income | $67,000 |

    Bill is a 20 percent owner of the S corporation and he performs services for the business as an employee. What is Bill's self-employment income?

    a.  $0.

    b.  $52,000.

    c.  $67,000.

    d.  $90,000.

3.  On August 1, 2010, Jack bought a 5 percent interest (5 shares) in XYZ, an S corporation that files as a calendar-year taxpayer. In 2010, the S corporation income was $160,000. How much will be reported to Jack on his 2010 1120S Schedule K-1?

    a.  $0.

    b.  $3,333.

    c.  $3,353.

    d.  $8,000.

4. At the beginning of the current year, Donna's basis in her partnership interest was $100,000. At the end of the year, Donna received a K-1 from the partnership that showed the following information:

| | |
|---|---|
| Cash Withdrawn | $31,000 |
| Partnership Taxable Income | $60,000 |
| Charitable Contribution | $1,000 |

What is Donna's basis in her partnership interest at year-end?

    a. $128,000.

    b. $129,000.

    c. $159,000.

    d. $160,000.

5. Cobalt, a calendar-year S corporation, was incorporated in 2007. The company had the following taxable income and distributions each year:

| | Taxable Income | Distributions |
|---|---|---|
| 2007 | ($20,000) | $0 |
| 2008 | ($30,000) | $0 |
| 2009 | $150,000 | $60,000 |
| 2010 | $400,000 | $175,000 |

Cobalt has a single shareholder. His original basis in the stock was $150,000. What is the shareholder's basis at the end of 2010?

    a. $150,000.

    b. $250,000.

    c. $415,000.

    d. $650,000.

6. Which of the following statements is/are true?

    1. Partnerships offer limited liability protection to partners.

    2. LLCs offer limited liability protection to members.

    a. 1 only.

    b. 2 only.

    c. Both 1 and 2.

    d. Neither 1 nor 2.

7. Which of the following statements is/are true?

   1. LLCs offer limited liability protection to members.
   2. S corporations offer limited liability protection to owners.
      a. 1 only.
      b. 2 only.
      c. Both 1 and 2.
      d. Neither 1 nor 2.

8. Which of the following statements is/are true?

   1. It is necessary to register with the state when forming a proprietorship.
   2. It is necessary to register with the state when forming a partnership.
      a. 1 only.
      b. 2 only.
      c. Both 1 and 2.
      d. Neither 1 nor 2.

9. Which of the following statements is/are true?

   1. Partnerships require registration with the state.
   2. Limited partnerships require registration with the state.
      a. 1 only.
      b. 2 only.
      c. Both 1 and 2.
      d. Neither 1 nor 2.

10. Which entity does <u>not</u> have all of the following characteristics?

    1. Limited liability.
    2. Ability to distribute in-kind appreciated assets to owners without gain recognition.
    3. Can have foreign investors.
       a. LLC.
       b. S corporation.
       c. Limited partnership.
       d. LLP.

11. Which type of entity could possibly file any of the following forms?

    1. Form 1040.

    2. Form 1065.

    3. Form 1120S.

        a. Partnership.

        b. Limited partnership.

        c. Proprietorship.

        d. LLC.

12. Which entity will meet the following requirements?

    1. Flow-through entity.

    2. Limited liability.

    3. Can have foreign investors.

        a. Proprietorship.

        b. Partnership.

        c. LLC.

        d. S corporation.

13. Which entity will meet the following requirements?

    1. Disregarded entity.

    2. Limited liability.

    3. Self-employment tax on all income.

        a. Partnership.

        b. Single-member LLC.

        c. S corporation.

        d. Proprietorship.

14. Which entity will meet the following requirements?

    1. Unlimited number of owners.

    2. Limited liability.

    3. Self-employment tax on all income.

        a. Proprietorship.

        b. Partnership.

        c. LLC.

        d. S corporation.

15. Which entity will meet the following requirements?

    1. Availability of preferred returns for certain investors.
    2. Considers loans from third parties in basis of owners.
    3. Limited liability.
        a. Partnership.
        b. LLC.
        c. S corporation.
        d. C corporation.

16. Which of the following can file as a corporation or partnership?

    a. LLC and LLP.
    b. LLC only.
    c. LLP only.
    d. LLC and S corporation.

17. Excess distributed income over reasonable compensation:

    1. is treated as self-employment income in a LLC.
    2. is treated as dividend income in a S corporation.
        a. 1 only.
        b. 2 only.
        c. Both 1 and 2.
        d. Neither 1 nor 2.

# Quick Quiz Explanations

### Quick Quiz 16.1

1. True.
2. False. To avoid piercing the veil, the entity should keep books and records separate from the personal books and records of the owners, segregate activities of business from personal affairs, follow corporate formalities such as meeting requirements and filings, and address all content in contracts and correspondence from the viewpoint of the business entity (rather than the viewpoint of the owners).

### Quick Quiz 16.2

1. False. A proprietorship may be required to obtain a local business license or register with the state or local taxing authority if it will be collecting sales tax.
2. True.
3. True.

### Quick Quiz 16.3

1. False. General partnerships are governed by the laws of the state in which they are formed.
2. False. A principal disadvantage of the general partnership arrangement is that all general partners in a partnership are jointly and severally liable for the debts and obligations of the partnership.
3. True.

### Quick Quiz 16.4

1. True.
2. False. Limited partnerships offer limited liability for the limited partners. The general partners run the business and are exposed for personal liability.

### Quick Quiz 16.5

1. True.
2. False. If the LLP is comprised of only licensed professionals, transfer of an interest will usually be more difficult because such interest may only be transferred to another similarly licensed professional.

### Quick Quiz 16.6

1. False. Only a general partner can manage a family limited partnership.
2. False. Upon creation of the partnership (FLP), there are neither income nor gift tax consequences because the entity created (the limited partnership and all of its interests, both general and limited) is owned by the same person, or persons, who owned it before the transfer.

### Quick Quiz 16.7

1. True.
2. True.

### Quick Quiz 16.8

1. False. The corporation's purpose may be broad (e.g., to engage in any lawful activity) or specific (e.g., to sell textbooks).
2. True.

### Quick Quiz 16.9

1. True.
2. False. Additional distributions to shareholders beyond reasonable compensation are treated as dividends not subject to payroll tax. In-kind distributions of appreciated assets will be treated as a deemed sale; thus, such distributions will generate a capital gain in the case of an S corporation to all shareholders in proportion to their ownership even if the asset was only distributed to one shareholder.

# Tax Rate Schedules

### 2009 SINGLE - SCHEDULE X

| If taxable income is over-- | But not over-- | The tax is: |
|---|---|---|
| $0 | $8,350 | 10% of the amount over $0 |
| $8,350 | $33,950 | $835 plus 15% of the amount over $8,350 |
| $33,950 | $82,250 | $4,675 plus 25% of the amount over $33,950 |
| $82,250 | $171,550 | $16,750 plus 28% of the amount over $82,250 |
| $171,550 | $372,950 | $41,754 plus 33% of the amount over $171,550 |
| $372,950 | no limit | $108,216 plus 35% of the amount over $372,950 |

## 2009 MARRIED FILING JOINTLY OR SURVIVING SPOUSE - SCHEDULE Y-1

| If taxable income is over-- | But not over-- | The tax is: |
|---|---|---|
| $0 | $16,700 | 10% of the amount over $0 |
| $16,700 | $67,900 | $1,670 plus 15% of the amount over $16,700 |
| $67,900 | $137,050 | $9,350 plus 25% of the amount over $67,900 |
| $137,050 | $208,850 | $26,637.50 plus 28% of the amount over $137,050 |
| $208,850 | $372,950 | $46,741.50 plus 33% of the amount over $208,850 |
| $372,950 | no limit | $100,894.50 plus 35% of the amount over $372,950 |

### 2009 HEAD OF HOUSEHOLD - SCHEDULE Z

| If taxable income is over-- | But not over-- | The tax is: |
|---|---|---|
| $0 | $11,950 | 10% of the amount over $0 |
| $11,950 | $45,500 | $1,195 plus 15% of the amount over $11,950 |
| $45,500 | $117,450 | $6,227.50 plus 25% of the amount over $45,500 |
| $117,450 | $190,200 | $24,215.00 plus 28% of the amount over $117,450 |
| $190,200 | $372,950 | $44,585 plus 33% of the amount over $190,200 |
| $372,950 | no limit | $104,892.50 plus 35% of the amount over $372,950 |

## 2009 MARRIED FILING SEPARATELY - SCHEDULE Y-2

| If taxable income is over-- | But not over-- | The tax is: |
|---|---|---|
| $0 | $8,350 | 10% of the amount over $0 |
| $8,350 | $33,950 | $835 plus 15% of the amount over $8,350 |
| $33,950 | $68,525 | $4,675 plus 25% of the amount over $33,950 |
| $68,525 | $104,425 | $13,318.75 plus 28% of the amount over $68,525 |
| $104,425 | $186,475 | $23,370.75 plus 33% of the amount over $104,425 |
| $186,475 | no limit | $50,447.25 plus 35% of the amount over $186,475 |

## 2009 ESTATES AND TRUSTS

| If taxable income is over-- | But not over-- | The tax is: |
|---|---|---|
| $0 | $2,300 | 15% of the amount over $0 |
| $2,300 | $5,350 | $345 plus 25% of the amount over $2,300 |
| $5,350 | $8,200 | $1,107.50 plus 28% of the amount over $5,350 |
| $8,200 | $11,150 | $1,905.50 plus 33% of the amount over $8,200 |
| $11,150 | no limit | $2,879 plus 35% of the amount over $11,150 |

## 2010 SINGLE - SCHEDULE X

| If taxable income is over-- | But not over-- | The tax is: |
|---|---|---|
| $0 | $8,375 | 10% of the amount over $0 |
| $8,375 | $34,000 | $837.50 plus 15% of the amount over $8,375 |
| $34,000 | $82,400 | $4,681.25 plus 25% of the amount over $34,000 |
| $82,400 | $171,850 | $16,781.25 plus 28% of the amount over $82,400 |
| $171,850 | $373,650 | $41,827.25 plus 33% of the amount over $171,850 |
| $373,650 | no limit | $108,421.25 plus 35% of the amount over $373,650 |

## 2010 MARRIED FILING JOINTLY OR SURVIVING SPOUSE - SCHEDULE Y-1

| If taxable income is over-- | But not over-- | The tax is: |
|---|---|---|
| $0 | $16,750 | 10% of the amount over $0 |
| $16,750 | $68,000 | $1,675 plus 15% of the amount over $16,750 |
| $68,000 | $137,300 | $9,362.50 plus 25% of the amount over $68,000 |
| $137,300 | $209,250 | $26,687.50 plus 28% of the amount over $137,300 |
| $209,250 | $373,650 | $46,833.50 plus 33% of the amount over $209,250 |
| $373,650 | no limit | $101,085.50 plus 35% of the amount over $373,650 |

## 2010 HEAD OF HOUSEHOLD - SCHEDULE Z

| If taxable income is over-- | But not over-- | The tax is: |
|---|---|---|
| $0 | $11,950 | 10% of the amount over $0 |
| $11,950 | $45,550 | $1,195 plus 15% of the amount over $11,950 |
| $45,550 | $117,650 | $6,235 plus 25% of the amount over $45,550 |
| $117,650 | $190,550 | $24,260 plus 28% of the amount over $117,650 |
| $190,550 | $373,650 | $44,672 plus 33% of the amount over $190,550 |
| $373,650 | no limit | $105,095 plus 35% of the amount over $373,650 |

## 2010 MARRIED FILING SEPARATELY - SCHEDULE Y-2

| If taxable income is over-- | But not over-- | The tax is: |
|---|---|---|
| $0 | $8,375 | 10% of the amount over $0 |
| $8,375 | $34,000 | $837.50 plus 15% of the amount over $8,375 |
| $34,000 | $68,650 | $4,681.25 plus 25% of the amount over $34,000 |
| $68,650 | $104,625 | $13,343.75 plus 28% of the amount over $68,650 |
| $104,625 | $186,825 | $23,416.75 plus 33% of the amount over $104,625 |
| $186,825 | no limit | $50,542.75 plus 35% of the amount over $186,825 |

## 2010 ESTATES AND TRUSTS

| If taxable income is over-- | But not over-- | The tax is: |
|---|---|---|
| $0 | $2,300 | 15% of the amount over $0 |
| $2,300 | $5,350 | $345 plus 25% of the amount over $2,300 |
| $5,350 | $8,200 | $1,107.50 plus 28% of the amount over $5,350 |
| $8,200 | $11,200 | $1,905.50 plus 33% of the amount over $8,200 |
| $11,200 | no limit | $2,895.50 plus 35% of the amount over $11,200 |

## BASIC STANDARD DEDUCTION AMOUNTS

| Filing Status | Standard Deduction Amount | |
|---|---|---|
| | 2009 | 2010 |
| Single | $5,700 | $5,700 |
| Married Filing Jointly/ Surviving Spouse | $11,400 | $11,400 |
| Head of Household | $8,350 | $8,400 |
| Married Filing Separately | $5,700 | $5,700 |

## ADDITIONAL STANDARD DEDUCTION AMOUNTS

| Filing Status | Additional Standard Deduction Amount | |
|---|---|---|
| | 2009 | 2010 |
| Single | $1,400 | $1,400 |
| Married Filing Jointly/ Surviving Spouse | $1,100 | $1,100 |
| Head of Household | $1,400 | $1,400 |
| Married Filing Separately | $1,100 | $1,100 |

## PERSONAL AND DEPENDENCY EXEMPTIONS

| 2009 | 2010 |
|---|---|
| $3,650 | $3,650 |

# *Topic List*

The following is the topic list for the CFP® Certification Examination.

## INCOME TAX PLANNING

### INCOME TAX LAW FUNDAMENTALS
A.  Types of Authority
   1)  Primary
   2)  Secondary
B.  Research Sources

### TAX COMPLIANCE
A.  Filing Requirements
B.  Audits
C.  Penalties

### INCOME TAX FUNDAMENTALS AND CALCULATIONS
A.  Filing Status
B.  Gross Income
   1)  Inclusions
   2)  Exclusions
   3)  Imputed Income
C.  Adjustments
D.  Standard/Itemized Deductions
   1)  Types
   2)  Limitations
E.  Personal and Dependency Exemptions
F.  Taxable Income
G.  Tax Liability
   1)  Rate Schedule
   2)  Kiddie Tax
   3)  Self-Employment Tax
H.  Tax Credits

I. Payments of Tax
    1) Withholding
    2) Estimated Payments

## TAX ACCOUNTING
A. Accounting Periods
B. Accounting Methods
    1) Cash Receipts and Disbursements
    2) Accrual Method
    3) Hybrid Method
    4) Change in Accounting Method
C. Long-Term Contracts
D. Installment Sales
E. Inventory Valuation and Flow Methods
F. Net Operating Losses

## CHARACTERISTICS AND INCOME TAXATION OF BUSINESS ENTITIES
A. Entity Types
    1) Sole Proprietorship
    2) Partnerships
    3) Limited Liability Company (LLC)
    4) Corporations
    5) Trust
    6) Association
B. Taxation at Entity and Owner Level
    1) Formation
    2) Flow through of income and losses
    3) Special Taxes
    4) Distributions
    5) Dissolution
    6) Disposition

## INCOME TAXATION OF TRUSTS AND ESTATES
*These issues are covered in greater depth in Estate Planning for Financial Planners by Michael A. Dalton and Thomas P. Langdon.*

A. General Issues
    1) Filing Requirements
    2) Deadlines
    3) Choice of Taxable Year
    4) Tax Treatment of distributions to beneficiaries
    5) Rate Structure
B. Grantor/Nongrantor Trusts
C. Simple/Complex Trusts
D. Revocable/Irrevocable Trusts
E. Trust Income
    1) Trust Accounting Income
    2) Trust Taxable Income
    3) Distributable Net Income (DNI)
F. Estate Income Tax

## BASIS
A. Original Basis
B. Adjusted Basis
C. Amortization and Accretion
D. Basis of Property received by gift and in nontaxable transactions
E. Basis of inherited property (community and non-community-property)

## DEPRECIATION/COST-RECOVERY CONCEPTS
A. Modified Accelerated Cost Recovery System (MACRS)
B. Expensing Policy
C. Section 179 Deduction
D. Amortization
E. Depletion

## TAX CONSEQUENCES OF LIKE-KIND EXCHANGES
A. Reporting Requirements
B. Qualifying Transactions
C. Liabilities
D. Boot
E. Related Party Transactions

## TAX CONSEQUENCES OF THE DISPOSITION OF PROPERTY
A. Capital Assets (Section 1221)
B. Holding Period
C. Sale of Residence
D. Depreciation Recapture
E. Related Parties
F. Wash Sales
G. Bargain Sales
H. Section 1244 Stock (Small Business Stock Election)
I. Installment Sales
J. Involuntary Conversions

## ALTERNATIVE MINIMUM TAX (AMT)
A. Mechanics
B. Preferences and Adjustments
C. Exclusions Items vs. Deferral Items
D. Credit: Creation, Usage, and Limitations
E. Application to Businesses and Trusts
F. Planning Strategies

## TAX REDUCTION/MANAGEMENT TECHNIQUES
A. Tax Credits
B. Accelerated Deductions
C. Deferral of Income
D. Intra-Family Transfers

## PASSIVE ACTIVITY AND AT-RISK RULES

    A.    Definitions
    B.    Computations
    C.    Treatment of Disallowed Losses
    D.    Disposition of Passive Activities
    E.    Real Estate Exceptions

## TAX IMPLICATIONS OF SPECIAL CIRCUMSTANCES

    A.    Married/Widowed
        1)    Filing Status
        2)    Children
        3)    Community and Non-Community-Property
    B.    Divorce
        1)    Alimony
        2)    Child Support
        3)    Property Division

## CHARITABLE CONTRIBUTIONS AND DEDUCTIONS

    A.    Qualified Entities
        1)    Public Charities
        2)    Private Charities
    B.    Deduction Limitations
    C.    Carryover Periods
    D.    Appreciated Property
    E.    Nondeductible Contributions
    F.    Appraisals
    G.    Substantiation Requirements
    H.    Charitable Contributions by Business Entities

# Glossary

## A

**Above-the-Line Deductions** – Deduction for adjusted gross income, also known as adjustments to income.

**Accelerated Depreciation** – Allows the owner of an asset to front-load the depreciation deductions so that more of the depreciation deduction is taken in the early years, and less is taken in later years.

**Accountable Expense Reimbursement Plan** – A plan under which an employer reimburses employees for certain actually incurred expenses and requires the employee to substantiate the expenditures by producing receipts.

**Accrual Method** – An accounting method under which income is reported when it is earned rather than when it is received in cash, and expenses are reported when they are incurred rather than when they are paid.

**Accuracy-Related Penalty** – A penalty of 20 percent of the underpayment amount imposed on taxpayers who file incorrect tax returns in certain situations.

**Acquisition Indebtedness** – Indebtedness that is secured by the home and is used to acquire, construct, or improve the taxpayer's primary residence and one additional residence.

**Active Participation** – Requires participation in making management decisions concerning the property, but is not substantially and continuously involved in the operation of the activity (the standard that applies for material participation).

**Activities of Daily Living** – Eating, bathing, dressing, toileting, transferring (walking), and continence.

**Additional Child Tax Credit** – The refundable portion of the Child Tax Credit.

**Adjusted Gross Income** – Gross income less above-the-line deductions.

**Adjustments** – AMT changes made to regular taxable income that either increase or decrease AMTI.

**Adoption Assistance Program** – An employer plan that assists employees with the cost of adoption and may not discriminate in favor of highly compensated or key employees.

**Adoption Expenses Credit** – A nonrefundable credit allowed for qualified adoption expenses paid by an individual to adopt an eligible child.

**Alimony** – A separate maintenance payment that is intended to replace income lost by one spouse as the result of a divorce and must be included in the gross income of the payee.

**Alimony Recapture** – Rules designed to prevent taxpayers from transforming property settlements into deductible alimony payments.

**Alternative Minimum Tax (AMT)** – An anti-abuse technique designed to change the timing of tax payments.

**Alternative Minimum Taxable Income (AMTI)** – Regular taxable income plus or minus certain adjustments and preferences.

**American Opportunity Tax Credit (formerly Hope Scholarship Credit)** – A credit (a portion of which is refundable) allowed for the qualified education expenses of an eligible student during the first four years of post-secondary education.

**Amortization** – Cost recovery deductions for intangible assets.

**Amount Realized** – The amount of money plus the value of property received in the sale or exchange of an asset.

**Annuitized** – When regular periodic payments on an annuity contract begin for life or for a specified period of time in excess of one year.

**Annuity Contract** – A contract under which an individual invests a lump sum or stream of payments with an insurance company and the income on the investment growth is deferred until the owner begins to take distributions from the annuity.

**Archer Medical Savings Accounts (MSAs)** – Tax-favored savings accounts for medical expenses that were established by HIPAA in 1996, but cannot be established after 2005.

**Articles of Incorporation** – The charter document for a corporation that must be filed with the Secretary of State in the state of organization.

**Articles of Organization** – The charter document of an LLC that must be filed with the Secretary of State in the state of organization.

**At-Risk Rule** – Provides that a taxpayer may not deduct, in the current tax year, more than the amount that he or she has at risk.

**Bartering** – An exchange of property and/or services for other property and/or services.

**Basis** – Represents the total capital or after-tax income used by a taxpayer to purchase an investment.

**Basis Limitation** – Provides that the maximum allowable loss that the taxpayer can deduct is equal to his or her basis in the investment.

**Below-the-Line Deductions** – Deductions from adjusted gross income, also known as itemized deductions.

**Bona Fide Resident Test** – Requirement for the Foreign Earned Income exclusion that requires the taxpayer to generally intend to work and reside in the foreign country for an indefinite period of time.

**Boot** – Non-like-kind property received in a Section 1031 exchange, usually cash or debt.

**Cafeteria Plan** – A written plan under which an employee may choose to receive either cash or taxable benefits as compensation or qualified fringe benefits that are excludable from wages.

**Capital Asset** – All assets that are not specified as ordinary income assets or Section 1231 assets.

**Cash Receipts and Disbursements Method** – An accounting method under which income items are reported for the tax year in which they are received in cash and expenses are deducted in the year in which they are paid with cash.

**Casualty Loss Deduction** – Deduction allowed for losses or damages to a taxpayer's property resulting from a sudden or unexpected event, such as fire, storm, shipwreck, or theft.

**Checking the Box** – When an eligible entity chooses to be taxed as either a corporation or a partnership.

**Child Tax Credit** – A nonrefundable tax credit of $1,000, which is available to an individual taxpayer for each qualifying child under the age of 17.

**Community Property** – A regime in which married individuals own an equal, undivided interest in all of the property accumulated, using either spouse's earnings, during the marriage.

**Compensation** – Salary, wages, and fringe benefits received in exchange for providing services to an employer.

**Compensatory Damages** – Monetary award intended to compensate for damage to property, for recovery of expenses incurred, for income lost, or for personal injury.

**Conventions** – Rules that govern the amount of depreciation that may be deducted during the first year that an asset is put into service.

**Corporate Recapitalization** – Restructuring the equity interests of a corporation, often in an effort to achieve estate planning or business succession goals.

**Corporations** – Chartered legal entities formed by one or more individuals by meeting state statutory requirements necessary for the formation of a corporation.

**Cost Basis** – Initial basis an investor acquires in an asset by using capital to purchase the investment.

**Coverdell Education Savings Account** – Plan similar to a college savings plan that allows taxpayers to contribute up to $2,000 per beneficiary per year to an account.

**Credit for Child and Dependent Care Expenses** – A nonrefundable credit intended to provide some financial relief to individuals who incur employment-related expenses for the care of one or more qualifying individuals.

**Credit for Increasing Research Activities** – A component of the general business credit intended to encourage businesses to conduct research and increase their research expenditures.

**Credit for the Elderly or Disabled** – A nonrefundable credit intended to provide financial assistance to elderly or disabled individuals with modest incomes.

**Credits for Taxes Paid** – Refundable credits generated by federal income taxes paid in advance.

**De Minimis Fringe Benefit** – Fringe benefits that are so small or insignificant that accounting for them would be unreasonable or administratively impracticable.

**Deductions** – Items that are subtracted from gross income, either below or above the line, in order to arrive at taxable income.

**Deferral Items** – Adjustments and preferences that result in a tax credit that can be used in future years equal to the additional tax that must be paid in the current year.

**Dependency Exemption** – A deduction from adjusted gross income that is allowed for each person who is a qualifying child or qualifying relative of the taxpayer.

**Depletion** – A form of depreciation that applies to natural resources.

**Depreciation** – A return of capital to a business that results in a reduction in the basis of the asset for the amount of depreciation that is claimed.

**Depreciation Recapture** – Special tax consequences that occur when a Section 1231 asset is sold for an amount greater than its adjusted basis.

**Determination Letter** – A letter issued by a district director of the IRS advising a taxpayer on how to report a transaction for tax purposes.

**Disability Insurance** – Provides benefits in the form of periodic payments to a person who is unable to work due to sickness or accidental injury.

**Disabled Access Credit** – A component of the general business credit intended to encourage small businesses to make their buildings accessible to persons with disabilities.

**Disallowed Losses** – Losses that are realized, but are not permitted to be recognized, including losses on the sale of personal use assets (except for casualty losses), losses on the subsequent sale of property gifted or sold to a related party when its FMV is less than the original owner's adjusted basis, and losses associated with a wash sale.

**Discriminant Inventory Function System** – A computer program used by the IRS to identify tax returns for audit.

**Distance Test** – In order to qualify for a moving expense deduction, the distance between the taxpayer's old home and new job location must be at least 50 miles greater than the distance between the old home and the old job location.

**Dividend Income** – A distribution of corporate earnings to shareholders, usually in cash.

**Doctrine of Constructive Receipt** – A cash method taxpayer must report income when it is credited to the taxpayer's account or when it is made available without restriction.

**Double Basis Rule** – A rule that applies to gifts and related party transactions where the transferee has a basis of the fair market value for losses and the transferor's basis for gains. The rule applies when the asset that is transferred has a fair market value less than the transferor's basis at the time of the transfer. This rule does not apply to arms-length unrelated party transactions. This rule may also be referred to as the split basis rule, dual basis rule, or bifurcated basis rule.

**Double Declining Balance Method** – An accelerated depreciation method used for MACRS assets with a 3, 5, 7, or 10 year class life in which the annual depreciation percentage is twice the annual depreciation percentage under the straight-line depreciation method.

**Earned Income** – Income received by a taxpayer in the form of wages, salaries, and income from the conduct of business activities.

**Earned Income Credit** – A refundable credit intended to reward lower-income taxpayers for earning income.

**Educational Assistance Program** – A separate written plan that establishes a program through which an employer provides educational assistance to employees.

**Employee Business Expenses** – Expenses that include professional and union dues of employees, travel, supplies and services, professional books and journals, job related educational expenses, work clothes and uniforms, and job hunting expenses in the same line of work, which may be deductible as a miscellaneous itemized deduction subject to the 2 percent floor if they are not reimbursed by the employer.

**Employer-Provided Child Care Credit** – A component of the general business credit intended to encourage employers to help provide and promote appropriate child care for their employees.

**Endowment Contract** – A type of insurance contract that pays a specified death benefit to a beneficiary upon the death of the insured owner, but also pays a specified benefit (in lieu of the death benefit) to the owner of the policy if the insured person lives to a specified age or date.

**Estimated Tax Payments** – Quarterly payments that are paid to the IRS and may be claimed as a credit against tax.

**Exclusion Items** – Adjustments and preferences that result in a permanent increase in tax.

**Exclusions** – Income items that are specifically exempted from income tax.

**Failure to File Penalty** – A five percent penalty of the unpaid tax balance for each month or part thereof that a tax return is late.

**Failure to Pay Penalty** – A penalty of 0.5 percent per month or part thereof that a taxpayer fails to pay tax that is owed.

**Family Limited Partnership** – A special type of limited partnership created under state law with the primary purpose of transferring assets to younger generations using annual exclusions and valuation discounts for minority interests and lack of marketability.

**Federal Insurance Contributions Act (FICA)** – The amount withheld from an employee's pay for OASDI benefits.

**Final Regulations** – Regulations issued by the Treasury that have been adopted formally after compliance with the requirements of the Administrative Procedures Act.

**First-Time Homebuyer Credit** - A refundable tax credit available for the purchase of a main home by first-time homebuyers.

**5-Year Lookback Rule** – A net Section 1231 gain in the current tax year (which should be taxed at capital gain tax rates) will be taxed at ordinary income tax rates to the extent of any unrecaptured Section 1231 losses claimed during the last five years.

**Flexible Spending Account (FSA)** – A type of cafeteria plan that is funded through employee salary reductions.

**Foreign Earned Income** – Income earned by a qualifying citizen or resident of the United States in exchange for personal services rendered in a foreign country.

**Foreign Tax Credit** – A nonrefundable tax credit available to qualifying taxpayers who pay income taxes to a foreign country on foreign source income and also pay U.S. income taxes on the same income.

**Fraud** – Implies that the taxpayer intentionally disregarded tax rules or misstated information included on the return.

**Fringe Benefits** – Non-cash benefits provided to an employee by an employer in addition to wages and salary.

**Functional Use Test** – Requires the replacement property to serve the same functional use as the original property.

**General Business Credit** – A combination of more than thirty different nonrefundable tax credits that must be considered in a specific sequence.

**General Partnership** – A joint business venture among two or more persons/entities to conduct business as co-owners in which all owners have unlimited liability with regard to the debts and obligations of the partnership.

**Gross Income** – All income from whatever source derived unless it is specifically excluded by some provision of the Internal Revenue Code.

**Head of Household Filing Status** – A filing status that provides a basic standard deduction and tax bracket sizes that are less favorable to the taxpayer than those for the surviving spouse status, but more favorable than those for the single filing status.

**Health Reimbursement Arrangements (HRAs)** – Employer-funded plans that reimburse employees for medical expenses and allow employees to carry any unused balance forward to be used in future years.

**Health Savings Account (HSA)** – Accounts that allow individuals who have high deductible health insurance plans to save on a tax-free basis to fund their medical expenses.

**Highly Compensated Employees** – Those employees that are either a greater than five percent owner or have compensation in excess of $110,000 (2009 and 2010).

**Hobby Activity** – Any activity that a taxpayer engages in without a profit motive.

**Holding Period** – The period for which a taxpayer owns an asset.

**Home Equity Indebtedness** – Additional debt secured by the home that exceeds the amount of acquisition indebtedness.

**Hybrid Method** – An accounting method that includes any other method of reporting that is permitted by the Code and regulations as long as it is deemed to clearly reflect income.

**Imputed Interest** – A payment deemed to be made by the borrower to the lender when the interest rate on a loan is less than the applicable federal rate.

**Incentive Stock Option (ISO)** – A stock option that meets certain requirements and is granted by a corporation to an employee to purchase the stock of that corporation.

**Income** – Broadly defined as the gross amount of money, property, services, or other accretion to wealth received, but it does not include borrowed money or a return of invested dollars.

**Individual Investor Exception** – Allows individual taxpayers who actively participate in rental real estate activities to deduct up to $25,000 of losses from that activity against non-passive income for the year.

**Interest Income** – Gross income generated by a variety of debt instruments, including bank accounts, money market instruments, and bonds. This is income to the lender and a gift to the borrower.

**Interpretive Regulations** – Official interpretations of the Internal Revenue Code by the Treasury.

**Inventory** – Assets that are held for resale to customers in the normal course of business.

**Investment Credit** – Part of the general business credit consisting of the sum of four different credits, (1) the rehabilitation credit, (2) the energy credit, (3) the qualifying advanced coal project credit, and (4) the qualifying gasification project credit.

**Involuntary Conversion** – A realization event that occurs outside of the control of the taxpayer.

**Keogh Plan** – A qualified plan for a self-employed person. An important distinction of Keogh plans is the reduced contribution that can be made on behalf of the self-employed individual.

**Key Employee** – An employee who is (1) a greater than five percent owner, (2) a greater than one percent owner with compensation in excess of $150,000, or (3) an officer with compensation in excess of $160,000 (2009 and 2010).

**Kiddie Tax** – A tax at the parent's marginal rate on the net unearned income of a child.

**Legislative Regulations** – Regulations in which the Treasury determines the details of the law.

**Life Insurance Contract** – A contract under which the insurance company promises to pay a specified amount upon the death of the insured.

**Lifetime Learning Credit** – A nonrefundable credit available to taxpayers who pay qualified tuition and related expenses to an eligible institution for themselves, their spouses, and their dependents for whom a dependency exemption is claimed.

**Like-Kind Assets** – Property of the same nature and character that may be exchanged in a like-kind exchange.

**Like-Kind Exchange** – A tax deferral technique in which assets held for productive use in a trade or business are exchanged.

**Limited Liability Company** – Separate legal entity formed by one or more individuals by meeting state statutory requirements necessary for the formation of an LLC that may be taxed as a sole proprietorship, partnership, or corporation.

**Limited Liability Partnership** – A hybrid entity generally comprised of licensed professionals that provides partial liability protection to its members and may be taxed as either a corporation or partnership.

**Limited Partnerships** – Associations of two or more persons as co-owners to carry on a business for profit except that one or more of the partners have limited participation in the management of the venture and thus limited risk exposure.

**Listed Property** – Suspect property that is easily used for both business and personal purposes.

**Long-Term Care Insurance** – Provides benefits when the insured is unable to perform some of the activities of daily living.

**Long-Term Holding Period** – Occurs when an asset is owned by a taxpayer for more than one year.

**Low-Income Housing Credit** – A component of the general business credit intended to promote the construction of housing for low-income residents.

## M

**Managing Partner** – A partner named to have responsibilities for specific tasks or for day-to-day operations.

**Married Filing Jointly Filing Status** – A filing status that allows married couples to combine their gross incomes and deductions.

**Married Filing Separately Filing Status** – A filing status used when married couples do not choose to file a joint return.

**Material Participation** – Requires involvement in the conduct of the trade or business on a regular, continuous, and substantial basis.

**Medical Savings Account (MSA)** – Accounts authorized by HIPAA 1996 which allowed contributions to the account to grow tax-free if funds distributed from the account were used to pay for medical expenses.

**Mixed-Use Rental Activity** – Rental activity in which the real estate is rented for 15 days or more per year and the owner's personal use of the property is more than the greater of 14 days per year or 10 percent of the rental days.

**Modified Accelerated Cost Recovery System (MACRS)** – An accelerated depreciation system under which assets are divided into specific classes according to their useful lives.

**Modified Endowment Contracts (MECs)** – Life insurance contracts that do not pass the 7-pay test or the corridor rule.

**Municipal Bonds** – Debt instruments issued by states and their political subdivisions, the interest income from which is generally excluded from federal gross income.

N

**Necessary Expense** – An expense that a prudent business person would incur in the conduct of business.

**Net Operating Losses** – Occur when trade or business activities generate higher expenses than income in a given year.

**Net Unearned Income (NUI)** – The amount of unearned income of a child that is subject to tax at the parents' rate. NUI is equal to the unearned income of the child, less $950 (minimum basic standard deduction) and the greater of $950 or the amount of the deductions allowed in producing the unearned income (2009 and 2010 thresholds).

**No-Additional-Cost Services** – A fringe benefit provided by employers that may be excluded from the employee's gross income if the service is (1) offered for sale to customers, (2) in the line of business in which the employee works, and (3) does not cause the employer to incur any substantial costs (including foregone revenue) in providing the service to the employee.

**Non-Accountable Reimbursement Plans** – Plans in which the employer gives the employee a specified sum of money out of which the employee will cover all of the business related expenses.

**Nonqualified Stock Option (NQSO)** – A right to purchase shares of company stock at a given strike price (generally set at the market price of the stock on the day the option is granted).

**Nonrecourse Debt** – Debt that is secured only by the asset pledged as security and not by any personal guarantee of the debtor.

**Nonrefundable Tax Credits** – Tax credits that can reduce the tax on taxable income to zero, but cannot generate a tax refund.

**Nontaxable Rental Activity** – Rental activity in which the real estate is rented for less than 15 days per year.

**150 Percent Declining Balance Method** – An accelerated depreciation method used for MACRS assets with a 15 or 20 year class life in which the annual depreciation percentage is 150 percent of the annual depreciation percentage under the straight-line depreciation method.

**Operating Agreement** – A written agreement similar to corporate bylaws that specify the rules and regulations for the operation of an LLC.

**Ordinary Expense** – An expense that is typically incurred in the normal, usual, or customary conduct of businesses in the same line of operations.

**Ordinary Income Assets** – Accounts receivable, copyrights, and inventory, all of which generate gains that will be taxed at ordinary income tax rates.

**Original Issue Discount** – The difference between the redemption price at maturity and the purchase price for debt instruments issued at a discount.

**Original Issue Discount (OID) Bond** – A bond that is issued for a price that is less than its face amount or principal amount on which interest is usually paid only at maturity.

**Passive Activity** – Any activity in which a taxpayer does not materially participate, that is a limited partnership interest, or that is a rental activity (even if the taxpayer materially participates in the activity).

**Passive Activity Loss Rule** – Provides that passive losses may only be used to offset gains from passive activities and may not be used to offset other types of income.

**Passive Credits** – Non-refundable tax credits designed to encourage individuals to engage in certain types of passive activities. Passive credits may be used to offset any tax attributed to taxable income.

**Passive Income** – Income received by a taxpayer including income generated from investments in real estate and income generated by business entities in which the owner does not materially participate.

**Pass-Through Entities** – Legal business forms that are not treated as separate taxable entities for income tax purposes. The income of a pass-through entity is taxed to each of the owners in proportion to their ownership interest.

**Personal Exemption** – A deduction from adjusted gross income that is allowed for the taxpayer and the taxpayer's spouse.

**Personal Property** – Any property that is not real property.

**Physical Presence Test** – Requirement for the Foreign Earned Income exclusion that requires the taxpayer to be present in a foreign country or countries for at least 330 full days during any period of 12 consecutive months.

**Piercing the Veil** – Occurs when a court disregards the status of the entity that gives the owners limited liability because the owners failed to maintain a clear and consistent identity for the entity.

**Portfolio Income** – Income received by a taxpayer through the investment of capital, such as dividends, interest, and capital gains.

**Preferences** – AMT changes made to regular taxable income that increase AMTI.

**Primarily Rental Use Activity** – Rental activity in which the real estate is rented for 15 days or more per year and the owner's personal use of the property is less than the greater of 14 days per year or 10 percent of the rental days.

**Private Activity Municipal Bonds** – Securities issued by or on behalf of local governments that bear tax-exempt interest for regular income tax and are used to provide debt financing for private projects. Private Activity Municipal Bond income is an AMT preference item.

**Private Charities** – Corporations or trusts structured to further the charitable intentions of a donor or the donor's family.

**Private Letter Ruling** – Rulings issued by the IRS that are binding on the IRS only with respect to the transaction and the taxpayer that are the subject of the ruling.

**Procedural Regulations** – Housekeeping instructions indicating how the Treasury and IRS will conduct their affairs.

**Profit Motive** – An actual and honest, even though unreasonable or unrealistic, profit objective in engaging in an activity.

**Proposed Regulations** – Regulations that have been drafted by the Treasury, but have not yet been adopted.

**Public Charities** – Charitable organizations that receive support from a wide cross-section of the population, such as the Red Cross or the YMCA.

**Punitive Damages** – Payments intended to punish the offending party.

**Qualified Charitable Organization** – An organization that is operated exclusively for religious, charitable, scientific, literary, or educational purposes, or for the prevention of cruelty to animals or children.

**Qualified Dividends** – Dividends subject to favorable tax rates.

**Qualified Education Expenses** – Educational expenses that receive favorable tax treatment. Such expenses may vary depending on the type of program or tax benefit.

**Qualified Employee Discounts** – Employer-provided discounts on qualified property and services that can be excluded from an employee's gross income.

**Qualified Moving Expense Reimbursement** – Direct or indirect payments by an employer to pay the cost of moving an employee's family and belongings.

**Qualified Residence Interest Deduction** – Tax deduction that permits taxpayers to deduct the interest on up to $1 million of home indebtedness and the interest on up to $100,000 of home equity indebtedness.

**Qualified Retirement Planning Services** – Any retirement planning advice or information provided to an employee and his spouse by an employer maintaining a qualified employer-sponsored retirement plan.

**Qualified Transportation Fringe Benefits** – Benefits in the form of (1) transportation between an employee's residence and the place of employment in a commuter highway vehicle, (2) any transit pass, or (3) qualified parking.

**Qualified Tuition Programs** – Also known as 529 Plans, permit taxpayers to save for post-secondary education of family members in a tax-favored manner through either a prepaid tuition program or a college savings plan.

**Qualifying Child** – A person who meets the relationship test, abode test, age test, support test, joint return test, and citizenship test, and may be claimed as a dependent of the taxpayer.

**Qualifying Relative** – A person who meets the relationship test, gross income test, support test, joint return test, and citizenship test; is not a qualifying child of the taxpayer; and may be claimed as a dependent by the taxpayer.

# R

**Real Estate Professional Exception** – Provides that if a taxpayer meets certain requirements, he is considered a real estate professional and may treat a real estate activity as an active trade or business.

**Real Property** – Land and anything permanently attached to it (such as buildings, trees, and swimming pools).

**Realization Event** – Generally occurs when an asset has been sold or exchanged. Gains on capital assets are subject to tax only when there has been both a realization event and a recognition event.

**Recognition Event** – Occurs when a realized gain is included on a taxpayer's income tax return. All realized gains are generally recognized unless a provision in the Code provides otherwise.

**Recourse Debt** – Debt that the taxpayer is personally liable to repay regardless of whether the investment produces a return for the investor.

**Refundable Tax Credits** – Tax credits that can be used not only to reduce or eliminate the current year's tax, but also to generate a tax refund.

**Reinvestment Period** – Period during which the taxpayer must acquire replacement property.

**Related Party** – Anyone defined under Section 267(b) including brothers and sisters (of whole or half blood or adopted).

**Reserve Method** – A method of deducting bad debts used by some businesses in which bad debt deductions are taken based on a percentage of accounts receivable representing the historical percentage of accounts that go bad.

**Residential Energy Efficient Property Credit** – A nonrefundable energy tax credit that helps an individual taxpayer pay for qualified residential alternative energy equipment.

**Residential Energy Property Credit** – A credit that increases the energy tax credit for energy efficient improvements made to a taxpayers existing home.

**Retirement Savings Contribution Credit** – A nonrefundable credit intended to encourage lower-income taxpayers to save for retirement.

**Revenue Procedures** – Statements issued by the IRS which details internal practices and procedures within the IRS and makes important announcements to taxpayers.

**Revenue Rulings** – Rulings issued by the IRS based on a set of facts common to many taxpayers and binding on the IRS.

**S Corporation** – A corporation formed under state law that elects to be taxed under Subchapter S of the Internal Revenue Code.

**Sale or Exchange Requirement** – One of the requirements for a gain to be subject to income tax.

**Section 1231 Asset** – Depreciable property or real property used for productive use in a trade or business or for the production of income.

**Short-Term Holding Period** – Occurs when an asset is owned by a taxpayer for one year or less.

**Single Filing Status** – A filing status used by an unmarried taxpayer who does not qualify as a surviving spouse or head of household.

**16th Amendment** – Amendment to the U.S. Constitution adopted on February 25, 1913 that gave Congress the power to lay and collect taxes on income.

**Small Corporation** – A corporation with average gross receipts of $7.5 million or less for the past three years.

**Small Employer Pension Plan Startup Costs Credit** – A component of the general business credit intended to encourage small employers to set up retirement plans for employees.

**Sole Proprietorship** – A business venture owned and operated by a single individual.

**Specific Charge-Off Method** – Allows businesses to deduct bad debts as an ordinary loss in the year in which the debt becomes partially or wholly worthless.

**Standard Deduction** – A standard amount that is specified by Congress and includes inflation adjustments. Taxpayers may deduct the greater of the standard deduction or allowable itemized deductions.

**Statute of Limitations** – Specified time within which the IRS may examine an income tax return.

**Step-to Fair Market Value** – The basis of inherited property, which is equal to the fair market value of the asset on the date of the decedent's death, or, if elected by the executor of the decedent's estate, the alternate valuation date.

**Straight-Line Depreciation** – A depreciation method under which the purchase price of the asset, less its expected salvage value, is divided by the expected useful life of the asset to determine the annual depreciation deduction.

**Substantial Omission** – An omission from a tax return of more than 25 percent of the gross income reported.

**Surviving Spouse Filing Status** – A filing status for a surviving spouse with a dependent child that affords the same basic standard deduction and tax rates as the married filing jointly status.

**Tax Court** – A special purpose court that sits in Washington, D.C. and only hears tax cases. The judges within the court travel throughout the U.S. to hear the cases.

**Tax Credit** – An amount that reduces the calculated tax liability of the taxpayer.

**Tax Year** – Normally a period of 12 months.

**Taxable Income** – Determined by subtracting allowable deductions from income.

**Taxpayer Use Test** – Requires that the replacement property be used by the taxpayer within activities which is treated the same for tax purposes.

**Temporary Regulations** – Regulations that have the same authority as final regulations and are issued when guidance must be provided quickly to taxpayers.

**Transfer for Value Rule** – An exception to the general rule that life insurance death benefits are received tax-free.

**Treasury Regulations** – An administrative source of tax law that are official interpretations of the Internal Revenue Code and give taxpayers insight as to how the Code will be enforced by the IRS.

**U.S. Court of Federal Claims** – Court that may preside over tax controversies and only hears cases in Washington, D.C.

**U.S. District Court** – Trial court of the federal judicial system which has general jurisdiction and is the only option for tax controversies in which the taxpayer would like a jury trial.

**Unrecaptured Section 1250 Depreciation** – The portion of gain that is attributable to non-recaptured depreciation (up to the amount of straight-line depreciation deductions taken) for depreciable real estate that is taxed at 25 percent upon the sale or exchange of the property.

## W

**Wash Sale** – Occurs when a taxpayer sells a stock or security at a loss, and purchases substantially identical stock or securities within a 30 day period before or after the sale.

**Work Opportunity Credit** – Part of the general business credit intended to promote the hiring of targeted groups of people who have special needs or high unemployment rates.

**Working Condition Fringe Benefit** – Any property or service provided to an employee to help the employee perform his job better.

## Z

**Zero Coupon Bond** – A bond that is sold at a deep discount, pays no coupons, and matures at its face value.

# Index